C000137273

GHOST BOY

a playwright's progress

by

RICHARD CRANE

Copyright 2020 Richard Crane
All rights reserved

No part of this book may be reproduced, or stored in
a retrieval system, or transmitted in any form or by
any means, electronic, mechanical, photocopying,
recording, or otherwise, without express written
permission of the publisher.

Cover design by Leo Crane.
Image for Act Two by John Birley,
for Act Three by Gered Mankowitz,
for Act Four by Leo Crane
and for Act Five by Roger Pearson.

*

by the same author
RUSSIAN PLAYS:
Brothers Karamazov
Vanity (Eugene Onegin)
Gogol
Satan's Ball (Master and Margarita)
Oberon Books 2011
UNDER THE STARS
Samuel French 1994
GUNSLINGER - a Wild West Show
Heinemann 1979
THUNDER - a Play of the Brontes
Heinemann 1976

CONTENTS

ACT ONE
Education 1952-58
. . . . 5

ACT TWO
Breaking Through 1961-66
. . . . 75

ACT THREE
On The Road 1966-69
. . . . 173

ACT FOUR
Free Fall, Free Flight 1969-72
. . . . 293

ACT FIVE
Making It 1972-74
. . . . 387

FINALE
. . . . 525

Acknowledgements
. . . . 533

to the 'Successor'

(See Act Five)

ACT ONE
Education: 1952-58

I am for him when he
walks in his golden slippers,
in the sunshine and with applause.
- Pilgrim's Progress

*

No eye his future can foretell
No law his past explain
Whom neither Passion may compel
Nor Reason can restrain.
- Rake's Progress

Scene One
KINGSTANDING ROAD

I remember stepping off the kerb, the screech of brakes, the towering, tiger-coloured double-decker bearing down on me. It blanked out the sun and rooted me to the tarmac, or I would have stepped back. I remember the driver jumping down from his cab, running towards me, bobbing down to my level: 'Jesus, dear God, you are the luckiest ruddy kid! Some angel must be watching over you.'

People were creeping round the bus: 'Oh my... so tiny... such a mite... surely can't be more than five...'

I wanted to say: It's all right. It didn't touch me. There's no need for this kerfuffle. And I'm not five. I'm nearly eight. I cross Kingstanding Road every morning. I have to escort my sister Judith (4¼), down the slope to the road and *at the kerb halt! Eyes right! Eyes left! Eyes right again! Then if all clear, quick march!* Judith then joins her friend Jane who is waiting at her gate with her mother Mrs Nicholls, and the two go skipping along to Peckham Road School and Mrs Nicholls returns to her kitchen at the back of the house. Then job done, I spin around, step off the kerb and WHAM!!'

Or nearly wham...

'Tell us your name son,' said the driver.

'Where's home?' said the conductor, stepping through the crowd.

'Do you live on Kingstanding Road?'

'What number?'

I said: '686.'

The conductor began shooing the people back onto the bus, as the driver took my hand, and with hardly an 'eyes right, eyes left...' quick-marched me across the road. Safe the other side, once again he bobbed down, but I was calm now.

I said: 'Thank you, you can go.'

Half-way up the long slope, I stopped and looked back. The bus had moved on. The traffic was flowing. The sun had vanished. Big heavy drops were beginning to fall. Then as the rain tipped down and thunder cracked, I knew for certain: *the bus hadn't stopped. The driver didn't see. The tiger had crushed me. I stepped off the kerb and in the blink of an eye, it cracked my skull, drew me in like a mangle, flattened me into a streak on the tarmac. And the rain washed me away.*

As I walked up the slope, I knew I was a ghost. I was different. I was acting. I was an actor and always would be. I was immune. I couldn't be hurt. And I had to keep it up, for as long as the person I no longer was, might live. And no one must ever know.

I clicked the latch of our gate, walked up the little path, by the dahlias and rhododendrons, hurried along the side of the house, on borrowed feet; could have passed through the closed back door but knew I must not draw attention. So I opened it and went in.

My mother was rolling strips of pastry. 'Well done Witty. Is it raining? Did you get wet?' I heard myself say: 'No I'm fine, honestly Mother. I ran between the drops.'

Then I went through to the hall, into the front room to do my piano practice.

THE HITLER ROOM

If this was death, what did living amount to? Life till then had been a house far away: a red-brick, sheer-sided giant of a house, the last house in the village, standing alone against the onslaught that came howling across the salt marshes of the Humber estuary. We gazed out on flat farm land, as far as the eye could see, stripped of trees and irrigated by dykes. We had damp, high-ceilinged, uncarpeted rooms, uncurtained sash-windows, still with blinds from the war. Day was day and night was night and winter was mostly night. Electricity didn't come to Laxton till just as we were leaving. We didn't have sewerage either. Ours was the only house in the village with a plumbed bath, flush toilet and cess-pit in the garden. Everyone else had a zinc tub by the fire, and an elsan pan down the garden or in the yard, which once a week the singing dustbinman would carry, slopful, on his shoulder, and tip into the teeming tank on his truck. Elsan I was told was a corrosive acid which dissolved solid matter. I once imagined committing suicide very slowly, by standing in the bucket and inch by inch being eaten away.

I could take you through the house, room by room, and it's the sallow light and echoey sounds that would stick, along with the distances, unsteady on little legs, crossing the hall, then clambering step by step up the wide front stairs, toddling along the landing, and slithering, clumping down the bare back stairs, into the tiled back hall, with its row of bells high up, each wired to a bell-pull in one of the main rooms, and to the front door and the back door.

The only really warm room was the front kitchen. Here was the coke-fuelled range with hobs where flat-irons could heat and dough could rise. High up in the ceiling was a clothes rack on a pulley. There was a farmhouse table, a rag rug on the floor, wooden chairs, a stool, an antique high-chair, and a utility cabinet with cake-tins, crocks and earthenware jars. Beyond the front kitchen was the back kitchen with sink and washboard, mangle, pantry and larder, and a boiler 'big enough for boiling children in' (as our daily used to say).

Every evening, my father would stand on a chair, and release the hiss of gas as he struck a match to ignite the cylinder. Then we would stand around the table, eyes closed, hands together, truly thankful for what we were about to receive, which might be a 'shell' egg, or spam fritters with 'puffs' (fried flour balls) or beef dripping on toast. Then sometimes my father would go out into the night, with the sacrament under his cloak, cycling in the light of his dynamo to lonely cottages, and my mother would worry about him being blown into a dyke.

My father presides, my mother provides. His sanctuary is his study. Hers is the front sitting-room, overlooking the little lawn, where she sometimes goes to write letters at her davenport or listen to plays on the wireless. My father in his study says the Office twice a day, followed by Bible study and contemplation. The crucifix above the prayer-desk is the focal point, with its nude, twisting figure, feet crossed, arms stretched, real nails attaching the bare body to the wood. I once slipped in and my father was kneeling, looking up, beating his breast, then bowing, speaking softly all the time. I crept out again.

Another time I went in when he wasn't there; nor was the crucifix – my mother had taken it for polishing – and the room seemed lighter. I looked at the shelves of brown-backed books, and the framed prints on the walls, telling my father's story: Ashby Castle, Repton School, Clare College Cambridge, York Minster. There were pipes in a pipe-rack, glacier mints in a jar, rough paper, torn in quarters, trapped in a clip, and receipts, confessing to the spending of scarce resources, impaled on a spike. Central on the desk was the typewriter, with its shiny black casing and upstanding keys. I pressed one which thwacked onto the cylinder, then two more which jammed. I tried to separate them, dislodging the ribbon, and – PING! – the carriage shot to the right. 'Wit?' said my father, standing over me. 'What are you writing?' He kissed me on the head, flicked the keys back into place and realigned the ribbon. Then he picked up a book called *Juniper Jinks*, about a mongoose who worked for the Universities' Mission to Central Africa, always getting into scrapes. 'Shall we read?'

He writes his sermons in a microscopic hand. He types his schedules: pastoral, spiritual, domestic, recreational. Every morning, half an hour before dinner, he sits on the step by the back door, puts on his boots and goes out to do the garden. Gardening has its own typed schedule through the seasons: mowing the big lawn, the little lawn, scything the long grass, digging potatoes and carrots, picking apples for storing and plums for bottling. After dinner, he goes to bed and sleeps soundly for twenty minutes. His 'rest' is sacred. If ever there is talking, he comes in, says quietly: 'Hey, you're making a lot of noise'. The more troubled he is, the more quietly he speaks. Elizabeth, my older sister, remembers being taken out of the kitchen after 'making a lot of noise' and being led by the hand up the back stairs to her bedroom. 'Just for a short time,' he whispers compassionately. Then he goes out, shuts the door, turns the key.

Next to her room is the Hitler Room. She can feel pure evil imprisoned in a room from which all life has been sucked dry. One day she dares to go in there. The windows are never opened so the air is musty: bare floorboards, bare walls, a pale shaft of sunlight. On the mantel-piece, arm raised in salute, is the little painted statuette: his baggy brown trousers tucked into brown shiny boots, his arm raised as if about to slap you, and his face with his tiny moustache, flattened hair, frowning eyes, tight mouth, saying: *Don't ever presume there is not evil in the world. I am evil. I am here. I am in the next room.'*

Once when I was three and she was five, we were in her bedroom and she was reading me the story of St Theresa and her brother Francis. There was a picture of them climbing out of a window to seek martyrdom. Suddenly she stands up, sniffs the air. 'Francis! Can you smell it?' Sin is seeping out of the Hitler Room like gas! If we want to be Six O'clock Saints and seek martyrdom, we have to leave now! She drags me down the front stairs across the hall, into the playroom. 'What's martyrdom Libbety – I mean *Theresa*?' She sighs: 'Martyrdom, Francis, is dying for your faith, as Daddy tried to in the war. But God allowed him to come back to us. That's why he is sad.' She is half way through the window. The picture in the book showed Francis hanging back, having to be pulled through by his sister. I protest: 'Why can't we go through the front door?' She freezes, as I fall into the flower-bed. Someone is coming up the drive on a bike. It's Daddy. He is smiling.

MY FATHER...

... was born, Robert Bartlett Crane, in 1914, second son to Charles 'Chas' Crane, founder of Crane & Walton Solicitors, Ashby-de-la-Zouch: Freemason, Church Warden, Clerk to the Magistrates and the Wisest Man in Leicestershire. An older boy Michael had died in infancy, so it fell to Rob to assume the duties of Heir Apparent, and be an example to his younger brother Arthur ('Arch') and sister Catharine ('Girl').

Sensitive, cheerful, honest and stubborn, Rob was miserable at school, forced as a left-hander to craft his letters with his right hand, then sent, at thirteen, to Repton School. The headmaster was Geoffrey Fisher, later Archbishop of Canterbury, described by Roald Dahl, Rob's contemporary at Repton, as '*a rather shoddy, bandy-legged little fellow with a big bald head and lots of energy but not much charm*'. His beating technique, as recounted by Dahl, had the boy to be punished, drop his trousers and pants, then kneel on the sofa, the top half of him hanging over. The cane would then swish on the bare flesh, Fisher pausing to fill his pipe, then swishing again, then striking a match to light the pipe; then another swish and a relighting and a puffing on the pipe, and so on until ten strokes, with intervals, had been delivered and the pipe was burning nicely.

If Repton was hell, home life was no easier. Rob's duty to his father and the law, was clashing with his attachment to his mother (Ma) and the church. Chas himself had come from a vicarage family, as had his father, and Ma herself; and several of Chas's nine siblings had gone on to become priests or nuns. Chas wanted to break the cycle and found a dynasty of lawyers. No son of his was going to take shelter under a leaky vicarage roof, and raise his children on charity. Be a church warden, a Freemason and

Pillar of the Community, instil fear in priests, as God Himself instils fear, but don't *be* a priest, for God's sake!

I have a memory, years later, in 1963, as we were carrying my trunk through the cloisters of Jesus College, on my first day at Cambridge: my father skipping, thirty years falling away, saying: Wit! These years will be happiest of your life! He had been at Clare in the thirties, where defying his father, he had read history, not law. As one of the first generation to grow up after the Great War, all dreams seemed attainable: the Spanish Fascists would be defeated by the power of free thought; George Bernard Shaw was hailing Stalin's Russia as the 'Land of Hope'; Mussolini was rebuilding Italy like a Caesar, and beyond all belief, a new socialism was rising out of the ashes of Germany.

*

It was heady time to be at Cambridge. Wittgenstein, former schoolfellow of Hitler, was teaching at Trinity. His students, Burgess, Philby and Blunt were going down just as Rob Crane was coming up. William Empson, expelled from Magdalene for gross turpitude (having a girl in his room), had championed ambiguity. Absolute truth is riddled with uncertainty! *All those dreams by which men long live well/ are magic-lanterned on the smoke of hell...* But it was Fred Hoyle, at Emmanuel, and his discoveries beyond the stars, that were opening Rob's eyes. Nothing comes from chance! Everything, from the tiniest microbe to the mightiest cosmos, operates according to set laws which must emanate from One Supreme Mind! This led to the proofs of St Thomas Aquinas, and a certainty that the Church, not the law, would be Rob's calling.

But returning, BA Hons Cantab, to Ashby, where as Heir to the expanding empire of Crane & Walton (they now had offices in Leicester and Coalville), he was expected to toe the line, become articled and sealed into his inherited career; finding he had no words to appeal his father's verdict, that the boy who had dared to didain law at university, must now start from the ground up, running errands for colleagues, making tea for clients; having no one to speak for him, Rob could offer only silence - dumb insolence! - regressing to neurasthenia, mental numbness bordering on idiocy.

'What do we do,' said Chas one night, to Ma. 'If I and Repton can't make a man of him, who can?'

Ma had a cousin Mo, who was a bishop in Africa, just then setting off for the Austrian Alps with a group of young ordinands. The clear mountain air, the Christian energy of Mo, might not these, said Ma, be just the tonic for Rob? A grunt from Chas signalled a flurry of arrangements, and before anyone cold say *knife*, Rob was bound for the peaks, where tumbling in the snow and joining in the laughter, he found his voice returning. And in long mountain walks, and long talks with Mo, he found the curtain of doubt lifting and a new clarity, for his own and the world's future, shining forth. This was 1937, just months before the Anschluss. Suddenly after so much despond, there was real hope.

Uncle Mo Gelsthorpe was the eleventh of thirteen children. He grew up a keen cricketer, rugby-player and scout. Twenty-two when war broke, he volunteered and fought at Passchendaele. In a letter written after the war to a fellow soldier, he wrote: *'Those years in the Ypres salient, were the happiest of my life... because of the qualities of comradeship and the self-sacrifice which transcended all other human emotion.'* He was awarded the DSO for valour, pushing through to a hard-won victory; was sent to join T E Lawrence in Mesopotamia; fought with distinction at the Battle of Sharagat, winning a bar to his DSO; then personally conveyed the envelope containing the surrender of the Turks to British HQ in Baghdad. Ordained after the war, he worked as a priest in Nigeria, then Egypt, Abyssinia and Kenya, becoming Bishop of the Niger, then Anglo-Egyptian Sudan. His Christianity was robust and joyous, as reflected in a poem by one of his ordinands at Bible Camp:

> *A fading sky, a setting sun,*
> *a golden pathway on the sea,*
> *three children playing on the sand*
> *beside the shores of Galilee.*
> *Clambering over rock and stone,*
> *Simon reckless leads them on;*
> *laughing run the brown-limbed boys,*
> *Jesus hand in hand with John...*

When Rob came home from Austria, he told his father he was leaving the firm. He enrolled at Queen's Theological College Birmingham and in May 1939 was ordained deacon by Archbishop Temple in York Minster. As curate at Acomb parish church, he married the vicar's daughter Nowell, known as Nan, and in May 1942, they had a child Elizabeth. He was called up in February 1944, to serve as chaplain in the Royal Navy. In June he took part in the D-Day landings, ferrying troops across the channel. In December, he left his ship HMS *Wildfire*, moored at Sheerness, and raced to York just as I was being born. Then he was away again in Belgium with the advancing allied armies, and on through the ruins of Germany with the Royal Marines;

then just as he was hoping to come home to his young family and a new life as a parish priest, he was posted for nine months to Hong Kong.

My parents wrote to each other every day, from February 1944 to September 1946. The letters were stowed away in an old ammo box in the loft. Elizabeth knew about them and told me we must never read them or we might learn the truth about our parents. That truth, which we never knew, was that they were passionately in love. There was a beating heart in the Ammo Box, and as long as it was there, the power of that secret love in the loft, could counter the evil of the Hitler Room. Whatever the motive in acquiring the statuette, the little man with the raised arm addressing no one in the empty room, was now Satan on Earth: the obverse to the twisting Christ on the cross. These two powers were still at war. Even though Hitler was dead and the Japanese obliterated, the spores from millions of corpses were in the air, and it was having to guard against despair, and to search one's soul, and at the same time, navigate back into the heart of a young family, that had grown used to being without you, plus a reticence in adversity, and the chill in the house, and the routine of daily offices, visiting, gardening etc, on my father's part, and washing, baking, brass-cleaning etc, on my mother's part, that were giving them little time for expressions of love.

I imagine them driving into Laxton on the first day, in the rackety blue Hillman, over the railway which forms the boundary of the village, past the newly built Victory Hall, up towards Front Street, past the pub and the forge, the shop on the left, the school on the right, and on past the turning down into Back Street, to the far end of the village and the two churches: the ruined fourteenth century chancel, surrounded by graves, and the Victorian replacement with its yew trees and iron railings. And beyond all that, the last outpost of the village, raw against wind, rain, mist and snow, the lonely giant: Laxton Vicarage.

BOYHOOD

My earliest memory is here. I'm in my room upstairs, down the side of the house, in my bed, in the cold. Every breath I drag in is like rust in my chest. It scrapes my throat, burning down into my lungs, then exhaling like a death rattle. I can hear feet on the boards of the corridor coming closer. My mother has the medicine. My father, in his cassock, kneels by the bed. I can smell the damp of his clasped hands, and the fear in his prayer: '*Thy Kingdom come... Thy Will be done...*' and my mother lifts my head so I can swallow the white liquid.

The prayer is answered. The medicine works. I am brought back from the brink, and given a kitten called Timmy, pitch black and nervous even though he is a farm cat. Elizabeth loves him, even more than she loves me. She goes to school now, skipping down the road every morning, then skipping home in the afternoon, to play with Timmy.

We had him for less than a week. One chilly evening, my father was backing the car across the yard into the garage, and didn't see Timmy. Elizabeth found him in a corner. He couldn't move his legs. She brought him into the back kitchen. My mother put him in a box. We knelt over him in a family group: my father, my mother, my sister and me, and Timmy in the box. Then in the morning, before Elizabeth went to school, we buried him, under the black tree by the hedge.

Timmy was succeeded by his brother Poozum who was altogether more canny. He grew rapidly into a little panther, prowling the fields for mice and frogs. Once he disappeared for three days and when he returned, there was a red hole where one of his eyes used to be. He stayed with us nearly all our time at Laxton and we were just thinking Birmingham with its buses would surely be the death of him, and we should return him to Beeton's farm where he came from, when Mr Beeton shot him, mistaking him for a fox.

Poozum was the feline equivalent of Trevor, Farmer Beeton's boy, who I was told not to play with. I could play with the Sweeting boys, the Kirk girls and Gloria Kendall but not Trevor Beeton who was rough and had the devil in him. He knew the farmyard facts of birth and death, and was given to mischief and trespassing. Once, when I'd gone over with the Sweetings to the Beeton farm and we were playing in the yard, we saw Trevor's brother coming towards us, carrying a hen by its legs. It was flapping upside-down and squawking, as if to say: 'Why are you doing this? You feed me and I give you eggs. Why are you now going to kill me?'

'Come and watch,' said Trevor.

We went into the barn, and watched Trevor's brother, chatting and laughing all the while, give such a twist to hen's neck, the head came clean off. He then dropped it on its feet and it went scuttling around, pouring blood and crashing into things, till it realized it was dead.

Another time, we were walking in a field with cows and there was a bull with them. 'Watch him,' said Trevor. 'He's going to foot them.' I wasn't sure what 'foot' meant but imagined it was something to do with feet and this was confirmed when the bull got up on its hind *feet* and began hugging one of the cows from behind in a clumsy way, while we watched and cheered. Later at school – this was my second to last term at Laxton Primary (I was six, Trevor was seven) – he said: 'I've got three girls to come to woods in playtime and we're going to foot them'. I said okay.

I was in Transition, the centre row between Kindergarten and Standard One. Trevor was at the back of Standard One, behind Margaret Kirk. Next term they would go up to Standard Two in Mr Womersley's room, then work their way up year by year to Standard Five, after which, at age eleven, having taken the 'scholarship', they would leave the village and go to either Goole Grammar or Goole Secondary Modern.

Our teacher, for our first three years, was Miss Wilson. She was probably quite short, but to us she was tall as a lamp-post with her luminescent perfectly permed white hair, and her long knitted dresses. Each year she knitted a new dress which she then wore every day. She was always clean as a new pin though I knew for a fact that she had no bathroom or lavatory. Later I would go to her house once a week for singing lessons, after which she and I would sit at table and have tea from her Clarice Cliff tea service: sandwiches and fairy-cakes, and tea poured through a strainer from a teapot shaped like a house. I once asked her how she managed to eat an iced cake without ever licking a finger, and she pursed her lips then smiled, then pursed then smiled and broke into her ripple of laugh – hohoho (with a short 'o') – which rocked her whole body but did not disturb a crumb.

She was the church organist and choir mistress, secretary to the Parish Council, Sunday School teacher and child-minder to the Vicarage. She was firm, but never strict. She was my first and best teacher. She taught me to read, write, count and sing.

When playtime came, we jumped the wall: Trevor, me and the Sweeting boys. We ran across the field to a clump of trees. The girls were already there. They stood, arms folded like little Yorshire housewives. Trevor said: 'Right. We only got ten minutes. Who's going to show?' 'Show what?' said the girls. On the cue from Trevor, we dropped our pants and he was expecting the girls to do the same. But they weren't impressed. 'Come on,' said Trevor, 'we done it, so you do it.' The girls shrugged. Then Mary said: 'Well, I will if Gloria will.' Gloria said: 'Well, I will if Margaret will.' Margaret said: 'Well, I will if Mary will...' And so it went on. I was thinking about Sunday School and Adam and Eve knitting skirts out of fig leaves, as Miss Wilson knitted dresses. And I thought about my teacher, my best of all teachers, never again laughing her ho-ho-ho, *never looking at me again*, if she knew what we were doing.

Then the bell rang and we ran for it.

LEAVING LAXTON

My sister Judith was born June 1948, and as she grew, and began to speak and assert herself in the house and in the garden – she would rock her cot till the bottom fell out, and rock the old high chair till the back fell off, and bury her face in the mole-hills on the lawn, and pull chunks from Sheena the scottie we now had, because Poozum was always away; as Judith began to dominate, the house, it seemed, had to soften around her: we acquired some carpets; we took down the blinds; the Hitler Room became a store-room for the furniture of my father's friend Mr Wilkinson, who with Mrs Wilkinson and their daughters, Rosalie and Francesca, was leaving to become vicar of Tristan da Cuhna, the world's loneliest parish.

And electricity was on its way; the poles were going up, like giant stilts across the landscape. The old house was wired and suddenly at the flick of a switch, there was light! Electric fires, electric irons, electric kettles brought warmth and sophistication. People started to travel. There were more cars, fewer horses. Lorrie Fox, the blacksmith, was having to turn from horse-shoes and farm machinery to wrought-iron gates. His furnace, that we passed on the walk to school, with its hammering of white-hot metal, and him with his leather apron and blackened hands and face; the forge, for centuries the sweated heart of the working village, was looking out-of-date, even quaint. It still had years to run, but its days were numbered. It would be the first pillar of the free-standing village to fall, followed by the school, the shop and finally the pub, with only the church and the station left standing. (Somehow Dr Beeching missed this branch line in his revision of the railways, and it continues to this day).

Laxton was no longer the centre of the world, where you could be born, grow up, get wed, have children, labour on the land, grow old and die, without ever having to leave. Going to Goole on the train was like going to London. The gas works, the rows of red-brick terraces, Goole Grammar and Secondary Modern: this was a grown-up world, that we were allowed a glimpse of, before chuffing our way home. Now, after four years as Vicar of Laxton and adjoining villages, my father felt he had served his apprenticeship and was impatient for bigger challenges; and my mother even more so. They weren't going to go the way of the Wilkinsons to Tristan da Cunha. Loneliness was furthest from godliness in my father's book. Ministering to the masses in cities was God's plan for him, and he set about preparing his family for the wider world.

First Elizabeth was sent away. Having completed three years with Miss Wilson – or Milson, as Judith called her – she now left Laxton primary and was put on the train to York as a new girl at our mother's old school, York College. She would leave Monday morning and come home Friday evening, staying the week with Rev and Mrs Lemmon and their daughter Susan.

And plans were being made for me.

*

My godfather was Gerald Ellison. Once Chaplain to Archbishops Temple and Garbutt, now Suffragan Bishop of Willesden, later to be Bishop of Chester and finally London, Uncle Gerald was everything in the Anglican Church that my father was not. 'Born to the purple, (as it would say in his obituary), devoted to the establishment, a staunch defender not only of the faith but of the status quo,' he was athletic, ambitious and dashingly handsome, and my mother was in awe of him. During the lonely post-war years when my father was in Hong Kong, Uncle Gerald would sometimes pop round for tea, to see his godson, always at only an hour or so's notice, plunging my mother into a flurry of scone-baking. Sometimes he didn't come, and she would be left, sitting on the edge of the settee in her new costume. I don't remember any of this of course; it's a legend laughed about in the letters. My first and only remembered meeting with my godfather, was a disaster.

It was 1951. Uncle Gerald had heard that his godson (now six) was possessed of a 'skylark singing voice'. He had written to say that the boy, being of an age to audition for St Paul's Choir School, should come to London and sing. He would not presume, as Bishop of Willesden, to be in a position of influence, but he did 'know the people', and Rob and Nan knew that no one in any field had remained unpersuaded when Gerald Ellison espoused a cause.

We were motoring down the A1, windows open, and I was singing. Every Friday after school, for six weeks now, I'd been going to Milson's for tuition and tea. She would sit upright at her piano in the front room and we would sing scales and arpeggios, and the lower, middle and upper notes of a chord. Then we would work our way through *Sixty Songs For Little Children*, and my skylark voice could be heard down Front Street:

> *If you wash you face*
> *in the pearly dew*
> *on the first of May*
> *as the sun breaks through,*
> *blythe and bonny you will be*
> *and happy too...*

I was feeling sick. They stopped the car. I was half out of the door when it came up. 'Oh Witty,' said my mother, 'you were doing so well.' We pulled in at a café to mop and tidy up. The audition was this afternoon, and it was already one o'clock. My father tried to telephone but the line was engaged. 'He's probably on one of his *persuasive* calls,' said my mother, as we motored on. I fell asleep.

Suddenly my mother leant round and shook me. 'Look! Witty look! *You must look!*' I woke up. A vast, curved castle wall was blocking the view, so close we were almost scraping it. 'It's Windsor,' said my mother, 'where the King lives and the princesses! I had to wake you to see it! You can sleep now.' But I didn't sleep. I felt cold. I smelt of sick. I didn't want to be here. I didn't want to be with boys who didn't talk as I talked. I wanted to be in Yorkshire with my sisters and the Sweeting boys.

The castle wall was like a sign saying: 'YOU ARE NOT WELCOME. KEEP OUT!'

Uncle Gerald and Auntie Jane had two daughters and a baby son. The girls had been allowed to stay up with the promise that I would sing to them, before bedtime, but I was so sleepy myself – it had gone eight o'clock; we'd been travelling for eleven hours, and my mother was uncomfortable. She was thinking: how did Jane, who is so *plain* and flat-chested, inveigle Gerald into marrying her and why is he so *rude*, still stuck in his study on the telephone – she could hear him *persuading* someone who didn't want to be persuaded but would be, because Gerald was a Pastmaster Persuader? (How much did it take to *persuade* Jane? she wondered.) Then like a blast of warmth, he breezed in. He wore episcopal gaiters and purple stock with starched white bands. He shook Rob's hand, nodded to Nan, frowned at me: 'You are the luckiest future chorister. I've just *persuaded* the Choirmaster to hear you 7.30 tomorrow.' 'Oh crikey,' said my father, 'we have to leave in the afternoon'. 'In the morning,' affirmed Gerald. 'Early breakfast Jane, all right?'

I was sent to bed. I could hear them talking. My mother seemed to be getting cold feet about abandoning me. She was talking about the fees. 'All taken care of,' said Gerald. 'As they have been since 1123 when eight boys, in need of charity were taken in by the Dean and given home and education in exchange for singing the Cathedral Office.' 'Which I haven't yet said,' said my father. 'The Office, I haven't said it. Have you said it?' 'No!' exclaimed Gerald. 'Let's say it together!' And they slipped away like eager boys, leaving my mother and Jane to skirt around the issue of what it was like being married to Gerald.

I was awake at five. I wanted to sing, but the house was silent. I mouthed the words of *'If you wash your face...on the first of May.'* But it was November and it was raining. I didn't want to sing this, or any of the *Sixty Babyish Songs*. I wanted to do *'O For the Wings of a Dove'*, but I hadn't practised it. Milson had said it was 'too old' for me, and we hadn't brought the music. I could sing it without the music and tried to, very softly, but no sound came. When my mother came in at six, I didn't speak. I was silent through breakfast and all the way in the car to the school. 'Sing a scale Witty,' said my father. 'He's saving his voice,' said my mother.

When we got to the school, the Choirmaster was waiting. He made a joke of our missing the audition yesterday but he liked to get up early and sing with the lark, as we obviously did too! We were led into a panelled room where my parents were invited to sit, while I went through into the music room with the Choirmaster, and the door closed.

Five minutes later, it opened. The Choirmaster was puzzled: 'Couldn't get a squeak out of him. Is he normally so quiet?' 'Perhaps,' said my father, 'we could come back this afternoon? We don't have to leave till – .' 'I'm afraid that's not feasible,' smiled the Choirmaster.

We didn't go back to Willesden. They'd said we should stay for lunch and tell them how it went, but we decided to go home. The weather was not good and we had to pick up Elizabeth and Judith from Ashby. No one spoke much on the journey. 'Stop the car,' said my mother. She got out, spent a penny by the road, then got in the back with me and I snuggled into her. We stayed like that till we got to Ashby.

Elizabeth and Judith were with our cousins next door. Uncle Arch, now a partner and Heir Apparent to Crane & Walton, married to Auntie Joan with two daughters Mary and Ninny, had bought the large rambling house that abutted onto Thorpe House; and Auntie Catharine, now a doctor, had married Uncle Mike, another partner in the firm, and they lived just down the road, with their two daughters Margar and Tisha, making six girls in all, aged from nine down to three, playing girls' games next door.

I went up to the attic.

*

Pip was a dog, Squeak was a penguin, and Wilfred was a rabbit with long ears, who could only say 'gug', 'nunc' and 'gugnunc'. They were orphans, looked after by Uncle Dick and Angeline; surviving by side-stepping the rules which would otherwise have excluded them. Life with no security, in the teeth of fate, was 'luvly' according to Squeak, who had been hatched on the South African coast, then brought to London Zoo, where she didn't fit in, being too talkative and opinionated. Highly strung, ever hopeful, hyperactive and motherly, she stood in direct contrast to Pip, who was genial and dogged as any dog. Arrested for begging on the Thames Embankment and sent to a concentration camp (dogs' home), he was rescued by Uncle Dick, who bought him for half a crown. He would have married Squeak if she had been a dog not a penguin, and the two of them would have adopted Wilfred who had wandered off from his burrow, having been rejected because of his ears, if it had been legal for cohabitees to adopt rabbits.

Reading my father's old annuals in the attic, I thought if we could view the trip to London as just another PipSqueak adventure, catastrophic yet survivable, it wouldn't matter so much. My father like Pip, was firm in his faith that bad things are sent to try us, that disasters are God's Will, and that regularity and pluck will see you through, though you may die first. My mother, like Squeak, was assertive, obsessive, given to outbursts of jealousy and joy in equal measure, ruffling feathers – mostly her own – bossing Pip, despairing of Wilfred. And I was a silly rabbit with big ears who couldn't speak.

It was getting cold in the attic. These were old books and I could see now why they had to be locked away; why my father had to leave Ashby, passing on the inheritance to his brother and brother-in-law. We used to come here from time to time and it was always a treasure trove, a sink-hole into the past. Aside from the annuals, train set and porcelain dolls in the attic, there was the mystery of the Russian matryoshkas in the master bedroom: the old man and the old lady, with progressively smaller, younger men and ladies, boys and girls, down to a bean-sized baby deep inside. We would play Cannibal Happy Families, where the parent eats the child and the grandparent eats the parent and on through the generations; while Granny Ashby watched over us from her bed – she was always in bed – in her mob cap, with her big eyes, behind bottle-end spectacles, and a wide false-teeth smile. That was Ashby, musty, tobacco-brown, shrouded in creeper, with family portraits on the walls; the steady tick-tock of the grandfather clock and a four-tone gong for meals; and Sarah the maid, swabbing the brick floor, collecting eggs from under hens; and old Harper in the garden tending marrows and beans. This was security, longevity, eternity: everything you'd ever need, from A for Ashby to Z for Zouch, so long as you toed the line.

I closed the book, put it away, shut the box, left the room, closed the door, went down the stairs, went next door to my sisters and cousins, not to play with them but to tell them (with a look – I wouldn't *say* it) that it was time to go, that it was *dangerous* to stay: Thorpe House was a swamp you had to drag yourself out of. Granny Ashby had been eaten by a wolf who would eat you too. The war was over, with ration-books and cesspits soon to follow. The second half of the twentieth century had begun. We were the future. We were going to Birmingham.

THE TWIDLES

I remember the day we moved. We'd been sent to stay with the Twidle grandparents in Burton Agnes, while the packing up was being done. Burton Agnes is a pretty village in the East Riding, mid-way between Driffield and Bridlington, with its own Elizabethan stately home owned by millionaire art-collector Marcus Wickham-Boynton. The church dates back to the Plantagenets and the Jane-Austenish Rectory is white-washed, large and rambling: home to the Rector, Arthur Edwin Twidle, known as the Admiral, or the Ad, because of his exploits at sea. He came here from the living of Thwing in the Wolds, before which he was Vicar of Acomb, on the outskirts of York; leaving there shortly after his younger daughter Nowell had married his curate Robert Crane and his elder daughter Maureen (known as the Morgue) had taken off with a squadron leader. The Ad had come to York from South Queensferry in Scotland where as Priest in Charge of the Priory Church of St Mary of Mount Carmel, he and my grandmother Edith had raised three of their four children, against the buffeting winds of the Firth of Forth, and the trio of hundred-and-fifty-ton piers of the Forth Bridge. Legends of the Firth and the Bridge abound, from St Columba and Macbeth to Jamie Balfour, Richard Hannay and the Ad himself. He had fought at Jutland, been torpedoed and sunk; recounting the bumpety-bump of the rivets as he slid down the listing deck of *HMS Nottingham*, into the icy North Sea. Was he holding aloft the icons he had rescued from the monastery at Archangel, besieged and desecrated by the Bolsheviks? Or was it the icons themselves that raised him from drowning? Or was that another time, another sinking, another miracle?

I have a photo of him with the Twidle family from the 1890s: staunch Methodists from Hull. There are seven boys and three girls, and my grandfather is the youngest. He is sitting at his father's feet, aged about six, with a broad, flat head (like mine), looking straight at the camera. I imagine him growing up, indulged by his nine older siblings, sternly watched over by his mother, morally guided by his father. He excels at school, especially in maths. He sits through sermons in chapel, wishing it wasn't so *undramatic*. He looks across the vast expanse of the Humber, at the dockyards and fishing boats, and dreams of going to sea. He's eighteen now and articled to an accountant, but this isn't his vocation. He passes Holy Trinity church on his way from work, cathedral-size, the largest parish church in England; and one day he goes inside. The hush, the height, the peace of this holy place, enfold him. He sits down, then kneels – something Methodists never do. He feels comforted and rebellious. He is not content with the closed walls of his family, the dullness of chapel. He wants mystery, candle-wax, vaulted ceilings and monuments.

He gets up and walks down the side aisle, looking at the inscriptions. He stops before a white marble plaque, reads aloud:

HARBORD HARBORD
HARBOURMASTER OF HULL
DIED 1888

'They had so many children they ran out of names,' says a voice. 'He was our uncle.'

Beside him are two girls: one about fourteen, with rosy cheeks, her straggly hair escaping a loosely tied bun; the other twelve, with a stern expression and a long blond pigtail. The older one continues: 'He squared the circle. They said it couldn't be done, but he did it. He was a mathematician.'

'He died the year I was born,' my grandfather says.

'Are you staying for the service?'

He stays for the service. He sits within sight of the Harbord pew. There is a mother, round-faced, with smiling eyes, who nods to him, and a father with a bushy beard and eyebrows that spring out like brushwood obscuring his glasses, and the two girls who he hopes will look round, and then the younger one does, straight at him, with an unblinking stare. He drops by again the next day and the next and every day, on his way home, just to walk up the aisle, hear his foot-steps echo, catch the sun slanting through the stained glass, and kneel and look up at the high curves interweaving in the vaulted roof. Here prayers can be heard. Here the circle can be squared. Here, he feels sure, his future lies, his vocation, his happiness. And on Wednesdays he stays for evensong, and sometimes he comes here after chapel on Sundays. He meets the girls again, Rosie and Edith, who introduce him to their parents, and to their brothers Dick, Vic and Billy, younger versions of their father, bushy-haired, sturdy-legged sailors all. Then one Sunday, a fourth brother, the oldest, is there. 'Arthur, this is Arthur,' says Rosie, introducing him to a young mariner with a weathered face and keen eyes. 'He can put *both elbows* on the table, having rounded the Horn *twice*! And he has been *very nearly*, to the South Pole. Mr Shackleton said he can go with him again, next time he tries, because he is the *best* First Officer...'

'Are you a sailing man?' says Arthur Harbord.

'I should like to be,' says Arthur Twidle.

I imagine my grandfather, in the stillness of Holy Trinity, impelled by three forces, which would tear him from his family and set his soul free: the Church, the Sea and the Harbords – especially Rosie: her little-bird face, her bright eyes and the way her voice soared when she sang; like a nightingale, he thought. He wrote out what he remembered of a poem about a nightingale, and one Sunday, gave it to her:

> *My heart aches, and a drowsy numbness pains*
> *my sense, as though of hemlock I had drunk,*
> *or emptied some dull opiate to the drains...*

She scanned it quickly: 'I didn't know you were a poet.'

'It's by Keats.'

'I love poetry.'

She gave it back to him. He had wanted her to keep it. He was going away the next day, to Theological College in Warminster, and then into the Navy. He wanted her to have something written, as a memory of him, but he wasn't a poet or a writer of anything except sermons and she was disappointed, he could tell. He wouldn't see her for four years, during which time, the world would go to war and few people would listen to nightingales.

Just before his ship sank, he had a message from Edith, saying that Rosie was now married and expecting a child.

When he was in the water, going under, freezing, swallowing oil, he tried to picture Rosie. If he was dying, then it was Rosie's sweet face that he wanted imprinted on his mind, but the more he tried to picture her, the more she faded, and the more *Edith's* face appeared: stronger, closer, lifting him up. If he was to live, it would be for *Edith* – the knowledge came like a thunderbolt! – and he *would* live because just the thought of her, was willing him to survive. The girl with the long pigtail, and the quiet, no-nonsense loving eyes, was now a woman of eighteen.

When he knew he was coming home, he wrote to her and asked if she would meet him at the station. He was still physically and mentally weak, with troughs of despair offset by euphoric hopes. Even though she hadn't replied, he knew she would be there waiting, because if she wasn't, it would be the end, they would lose the war, there would be no salvation, the devil would have won. So when the train pulled in, and he couldn't see her in the crush, he climbed a pillar and called out her name across the concourse: 'EDIE! EDITH HARBORD, ARE YOU HERE? *WILL YOU MARRY ME?*' She was just a few feet away and against roars of male laughter, was trying to get out of the crowd. He followed her. She wouldn't speak to him, even though he was insisting: *he did really mean it* – all the way on the bus, till they got to his brother's house, where he would be staying. 'Please Edie, you're the one. I want to marry you.'

She agreed to come in just for a moment. She had something to tell him. She would just say it, then go.

'Say what?'

'About Wilfred. Rosie's husband. He was killed. He was a poet. He was twenty-four. He wasn't killed by the enemy. It was just a gun that went off and he was wounded, then killed. We know this because his friend came to see Rosie, and brought his diary. You can read it. Everything he did, every day, and his hopes...'

He wanted her to stop talking. He'd only heard of Wilfred as a rabbit with long ears, who couldn't speak, let alone write poems. And if he was dead, he was dead. So were hundreds of thousands of others at the front. Only love could stop the guns, and bring sanity to the world. And he was discovering the power of that love now, for the first time, as he held Edith to stop her crying. She was saying, through her tears, that she supposed he would now want Rosie to marry him and she would, most definitely, not because she loved him – she only ever loved Wilfred – but because she needed him to help her, and be a father to little David... She was sobbing now, choking on the words, and he was holding her, looking into her face which was fuller and softer than Rosie's ever was, in fact more like a rose, with the sweet scent of a tea-rose. He said: 'Edie...' She stopped speaking. He folded her in his arms, felt her heart beating against his, and filling his own emptiness, as his lips touched her closing eyes.

They were married on his next leave. Peace broke out. He was demobbed. She had a child and they moved to South Queensferry. She had two more children, then moved to Whitby then York, where a fourth child was born. She was a working vicar's wife, running the local Mothers' Union, cleaning brasses, teaching Sunday School and bringing up four children in gaslit, uncarpeted vicarages and rectories, then seeing her daughters married and having children of their own, and relaxing into grandmotherhood: bosomy, with twinkling eyes, a how-do-you-do chin and a ready, wheezy laugh, sitting solidly in front of the fire, feet firmly planted, knees apart.

*

My father came to Burton Agnes and we left straight away: Elizabeth and Judith in the back; me in the front because I might be sick. We sang Grandpa's song which he used sing, galloping round the rectory with Judith on his shoulders:

> *... All the girls declare*
> *that I'm a gay old stager!*
> *Bumpety-bumpety-bumpety-bump,*
> *here comes the Galloping Major!*

We drive through Driffield, York, Doncaster, down through Derby, Burton, Lichfield, the girls asleep, my father at the wheel, excited, as he starts to thread through the complexity of suburbs, the hugeness of Birmingham; no more wide flat farmland and lonely cottages. Here people are living twenty thousand to the square mile and he is plunging in amongst them. God is guiding the wheel – he hasn't got lost once! – as he turns out of Sutton Coldfield, onto Kingstanding Road.

The house is tiny, crowded with bulky furniture: a between-the-wars semi, high up in a ten-mile long line of similar semis, broken up with bombsites. We will live here for at least a year, technically outside the parish, while the new Vicarage is being built. Kingstanding Road is the boundary between *us*, the privately owned, three-up-two-downers, and *them*, the ten thousand council-housed young working families who will be my father's flock. The parish is designed like a clockface, with radial roads linked by crescents, all bearing the names of London districts: Finchley, Peckham, Caversham, Carshalton, Hornsey, Hurlingham... and in the centre, St Luke's Church, brown-brick, with a one-bell tower: the living heart of Kingstanding.

But this isn't to be my home, so I mustn't get used to it. I had thought, after the Choir School Disaster, that I would go to a day school, like my sisters. But Ashby had other plans. If he is to *'keep his head ... meet with Triumph and Disaster... talk with crowds and walk with kings...'*, then the boy must board, and if he wasn't to go to Repton – Ma never forgot Rob's agony under Dr Fisher – then there was a school at Leatherhead in Surrey, where the sons of the Vicar of Ashby were to go, which gave bursaries to clergy; and there was a preparatory school in Buckinghamshire with a clerical head who likewise favoured clergy boys, which would take the boy at seven. All balance of fees, cost of uniform, books and any extras would be met (with a wink from behind the bottle-end specs), from Ma's personal account. Then, who knows, maybe Master Crane would go up to Cambridge to study law, with a view to taking his place, in the absence as yet of any male issue from either Arch or Girl, as the Rightful Heir to Crane & Walton.

I sometimes dream that I'm walking with Judith down the grassy slope to Kingstanding Road. The black clouds have descended and we're slipping and skidding down the slope in a thick fog. We can hardly see the road, just the blur of distant head-lights gliding towards us and disappearing. We come down to the kerb and wait as if at the sludgy edge of the River Styx. On one side is the past, the known place where we live *pro tem*, where our furniture, books and toys remain. And on the other side is the future: the new house soon to be built; Peckham Road School, St Luke's Church; hundreds, even thousands of children of all ages; the swimming pool, the cinema, the library, the shops, and our parents at the heart of it. That's the future for Judith, and I have to see her safely across the river of death, so she can live. We're holding hands in the fog. We look, listen, do '*eyes right, eyes left... der di der... quick march*' . Then we walk across the water and she joins Jane Nicholls. That's the last I see of her.

And I step off the kerb, out of the future into the present, and the roaring, tiger-coloured bus is towering over me. I smell the oil and scorched rubber, feel the heat, hear the shrieks. I'm going down under the wheels, through the mangle, into the tar. And then everything goes black.

Scene Two
INTO SPACE...

The journey if one went via Meriden – geographically the *omphalos* or 'tummy-button' of England – was seventy-eight miles, and this, my father calculated, would take just over two hours; so we should aim, he tapped his watch, to leave at one o'clock, after a quick lunch, allowing say, an hour or so for stoppages. The tuck-box and grip should fit neatly in the boot; the trunk could be either lashed on the roof-rack, or if it looked like rain (which it did), laid across the back seat. But hang on, where would Witty then go, except bumping along in the front, on Mummy's lap, eh Wit? (I wished he wouldn't call me that.)

My mother was wearing a new blouse and skirt with a navy jacket, her hair permed and slotted into a new felt hat. Her face was pinky-white, with a gash of lipstick. 'One must make an impression,' she had said, urging my father to wear his dog-collar and a cassock. It was awkward on her lap. She couldn't hug me because of the jacket. She couldn't kiss me because of the gash. But, sensibly, I was less likely to be sick in the front. Did I want the window open? 'He'll say if he does,' said my mother.

Castle Bromwich, Coleshill, Coventry, Daventry... we were copying the journey we had made in the Easter holidays. It had been jolly on that occasion because nothing was yet fixed. We had been shown round the school, then my parents had had tea with Mr and Mrs Flynn, while I took my orangeade into the library to do the Test. I finished it in ten minutes and got ten out of ten. Then Mr Flynn asked me questions. What sports did I prefer? I said I enjoyed the egg-and-spoon race and I quite liked the three-legged race, but only if one was paired with a partner one's own size. Mr Flynn had a purply, spongey face, which squeezed when he laughed, till it was running with tears, and thick beefsteak hands with which he slapped his legs twice, and then mine, locking his hand on my bare thigh, and saying: 'Horse-bite! *Grus Grunculus*, (Crane, Little Crane) does he like a horse-bite?' I said: 'No sir! He does *not* like a horse-bite!'

I could feel her heart beating. My own was still. No one had said anything about the bus. I just didn't leap up the next morning when the clock struck eight. Judith said: 'But why isn't Witty...?' as Mother, pulling her coat on, was bustling her through the hall. Elizabeth had left, as she always did, at twenty to eight. My father walked her to the bus; he said he had to go into town, so might as well go with her. Elizabeth and I had done the journey on our own, all through the spring and summer terms, taking one bus to Corporation Street, then another to Five Ways, where we did '*Eyes right, eyes left...*' then skipped all the way down Calthorpe Road to Edgbaston Church of England College for Girls which for just two terms, had agreed to take one boy. I remember the journey but very little about the College. The journeys were the education. Birmingham was booming; rationing was ending: the Bull Ring piled high with fruit and flowers and chickens and bananas; black people from Jamaica, Chinese from Hong Kong; trams phasing out, being replaced by towering, tiger-coloured buses.

Years later, my mother told me, the driver had called round, in the evening, after I was in bed. He had been ushered into the front room, had affirmed that what had happened, or nearly happened, that morning, would live with him for ever. He said he had children of his own, one of whom had polio, and he would never allow any of them, able or lame, to cross a main road unattended. He had been thinking he would have to report the incident to his superiors who would then inform the police. But he didn't like to do this. He wasn't a church-going man; all the same he did believe in charity: that a parent should be willing to pay the price of a child's life, to help another less fortunate and (he winked) let sleeping coppers lie...

It was getting dark.

'Let us pray,' said my father, dropping to his knees. My mother, glancing at the driver, also knelt.

'Almighty God,' said my father, 'you have shown that the life of a child is beyond price...'

'Jesus...' said the driver.

*

We didn't stop at Meriden. We had to press on. The car was straining under my mother's depression. I could sense her wishing she'd stayed behind and done the things she always did when the 'blues' came on: cleaning brass and silver, washing shelves and skirting, and wishing Bee would go away. She called him Bee, short for Bob, never Rob, which was his Ashby name. She felt Ashby was like a web, which clung to him whenever he went there. He often went on his own – 'Go then! Go to your mother!' – and when he returned, she had to brush the 'Ashby' off his clothes. She herself didn't *dislike* going to Ashby. She liked the comfort, the sleepiness, the ambling pace of Sarah doing the housework and Harper doing the garden. She liked Pa being gracious to her and Ma being overwhelmingly kind, in her bed of pillows. These were blessings, but they always cloyed after a few days and she longed to be home again.

'When we get a new car I will have driving lessons', she says suddenly. She distrusts a father setting off with his son, like Abraham making Isaac carry the firewood up the mountain. I'm hoping she won't say: 'Turn around! We're not going! *My* parents would never do this!' But she bites her lip. It's a Twidle trait, not to express rage but to sink it deep into the silt of the river-bed. Like the piers of the Forth Bridge, NOWELL CHAMBERLAIN HARBORD galumphs unchallenged across the raging Firth. Though no one uses her names, they stand riveted, rust-red: guarantors of her slight frame. To the world, she is Nan, having been Nanny to Little Bob, the baby brother who bobbed up when she was eleven, to be her nurseling. He remembers her playing Owl to his Christopher Robin in the Hundred Acre Wood; deaf in one ear (from a childhood accident), which she 'turns' to whatever she does not wish to hear; being wise and strict, and witty and cross.

My father is humming. The next town is Towcester. We could stop here and 'have some toast' but no one responds. We drive on to Stony Stratford. Here, he tells us, is a tower without a church, standing alone among the graves, on one of which, he laughs, is a very *grave* epitaph (if he remembers it correctly):

> 'Here lies a body who did no good,
> and if it had lived, it never would;
> where it has gone and how it fares.
> nobody knows and nobody cares.'

We plough on to the village of Nash, where there is a little church, probably locked. 'Nash,' says my father, 'where you *gnash your teeth* as you drive on through.' The sky is clouding over. The sun disappears. The whole landscape is grey. My mother opens the window: 'He's feeling sick,' meaning *she* is sickened. In the time since coming to Birmingham, instead of new life springing up through new soil, the buds have been nipped: first the King dying, younger than her own father; then a month later, the telephone-call saying Maureen's squadron leader husband has been killed in a plane-crash, leaving her pregnant with her third. And the pall persists: work on building the new vicarage delayed; no coronation till next year, the Queen traipsing uncrowned round the tottering empire while the world falls to pieces. 'I'm fed up with this *wretched* business in Korea,' she mutters behind the *Telegraph*; then Maureen having her baby, not wanting help when it was offered, then *wanting* it when it was no longer convenient.

She knows now why she came today; why she doesn't want to break the journey. If she were Sarah, wife of Abraham, she would tell the angel *his ram is not needed*. What God wants, God gets, and here the boy is, like a dead thing: we're handing him over. This stiff creature on my lap in its outsize clothes, must be deposited out of reach. I will write to him of course, we will start a lifelong correspondence, but I will never again cut his nails, wipe his nose, kiss away his tears.

And now we're passing through the picture-book village of Little Horwood, except it isn't pretty any more. The rose-trellised cottages, the pond with its ducks, are twee beyond words, bleached out, like a plague village. Last time we stopped here, we picnicked on the green, then looked in the church and admired the recently uncovered, pre-Reformation fresco of Christ Resurgent. Now we chunter straight through. We're an hour and a half early.

I can feel her heart. I can enter her mind. A memory flashes through: how once upon a time Robert Crane came to Acomb. Two teenage girls are peeping through the banisters as the curate steps out of the rain: the giggling, the blushing, the dreaming, the despairing: how everyone says, if there is to be a wedding, then the older girl should be preferred. Then one day, on the bus coming home from school, she sees him at the bus-stop; he gets on and without realising, plonks himself beside her! They laugh so much, she could die, and what bliss that would be, because never again could she be so happy! He says: 'Let's get off at the churchyard. I want to ask you something'. But they get off a stop too early, still giggling, almost running. They stop by the railway. She says: 'I can't wait till the churchyard. Ask me now.' She looks up at him. He isn't laughing any more. His once neatly combed hair is all over the place. His lips part, as if about to cry. Then a train thunders past, plunging headlong into the future, drowning his words. She thinks: he is dumb, I am deaf; we are made for each other.

We've reached the lodge. The triangular white wooden sign says:

THE OLD RIDE
Preparatory School for Boys

She remembers it now, but this time it also reminds her of a photograph, published after the war while Bee was still away. She feels her blood freeze and her hands grip the child so tight she can feel his bones: just a lodge, brick-built, slate-roofed, with neat, two-storey accommodation either side. But blink and there's a tower on top, extensions either side, and a railway running through, along which, so it said under the photo, trucks carried daily consignments of the Children of Abraham, streaming to their deaths.

THE OLD RIDE

The house looms towards you as you pass under the lodge and motor down the straight avenue of lime trees. It looks Jacobean with its steeply gabled roof, leaded windows and tall chimneys. Shadowy, being north-facing, and covered in creeper, it has an ominous air. Maybe once long ago, it was the seat of an earl who fell on hard times, was murdered and still stalks the panelled corridors, his legend kept simmering by Mr Flynn, who with his leaky face and spongiform hands, would seem to be a feature of the building.

But it's all a hoax as any detective will tell you, pointing up at the date embossed in the guttering: 1911. The house is not even Edwardian, hardly forty years old. It was built by the pork and bacon king F A Denny, as his country seat. First he knocked down the existing old house which *was* Jacobean, then instructed Cubitts the builders to create a replica of a mansion he admired in the west country, using antique bricks imported from Holland, and some of the fireplaces and panelling from the old house. And how well it worked! Horwood House, as it then was, became instantly historic, even haunted, by the owner of the original house, Colonel Daucy, whose health had crumbled along with his ancient home.

You click open the studded oak door and enter a chill flagged hallway unwarmed by the sulky log fire in the inglenook, attended by exhausted tapestried sofas; frosty landscapes and pale portraits on the high panelled walls.

We're too early for my luggage to be taken up to the matrons, so the hunch-back maid with the crooked smile and huge hands, who let us in, says: 'Leave it by the door'. We stand in the hall, waiting for someone in authority, to rebuke us for our bad timing. My father smiles and hums. 'Don't hum,' says my mother. 'There are three things we can do,' says my father. 'Let's wait,' says my mother. 'We can go away and come back later. We can shout "Cooee! Anyone home?" Or we can –' '*Wait*,' repeats Mother. There's a black-and-white liquorice-all-sort thing sticking out of a brass plate on the wall. 'Don't fiddle Witty,' says my mother. 'It's a light switch,' says my father. I push it in, a light comes on, a bulb pops and it's dark again. 'Witty!' hisses my mother. '*Never*,' I hiss back, 'call me that again! I'm not yours to be called *anything*! You've delivered me. Why can't you *go*?' And the 'veil of tears' crashes down, cutting off all sense, so I don't see the lady in white coming down the sweep of stairs in the second half of the hall, carrying a tray stacked with cups. 'Hello!' says my father. 'What do we do with a new boy?' The lady squints at my face. 'What's his name?' 'Crane,' says my mother. 'Come with me then, Crane,' says the lady. 'Do your parents want to come too?' 'No,' says my voice, from behind the veil.

We set off through a narrow passage, down a short steep flight, along a scrubbed corridor into a back hall. 'Wait here,' says the lady and disappears through a swing door into a clanking kitchen. I wait, looking up at names of scholars going back to 1937, inscribed high up on the wall. Then I go for a wander. If the school was a body, I've come in through the mouth, been golloped down the gullet into the stomach which is this hall, and now I'm swilling through intestinal passages, past doors into formrooms, with rows of single desks with seats attached, like sledges. Then I turn right and enter a big room with an army of orderly double desks: six rows of five equals thirty, times two equals sixty, and a row of twelve chairs down the side without desks, equals seventy-two total, and a tall desk in the front with its own tall chair. If the school is a body, this room is the bowel; it smells of bleach, as I walk through to a door, into a lobby, and through another door, where there is a row of six lavatories with doors but no locks and a trench for a urinal. I go back through the lobby, through another door and I'm outside. To the left is an orchard. Straight ahead is a track leading to a low, windowless brick building. I start to walk down the track but there's a child coming towards me, a small boy in blazer and shorts, smaller than me. He stops. He's staring at me with fierce little eyes. I turn back, walk away, through an arch into a stable yard, which has split stable-doors leading into formrooms with sledge-desks. The roofs are thatched and there's a bell under an arch on a wheel with a rope which I pull but it doesn't move.

I know he's behind me but I don't turn. I walk on through another arch and I'm in the forecourt again. And the first thing I notice is the Hillman isn't there. They've gone. They might crash and I never said good-bye. They might not crash, not talk, not stop at churches, all the way home, like returning from a funeral.

'What nation are you in?' says a fierce little voice behind me.

I glance round. He's there, in his long shorts and outsize burgundy blazer like me, and a cap down to his eyes.

'What do you mean "nation"? I'm British.'

'I'm a Spartan,' he says. 'My father is Master of the Spartans. The Master of the Britons is Mr Brooks. The Master of the Vikings is Mr Horne. The Master of the Trojans is Mr Wheeler. How old are you?'

'Seven years, nine months.'

'I'm six. I'm the youngest in the school.'

There's something unpleasant about the frown, the piercing eyes, the lips pulled back over jutting teeth, as he spits the words.

'What form are you in? I'm in Form One with Mrs Watt. In Form Two you have Mr Horne. In Form Three you have Mr Lawson and Mr Wheeler. In Form Four A, you have my father. He was wounded in the war. He's half blind and slightly crippled *but you must not mention this*. What's your name?'

'Crane.'

'My name is Susan.'

She pulls her lip over her teeth in a kind of smile, then goes rummaging among the conkers under a group of trees. If she's being George in the Famous Five, then I'm Dick and I don't like her.

There's a large car coming through the lodge at the far end of the drive and another one behind it. I'm not ready to meet people. I click the latch on a small door in the garden wall and slip through. 'You can't go in there,' says Susan.

It's peaceful and damp, smells sweet; there's a bird singing. There are beds thick with flowers and a blast of late sun from the south side of the house. Straight ahead is a high yew hedge clipped square like a castle wall with turrets. I enter and all sound dies; air chills, light fades. There is flagged paving round a rectangular pond, with curved ends. The surface is tangled with lily leaves, and roots like wiring. I walk round the edge and leave through the exit at the far end, onto a broad close-cut lawn, overshadowed by a cedar tree. In the centre, too old to stand, is a basket-shaped Spanish chestnut, with a mass of nuts on the ground. I cross the lawn to a gate leading down to a sunken garden, and there's a pond in there and greenhouses. I walk past, to the very edge, where the lawn ends with a sudden drop. I am looking out across a field, beyond which are long grass and bushes, beyond which is a wood, beyond which I can see the plume of smoke from a train, like a boundary between earth and sky.

I know I'm being watched; being wondered at for my trespassing. She mustn't know that I know she's watching, storing the evidence. But the watcher, the silent approacher, is not her. I'm standing on the haha's edge, as if on a stage, and there's a presence looming behind me. I'm daring to perform from the forbidden platform of the designed garden, to the gentle wildness of the open field, and a dark shadow is rising behind me.

TOBY FLYNN

... was born in Cornwall, 1885, his Romano-British forebears once lords of Britannia, pushed to the margins by invaders. Now in the dawn of the twentieth century, like an Arthurian holy man set to return, or an old oak, rising out of the mists of legend, he uproots himself, fungoids and all, and heads east, via Harrow School and Corpus Christi Oxford, till he comes to Brighton. Here, as a young priest he joins the staff of William Rodgers Dawson, the new head of Brighton College, the 'new broom' appointed to sweep the College out of penury. No scholar, Dawson knows every boy by name, takes the top and the bottom forms once a week for an Open Lesson on 'everything under the sun'. In the holidays he travels the country, stopping parents with boys and selling them the Greatest College in All Britain. Within three years, recruitment has doubled and Brighton College is in the black.

Toby Flynn is his disciple, a Peter to Dawson's table-turning Christ. Where Dawson is mercurial, Flynn is solid. Where Dawson leads from the front, Flynn chivvies up the rear. We're in the Age of Heroes and Toby's heart is on fire. Enid, Dawson's daughter, though fifteen years his junior, has fixed him with her eye, and this spurs him, when war breaks, to enlist in the Royal Horse and Field Artillery. He watches her grow through the war years: neither tall nor slim – a cad would say 'dumpy' – with jutting teeth and wild hair. But she loves him and he thinks he could love her when she is older. He writes to her from Flanders, keeping hopes high for victory, but the carnage is seeping into his skin, his face reddening as if flayed. When he comes home, he still doggedly believes in the old values. An Asquithian Liberal, 'wait and see' is his maxim, even now when name after name of cherished boys is listed among the fallen, and 'squiffy' is his too frequent state, to ease the pain. But Enid is there to fix him with her eye and pour the whisky down the sink. They marry quietly in 1920.

They dig in their heels as the world is changing. A lethal cocktail of atheism and hedonism is undermining the College. Enid's father has a stroke. He continues his maverick rule, but as a parody of his former self. Morale slips. Numbers fall. By 1933 the role at Brighton College is back to what it was in 1906. But the Flynns have moved. With their sons, Thomas and Mark, they purchase a property in Bournemouth and open a school. Based on Dawson-Flynn principles, with Enid at the helm, The Old Ride, will prepare boys not only for the best public schools, but for *life*. Like Noah's family on the Ark, they weather the gathering storm of the thirties and the deluge of the forties. Then as peace returns, and their son Thomas comes home half-blind and lame with a Military Cross, they make the move to Little Horwood. The symmetry of the house, its seeming antiquity built on modern foundations, the stables convertible into formrooms, the paddocks into playing fields, the cottage, the bluery, the lodge, the bothy, making suitable accommodation for newly demobbed masters and keen, young matrons; the whole horticultural pile, created for the Pork and Bacon King by Harry Thrower (father of Percy, the BBC gardener, who was born here); this Other Eden, demi-Paradise, self-sufficient and removed from the world, is a gift from God, as if the Flynns and The Old Ride have belonged here for ever.

IN MY BUBBLE...

I go where I like, till I'm told not to. Then if I want to, I go there again. I like the lily-pond and the sunken garden, and the lawn with the Spanish chestnut. I like to stand, with Paynter, an American boy, on the edge of the new world, looking west across the prairie, to the Bicester-Bletchley railroad; till Mr Thomas, with his caliper-boot and thick smoked glasses, comes hop-skipping up the haha, hoiking each of us under his arms like piglets: 'Lawn and pond out of bounds to squealers, on pain of cane!'

And in the long hours of light, lying in bed from six-thirty, I like to whisper to Pearce, the farmer's boy ('Have you ever strangled a chicken?

Have you seen a bull "footing" a cow?'), till Mrs Flynn pads in, in her silent pumps. She warns us the first time. There won't be a second time. And the moment she's gone, I'm whispering to Pearce: 'Did you see a chicken footing a cow?' and giggling. And she comes in again. 'Who was it? Who was talking?' 'I wasn't,' says Beardsley, across the room. 'Explain that to Mr Flynn, tomorrow,' says Mrs Flynn. Silence falls. I thicken the bubble around me, till all sound goes white. Beardsley isn't sleeping, trying to work out how to explain he wasn't talking, without talking. Mr Flynn likes puzzles – 'There is only one rule: never obey rules, including this one'. But he also likes and *needs* to beat boys, and Beardsley was born to be beaten. His father is an artist with shoulder-length hair. Once during Latin, someone said '*Mater meus...*' and Mr Flynn said: 'Who here has a masculine mother?' Someone piped up: 'Beardsley has a feminine father!' and everyone laughed. When, two years later, I was in the sick-room having nightmares, they brought Beardsley in. He'd been so beaten, he couldn't stand. His bum was bleeding. He just lay looking at the ceiling. I said: 'What did you do? What is you always do Beardsley?' He said: 'I owned up.'

✳

They put me in Form Two but I wanted to be in Form One, with Paynter, Pearce and Williamson-Noble (known as Woble); and Susan Flynn sitting at the back, like a spy. But they put me in Form Two, with boys aged nine. I sat in a sledge-desk in my bubble, by the window looking out across the yard to where Form One were singing their times-tables with Mrs Watt. I was homesick now. I was missing Judith and Elizabeth, and Sheena who had mange; and the *Eagle*. Every week, at home, the great bird in its red sky, would come winging through the letter-box, bringing Dan Dare and the Mekon, Harris Tweed and Boy, PC 49 and the Terrible Twins, and on the back page the adventures of Saul who became Paul, and John Mark, the Boy Disciple. They were the stuff of The Old Ride. They were the heart of my education. But classed as 'comics', they were banned.

At the end of break, in my space-helmet, I went wandering. I could hear my breathing and the thudding of my heart, as I crossed the yard to Form One. Mrs Watt said 'Hello stranger. I hope this is this official?' I was put on a table – there were no desks in Form One – with Pearce, Paynter and Woble, making plasticene figures: Treens in green, Venusians in blue. Then I noticed Susan wasn't there. She'd been sitting at the back, then she'd gone, leaving a chill. Moments later, she returned, sat back in her place, teeth jutting in a grin, as two Second Form boys, Maclaurin and McLauchlan, knocked, came in, conferred with Mrs Watt, then came and stood over me. Mrs Watt said 'You have to go'.

After lunch, the space-bubble, thicker than ever, wafted me to Form One again. Mrs Watt gave me a hug, and instructed me to read aloud from *Bill Badger and the Pine-Martins*. But just as I was starting, Mrs Flynn came in. She spoke over me to Mrs Watt. 'Why is the boy here? He knows he is in Form Two.' In the silence that followed, she addressed the form: 'What is the first sin?' Woble's hand shot up: 'Disobedience!' 'And the second?' 'Feebleness Granny?' offered Susan. 'Sneaking,' said Pearce. 'Is it sneaking?' 'Sneaking is second equal with feebleness,' said Mrs Flynn, looking at Susan whose head was bowed. 'Excuse me,' said Paynter, 'but why does Crane have to be in Form Two when he's only seven?' Mrs Flynn ruffled his red hair and tweaked his freckled nose, as he snuggled into her (I hated him!): 'Because Crane has a brain growing faster than his years, and *does not need reasons to obey*.' She padded back across the yard to Form Two. I followed. But the next day, after dreaming that my head had swelled to twice the size of my body, and the bubble-helmet had ballooned into the cranium of the Mekon, I found myself zooming again across the yard into Form One. *I go where I like, till I'm told not to. Then if I want to, I go there again. I am the Mekon.* Mr Flynn came in. Mrs Watt went white. I followed Mr Flynn, not to Form Two, but to the study. He shut the door, opened his cupboard. Clipped to the wall was a rack of canes, from short and swishy to knobbled and thick. He chose a middling one, tested it, put it back, chose a swishier one. '*Homuncule Gruncule*,' he said with a sigh, 'what did the Lord say to Adam when he disobeyed?' I would have said: 'I don't know sir. I am not Adam. I am the Mekon. I can destroy you.' But the Veil of Tears was gagging me. He sighed again, gestured to a greasy chair with a sunken seat. I sat in it. 'No!' He yanked me up, tried to bend me over. I sat on the floor. He tried lifting me bodily but I was curled up and screaming. I went on screaming while he stood there, his face redder and hotter and bloodier than the sun.

I got up as, defeated, he was clipping the cane back into the cupboard. He let me walk on ahead of him, down the steps, along the corridor. Mrs Flynn was in the small hall. She smiled as we walked by; or was it just the skin of the upper-lip retracting to reveal the incisors?

I crossed the yard and went to Form One. Mr Flynn reached in front of me. Opening the door, he exchanged a glance with Mrs Watt as if to say 'Your days are numbered Boy-Hugger', and let me go in.

*

The next term, January 1953, Mrs Watt had gone. I was firmly relocated in Form Two. This was the start of my school career. I began keeping a diary, one sentence per day, with a one-word summing-up: good, middle or bad:

I scored a goal today. Bad.
Paynter got wacks today. Middle.
Queen Mary died last night. Good.

I learnt to make my bed with hospital corners. I learnt to like porridge with bemax, and prunes with junket. I learnt to appreciate Elgar and Beethoven played on the radiogram every day during lunch. I learnt in Latin: *I love, you love, he loves the table* and *the girl will kill the farmer.* I learnt to be top of the form and win a book tally every week. I learnt the Ten Commandments (Obey, Don't Sneak, Eschew Feebleness, Own Up, Play the Game, Be Prepared, Love your Country, No Bullying, No Cheating, No Talking After Lights-Out.)

There is a secret panel in the playroom. Good.
I had some of Ellington's cake today. Middle.
We went to church today and I nearly broke my Lent Rule. Bad.

Sitting next to Mr Flynn – he would queue with us, then squeeze into a different place every day, obliging us to budge up – I learnt to anticipate the horse-bite and not leap up with a yelp. In the summer term, I learnt to jump in a cold bath, jump out again, run shirtless to the lodge and back before breakfast, after which I learnt to line up in the Big School Room, till 'Place!' was called by the duty Nation Leader, and my turn came to to go to the Six to 'pass a motion', after which I learnt to wait for my name to be called by the Duty Master at the high desk, and to answer 'Yes sir!' or 'Couldn't go sir!' I learnt how to earn plusses and how to avoid minuses, and when I broke the Eleventh Commandment (Thou Shalt Not Be Found Out), how to bend over the greasy chair and take stick like a man.

Today I went with Paynter to Whipsnade Zoo. Middle.
We had a film today called 'The Marx Bros go West'. Good.
A new master came today called...

MR FRIED-EGGIE

Mr Carneggie took us for French. We gave him a bad time. He gave me a bad time. He was Scottish. Mr Flynn liked him. He lasted less than a term. That is all I know about Mr Fried-Eggie.

But in the long, light nights, I imagined his story: how he fought alongside Toby in the trenches, suffered shell-shock and was sent home; how in the Second World War, as an air-raid warden, dragging bodies from bombed buildings, he had suffered nightmares and neurasthenia. 'Those who can, do;

those who can't, teach,' as the saying goes; so he applied for the job of French teacher at The Old Ride. 'Don't take him,' said Enid. But Toby, believing Dawson-Flynn principles may turn even a shell-shocked wreck, defied her and took him on.

He did talk to me once. It was his worst teaching day. Amid cat-calls and the hail of chalk, I crept up to the blackboard and scrawled: 'FRIED-EGGIE IS A DREGGIE', then ran back to my desk slamming the line of raised desk-lids, like machine-gun fire. When the bell went and everyone ran, I stayed behind, to wipe the board before Mr Flynn came by. The Egg was sunk at his desk, head in hands, and I thought he hadn't seen, but when I turned, he was standing over me. He grasped my shoulders. I thought he was going to cry, but his voice, when he spoke, was measured.:

'Boy...'

'Sir?'

'What will you be when you grow up?'

'I don't know sir.'

'A general, a bishop, a judge?'

'Do I have to choose now sir?'

He stooped till his face was inches from mine: 'You will be none of these things. You will make no mark. You are a fool who will fool no one. You may think you're ahead of the field, but they're sheltering behind you, exposing you to the guns. You may have dreams of happiness but when the moment comes, you will dry up, go blank. You don't believe me? Look at me. *I am you grown old.* Alive or dead, what's the difference? When the earth opens and swallows you, what will remain?'

I was looking at the yellow eyes – up-and-over, not sunny-side-up, as Paynter would say – and they were watery at the edges. I thought he was going to soften and there was a flicker in the crow's feet, as if he was about to say: 'and yet...' or 'if only...' But he went silent. Then I saw him raise his hand and I thought he was going to redeem all with a touch of my cheek and was just closing my eyes and feeling the tears come, when a stinging smack on my ear sent me crashing into the blackboard.

At supper, Mr Flynn announced that Mr Carneggie had left, and that Mr Lawson and Mr Thomas would be sharing the French teaching until a new appointment could be made. No one asked about my red-hot ear, and I wasn't going to sneak. The horrid creature had gone. The Fried-Eggie had been flipped out of the frying-pan into the fire, and I had some imagining to do.

*

He lugs his broken revelation, held closed with a length of cord, the half mile up the drive. He turns right out of the lodge along the winding road, towards the bridge, humping the case all the way to the station. There's no one there, no office to buy a ticket from. He waits on the platform for the train to Bletchley which is empty. He changes trains for Birmingham, then gets the last train to Edinburgh. No one asks for his ticket. No one acknowledges his existence. He still has the key to the flat of the friend who once let him stay. The train pulls into Edinburgh just before midnight. It's raining. There are no buses. He walks to the old tenement building in Guthrie Street. No one answers when he knocks on the door of the top-floor flat; finds the key won't fit, and he's glad in a way. This has helped him decide. He unties the cord from his case, ties one end of it to the light-fitting in the ceiling which seems strong enough, and makes a rough noose with the other end; wriggles his neck into it, but when he jumps, the fitting gives way and he falls forty feet into the well.

NIGHTMARE

Most Saturdays in the winter and spring terms, Mr Wheeler and Mr Lawson showed films in the library. The big table was pushed aside, chairs laid out in rows, and blankets spread out in front for the young'uns. If you were in Form One, you had to go to bed after half an hour; in Form Two, after an hour. Only from Form Three onwards were you likely to see the whole film. So I never saw beyond the first reel of *The Scarlet Pimpernel*, or beyond Harpo playing the harp in *The Marx Brothers Go West*, or beyond Paul Robeson singing 'Ay-ee-o-po, ay-ee-o-po...' in *Saunders of the River*.

One Saturday, when I was ten and in Form IVB, we were due to see *The Four Feathers*, but as it was a long film, we were to have the first two reels one week and the second two the next. When we were all assembled and ready to go, on the first Saturday, Mr Wheeler discovered that they'd sent the wrong reels, but it was too late to return them, so we went ahead anyway, straight into the full heat of the Sahara: Ralph Richardson staring into the merciless sun as he lures the Khalifa's army away from Omdurman. He raises his field-glasses straight into the magnified disc, which blinds him, sends him staggering towards the camera, his sightless eyes staring through you, *as if you were to blame for even watching*. And that was the beginning of a week of nightmares. As soon as my eyes closed, I'd see Richardson bearing down on me. I didn't know the story, so it was personal between him and me. His eyes were frying in the sun till they blistered, and though he couldn't see me, I could never get away. My feet dragged in the sand, and whenever I turned, there he was, coming closer, arms reaching out. I was afraid to shut my eyes and would try to stay awake the whole night. But always, he came, even when I thought I wasn't asleep. One night, with supreme effort, I managed to drag my feet out of the sand and walk across the dorm, out of the door, down the passage to the sitting-room, where Head Matron was at her desk, checking laundry lists. I said: 'It's the war. I should have warned you...' She turned to look at me, horrified. I stared but couldn't speak. She got up, gently took my hand and led me still asleep back to the dorm and my ruffled bed. The next day, I was moved to the sick-room, where I stayed for four more days, doing puzzles from *Hello Puzzlers* and reading *Man-Eaters of Kumaon*. So I never did see the first two reels of *The Four Feathers* but Woble told me it was about cowardice.

'HUMAN GROWTH'

School was home and home was holiday, relief surging in like a tide when I came back to Birmingham. I was acting being me; they were acting not noticing, pretending I belonged. It meant I never had the clashes my sisters had with my mother, and I didn't have to seek physical affection from my father. If school was the main drama, home was a *divertissement* between the acts, with real plays beginning to put theatre in the blood. Every December we went to the Christmas play at the Rep, featuring rising classical actors: *Beauty and the Beast* with Derek Jacobi; Ian Richardson as First Thief in *The Royal Astrologers*; Albert Finney as Bamboo the Fisherman in *The Imperial Nightingale*. Albert was 'our lad'. Down from the north like us, we knew he would be famous; he didn't have to put on an 'acting voice', scorned snobbery, had the devil in him. And soon he was playing Macbeth and Henry V, going to Stratford as Cassio to Paul Robeson's Othello, and replacing Laurence Olivier as Coriolanus. Elizabeth had a crush on him. She was nearly thirteen and had been given a book by our parents called *Human Growth*. Every time I came home she was moodier, womanlier, and I learnt not to comment on the bloody pads in the bin. Once she summoned me into the bathroom. Naked among the bubbles, she said: 'Behold a slender bare lady!' She had friends who had boyfriends and one who had a friend who was as old as her own father, who had said to her when they were alone: 'Come here my darling', and she went to him and he crushed her in his arms and pressed his rough, whiskery lips on hers.

Judith was growing too, keeping pace and overtaking me in height and weight, still my 'Terrible Twin', playing rough on the wasteland. But we were less terrible now, less like twins, and there was less call for tramping the wasteland, since Sheena, the mangey scottie, was dead. We were moving anyway, crossing the road, to where kids played in the street, and we were not to join in. As children of the Vicarage, we could be gracious, even friendly, but shouldn't get involved; should avoid adopting the brummie accent, except for amusement at home. We were the prime Christian family, the heart-beat of the parish. We sang in the choir and in the bus on parish outings. We sold raffle tickets at socials, served tea at beetle drives, sorted, priced and purloined jumble for jumble sales. (I got a top hat, white tie and tails, a cricket bat and full sets of Hardy and H G Wells). Then most days we went over to the Caversham Road site to observe the new Vicarage as it rose, like a consort beside the church. It was our place. It had our names in it. We sealed them in bottles with our ages and a message, then had them bricked into the wall, for discovery in a thousand years.

Only my mother didn't seem to change. We wrote to each other every week so the changes were gradual. I hardly noticed, for instance, when she became pregnant again. She didn't mention it, except obliquely: that she was resting in the afternoons, cutting down on parish meetings, brass cleaning and services, and delaying taking driving lessons, even though we had now swapped the old blue Hillman for a brown Bedford van.

Monica was born on Shakespeare's birthday 1954. I had prayed for a brother. I had wished with every wish-bone that it wouldn't be a girl. If there were to be six in the family, it had to be three against three, especially as my father was professionally *hors de combat*, and I was mostly away. But more than that, I didn't like the physiognomy of girls or their habits. The whole Terrible Twins thing was a effort, to turn Judith into a boy, not like Susan Flynn (who had now left the school anyway), but a *real* boy who could fight with fists and not pull hair. So when Monica arrived, it was like a snub from God. The rancour needled into me, so that everything the new baby did was an annoyance. I wasn't home that often, so to have the cot permanently in *my* room, even in the new house, was an insult. The crying, the having to appease the little imp who would go purple with rage, was intolerable. I was trying to read *Pickwick Papers* which someone had given me and that was punishment enough. The rancour went in so deep, it would be years before I could accept Monica on anything like equal terms. I used to practise horror movie techniques, creeping up on her, as a swivel-eyed, dribbling zombie, and when she screamed, I went normal, and when she stopped, I went zombie, switching on, switching off. That's what I remember, but there are photos of me holding her and rocking her and loving her; which you will say was 'acting', and it was, except acting, when your ghosthood depends on it, *has to be truth*, so it was true, absolutely. I was good, I was bad. I was there, I wasn't there. There are no wholly bad people or wholly good people. Not even Jesus was completely good. Read the Bible, those bits that are usually glossed over, where he loses it: 'If anyone does not *hate* his father and mother, his wife and children etc, and does not *hate his WHOLE LIFE*, then he cannot be my disciple'. Luke 14, 26…

'Whosoever offends one of these little ones... *hang a millstone round his neck and drown him in the sea...*' Matthew 18, 6 (a bit steep I thought, even for Archbishop Fisher and the Flynns)... '*ELOI ELOI LAMA SABACHTHANI?*' Matt 27, 46. And do you wonder? But I liked all that. It showed Christ as a human being, at odds with his father. It allowed me in those days to sing my heart out as a believer, and do bad things as well. My Christ was not gentle, meek and mild; he had Satan at his shoulder, was left to get on with it by his Pa who abandoned him, although he loved him. So even God had goodness and badness in his Being, which confused me, because my image then of the Father we prayed to, was my own father, who more than any priest I ever heard, could speak the liturgy both publicly and intimately, without a trace of performance. His tone was vulnerable and authoritative, compassionate and stern, stubborn and open to change. I longed to serve him at the altar, and receive the Host from his hands. But even as I tasted it and sipped the wine from the cup, I knew the God image was shifting, as it had to, towards the more Old Testament style of Mr Flynn who was capricious and, ultimately, senile. If I could survive his (and Mrs Flynn's) domination, having learnt survival like a jungle animal, then I'd be able to return, as an adult, to the comfort of my own father (and mother). But there was a long way to go yet.

*

In 1955, we went to the YMCA Lowestoft for our summer holiday. I'd just had the plaster removed from my arm, which I'd fractured falling in the high jump at school. The sun was blazing, the sea was blue and I now had two arms, which could cut through the waves. No one taught me to swim. Like Jesus walking on the water, I just did it. Then in the evenings, there were barn dances, films, housey-housey and talent shows. On our last night Judith and I did a comedy routine, and I sang *O For the Wings of a Dove*. My prize for Best Song was *The Lion, The Witch and the Wardrobe* by C S Lewis. I read it in a day; then, as soon as I could get hold of them, all the other Narnia books, in an avalanche of reading. This was my world. Every time I went through the arch of the lodge, at the beginning of term, I was entering a different time-frame, another kingdom, which even though founded on prayers and the Bible and ruled by a clergyman, was largely free of the Christian message. Redemption was not offered because our Aslan was *married* to the White Witch and together they had woven Good and Evil into a sail that blew with the wind. This made our adventures far more dangerous than any fiction, there being laws applied on a sliding scale of brutality, but no absolute standard. And this term, going up into Form Five, I would learn what lay beyond those flailing laws. The Fifth and Sixth forms were permitted, on Sundays, to go down to the woods. Here by tradition, no masters would go. There were camps in the trees with rope-swings, booby traps and pea-shoot patrols. Then if you went down deeper into 'Dago' and beyond, you'd find laws and loyalties decomposing into savagery, sexual acts and human sacrifice. (A boy was once rumoured, before my time, to have been tied to the railway and to have had his feet severed by a train.)

But I was ready for anything now. If there was a turning-point at TOR, this surely was it. I could swim, I could sing, I could win prizes. This was my future. And there, as if he'd dropped out of a clear blue sky, was the man to make it happen.

MR LUDO

… was black. He was Spanish. He taught music and geography. He played the piano like Fats Domino. His stubby fingers raced across the keys like rabbits, and he chuckled as he sang. Replacing Mr Lawson as chooser of records, DENZIL S. LUDOWYK sneaked jazz into the repertoire of music to eat meat by, and even the Flynns were amused as table by table clattered cutlery in rhythm. Opportunities rolled out before Mr Ludo like a banquet. A new Big School Room had been created during the summer holidays, through the removal of a wall and the roofing over of a yard, and a theatre-owning mother had donated swags of burgundy-coloured drapes for the new stage, and a tapestry-making mother has embroidered *TOR* in giant golden cursive capitals at either end of the velvet pelmet.

All was in place, and ready for Ludo to rise like a rocket and light up my sky, then vanish in a fizzle of sparks.

He was a star without trying. His tales were tall as trees. He had produced operas in Germany, played in jazz bands in Italy, given organ recitals in cathedrals across Spain. He wasn't boasting, just 'happening to mention' as his hands travelled the keyboard. He taught me piano twice a week and at the end of each lesson, I would sing and he would play, as Milson used to do, only richer, gutsier, stretching my range, finding the emotion that underlay a love song or a lullaby. I became chief chorister and soloist and it was understood that when it came to the Carol Service in Little Horwood church, it would be my pitch-perfect *a capella* that would be heard, unseen from the back of the nave, singing *Once in Royal David's City*. When this was given to Williamson-Noble, whose voice was weak and would crack on the high notes, I felt betrayed and when Mr Ludo came up to me, I shrugged him off. But he wasn't having that. He took my head in an arm-lock – 'Ouch sir! You're hurting!' – marched me to the music room, sat me down, said 'Learn this.'

> *Lully lullay*
> *Thou little tiny child*
> *Bye bye lully lullay...*

I thought it was a sop. There was no range in the tune. It was dreary, with no drama in it. But as we practised it, and he told me the story behind it, how it wasn't sung by Mary but by an unnamed mother in Bethlehem trying to keep her baby quiet, because there were soldiers downstairs; and as we practised the song, I found my voice filling out, enriching the semitones, leaning on the notes, like putting a hand over a child's mouth to save his life, all the time knowing that he wouldn't be saved; the soldiers would hear and come up and kill him, because the Gospel says only One Child got away. This was the underside of Christmas that I'd never considered. I knew about the Three Wise Men – I had been Frankincense in Mrs Watt's Form One Nativity Play in the same church at the end of my first term and she had allowed me to be Chinese so I could wear the dragon dressing-gown and coolie hat my father had brought back from Hong Kong. And I knew about Herod and about Mary, Joseph and the Babe fleeing to Egypt, but I had never imagined the massacre. And of course, when I stepped forward, after the lesson about Herod 'sending forth and slaying all the children of two years and under', read by Susan Flynn, back just for the service in her schoolgirl uniform, as if it was the jolliest thing; when I stood centre on the chancel step, the eyes of all on me, and I started singing the low lullaby words, with no accompaniment, they knew something was wrong; this wasn't a happy story; there was darkness at the heart of Christmas.

I was sick on the journey home. It wasn't the usual car-sickness. It lasted on and off all over the holiday. I tried to eat Christmas dinner, then brought it all up again. The doctor said I shouldn't go back to school, and it was two weeks into the term before I was well again. As we passed through the arch of the lodge into Narnia, snow feathering down and covering the earth in quilted silence, I felt gloriously sad: weakened from sickness, but resolute in the new dawn of 1956, like a prince coming home, to assume his inheritance.

*

Ju Ju is eighteen. Her father, Emperor Hokipokitipitoptop, has planned a festival in her honour. A wisewoman has foretold that a Prince will come to claim her as his bride. But when O Shee Ma Guin arrives with his companions Fu Shu and Go Bang, disguised as a beggar minstrels, having been robbed by bandits of all their jewels and documents, they are immediately arrested, as murderers of the true prince, and condemned to be executed. But Ju Ju has fallen in love with O Shee, which proves, she sings, that he *is* the true prince. Defiant, she slips out of the castle in disguise, into the woods, at the dead of night. She cries out to the moon, as she makes her way to the hovel of Abud Hiram the magician who alone can help...

> *A little Jap's heart is breaking*
> *and all for a lover true.*
> *The day that awoke so gaily*
> *has turned to bitter rue.*
> *The sun which arose so brightly*
> *has turned to shadow grey.*
> *The moon over a weeping maiden*
> *now casts a pitying ray...*

I went straight into rehearsal as soon as I arrived, just as Mr Ludo was giving the part of Ju Ju to Woble. It was like the third act of the play, where I burst in singing – *Ah stay your hand! Stay your hand!* – to the executioner whose axe is raised over the neck of the Prince. A second later, his head would have rolled and my part would have gone. Mr Ludo, beaming, said: 'Take it from the top!' and the cast broke into the opening chorus: *Welcome to the Princess Ju Ju! Welcome from her subjects true true!* Knowing nothing in advance, I didn't have to act to show Ju Ju's delight, which then transmutes into grief, defiance, persistence, nightmare, discovery and vindication. It was a complex intellectual journey. Mr Ludo drew me deep beneath the *Mikado*-ish facade into the entrails of the story. Here were stirrings of rebellion and confusions of love that you begin to be excited and disturbed by when you're eleven. Writ large in the play, they matched the enormity of the Flynns' rule at TOR: tyrannical unfairness, execution with no appeal, jubilation turning instantly to misery and fear. I now had permission to voice rebellion in public, and on a broader scale look at the justice system that continued to send innocent people to their deaths: Timothy Evans in 1950, and more recently Derek Bentley. This latter case had become a feature of my new best-friendship (Paynter having returned with his family to the US) with two older boys: Michael Bentley and Nigel

Buchanan. Bentley was the son of a country squire in the Lake District. 'Knighted' by Mr Thomas as Sir Bertram Bunt, he liked to re-enact Wodehousian scenarios – I was Jeeves to his Bertie – but when it came to our namesakes Bentley and Craig (just one consonant different), we took it seriously and made a cause of it. Christopher Craig, aged sixteen, had shot a policeman, but was too young to hang. Bentley, nineteen, epileptic and feeble-minded, had said 'Let him have it Chris' meaning either 'Let him have the gun' or 'Shoot him now'. We went on re-enacting this scene long after the hanging, convinced Bentley was innocent and hanging under any circumstances, was wrong. Buchanan was the policeman who said 'Come on boy, hand it over, give me the gun', prompting Bentley's famous line; then, in the next scene, he was Lord Chief Justice Goddard, putting on the black cap. Buchanan's father was Canon Buchanan, Vicar of Chesterton, Cambridge, who loved churches and church matters, a rotund black-suited cleric straight out of Trollope. I would later go and stay with the Buchanans in Cambridge and visit all the chapels in all the colleges; and subsequently they took me, as Nigel's companion, on their summer holiday to Edinburgh, taking two days to get there, stopping at churches, abbeys and cathedrals all the way.

Neither Bunt nor Butch, as we called them, had a part in *Ju Ju.* I can't remember why, as they were both natural actors. But it was good for me to have friends who weren't caught up in the hurly-burly and were fairly grown-up about rebellion and things that went on in the woods. I had been a Vth-former now for a whole term, that is twelve Sundays, and hadn't been over-impressed with the woods. I never joined any of the camps, and whatever went on down in Dago remained a mystery. However one Sunday in February, when we had been rehearsing the scene where I fall in love with the prince, and Mr Ludo had told us to *go away and learn our lines,* O Shee Ma Guin said to me 'Let's go down to the woods.' So we changed and walked briskly, going over the lines, down to the big field, through the long grass into the woods, past the camps and down to Dago. When we had finished the lines, we walked on in silence, O Shee leading the way, down to the stream – he helped me over – and deeper down to the bamboo clumps. 'Where Toby grows his canes,' said the prince. 'Sort of Japanese,' I said. 'Bamboos, like in Japan.' He put his finger on my lips. He was tall, with soft features and a voice close to breaking. 'What if we kiss,' he said, 'in the play? When you save me. It would be the natural thing.' I said: 'I think we should just hug.' And in the crowd of canes, we undid our shorts and hugged, just for a moment, till we heard someone coming. Then we buttoned up and O Shee led the way back out of the bamboos, up past the camps, over the fence into the long grass, and onto the big field where he ran on to join his friends and I ran to join Bunt and Butch, sitting on the ha-ha.

*

Ju Ju was a triumph but it was the end of Mr Ludo. He had written in the programme: 'I have had several things to battle against... the main obstacles being shortage of time and lack of money...' and in a speech at the curtain call he had said this wonderful show, to which so many had contributed, could not have taken place without his personal subsidy; to offset which there would be buckets at the door for a silver collection. This on top of charging two shillings for the programme, sent the Flynns into a rage. But the applause was so great and the clatter and flutter of coins and notes into the buckets, so complete, they had to bottle their feelings and distil them for later lethal use, which in any case was their preferred way.

He came to stay with us in the holidays. My father had invited him to give an organ recital in St Luke's on Easter Sunday. He played a medley of Bach organ pieces, and I sang *Panis Angelicus*. Afterwards, in the vestry, as my mother was counting the Easter Offering – traditionally the parishioners' annual bonus for the Vicar – Mr Ludo made the mistake of requesting a fee. He said he was usually paid twelve to fifteen guineas, but in deference to 'Ju Ju' would settle for ten. The room went silent. My mother went on counting. My father said: 'Let us pray...' But Mr Ludo wasn't going to be bowed into 'seeking no reward save the joy etc...' He quietly left the vestry, went to talk to his departing audience, was his normal laughing self over dinner, and was away first thing in the morning. I never saw him again.

He wrote to me a few times, from Spain – 'Here I am in Toledo, invited to sing in the cathedral choir where I sang as a boy...' – then from Germany – 'Tell your father tonight I press the organ pedals once pressed by the feet of J S Bach...', but I was told not to reply. In a letter at Christmastime, he said: 'Would you care to spend two days with me in London? I could take you to the theatre and be responsible for you.' And in a different 'ghost universe', I imagined taking the train, being met at Euston by Mr Ludo: 'I will show you the world you are destined to step into!' and off we would go into the buzz of 1956 theatreland: *Look Back In Anger* at the Royal Court, *Romanoff and Juliet* at the Piccadilly, *A View From The Bridge* at the Comedy, *The Quare Fellow* at Stratford East... All these, aged eleven, I could have blinked at in wonder and stored as seeds for future growth. Diaghilev, Walter Mitty, Harris Tweed, Fats Domino, whoever he was, it was Mr Ludo who got me started. However tall his tales, I believed them and wanted more. Was he real? What became of him? Imagining, I drew a blank. I just hear his chuckle and his lightning fingers on the keys. *Ludo, ludamus*: let us play.

Scene Three
IF YOU GO DOWN...

Mrs Flynn called us to her sitting room. She had two things to say. The first was about Mr Flynn. Then she paused, just as the Old Man had taken to pausing, sometimes for ten minutes, during Scripture, which he took us for once a week. We were Sixth formers now, just the six of us, Nation Leaders and scholarship boys: Bunt, Butch, Pearce, Woble, a Greek boy called Fafalios, and me.

'You may have noticed,' she resumed, 'that Mr Flynn has been slowing down. The doctor has told us this is not a normal slowing, but a gentle slippage of the brain.' She paused again and I thought for a moment she was going to cry. 'He suffers a sequence of little strokes,' she continued, 'which each time deprive him of a small piece of his memory.'

'You mean like losing his marbles one by one?' suggested Bunt.

She continued: 'And this condition has been exacerbated by a letter we have recently received from British Railways.'

We leaned forward. What was coming? In his confusion had Old Toby failed to buy a ticket, or lost some luggage?

'They are seeking,' she went on, and there were real tears in her eyes now, but her voice was steady, 'compulsory purchase of the school and all its grounds for demolition and conversion into a marshalling yard. Everything we have built and cherished will be destroyed. There will be no appeal. The school will have to move.'

In the silence that followed, darkness fell. Mrs Flynn, her flat pumps hardly touching the ground, was growing smaller and feebler, as we were growing larger. That the scourge of the feeble should herself become feeble, seemed sad, more than just. We went back to our formroom to do our prep. We didn't speak. There was comfort in the presumption that we at least, with just one or at most two years left to run, were unlikely to be touched. But it would spell the end for old Toby and diminution to the point of disappearance for Mrs Flynn. In our formroom, the former drawing-room off the great hall in the main house, we were safe for the moment, privileged and warm, like grown-ups in a home setting, having swapped the sledge-desks and one-bar fires of the stable-yard, for radiators, a carpeted floor, separate chairs, modern desks and a view, through mullion windows, of rose-beds, yew hedge and a glimpse of lilies. And for diversion, at times of siege, there was the glass-framed book-case housing board and card games, the Children's Encyclopaedia, and two giant antique morocco-bound illustrated volumes of *Pilgrim's Progress* and *Paradise Lost*.

We were a school within a school, taught almost entirely, by three masters. Mr Stoddart (Latin and Greek) brought a context to the languages, and a voice to the people who wrote and spoke them. In Latin, we read Petronius and Pliny; learnt about Nero the boy emperor, who did so well till he murdered his mother. He was an actor who believed in government through the arts, not the military, and died at thirty, crying: '*Qualis artifex pereo!*' In Greek we read Plato's *Symposium*, about the dinner with Socrates where guests included Alcibiades and Aristophanes. Alcibiades, amoral superstar politician, led Athens to defeat, then defected to the enemy; helped Sparta win the war, then as the knives came out, defected to Persia, all-time enemy of all the Greeks, finally returning to Athens, becoming a general again and getting exiled again. This was the kind of person we were taught *not* to be, but Mr Stoddart pointed out that Churchill had also traded loyalties, as had Robert the Bruce. Then he turned to Aristophanes, the comedian, who answers the question 'Where does love come from?' with the tale of four-legged, four-armed, double-faced, cartwheeling humans, sliced down the middle by Zeus and sent searching for their 'other half'.

That is what love is. It can be male seeking male, or female seeking female, or a freakish search for a hetero-pairing. Whatever the original construct – and you won't know it till you find it – somewhere out there is the perfect match, seeking you with the same intensity as you are seeking him/her.

Mr Stoddart was joined by Mr Britten, successor to Mr Ludowyk, and Mr Bernau successor to Mr Wheeler who had run off with a matron. Mr Britten was the younger brother of Benjamin Britten: casual and wise, a little burdened by his brother's fame, a musician who loved the 'tidal surge' of choral singing and the 'lark in the clear air' of the boy soprano. Mr Bernau was a former actor and Friend of London Zoo. He took Form VI into the snake house and draped us with pythons, then to the Old Vic where he had once acted, and after seeing *Hamlet,* we went backstage and met Coral Browne and David Dodimead (who ten years on would be my landlord and lover at the Nottingham Playhouse). On the Big School Room stage, Mr Bernau produced *Scenes from Macbeth.* Storm music from Mr Britten's brother heralded the entrance on the battlefield of King Duncan, played by Butch, myself as Malcolm, and Sir Bertram Bunt in a cameo role as Prince Donalbain.

*

On the morning of my twelfth birthday, 4th December 1956, I was summoned out of breakfast to take a telephone call.

'Richard?' said my mother, ominously. It would normally be 'Witty' or 'Wit' on my birthday. And why didn't she say 'Many happy returns' – though she wouldn't normally ring me up to say that; trunk calls were expensive.

'Yes?' I said.

'I have some very sad news. Granny died this morning.'

'Which one?'

'Granny Ashby.'

'Oh good.'

'Did you hear what I said?'

'I mean it's good it wasn't Granny Twidle. I mean it's not good at all. It's my birthday and you've just ruined it!' I put the receiver down.

What I should have said was: 'Actually you *haven't* ruined it. By not mentioning it, not sending cards or a cake, I might just get away with no one knowing. No bumps, or tossing in a blanket – I couldn't have taken that stupidity with my grandmother lying cold. It gave me time to think of her. If the family were the solar system, Granny Ashby was a sort of wintry sun. Everything revolved around her, as she radiated light, fuelled by an unseen religious furnace. With Uncle Mo she had enabled my own father to break free, and had continued to support him when he was cut off from the firm, paying my school fees, funding holidays, sending hampers at Christmas. She was the queen bee, immovable, except when, pillowed and blanketed, she was driven in the Bentley to take the waters in Matlock or Buxton: my granny in her mob-cap and bottle-end specs, who could invalidate any wolf.

*

The pool in the sunken garden was drained, reclaimed and filled, in time for the summer. We called it the Puddle, and swirled about in it naked like fishes in a bowl, supervised by the duty master. Two thirteen-year-old twins had come just for a term, to be got through Common Entrance. The first time they jumped in the Puddle, they had erections, and began splashing and fooling. Mr Bernau told them sternly to get out and not come back till they'd got a grip on themselves. No way nonplussed, they went down to the woods – it was a Sunday – and set up camp. We followed later, and when we saw what they were doing, Bunt said: 'Bloody kids!' and Butch said 'Leave them to it'. And the three of us walked over into the long grass to look for mushrooms.

I wandered back out of curiosity. At the twins' camp, several Fifths had turned up and a 'mass turbation' was in progress. When they saw me watching they beckoned me to join the circle. I was going to slip away but one of the twins caught me. I said 'Hey steady! Keep your shirt on', and everyone laughed because that was all he *had* on. And to myself I said: 'If they force me, I can't be blamed, and if the only way to stop them using force is to comply, then that isn't my fault either.'

They didn't use force and the threat was nominal. I paused, just long enough to flip a coin in my head. Odd, I reflected, as I joined the circle, that something the aim of which was to prove adulthood, should appear so childish. To make babies, it seemed you had to become babyish yourself. Surely intelligent, God-fearing people didn't do this. Did Jesus do it? *Except ye become as little children...* He said that. Sperm is the seed, which must die and be buried before it can bear fruit. Bed it down under concrete or indulge it like an animal: is that the choice? Who then bears fruit? At the zoo with Mr Bernau, we had seen monkeys doing it. Reverse evolution. Except ye become as little monkeys...

We drifted. I didn't tell anyone, but later I did indicate to Woble who said the twins had niggled him to do the same, but he had declined. He had mentioned it to his older brother, who had said, if it happened again, he would tell their parents who would tell the Flynns. And maybe that's what happened because suddenly in the middle of lunch, Old Toby, in a rare moment of authority, rapped the table, got up and said from now on, the woods would be out of bounds. There was no explanation.

But the twins had bikes, which were allowed in the Fifth and Sixth. And the next Sunday, we were off down a lane, dumping bikes behind a hedge, and doing it openly in a field. Or trying to. I was twelve; my voice was cracking; I had spots and some hair. Surely any time now... So every night, when all the squits in the dorm of which I was captain, were asleep, I would try, try, try, like the traitor Robert Bruce...

Then one long night, at ten past eleven, 14th July 1957 (it's in my diary), I struck oil, just a drop. I expected shame to descend, with promises attached: *never again, so help me God!* But instead of slipping out of bed onto my knees, I lay prone, uncovered, ecstatic, like sculpted marble.

But the net was tightening. Woble, who had heard about the twins and their bikes, had hinted to his brother, who had mentioned to their father, who had side-stepped the Flynns and reported straight to Mr Thomas, who that week had just returned to the school to assist, as *de facto* headmaster. He had been away for two years, working in the City – a man of ambition can only serve for so long under autocratic parents. But now the Old Man was ailing and Mrs Flynn was weighed down by the Railways' purchase order, Thomas agreed, to return pro tem, expecting his brother Mark to stand by to do the same after a year.

So when, on his return, Thomas found the school in the throes of a moral sickness, he set about purging it without mercy. One by one, the suspects were called to the study to be interrogated, then beaten. As the air chilled in the corridor, I felt my skin thicken, so that when I entered the panelled room with its cane cupboard and greasy chair, I was insulated from fear. I could observe the man sitting at his father's desk, cane in hand:

his round, metallic face burnished to a sheen as if he never had to shave; his smoked glasses like shutters to his soul. There was a photograph of him in Mrs Flynn's sitting-room, aged about twelve: a self-possessed boy, sporty and bright like his grandfather Dawson, who had saved Brighton College. Would Thomas now save The Old Ride, from lechery and also from the railways? One thing we knew: there would be no 'Wait and see' for Major Thomas Flynn, who had won the Military Cross in the Far East, captured (as I imagined) and sent to work on the Burma Railway, his skin burnt to old gold, his eyes bleached in the sun like Ralph Richardson in *The Four Feathers*. Escaping with a wounded comrade, was he shot in the heel as he crossed the infamous line? I looked at him; he looked at me. He expected my help and I was giving it freely: what happened, when, how often, with whom? I was answering like an automaton as he made notes for a letter to the father of the twins. At the end he thanked me, shook my hand, didn't beat me. That was my punishment: to be reprieved when others, braver than I, had been disgraced; to be the source of information which others had not divulged.

The twins were sent to the sick-room, to await their parents. I saw them as they were leaving. They looked tired and much younger: just kids. I envied their going. I was longing for the end of term. The Old Ride had a bad smell to it, and there were new, exciting developments at home, which I wanted to explore.

BALSALL HEATH

...was a square mile of inner city Birmingham, housing twenty thousand people. Originally, well-to-do, grandiose mansions looked out on a real heath going down to a babbling river with grassy banks. As Birmingham prospered and expanded, neat red-brick back-to-back terraces sprang up, creating a bustling street community, and a vibrant congregation for the new neo-Gothic St Paul's Church, built grandly and economically in just twelve months, its tower capped with battlements and ringed with gargoyles. But the nave with a capacity of a thousand souls was just not big enough, and five years later had to be expanded into a side-chapel, then extended again after ten more years, by which time the vicar, the Reverend William Bradshaw Benison, was packing in upwards of sixteen hundred on a good Sunday. It was a working people's church that blessed the beneficiaries of the Birmingham miracle, standing proud on the Moseley Road, looking along to its newly built neighbours the Public Library and the Public Baths; soul, mind and body amply cared for, as Balsall Heath swelled and Birmingham spread, engulfing the suburbs, until the heath was bricked over and the river piped underground, and extra houses had to be backed onto the back-to-backs, bringing poverty, indolence, disease and crime. By the time my father came here in 1957, Balsall Heath was a by-word for the grimmest of slums. Decent people moved away selling their grandiose mansions to Rachmanesque landlords, who filled them with the poor and lonely, and the newly arrived from Jamaica and Pakistan. The once bustling street community in the closely-packed terraces became a red-light, drug-den, gangland jungle. And the church struggled on, its fabric betraying the cheap materials it was built from, and the hubris of its size. It was the bleakest of places in the bleakest of times, with bleaker times to come.

Why did my parents want to move? Kingstanding had been a resounding success: young families enrolled, a new social scene nourished, weddings and christenings outrunning funerals three-to-one. As a choirboy in the holidays, earning 1/6d a wedding, with up to a dozen weddings on a Saturday in the spring season, I earned enough to buy a camera. I photographed our new house on the hill; our newly springing-up lawn and vibrant shrubbery; my conker-tree, grown from conkers saved in my pocket for a whole term – everything took root and shot up at St Luke's, like the lamp-post in Narnia. I took snaps of the choir outing to Llandrindod Wells, the World Scout Jamboree in Sutton Park and our own straight-backed, chins-up, exemplary happy family: Father, Mother, Elizabeth, Judith and Monica, in descending order, in front of the relief of the Bull of St Luke in the wall by our front door. I wasn't in the picture (being the photographer) and I missed the debate about moving which may have gone something like this:

MOTHER: We're just beginning to enjoy ourselves here and you want us to move.

FATHER: When called, we have to move. Success is of the devil. A priest must learn to fail as Our Lord failed.

MOTHER: Excuse me Bee, but I thought He triumphed.

FATHER: There is no resurrection without descent into hell and Balsall Heath is calling.

MOTHER: If Our Lord had been married with four children he might have thought twice about descending –

FATHER: (*laughing*) *Ut Migraturus Habita!* Live as a Pilgrim! The family motto. Better translated as 'Be ready to fly', like the migrating crane. If we stay here, we will grow contented like Mr Worldly Wiseman.

JUDITH: Who is Mr Worldly Wiseman Daddy?

ELIZABETH: (*sternly*) If you'd listened to Daddy's Lent Talks on *The Pilgrim's Progress*, you'd know that Mr Worldly –

MOTHER: All right then! Tell us what's good about Balsall Heath.

ELIZABETH: It's dirty, it smells, it's crowded, it's ugly and full of bad people.

MONICA: I want to go to Boresaw Eef! I want to go to Boresaw Eef!

FATHER: I haven't told you about Colonel and Miss Piggott, and Moseley, and Trafalgar Road, and the Vicarage, which is sited a good mile from the church, on the border of Moseley Village, Trafalgar Road being the boundary-line. One can work in the day bringing Christ to the Balsall Heathens, then retreat in the evening to the Delectable Uplands of Moseley where Colonel and Miss Piggott reside. 'Clive', as he likes to be known, has been church warden at Balsall Heath for as long as anyone can remember. Ex-Grenadier Guards, he stands six foot four and with his sister Margaret (six foot one) will venture into the Heart of Darkness every Sunday and some week-days too, then motor back to Moseley. Does that settle it love? Don't be cross. Take it up – the Cross! – and follow!

*

I wasn't there when my family left Kingstanding and I didn't see Balsall Heath Vicarage, till it was all kitted out. I came home for the Christmas holidays by train, luggage sent in advance. I got the bus to Trafalgar Road, shouldered my bag past the grandiose mansions, till at the bend in the road, as it began to climb, I saw it: St Paul's Vicarage.

It was bigger than Laxton, the biggest house in the road, with the largest garden. Counting attics, cellars, hallways, landings, outhouses, coal-houses, it had twenty-four rooms. There was a front door, a side-door, a back-door, a brick-floored yard, a garage, a workshop which became our table-tennis and storage room, leading out into the garden with two croquet-sized lawns, a rockery, a rose-garden, a kitchen garden and orchard with plum, pear and apple trees. And in the midst, like the Tree in the Garden of Eden, *Mespila Germanica,* the medlar-tree: as old and as rude as Shakespeare (so we told visitors) who dubbed it the 'open-arse' fruit, because when 'bletted', or going rotten, which is the only time to eat it, a sweet mushy mess exudes from it like shit.

My bedroom was the last room at the end of the north wing. It had three exterior walls, a rug over bare boards, my book-cases, table and chair, utility tallboy and wardrobe, and a high, Edwardian queen-size bed, with eiderdown, counterpane, blankets and sheets that crinkled on a frosty morning. Heating was from a popping gas fire with cast-iron surround, which barely heated itself, so you had to squat right over it once lit, having peeled yourself out of bed, still in jumper and balaclava. But this was nothing, I reflected, to what Uncle Arthur had endured, in Artarctic waters, on the *Nimrod* with Shackleton. In his honour, and to prolong the coldness, I painted the walls ice-blue.

You couldn't grow up in this house and not be creative. The first thing Judith and I did, on moving in, was write the guide-book and arrange tours. But when parishioners began believing in the ghost in the coalhouse and the body under the floorboards and the jaw-bone of a lion from a Roman amphitheatre in the garden, we ducked out and turned to drama. There was a natural stage on the front landing with a step down into an auditorium that could take two rows of seats. Doors off to three bedrooms provided entrances and exits, or you could 'break the fourth wall' and exit grandly down the stairs. Here Judith and I staged *The Life of John Bunyan,* myself as the imprisoned preacher, Judith as everyone else; the play researched from *Proud Heritage,* a tiny book of British monographs, which had been award-ed to me on my first Speech Day at The Old Ride.

And there was a 'priest's hiding-hole' in the attic leading through the roof-void where apples were stored, to an enclosed V-shaped space be-tween the double-pitch of the roof. Here snow had to be scooped before it melted and came through the ceiling. Here on a summer night, when the house was asleep, you could come up with a blanket, lie out in the valley, naked and undisturbed, and like Amun-Ra, Creator God of Egypt, shoot sperm at the stars.

Thirty years on, when I was Writer-in-Residence at Birmingham Polytechnic, I came back to Balsall Heath. The church had long disappeared, razed to the ground to become a car-park and I half expected the vicarage to be gone as well. All the time we were there, we were losing the battle of dilapidation: dry rot, roof leakage, erosion of foundations by roots of trees – not least my conker tree, brought in a pot from Kingstanding and replanted in the front garden, where it grew like the mustard-seed, into a full-size, foundation-rocking, bird-sustaining tree.

Coming back after a generation, I had to check the road sign, because so much had changed. Many of the grandiose houses had been replaced by play-areas and low-rise blocks. The vicarage, structurally the same, had been reconfigured to suit the new landscape. Sand-blasted, repointed, reroofed, brightly painted, it was the Disney-version of our house. Now divided into thirteen flats, its future was assured. I felt like a time-traveller, a true ghost from a previous era, as I touched the stump that was once my tree, and walked down the newly tarmacked road that cut through the garden, to a row of neat maisonettes where the orchard used to be.

Looking up at my bedroom window, for a second I saw the face of a boy, pressing his temples against the glass. It was cold then, but even frost couldn't cool the pain. I was looking out on my future self and he was look-ing at me. I pulled back from the window and tried to connect my hand to the door-knob, racking my brain as to how to turn it. I'd been reading in my room, but the book had gone mad. The words, the letters I'd so diligently unpicked, had twanged back into hieroglyphs. I was floating in my skin, on Frankenstein legs, slowly passing Judith's room, with its blast of heat from the boiler, then clump by clump down the wooden hill of the back stairs, to the front kitchen, which could have been the Laxton Vicarage kitchen, with its coke-filled range and clothes pulley against the ceiling. I could have been five years old, or fifty. I was out of time, with an axe in my head and blinded eyes.

They sent me to our family doctor, Dr Fraser-Brown, whose surgery was in Moseley. A big bluff man who resembled Jack Hawkins in *The Cruel Sea*, he sat me down, looked me steadily in the eye. Then very gently and frankly he told me the facts of my teenage life. Masturbation is natural. It's only *worrying about it* that sends you blind. The best cure is a brisk walk, to shake up the liver. If the light is too bright, wear dark glasses.

I went home, up to my room. The virtue of a large house is that you can easily avoid people. I put on my shades and duffel-coat, put up the hood and left the house. It was four o'clock; already dusk was descending. I walked up to the top of Trafalgar Road, turned left, and on till I got to Ladypool Road, once a pool called the Lady Pool, after a lady who fell foul of Mr Bradshaw Benison, so our guide-book had it, and drowned herself. Now the houses, once grandiose, are crumbling and multi-occupied. There are cooking smells and noise. I walk through it like a blind man. A Jamaican lady asks if

I'm all right. I don't see her. I've turned into Runcorn Road, zig-zagging through darker, foggier, narrower streets of back-to-back terraces, until I see it, looming up, like a tottering giant. We were told not to stand under the tower because once, recently, a gargoyle broke loose and nearly killed a child. So I don't linger; I go straight up to the big west door which is always open, daring you to go in. The candlesticks were stolen long ago and there is nothing in the charity box, so robbers don't come. Crime anyway in Balsall Heath is not so petty. It goes deeper, has its own moral code which forbids offending against the defenceless, including churches.

There's fog inside, like toxic incense. The church is hugely, infinitely empty. I'm walking up the side aisle, trying not to make a sound, but my foot-steps still echo. There's something massively frightful in here, either a presence or an absence. I am drawn towards the only light, a little red glow from the reserved Sacrament suspended in a boat on three chains, in the Lady Chapel. But it's not ominous or fearsome, because I know what it is. The presence, or the absence is unknown, uncontained, inhuman, engulfing. Any moment the great west door will slam shut and I will be confined here for ever. I can just make out the figure in the stained glass: St Paul in his toga, hand raised in blessing, standing on the tramlines in the middle of Moseley Road. On either side of him, in the distance are the Library and the Baths. Not much has changed since Roman times, except for the tramlines, and they're gone now. What's to say his gesture isn't the same as Hitler's, that we used to be so afraid of? Was Paul's moment of revelation on the road to Damascus, the same as my father's in Austria when he bought the statuette? Who's good? Who's bad? Who has the answer?

The hand on my shoulder is my father's. He has been visiting and now he has come in to lock up. But first he must say the Office. Would I like to say it with him?

GONONSAFARI

My diary entry for 1ˢᵗ January 1958 says 'TURNED OVER NEW LEAF.' For my final months at The Old Ride, that leaf remained firmly turned with a few flutters, and one complete flip in my final days, that nearly ruined everything. Butch and Bunt being older, had left, as had Pearce and Fafalios. I was top of Form Six and Nation Leader of the Britons. I had hoped to be Head Boy, but that went to Woble. After a week of annoyance, I conceded that this was actually a good thing. I didn't have to speak with the voice of the Flynns and I had time to revise. With Mr Stoddart, Mr Bernau and Mr Britten to guide me, I structured a steady revising programme, practising from previous papers, doing mock exams within the time-limit, till my head was stacked with retrievable knowledge, to be unloaded with flair. I concentrated till I cracked, then went for a brisk walk. I even stopped writing to Paynter in America. His world was not mine. He was saying things like 'Right now, we have a craze called Rock n' Roll... you can hardly move before you hear of a man call ELVIS PRESLEY. The girls scream, sob and yell whenever they see him. It seems like they've gone mad!'

I was meant to go to Leatherhead to take the scholarship, but they had a flu epidemic, so an outside invigilator was brought in and I did the papers in the library. It all went as planned. I knew I had done well, and when the result came through, it was almost an anti-climax. Mr Thomas called me to the study. He had already set up the call and the phone was ringing. He handed it to me. He said: 'Talk to your parents.' I said: 'What about?' He said: 'Tell them you've won the Albany Scholarship to St John's Leatherhead.'

After lunch, I had to stand on a chair and tell the whole school they would have an extra half holiday. It was a balmy, sunkissed, idle afternoon, and I felt quite spare with no revising to do, in fact no really necessary work for the rest of term. I did some batting in the nets, then went for a walk in the long grass with Woble. I suggested he might like to suggest to Mr Thomas that, since I didn't any longer have anything much to do, I might take over as Head Boy, just till after Common Entrance, to allow Woble to swot. I was just offering, it didn't bother me one way or the other, just helping out, if he wanted. He said that was fine; he meant fine for me to help, and he would definitely take me up on that. There were lots of things I could do to take the weight off, like marshalling the squits in their toilet queue and ordering the swabbing of the bathroom after games; but he didn't think the Flynns would want him to relinquish the actual Headboyship, because that might look like abdication. I said fine, that was fine, though, come to think of it, I did have quite a lot still on my plate, so my helping out would be strictly limited. He said 'But you offered and I accepted'. I said 'I offered to be Head Boy and you *didn't* accept. So let's leave it at that now.' He said: 'I don't think we can just leave it Old Crane. I'm Head Boy and I'm ordering you to do the squits and the swabbing, and while you're at it, get Gononsafari to change his pants.' He burst out laughing and I knocked him over and pinned him down then rolled over till we were both lying on our backs, crying with laughter.

(Gononsafari was Ghazanfari, a Persian boy who like the twins last year, was only here for one term. He came to lessons when he wanted and often wandered off for a whole day, prompting Mr Stoddart to re-name him in response to the question: 'Where's Ghazanfari?' [He's gone on safari.] He was nearly fourteen but looked nineteen, with a growly voice and moustache, like a man in boy's clothing, and he had never been seen to take his pants off, not even in the bath.)

When everyone went into prep, I stayed on the big field. I sat on a bench opposite the ha-ha, looking at the school. Quiet in the dwindling light, it looked doomed and old: the ancient cedar and Spanish chestnut, which must date from the original Jacobean house, standing like aged retainers on their last legs downstage; the yew hedge hiding the lily-pond, ominous in the middle distance; exits stage left into the spinney, stage right through the wrought-iron gate, into the sunken garden. All this will be bulldozed by the Railways: trees, yew hedge, pond, gardens, lawns and house, till not one stone stands on another or one root remains. Put another way, it's done its time. It's seen me through. I no longer need it. Like a chrysalis that's nurtured me for six years, it's about to be peeled away, as I shoulder my way out of it. Prep school is an understatement. This has been a whole education. I have learnt all I will ever need to know – anything extra will be a bonus – not just subjects, but survival, navigation on a rocky moral sea, how to play a part in a closed society, how to leave when the time comes.

The sun sinks. Shadows lengthen. The railway lines are marshalling like snakes, to lash the memories into the ground. There will be no return to this place. No one will remember it.

I get up and for the first time since my earliest days at the school, walk up the steps onto the forbidden lawn. I feel weighed down with age and experience like the house, and like the house which in reality has only ex-perienced half a century, I am pretending and I know I am. But that doesn't stop me feeling overwhelmingly sad.

But it isn't over yet. There is one more trial which will test me to the very edge.

*

Ghazanfari wouldn't turn his mattress. He was in my dorm and it was my duty to ensure the weekly turning. To my knowledge his mattress had never been turned and each week I endeavoured to have it out with him, but he would just look blank, as if English was not his language. So I went to Mr Britten and asked him to translate 'Please turn your mattress!' into Italian, because I knew Ghaz had been brought up mainly in Italy and had been heard speaking Italian on the phone. Then the next time it didn't happen, I went up to him and *con gusto*, so the whole dorm could hear, I said: '*Gonosafario, prego di girare il materasso!*' But he just curled his moustachioed lip and looked askance with heavy, half-closed eyes.

*

Colonel and Miss Piggott came with my parents to Speech Day, two weeks before the end of term. My father wanted some off-duty time with the twin pillars of the parish, whose *hauteur* he had yet to bend. My mother wanted to dazzle them with the brilliance of her scholarship-winning son and at the same time impress the Flynns by driving up in the Colonel's Daimler instead of the rickety vicar's van. They arrived in good time, parking impressively among the more parochial cars, under the limes along the drive. It was a serenely warm day with a light breeze that ruffled my mother's new gaily-coloured dress and threatened to lift off her hat, as she stepped out of the car and walked with my father, in his dog-collar, light flannels and blazer, followed by the Piggotts, too hot in matching tweeds.

Stack chairs had been laid out in rows on the south side of the house, below the terrace on which stood a long table bearing books and trophies. Boys sat on rugs on the grass in front of the chairs and there were benches either side for masters and prize-winners. When all were gathered, the Flynns entered and took their places at the table: Mr Thomas in the centre, affable, businesslike, guiding his father, who looked surprised then puzzled, to the seat on his right. Mrs Flynn looking small and drop-shouldered beside her muscular son, took the seat to his left; still a force to be feared, till you remembered you were leaving in two weeks, having raised the school to new scholastic heights, and obliged her to chew up, swallow, digest and excrete her previous low opinion of you. I glanced at her each time I went up to receive a record number of prizes, and each time she returned the glance with a tiny smile, which melted into a horrible fully-toothed grin – something I'd never seen before – when Mr Thomas said my parents were going to have to hire a van for all these books! I wanted to reply that the Daimler should be big enough thank you, and on a more serious note, to add that if anyone should be credited as the source of my success, it was Mr Ludowyk. Shocked silence. Grins feeeze. Sun goes in. Sky darkens. And far away, in the inner reaches of my heart, I hear the black man chuckle. But only the Head Boy is to speak on Speech Day, and I have to admit Woble spoke impressively, only once glancing at his notes. He said he owed everything to Mr and Mrs Flynn, who had created and given their lives to the school and he urged all parents to campaign to stop British Railways knocking the house down, because it was so good here, it was unique, it was the best start a boy could have.

We had a picnic lunch on a rug on the lawn, the Piggotts squatting on low-level folding stools. Gononsafari, at a loose end, was haunting people's lunches, till he caught the Colonel's eye, and sidled away to our relief. The Colonel noting the loping stride of the sinister Persian observed that he had encountered many such in the Middle East; that they were not to be trusted.

The next day was a visiting day, and after church in the village, parents took their sons away for the day. Mine had left the previous evening and I was happy to be free to read and wander. Walking back from church, with the dozen or so boys whose parents were abroad or busy or in trouble, I was joined by Ghazanfari. He seemed to want to be friends and thinking of Mr Ludo, and the Jamaicans in Balsall Heath, and the natives in *Kim* by Rudyard Kipling which I was currently reading, I felt I should broaden my horizons and get to know more about people from other lands. I was also puzzling over Mr Flynn's sermon about a rich man entering Heaven, being like squeezing a camel through the eye of a needle. He seemed to be saying it was all right to be rich because Jesus could fix anything - raising the dead, threading camels through eyes of needles, no problem for the Son of God! I asked Ghaz how he felt having super-rich parents who never visited. Did he even know where they were? He said they were either in Rome or Teheran. He hadn't seen them for a year. In the holidays he was looked after by his uncle in Italy. He liked Italy. He had a good time there. He didn't like Persia. It was too strict. His father worked for the Shah who expected him to join the army, which his uncle said he didn't have to. I said I would like to go to Italy one day, to see the forum and the colosseum, to read the Latin inscriptions and see where Caesar was assassinated. He said he would take me to Rome but not to the ruins – they were dull – but to the heart of Rome, to the *terme* and *locali notturni*, where boys and men play. I said: 'You mean like in *The Satyricon* by Petronius?' He said: 'I mean *nella casa dei cazzi.*' He laughed: 'Do you know what that means?'

Later, in the Big School Room, we were meant to be writing letters home. I was excused having just seen my parents, so I sat and read *Kim*. Ghaz came and sat next to me, not reading anything. He scribbled a note, nudged me, flicked it along. 'One day I take you *nella casa dei cazzi.*' I scribbled back: 'What does that mean? I know *casa*, but what is *cazzi*?' He wrote: '*Cazzi* is the plural of *cazzo*. Do you have a *cazzo*?' I wrote: 'No I don't, but we used to have a *dogso*'. We both collapsed laughing, Ghaz rocking into me and pushing me, scribbling in huge letters: 'YOU DO NOT HAVE A *CAZZO!!!!*' – and pummelling me in the stomach, till I thought Mr Britten, half asleep at the high desk would notice and want to be 'acquainted with the joke'. But he didn't stir. I screwed up the paper, Ghaz snatched it back, unscrewed it, wrote: 'I show you *cazzo*. Okay?' He watched me as I read it, caught my eye as I looked up. Then he rose with a smile and went out towards the old big school room and the 'six'. I went back to reading. Any moment, Mr Britten would cast a weary look and I'd just be flipping the pages of *Kim*. But he was dozing. The air was heavy. No one seemed to notice anything. So I closed the book, put it down, got up quietly.

The 'six' is a line of six lats in cubicles, with doors but no locks. I walked down the line to the last door which was closed. I pushed it open. He shut it behind me.

What happened next was like when the bus was towering over me: a marker beyond which nothing would ever be the same again. It wasn't rape because I knew very well what a *cazzo* was, and I wanted him to show me. The shock was being turned around, face to the wall, while he worked and chiselled, like *squeezing a camel through the eye of a needle*... It couldn't be done, yet it *was* being done, and I was willing him to persist, quickly quickly, before someone came. Then suddenly, catastrophically, the camel was in, the whole hump, elasticating me to tearing-point. I would have yelped but he was gagging me, risking our lives as he plunged and plunged. I once saw two cats 'footing' on Beeton's Farm, the upper one with the scruff of the lower one in its teeth, spreadeagling it as it howled. But a cat's *cazzo* is not a camel, more of a needle you might say, injecting its stuff then pulling out, all in a moment. I remember watching Old Tom lope away, job done, while little Minnie began the clean-up, none the worse if you're asking, *c'est la vie*, what are you looking at?

Two squits came in suddenly, voices I recognised, signalling the end of letter-writing and the advent of hordes who might kick the door open. I listened petrified, as just inches away, two angels chatted as they pissed, while we devils held our breath.

Ghaz had gone cold. I shat him out like a turd. He seemed to be blaming me. I couldn't get away fast enough. I walked down to the Big Field, tunnelled out, as if disembowelled. Mr Bernau was in the pavilion. I helped him stack the stack-chairs from Speech Day and we talked about what I wanted to be. I knew as soon as I said the word, that I was one already. I was playing a part and he knew I was, because he had also been an actor: 'But it wasn't enough. It was an excuse and quite selfish: *not being* instead of *being*, like Hamlet who also saw himself as an actor, until real life got in the way.' He took my head in his hands, as if holding a mask and looking through it: 'But do it, boy, do it. You might make it, who knows? Or you might – I have to say this – only *half*-make it, which is worse, believe me, than *not* making it. I've seen them, like ghouls, the half-made actors, trading hope for envy, ambition for bitchiness, empty of heart and dead behind the eyes. That is limbo, living death, the ghost world, *not being.'* Stacking the last of the chairs, he caught my eye: 'Are you all right chum? You look sick.'

LOSING PARADISE

I made a decision. If it was 'being' or 'not being', I would *be*. More than that, I would *do*, and do *good*. I would lead, not follow; look ahead, not back. I would go straight to Form VI and read *Pilgrim's Progress* from the big leather-bound book in the glass-fronted book-case. I wasn't going to leave The Old Ride, brought down at the last fence by my own feebleness. I would tread the memory of Gononsafari under my heel and go proud, head high. Strive, seek, find and not yield! *Ut migraturus habita! Be ready to fly!*

There was just a fortnight to go. It wasn't a long book. I calculated if I read fifteen pages a day, and didn't linger over the illustrations, and wasn't tempted to transgress into *Paradise Lost* (the other big leather-bound book) with its writhing, anguished, sensuous, black-muscled coils of Satan; if I eschewed the fiend and cleaved to the pilgrim, I could be up there, safe in the Celestial City, just as the landrover mosied off on the Monday morning, with me and the train boys, to get the 9.49 to Bletchley, for the last time.

And when I wasn't reading, I would do my garden. In the past year, on the initiative of Mr Stoddart, and in the spirit of Percy Thrower, who had been born in the cottage where Mr Thomas now lived, Arthur Venn, the current gardener, had been instructed to plough up an area of the long grass that linked the Big Field to the woods, and create a row of allotments which boys could then cultivate, in pairs: an older boy with a younger 'apprentice'. My apprentice was a odd-bod known to everyone as (Just) William, whom I, as Nation Leader, had been deputed to keep an eye on. He was eleven, unsporty, spindly and shy, with pale blue eyes and ash-blond hair and no feeling for horse-breeding which was his father's multi-million-pound business. But he was very good at gardening and, being otherwise busy, I generally left him to it. He grew radishes, lettuces, carrots and spring onions, which he offered to me to eat or trade, as we were allowed to, at Sunday tea. Now in the final fortnight of term, having some time on my hands, I took to joining him at the plot during free time. I had helped create the garden at Kingstanding and would do my turn among the roses and raspberries at Balsall Heath. So it was pleasant to get my hands in the soil again, and soon I was wishing I'd spent more time there, growing things and harvesting, and being friendly with William. He was a natural partner: I hoed, he weeded; I dug, he sifted. We could talk, or not talk, about anything or nothing. He was the younger brother I'd never had, and I developed an overwhelming urge to protect him. Once I caught an older boy twisting his arm, and fetched the bully a crack across the head. 'Just tell me,' I said to William, 'if anyone else attacks you. It's not sneaking; it's justice.' I felt in those final weeks, I was helping him grow, just as he and now both of us, had coaxed our produce to its vibrant maturity. He seemed to be broadening by the day, his hair darkening, his voice deepening. He was the age I was when I played Ju Ju, and like me had now probably reached the turning-point of his school career. I was seeing him in a different light, wanting to be in his orbit at all times, even hug him if occasion arose. This was love, but the dreamy sort, as enshrined by Plato and sung of by the Everly Brothers – *only trouble is, gee whizz...* I was a Nation Leader, reading *Pilgrim's Progress*. I shouldn't be dreaming my life away. (*But wasn't that exactly what Bunyan was doing? Dreaming himself out of the mire of 'real life'?*)

On the last Sunday of term, I didn't go down to the garden. I was struggling with Bunyan, wanting to shut out intrusive thoughts. This was my father's favourite book. It plotted his life. He'd done a series of Lent talks on it, which I had missed, being at school, but he'd given me his notes. There are no chapters in the book but the notes broke it into sections, and I saw this as a distraction. Having breaks is like stopping on the journey to reconsider. Do I actually *want* to 'progress'? Is this world really so doomed? Why are all the adjective-named characters – Obstinate, Pliable, Faithful, Hopeful – incapable of change? Isn't it all Puritan propaganda? And why is Christian such a prude? I'd got to where he and Faithful are in Vanity Fair and obviously not enjoying it. Here are '*delights of all sorts, as harlots, wives, husbands, children, blood, bodies and what-not; and jugglings, cheats, games, plays, fools, rogues...*' I felt basically that Chris and Faith, when they were arrested, were asking for it, '*putting their fingers in their ears and crying "Turn away mine eyes from vanity!"*'. What did they expect? This was a fair like any other, only *vain* if you consider all human life vain. I felt Bunyan, aptly named, must have pains in his feet as he trampled through life's pleasures, listing 'plays' and 'games' alongside 'harlots' and 'cheats'. I kept wanting to put the book aside and turn to *Paradise Lost* which had Satan as the lead. This was stuff I could read aloud and be staggered by: the darkness of rebellion, the subtleness and sinuosity of the threat from fallen angels, the terrible *humanness* of evil. But I knew this was wrong, mustn't let it get into my skin, must learn to love Christian and follow his lead. Back in the *Progress*, I read on, wincing at the goody-goody, masochistic tone: Faithful dead, tortured and executed in the grisliest manner; Hopeful, springing from nowhere to join Christian who suddenly (with one bound he was free!) was on the road again, getting bogged down with By-ends and Money-love and Hold-the-world.

I stopped reading. I needed a break. It was the last full Sunday of term. (Next week only a rump of train boys would be left.) I went down to the Big Field for a final check on the garden. Most boys had gone in, but William was still there, crouching and pulling up the last of his carrots. My heart leapt at the thought of just sitting with him and talking as we contemplated raking over the allotment so it could lie fallow over the holidays. Next year he would have his own apprentice, maybe a new boy. He was growing fast in so many ways, less of a mouse, more a mongoose, and I was happy to expect some of the credit for his transformation.

I hadn't noticed the figure squatting on the ground beside him, so low he was almost lying, merging with the soil, like a serpent. He seemed to be annoying the boy, prodding him, even tickling his leg, till he fell over, clearly aggravated, not amused, keeping cool, pretending to laugh. I was walking down past the haha, skirting the field, so as not to be seen, determined to intervene if need be, but at the same time confident that the new William could handle this. Rikki-Tikki-Tavi could see off Nag the cobra, I was sure of that. He just had to get up, gather his carrots and run back to school – it was time to go in anyway – and if Ghaz followed him, I would have no hesitation in collaring him, telling him to back off.

In the dip of the haha I could watch them unobserved. Ghaz seemed to be saying something. William seemed not to be listening. Then Ghaz seemed to give up and start wandering towards the woods. I was about to go over and congratulate William, on his last harvest, and also on seeing off the Persian, when suddenly up he jumps, like a rabbit, looks around and, leaving his vegetables, skidaddles into the long grass, following Ghaz, who is just now vaulting the gate into the woods. I feel my blood run cold. I should be speeding after them like a rocket, stopping them in their tracks. But my feet won't move. I know exactly what they're doing, and it's no longer a mongoose putting paid to a cobra. It's a child being raped and I am incapable of stopping it. I wait ten minutes, then another ten, till the sun is sinking and long shadows are falling and it's too late to stop anything; as if I want it to happen and maybe, deep down, I do. (What am I *saying*!) One person with one deed, may think he can stop the tide, but it crashes back next time with deadlier force. I am a coward; I am a realist. You can't change your nature. Let the sad sink in Despond. Let the stupid rot in Doubting Castle. You are who you are and so you perish. Bunyan confirms that.

I don't know when they returned. They were both there in supper: Ghaz on the Trojan table, hollow-eyed, slack-jawed; William on the Britons' table, the far end from me, silent and paler than I'd ever seen him. 'Is anything wrong?' I asked as he was stacking his plate after the meal. 'Did you go in the woods? What happened? You can tell me.' He walked away. I ran after him, grabbed his arm: 'Was it Ghazanfari? What did he do?' He wouldn't look at me. I pulled his head back by the hair. 'I'm talking to you William. *What did that bastard do to you?*' He was looking at me now. He was different, dishonest, corrupted, grown-up. He smiled showing big teeth, which I'd never seen before, because he'd never smiled that way before. He said: 'He was nicer to me than you are.'

I knew he was lying. The look in his eyes, contradicting the toothy grin, was alien and terrified. This was more than just the wickedness of Ghazanfari. Something much bigger was going on. I'd sensed it in the haha when I was unable to move: the old deathliness descending in a great paralysing cloud, evil leaking like gas under the door of the Hitler room. You know it's there, yet it always takes you by surprise, and once acknowledged, becomes thicker than ever. It blurs your reasoning, fogs up your memory. What if I *did* follow them into the woods, saw the struggle, heard muffled screams, witnessed the murder of the child and his resurrection as a different, depraved, corrupted *man*. What if, *even then*, I couldn't stop it, rooted in the slough of the realist and the coward? It was like the nightmare of *The Four Feathers*, except this time I was awake, not being pursued but pursuing, determined to *do something*, to *tell someone*; to save myself, if no one else.

I went to see Mrs Flynn. I didn't wait till the morning. It was half-past ten; I'd just heard the clock. I slipped out of bed, put on my dressing-gown and slippers, crossed the landing to her sitting-room. As my knuckles touched the door, so softly only the keenest ear would hear (and I knew she was slightly deaf), I was praying she wouldn't be there, but she must have been standing just the other side of the door, because it opened immediately. I don't remember the conversation, except that I was in there for about an hour. She was in her dressing-gown as well, softer, smaller, uncommonly like Granny Ashby, but without the bottle-end specs. Her eyes were eagle-sharp. Her teeth were just visible. She hardly spoke at all; I did all the talking, and I remember feeling quite hoarse when it was over. How did I put it, the actual details? Did I admit to my own willing participation or did I make out that I was forced? Whatever I said, she understood completely. She had been here before, the previous year, with the twins. She knew when a boy was lying, and *I was not lying*. She had never heard such a flood of words! Did I talk about William? I must have done. Did she sense my own dream-love that went beyond the usual responsibility of the Nation Leader? She must have gathered all that. She had been associated and involved with growing boys all her life. She knew the nobility of love that with one quake of mistrust could subside into contagion, and Toby had been a prime example, stationed in the borderland between valour and vice

– what else were horse-bites about? She had only to look into a boy's eyes, to adjust the balance, and she did that with me, bridging the gulf between us, with a stare that could petrify. She was never going to crush me to her bosom as she did with Paynter, and I wouldn't have wanted that. What she gave me now, was the best thing: she listened. She had made me. She was proud of me. When I left the room, I felt drained of all badness. I was not the betrayer; I was the testifier, the penitent. I could leave the school with good report.

The last thing she said – and I do remember this – was: 'Thank you for coming clean. You can leave it to us now. There's no need to talk to anyone.'

The rest of my last week at The Old Ride were the best days. The sun shone; we swam in the Puddle; with Woble, I won the tennis doubles tournament; we both presented our leaving gifts and made speeches. His was a new Victor Ludorum trophy; mine was a new hand-bell, with my name engraved on it. I was aware of William hovering, avoiding me as I was avoiding him, for *his* sake more than mine, and I was aware that Ghazanfari, had gone on his last safari, disappeared from view, though there was still a whiff of him in the air. Following my revelation, Mrs Flynn would have talked to one, Mr Thomas to the other. Mrs Flynn would have said to William: 'What you have been subjected to is unfortunate, and it is to your credit that you didn't report it. Now the best thing you can do is forget and carry on. Your parents will only be upset if you tell them. A trouble shared is a trouble doubled.' And Mr Thomas would have said to Ghaz: 'It was wrong for you to have come here. You are not suited to The Old Ride. My father would have caned you and wiped the slate clean so you could carry on in the school. I am not going to do that. I believe you should go back to your own people and let them deal with you, over any future offence, according to their laws which are much stricter than our own. I am not going to inform your parents because in a few days you will be leaving us and, may I say, with good riddance. Until that time, you will be confined to the sick-room with no access to anyone.'

On the final Sunday, in Little Horton church, to a congregation of parents, masters, matrons and boys, with Mr Britten on the harmonium, I sang Brahms's *Lullaby*. My voice cracked a bit which just added to the emotion. I was singing it as a last farewell to the school, to the Flynns and all staff, present and gone, and to the friends I'd made, from Paynter to Butch and Bunt and Woble, and yes even William who I could see in the second row, head bowed, cinched in, like a wingless butterfly. But it was old Toby who surprised everyone. When I'd finished singing and was standing there in the silence, he got up from his stall, in his robes, came and stood over me, just as he had done years ago when I was standing on the haha. He made me bow, and bowed himself; people applauded (even in church) and there was a ripple of laughter, as the old man led me by the hand, back to my place in the choir. And that was it, end of show.

In the afternoon, I played tennis with Woble. We played game after game, until the sun went down. As we walked back to the house, I looked up to the barred windows of the sick-room, expecting to see Ghaz. But the window was blank. He'll be sitting on the floor, I thought, in the semi-dark, like Lucifer in chains, and for a second I wanted to risk all and go to him; but not now, maybe later, after dark, when everyone is asleep, I might somnambulate to the sick-room, ease open the door and be hit by the shit smell, the gaseous, intestinal coils of sadness that thicken the night. 'Ghaz?' I whisper, '*Gononsafario*? *Sei qui*? I just came to say good-bye. If you're with the train boys in the morning, I might not speak to you. I've done with you. I've extricated myself from your hell, you'll be glad to know, and learnt from it too. In a sense you did me a favour. You opened me up, if I can put it that way, to the fundamentals of evil. There was a master called Mr Ludowyk (what would he have made of you I wonder?) who taught me that discipline and scholarship are not enough: one has to have flair, wings of a dove, eyes of a hawk. Then you came and added something extra, you killjoy, something leaden and bleak, which I'm not going to let spoil the party, but will keep stashed away because you made me aware of it: a sense of death, *memento mori*, tinged with disgust, just an inkling, just a shiver to take the shine off, which I'll nurture for future use, to offset the razz, and when the abyss opens, I'll think of you.'

I put the light on. He wasn't there. Nor was I. I was in bed. It was my last night. In the morning, on the train, I would be rocketing into the future, and with no one to sustain it, no one with my scholar's discipline and sympathy for the devil, the school would fall.

The Old Ride was saved by Dr Beeching. When the Bicester-to-Bletchley branch line was axed in 1962, the scheme for a marshalling yard fell by the way. Mark Flynn came home, and there was a family discussion. The night-mare was over. They could soldier on as planned, the brothers taking turns to assist their father, Thomas returning to his job in the City, Mark stepping in pro tem, carrying on; or they could seize this chance for a new start in a new place. The purchase was agreed; the price was good; they didn't need to go back on it, and Mark, scouting about for a new location, had found a suitable house in Wiltshire that they could move to within the year. But only, he stressed with a sudden fieriness in his eye, if he were *sole headmas-*

ter, not subject to any authority or partnership. This is how I imagined the discussion, over dinner in the private dining-room, the dark panelled walls absorbing the shock, as the younger man deftly outsmarted his brother and took the birthright.

ACT TWO
Breaking Through: 1961-66

*You never reach any truth
without making fourteen mistakes and
very likely a hundred and fourteen.
And a fine thing, too…Talk nonsense,
but talk your own nonsense,
and I'll kiss you for it.
Truth won't escape you.*
- Dostoyevsky

*

*You're only young once,
but you can be immature for ever.*
- Germaine Greer

Scene One
JAMAICA!

I'd done sodomy and the lash; now it was time to try rum. I was sixteen and had just run away to sea with my parents and two of my sisters. They came to get me from Leatherhead on Saturday 15th July 1961, and we drove straight to Southampton. Now a day into the voyage, in the upper bar of the storm-tossed *TV Ascania*, bound for Jamaica, I raised a tot with my father.

'To Uncle Arthur!'

'Uncle Arthur!'

It shot through me like a flame. Was this how the apostles were reborn at Pentecost? Now we can work miracles! Now we can talk in tongues! This was so clearly *meant to be*. Uncle Arthur, who had sailed on the *Nimrod* with Shackleton, had died leaving a legacy that just covered a look-see voyage to Jamaica for the five of us. Elizabeth, now nineteen and a student nurse in London, would stay behind. I would be sprung from school, missing Latin A-level, which being a scholar and a year ahead, I could take next July. My father would stand in for a month as Rector of Marley near Montego Bay, and have talks with the Bishop about a more permanent post hereafter. Balsall Heath, now more of a West Indian than a Brummie parish, would be left with a locum for six weeks, Pa then flying home, while we came back, in our own time, on the *Ascania*.

'We may be sailing against the tide,' Pa had said from the pulpit, 'but God calls us in different ways, and now, through your joyous faith, He is calling me, Nan and the family, to discover the source of your joy and to be the link between you and those you have left behind. We have summer dresses...'

'... and sun-hats and flip-flops,' said Mon as we walked home.

'I think he meant "some... addresses",' advised Jude.

'What was the name,' I quizzed, 'of the Frenchman who invented the open-toed sandal?'

Jude knew the answer: 'Philippe Pheloppe.'

'I don't get it,' said Mon.

Now in the tumult of the Bay of Biscay, Pa and I were in the bar, while Ma and the girls were still groaning in their bunks. 'Staying below,' said Pa, 'is no way to get sturdy, heart-of-oak legs. You have to be on deck, to feel the roll of the wave.' And I had done just that. Before dawn, on the first morning, I had left everyone sleeping and gone up to watch the sea. In the last lesson before they came for me on the Saturday, we had been translating in the *Odyssey*, where Our Hero is washed up and held captive by Calypso. In the north-facing, sunless Classical Sixth, it was impossible to imagine detention in the arms of a nymph-goddess on a magic island. Now suddenly, in the light of rosy-fingered dawn, as we surfed the waves of the wine-dark sea, Homer's vision was revealed. I was heading at speed towards a new Calypso island. It was delectable. It was dangerous.

We rounded Finisterre and fell into the blast of the Bay of Biscay. My father and I were the only ones in breakfast, having just said seven o'clock Mass, as celebrant and server. We had the chapel to ourselves and had to hang onto the altar and scrabble to find the Body of Christ, which shot across the floor. The chalice, when I was offered it, slurped Blood in my face, as my father landed on top of me. Anyone else would have collapsed laughing and given up, but we saw it through to the end, getting up, falling over, hauling ourselves up again, being thrown, clinging on, as seriously as if these were our Last Rites and we were drowning.

*

The *Ascania* was a much-battered, much-patched-up old lady of the sea. Launched in 1926 as the two-funnelled paquebot *Florida*, she criss-crossed the Atlantic through the great age of the liner Queens, till she was torpedoed in the war. Raised and refitted, she was relaunched with one funnel and a four degree list to starboard, first as a French troop ship, then as the *Ascania*, flagship of the Italian Grimaldi-Siosa line, carrying 183 first-class and 932 tourist-class passengers. As on the *Titanic*, most passengers below decks were migrants: outward, Spanish and Portuguese seeking new lives in South America; and West Indians, coming in great waves the other way.

In 1961, the *Ascania* was doing record business, especially on the homeward run, creating an unofficial extra class of 'deck passengers', uncatered for in the dining-room and beyond the capacity of the lifeboats. All would be well, if the voyage was not extended, if the sea was not too rough, if the beer held out, and the passengers kept dancing. The man responsible for harmony on board was Alvin Bennett, Chief Purser and Welfare Officer. Raised in Jamaica, he spoke Spanish and Portuguese, as well as patois and 'proper' English. He showed films, hosted bands, refereed deck games, compered talent shows, took the brunt of complaints and cheerfully kept the peace. But privately, he was seething against the double standards of the exploiters, from Enoch Powell, who as Health Minister had gone to Jamaica to recruit nurses, to Grimaldi-Siosa, who were whistling up a vision of mother-country welcome, and fortunes to be made. Mr Bennett had written a novel, published two years earlier, which hadn't yet (he laughed) come to the notice of his employers. *Because They Know Not* was about a family awaking to the truth of a grey-skied, cold-hearted mother, who feared being swamped in alien blood. The return voyage, buffeted by hurricanes and extended by four days, would test Mr Bennett to the limit, but the outward voyage with its manageable passenger list and well-scheduled entertainments, gave him time to talk (my mother taking notes for a series of articles for the *Birmingham Post*): about the violence of Jamaican politics; the dismantling of the colonial status of the church; the dream of Federation – to join all the islands like a Caribbean Indonesia – blown apart by Jamaica's surge for nationhood. He was now working on the book which would release him from the shipping line and establish him as a writer. *God the Stone-Breaker*, published 1968, would tell of the crushing of Jamaican hopes in the colonial period, and the inevitability of rebellion.

*

Managing life on a ship, keeping order in a school, Alvin Bennett was the obverse to my housemaster 'Tick' Turner. Mr Bennett rolled with the waves; Mr Turner revolved mechanically, cog by cog. Mr Bennett had weathered skin and rope-tackle hands; Mr Turner's knuckles were bone-china that cracked as he smacked a fives-ball to victory (he was an Oxford half-blue). There had once been two Mr Turners, both sticklers for precision: one known as Tick, the other as Tock. Together, I imagined them as Aristophanes' double man, cart-wheeling in unison; till Tock went away and left us with only Tick. Cruelly halved, but still turning, Tick Turner cut a lonely figure, sustained by routine and his Christian faith. As my housemaster, and for four of my five years, my form-master, I had Tick and only Tick, around the clock, thirty-six weeks a year, and like a cloud over the holidays; and it was only now, on the high seas, contrasting him with Mr Bennett, that I began to realize, taking the 'road less travelled' - the dusty B-road into the past, instead of the sea-lane into the future - might have been the wrong choice. I should have listened to Munro. He and I were both scholars, well advanced in the classics, and in our first week, had to choose Greek, Spanish or Science as our optional subject. Go Greek and you move straight into the fifth form, do O-levels within the year, then go up, at fourteen, into the Classical Sixth. Go Spanish or Science and you stay down in the Fourth, marking time in all subjects, till the non-scholars have caught up. As a clincher, with Greek comes release from a year's fagging, because how can you study desk-to-desk with a prefect, then come running when he calls 'BOY!'? How can you debate Justice and Valour with a corporal or petty officer, while at the same time, blanco-ing his webbing and spoon-polishing his boots? To follow Greek is to prepare for revolution. Fagging is feudal. The 1960s are round the corner. By the time we are prefects - Munro, are you taking this in? - the ground will be laid: no more fagging, or deference just because a boy may walk in the puddles of the Prefects' Path and can cane you if he wants. We'll abolish caning as well! *'Leaders of the mail-clad Argives, would that all had your fiery hearts!'* Who says Classics can't change the world?

Alexander (the Great) Munro is classically proportioned. Tall, tight-muscled, with bronze, curly hair, equine nose and a slight curl to the upper lip; he listens, takes it in, nods, uh-huh. He has already spoken to Mr Turner. He has chosen Spanish.

*

Vigo is a small port just inside Spain, on the border of Portugal. Captured by the British in 1719, it was occupied for just ten days, before the fleet, flush with victory, billowed out and moved on. Our own little invasion (17th July 1961), was over in three hours, just long enough to feel foreign for the first time, to see poverty as a fact of life, to buy twenty Ben Hur cigarillos for six pesetas (9d) and to know that Jude (13, but looking 17) should *not* be wearing those shorts on the quayside.

We were a grumpy little group, going ashore at siesta-time: my father puzzling over the map, my mother wondering when this 'adventure of a lifetime' was due to begin. Bee had travelled through Europe and to the mysteries of the East; Joan, his sister-in-law (my godmother), had been stranded in occupied France, escaping like Ingrid Bergman in the film, through Casablanca and Lisbon (where we would dock tomorrow); my mother's father had rescued icons in Archangel, had been sunk and come up again, at Jutland; her Harbord uncles Arthur, Billy, Dick and Vic, had sailed to the ends of the earth... while she herself, for all her love of adventure books and films, had only ever crossed to the Isle of Wight.

I bought a newspaper in Vigo, with world news I could identify, as an aid to the language: Elizabeth Taylor, dumping Eddie Fisher for Richard Burton, and putting *Cleopatra* at risk; Marlon Brando, filming *Mutiny on the Bounty* on Tahiti, insisting it was *not his fault* the film was rocketing over budget: the script was unusable, he was having to buy an island and invent his own lines. I read this in Spanish, in my bunk on the high seas: epic films teetering on ruin through the caprice of stars: art merging with life, destabilizing empires, provoking mutinies, through *acting. I* could do that. Mr Turner had said I could produce the next House play, if a suitable script could be found and I had flicked through *One-Act Plays for Today* ('today' being twenty years ago) but had found nothing of note. So I had decided, as 'homework' on the boat and on the island, to WRITE MY OWN PLAY.

FIRST LOVES

We docked at Lisbon in the morning and would have six hours ashore:L my father and I in long trousers, mother and the girls in long-sleeve blouses and knee-length skirts, because there were churches to be visited. I knew about these churches from a lecture I'd been to in the History Soc at achool, given by Rupert de Horsey Girling, a senior classicist, entitled *William Beckford and the Churches of Portugal.* He had shown pictures, on the epidiascope, of abbeys and cathedrals, as discovered by the maverick 18th century art collector, raconteur and gothic novelist, who had gone ashore at Lisbon in 1793, en route to his sugar plantations in Jamaica. Churches visited included: Belem Abbey, built by Dom Manuel the Fortunate who had promised the Blessed Virgin if Vasco da Gama were successful in bringing from the Indies a fortune in peppercorns, he would build her a monastery 'not to be sneezed at'; and Batalha Abbey, built by Dom Joao I, who had promised the Blessed Virgin if she were to grant him victory over the Spanish (she obliged), he would build her an abbey bigger than anything in Spain; and the convent at Mafra, built by Dom Joao V, who had promised the Blessed Virgin, if she would grant him a male heir, (*Lady, please do not grant this!*) she should have a basilica with fifty bells served by 300 monks and library with 35,000 books; and the magnificent, multi-turreted monastery at Alcobaca, built by Dom Henrique who had promised the BVM (*Mother of God! Deny me! Stop this cycle of over-spending!*) etc etc...; and Sintra where Beckford himself built his own gothic wonderland, housed in a classical landscape with a Claude Lorrain waterfall, and sheep shipped in from England. He never made it to Jamaica.

*

We were flicking notes in prep.

'Would you care to hear more about Beckford?' Wrote RdeHG.

'Yes please!' I wrote back, screwed it up, flicked it across.

'It's not pleasant,' he wrote.

'Then I definitely want to hear it!'

'So then...' Tapping his pursed lip with his Parker pen, the bluff entertainer (Albert Finney could play him) began writing:

'William Beckford is a forgotten hero. He was tall, imperious, musical, athletic, an art lover, raconteur, bon vivant... you know the sort?...'

He screwed up, flicked.

'A bit like you then?' I flicked.

'A multi-millionaire through sugar and slaves, in fact the richest man in England. His destiny, if he stuck to the straight and narrow, was assured. If he wasn't going to be a concert pianist (his piano-teacher was Mozart), then the next Prime-Ministership-but-three was his for the asking. (He was a schoolmate of a nasty little swot called Pitt Minor.) But first, to make a match, he was taken by his mother on a nationwide wife-hunt. The last port of call was the Earl of Devon who had six daughters, and a son. Surely something would happen here! But WB was in a mood and, hardly glancing at the girls, went off for a walk with the boy, whose name was Courtney...'

I kept all RdeH's notes in a locked box in my locker for two terms. Then I burnt them. The above dialogue is an invention, but the wisdom and wit of Rupert de Horsey Girling (not his real name) are absolute and real. With his springy, swept-back hair, his peach-soft skin with incipient whiskers, his Michelangelo limbs and torso, which in middle years might go to fat, but for now were godlike, he was every boy's *beau ideal*, whether sprinting down the wing for the 1st XV – 'On Johns! On John's!' – or playing Count Jean de Dunois, the Bastard of Orleans in *St Joan*, in my first term. I had been cast as Joan, and together, with RdeH's battlecraft and my Maid's faith, we could have wiped out the English! 'But that would have changed history,' said Mr Turner, having called me to his study, his face cracking a smile, then shattering into a honking, donkeylike laugh as he concluded: 'and North House could not sustain that!!!' He had reflected, he continued, stone-faced now, and concluded that a scholar in his first term, should not imperil his career for the lead in a school play. *Ergo*, (a cold hand on my shoulder), he had spoken to Mr Shaw, the director, who had said he would recast me, in the smaller role of Dunois' page.

*

We saw four or five churches in Lisbon, including the Cathedral, but I was actually more interested in the families coming aboard. There were kids my own age, adventurous and curious, most like me having never before set foot on ship. Language was not a barrier. There were deck-games, card-games and table-tennis we could play, and siesta-time on loungers when we could trade phrases and jokes, plus swimming in the first class pool (when Mr Bennett allowed) and film shows, socials, a talent show and dancing. Mr B got Jude and me and Antonio and Felipe and Maria and Celestina, doing the samba, to the ship's steel band, which featured Carlos (Jude's favourite) on double tenor pans, and Not-Carlos-But-The-Other-One (Mon's favourite) on ping-pong. I had learnt the samba at Janet Cranmore's School of Dancing in Edgbaston where Elizabeth and I used to go on Saturdays. Quick-step, waltz and foxtrot were the staples, and some barn dancing and reels. Latin dances were just coming into the frame and Miss Cranmore taught them as an extra. She drew the line at the jive which she said was not ballroom: it was far too enjoyable! Dancing was a skill to be learnt the hard way; and it was a mark of distinction when she said to Elizabeth and me after a neat quick-step: 'You've learnt it, now enjoy it!' I tried to teach the basics to Jude on the voyage, but she dug her heels in. *Yellow Bird* and *Island in the Sun* were not ballroom. Janet Cranmore was yesterday. Elizabeth had missed the boat. Alone in London, she wasn't enjoying nursing, hadn't got a boyfriend, was meant to have met me for tea, on my way to school, at the beginning of term. I'd said 'Let's meet at Waterloo station', and put the phone down (I hate phones), without saying what time or which *part* of the station; so we'd spent all afternoon wandering and not meeting, till it was time for the train to Leatherhead. To make up, I had tried to introduce her to Girling. It was the custom in the Classical Sixth for an older boy, enamoured of a younger boy, to ask the Beautiful One if he had a Beautiful Sister (I had three). So as a peace offering to Elizabeth, and rekindler to RdeH (whose ardour been cooling, I didn't know why), I set up a tryst for the two of them, at Waterloo Station, one Sunday. And they *did* meet, they must have done, and I have to presume it was a disaster, because neither ever mentioned it; in fact Girling never mentioned *anything* to me, ever again. If we met in a corridor, he would walk straight through me, as if I'd never existed. And it was worse with Elizabeth. I wrote to her all cheerful: 'How did it go? Isn't he wonderful...?' But she never replied. We were going half way across the world and she wasn't even saying good-bye. It was as if I'd lured her into a trap, and she'd been lucky to escape; or worse, there had been no drama, just awkwardness. How things change, I thought. How distance dulls the music. Just weeks earlier we'd been winding up the old jumble-sale gramophone and dancing across the landing, to *South Pacific*: *I'm gonna wash that man right outa my hair...* (quick-step); *Happy Talkie-Talkie, Happy Talk* (cha-cha-cha), and as a Viennese waltz:

> *You've got to be taught*
> *to be afraid*
> *of people whose minds*
> *are oddly made*
> *and people whose skin*
> *is a different shade...*

The song still chills. It says: FEAR is the thing. *Trust no one*, least of all dark-skinned people. Build walls, be suspicious, stick to your own or you'll regret it. Of course it's ironic, sung by the Lieutenant who is in love with a Polynesian girl and is merely quoting his parents. But their views are real, and all the more crushing when voiced with reason and understanding. At least, with my own mother, when the blast came, it was with full fury: ice-cold and final. I'd been to the Christmas youth club dance and was late home. She'd been waiting up and I'd gone straight to my room, radioactive with forbidden love. Several days went by and nothing was said, about the dance or my increasing moodiness. I always tried to be first to get the post, but one morning I found someone had beaten me to it. I was summoned into the front room. She had the letter in her hand. Her frown was fixed, her face drained of colour. I said: 'I think that's my letter. Why did you open it?'

She spoke over me: 'What on *earth* were you playing at? Did you have any *thought* for this girl? Do you know how *old* the child is? Have you any *idea* about West Indian families? Have you thought how *difficult* it will be when someone *complains to the Bishop?*' She stopped me replying: 'You don't have to tell me anything. It's over now, the letter says so. She says her mother has said she's too young to be taken out. And *your* mother says the same.'

'Are you going to give me the letter?'

'If you promise to destroy it.'

I still have it, in front of me. Written in a child's hand, it says

> *Dear Richard*
> *I am sorry to disappoint you but I cannot come tomorrow because Mother said she doesn't like me to go out with boys, as yet I am to young. I got your postcard. I wanted to see you myself and tell you I couldn't come. I must close my letter but I hope you can get my letter in time. I hope you forgive me.*
> *I love you*
> *Yours ever*
> *Bella Mills*

I had walked her home after the youth club dance. It was frosty and she was cold, so I put my arm round her. She nestled into my shoulder and I could feel her heart beating. When we got to her door, she looked up at me, her eyes glistening in the moonlight, her mouth slightly open. I had never touched anyone's lips with my lips, and it only lasted a second, but the softness was heaven on earth. She giggled. I kissed her nose. She shut her eyes. I kissed her eyes. She was my angel. She smelled lovely. She was black. She was thirteen. She was my first kiss.

A SHIP IN THE NIGHT

He has HATE tattooed on the knuckles of his right fist; LOVE tattooed on the knuckles of his left. The hands come together in a death-struggle clasp, independent of the preacher, HATE gaining the advantage, but LOVE enduring, forcing its will, till with a saint's tenacity and the power of faith, LOVE prevails, as it must.

We are watching a mirror image of the contest which traditionally has LOVE on the *right* fist, and HATE on the *left*, because the screen like a great sail has been hoisted amidships and half the audience are on one side, half on the other. The film is *The Night of the Hunter*, Charles Laughton's only film as director, starring Robert Mitchum as the preacher. It's night, the moon is full, the stars are brilliant across the sky, the sea is choppy, the air is warm.

'*Leeeeeeaning, leeeeeaning, safe and secure from all alarms…. Leeeeeeaning, leeeeeaning, leaning on the eeeverlaaasting arms…*' sings Mitchum on his horse, his shadow falling across the window where the children are not sleeping.

We are in a dangerous, destabilized, back-to-front world.

We left Madeira yesterday after a day of fortified wine, steep streets and jacaranda trees, and wouldn't touch land again till Venezuela in ten days' time. Some Portuguese had disembarked, some more came on board. We were set fair for the tropics, every day a little hotter, the sea a little bluer, the night sky a little more star-filled and dazzling. Soon there would be flying fish, sporting dolphins and maybe whales. Could anything in heaven surpass this? I had read about Jamaica in *You Only Live Twice* and *Doctor No*, and mugged up on the islands – Curacao, Grenada, St Lucia – that we would visit on the way. Montego Bay, Negril, Dunn's River, Blue Lagoon were all shiny in the brochures, waiting to delight. But for now, there was bliss enough. Being rocked on the deep, watching horror, on a flapping screen, was ecstasy and we could pause.

I stayed on deck after the film had finished, lying back, looking at the sky. I'd never seen so many stars. I'd never felt so small, so safe, so invisible, such a spec in the ocean, such a pinprick in the universe, such an absence, such a ghost.

Ships pass in the night and you don't know it till years later, when you say to the woman who will soon be your wife: 'Where were you in the summer of 1961?' And she says: 'I was crossing the Atlantic. New York to Southampton. I was alone in the state cabin of the SS United States. *It was the turning-point of my life.' And you say: 'That is weird. It was a turning-point for me too, though on a much lesser scale. State cabin! We weren't even above deck! Though we did have permission from Mr Bennett the Chief Purser to have lunch in First Class, provided we had it at 11 am. That meant breakfast at 6.30 so it would go down in time for a full lunch which on the ship was the main meal of the day, with wine and rum to follow. What did you eat in the state cabin?' 'Nothing,' she says laughing. 'I was broke. I wasn't meant to be there. I was escaping. I was on the run.'*

HEAVEN AND HELL

We disembarked at Kingston on Tuesday August 1st. We were met by the Bishop's chaplain, Father Campbell, who drove us and our luggage, down streets with names that I recognized from Ian Fleming. At Bishop's Lodge we were welcomed by Archdeacon Price and his sister who gave us lunch on the veranda after which Jude, Mon and I fell asleep on the swinging sofas. When we woke, Percival Gibson Lord Bishop of Jamaica, in full purple, was standing over us, rocking with laughter, and all the white clergy – my father, the Archdeacon, Father Campbell – in their shorts and sun-hats, were chuckling on the periphery. The first ever black face at the Lambeth Conference, scourge of indolence and corruption, champion of the dispossessed and educator of any child from any background that showed promise, was welcoming us *on his terms* – no alcohol, loose talk, old-country banter or abstruse theology! God was the Stone-Breaker. Jesus was Jamaican. It never snowed at Christmas. We were honoured albino curiosities whose days were numbered.

We stayed the night with the Bishop then set off over the mountains for Montego Bay. There we were joined by Paul Burrough, Chaplain to Overseas People for Leonard Wilson, Bishop of Birmingham. Serving in Malaya during the war he had been captured and spent three years as a POW in Changi prison with Wilson, who at that time was Bishop of Singapore. Together again in Birmingham, Wilson and Burrough now led the Church's welcome to new Caribbean families, denouncing prejudice and fear, as they eased hallelujahs into stiff-backed Victorian parishes. Tall and supple like a tree that could bend and stay standing against the wind, Paul Burrough was a generous, entertaining Christian. An Oxford Blue, he had rowed in the winning eights of 1937 and 1938, scraping a degree in English, then going off to coach rowing in Argentina, until the war came. Ordained in 1946, he returned to the Far East, as a missionary in wartorn Korea. Later he would be appointed Bishop of Mashonaland in Rhodesia during the time of UDI. He was a clerical hero in the mould of Uncle Mo and Uncle Gerald, and my father looked to him as a beacon in an increasingly murky world. When he told him he was thinking of taking the family to Jamaica, Burrough said hurrah! He would square it with Bishop Wilson, then write a letter of introduction to Bishop Gibson in Kingston who would be sure to provide work and quash any thought of 'holiday'; then Paul B himself would pack his trunks and be on a plane to join Bob, Nan and the children, on Doctor's Cave beach!

He never lay in the sun. He would sit fully clothed talking priest-talk, Oxford, rowing and college choirs, then in a flash he'd strip and his long white limbs would be striking out across the bay as we paddled after him to the anchored raft, from which you could dive down among the multi-coloured fishes. Then he'd be dressed and off again, to the bad side of town, just a stone's throw from the millionaire holiday apartments. We once saw him walking straight into a group of Rastafarians; they were arguing and gesturing and he was nodding and listening and they were dancing and he was offering up a prayer and they were chorusing in response, and waving arms as he was blessing them.

My mother was in heaven. She had a maid to do the housework; three articles to write for the *Birmingham Post*; and with Jude, Mon and me in our own apartment next door, she could enjoy child-free 'intelligent conversation' with her two men, over rum-and-cokes on the veranda. When Paul was not there, and she and Bee were in bed, she could imagine the long bleached limbs and stubbled lips, and even cry aloud, without the children being disturbed. And when Paul *was* there, popping in with no warning, she could just bask in his warmth, his boyishness, his *unmarried* state of grace. He was the best thing to happen since she didn't know when, and Bee loved him as a brother and was tickled that his wife could be flirtatious with his friend.

Then suddenly they were gone. Paul disappeared into the night and Bee was on his plane. She was left feeling old, a childminder again, a housewife with no housework because the maid did it all (so *slow* – she could have slapped her!). And the sun was clouding over, there was bucketing rain, and the beach when they could get to it, was infested with gangs of near-naked youths and Judith egging them on; and Richard (since he no longer answered to 'Wit', all her children now had their full names as christened) being bored on the beach, saying he'd rather stay in the apartment writing his 'play'; and Monica whimpering, her eczema pussing and breaking out in the sun, and scratching till she bled; and Elizabeth who had only written one letter the whole time, clearly wretched on her own, uncomforted by the Twidle grandparents, who had been deputed to keep an eye on her. She had thought in the few days left, after Bee went, she would be able to get down to the articles at last, but somehow she'd lost the knack. Her previous pieces for the *Post* had been vivid exposures of injustice and squalor in the back-streets of Balsall Heath, provoking debate on the letters page and praise from the editor who was looking forward so much to Nan Crane's Jamaica series!

She put the writing aside. She busied herself packing. They were leaving in two days. Monica's skin was blistering; she was crying all the time. Judith and Richard were arguing over ownership of the conch shells (which were too big to pack anyway), and each claiming *both* the maraccas, not one each. Back in the days when Bee and Paul were here, they had talked about forming a family skiffle band to play at socials on the boat home – Monica on washboard, Judith and Richard (taking turns if you can't decide) on bongos and maraccas. Nan was dreading the voyage home and it fully lived up to her dread. It was hell on earth, like a slave ship. There were whole families with nowhere to go except on deck, and nothing to do except drink beer. One had to step over them lying head to toe like sardines. Then the hurricanes began, or the *avoidance* of hurricanes, the altering of course and prolonging of the voyage *by three days.* Honestly, she said to Vernon Forbes, the white overlord from Hampden Sugar Estate who was getting out before the blacks *kicked* him out: 'Honestly Vernon, it would be better to sail straight into the heart of the hurricane, instead of simpering round the edges, then at least we might sink!' Then the beer ran out, which led to riots on deck. She took to staying in the cabin with Monica wailing because the eczema was now ravaging her scalp. They went to see the ships's doctor who said all the child's hair would have to be shaved, so he could bandage her, and Nan had to go through all this on her own, with no help, because Richard and Judith were away trespassing on the upper deck, going to dances with first class girls and the two naval cadets whose names were Philip (he was English) and Urban (Trinidaddian though he lived in Stoke Newington). They seemed nice boys when first introduced, and reliable companions for Richard and Judith, but now she wasn't so sure. They were staying up, going to areas that were legally out of bounds, and waking poor Monica with their noise, when they came in bickering and arguing at midnight or one o'clock. So they *weren't* enjoying themselves! That was evident from the harshness of their voices, which was comforting in a way. If they'd come in happy, it would be unbearable.

Then one night, at nearly two o'clock, Judith comes in alone and she was crying.

'Oh Mummy – '

'What is it?'

'It's Hair-zoose. You know, *Jesus,* but he's Spanish so it's pronounced Hair-Zoose. He's our waiter.'

'What's he done?'

'I don't know.'

'What's he done to *you?*'

'He's done *nothing*! He's disappeared! He's gone overboard! I know he has. Because Witty said I wasn't sixteen, as I'd told him I was. Oh Mummy!'

'Stop crying.'

'I've lost him!'

'How old did Richard say you were?'

'Twenty-eight! He said I was married with three children! They were mocking him. He didn't understand. So Philip translated – he speaks Spanish. Then Jesus went away.'

'Which is a very good thing if I may say so.'

'He gave his life for me.'

'No, that was the other one. Where is Richard?'

(*Crying again*) 'I don't know! Philip was being stupid. He was saying: Man overboard! Man overboard! So Urban went to look and Witty followed and now *they've* gone. They've vanished! Oh Mummy what have I started?'

'Did you look for them?'

'I looked for everyone everywhere but no one was anywhere! I wish I was dead!' (*Deep sobbing and choking; Mon, with her bound-up head, like a nun, bewaaaaailing and squeeeeealing; Mother hugging her and cursing THIS BLASTED SHIP!*)

At this point I came in.

THREE SURPRISE TWISTS

We docked on Thursday 14ᵗʰ September. I'd seen the world, written a play, learnt to jive and play bongos; loved every selfish minute. I'd imagined clouds would come down, real and emotional, the moment we got back to the drizzle of Balsall Heath, but the night was hot, almost tropical, when my father, who had met us on the quayside, bought us coffee and hot dogs, then sped us in the new Morris Traveller, 'Ben-Huring' (racing three abreast!) up the new M1, and talking all the way. We now had Jamaicans on the Parish Council; a curate maybe two, would join the team in the new year; and future dreams - top secret! - Paul B was talking to Bishops Leonard (B'ham) and Percival (Jamaica) about a posting, an actual *cure* on the island on a four-year renewable contract! Coo! How about that for a calling, eh love?

After the 'blasted ship' and the 'voyage through hell', you'd have thought my mother would be tight-lipped about new ventures. But the first of three surprise twists in the family narrative was her eagerness to get going on a host of schemes. She didn't yet know that she was pregnant, which would have explained her joy at resuming 'intelligent conversation' with the man she had missed so much! He was busy, she was busy, with joint and separate to-do lists, top of which were the *Birmingham Post* articles, which she set to with gusto, as soon as we'd unpacked, got the washing going and the hoovering, and tried to contact Elizabeth - top of the Worry List, but not so as to dampen her spirit! I also had a deadline, to type up a final draft of the play and it helped to have Mother tap-tapping on her own typewriter in the kitchen: *FROM BALSALL HEATH TO MONTEGO BAY; WEST INDIAN 'RALLY OF THE PRIESTS'*, and *WHY MIGRANTS TAKE A CHANCE ON LIFE IN BRITAIN* to be splashed week by week across the Mainly For Women page, headlining full-page features.

The second surprise twist was Elizabeth. What was she playing at? We hadn't heard from her at all. When we rang the Twidles in Yorkshire, where she had been staying, they were hesitant. 'She's gone,' said my grandmother. 'She's on the road, in a car... (*but she hasn't got a car!*), will be stopping off in Birmingham on her way back to London, and that's all we can say.'

Just as my mother put the phone down, a car pulled into the drive. Elizabeth and a man in a dog-collar got out.

'This is Roy,' she said, when we opened the door. 'He wants to marry me. I said yes.'

She had been staying at Bishop Burton, where my grandfather, had the living. She had confided in my grandmother that what she wanted most was to serve God, to marry a man who shared her faith and to bring up children to do good in the world. But this, she concluded, was setting an impossibly high standard and she was resigned to being a spinster.

Roy Lambert was the youngest of the sons of Canon Lambert best friend of Canon Twidle, since their theological college days. He had four sons, all of whom had taken Holy Orders, and all but one of whom were married. Roy was his 'Benjamin', his most beloved: a boy (now 35) who, setting impossibly high standards for a spouse, had concluded that marriage was not God's will, and was resigned to being a bachelor.

Canon and Mrs Twidle exchanged a wink as the Lamberts entered. They were invited to dinner, and it was arranged, using place-names, that Elizabeth and Roy should sit elbow-to-elbow, knee-to-knee. Later, after the beef and home-grown veg, home-baked apple pie and Yorkshire cheese, the young ones were encouraged to walk in the garden, and then, if they so wished, to cross to the church, and finding it open, as the sun went down, to slip inside, and on an impulse, kneel, hand in hand, heart to heart, and with a kiss, thank God for this moment.

A year later, in the draughty, unheated St Paul's, I would walk my sister, in her white velvet and veil, up the aisle to join Roy. We had played this scene years ago, as Ditcher and Liberty-buff, in Laxton church, and it still felt like a children's game: my father in his robes on the chancel step, canons to left of him, and right of him, surpliced clergy all around.

And half a century on, in another, warmer church, before their four children, daughters- and sons-in-law and twelve grandchildren, Roy and Elizabeth, hand in hand, heart to heart, and with a kiss, gave thanks for this fifty-year wink of God's eye.

*

The third twist was The Twist. I took time off typing and went to the youth club in my final week, hoping to see Bella, and with my new dexterity, to jive jive jive! But the moment I set foot in the hall, it was clear: the tune had changed. Chubby Checker was king. The new dance was banal, unskilled, unromantic and damaging to the spine. I looked around for Bella. She would be fourteen now, the age Juliet was in the play, and the Virgin Mary wasn't much older. How could anyone object? There were just two years between us – and *six* between my parents, *sixteen* between Elizabeth and Roy. How could anyone be appalled? Then I saw her, or someone I assumed was her. I went over to her. She said: 'Let's twist again.' I said: 'How can we, if we've never done it before?' Then she giggled in a high-pitched way. She'd put on weight, was full-bosomed and her twisting legs were beefy and un-natural. I kept thinking of Urban on the boat, the night we went looking for Jesus, leaning on the rail, watching the waves. I glanced over at him. His face was sculpted, with a sheen to it, as Bella's had been when I kissed her in the moonlight. I thought: if he looks at me, if our eyes meet, our hands touch, and nothing is said... Then I felt a presence behind me and we both turned. It was Jesus.

I returned Bella to her friends and was aware of a blond, leggy girl call Sally Blick, approaching through the twisters. We jigged a bit like idiots, till she said: 'Let's go.' I walked her home and we had a long, tongue-filled snog, like an over-sauced meal, till I had to pull away. I said: 'Sorry, I'm not well. I feel sick.' And I *was* sick, after she'd gone in. I was sick in her front garden. It all came up, in a big rush, all the churchy, youth club, twist-induced gumf, till I was empty and completely purged.

Scene Two
THE BASTARD'S RETURN

The play opens in the dark. A fist-fight is in progress: thwacks and biffs, muffled groans and crashing furniture. Finally, the sound of a knife entering flesh and a death-moan. Feet exit swiftly. A door slams. A light is switched on. The baronial dining-room of a Jacobean country house, some chairs overturned. Downstage, the body of a well-dressed middle-aged man in a pool of blood with a knife in his chest. Enter Elsie, the short-sighted maid, carrying a tray of cups and saucers. She almost trips over the corpse – 'Clumsy, clumsy...' – and exits with the tray. Re-enters staggering under a large pile of plates. This time she sees the corpse, registers shock, hurries to the sideboard, puts the plates down and screams.

The Bastard's Return is a play in two acts about vengeance in the family. It began as part two of the *Oresteia* as retold by Agatha Christie. But as the Jamaica days lengthened and the typewriter tapped along, it acquired a style and story-line of its own. More farce and *grand guingol* than tragedy, it was theatrical first and foremost: risque, rude and juvenile, why not? I was younger than Shakespeare ever was as a playwright. I should be allowed an 'early period'.

When I got back to St John's, with its Broadmoor-like facade, and H-block shape, with wings housing fifty-bed dormitories, which still hosted House Prefects' beatings, when the whole house would gather, to witness a boy bent over, and swished with one swish of the cane from each prefect; as I passed through the portals, with the West Indies in my travelography and *The Bastard's Return* in my bag, I felt ready to face any music. Tick Turner would require my script for perusal, and if I wasn't robust in its defence, would unpick it till it fell to pieces. No one had ever yet bested him in argument – he would grind on till your spirit died – so I resolved, if it was to be attritional, in the last resort, to employ subterfuge. There was unrest in the air, youth rising, old ways hardening. Christine Keeler, the same age as my eldest sister, was just beginning to dismantle the Macmillan government. J F Kennedy as the new, youngest ever US President, despite ramping up the Cold War, adding billions to the defence budget, provoking the building of the Berlin Wall and sowing the dragon's teeth of Vietnam, at least supported civil rights, inaugurated the space race and alone of world leaders (Kruschev, Adenauer, de Gaulle, Macmillan) still seemed to be having sex.

*

I'm standing outside Tick's door. I'm early. I know he's reading my script because he said he would set aside half an hour after lunch and I should come to him at two. I can almost hear him, the other side of the door: the squeak of the knuckly fingers, stiffly turning the pages. Then suddenly, like a fire alarm, the horrible honking hee-haw, which is a Good Sign, I remind myself, a Very Good Sign. Long may it honk. Then too soon, it goes quiet, as death, and that is *not* good. I can almost hear the sucking in of breath through twisted teeth. I knock and go in..

'Ah Richard,' he says. (When did he ever call me that?) 'Sit down. I have read your play.'

He is thinking: this boy is my project. He has aptitude and ambition, marred by immaturity. To achieve *sophrosyne* (moderation) which is the key to steady progress, one must chip away, chip by chip, at the crude marble. Like Praxiteles, one may sculpt him; then like Pygmalion, breathe life into his lungs. A year from now, having filled the 'Jamaica crack' with concrete study, he will have achieved three S-levels topped with a State Scholarship: of which, in this the last year of the award, there will be a thousand or so offered: surely a wide enough field! However, should he fall short (should the sun not rise – *honk!*), then the Rustat Foundation to Jesus College Cambridge, exclusive to St John's Leatherhead, will be his for the tapping into. And if that should fail (if hell should freeze – *hee-haw, hee-*

haw!), then the Oxford open scholarship in the spring is distinctly possible. But first we must tackle his play.

'You don't like it sir?'

'On the contrary, your work has an inevitability, such as one finds in the Greeks, but you spoil it with coarseness.'

'But sir, did not Aristoph – '

'Aristophanes,' he interposes, 'was coarse to a purpose, and shocking as well. Whereas your humour works only on a scatalogical level.'

'But you laughed sir. I heard you.'

'Not at the location of the disposal of the body.'

'But *The Body in the Lavatory* is my alternative title: a take on Agatha Christie. Surely that could be funny sir.'

He said: 'We'll come to alternative titles later.'

I was with him for an hour, identifying and extracting all low-level lines. I fought for each victim, but the inexorable mangling wore me down. So the body was not to be stowed in the bog, obliging the incontinent Colonel to stagger on with crossed legs, but in the loft whence at a key moment, it might 'fall through the ceiling and crush the murderer!', offered the self-styled *artifex*. 'That would be dramatic as well as funny, not in a low but a *lofty* manner!!! And the predatory clergyman, (based on Mitchum in *The Night of the Hunter...*) does it not spoil the tension, to have him loosen his trousers and chase the girl round the room, only to be felled by an unlikely axe-wielding twelve-year-old?'

When the script was in shreds, he said finally: 'And now the title: *Bastard*, do we need that?' I should have retorted: 'But Shaw has the Bastard of Orleans in *St Joan* and Shakespeare in *King Lear* says: 'God stand up for bastards!'

His eyes lit up: 'Let's call it *The Return of the Prodigal Son*.'

*

Thenceforth, week by week, I would bring my revised text to be gone through line by line. Having the body crash through the ceiling onto the head of the murderer, was deemed technically unachievable; but the loft, not the lavatory, remained its location, provoking no laughs. Likewise the vicar no longer lusted for the ingenue; he just strangled her, which was morally okay (but not funny). At our final session, at the end of term, Tick referred to himself as my 'partner in crime'. Excess moderated, together we had chiselled at the rough stone, and crafted a thing of 'proportion and some beauty'. The pedagogy of the Classical VIth, so often sniped at, had been vindicated. Boys seated, in a cave, as if in chains, drained of colour, watching shadows perform, might now turn and see the real show for the first time. We could invite them (he cracked his knuckles) to step out of Hades, into the light of day; out of lifeless texts, into the sunshine of new work. He stood, swished open his curtain, looked out at the early-rising, rosy-fingered dawn. He would never be Michael Shaw, who had directed *St Joan*, and last year's *Tartuffe*, (R A Crane as Elmire, the seductress who exposes the lustful preacher – he found this disturbing); and he would never teach languages with Shaw's *brio*, nor be first off the blocks when holidays came, jetting off to Patagonia, as the man did, writing travel books and articles; and he would never be Derek Pitt, teaching history as Plato taught in the olive groves: no boys in rows, but desks pushed back, allowing space for perambulation. Pitt had played the Inquisitor in *St Joan*, arguing at length for the damnation of heresy; then the following year directed *Richard II*, Shakespeare's most iconoclastic play. No, Tick would never be bombastic or double-sided, like Shaw and Pitt. And he would *never* be like the modernizing new bloods now coming in, following a purge of the priests. There had been three chaplains in the Common Room; now there were none. Tick had stood up for them (he himself was privately in the grip of a vocation), and had gone over the head of the Bod, so to speak, and spoken to the Field Marshal. Montgomery, as Chairman of the Governors, had always said 'Lobby me, any man-jack, any time!' and as a militant Christian, knew the value of padres. At the same time, he was 'a weather-vane for the Wind of Change', and told Tick that no posse of priests should block a boy's path. (Were there not loose priests enough in the region to do services?) Tick had come away feeling, on the one hand, stung as Rommel had been at Alamein, yet on the other hand, encouraged, in the new fresh breeze, to tack along or sink. Now, as 'partner in crime' to a boy-playwright, he might just steal a march on Shaw and Pitt, and put a spike in the new brooms. Monty and the Bod might also take note that their 'stuck-in-the-mud dullard', was at last extracting his boots from the slough, and marching to the new music. Very soon he would announce that he was planning an excursion for the Classical Sixth: a two-week study tour of Rome and Pompeii, in the summer vacation, *which he himself would lead*. That, he mused, should set a seal on the new Tick.

A MUTINY

There was a boy called Boyle, who had boils all over his face, neck and back. He was sporty and pugilistic. A Crusader for Christ, and a sergeant on the fast track to becoming Drum Major in the Corps of Drums, he turned up to audition for *The Return of the Prodigal Son*, enthused by the Biblical title. He had trouble reading the lines, seemed to be paraphrasing deliberately, as if censoring as he went along. The script, he judged, was 'bloody brilliant, I tell you!' and he would kill to play the lead. By asking him to read the murdering vicar – could he not just *punch* her instead of strangling her? – was I not confirming, that the part was written with him in mind! Eyeing the flaming craters, I said: 'Not so fast Boylsie! There's a queue of vicars here.' He gave me a shoulder-hug. 'Tell you what, Dickie love (actors' talk! La-di-da!), we play ball and I'll forgive you'. 'Forgive what?' 'The *try*, remember? When you lost us the cup. Last year, the house tie against West. You can't have forgotten. You were standing in front of the goal' he chortled viciously. 'Just seconds from the final whistle! We were winning 15:13! Just you standing alone and de Horsey Girling charging towards you with the ball! You could have brought him down. You were our ace defender. But you funked it. Why?'

Fade to a frosty, foggy day on the rugger field. I'm shivering in shorts, on rucked-up grassless ground, hard as iron. There's just me between the goal and the charging RdeHG. One leap at his legs - I'm a ace defender! - and he's down! I've saved the day, while at the same time pressing my cheek to his thigh, a thing that could only happen in sport, and then only in the manliest of collisions, never love. But we haven't spoken for weeks. I'm a midge in his world. He is resolved, in his yellow-and-black West House colours, to bowl me bus-like into the turfless pitch. Will I launch myself, risk death, gain glory? Or pretend I hadn't seen?

I didn't cast Boyle, and he vowed, with his piggy eyes, to shame me, but not yet. I assembled a strong cast and felt confident enough to hand over the original *Bastard's Return* to Tick, to be destroyed, keeping a copy in my locker, should anyone wonder where the laughs had gone. There was rebellion in the air, soon to erupt in revolution, and it had *acting* at its heart! Five years on, I would audition for the film *If...* about an armed insurrection in a public school. I didn't get the part, and when I saw the film, I found it dishonest. Machine-gunning masters and parents from the chapel roof, was not the way to effect change. Things certainly *needed* to change and *my* year in *my* house at St John's did achieve revolutionary change without blood in the quad. The tipping-point came with a scandal that pitted the theatre against the army. Twelve of us had founded the Drama Circle, dedicated to the overthrow of staff-run plays. Our leader was

David Collins. He had written a play called *One* which he would star in and direct, with me as the female lead. We rehearsed during corps time, so regularly skipped parade. At first this was hardly noticed. An absence of twelve out of five hundred cadets wasn't going to make waves. Then someone, seeking an *If*-like revolution, must have tipped off the *Daily Express* and given an unattributed interview. 'MUTINY AT MONTY'S SCHOOL!' was splashed across the society page: not a section the Field Marshal regularly turned to, but someone alerted him and he summoned the Bod. This was the new Bod, Ian Sutherland, just a term into the job, a mild man in his early forties, who we all thought would never measure up to his predecessor, the Saxon-blooded Hereward Wake. But we were wrong. Sutherland came in like a breeze, with Monty behind him, to speed the school into the post-war era. First to go were the priests, making way for three new brooms to sweep in. Ross, Hamilton and Chubb, hardly older than the oldest of the boys, would shake the curriculum to its roots. Soon science would lead, leaving Greek for the stragglers. To Spanish and French, were added German and Russian. Old practices – prefects' beatings, initiation rites, compulsory CCF, even fagging – would be history within a decade.

On the day of the *Daily Express* exposure, the whole school was summoned. The Bod came on stage, billowing in his gown into a down-stage spot. Slowly he raised his head, seeming to fix each one of us with his steely eyes.

'I am...' he began, 'by nature... (pause)... slow to anger... (long pause,) ... but what I have seen today... (longer pause)... has made me.... (*sotto voce*, hold the stare)... *very angry*...'

We were spellbound. This was *acting*: a masterclass the Drama Circle had provoked and should learn from, both the voice and the message. Modernising, he said, was his mission but on *his* terms. No new ethos for the school should compromise the duty of obedience that lay at its core. No boy should at any time, whatever the provocation, go sneaking to the press. 'This act of sneaking is worse than sneaking on your fellows, because it un-pins our society and brings the whole school down. Revolution is not ro-mantic. Though born of high ideals, historically it ends in chaos which leads to terror. As long as rules are in place, they must be adhered to. They can only be questioned from the position of trust. This trust is the force that binds us and it has been broken. A mistake has been made. It will not be repeated.' He would see the twelve members of the Drama Circle, this evening, in his house.

We thought we were going to be expelled, and were planning to leak the story to all the papers this time, but when we were gathered in his sitting-room, and he made his entrance, he was relaxed, not a angry at all; he hardly spoke of the scandal. He said he had been most impressed by *One*, and wanted to know what we were planning next. Collins piped up: 'It's a verse play by Richard Luckett (South House, History Sixth), called *The Making of Mordred*, about rebellion in Camelot. It's anti-war, anti-establishment, and we have the support of CND.' The Bod essayed a smile. He would like to read the script and looked forward to seeing the play. He could offer the library as a venue. Meanwhile Collins should come and see him to arrange a rehearsal schedule that did not clash with the CCF.

He asked me to stay behind (or did I dream this?). When the eleven had gone and the door was closed, he turned to face me. I thought he would invite me to sit down, but we remained standing. He said he had proof that it was I who had leaked the story to the press, and for this I would be expelled. But first it was proper that I should own up.

'Why sir, if you have already decided that I did it?'

'I need to hear it from your own mouth.'

'From my own mouth sir, I will tell you: I did not leak the story.'

He looked at me, boring a hole in my brain, and finding it empty, slowly pursed his lips and tapped them with his finger. He didn't believe me; he didn't disbelieve me. I was in limbo. I held his gaze till he turned to face the window, so he didn't see me walk through the door without opening it.

THE FIGHT

My head being empty was ready to fill with resolutions for '62: three S-level passes and the last of the State Scholarships, crowned in December by the Rustat Foundation Scholarship to Jesus, allowing me to leave school at Christmas and go straight to the stage door of the Birmingham Rep just as a junior actor falls ill, and they take me on for nine months, encouraging me to stay, but I tell them so sorry, off to Cambridge don't you know, acting all the way and with a Equity card! All this factored onto a golden final Leatherhead year, begun on the wings of raves for my Joseph Surface in Derek Pitt's *School for Scandal* - '... *Crane's outstanding performance. How civil he was! Such elegance of gesture, such exquisite philandering! Such a voice! Such a figure! Such a Surface!*" - then straight into rehearsals for *The (Bastard's) Return*, while also prepping Guinevere for the Drama Circle in the Easter hols, and co-writing and directing the summer term's Sixth Form Revue, which would feature me as Tick Turner and at the end popping up *ex machina* (helicopter) as Field Marshal Viscount Montgomery of Alamein.

*

It was the third Saturday of term. We'd been rehearsing and getting nowhere. Boyle had appointed himself prompter, and was crowding me. His campaign to 'take me down a peg' was causing me to lose confidence, and whenever I suggested feeding in some of the forbidden lines, he would suck in his teeth and go tut-tut-tut. Finally I cracked and said: 'BOYLE, WILL YOU *FUCK OFF!*' He walked out without a murmur. We were free now to re-incorporate, one by one, the lost lines, and suddenly like twigs burning, the big laughs began to come. The body returned to the bog, the colonel staggered on, in an agony of incontinence and the vicar, lusting for the ingenue, was axed to death with his trousers down. I swore everyone to secrecy. Defying Tick was a beatable, even expellable offence. But we'd crossed our Rubicon, and no one would know till the first night which would be electric. (Whatever one might think of Boyle, he would never sneak.) And if I had to go, which I would, if there was a threat of caning – I was seventeen for chrissake! - then, forsaking S-levels and university, on the back of Guinevere who was emerging as the lead character in Luckett's play, and second only to Helen of Troy, as the Bitch-Queen of history, I would get the pros along to see it, and go straight into the business, so help me.

*

I was called to a meeting in Collins's study, before breakfast on the Sunday morning. I had ducked being a member of the triangle within the Drama Circle, seeing myself as more of a Scofield than an Olivier, ie preferring not to compromise my acting with organizing, so had no idea what this was about or why the air seemed thick with embarrassment the moment I entered. Collins was posing, elbow on mantel-piece, chin in hand. Munro, the general manager, perusing papers, wouldn't look at me. Luckett, the author, was all smiles, but of the pitying variety.

Collins said: 'Thanks for coming chum. We've only got a moment. Luckett will you explain?'

'The fact is,' said Luckett, pausing, 'while it's true I wrote Guinevere, with yourself in mind, the way the play is going, she's emerging, how shall we say, as more *feminine*, younger; not so much Lucrezia Borgia, as Jackie Kennedy.'

'Fine by me,' I agreed. 'I can do feminine, young, (grin, blink) Jackie K.'

Luckett passed a glance to Collins.

'Sure you can,' said Collins. 'This isn't about skill. It's modernity, how we see ourselves, free from the sexual shackles of school.'

'We're going to cast a girl,' said Munro. The penny dropped. 'And we've found one,' he went on, extracting a photo from his papers. 'Sophie Kingsley, goes to Guildford High. Has played Juliet and Cressida. What do we think?'

'She's gorgeous,' said Collins.

'When can we see her?' said Luckett.

'So that's it,' said I, as the bell rang for breakfast.

*

I was of a mind to give up everything. The fuckers had been seeking out *girls* behind my back, getting photos, assessing gorgeousness. I was in a mood to punch someone, with wit not fists, and the punchiest person, seated diagonally down the table at breakfast, was Boyle. He was joking with Munro, prompted by the Drama Circle casting, about the bustiness and legginess of the girls at Guildford High. So I started my own conversation about the *spottiness* of girls, the *spunkiness* of boils. Was it semen that spurted when you discharged them at the mirror? Was squeezing them akin to tossing off? In the battle of the conversations, my own was winning with laughs all down the table, and soon Boyle was backing off.

I came into the day-room ten minutes before chapel bell. The room was crowded and silent. In the centre was Boyle with his jacket and tie off and shirt-sleeves rolled.

'Uh-oh!' I spun around.

'Don't let him go!' barked Boyle.

Two of his cohort grabbed my arms.

'What's this about?' I protested. 'Is it my birthday?'

'Say it again, what you said,' said Boyle.

'What I just said?'

'What you said at breakfast.'

'Oh God, I said so much. "Pass the butter... Marmalade anyone?"'

I hardly felt it: the crack of knuckle on tooth, then the whole side of my face ballooning. I was on the floor, curled up.

'Stand him up!' said Boyle. 'Get his jacket off.'

I stayed in the floor, yelling: 'Sorry sorry sorry! I didn't mean to prick fun at your spunky volcanoes! You blistering fascist fucker!'

They dragged me to my feet, got the jacket off me, loosened my tie, squared me up.

'Boyle,' I said. 'Are you a Christian?'

His face was a furnace. Only his fists could speak. I raised my ballooned-up cheek and turned the other one. He smacked it hard. I fell back. There was blood, a loose tooth. I was crying now. 'Okay,' I blubbed. 'I apologize. I didn't mean you any harm, you poxy idiot. You can't help it, you're stuck with it, being an ugly bigoted fucking pus-pisser! *Don't hit me!*'

The chapel bell rang.

Weirdest thing: no one mentioned my face. I went through the whole day, with a stuck pig's head and garbled speech, and no one seemed to notice. We had Quintuple Tick – five Tick lessons in a row – and all he said at the end was : 'How's the play coming along?' I said: 'Fine sir.' But he couldn't have heard me, mangling the words through blood-blocked, pumped-up, tooth-chomped lips.

A TICKING OFF

We couldn't restore the title because it was already publicised and to change it would have alerted Tick and got the play banned. But everything else was exactly as writ in *The Bastard's Return*. Not a word of Tick's amendments remained. There were two performances, a matinee and an evening. The audience hooted and brayed. They guessed the murderer in the first minute, but that didn't matter. It was comedy all the way, and the actors rode their laughs like jockeys. People were stamping at the end. I was dragged on stage and forced to bow on my own, with all the actors applauding. It could have been the high-point of my life to date, nudging even *Princess Juju* into second place. But I was petrified about Tick. And with good reason. He came to the second show. He sat in the front row, between Pitt and the Bod. I watched them from behind. Pitt was vastly amused; I could see his shoulders shaking with laughter. The Bod was poised. Was that a laugh or a cough? Inscrutable, unmoved, either one way or the other, he sat it out, was gracious, when I went up to him afterwards, though he didn't shake my hand.

But Tick, once the truth sank in, the shattering of the dream, once he knew I had abused his trust, made a mockery of his transformation into a 'partner in crime', he sat like death. Even in the heat of mirth, you could feel the iceberg of betrayal, that his hopes now foundered on. I learnt later that that very day, his aunt who had been a parent to him and lived in a cottage behind the school, had been rushed into hospital. Over the next nine months, till her death, she would require Tick's regular care. He would have to hand over the supervision of the study tour of Rome and Pompeii, to Bill Chubb, a younger man, less demanding of discipline, less classically trained.

He didn't ask to see me. He no longer called me Richard. He was formal in lessons, not singling me out, not responding to witty or astute observations, never again bursting into the honking laugh. He was civil, if we met in a corridor, unsmiling and distant if I tried to open a conversation. He had done with me. I was immature, weak-willed, lacking in leadership, a moral coward and a fool. He said as much, in my report, with all the authority of a man betrayed.

THE LAST DAYS OF...

I'm walking fast down an empty street of roofless houses. The sun is going down. All the living have left. I went to find the brothel which I knew was here, but wasn't mentioned by the guide. I'd been in the bath-house, where slaves massaged the flabby limbs of merchants. I'd been to the 5000-seat theatre, sat at the back and heard a whisper from the stage. I'd been to the amphitheatre where Spartacus fought his brother gladiators to the death. But I hadn't found the Lupanare Grande, the Great House of the She-Wolf. This was Gononsafario's *casa dei cazzi*, as old as the wolf who has suckled Romulus and Remus. But why had she turned to prostitution? Was that just the way of the world, the way language turns, the way the sacred and iconic are just a breath away from the sensual and sordid? Was someone laughingly asking that question of the girl whose lupine lips couldn't reply, being gagged with *cazzo*, in the early morning of 24th August 79 AD, as the earth shuddered and shook and the mountain spumed fire and the sky rained ash?

It was dark now. They'd all gone. I could hear a train in the distance. Was there another one back to Rome that night or should I wait till the morning? In the long arc of time that we ghosts had walked these streets, getting back to mortality hardly mattered. I was among my own people, non-beings, unremembered: the void human shapes that can be filled with plaster to show the last terrible attitude of a body snuffed out in the pyro-clastic surge.

They didn't see the mountain. I didn't see the bus. They were buried; I was washed away.

∗

I still see Bill Chubb. He's in his eighties now. He was the first teacher I had who didn't seem to be standing on the other side of a gulf. Going to Rome with him, instead of Tick, was a twist of fate that completed my schooling. If you can leave having, just once, bridged the divide between teacher and pupil, you will be equipped for university, where dialectic is the key. Bill recalls that I did him a favour on the Rome trip. I asked him to join us in our compartment on the train: perfectly natural now; unheard of then. No deference - we called him Bill - we were at ease on the same journey. And I thought about Tick: how he was missing all this; how his last chance to break free was scuppered, on the one hand, by me, dismissing his revisions (re-reading them you can see how he was trying to move the play towards tragedy, and ten years on I would do just that with *The Blood Stream*, my modern *Oresteia*); and on the other hand, by his auntie, whom I never met but imagined to be the cause of his emotional immaturity. He called me immature, but even at seventeen, I'd already had a richer life/death to be spurred on by. When had he sung solo in church, skipped exams to cross the ocean, been beaten, buggered and biffed into a balloon-face, staked his life in a play?

We patched up a kind of relationship, to get me to university. I achieved three good S-Levels, but not the State Scholarship. I was offered a place at Jesus College Cambridge but without the Rustat Foundation. He hoped I would try for the Oxford Open Scholarship but I'd had my fill of exams. Culturally, he nodded along to the Incidentals, the North House close harmony group of which I was a member, but was unamused by my impersonations of himself and Monty in the Sixth Form Revue.

Half way through the spring term, he finally made me a House Prefect, and against his advice, we began rushing through reforms: no more dustbinizing of new boys; no more boy-on-boy beatings or unpaid personal fagging. It was a good final term. I was signing off with a light heart. Tick also was moving, placidly, towards his own signing off. With auntie deceased, he was free at last to pursue his vocation. He would leave, return to college and pledge himself to the church. If it wasn't too late he would find a new life, that was more enriching to the spirit and more useful to the world. But it *was* too late. He did get ordained, he did take on parish life, but he missed the daily discipline, the teaching and the boys. Dwindling congregations, the politicking of councils, the intimacy of pastoral care and the constant intrusion of the secular world, made him ill and depressed. He lost contact with the school. No old boys sought him out. There is no record of what happened to him after he left his parish, where he went or how he died.

RETURN TO T.O.R.

I had a term before Cambridge. I wanted to teach. I wrote to Mark Flynn at The Old Ride which had now moved to Bradford-on-Avon, Wilts. He said there was a junior master they were trying to get rid of, and if they succeeded, a place would become available, to teach geography, junior maths, PT and games. I should come and visit them anyway. Old Mr Flynn was dead. Mrs Flynn was still active. Mr Thomas was back in the city. Mark Flynn was sole head.

Grandpa Twidle, having retired, had moved with Granny Twidle to Bath. I drove with my mother to help them settle in, then continued on my own, for six miles to Bradford-on-Avon.

The new Old Ride had an ivy-covered lodge and a winding, leafy drive, not at all forbidding. The house itself was similar in style to the previous house, but softer and warmer, with curtained leaded windows, higgledy-piggledy chimneys, more shrubs than trees, and instead of the dark Jacobean studded oak, a bright green panelled door with a plant-filled porch, and a buzzer for a bell.

I was greeted by Mark who led me swiftly to see Mrs Flynn in the sitting-room. She was sitting on the chintz-covered sofa like a child. Her bosom, once ample and upheld in a sort of sling, was now loose as if punctured.

'I was sorry to hear about Mr Flynn,' I began.

'He doesn't like it here.'

'I mean old Mr Flynn. I'm sorry he died.'

'I don't know. He's always wandering. Why are you here?'

'Mr Mark said there might be a teaching post going for just a term.'

She had fallen asleep. A maid, not one I knew, brought in the tea, set it down, tip-toed out again. I poured a cup, drank it, thought I might look around, got up, went to the door.

'Where are you going?'

'I thought I might – '

'If you see Toby will you tell him?'

'What should I tell him?'

I was standing in front of the door which opened suddenly. Mark came in.

'Ah tea! Have you had some? What, no buns?'

'Yes thank you,' I said. 'I've had a cup.'

'This boy...' began Mrs Flynn, puzzling it out.

'We were hoping he'd be our new junior master mother.' Then to me: 'I'll show you round.'

We walked swiftly through the house, through dorms and formrooms, changing-rooms, play-room, big school room, halls. He showed me the scholarship board, pointing high up to:

1958 R A CRANE
St. John's School Leatherhead

He allowed me a moment to reflect and feel proud, but my eye had been drawn to the name below mine:

1960 W S LANDA
Marlborough College

Just William! My co-gardener! I felt tears prick my eyes. Whatever had happened with Gononsafari, he had survived it and won a scholarship. As had I. But to what end? There we were, our names permanently inscribed, as on a gravestone. We could be dead and who would know?

'Shall we hurry on?' said Mark.

As we walked out onto the terrace into the garden under a grey sky, he explained he'd actually been unable to dislodge the damn-fool junior master, so there wouldn't in fact be a teaching post available. But it was always nice to see an old boy nonetheless! We crossed the lawn, taking in lily-pond, trees, a walled garden, down to a shallow ha-ha, as if someone had recreated Horwood House but a softer version, with no long grass or woods. Mark himself was a smoothed-out version of his father, without the horse-bites and crumpled cassock, and none of his brother's hop-skip *elan*, or his mother's eagle-eye. Standing for a moment on the edge looking out, I felt relieved that I didn't have to consider coming back here. My memories had been homogenized, removing both harmful and life-giving bacteria, and straining off the cream: no sun, no rainbow, just a dampness in the air.

SKIRTING THE VOID

I got a job in the Easter holiday working nights for Bird's Custard, and on the bus to and from the depot, in smoke breaks and at home when I couldn't sleep in the day, I read the whole of *Crime and Punishment*. It was written in a month; I read it in a fortnight. The blank term before Cambridge, I now knew, could be filled, and tolerated. I had discovered Dostoyevsky! I didn't need to go anywhere. Bird's would keep me on, packaging, labling, stacking and loading, through nights and months, unaware they were harbouring an axe-murderer who believed that to do good in a bad world, the *ubermensch* must first exterminate the vermin. I was crossing the void, from school to university, boyhood to youth, via St Petersburg, built by Peter the Great on the bodies of his workers. Can you create a modern, westward-looking city on the backs of tens of thousands dead? Can you wash off the blood and not have it seeping back into your dreams? I was ready to rebel, but silently, so that only *I* would know I was cutting free from 'salvation'. Others could continue in the lie; that was their comfort. Only I possessed the truth. I stopped singing the Creed. It was Easter Sunday. The church was full. As crucifer, robed in cassock and cotta, I led the procession, flanked by candle-bearers. The music was sublime. The words had age and poetry at their heart. The living flame, the smell of wax, my father's clear tenor ascending to the vaulted ceiling, the choir stretching their mouths and singing their hearts out, the congregation following shambling along, all were saying: Join us! Accept that you are sinful, child-like and in mortal peril, and sign up to be cleansed. The price is complete surrender to these fixed articles of faith. Join us, believe with us in the Absolute Authority of the Incomprehensible, and you will have protection for ever.

Walking home with me, my mother said:

'You weren't singing the Creed. People noticed.'

'I was thinking about what I was being required to believe.'

'It creates a bad impression.'

'*Very God of Very God, visible and invisible, begotten not made...*'

'I had to tell them you weren't well.'

'*Incarnate of the Holy Ghost of the Virgin Mary...* I find it really hard to believe all that stuff. Does it matter if Jesus wasn't physically the son of God? Did he ever claim to be? Wasn't he much more concerned with dismantling institutions and oppressive dogmas like the Creed. It doesn't even *mention* what he taught, his humanity, how you should love your neighbour, turn the other cheek etc, and not be a hypocrite!' I was in my stride now. 'The Creed is just a list of impossible things written by monks hundreds of years ago, for political reasons. If you don't switch off your brain and sign up, you won't be saved. Well actually, I'm not really bothered about salvation. It's what you do *here* that matters, and you can do loads of good without having to kowtow to autocratic nonsense. Sorry Mum.'

She was biting her lip, not speaking and I knew she was probably with me on all this, but could never say so; not only because as vicar's wife, she had to toe the line, but because *belief is all we have*. In the beginning, the earth was without form and void, and it still is. All we've done is build a platform of beliefs and it's wafer thin. If you pick holes in it, very soon it'll give way and we'll all go plunging into the void! We could have discussed all this, but she was turning her deaf ear. We didn't speak all the way home. I went up to my ice-blue room and locked the door. I would have thrown myself on the bed and sobbed my heart out, but I was beyond acting now. I sat on the floor like a prisoner, condemned for telling the truth. God was dead. There was no plan. The Creed ignored the only virtue I clung too. Sure of this, after an interval, I would now go down, put on a face, make an entrance. She would have told my father who would raise his eyebrows as if to say: 'Wit, let's talk.' But I would avoid him, slip away, go for walks instead of sleeping, zombified by the night shift, the clangour of automation, the custard that coated you in vanilla and turned the bath water yellow, the smoke breaks in the smoke room where you were considered unsociable if you sat there reading. I'd finished the book anyway. Raskolnikov was in Siberia.

I felt ancient, bulky, invisible, brain-dead.

STRATFORD DAYS

A letter came from Gabbitas-Thring, the Educational Agency, on whose books I'd forgotten I was. A junior post had suddenly come up at Idlicote House Preparatory School at Shipston-upon-Stour, near Stratford-upon-Avon. I had decided on the principle of 'Those who can, do; those who can't, teach', to stay away from schools. But this was a chance to leave home and I leapt at it. I drove with my mother in the Morris Traveller for the interview. I didn't want her there, but actually it helped. Mr Parsons, the headmaster, had a mother, aged ninety, a permanent presence in the staff drawing-room, whose hand poured the tea and whose opinion was law. As Mr Parsons showed me the school, holding my arm (he was blind), the two mothers were conversing. Mrs Parsons had been companion to the late Queen Mary, and had inherited her dresses. With her toque, her pearls, her raised coiffure, rounded bosom and erect bearing, she was the double of the dowager queen and had in fact stood in for her on a number of occasions. It was rare she had the chance to give audience to the mother of a candidate master, and this mother was so sweet, so engaging, so natural, henceforth she would insist on the mother, if there was one, being the deciding factor on whether or not to employ.

I got the job. I began immediately. My fiefdom, said Parsons (known as Stinker from his initials LAMP, which is 'oil lamp' in naval slang) will be Form II, a class of ten eight- and nine-year-olds. I would take them for everything: English, Latin, Scripture, Maths, French, History, Geography and Art. I would also coach cricket, and organize athletics. My duty days would be Monday and Thursday and every third Sunday. Every Saturday except Speech Day, would be free.

The aim of the school was to provide a liberal education, treating every boy as an individual (fees 74 guineas per term). The duty master should never 'supervise' – a dead word! – but should personally encourage new activities, never lingering in one area but fluidly moving across the whole school. Dialogue and debate were the school's life-blood, with weekly forums, and regular talks set up to keep it coursing. All boys should do sport, whether they were good at it or not, the emphasis being on 'playing the game'. There was no corporal punishment. Boys should learn to right the wrong, to meditate on misdemeanours and be corrected through physical tasks, such as cleaning and digging. Every night there would be staff dinner and the rules were strict: jackets and ties even in the summer, no 'boy talk' or politics. And at no time should there be any deference or even *reference* to the blindness. Mr Parsons and his sister, Miss Parsons, who taught dancing and drama, and was also blind, could 'see' (with ears, noses, fingers and the eyes of others), as well as any sighted person. Having them take your arm might give an impression of dependence, but this was false. There was not a chink of dependence in the armoury of the Parsons family, and generally when your arm was gripped, it was to control and steer *you*.

I enjoyed my teaching. There was no set curriculum in Form II. As long as work was set, completed, marked, reworked and reported on, and the individual flourished, Mr Parsons was pleased. I came ignorant and fresh to most of the subjects and he liked that: the teacher setting off into *terra incognita* alongside the pupils. I found I could do most of it on the hoof, debating the problems even in maths, with books mostly kept closed and red herrings aplenty. Innovation scored when it came to art and we did action painting, pushing all the desk to the side, on a sheet on the floor, using foot-prints, beetroot and eggs and riding my bicycle over it. I only once failed completely. We were doing Scripture and discussing the transfer of devils into the swine. Suddenly the class tipped over into chaos. I was screaming myself hoarse as Fried-Eggie used to do, then sitting with my head in my hands praying for death. The room fell silent. I blessed them all. They understood, in a way we had never understood Mr Carneggie. Then I looked up. They were seated good as gold in their rows. Stinker Parsons was in the doorway.

*

On Saturdays when I was free, I would cycle the nine miles into Stratford, go straight to the theatre, book my ticket for that night's show, have egg and chips in the transport café by the cinema, see a film in the afternoon, walk by the river, have a sandwich, see the play then cycle home. I saw *Barabbas* with Anthony Quinn; *The Tempest* with Tom Fleming, Roy Dotrice, Ian Holm; *Porgy and Bess* with Sidney Poitier; *The Comedy of Errors* with Alec

McCowan, Ian Richardson, Diana Rigg; *Heavens Above* with Peter Sellers; *Julius Caesar* with Kenneth Haigh, Tom Fleming, Cyril Cusack and Roy Dotrice.

On the day I saw *Caesar*, for some reason I was without the bike, so I hitched into Stratford. It was a cloudy day threatening rain. I saw *Heavens Above* in the afternoon, about a vicar who upsets the parish by appointing a black dustman as church warden, and giving charity to gypsies. An expert in this field, I thought it was mild and rather cliched, compared with the Piggotts and Balsall Heath. *Julius Caesar*, which I was looking forward to for the politics and the history, having rebelled against and also *played* a conquering general (Monty) and having stood in Rome on the spot where Caesar lay and Antony made his speech; but the play, which I'd set such store by, as the last of my Stratford jaunts, was dreary beyond words, except for Caesar himself, played by Dotrice, who was electric, almost literally. He lit up the room, the way Monty does – you have to notice him and be amazed! He insists on that! – so that when he is snuffed out, there's no fire left in the play. I would have left, except I knew that his ghost appears near the end, and might perk things up. And he did for a moment, then there was just the killing oneself because one has blown it. I didn't wait for the curtain call.

It was raining when I came out. There weren't many cars on the road and no one was stopping. I walked for about half an hour. I estimated if I walked the full nine miles and the rain didn't stop, I'd be as wet as if I'd swum home up the river, in all my clothes, like Cassius plunging 'accoutred as he was' into the Tiber to save Caesar; and I also estimated, taking account of the slowness of walking when water-logged, that I might just about get back to Idlicote in time for breakfast.

A car pulled up. It was dark. I couldn't see who was in it.

'Where are you going?' said the driver. He was alone in the car.

I said: 'Idlicote, but you could drop me at Shipston. I can walk the last bit.'

'You're soaked.'

'Soaking your car. Sorry. You're really kind. Thank you.'

We drove on. It was a smooth, soft-seated, purring foreign car, wide enough for the driver to be just an outline from the passenger seat. He was sitting back, driving fast, steadying the wheel with an idle hand, as the rain lashed against the wipers.

'What took you to Stratford?'

'I saw a play, *Julius Caesar*.'

'What did you think of it?'

'Not much.'

'I just played him.'

'No!'

He laughed.

'You're Roy Dotrice! You were magnificent! I only stayed because I knew you were coming back as the ghost! I saw you as Caliban as well. Oh God, can you believe this?'

'You saw *The Tempest.*'

'It was fantastic. You weren't the normal sort of Caliban, if there is a normal sort. You were intelligent. You played him aboriginal, with a deeper intelligence. Was that you or the director?'

'It was Peter Brook.'

He took me all the way back to school, right up to the door and even then, he stayed, with the engine purring, till we'd finished our conversation. I'd said I wanted to be an actor and was going to Cambridge in October. He said: 'Most of the leading actors and all the directors at Stratford went to Cambridge, except Brook – he went to Oxford. If you want to act, you should follow Jacobi and McKellen into the Marlowe Society, or Frost and Miller and Cook into the Footlights.' I asked him about drama schools. Did he go to one? Where did he train? He said his training was three and a half years in weekly rep, and singing songs during the war.

'Were you in ENSA?'

'I was a POW. Shot down over France. It was how we survived: doing shows, singing songs. That was my drama school. A good school is a good school, but acting only starts when you're out in front of an audience. That's why Caesar is a great part. He's performing all the time. Necessity. You *have* to do it.' He shook my hand. 'Good luck Richard Crane. I hope we meet.'

COLIN CORNELL

We always told Colin Cornell he would be late for his own funeral, and he was; in fact he missed it completely. He's even late for inclusion in that part of the story where he belongs (I forgot about him). He was in North House at St John's, same year as me, and I suppose the nearest I ever got to a Best Friend. My uncle, Bob Twidle, says in the course of your life, you meet your six pall-bearers: dull but reliable, constant friends, who you don't see very often but can call on in a crisis. Well, Colin would definitely be one of my six (if he remembered), and I would have happily/miserably been one of his (if there'd been a coffin). We even talked about it, sitting in a boat on a lake, going nowhere, sails hanging down, on the stillest day of the year. That was the only time I went sailing with Colin. He was one of those friends you tend to go with when there's no one else. If I had nothing better to do on a wet Sunday, for instance, we'd go and have tea with his parents in Ashtead, down the road. Then one day we went sailing. It could have been brilliant if the wind was up, but we were stuck in the doldrums, talking about funerals. I was on the point of telling him I wouldn't actually be having one, because I died when I was seven, but just then, a whisper of wind came to shut me up, and we got to our stations. Then it disappeared again. He said I should join the Naval Section of the CCF. He was a petty officer and saw this as the first step in a naval career. He was also a crack shot in the shooting club, and a champion long-distance runner, but he never put himself forward so his successes passed you by. He really wasn't noticeable even when he won. In fact I hardly remember him. The photo is of a tall, soft-face, gangly boy with big feet, wearing a mob-cap, laddered black stockings and a short black dress to emphasize the knobbly knees. He didn't find the part of the myopic maid in *The Return...* at all funny, just did what it said in the script and got his laughs. He was my best support over the trouble with Tick, even offering to come with me if I was summoned after the performance (but that never happened). And if he had been there over the Boyle business, it would probably have blown over – he would have stopped me saying those stupid things, or would have diverted Boyle into talking about boats. But he was away on a two-day shooting camp, didn't even remark on my face when he came back. I went off him a bit after that, I must say; he seemed to be getting too friendly with Boyle. He even got him to go sailing. In fact they seemed to be really close and that was annoying. With me, as I said, he was only a 'best friend' by default. We had absolutely nothing in common. He was a scientist, he loved the corps, he loved shooting and running and trains and boats. Come to think of it, he and Boyle were made for each other. And so it was, in the summer holidays, when we were in Rome, Cornell and Boyle set off for Ireland. They were to pick up the boat in Bantry Bay and spend a week on the water. But the first day they were out, a squall blew up. Colin must have loved it: full sail, big waves, leaning back, close-hauled – this was the life! Till a wave as big as a house came up – which was how Boyle described it. Was it really so big, or was he covering himself? He had no experience of rough seas. He was probably panicking, pretending he knew better; probably argued with Colin, might even have punched him. Colin was always the better swimmer, yet when the boat capsized, it was Boyle who swam to shore. Colin's body was never found.

I still think one day he might just appear, as he used to, late. Maybe he was washed up in Donegal, having lost his memory; taken in by a shepherd, who restored him to health, till one day his memory began to return.

But do we *need* to know him? Haven't we all moved on? Living in the past is for old people. I remember him saying that. So he won't be coming back, dead or not dead, not even as a ghost.

THE WORTHING AUNTS

G reat Auntie Cis and Great Auntie Dick were numbers seven and eight in the ten-strong line of siblings of which Chas Crane was number four.

The culling of young men in the Great War and the sisters' ugliness – each sported the aquiline Crane nose – meant they would never marry, which was good in a way, because it also meant they would never be parted. They trained as Norland nannies and side by side, wheeled the high prams of the mighty, from London to Shanghai, keeping diaries, writing letters, despatching 'pieces' to be published in the monthly Crane paper *The Geranium*, which they took turns to edit. Having done their time nursing other people's babies, in 1938, just as Rob Crane was finding his voice in the Austrian Alps – 'and writing about it please for *The Geranium*! Come along Rob!' – the aunts packed away their uniforms and set up home together in Padstow. Here, as supplements to the family paper, which now ran to six pages, they began excavating the genealogy and assembling the dynastic archive. Their discoveries and the accumulation of boxes, trunks and filing trays meant the Padstow house was filled to bursting. So they moved to Worthing, to a house with a conservatory for breeding actual geraniums alongside the flourishing eponymous newspaper, but whether it was the stress of the move, or the dead weight of centuries overpowering the genealogist, or the lugging of the luggage, the dragging of trunks, unpacking of particulars and placing of every little thing in its new little place, whatever it was, as soon as she sat down, with a sigh, Dick died. My dickle sister, wept Cis, just downed and died. My darling Dick, whose real name was Florence, but we called her Dick because she was our dickle one, just downed her darling head and died. And *The Geranium* died. How could Cis keep it on? For her, geraniums were things in pots to be multiplied and talked to, and this was her life now: cutting and rooting and potting by the hundred till the conservatory was a blaze of red. The archive and genealogy she preserved but didn't alter. This had been Dick's domain, rolling the family right back to the Plantagenets and there was a claim to the throne here: more direct, more legitimate than the Saxe-Coburg-Gothas! 'So whatever kind hearts', she wrote in a stream of postcards, 'were curious to topple the monarchy, (Stafford Crane, the only son of her deceased older brother Arthur, was the pretender [if he did but know it!] followed by Chas – King Chas! – and then Rob and Rob's son), whoever wanted to browse and learn and topple and swim and walk on the sands, should come to Worthing; bring the family.

We were short of money that summer, so we went to Worthing for our holiday. The house was large enough to accommodate Auntie Cis and all five of us; just yards from the sea and the sandy beach. My father took the opportunity, to corner me and sit me down for half an hour each day, and lead me gradually along the *Quinque Viae*, the Five Ways Towards Proof of the Existence of God, as pronounced by Thomas Aquinas.

There would be seven sessions in all:

1) The First Argument: the Unmoved Mover
3) The Second Argument: the First Cause
4) The Third Argument: Contingency
5) The Fourth Argument: Degree
6) The Fifth Argument: Teleology
7) Conclusion: Binding the Five Together

This was work, but it was worth it, because eternal life was at stake. I waded straight in and asked what he meant by 'eternal life'. He said it was *my* eternal life and if I denied it to myself, then it would not be made available. I said: But what if I am not interested? The great thing about this life and the only thing we know, is that it's finite, and I'm happy with that. He said: But what if death is not the end? What if we don't have to succumb to it? What if Christ has broken the chains of mortality, and we don't have to die? I said: But we *do* have to die. There is no one alive that won't die. We know that. He said: God knows our knowledge is limited by our pride. If we bring down our pride we will see God and be granted a share in His knowledge. I said: *If* God exists. He said: And that's where the proofs come in.

We worked through them day by day, for seven days. As he explained these were rational arguments, not coercion through miracles: just a seed sown, which might take root when I got to Cambridge and began thinking. About the Creed, he had no objection to my not joining in; there was a time when he himself couldn't say it – couldn't speak at all! One had to clear one's head and let one's thoughts run free, but with guidance, and a clear map.

The Unmoved Mover and the First Cause, he explained, were both arguments against the evil of infinity. You can't have a thing which is moved by a thing which is moved by a thing which is moved by a thing, without the original thing being fixed and *un*moved. Likewise you can't have an effect from a cause which is caused by a cause which is caused by cause, without the first cause being absolute, and *un*caused? Simple! Then the arguments for Contingency and Degree suppose that everything either is or is not, or is more or is less. So that if everything that is, once was not, as we know it was, then once there was nothing, so how do we have something out of nothing, except through God? And if everything is on a scale of either bigger or smaller, or prettier or uglier, what is the standard we're judging by? Where does the absolute come from, except from God? And the final argument asks: Why is there order in the universe? Where do the laws come from that lead non-intelligent objects towards their end? Who made this order and these laws, if not a super-intelligent single Being called God?

He was happy with our sessions. He felt the spirit was with us. He felt the proofs were slapping down the devils of doubt. I had lots more questions, valid and combative, but he was looking at me, as if to say: 'So you see, it's proved. QED. Let's have a swim.' And suddenly I wanted to throw my arms round his neck and say I believe in everything you believe, because I love you. But he wouldn't have accepted that. He wanted a grown-up argument which he knew he would win. And I wanted him to win. It wasn't worth chipping away at every flint in his Temple. If he believed in eternal life, and the vanquishing of death, then bully for Jesus! There are no proofs of belief because belief is unprovable. And yet rational people, intelligent, scholarly, *thoughtful* people like Paul Burrough, Uncle Gerald, Grandpa Twidle, the Bod, all believe these things, with passion and intellect. They have made the leap. They have found the grand unified proof of religion which allows them to act for others because they don't have to dread death. Maybe if I wasn't having to pretend, if I could somehow tell someone: I am not here; I am an intruder – then all would be clear. They would carry on; I would vanish. But if it turned out that I *was* here, and I told them that nonsense about the bus and the *acting*, they'd be desperately worried. I'd be sent to some shrink to be electrocuted and trepanned. It wasn't the time for revelation. We were nearly at the beach. My father was still talking, throwing me looks, raising his eyebrows, even now expecting questions which he was ready to play with a straight bat. ('Come on Wit! Bowl me one!') He couldn't see the great emptiness I was slowly falling into. I just wanted him to go on talking.

Scene Three
CAMBRIDGE

Tucked away up Jesus Lane, off the tourist track, with its own cricket ground, hockey pitch and boat-house, the former nunnery – the first Cambridge women's college – having disgraced its patroness St Radegund the Virgin, with sex and money scandals, and having dwindled to just three worn-out nuns, was reinvented as a men's college, in 1496 by Bishop John Alcock, prompting the college crest of three black-faced, red-wattled cocks, or roosters, facing left in a shield, with a cock rampant on top. Symbolizing the sporting virility of the college, these birds also formed the motif for the signature Jesuan institution, the Roosters, whose objects were 'to study, maintain and extend the art and mystery of Roosting', and to perpetuate the memory of Bishop Johnny All Cock. In practice the Roosters were a reverse debating society, where members gathered once a term, took a vote, had speeches from the floor, heard the motion seconded, then proposed, then finally decided upon. There was a complaints book in the Junior Common Room, where waggish comments were recorded about not enough time being wasted. 'There hasn't been a good complaint for ages – (signed) Sister Brady', wrote my friend Andy Mayer.

I met him on my first day, and told him what my father had said to me as we lugged my trunk across Pump Court: that these three years would not come again; one should fill every moment, join in, play the game and *not miss the boat.* So when oarsmen came seeking new talent to keep us 'Head of the River', Andy and I consented to go and find out more about the Jesus College Boat Club (JCBC). I would cox, being lightweight, and possessed of an 'actor's voice'; Andy would row, but preferably near the front as he had a hearing problem. And so it was, the next morning, Andy, I and a German called Jurgen, went down to the river, and were instructed to sit, three men in three tubs, secured to the bank. Heaving, straining and going nowhere, I sensed boredom setting in. At least I, as a cox, would soon assume command of a boat, but Andy, doomed to be a galley-slave, wasn't sure he would last. He said he might give it a week, or even a day, as we walked that afternoon to the Societies' Fair: an open market for Freshers to decide on extra-mural activities. I'd said I wanted to do acting. He said he wanted to do comedy. I said I once hitched a lift with Roy Dotrice, who said Cambridge was the best drama school and if I wanted to act, I should follow his friends Jacobi and McKellen, and join the Marlowe Society. Andy wasn't so interested in the Marlowe, which specialized in high-calibre Shakespeare (and Marlowe), so he drifted off. I by-passed the Amateur Dramatic Club (ADC) – I didn't see myself as an amateur! – and the Mummers, which sounded like 'mumming', ie not speaking, and I wanted not only to speak, but to sing; to get back into proper singing, having missed out at Leatherhead, though I had been a member of the Incidentals, incidentally.

There was no Marlowe stall. When I enquired, I was told they were so famous - alumni including Peter Hall, Trevor Nunn, McKellen, Jacobi etc – they didn't need to tout, and anyway there wouldn't be a Marlowe produc-tion till the Lent term. I should apply then if want the humiliation of being rejected.

Andy was at a booth that said FOOTLIGHTS CLUB. Two men behind the table, one long-faced, like a bloodhound, the other scrunch-faced like a pug, were both yapping and not noticing. 'How –' began Andy. 'How,' said the pug, raising a hand, Indian-style. '...does one join - ?' 'One doesn't *join,*' said the hound. 'One writes a sketch, and if we like it, one auditions, and if we're amused, we invite one to perform at a Smoking Concert.' 'At which,' continued the pug, 'if one makes us laugh an enormous amount, we consider whether or not to invite one to become a member.'

Like the Marlowe, it seemed the Footlights were flush enough, to be able to set the bar so high, aspiring members, jumping up, would have to fall in a truly *satirical* way to provoke even a titter; unlike the Boat Club, from which the more one tried to distance oneself, the more they came knocking, till one had to sign up, and like the Sons of Thunder, give up all to follow Jesus. To be a cox, was to set the heart-beat of the college, because rowing was its life-blood. It was more than just yelling and steering, though that was hard enough; you had to organize the crew, draw up training schedules; make sure everyone got double breakfast and slabs of red-blooded meat in Hall; drum up towpath support for the Bumps each term; associate (like a spy) with coxes in other colleges; order beer for the binges and not get so drunk you couldn't do the clean-up.

On the day I took out my first eight, I was cautious. Stroke fed me the commands and I yelled them out like an actor. We meandered half a mile downstream, then did a zig-zag turn and ambled home. On the second day, I yelled the commmands unprompted, went about a mile downstream, then slowed to do the turn, matching fore-paddle to back-paddle, then streaked confidently home. On the third day, a bright sunny autumn day, we ploughed the Cam a mile and half, to where the river bends sharply, against a concrete wall. A coxless four was heading towards us and river lore requires a coxed boat to give way; but I saw space we could slip through and took the boat at speed between the four and the wall; then just as we were passing, the four swerved, I steered in, my 'EASY! SHIP OARS!' drowned out by the noise of starboard blades splintering against the concrete, and port blades tangling with the furious four, who were *blues* – 'Oh Jesus!' was all I could yell, as we limped home. There was a general meeting that night, at which it was decided I should make reparations (£30), or be thrown off the bridge after the Binge that followed the meeting. Succombing to the heartiness, I drank my yard of ale, drank a pint standing on my head, olly-ollied with the best through the beer-drinking relays, till I lost consciousness and had to be carried to my rooms. I was sick all through the night, and still trying to mop up when Mrs Shipp, my bedder, sailed in, at 7.30 with a jug of hot water – there was no plumbing in Pump Court – and a 'Chilly morning again Mr Crane!' as she flung up my window overlooking the smug river.

I decided to quit. I just stopped turning up. If I saw anyone from the Club, I would hurry on by: 'Sorry! Late for rehearsal!' I was acting all the time now. This was, let's face it, what I'd come to Cambridge for, and if JCBC and stage didn't mix, then Jesus would have to go; and if the Footlights and the Marlowe weren't knocking on one's door, then surely the way forward was to to *get famous first*, so that when, next term, one went to Eric Idle and Graeme Garden with one's script, ready to audition, they had at least heard of one. Ditto with the Marlowe, which like a sleeping giant, wouldn't be waking till after Christmas. So I drifted downstream to the ADC and the Mummers. I suppose I was blasé. It was all a bit beneath me. The auditions were, technically, for Freshers' productions or 'nurseries', as well as for membership, and I suppose I looked bored. My audition for the ADC, I was told afterwards, was so bad, I just missed becoming the first person ever to be rejected and have his sub returned.

But they needed my money and I needed to show them there was light under this bushel, which could fuel a revolution. I had read the Freshers' Supplement in *Varsity*, the student newspaper, which lambasted the 'monopolistic, rat-race-promoting oligarchies' who controlled the drama societies:

> *It is not unusual for one director to collect most of the major productions in one year, for one actor to play many of the leading roles, for a producer to preach about Chekhov or Sophocles, without the faintest knowledge of Russian or Greek theatre...*

*

In the ADC nursery – extract from *The Merry Devil of Edmonton* – I had no lines. In the Mummers' nursery – *A Jubilee* by Chekhov – I had one. In the two Mummers' experimental productions that followed the nurseries – *Leonce and Lena* by Georg Buchner and *The Lunatic View* by David Campton – I had twenty lines in one and at least seventy in the other. I was making my mark, I was meeting the right people, I was going to 'bird and bottle' parties (with or without the 'bird'), and to lectures, hardly ever. I could as easily skim a lecturer's book, then dash off an essay or a translation after midnight, even skip a supervision. There were films to be seen at the Rex, Kinema and Arts Cinemas, more educational than lectures: European *nouvelle vague*, classic Hollywood and *film noir* as well as health-and-beauty nudist films, which soon had me popping in three or four times a week.

*

Take Off Your Clothes And Live! was showing at the Kinema in a double feature with a Spanish film called *Los Olvidados*. I had just opened in the Mummers' *The Lunatic View Part Three: Getting and Spending*, playing a silly husband whose life flashes by, all chances missed due to little avalanches of DIY jobs about the house. There was a final performance that evening in the Chetwyn Room at King's and it was rumoured that Graeme Garden, President of the Footlights, and George (Dadie) Rylands, *eminence grise* of the Marlowe Society, would be coming.

So I decided to skip Dr Shackleton-Bailey's lecture on Cicero's *Letters to Atticus*, and allow myself a film. I hadn't been to the cinema since the previous Friday when I'd seen *The Lady Vanishes* at the Rex, then *Singing in the Rain* at the Arts, both of which would be fodder for my first Footlights sketch, which was growing in my head like a second brain.

*

His mother can't feed him. He wants to be good. He didn't steal the knife. He is sent to the farm school. He massacres the chickens. The Head decides to trust him and sends him with fifty pesos to go buy some cigarettes. 'If only,' says the Head, 'we could imprison poverty instead of children.' This is the moment your heart cracks and it's in pieces by the end of the film. You can't summarize *Los Olvidados*; you can only go back the next day and see it again, and again the day after. I saw it three times. I still couldn't believe it would end the way it did. The nightmare scene, where Pedro says to his mother 'You never give me meat' and she comes wafting across the bed, swinging a slab of raw flesh: the film like the meat is rotten through and through. Life is a tip and all too soon, your young carcase is under a rug on the donkey and your mother passes you, going the other way, searching. And they drag the donkey to the edge of the pit and tumble you into it. *Fin.*

THAT WAS THE WEEK...

'They've shot Kennedy,' someone said, but I don't remember precisely where I was or who said it; something more devastating and closer to home happened that evening.

A few weeks before, when I was still in the JCBC, I'd been to a gathering of coxes in the Blue Boat-house and had met David Prust. He was a new cox in Clare, my own height and build, with lank hair like mine, had done some acting and singing, was my equal in age, a classicist and he was from Solihull. We immediately slipped into brummie accents and talked coxing. He wasn't sure if he would continue. Like me, he'd smashed a boat and been threatened with depontification, but Clare needed him in the Bumps so he was staying till the end of term, possibly. He said we should keep in touch. If I left, he would leave, and I agreed vice versa. We were blood brothers, we were twins. I never saw him again.

On the night of November 22nd, I'd been to a rehearsal of *Leonce and Lena* followed by a party in Newnham, and was walking back across King's Bridge, humming *That Was The Week That Was* which I'd seen the previous Saturday. Andy had said, if England were to have a revolution, as in Cuba, it would be through satire. Just three years before, David Frost had been reading English at Caius. Now he was leading the mob that was chiselling away at deference and only a month ago, had toppled Harold Macmillan.

I noticed a row coming from Clare Bridge: shouting and whooping, someone yelling and then a splash. It was the sort of *ancien regime* crap that would surely be flushed away in the coming deluge. In my slightly drunk state, I was linking D Frost to D Prust. If Frosty could do it, sure as hell Prusty, my twin, my other self, could follow suit. I would contact him tomorrow, ease him out of his boat and onto the boards where we could play the Dromios in *The Comedy of Errors* for the Marlowe, and for the Footlights recreate the sensational, sand-dancing Cox Twins (*sic!*), Fred and Frank, singing a song Andy and I would later write:

> *As you bowl along the highway,*
> *Don't forget to say good-bye.*
> *Keep a smile upon your face*
> *And wipe the tear-drop from your eye.*
> *We may never ever meet again*
> *Until the day we die,*
> *So au revoir, auf wiedersehen*
> *And hold your head up high!*

The next morning, the news was out. David Prust (18), had been thrown off Clare Bridge and failed to surface. He was drunk and it was thought, had choked on his vomit. There would be an inquest, a bowing of heads, a discreet funeral (no press), and an unsung tumbling of the body into the pit.

And J F Kennedy was dead; and C S Lewis and Aldous Huxley.

That was the week that was,
It's over, let it go...

MOSES FINLEY

Home for Christmas, I worked for the Post Office to get cash; went to church, said the Creed, even served at the altar. Relief at being home again after a choppy first term, was enriched by two factors bringing joy to the vicarage and keeping Aquinas at bay. The first was the surge of West Indians into the parish, and my father's plan - still under wraps! - to move to Jamaica in two years' time. The other was the impact on all of us of the two new curates Malcolm Goldsmith and Neville Chamberlain. Malcolm was a bluff, jazz-trumpet-playing Northerner; Neville, named in deference to the appeasing Prime Minister, was an iconoclast, sworn to bringing down the establishment. God's wide boys - 'bolshies', in my father's eyes - they were disciples of Bishop John Robinson author of the 'heretical' *Honest To God.* 'Our Father in Heaven' was homogenized into the Ground of Our Being. Jesus was dethroned from Son of God into the Man for Others. Virgin Birth, Resurrection, these had the truth of myth, not fact. You could be a Christian without ever having to prove the existence of the Deity. Fine by me, I argued, but how does this square with the Creed? The Creed, said Malcolm, is a cage you have to be confined in if you want the strength - and RAGE, added Neville - to take on this SIN! meaning planned urban decay, forced resettlement of communities to out-of-town tower-blocks. These were sins worse than drugs and prostitution. They were like big brothers to me, just a few years older, explosive arguers, unrestrained jokers. My father had introduced them to contemplation, which they practised in church after saying the Office, and Mal told me how once, seated correctly, upright, slightly forward, eyes closed, knees apart, the church toilet had flushed and the two of them had broken into hoots of laughter. My father had stayed still.

Another time, when we were walking across the wasteland of Balsall Heath where whole streets had been erased in advance of urban motorways, Neville, keen to know if I'd met the new left at Cambridge, asked me who my teachers were. When I said 'Moses Finley', he stopped dead.

'He teaches ancient history,' I added, thinking this was about as unbolshie as you could get.

'What do you know about him?'

'I know he's American.'

'Wrong! He's *un*-American. He was dismissed by the House of *Unameri-* can Activities, for being a red. How does he teach you? What's his style? Is it catching on?'

I found myself mumbling that I didn't often go to his lectures, and in his seminars when you read your essay, he was always interrupting saying 'How do you know that?' and 'Prove it'; though I did remember once someone saying, in answer to a grilling: 'I plead the fifth amendment' and Moses frowning as if struck by a whip.

I should have known. This was the man who had stayed silent under interrogation and been stripped of his career. Back at Cambridge, I went to his lectures, which were standing-room-only, like rock concerts for the left. Assassinations, imperialist wars, slave rebellion, theatre as indictment of tyranny and genocide: the classics were suddenly a banner for change. Malc and Nev's platform was the pulpit; mine should be the stage. But first I had to get onto it, and time was racing. The exodus of my family would coincide almost to the day with my leaving Cambridge. I could go with them of course, do a Masters at the University of the West Indies, or try journalism or broadcasting (as my mother hoped to do) with the *Gleaner* or JBC; or be a Jamaica-based writer like Ian Fleming or an actor/writer like Noel Coward with property on the island...

Or I could stay here; be independent, begin to be a shifter of the cultural tectonic plates, like Peter Hall in theatre, David Frost in TV, John Robinson in the church. Now more than ever, was the time to *act* in every sense, and I had just eight terms to break through.

THE MARLOWE AND THE FOOTLIGHTS

I'm in a crowded compartment, like Margaret Lockwood in *The Lady Vanishes*. I've been hit on the head and the people opposite and beside me are blurring into political figures. I have three accents I can use: Yorkshire, brummie and posh. Yorkshire is Warold Hilson; posh is Alec Humourless-Dug (a serious tit) and brummie, the only Brummie politican I can think of: Cheville Name-Boleyn who keeps talking about 'purse in or toim'. Hilson and Doug can't make him out, think he's talking about the economy. This gives them an opportunity to argue the capitalist and socialist corners, until it's revealed that Chamberlain, who is dead and never did speak brummie, is symbolically, the spirit of middle England which both parties have to win, and when they run out of steam (and the train stops and it starts raining) all three coalesce into Gene Kelly 'singing and dancing in the rain'. Glorious feeling. Babum. All over in two minutes.

On the page it looked crazy, but when I tried it out on Jude and Mon, rattling through it on the landing where we used to do our plays, they were bemused, thought it was rubbish; then they laughed, fell about, sending me up, but so what? They didn't understand politics but they loved the accents and the dancing. So when I did it to sophisticated Footlighters, the very chaps whose predecessors had invented *TW3* and *Beyond the Fringe*, it would be sensational, I told myself.

On Thursday 22nd January 1964, I took *Train of Thought* to Graeme Garden in his rooms in Emmanuel and he was nice about it. I said: 'But you haven't read it yet!' He said: 'But I haven't read it yet.' Later I was called to the Footlights' Club to perform it to Jim Beach and Tony Buffery who would be chairing the Smoker on the 6th of February. They said it was too complicated, would I simplify it and bring it back tomorrow? That was the day I had my audition for the Marlowe's *Troilus and Cressida*, so I was up all night re-routing the 'train' and at the same time, trawling through *Troilus* for the part I wanted. There were four speaking parts as yet uncast but they hadn't said which, so I thought one of them might just be Troilus. A new star in the lead would be in the spirit of the times and it was right up my street: love tangled in war; loyalty bent into treachery. I learnt the short speech, just before the love scene with Cressida:

> *I am giddy. Expectation whirls me round.*
> *The imaginary relish is so sweet*
> *that it enchants my sense...*

I was to go to the Arts Theatre stage door, state my name and college, wait to be called onto the stage. If I had a piece I could do that, or I could just read from a page of script. When I walked into the light, I said I'd like to do a short piece of Troilus. A voice said: 'Okay.' I said: 'That is, if it isn't cast yet, Troilus?' The voice said: 'Get on with it.' I came forward, to the very edge, took my time, spoke softly. They would have to lean forward to hear me, and I felt they did. I ended mid-sentence.

The voice said: 'Is that it?' Then as I was going off: 'Do you fight?'

I said: 'Yes.'

'What in? What have you fought in?'

'Oh, lots of things. *Tartuffe* – we had a scrap. *St Joan* – there was fighting in that, though it was off stage...'

'If you're cast, there will be fighting.'

I said: 'Fine by me. Thank you.'

'I'll be directing the fights.'

Then, instead of slinking off, my destiny as a spear-carrier confirmed, nothing to lose, I found myself saying: 'Actually, I was hoping to be cast as Troilus. I thought casting a new actor, would be in tune with the spirit of the times.' The voice broke into peals of laughter. 'I'm serious! I'm not interested in walk-ons.'

'Then you'll have to come back and see Robin.'

'Robin who?'

'Midgley. He's the director.'

'Who are you then?'

'Sean Connery.'

What!!! I'd heard that the Marlowe had access to famous people who liked to drop by and pass on their skill to the next generation. But Connery! Doing the fights! Forget Troilus! I'd play the servant of Troilus's servant, to be taught fighting by Bond! If I could have cartwheeled, I'd have done so, as I hurried from the Arts to the Footlights, ran up the stairs two at time, found them waiting for me, so without even a cue, went straight into the sketch, reading the revised version because I wasn't yet sure of it. There was no response. Then some whispering. Then Jim Beach said: 'I'm so sorry, can you do it again? For Tony.' Enter Tony: 'I'm so sorry. Did I miss it?' 'He's doing it again.' I did it again, this time exaggerating the accents, with more clowning which they liked, applauding in the middle and even more at the end; said it was like nothing they normally had in a smoker; risky but they would go with it.

Meanwhile, I'd been cast as the Priest in Durrenmatt's *The Visit* which was the Mummers' main production: a nice cameo part: a conscious-stricken coward who colludes with the corrupt town and stands by as a good man is ritually killed. I'd been hoping this would happen before the Footlights and Marlowe auditions, so I'd be a bit more known, but that didn't matter now. I was on both the big thespian ladders: lowest rung, but surely, with lenten zeal, going up. The good man who is killed in *The Visit,* I was shocked to find, was David Collins. We'd acted together at Leatherhead: Joseph and Charles Surface in *The School for Scandal*, and his own play that had started the Drama Circle. Now at Cambridge, in just a term, he had shot up all the ladders and was playing leads, along with his girlfriend Sophie Kingsley, who had joined the Drama Circle when it was decided to have girls playing girls, scuppering my travesty career. Sophie wasn't actually *at* Cambridge, but like lots of girls who acted, became attached and because of the shortage of females, indispensible. She and David were quickly becoming Cambridge's golden couple. They would play Beatrice and Benedict in *Much Ado*, St Just and Marion in *Danton's Death,* Jimmy and Alison in *Look Back in Anger*, and gossiped about in Varsity, would be married before David graduated. Like the hare, I told myself, David was making all the running, but I was tortoising along behind. (An actual Hare, also called David, would spring up at Jesus, two years later, and overtake all of us.)

*

The Footlights Club was on the first-floor of a plain building in a back street in central Cambridge. There was bar at one end, a stage at the other. For a Smoking Concert, chairs were laid out in a dozen or so rows and the room soon filled with dinner jackets and smoke. This was a Men Only club, as were many of the clubs in Cambridge. Men played women in sketches, pantomime-style, except once a year, on Ladies' Night, when female guests were invited to attend and even perform. 6th February 1964 was a Ladies' Night, which slightly softened the ordeal. I didn't bring a guest; I didn't think I was allowed to, being a kind of guest myself. I still have the programme, stuck in my scrap-book alongside a still from a Japanese film of a man committing hari-kiri. Writing and acting credits, if you're a member, give only the surname: (Eric) Idle, (Richard) Eyre, (Graeme) Garden, (John) Shrapnel... Ladies and non-members sport full names. In the programme of that night, there are three Ladies' names and just one non-member. *JUST ONE NON-MEMBER!!* Did I realize that at the time? Was that why I was petrified? Is that why – shit shit – I cocked it all up?

In my weekly letter to my parents, I wrote:

> I had the Footlights thing on Thursday evening, which was an experience if nothing else. All the other sketches were very good. That was the trouble. The standard was so high, and I got in such a panic. I started off quite well, then I suddenly forgot my words, and had to skip a bit leaving out my best joke, about the Prime Minister. However I got into my stride again, was just beginning to enjoy it, when I got to the end. Still, some of them laughed, but I don't think I have been elected.

Then I go on to say how after the show, Tony Buffery bought me a drink. He said he liked my Birmingham accent; he was from Sparkbrook himself. He had been in *A Clump of Plinths* last year with John Cleese, Tim Brooke-Taylor, David Hatch and Bill Oddie, but had left when it went (as *Cambridge Circus*) to New York. The Footlights was his hobby; his career was Psychology. Before Cambridge he had been at Hull. I said: Did you know the chaplain, Roy Lambert? He said: 'Yes! Lovely man! I hear he married someone from Birmingham. 'That was my sister,' I said.

*

I was cast as Troilus's servant. I had three lines:

Sir, my Lord would instantly speak with you…
At your own house. There he unarms him…
No sir, he stays for you to conduct him thither.

Then just as he is about to expostulate on the rude sounds and monstruosity of love tangled with war, Troilus says:

Sirrah, walk (fuck) off.

From the start I felt there was a subtext here. Troilus calls him his 'varlet', not his servant. What exchanges they have are abrupt, and even when silent, the varlet is often there, in the shadows – I appeared in nine scenes – hoping to speak, but not allowed to; sometimes with flaming torch, sometimes battle-ready with sword and shield, sometimes armed with just his wits. This is the kind of part Shakespeare would expand later/earlier, in characters like Lear's Fool and Puck, speaking truth to power, and diverting the course of true love through mischief. Given access I might have pursued this master/varlet relationship with Troilus (Michael Pennington). There was so much hanging about while the heroes strutted, I found myself, as an apprentice actor, merging with the varlet and looking to Pennington as master, who in just over a year would be treading the Stratford stage. He was a keen, brittle-framed performer, who approached his role in the manner of James Dean. On the first night, just before curtain-up, while assembled lords were joshing in the wings, I saw Troilus, alone, leaning over a rail, mad with love and racked with doubt; his posture, if one didn't know him, inviting a slap and a 'Hey, break a leg Mike!' I held back, in awe. No one 'acted' in this production. They were who they were, the princely heroes, pumped up with the same follies that fuelled their student selves. 'Degree' at Cambridge wasn't simply what you got, having done your time; it was *'priority and place… office and custom… primogenity and due of birth…'* The Marlowe programme was anonymous, and if I hadn't filled in the blanks, I would have forgotten that Hector was Robin (TV's *Poldark*) Ellis, Paris was Carey (son of Rex) Harrison, Agamemnon and Menelaus were Tonys Vivis and Palmer (translator of Brecht, and filmer of Richard Burton), and Johns Grillo and Shrapnel with respected theatre and film careers ahead of them, were Ajax and Ulysses. Altogether eighteen of the thirty-strong cast, including servants and Myrmidons, went professional after Cambridge.

But discord was coming. 'Untuning that string' was what we below stairs were setting our minds to, and soon, with a twang, the mid-sixties would be upon us. *Troilus* was the perfect play for our time: deceit, inner rage, hypocrisy and disgust, finally exploding in butchery, staged with epic sweep by Shaun (not Sean) Curry (not Connery). In the end, the finest are gone; the inadequate survive. In Shakespeare's most modern play, the bad taste lingers on, in its closing line:

I ... bequeath you my diseases.

THE DREAM

The Beatles hit Hamburg in 1962. When the Marlowe arrived, two years later, with *A Midsummer Night's Dream* (I was Puck), in the 1700-seater Auditorium Maximum, it was like a Second Coming. In letters home, I wrote:

> *Everywhere we go, heads turn and voices whisper 'die Beatles, yeah yeah' because of our long hair. German students are all very smart and tidy and they boggle at anyone who looks scruffy, which is odd because they seem to have a morbid dread against baths and washing.*

I played Puck like Pan, with wild hair and horns, furry leggings with hooves and the rest naked with body paint. Shortage of water meant I might go days without cleaning up, soiling bed-sheets across Germany. In two and a half weeks we played the *staatstheaters* of eleven cities, mostly one-night stands, to huge sold-out audiences.

> *The place we are staying in is rather like a concentration camp. We live in huts and sleep in bunks, eight men to a room, and for breakfast they give us bread and cold cocoa, and whenever we have lunch here, we have sausages, German sausages, about a mile long...The night before last, after the show, after we had dozens of curtain calls, there was a party in the foyer. It was a bit of a let-down actually, as our hosts were not fans but university dons etc... At about midnight, we went to someone's flat for drinks & I thought things might hot up, but it was so crowded & I felt so tired and dirty & I had drunk rather a lot. About three o'clock I could hardly keep my eyes open, & we all went back to Auschwitz in taxis...*

Our *Dream*, directed by Shaun Curry, was everything *Troilus* wasn't. The superheroes we deferred to – Ellis, Shrapnel, Pennington etc – had moved on to higher stages; only Ajax and Thersites remained, to play Quince (John Grillo) and Bottom (Keith Mano). Grillo would go on to play Danton in *Danton's Death*, Mercutio in *Romeo and Juliet*, and later professionally, Rasputin, Verlaine and a string of film and tv roles; and he wrote plays too. Mano was American: an off-Broadway actor and graduate of Columbia, he gave a performance (said the Cambridge News) of 'limitless talent, depth, maturity and reason'. The production by the 'quite brilliant Mr Shaun Curry of the Royal Shakespeare Company... is unashamedly played for every laugh in the book... richly comic as only Shakespeare can be, with timing and performance that is rare for this play'. I wrote home:

> The performance last night, I thought, went very well, as least as far as I was concerned. I got the feel of it much more... The audience was hysterical with laughter at times, later absolutely still, & there were curtain calls galore, & after the show we had our first taste of fans & autographs. I had a long chat with one fan, I don't know what about, as he was talking German and I was talking English... Shaun thought the play was awful & he started blowing his top, but all directors do that once in a while. He then went off to a night club to drown his sorrows & came back at six am...

With his bashed-in face and surprised eyes, he had a benign, bruiser quality which suited his directing style. The first thing he said to us was 'I'm going to treat you like professionals. You've got to be body- and brain-fit, or the comedy will trip you up. It's dangerous and dark in that fairy-infested wood. There can be no pissing about.' I'd seen him at Stratford, the previous year, with Roy Dotrice, in *The Tempest* and *Julius Caesar*. Twenty years later, we would meet again, when he played the Bos'un in my musical *Mutiny!*, still steadying the ship, and swinging a whip with compassion. He knew what worked and what didn't, and when it didn't, he blew his top, or said he was going for a shit or a drink. Once, in rehearsal, it was late, we should have finished, but he wanted to get to the end, and I was alone on stage doing '*Now the hungry lion roars...*', when someone burped and there was a laugh. Shaun stood up: 'Okay! I don't have to stay here. I can get the next train home. If you can't respect *this most classic moment in theatre*, you can fuck off all of you and I will too.' In the silence that followed, I did the speech. It was my duty, exhausted, to call up the ghosts, not wake the dreamers, let the fairies dance and keep the mice quiet; then when all is done, '*with broom before... sweep the dust behind the door*'.

Shaun stopped me as I was leaving: 'Can I ask you two questions?' I said:' 'Fire away.' He said: 'Do you want to be an actor?' I said: 'I am an actor'. 'I think,' he said, as if I hadn't spoken, 'I *think*... you *could* ... you *might just*... (long, thoughtful pause).' I said: 'Thanks Shaun. What's the second question?' He raised his eyebrows, the way my father did: 'Are you queer?'

JEAN

The fact is, I wasn't anything. I hadn't had any physical relationship since Ghazanfari. But that was going to change. I'd just about got to where I wanted to be at the end of my first year. Puck would be a spring-board to the next dramatic level, and I was sure enough of my footing to be able, after Germany and a triumphant week at the Arts, to take a ten-day camping holiday in Florence. Jude came too; I wasn't sure about this, but my parents insisted. My friend Trevor Thomas, from school, who now worked for Premier Travel in Cambridge, drove us in his parents' car to his girlfriend's home in Geneva. Jude and I then went on by train to Florence. We camped on the slope below the Piazza Michelangelo, and every day, did churches, museums, piazzas and galleries. After a while, bored with Berninis and done with Donatellos, Jude hived off on a lambretta with 'Luigi' – she was sixteen; I was not her keeper – and I carried on alone. This was my world: Herculean musculature in living marble; Venus born from the spunky froth of the testacles of Uranus; David with huge hands, and incorrectly uncircumcised cock, up at which I was looking, when I heard a girl's voice: 'There are men trapped in the stone, forever struggling to be free...' She was staring at the four blocks of half-carved marble, flanking the David. 'Can't you *feel* their torment: abandoned half-created by an artist stopped in his tracks by death?' We got talking then went for a *vino* and a *minestrone* and I would have told her they weren't in fact stopped by death. Michelangelo lived on to eighty-eight, but I didn't want to spoil the story. She was doing art at Wolverhampton. Her name was Jean.

Back at Cambridge, I invited her to the Jesus Michaelmas Dance. I'd never actually invited any girl to any dance. I'd been to bird-and-bottle parties, where the bird was the optional part due to the shortage, and I'd gone to the Jesus May Ball, during May Week, (actually a fortnight in June), with a pay-in-advance blind date, who *was* almost blind with her bottle-end glasses, and blind drunk by the end, as I was, as the dawn came up and found us soaking in a punt. I was so bored and annoyed at the waste of money – TEN POUNDS! – back in my rooms I fell asleep, and dreamed I was running to get to Newnham, then waking up and *really running* to get to Newnham Gardens in time for the matinee of *Comedy, Satire, Irony and Deeper Meaning* by Christian Dietrich Grabbe, in which I was playing Second Naturalist and the Emperor Nero. I was an hour late but no one minded.

Back to now, my heart leapt because Jean had said YES to the dance, and to staying over. I was well up the thespian ladder, having played Puck; was cast (albeit in supporting roles) in *Danton's Death* and *The Merry Wives*; might even try again for the Footlights, or maybe not. The Marlowe was the thing and rumour had it the Lent production would be *Hamlet*. If I was to play the Dane, it would take all my concentration. The Footlights had originally been an offshoot of the Marlowe, designed to satirize the Bard, and prick his pomp. If one was honest about acting, one should avoid this distraction. Pennington and Ellis were not Footlighters. So I wouldn't be joining; even when Andy Mayer and two of the *Dream* cast – Matt Walters (Snug) and Chris Allen (Starveling) – all applied and were elected.

Great political techtonic plates were shifting too. Tory days were over; Mr Wilson was in Downing Street. The Age of Heroes, chipped away at by David Frost *et al*, was metamorphing into the Age of Equality and Sorority. All-male bastions were crumbling. The women of Cambridge were realising their strength. At a ratio of eight-to-one, (similar to the gender divide in Shakespeare's plays), if a woman made it to Cambridge, she must be eight times the worth of any man. And here they come now! A six-foot Australian post-graduate called Germaine Greer, applies to the Footlights. Rather than tell her 'sorry my love, this is a Men Only Club', they change the rules and let her in. Anne Mallalieu scales the ramparts of the Union to become the first woman President. Suzy Menkes becomes the first woman Editor of Varsity. Freja Balchin becomes the first woman President of the Marlowe. Sally Kinsey-Miles (later Beauman), Andrea Duncan (later Wonfor), Lisa Bronowski (later Jardine), Miriam Margolyes and Sue Ayling, are acting, writing, broadcasting, producing, driving a wedge into the male world.

Workwise also, it was going to be a good year. Refreshed by Italy, with Shackleton-Bailey gone to Caius, and Moses now my Director of Studies, I could become a Classicist again, even merge work with play by getting cast in the triennial Greek Drama, due to be staged at the Arts, and rumoured to *Oedipus Tyrannus*, directed by George 'Dadie' Rylands. *Hamlet* and *Oedipus*, the two greatest plays ever written, one at the beginning, the other at the end of the Lent term! So it would be possible to be in both, possible even to play leads, which was how it happened at Cambridge, where at the very top of the acting ladder there was room for only one.

Jean arrived by train. I'd booked her into a room over a pub, near my digs. I was out of college in my second year. I had a tiny bedroom with a sloping ceiling, and the dining-room downstairs for my study and daily use, in a small white-washed terrace house owned by Mr and Mrs Ison, a Jesus porter and bedder respectively, respectably: no 'guests' beyond the dining-room; the narrow bed under the sagging ceiling, suitable only for the lonely.

It was a mistake. We had nothing to talk about. The dance was a fiasco. Only Jesusmen were there: boat club and hockey club brutes that I was avoiding. We jigged about a bit to the Hollies and Matt Munro, then I said: 'Let's go for a walk.' Of course it was raining, so all we did basically was walk to the pub behind Jesus, which was just closing, so there was nothing for it but to go up to her room. I truly thought that her willingness to come to Cambridge and stay over, implied the possibility of completing what we couldn't quite get round to in Florence because I was stuck in a tent with my sister and Jean was in an all-women dorm in a hostel. So I truly thought this might finally be *it*. I had even, bravely, after walking round the block several times, bought a packet of three. I could feel them burning in my pocket, as the door clicked shut. In Florence one afternoon, when the door to the church of San Miniato, had clicked shut, just as we were approaching, we had both said together: '*La chiesa e chiusa*'. And in the laughter, we had kissed. She said it again now, and we both laughed and kissed again. But it was different out of Italy. Her mouth seemed loose; her lips were cold; her tongue was salivery. I've tried to block out what happened next. She was looking at me with her saucery eyes. I watched them change, from hungry and hopeful to shocked, in a few seconds. She saw through me. I wasn't acting. Going through the motions, out of politeness, was dishonest and impractical physically. I was about to make a complete eunuch of myself and should start negotiating an exit. She read this, and moved from shock to a kind of horror, unexpressed, because something much worse was happening. I was decomposing, like a mummified prince unbandaged, exposed to the light.

LINCH-PIN ROLES

T he Revolution was in full swing. Hot on its heels came the Terror. Heads were falling fifty a day. And still the people had no bread. Virtue sustained them. Virtue was the Republic's strength; Terror, the child of Virtue, its weapon. Without Terror, Virtue is paralysed. Without Virtue, Terror is a plague. The Revolution is the despotism of Freedom against Tyranny. *Le jour de gloire est arrive!*

Georg Buchner wrote *Danton's Death* when he was twenty-two. The original script, said Tony Vivis (21), translator of 'the best of six or seven versions I have read' (Malcolm Griffiths, director, 22), was unstageable. Vivis had modified the numerous episodic changes and cut the cast from seventy to fifty.

'There's a tremendous conflict of ideas, on an epic scale,' said the review, 'and such a range of feeling. This is the kind of theatre Cambridge should explore.'

'I like a play,' said Griffiths, 'where there is a lot of physical action. I get so depressed when I see production after production that is "fairly good". The audience has not got to sit back and see it from the outside, but to get right into it.'

Danton's Death was the ADC main production, the largest and most ambitious ever staged. We rehearsed four and a half weeks. 'As a new translation,' I wrote home, 'it counts as a world premiere; so the Lord Chamberlain has to censor it. Several obscene lines have had to go but no one minds really as (a) they are so obscure the audience wouldn't understand them and (b) it is excellent publicity. All the lost lines will be pinned up in the foyer, alongside the Chamberlain's licence. With a cast of fifty and a guillotine which actually works on stage, it should draw record audiences. We have got to have the theatre at least two thirds full throughout the ten day run, so it is quite a challenge. But I think we will do it because *Danton* has been the talk of the town for weeks. The latest hand-out mentions RC as one of the leading actors which is quite untrue but very good for my ego.'

I was Collot-d'Herbois, actor, dramatist, essayist, and member of the Committee of Public Safety. Having cleansed Lyon in the blood of two thousand traitors, including priests and nuns, I have returned to Paris to the chill of St Just (David Collins at his icy best) and the terrible virtue of Robespierre (Roger Gartland, a Jesus colleague, who had played the weak-willed Mayor in *The Visit*, now 'prissy, fanatical, auto-intoxicated' as the Incorruptible). But we were all – moralists and indulgents – getting swept away and we didn't know it. '*The Revolution made us,*' said Danton; '*not we, the Revolution. We are puppets strung on to unknown powers, in a pitiless universe. Nothing nothing ourselves!*' John Grillo's Danton, said the review, was acted with great power and tenderness, never slipping into sentimentality. '*Evil must come! It must! But who has decreed that "must"? The great void is the god who has yet to create our world.*' It's a bleak, urgent play, by a writer and about people, of our own generation, trying to plug the deluge while actually adding to it. I was given a drum in the final scene, to beat out the march to the scaffold, and play the death-roll as the blade rose and crashed down on the necks of my friends: Matt Walters (Camille des Moulins), Tim Davies (Lacroix), David Lascelles (Herault de Seychelles), and finally Grillo/Danton himself. The Age of Heroes had passed into the Age of Iron. We were on our own now.

*

Speeding along the autoroute in the south of France, heading for Switzerland, I could reflect that Collot d'Herbois, before the Revolution, had been director of playhouses in Lyon and Geneva. One of his biggest hits had been an adaptation of *The Merry Wives of Windsor*, a world away from the gore-fest he was about to soak his country in. And here we were now, in one of Trevor Thomas's Premier Travel coaches – Falstaff, Mistresses Ford, Page and Quickly, Shallow, Simple and the rest – roaring to a monologue by

Mrs Ford (Miriam Margolyes) about our Alpine hosts *who were yodelling the approach of their famous guests.* Miriam had left Cambridge two years earlier, but kept coming back to play plum parts like Mrs Ford, for the Experimental Theatre Group. I was under- and mis-cast as Master Page, but happy to be one of a genial team, being swept along by time. I was almost half way through Cambridge, coasting along, believing tides would turn and fate had a plan. We would play to full houses in big theatres in seven cities, and be home for Christmas, where Malcolm and Neville having both left, the bolshie-theology-revolution would be on hold, and my father, free from corpsing curates, could concentrate on Jamaica.

*

Zurich. Midnight. Heavy with *fondue*, I'm trying to find my way back to my digs, blankets of snow making all the streets look the same. No hat or scarf or gloves, I could die here and vanish, a puzzle beyond solving, which Falstaff, Mistresses Ford, Page and Quickly, Shallow, Simple and the rest would be baffled by, cancelling a performance, then after discussion – 'it's what he would have wanted' – carrying on with the tour (the director would play my part), but in a darker mood. Fuddled with gruyere, I insist to myself that being dead is not an option. I must keep up the fraud and trust to the script; till lo! Opening my snow-flecked eyes a crack, I see a street-name I recognize, then Christmassy and candle-lit, the Swiss family house where I am staying and they're waiting up! Is this pure chance or the grace of God? Is the narrative being forced to skew in my favour? All I know is KEEP ACTING, even non-parts like Page; even, returning for the Lent term, cast not as Oedipus, but as the Messenger from Corinth, in Dadie Rylands' Greek production, the part he explains that is the *linch-pin* of the drama, telling Oedipus the truth that will precipitate tragedy; and when the Marlowe replaces *Hamlet* with *Romeo and Juliet*, I am cast, not as Romeo, but as Balthazar, the part, as director Gareth Morgan explains, that is the *linch-pin* of the drama, when he misinforms Romeo that Juliet is dead, thus presaging corpses. 'If no one remembers you, then at least they will be touched by the consequence of your mistake.' But I want to be remembered! As errant linch-pin, I want to provoke laughter amid the howling, as Sophocles *and* Shakespeare demand, even if directors don't. Dadie's take on *Oedipus* is that the setting is not Greek but *Egyptian* Thebes, following Velikovsky's thesis that Oedipus historically is the Pharoah Akhenaten, Jocasta is Nefertiti and their sons Polyneices and Eteocles are the disgraced Smekhkare and the lavishly buried Tutankhamun. However tenuous this theory, it allows Dadie to have pyramid-tombs looming over the action and the Sphinx's riddle ('What has four legs in the morning, two at noon, three in the evening? Answer MAN! – ie MAN in opposition to GOD or FATE') to fuel Oedipus's *hubris*, which is how I would have played it, storming the pentameters till the very vileness of truth pops my bulging eyes! I wrote home:

> *My costume (as the messenger) is a raggy grey tunic, a blanket-type cloak, semi-bald grey wig, red hat, crook and body make-up – another dirty sheets week! The setting is Egyptian, so everyone is very dark. As the only 'foreigner' in the play, I thought I had better be darker still, so I blended in the remains of my Midsummer Night's Dream negro black. I thought if Thebes was going to be Egypt, Corinth might as well be Nigeria. I also cultivated some gory scars and bruises on my legs and arms and blacked out a few teeth.*

Discussing accents with Dadie, and putting Africa to one side (we were after all performing *in Greek*), I suggested that as Corinth was located in the Greek midlands, maybe I should lean towards brummie, and when I tried it and got laughs, he clipped me round the head (his way of giving notes). When I persisted and got more laughs, I thought he was going to sack me, but he just took me by the ear (his way of showing affection) and said: 'My dear, I hadn't realized this was your natural accent. It serves the text well.'

When discussing Veronese accents with Gareth Morgan – Balthazar's whiney tone suggesting he was from Solihull – before anyone could laugh, half my lines were cut.

*

Balthazar, being a Montague, has no scenes with Lady Capulet (Germaine Greer) but I had ample time in the green room to observe and be awed by the mould-smashing Australian; mentally placing her, alongside Miriam Margolyes, as the two who stood head and shoulders above/beneath the other great Cambridge women of the mid-sixties: the one caustic and tall, the other ribald and short; both born on the cusp of the 1940s, pioneers of gender politics, literary prodigies and iconoclasts, targets for some, role models for others, and brilliant comedy performers. Both read English at Newnham, one as an undergraduate, the other doing her PhD, missing each other by just two years. Coinciding, they might possibly have changed the face of British comedy: each starred in separate Footlights Revues, excelling as solo performer, but what might they have achieved as a double act, temperamentally and physically disparate (six foot by five), both razor-sharp and rude? And how might they have galvanized the two less-than-scintillating Shakespeares I was in, in my second year, if GG had been Mistress Page to MM's Mistress Ford, and if MM had played the Nurse (as she later did, in Baz Lurmann's film) to GG's Lady Capulet?

One afternoon, during the run of *Oedipus*, something happened to remind me that, however petty and overbearing the system might seem, I was no longer at school; I was twenty, should be smashing moulds, calling the bluff of the Sphinx and forging my own destiny.

I wrote home:

> *Yesterday I had the shock of my life. I met TICK TURNER in the mark place!!! He had come up with half the Classical VIth to see Oedipus and was all shaven and shorn and icy. I asked if we could meet up afterwards for a drink, but he said no, impossible, as the inmates had to be hustled back, in time for prep. I made cheerful conversation with this reptile for about five minutes, then rushed to Premier Travel to warn Trevor to STAY INDOORS, because the Turner Fiend was loose! Outside the theatre I met some wretched Classical VIthers who used to fag for me years ago (all bigger than me now). They were in their undertaker outfits and grey as grey. I nearly took two of them out for coffee, which would have been their THRILL OF THE YEAR, but there wasn't enough time and Turner would probably have caned them for associating with a tramp. I was really glad to be looking long-haired and weirdy when I met him.*

CATASTROPHE
(THE TURNING POINT)

I was slipping. Half way through my Cambridge time, I seemed to be back at square one. I wasn't getting cast except as 'linch-pins' which I knew was a sop because once I accidentally removed myself (forgot a matinee of an avant-garde piece of nonsense in college) and the edifice didn't fall; the cast skipped a scene, muddled through, got away early. I was dispensable, a loner. Bandwagons rattled by and I gave up even trying to jump on, having fallen off so many times. I no longer sat with a group in hall. I would eat quickly and slip away, go to grim films on my own (*The Trial, Victim, La Notte, Winter Light*), or spend hours in the library with the Dictionary of National Biography, tracing my ancestry back beyond Edward I, through the Saxon Chronicles, all the way to Woden. But no one was interested in acknowledging my godhead, not even God Himself, when I began going regularly to chapel and trying to pray. The Dean, Peter Baelz, who was my moral tutor and a friend of my father's, asked me, after chapel one Sunday, if I was enjoying Jesus. I said: 'Yes of course, it's fantastic, why do you ask?' He said: 'You seem to be on your own a lot.'

*

Dear Crane
Next time you are not able to come to a supervision, I expect to hear about it before *the beginning of the hour, not at the end of it, and don't consequently have to sit about on the off-chance of your showing up. As you have missed a supervision on Plato (What importance did he attach to his myths?) an extra one will have to be arranged next term...*

Hopes for better things in Classics, with Shackleton-Bailey gone, and Moses Finley as Supervisor, faded when Moses was taken ill and we were farmed out to tutors across the University. I had to go once a week to a young philosophy graduate in Churchill who was as tight as Tick and duller than Shack. An Aristotelian to his bones, he had only scorn for Plato, believing what *is*, is what is proved, all else being pie in the sky. I was just getting into Plato, and pie in the sky was the food I craved. I was half-way through re-reading the *Phaedrus*, where the soul is likened to a charioteer with two horses: one spiritual and good, the other carnal and bad. When the soul falls in love, it grows wings and flies, pulled upward by the good horse, downward by the bad horse. I understood this absolutely, though my own chariot had for so long been stubbornly grounded. But I knew this had to change for a very practical reason. In little over a year, my parents, with all their chattels and home comforts, would be setting sail for Jamaica. *I would not be going with them.*

I decided to change to English. Moses was back in his rooms and I went to see him. He was frail but still sharp. Before I could speak, he said: 'You want to switch disciplines. I think that's the right decision.' Then I went to see Peter Baelz who was more cautious: changing to English would not be easy; the workload would be immense; there would be no time for acting, unless I stayed for a fourth year, but for that the College would require a First in Part I. I should go and talk to Raymond Williams.

Raymond's rooms were above the post room, next to the Porters' Lodge, as if he needed to be ready, come the revolution, to be out manning the barricades. I imagined, from what I'd read, that he would be restless in an ivory tower and ill-at-ease with the silliness and conservatism of Jesus. The son of a railwayman from Abergavenny, he hadn't known he was coming to Cambridge; it was all fixed behind his back by his father and teacher. But being Welsh, there was never a problem with a working-class boy espousing high culture. He had come here, in the thirties, to feast on an education normally reserved for a social elite, and to campaign for working people to re-possess their culture. I thought he would be hardened against the dead hand of tradition, but he was relaxed, amused, long-faced, long-limbed, in his long leather chair, and a sweet fog of pipe-smoke. I sat opposite him, sinking into a similar chair, a gulf between us, but so comfortable I felt I could spill any artless truth and, with a nod of his crumpled face, he would consider it. The dialogue may have gone like this:

RW: Why did you come to Cambridge?

RC: I wanted to be an actor.

RW: Shouldn't you have gone to drama school?

RC: I was told by an actor that Cambridge was the best drama school because here you learn to think as well as act.

RW: How much thinking and acting have you learnt since you came here?

RC: Not enough because the two keep heading off in different directions, and I want to change that.

RW: What is acting all about?

RC: Acting is about being someone else; or about being a bigger, more interesting version of yourself.

RW: Does it help to be a scholar? Doesn't academic study get in the way?

RC: Only if it's not part of the same thing. When you learn, you sort of *become* the person you're studying; even if, *especially* if they are the opposite of what you are. You have to bring them to life. And that's what acting is, that's what *studying* is: bringing the dead to life. Without it, without being able to go forward in studying and acting, you're not really alive.

RW: Why did you choose Classics?

RC: It chose me, and I've grown out of it. As a subject, it wasn't helping with my career as an actor. I've done one Greek play, and Classics helped with that, but all the rest have been outside my area of study. I need to be more up-to-date with culture if I'm going to make any mark.

RW: Do actors need to make a mark? Are they not in the end just the voicebox of the playwright?

RC: I want to write as well.

RW: Ah, now we're getting somewhere!

RC: But to write plays, I believe you have to start out as an actor. Shakespeare was an actor.

RW: Perhaps that is why my own plays never get performed!

RC: I didn't know you wrote plays.

RW: I try not to, but sometimes one is compelled to do the thing one is no good at. I'm not an actor.

RC: That's not true! I've seen you giving lectures. You are definitely an actor!

RW: I deal in the second-hand. I stoke up the talents of others. I present them with impossibilities and make them turn them into art. For instance, how would you reconcile the impossibility of using English to sustain your acting career, when the hours you will need to devote to the new subject will preclude doing any acting?

RC: I can do both, because with acting you stretch the present moment. With thinking and studying, you can also bend time. It's like quantum mechanics.

RW: Maybe that's what you should change to. Seriously, why should theatre be the prerogative of English? Isn't it just as much about geometry, architecture, biology?

RC: Of course, but they wouldn't have me; I never did science. But I do read books, and in books, you can do all that stretching of the moment and bending time. That's why I want to do English. I want to act and I will act, and I want to do English. I want to, and will, do both.

*

I said I would apply for a fourth year and if that meant getting a first, I would get a first. I would work all through the vac and do no acting till after the exams; not difficult because for the first time, after auditioning for everything, I had been offered no parts, not even Puck in the ADC's *Dream* which was going to Stratford. I was just a student, swotting through the night, doing practice papers, not going to parties or films, cutting out lunch and only going to hall because you had to eat so much venison and potatoes, to get your degree. I did go to one film. Jean Cocteau's *Orphee* was showing at the Kinema, and I thought it would be a suitable good-bye to Classics. It was steeped in death, yet had a perversely happy ending, which I felt was a good omen. If Orphee can outsmart the motorbike henchmen, and be judged not to have died, and have love and happiness restored, then the hard slog was worth it and there would be a future beyond Cambridge.

Greek Prose Composition at 9 am Saturday 22nd May, was a piece from Housman about the spiritual death of the man who neglects knowledge. He may appear to be still alive, but he contributes nothing as he '*wallows in ignorance with the complacency of a brutal hog*'. Translation in the afternoon began with the servant in *Hippolytus,* telling of the towering bull that rises from the sea to mangle the youth who refused love, smashing the linchpin of his chariot. I knew the story. I knew all the words. I was heading for a first.

Then came Philosophy. At the end of the week, I wrote home:

> I think I had better give you the full story. I had a breakdown on Monday and walked out of the philosophy exam after forty minutes. I wish it had been a migraine, then I could have explained it. I had crammed myself with knowledge, and thought there was nothing I couldn't write about, yet when it came to answering the questions, I couldn't remember anything, though they looked easy enough. After half an hour I wrote a page of illegible nonsense, and then crossed it out. I felt all the work I had done had been a waste of time, and I couldn't go on sitting there any longer; so I left and went for a twenty mile cycle ride...

*

I remember vividly (or am I imagining this?) sitting at a small table, at the back on the left in the far corner of a vast room, in which fifty (or five hundred) gowned undergraduates were similarly seated, in strict rows, with strictly measured gaps between: a grid like a city, running one way, the other way: geometrically exact. A long-gowned invigilator sits at a high desk, the last words 'turn over' having been spoken, the only sounds now, a cough, a sniff and the scratching of nibs. The questions are give-aways; I could answer them all. *How convincing in today's world is Plato's myth of the immortality of the soul?* I could lead with the *Phaedrus*, relating it to themes of love and death in *Orphee, Romeo, Danton, Los Olvidados. Evaluate Aristotle's advice that one will never achieve anything in this world without courage.* I could relate this on the one hand to Alexander who was tutored by Aristotle, and on the other hand, to Oedipus whose courage led to self-blindness. And finally, the fun question: *Is life a thread, spun, measured and cut by the Fates, or just as long as a piece of string?* I could have set this as a topic for a Socratic symposium, with contributions from Alcibiades, Aristophanes... I could have flown with this paper and broken through into First Class. It was what I lived for, this discussion. But one needs a respondent, as a bowler needs a batsman. The road to truth is dialectic. Philosophy, like drama, is living speech. Writing it down fixes it in the past or for the future. You only really address the big questions in the active present. Socrates, Jesus, Buddha, did they write anything? They set the words rolling and we, in our time, take them up. I should have written this, but the clock was ticking, and rank upon rank of gowned undergraduates were nib-scratching against the time, getting all past knowledge set in ink for the future. I wasn't meant to be here. There was no point in putting down anything that would be held against me. I needed an opposing brain to hammer things out with, as an actor needs an audience. Dealing, as Raymond said, in the second-hand, fenced in by the possible, is a denial of quantum mechanics. There were infinite dimensions just a hair's breadth away and I could break through to them, with courage and a little madness. My sheet was blank, but I wasn't ready to go yet. I needed a moment of panic and bland writing. All the ranks of gowned vultures with acned necks, driving nibs across pages, were pushing me to try. Pen to page, black on white, I quoted Socrates' opening line: *'My dear Phaedrus, whence come you and whither are you going?',* then crossed it out. Being positioned at the back on the left in the far corner, I would have to cross the whole hall to get to the door in the opposite corner. The invigilator was watching, relaxed, content, superior, smug. It might take fifteen seconds to cut a path through the grid of tables to the door, if I went swiftly; half a minute if I sauntered. Or I could just sit still for a further two hours twenty minutes. Putting my pens in my pocket would be a step towards the Rubicon. Standing up would be stepping in. Walking would be the moment of no turning back, walking swiftly away from Cambridge for ever, into real life for the first time.

I put pens in pocket, got up, walked out. No one stopped me. I was free. I took a bike, not my own – couldn't find it, but to the *ubermensch* who quits an exam, negating two years of learning, everything is permitted: damn the law and the darkening sky! I set off, under black clouds, southwards out of town, towards Trumpington and Shelford. Rupert Brooke's Cambridge was never mine; the rat race ran through it. I'd never punted to Grantchester or had honey at ten to three. Now released from the curse, I could ride by the water, *green as a dream and deep as death.* I veered onto the Saffron Walden road, as heavy drops began to fall. A fleet of black-clad motorbike henchmen roared by, overtaking me, forcing me to skid off the tarmac, onto grit; and tossing me onto the verge, dragged the bike from under me, tangling with it, like wrestling with a puma, till one wheel was wrenched right round, flat against the other. I didn't wait for recriminations. There was cursing and revving from the disturbed swarm of bikes and the sky was bucketing. I set off across the field down to the river. There was yelling. I didn't turn. I was running, stumbling, waterlogged, thinking one missed footing and I'm in, under the wave, going down like Brooke, or was it Shelley?

> *Nothing in the world is single;*
> *All things by a law divine*
> *In another's being mingle.*
> *Why not I with thine?*

I walked home. Mrs Ison made me a cup of sweet tea and said the Dean had been round and she should telephone him if and when I returned. She gave me a fresh towel and some hot water and went to ring him. It was half-past eight when he came, in his gown, straight from hall, under a dripping umbrella, and nearly nine when the doctor came. They presumed I was suicidal, and made Mrs Ison guardian of the sleeping pills which I should take, one per night, through to the end of the exam week. Missing one out of nine papers, would rule out a first but would not necessarily mean a fail. I should concentrate on fulfilling what I had come here to do, and think about the future in the future.

Scene Four
TO RUSSIA

I did the remaining Classics Part I papers, got a 'fair' two-two, changed to Part II English, under Raymond, which I would complete in a year. To get to grips with English - papers chosen included Medieval Latin, French and Italian literature, the American novel (so not a lot of 'English') - I got a £25 supplementary grant to come up for the Long Vac Term. Back in college in rooms over the archway into Chapel Court, I set to wrestling with Tragedy etc, but *a ghost needs to act and to act is to travel.* So when the Dryden Society said they were short of an actor for their tour of Germany and Russia, I auditioned and was cast: as the cockney bruiser Bill Walker in *Major Barbara* and the Provost in *Measure for Measure.* We would open at the ADC, then play Oldenburg, Wilhelmshaven, Luneberg, Leningrad and Moscow. Both plays fitted my study of moral argument in drama. Does the end justify the means? Is arms manufacture to be preferred over soup kitchens, as the answer to poverty? Is loss of virginity a fate worse than death, when the death is your brother's, and valued above your own? It didn't matter that I was wrong for both parts or that Cambridge acting talent, with so many groups on the road, was wearing thin. I was happy to be a cuckoo in a nest of no aspiration. I could enjoy mangling Shaw's phonetic cockney vowels, without being judged; I could enable Shakespeare's cunning Duke to effect summary justice, without having to compete.

*

From letters to and from home:

ME: *We had a meeting yesterday and spent hours filling in visa forms. enclose a spare itinerary. You'll see it is quite extensive: 4,000 miles in 12 days.*

MA: *Roy has just telephoned. Elizabeth has been haemorrhaging again. If you are still in the habit of praying, (which I trust you are) remember E and Roy.*

ME: *We will be performing in youth clubs, but Russian ones shouldn't be compared with English ones. I should imagine they are compulsory. I have started reading* War and Peace.

MA: *I forget how well up you are about Uncle Mike… First they thought it was lung cancer, but now it seems he has got something almost as bad, namely Hodgkin's disease.*

ME: *We're on a limited budget and have to provide our own costumes. Could you lend me your 'fur' coat. Bill Walker is Edwardian working class, so I can't wear a duffel coat.*

MA: *E is back on injections. She is now 5½ months and says the baby is very lively. Judith has gone up to Saltburn to be with her, so Roy can see his parents who haven't been well.*

ME: *… and I was wondering if you could unearth that spotted red thing I used to put round my neck. I think I last saw it in the shoe box.*

MA: *I am complying with your requests. The fur coat was your grandmother's, so treat it with respect. The scarf may smell a bit shoe-polishy, but I have washed it.*

ME: Barbara *went up on Wednesday at the ADC. I am only onstage for about twenty minutes but I have two appearances in which I dominate the stage, by terrorizing the Salvation Army and later by telling a funny story about my conversion. The house was full on the first night and they all applauded like mad. The second night on Thurs was a bit marred by a bad review.*

MA: *This letter should reach you before you leave for Russia... Don't get involved with any spies! I don't want to read in the Telegraph: 'Mrs Crane was permitted to visit her son in the Gulag'.*

Even though both shows were the worst I'd ever been in; even though casting was a lottery (anyone could have played any of the parts just as badly); even though, as the first Cambridge group to cross the iron curtain, we were poor bearers of the legacy of McKellen, Jacobi etc; even though, in fact *because*, we were not stars, but students, like our audience, not responsible for the chasm that divided us, we were greeted with real warmth. The message of Shakespeare and Shaw – parental double standards, the hypocrisy of those with 'a little brief authority' – seemed to come through more strongly. We were on a level with our hosts, whether they were showing us treasures – the Hermitage, Tretyakov Gallery, Tolstoy's house – that like theatre could cross national boundaries, or sitting with us as we were instructed on the wonders of the Soviet system, much as Shaw had been in the thirties: here was a goal to be achieved through mass belief and the general will; a social fabric, though ragged at the edges, that at heart was still pure. Of course we weren't taken in, but we weren't dismissive either. It was like the argument in the plays, compelling yet insoluble; brought into sudden focus by the fleet of black cars, that sped past on the day we visited the Kremlin, in the grandest of which General Secretary Leonid Brezhnev was hosting President Gamal Abdel Nasser of Egypt, just as our hosts were hosting us.

Isabella in *Measure* was played by Jane Barry. The review said: '*She has a quick intellect, an immediate compassion and innate feminine grace.*' She also had smartly chopped Mary Quant hair (under her wimple); long, varnished finger-nails filed to a point; pale pink lip-gloss on knowingly pursed lips, and an un-nunlike fondness for innuendo. How could anyone be further from the virginal novice wishing 'more strict restraint'? You wanted to laugh and some did, only to be left open-mouthed at her demolition of both the despicably priapic deputy and her whining condemned sibling. You came away thinking: mis-casting works! This is Isabella for the sixties: a feminist icon cracking chastity as a whip for chastising men. Offstage, she encouraged me, with my Lenin flat cap and neat Lenin beard, to *be* Lenin about town. Passing in the mighty car, did

Brezhnev's piggy eyes in his cadaver face widen a fraction? Was Nasser's rictus grin, already stretched to its limit, now frozen in shock? We were making people laugh and on the long train and coach journeys began writing sketches. The Footlights were waiting. We would start at the beginning with a sketch about Adam and Eve.

BARRY, BATTY AND CRANE

Adam and Eve in their dressing-gowns, like Ron and Eth in the Glums.
EVE: Ho Adam...
ADAM: Yes Eve?
EVE: I'm fed up. We've been here for ever and what have we achieved except delving and spinning in our dressing-gowns. I feel ashamed –
ADAM: We're not allowed to feel ashamed Eve.
EVE: I want to sing beloved, I want to dance and go shopping for petticoats and panties.
ADAM: We don't have knowledge of underwear Eve.
EVE: We don't have knowledge of anything Adam. We're ignorant!
ADAM: I know!
EVE: You know we're ignorant. Well that's a start anyway.
ADAM: Ach!
EVE: What is it Adam?
ADAM: My ribs. There's a gap. There's one missing. And I don't appear to have a belly-button either.
EVE: There's so much that could be explained, if we just –
ADAM: If we just what?
EVE: Would you like an apple?
ADAM: What?!!
EVE: It might open our eyes to our nakedness beloved.
ADAM: But what's *He* going to say?
EVE: What's *Who* going to say?
ADAM: Him who said we weren't to eat apples?
GOD: (*off – as Jimmy Edwards*) Hello hello hello...
ADAM: He's coming!
EVE: Quick! Eat it! (*Stuffs the apples in Adam's mouth, eats her own*)
GOD: (*entering*) There was I walking in the garden in the cool of the day, as the Bible so eloquently –
ADAM: (*apple in his face*) Ur...ur...
GOD: Who do you think you are? A surrealist painting by Henri Matisse?
(*Post-apple Eve and Adam are transformed into scholars*)
EVE: It's Rene Magritte you ignoramus.

GOD: Unh?

ADAM: We have knowledge.

EVE: We know.

ADAM: About Eve -

EVE: O –

ADAM: Loo –

EVE: Shun.

ADAM: You didn't 'create' anything. (*Beat pause*)

GOD: Well, that's that then. Now am I dead, now am I fled, my soul is in the sky, as Hamlet so tragically puts it.

EVE: It's Bottom, you duffer.

ADAM: We're getting dressed.

EVE: We're getting out of here.

GOD: (*exiting*) I dunno. Student revolution. Would you adam-and-eve it? Take away their grants, that's what I say. Mother!

(*Blackout*)

*

As soon as I got back to Cambridge, I went to see Andy Mayer. Like me, he had tried for the Footlights in his first year. Like me, his first smoker had been a humiliating nightmare. Unlike me, he persevered, and for the next smoker, he wrote a monologue about a story-teller who gets tangled up in the detail of *Goldilocks and the Three Bears*. It was an inspired answer to the nightmare of having to remember your lines before a super-judgmental audience, and the way he delivered it stirred even the sniffiest of the dinner-suited elite, and got him elected. Clive James, who came up a year later summed Andy up thus:

> He had a weird sort of negative timing which made pauses go on longer that they should, except when, as he often did, he got a big laugh, which he would try to talk straight through, as if he couldn't hear it... A routine in which he pretended to be an American evangelist had me simultaneously roaring with laughter and breathless with admiration... There were only about a hundred words in the piece but it took him five minutes to get through it, so panic-stricken was the audience. They would hold onto each other and howl.

Andy had succeeded Eric Idle as President. The system remained the same, and you still needed to 'know people', but the tone was altogether more collaborative and friendly. Discussing cast, I said I'd like Jane Barry to play Eve and if Andy wanted to play God... Laughing, he said he wasn't that kind of President. But he did have someone in mind...

*

Call him Col. For a surname, give him the name he would later adopt for his children's entertainment alter ego: Mr Batty. Cast him as the fall-guy who in falling became my bridge of guilt into professional acting. Stretch him, with his new name – he was already six foot one – into a ganglier, sorrier figure that I can append motives to and amalgamate with others, fusing fact and imagination. See him: Col Batty, a stand-up, before the age of the stand-up, toppling over, getting up again, toppling and, unbelievably, still staggering up, till he disappears, via Butlins and the tv cop show *Juliet Bravo* into the wasteland of the jobbing actor. His comedy hero is Ken Dodd, but he lacks the fortification of teeth and can't sing. His theme is his own failure – with his career, with girls, in seeing the joke, in life generally. He was Starveling in the Marlowe *Dream,* who plays Moonshine with his lanthorn and dog, is ridiculed by the audience, loses his rag, feels redundant. He was a servant to the Capulets when I served the Montagues in *Romeo* and he would be Pompey, the tapster to my Overdone in the upcoming Marlowe's *Measure for Measure.* Later Col Batty would be my flatmate in London, till we parted without words; then friendship restored, my first-choice when casting plays with fall-guys, and through up-and-down personal times, my confidant and drinking buddy.

As God, Col Batty brought his own bravado and ineptitude to the Mr Glum original. As Eve, Jane was June Whitfield by way of Fenella Fielding, to her pointy finger-nails. And my Adam, once I got the apple in my teeth, neatly completed Barry, Batty and Crane (BBC): the trio that on Thursday 14th October 1965, at *The Coughing, Hawking, Spitting And Running Nose Smoker In Which New Faces Are Observed,* would bid for Footlights glory.

*

From the letters:

ME: *About my 21st, the party is going to be a month early because that's the only time we can get the Union cellars. We are limiting numbers to 150 and I am inviting 100. The two men I am sharing with, don't know as many people as I do. It will cost us about £15 each, plus 15gns for the Soulbenders who are the top Cambridge group.*

MA: *About your party, Judith and her friend Jane hope to come on the Friday & return on the Sunday. Will you book them somewhere comfortable but cheap for the two nights?*

ME: *I am working on getting elected to the Footlights. The first smoker is on Thurs and I am doing a sketch with J Barry and C Batty.*

MA: *Worrying news from Granny about Grandpa T. He was in terrible pain and was put on a heavy drug which has now stopped his bladder and bowel working.*

ME: *The smoker went well. Our sketch was towards the end, so the audience had plenty of time to warm up. I was scared stiff and continually fortifying myself with whisky. I felt a bit depressed the next day because I had a hunch we hadn't got in.*

MA: *Grandpa's complaint has a long name but means that his intestines have become wrinkled with age. He has to live on a low residue diet, so that everything 'glides through'. Granny tends to get rather morbid and makes heavy weather of it all.*

ME: *The big headline is that I AM NOW IN THE FOOTLIGHTS. That and the party have made this week the best in my whole life! Jude will tell you, Sue is the MOST BEAUTIFUL GIRL IN CAMBRIDGE! We went to a party in the Real Tennis Courts afterwards which lasted till two…Yesterday I took Sue to another party in the Footlights, and I am going to see her tonight before going to the Club to rehearse a sketch. Then she is coming to the smoker on Thurs. I hope to be doing three sketches, one with Batty, one with Barry and one large cast one in which I play Billy Bunter.*

MA: *I'd like to know more details about Sue. Full name? Age? Home town? Antecedents? Etc etc. So far, all I have gleaned is that you think she is the 'most beautiful girl in Cambridge'!*

ME: *Sue is 20. She is assistant editor of the Women's Page in* Varsity. *She is in New Hall which is much nicer than Jesus. I am thinking of moving in there.*

MA: *Now I think it's about time I congratulated you on your success in the Footlights. I know this is what you have been aiming at, so am really pleased. By the time we get back from Jamaica (if we ever get there!) you should have got over your struggling years, and made the name Crane a household word.*

ME: *As I foretold, academia has been getting me down. My last essay was disastrous and I have to have extra supervisions, because I am thick. Also Sue has been away this week-end so I am lonesome.*

MA: *I must say I am very distressed to think any son of mine is classed as 'thick'; so please concentrate on your work a little more and on other things a lot less, and achieve something to remedy that aspersion.*

ME: *Sue is coming round here in about an hour and we are going out to dinner and then to a revue at Queens', in which a song of mine is being sung.*

MA: *I have found my entire family very disappointing lately. Dad's been making stupid mistakes, which I have to tidy up; Mon is under the influence of her 'hellish' friend Helen; Judith is stubborn and pernickety over food and you are 'thick'. E is all right at the moment, for a change.*

ME: *Must stop now and write some more letters before Susan Mary Ayling comes.*

SUE

On Tuesday 25th March 2003, I opened the *Guardian* and saw her picture. It was the very same picture I used to have by my bed at Jesus: her short bobbed hair, her beautiful, intelligent smile, and the white polo jumper she often wore. I remember the evening when she came up to my rooms, after being away for the week-end. I was watching through my window as the sun went down and saw her walk across the quad, like Julie Christie, a slight swing of her hips, her bag slung on her shoulder. I lit the candles and turned the light off and was just uncorking the wine, as she knocked. 'It's open.' She came in. 'Wow', she said, in her soft throaty voice. 'We've got just about an hour,' I said, pouring the wine. 'I thought you were offering sherry,' she said. 'Would you like sherry?' 'I hate sherry.' 'That's why I'm offering you wine'. She laughed, and I should have kissed her then, but I was holding two glasses and she was wearing her white jumper. I said: 'Don't spill, it's red.' She smiled looking up at me, her eyes almost level with my nose. I said: 'Cheer ho.' We clinked and sipped. I put my glass down, went to the record-player. 'I bought this today.' I put on *Girl* by the Beatles. 'It's what we danced to at the party. Only then, it was the Soulbenders playing it. This is the real thing.' I took her glass, put it down and we danced a bit. 'It was the most brilliant night of my life,' I said, kissing her ear-lobe. She laughed: 'And you're not even twenty-one yet.' I said: 'I know, I'm still a child.' 'So am I,' she said...*She's the kind of girl you want so much, it makes you sorry...* 'Sorry for what? I don't understand these lyrics.' She said: 'I think what he's saying is she came to stay, then she went away, but he doesn't regret a single day.' I said: 'And I don't, not a day, not a month, not a lifetime.' She pulled away, ever so slightly: 'You don't have a sofa.' I said: 'I don't think Jesus does sofas. I don't think we're expected to have sofa-type company.' She said: 'How many rooms do you have?' I said: 'Just the three' and before she could say: 'Show me the others (show me the bedroom?)', I said: 'I often lie on the floor listening to music.' She lay on the floor. I lay beside her. I said: 'Don't worry. I'm not going to...' *When I think of all the times I've tried so hard to leave her...* She looked straight at me: 'Not going to what?' 'I am not going to take any kind of... if you don't want me to.' She kissed me on the forehead, then on the nose, then slowly, warmly, with the taste of wine, on the lips. I tried to sing, with the song: '*Oh girl...*' but her lips stopped mine, and we rolled over giggling. I could feel her heart through her jumper. This was the closest I had ever been to being joined to another person and I wanted to linger and I felt she did too. If she just wanted to lie here for the full hour, in the crook of my arm, I was absolutely happy with that. When I mentioned to Jurgen Martini, who was still in the Boat Club, that I was going out with the Most Beautiful Girl in Cambridge, and was just hoping I could keep her, he said: 'Fuck her. It's the only way.' I told him it wasn't that kind of affair. And anyway, from my experience (!), going to bed with someone, or trying to, was the best way of losing them. I was going to play this *my* way, and I knew instinctively (probably), it would be Sue's way too. This moment, on the scrubby carpet, not speaking, just listening, was for keeps; we could bottle it and keep it, with all the other moments, like when the Soulbenders played *Girl...* and my hundred friends suddenly knew they were guests of the most fabulous couple in Cambridge: the acknowledged Most Beautiful etc with the soon-to-be-acknowledged (on the Women's page in *Varsity*) Funniest Man in Town. I was one step away from the topmost rung of the ladder, bottling moments, not taking any kind of..., just lingering, as we had done (another moment) on her window-sill at New Hall, after the Tennis Court party at 3 am, as she was climbing in, one leg in her room and one leg out, like the hokey-cokey, and mine similar, poised for an eternity, on the cusp of the moment, in the full moon, under a starry sky... *and she promises the earth to me and I believe her; after all this time I don't know why*... She said: 'Rich...' I said: 'Sue...' She said: 'Will Tony P be at the cabaret?' I said: 'It's a revue and I haven't a clue.' She said she wanted to interview him for the Women's Page. I said: 'But he's a dinosaur when it comes to women. He was the only one, last year, who objected to women being admitted into the Footlights. She said that was why she wanted to interview him. She had talked to him at the last Smoker, when I was doing my sketch with Jane about Burton and Taylor. I said: 'But weren't you watching?' She laughed: 'Of course I was! I'm a woman. I can do twelve things simultaneously.' 'What was it about then, the sketch? What was the gist of it?' She said: 'It was a lampoon on a terrible film called *The Sandpiper*, which Liz and Rich both obviously hated being in, and hated each other for hating it. You were very funny, but I don't think Jane got it.' ... *She's the kind of girl who puts you down, when friends are there; you feel a fool...* I was beginning to feel this wasn't our song. I wished I'd bought *And I Love Her* or *Help!* Maybe Jurgen was right and I should just carry her into the bedroom and shag the shit out of her, like James Bond or Tony P, before both of us then slipped into our glad rags and, missing dinner, went to the cabaret at Queens'. 'What are you thinking about?' she said, still cosy and sweet in my crook on the floor. I said: 'I don't understand these lyrics: ... *that a man must break his back to earn his day of leisure.? Will she still believe it when he's dead?*'

And now she was gone, at fifty-seven, from breast cancer. It was in the Guardian. She had been a much-respected TV current affairs producer: married, two children, divorced, independent. Had she ever thought of me as I'd thought of her, on and off, with deep shafts of regret, quickly pasted over, because in our line of work you don't ever rely on anyone? Was that why she drove herself to an early death? Affairs are for 'taking advantage' and I could have done that; I could at least have known the physical inside of her, and bottled that as the supreme 'moment'. I hadn't seen her for thirty-eight years, not since the night when we'd snatched dinner and gone to Queens' and she'd hived off with Tony P after the cabaret.

ABOUT THIS TIME...

... something trivial happened which didn't *feel* of historical note, but somehow I remembered it. I had gone to my room after hall, intent on finally getting my head around *Moby Dick*. Swallowing the whale was my project for the night, digesting its blubbery mass then excreting it in an essay.

There was firm rap on my door. I wasn't going to answer; in fact I turned the light off and continued reading with a torch. The next rap was identical and I heard a low murmur of policemanlike voices: 'He's in... There was a light on...' It couldn't be the Boat Club; I had settled my score with them two years ago. It couldn't be Andy or Roger; they were at a party tonight that I hadn't been invited to (I was quite sore about that). It couldn't be anyone of importance, so I left it. There was no third rap. Had they gone? I switched the light on, switched off the torch, opened the door, just to check. Facing me, taller by half a head, his face cocked slightly to one side as if wrily examining me, recording what he found and filing it for future use – all in an instant – was the stringy-looking first-year boy I'd seen in the JCR and around the ADC, always wrily examining, recording, filing... and always with the boy, shorter, with glasses, now standing at his shoulder. I hadn't avoided them, just hadn't made a point of crossing their path.

'Hello. I'm David Hare. This is Tony Bicat. Can we come in?'

All they wanted was the lowdown on how to join the Footlights, and not only join, but *exploit* politically. There'd been a breach in the walls and a crack in the ceiling, but the house of privilege hadn't yet fallen. I was a friend of Andy Mayer whose father, they'd been told, was a car-park attendant. We were all obviously of the same ilk, and together, exploiting the prestige of the Footlights – how does one write for and get cast in the Revue? – we could *thespianize the struggle.* I said absolutely, I'm with you, or more correctly, you're with us – 'We're with each other,' Hare amended – but I'd just joined myself, and there really was only one way to get in, and get on, and that was the official way: submitting a script, auditioning for a smoker, getting elected, getting known. I agreed there was a mood of change in the air – 'No,' he expostulated, 'we *are* that mood! We *are* that change!' – and we should absolutely go with it, use it, *exploit* it, but just now (nodding to the book) I had a whale of a task to complete before tomorrow...

I hardly saw him again. We never acted together. He did join the Footlights, but it wasn't the platform he'd imagined. He had bigger fish to fry. Like the captain of the *Pequod*, he was driven and unstoppable, and recalling it now, some of that zeal stayed on, like a whiff of cordite, in the room, and stirred me to exploit, enjoy and *be* the mood of the class-cracking sixties.

THE FUNNIEST MAN

A Christmas Carol has always been too sweet for my taste; I felt there must be another side to it. Scrooge's conversion seems pure humbug in the age of the workhouse and 'surplus population'. For all his campaigning against the evils of poverty, and notwithstanding his own brush with family debt, Dickens's feet were always firmly planted above stairs; salvation for his heroes who have fallen down the class ladder, is generally to find that they are, through fate or pluck, truly bourgeois after all. Eight years on from Cambridge, I staged an alternative *Christmas Carol* where the story is told backwards. Scrooge is a reckless philanthrope in a strictly monetarist world. He is visited in the night by three ghostly financial advisers, who counsel him to tighten up. Benevolence will ruin him; Bob Cratchit is a conman who will bleed him dry; Tiny Tim is exploiting his disability and is not lame at all. The festive season is for piling high-interest debts onto the poor and peddling lies about redemption. In the morning Scrooge wakes and cancels Christmas.

The germ of this show was *The Truth About Scrooge*, a monologue I wrote for the Footlights Christmas Smoker 1965. I took my cue from Andy's *Goldilocks*, by now a cabaret regular, where you choose a well-known, dearly cherished tale and shred it, or let it shred itself. I don't remember planning *Scrooge* or doing drafts. I just postulated a twin brother, a fourth ghostly visitor and a flush toilet with a dodgy chain; then talked it to myself, pinning the words onto the page before they could escape. In performance I decided the effort of recounting Dickens's hero's catastrophically embarrassing adventure, would have exacerbated the asthma most Dickensians would have suffered from, living in smoky London, so that every line was preceded by a wheeze, allowing me a 'breather' to ride the laughs, and even generate more laughs just by wheezing. For tone I looked, partly to Kenneth Williams and partly to an emphysematic Balsall Heath spinster called Gertie Palser, whom we used to visit and then imitate. Structurally, the sketch was underpinned by lines like 'Now before I go any further, I must tell you... (something absurd)', which a few seconds later would lock into the story provoking a laugh, then, on activation, a bringing-the-house-down laugh. I didn't imagine this reaction, so when it came, the sheer surprise brought on even more gale-force mirth and clapping. In a decade or more of acting, I had never yet felt such mastery of an audience and the shared thrill of entertainment. There was defiance of the norm (the Footlights seldom did 'characters'), sabotage of an iconic story, dangerous detours into absurdity, and a flush of classic toilet humour. Afterwards, as I was heading through the crush, to have a pee, Tony Buffery said 'That was top-hole' and Germaine said 'You're a star'.

*

Being a star meant suddenly people were asking for me, and post-Sue not having emotional attachments to anyone, meant I could stretch my last months to include acting, writing, parties and work, to the giddy limit and beyond. In the runup to my finals, I acted in four plays, one film, wrote and/ or acted in three revues, five smokers, a dozen cabarets; read the absolute minimum of everything on the list; wrote a twelve -page essay on the Brontes, which Andy and I then transposed into an epic sketch; and another on *Measure for Measure* which metamorphed into a rediscovered fragment of a draft too carelessly bequeathed to the Bard's fool and his footlit descendants; built up the triptych of Barry Batty and Crane to the point where hell would freeze before the three of us – all for one; one for all! – were scooped up into the cast of the 1966 Footlights Revue.

Hell froze, as in my coldest moments I thought it might. I was working for the GPO pre-Christmas, humping mailsacks off trains at Snow Hill Station from five in the morning, and between trains, sitting duffeled-up in the waiting-room, reading *Anna Karenina*. When I heard that Richard Syms, a theologian at Christ's, would be directing the Revue, I knew Batty wouldn't be in it. Both were known to hold low opinions of each other's talent. Batty thought Syms, as a vicar-to-be was only in it to preach. Syms thought Batty's fall-guy persona was too true and not funny. So what would Jane and I do without Batty? What would *I* do if Jane herself didn't get in? What if none of us got in? *Drawing her head back into her shoulders, Anna fell on her hands, under the carriage...* But it wasn't my call. My ideal casting had B, B & C plus Andy, Germaine, and David Lascelles to do the music. But a star can't fix the placing of others in the universe. Syms had the power and some glory, having just played the martyred priest Grandier in *The Devils*. Batty and I were Adam and Manoury, the 'broker's men', tasked with bringing him down, then getting cold feet when the leg-breaking starts. People said we made a classic double act that should be seen on a wider stage. Would Syms, even under torture, remain unconvinced?

*

Elizabeth bore a son Nicholas on St Nicholas's day 1965 and we all went up after Christmas for the christening. As godfather I vowed to 'set him a good example by my own way of living'; then we came home, leaving Jude behind to help, and to give Mother a break from trying to force-feed an anorexic. On January 4th, at 4.45 am, Elizabeth rang to say Jude was dying, so she was sending her home. This was the day I went back to Cambridge; early because of rehearsals for *A True Widow* by Thomas Shadwell, in which I was to play Bellamour, a gentleman of the town who has retired into the country. Letters criss-crossed:

MA: *Daddy met Judith at the station. She looked tired and bewildered. I was desperately disappointed that E didn't ring.*

ME: *A True Widow goes at a cracking pace and is absurdly complicated, full of sword fights, people hiding behind screens etc.*

MA: *I wrote a long letter to E. I said I knew how she felt about J ...and what it was to get overwrought in the post-natal weeks.*

ME: *Thurs was the Footlights Smoker... The hit of the evening was* Why didn't they ask Cartwright? *which I did with Barry, Batty and Andy.*

MA: *We went to Thorpe House and found Grandpa in fine form: cracking jokes & eating really well! He is 83 on Monday.*

ME: *Barry knew her lines, but not her cues, so I had to knock her over every time she was meant to speak.*

MA: *But there is not such good news of Uncle Mike. He is having a real struggle with his Hodgkin's Disease.*

ME: *For the Revue audition, Lascelles and I wrote a song called* Burly Shirley *about a girl who gets run over on her wedding day.*

MA: *I'm afraid Grandpa Twidle is also going downhill. He now gets really dreadful pain and is so exhausted.*

ME: *Waiting waiting... but at least I have three plays, a college revue and several cabarets, to take my mind off - and work (almost forgot!).*

MA: *I had a phone call from Granny, very upset. G'pa had been rushed into a nursing home after a bad week. So I packed up hastily and drove here, in 2 ½ hours... We went to see him at 6 o'clock. He is really very ill and was just working up to another bout of pain when we left. He is having x-rays and tests, and they may have to operate.*

ME: *Did I tell you I am playing Third God in* The Good Person of Sechwan. *I don't have to do much except follow the Second God who follows the First God. Because of all my other commitments I have agreed with the director that I don't have to go to rehearsals.*

MA: *Uncle Mike died at 4.0pm today. It's hard to believe isn't it? Better news from Bath. Grandpa's xrays are all clear, so no surgery which is a blessing.*

ME: All too long on earth we lingered.
Swiftly droops the lovely day;
Shrewdly studied, closely fingered
Precious treasures melt away.
Now the golden flood is dying
While your shadows inward press.

Time that we too started flying
Homeward to our nothingness.
That is what we gods sing as we go off. It's hilarious.

*

And then:

MA: *At last! Good news!! YOUR PA IS TO BE RECTOR OF PORT ANTONIO JAMAICA!!! We had a lovely letter from Bishop Percival. He wants us to advance our sailing date, to make it the end of June.*

ME: *Finally it's out! I AM IN THE FOOTLIGHTS REVUE!!! There are three women (Greer, Barry and a first-year Newnham girl called Chris Mohr) and three Richards (Syms, Crane and Harris - not the one from* This Sporting Life, *though he looks like him), plus Tim Davies who was Diomed in* Troilus *two years ago, and Ray Elmitt doing the music. But no Lascelles and no Batty. So I am happy, but not totally, and Batty is in despair.*

'TALK TO MY AGENT'

We had time, in the dressing-room during the Marlowe *Measure for Measure* – I was Mistress Overdone; Batty was Pompey Bum (now there's a name!) – to talk about the future. I told him, in the toss-up between the Marlowe and the Footlights, I had originally leaned towards the former, but seemed now to have swung the other way; maybe the opposite was happening with him. His Pompey was generally taken to be his best acting performance. Harold Bloom described the part as 'a triumph of Shakespeare's art, a vitalistic presence who refuses to be bound by any division between comedy and tragedy', and Batty absolutely got that. Dadie Rylands, who directed *Measure* said he had a Will Kemp quality, telling stark and veiled truths to equal effect. Surely once that comic/tragic divide had been bestridden, no stage door would remain closed. George Robey had played Falstaff; Frankie Howerd and Benny Hill had both played Bottom. He should dump his grump about not being in the Revue and get agents to see his Pompey. He said actually he had already done that. On Dadie's advice, he had written and sent photos to John Penrose, who represented such divide-bestriders as Steven Berkoff, and he was coming to see the show. I said: 'You bugger! You never told me.'

That night I wrote and sent photos to John Penrose and also Noel Gay of NGA, Max Kester of Foster's Agency, Jack Molony of International Agents, and my own unknown distant uncle Gordon Harbord of the Gordon Harbord Agency. John Penrose replied briefly: 'Make an appointment to come and see me'. Noel Gay didn't reply, having been dead for twelve years, but his son Richard Armitage, said make an appointment etc. Max Kester wrote that he already had more people on his books than he could satisfy and advised starting with at least one year in a good repertory company, such as Coventry who were looking for people for their new season rehearsing late August; and I would have written to them straight off had not Jack Molony, no longer of International Agents, but heading his own new talent-scouting outfit, replied advising a young actor not to hide away in rep, but take a chance on stardom: I should come and see him and he'd fix some *attractive* photos, not those gloomy film-noir-ish efforts the Footlights had had done for me. Gordon Harbord replied that I was welcome to come and see him but warned that he didn't 'do family'.

✳

There was a group of playful, well-high-heeled girls, not attached to the University but intrinsically part of the acting scene, playing small parts in plays and hosting large parties; three of whom had taken a shine to me. Estelle Tudor-Landor, Maisie-Lou Glyn and Zanna Raleigh-King (pronounced Rollicking), when possible took me for rides in open-top cars and had me punt them to Grantchester. In advance of the 'season', Maisie-Lou was holding a cocktail party in Chelsea on Monday 28th March and begged me to go. I wanted to get the agent thing under way before the summer term, when I would have to be revising, so I made a string of appointments through the day up till 5 pm after which I would whizz to the party then get a late train back to Cambridge; the next day pack, revise a bit, see friends, maybe a film, and the day after go home for Easter.

I caught the nine o'clock from Cambridge, cocktail clothes in a bag, arriving London 10.15. My appointment with Richard Armitage was for twelve noon, so I located the office, and was just going off for a slow cup of coffee, when a tall man rushed past me and into the building. I followed him in, as fast as I could, and was with him in the reception area before the door closed. 'You're John Cleese,' I said. He said: 'Am I? So I am!' I said: 'I'm Richard Crane. I'm in the Footlights.' That was the sum of our conversation, because a door opened and he shot through it, closing it sharply behind him, as raucous laughter erupted. I told the receptionist who I was and that I was early and she said: Did I want to wait? For the next half hour, I read *Variety* and *The Stage*, made a mental list of plays I should have seen for these interviews – *America Hurrah!, Staircase, Saved, Eh?* – and films – *Blow Up, Who's Afraid of Virginia Woolf?, Georgie Girl, Alfie* – flipped through *Spotlight*, checked the NGA client list – Russ Conway, Manuel and His Music of the Mountains, the Swingle Singers – felt maybe this agency was a bit limiting, and I should creep away, but then the door opened and Cleese came out. He didn't seem in such a rush now. 'Richard –' (he remembered my name!). Richard Armitage came out. Cleese continued: 'It's *Gilliam*. Chapman, Idle, Palin, Jones and *Gilliam*. He's the one.' 'And Cleese,' joked Armitage. 'And Cleese,' said Cleese, and he was out. I went in.

'Footlights...' sighed Armitage, swinging his feet onto the desk. I said: 'I've just been cast in in the Revue. These are some of my sketches.' He flipped through them, took a phone-call – 'Hey Russ!' – continued reading while talking, finished the call, swung his feet down. 'They're good, but we're glutted with Cambridge jokers. You saw Cleese just now. There just isn't the audience. We need regular stuff for Arthur Haynes and Dickie Henderson. Can you do that?' I said 'Sure'. He was looking at my photos. I said: 'And I want to perform as well.' Not looking up, he said: 'You've got a face we could use. Tell you what?' He passed the photos and sketches back: 'Let's see some simple funny stuff, and we'll send you a preliminary contract form.' He stood up, shook my hand, showed me the door. I said: 'What does a preliminary contract entail exactly?' He said: 'It means NGA has first claim on you, but isn't obliged to find you work.'

I went to John Penrose for 2.30pm. This seemed more like my place and I would have Batty for company. When I went in and mentioned Batty, he didn't seem to have heard of him. Feet firmly on the floor, he said: 'Why do you need an agent?' I said: 'I suppose I need someone who will find me work and guide my career.' He said: 'I rarely take on actors who don't already have a job.' I said: 'I do have a job. I'm in the Footlights Revue, which will play professional theatres around the country and may transfer to the West End.' He said: 'Would you arrange for me to see that?'

Jack Molony's office was brand new and bright. He was a jovial, tactile, extrovert showman, and nimble despite his rotundity. Writer, actor, comedy, tragedy, variety, legit, he could launch and manage me as any or all of these. Tommy Steele, Tommy Courtenay, he was scouting for the next of either; didn't need my scripts, handed back my photos. 'I'll have David (Bailey) or Gered (Mankowitz) do proper ones. Meantime, book me for the Revue. Can't wait!' As I was leaving, a many-scarved, bouffon-haired dowager sailed in. 'Hermione G!' exclaimed Jack. 'Meet the next Cuddly Dudley!' 'Darling, he's gorgeous!' said Hermione. 'Are you going to fuck him?' And we all roared.

I just had time to drop in on Gordon Harbord. He was an upright, frail-looking patrician in a suit with a slight look of my grandmother. The musty, book-lined office reminded me of Mr Flynn's study at The Old Ride. There was even a forlorn leather chair, which he gestured for me to sit in it. Seeing a photo of a sultry blonde on his desk, I said: 'Is that Diana Dors?' He sighed: 'I'm trying to get her to go straight. There's much more to her than peroxide and the pyramid bra, don't you think?' I said: 'There's probably much more to most actors.' He brightened: 'That's well said. But these days, you have to fit your slot and stay in it. What do you see as your slot?' 'Gosh,' I said. 'I really don't want to fit into any slot.' He collapsed in a fit of coughing, recovered, upright again, as the phone rang. He shook my hand, simultaneously angling me towards to the door. As I left, he was answering: 'Diana, Larry called. He wants you for Jocasta.'

I was in a hurry now; it was after six and I had to transform. Finding a phone-box, I went in as Clark Kent and came out in a dinner jacket, with red cummerbund, bow-tie and a loose bag on my shoulder. The party was walking distance and I ran most of the way, arriving crumpled and sweaty. Tudor-Landor and Rollicking exploded at my attire. Hadn't I read the invitation? This was a *dressing-down* party! Anyone dressing *up*, would be given a good dressing *down*! Tudor-L was a baglady in swathes of torn chiffon; Rollicking, stick-thin, was a turbaned mystic in dhoti and bra. 'But he *is* dressing down,' exclaimed Maisie-Lou, sailing in as a heroin addict. 'You should see him in his regalia. He is the Prince of Comedy! He is the Funniest Man in Town!' Everyone crowed, demanding a monologue or song, so I gave them *Burly Shirley*:

> Shirley was a burly girl.
> Shirley was to be my bride.
> Shirley rose up early
> On the day she died...

It was a crap performance, inaudible and off-key because I hadn't eaten all day and strangely named cocktails – Paint Stripper, Toilet Cleaner – were going straight to my head ... And someone had put the Stones on, over-riding all sound. '*I see a red door and I want it painted black...*' sang Maisie-Lou, grinding against me, with poppies in her hair and a necklace of syringes; her boyfriend butting in with jerky Jagger moves - '*I want to see your face painted black, black as night...*' – had actually blacked up – no wait! He *was* black! My head was spinning. I had to eat if only to sick something up. There had been finger-food but I'd missed it. The last tray was spilt across the floor and I was stopped from sliding on it by Rollicking, who was saying we must all go to Joe Allen's, 'and then,' insisted Tudor-Landor 'to Mandy's (cheers!) where the Moody Blues were playing!' '*I want to see the sun blotted out from the sky. I want to see it painted, painted, painted, painted...*' The lights fused. Everyone screamed. In the black, I fumbled to the door where my bag was and slipped out, hailed a taxi – fucksake I was an actor eschewing rep, taking a punt on stardom! – got to Liverpool Street, just as the train was pulling out. The next one was the last one. I could have had a meal, except (a) I'd just blown my cash on the taxi, and (b) my innards were in turmoil. I fell asleep and woke just in time to jump on the last train. When I got back to Jesus it was after locking up. At night the college was like a prison: high walls topped with revolving spikes to prevent inmates climbing in. In my first year I once nearly impaled myself; then a friend showed me where there was a low, unfortified stretch of wall where one could hop over without injury. Jumping down, I took a detour to the post room, to check for post. There was a Footlights rehearsal schedule for next term, an Easter card from the chaplain and a telegram: GRANDPA DYING STOP COME TO BATH NOT BRUM MUM.

GRANDPA

I was fifteen when I saw my first dead body. My grandfather had come to stay at Balsall Heath and asked if I would like to go with him to the morgue. 'This is the luggage-room,' he said as we entered a chilly space where six or seven bodies were laid out under sheets. 'They are the empty cases, not wanted on voyage, but people have grown used to them, so our job is to dispose of them as decently as possible.' He pulled back a sheet and I saw a young woman, my age; so lifelike I thought, if he had said '*Talitha cumi!*' her eyes would have flipped open. On the way home, I said: 'Grandpa, I thought the body *and* the soul, went to Heaven, as it says in the Bible.' He said: 'Dick, we have no idea what happens. All we know is things fall apart, cells divide, bodies rot, become the mansion and the menu for a convocation of worms, who are then ett oop by t'ducks, who are then ett oop by us, in a most natural eucharist, (singing) *On Ilkla Moor Baht'At. On Ilkla Moor Baht'At. On Ilkla... Moor... Baht'... At.'*

I said: 'Grandpa?'

'Dick?'

'Do you really not believe in Heaven?'

He considered a moment: 'There has to be a distinction between believing and knowing. I do absolutely believe in God's Love which is Heaven. What I don't have, is *knowledge*.'

I wanted to say: 'But what about the proofs? Aquinas, the maths. If this, then that; if one thing, then the other. Is that true knowledge or just pasting over the void? Is the need to give comfort where there is none, more important that telling the *un*comfortable truth? Is that what love is: telling a lie because the truth is too upsetting? Can one do that and be a priest? Would Jesus have done that?' I wanted to ask him all this – things I couldn't ask my father because I knew his belief was proven and unshakeable; whereas Grandpa was *political*. A canon and a rural dean, he sat in Chapter, chaired committees, dwelt in the realm of the persuadable, like Uncle Gerald, now Bishop of Chester; except that Gerald *knew* that he didn't know, whereas Grandpa didn't know anything.

When I saw him in the hospital, I knew it was too late. We would never have that conversation. He had said to my mother, after months of pain, that he knew what it was to be crucified and he shared Christ's terrible doubts that he had been forsaken. He had preached peace for the dying, and a heavenly reward if one's life had been good. But had *his* life been good? Had he not, with the best of intentions, peddled lies? Looking now at the shrunken body, eyes closed in drugged sleep, I understood about the luggage. This was a carcase, not wanted on voyage. The skin stretched tight across the skull, the once dimpled cheeks and crinkling eyes, from seventy years of smiling, now taut as a drum; the once plenteous nose, now pared to a point, and the smell coming up, as if death was already biting and he was rotting while still alive.

His eyes flipped open.

'Dick...?'

'Grandpa...'

And closed again. I sat by him for a minute till my mother said: 'Do you want to go now?' I got up and was just leaving, when she said: 'Wait.' I looked back. He was raising his hand, as is if waving. I sort of waved back. She said:

'He's blessing you.'

*

Funerals have very little to do with death. They are mostly, solemnly, about glossing over the doubt. Everything was going to be all right after all. Grandpa's long dark night was over. He was now properly alive, in the arms of Jesus.

I was back at home when he died. My mother stayed on with my grand-mother. I took the call – it was after midnight – and went to tell my father who was sleeping in the spare room. There was a pause and I wondered if he'd heard me properly. Then he said: 'Was he in pain?' I thought that was an odd question. Of course he was in the most terrible, crucifying pain. I said: 'I don't know. He was unconscious when they left.'

'Was he alone?'

I went to make a cup of tea. When I came back my father was on his knees by the bed. His shoulders were shaking. He had failed his fellow priest. Even though he wasn't there, he could have rained down prayers, to help him through his darkest hour. This is when faith matters most, when you can offer it like a life-belt. The old Admiral, as they used to call him, had slid down the deck of *HMS Nottingham* into the icy peril of the North Sea, and been buoyed up by the faith and love of Granny Twidle, his future wife. With the sheer strength of another's prayer, he could now have been lifted from the slough, rung by rung, up the ladder to Paradise.

> *Bring us, O Lord God, at our last awakening*
> *into the house and gate of Heaven, to enter into*
> *that gate and dwell in that house...*

*

As we cruised in the cortege, in our best black, slowly down the winding spring-blossom-laden lane from Combe Down into Bath, men doffed their caps, regular traffic gave way; even as we descended towards the orderly, sunlit, sandstone terraces, everyone knew that this day, 4th April 1966, belonged to Arthur Edwin Twidle, Priest, Canon Emeritus of York, Rural Dean of Beverley, Incumbent of Thwing, Bishop Burton, Burton Agnes, Acomb, St John's Micklegate and the Priory Church of St Mary of Mount Carmel, South Queensferry...

We crossed the river into Pierrepont St, and came to a halt before the carved ladders of angels climbing the high West Front of Bath Abbey: a holy place since Saxon times, site of the coronation of the first King of All Eng-land, refashioned 1874 by Gilbert Scott at his most Gothic.

It was the Monday in Holy Week, so the whole Abbey was in mourning: all crosses veiled in purple, no flowers, no cottas for the choir. The air was still and hugely sombre. All the Cranes and Macks and sea-faring Harbords were there, but no Methodist Twidles (still unreconciled, after fifty-five years, with their apostate brother). My grandmother sat with her sons Hugh and Bob and daughters Nowell and Maureen. Her sister Rosie was absent. On the night the Ad died, Edie had rung Rosie, who had said: 'I think we're in the same boat.' After the death of her poet husband Wilfred Bone, in the trenches, she had married Gordon Blood, a one-legged missionary. He hadn't been well, and on the night my grandmother phoned, she had just come from closing his eyes.

> *Save us, O Lord, waking, guard us sleeping;*
> *that awake we may watch with Christ,*
> *and asleep we may rest in peace.*

As the choir sang of the heaven of God's love, I kept thinking of the devil: the creature that had lodged in my grandfather's bowel and eaten him from within. I thought less about the 'luggage' that was laid out in the coffin, waiting to be burned, and more of the coils of Lucifer, alive *within* the luggage, and soon to be released into his best hellish element.

LEE CLARE

There was one play, in my final run of plays at Cambridge, that I ducked out of and shouldn't have. Clem Vallance, a fellow Footlight, had come across a banned German play that had recently had two censored performances at the Royal Court in London. The Lord Chamberlain had instructed that 'there be no kissing, caressing or embracing between the two boys in the vineyard scene; that the words *penis* and *vagina* be expunged, and an alternative be found to the masturbation game in the reformatory.' Wedekind's *Spring Awakening*, written in the 1890s, was absolutely a play for us now. Reading it, I cast myself as Moritz, the neurasthenic student, traumatized by puberty, who shoots himself after failing his exams. In the last scene, he comes back as a ghost, head under his arm, and says to Melchior, his friend:

> 'We're high above you people. We smile at your little upsets. We can see through the whole thing. We see the virtuous stoking up their lust on their own and the wicked being inspired by great poetry... We join in when God and the Devil drink each other under the table... Come Melchior, join me. Just give me your hand. Just your little finger will do.'

The cast divides between the kids who are real and the grown-ups who are caricatures. The kids still have hope, mixed with ignorance and terror; the grown-ups are kept stiff behind their actors' masks. I was cast as one of the teachers, having proved I could do eccentrics; but I really wanted to be Moritz. At the read-through at the end of the Lent term, the actor cast as Moritz was away sick, so Clem said 'Richard, will you read?' So I did, I stunned them all, I *was* the desperate, dogged, misfit ghost-boy who loses his chance and is left floundering in limbo. Walking away up Jesus Lane, with the actor (Lee Clare) who was playing Melchior, I said I could kill to play the part. 'Then kill,' said Lee. 'The fault Richy-rich,' slapping his arm round my shoulder, 'is not in our stars, but in *ourselves* etc...' I said: 'How many did you kill to get where you are?' He said: 'For "kill" read "fuck". It's the better way. You want to hear?'

He was everything I wanted to be and wasn't. In his second year at Trinity Hall, he had come up, aged seventeen, with an Equity card and one play already written *and* performed on the Edinburgh Fringe. He had joined Ipswich Rep at fourteen as a student actor, working with the likes of Ian McKellen and Hildegard Neil. One midsummer night, after a dress rehearsal of the *Dream*, he stayed behind with Titania to hear her lines. The stage manager, presuming everyone had gone home, had locked them in. The stage was pitch dark. It was magic, it was a lark, it was naughty, it was pure theatre. In the Fairy Queen's bower, before a full house of empty seats, he fed her the lines, '*... with apricocks and dewberries... purple grapes, green figs and mulberries... honey bags, humblebees, waxen thighs... to have my love to bed, and to arise...*

Mustardseed rogering the Queen of the Fairies in her own bower! Would it ever get better than this? Yes it would! Larks and girls and giggles and queens, were falling into his lap, and he was still only fifteen! Was he telling me all this as we as we crossed the quad to my staircase? Was he following me, gangly, with a bounce in his step, into my rooms, flopping down, while I poured whiskies, lit two cigarettes, then handed him one, like Paul Henreid obliging Bette Davis in *Now Voyager*? And were we now doing the lines... '*Let's lie under this tree... feel the warm wind blowing down from the hills. That's where I'd like to be now...*'

And did I then kiss him?

He'd just taken a drag and choked: 'Richie-rich... What are you doing?'

'Shit, sorry. Wrong scene. Forget it. Shall we go on? *Did you ever feel shame?* That's the line, and you answer.'

We lay on the floor looking up as it grew dark: best friends, poles apart: Melchior, the genius, atheist, rebel; Moritz, the fatally hopeful non-person, who when Melchior's mother (Germaine Greer) refuses to fund his passage to America, takes a gun and blows his head off.

I wouldn't be playing that part.

THIS WAY OUT

MA: *I hope you have a really good final term. It's odd to think that you won't be coming home again...*

ME: *We have been Footlighting all week. The dates, for your diary are: Cambridge June 6th-18th, Oxford June 20th-25th, York 27th-July 2nd, Averham 4th-9th, Bury St Edmunds 11th-16th.*

MA: *Daddy will be giving you £200. Please spend it thriftily, as it is really an advance for your fare to come and visit...*

ME: *All Footlights members can suggest a title for the revue. Andy proposed* The Black and White Nostril Show. *Col Batty proposed* Why the f*** aren't I in it? *The chosen title is* This Way Out (TWO). *It's supposed to be ironic.*

MA: *Uncle Sam died last Friday, only 65. Isn't it strange? Between us, Daddy and I have lost a father, a brother-in-law, two uncles and one great-uncle in the past two months. Grandpa Ashby continues to keep very well.*

ME: *We have just one week to go now before the exams and I am planning to work very hard.*

MA: *When G'pa does go – this next bit is TOP SECRET! – Daddy will get Ma's estate (about £6,000) plus £15,000 legacy... So you should not have to worry about your parents in their old age...*

ME: *I have spent the last three evenings in a dinner jacket and each time didn't get to bed before two. On Thurs was the last Smoker. Andy, David & I had written a sad song which closed the show:* The spring of youth is over now... *Two of the girls in the audience cried. On Friday I went to London to do a cabaret at the Guy's Hospital Annual Ball at the Grosvenor Hotel in Park Lane. Then yesterday, we pootled down to Brighton for the opening of the Pussy-Cat Club. We shared a dressing-room with the Kinks who sang their new hit* Sunny Afternoon, *even though it was night-time and raining!*

MA: *I have now completely packed the big zinc trunk, the brown tin trunk, the old brown cabin trunk and four tea-chests (all sewn up in sacking). These are for the heavy Not-Wanted-On-Voyage baggage...*

ME: *I went to be measured for a made-to-measure suit: grey mohair with four buttons. We are also getting shirts, ties and shoes – there is a budget of £200 to spend on clothes!!!*

MA: *We are looking forward very much to June 9th and to seeing you in your new mohair suit! Did you manage to get extra tickets for U Arch and A Joan?*

ME: *I finished my exams yesterday. I would prophesy a tutu (2:2) for myself, which I will be wearing in the revue!*

MA: *Well, what a show that was! I think we enjoyed it – U Arch and A Joan were very complimentary about the suit! – but not sure about the mangling of* Land of Hope and Glory *by the Australian woman.*

ME: *I'm so glad you appreciated the revue...We're still rehearsing and I think you'll notice a difference next week!*

MA: *I am writing this at Milson's where we are staying the night on the way back from Saltburn... then tomorrow up to York, where we will see* This Way Out *for the third time. Our final exit!*

ME: *I'm sorry about York. I didn't mean to get upset.*

MA: *This is to greet you at Averham in your 'country house', and to wish you and all the cast a very successful penultimate week.*

ME: *Richard Syms has been murdered. Andy Mayer is investigating because he is the detective. Germaine Greer is in the conservatory reading Hercule Poirot's Christmas. Why were eleven people with no apparent connection, strangely invited to spend a week in this eery house?*

MA: *Well, we are now homeless. We reached Gran's as planned at 5pm after a really busy day closing down our life at St Paul's. I lit my bonfire at 6.30am & kept it going till 1.0pm, when I finally stripped off my frock & threw it in the flames...*

When Richard Syms was directing my Bronte play *Thunder* in London in 1994, he mentioned he had a recording of the Footlights Revue he'd directed and acted in, twenty-eight years earlier. He'd had it transferred from reel-to-reel to cassette and gave me a copy. I was wary about listening to it; I didn't want any doubt rocking the certainty that *This Way Out*, as confirmed by the critics, had been the grand finale of my Cambridge years and my springboard into professional theatre:

> *Of the actors, Richard Crane and Andy Mayer run away with the honours... Mr Crane has written some of the best numbers too...*

> *...a fresh sense of humour seen at its best in* The Truth about Scrooge, *where he adopts with deceptive ease and a voice that needs oiling, the character of a male Irene Handl...*

> *With Mr Mayer, he has written a delectably comic onslaught on the Brontes, in* The Tenant of Wutherfield Grange, *in which the very stones of Haworth Parsonage shake beneath the attack...*

Miss Greer, as a vocal comedienne is probably the most professional performer in the show, but Mr Crane runs her close... He has an expressive comic talent, can sing, and given the opportunity, by his fleeting exhibition in Hey There Lady! *could even dance...*

This was what I'd come to Cambridge to do and step by step I'd done it. Of the Marlowe and the Footlights it turned out in the end that the latter was my niche. Our style was subversive yet inclusive, whimsy-free yet juvenile, less Stones, more Beatles (in our made-to-measure suits), swinging humour like a glitter-ball against cultural monuments. 'You're only young once, but you can be immature for ever,' said Germaine, and six feet tall, hers was the pinnacle we aspired to. In the eight-to-one mismatch of the sexes in Cambridge, her voice was ringing out for gender awakening ('Aw Germaine,' said I, 'do stop yacking on like – I dunno – some *female eunuch* [ping!]; write the book for chrissake!!') Lee Clare who was her student and came with us on the tour, tells how he met her at a party, wearing high-heeled boots, and a dress slit to the thigh. Every boy's oedipal wet dream, she played along, whipping out a diary and cooing: 'Let's see where we can *fit you in...*' And the next day, at the appointed hour, he turned up at her little town-centre cottage in the square behind the Arts, expecting full-on, fish-net, fairy-queen sex. He knocked, the door opened and there she was, in her cardigan, tweed skirt, flat shoes, half-moon glasses, sitting him down and quizzing him line by line through his essay on *The Ethics of Love and Marriage in Shakespeare's Early Comedies.*

There was one review of *This Way Out,* that I kept folded over in the scrap-book and was the reason why I was wary of playing Syms's tape. '*FOOTLIGHTS FALTER,*' was the headline in *The Stage:*   '*... a patchy concoction... pleasant but unremarkable... peters out listlessly... occasionally it rises only a little above schoolboy level, which would not matter if the presentation were slick and pithy...*'

Twenty-eight years on, alone in the car driving home from Clacton, in thin June sunlight, I slipped Syms's tape into the slot and pressed: Play.

It was a terrible recording: creaky, muffled with elephantine dance-steps and shrieking voices, one of which was mine. Pure juvenile tosh was the kindest description and I was grateful to be alone. I pulled over into a lay-by, sank head in hands and let the thing run. It was ghastly, beyond embarrassing. So why were the audience howling with laughter, and cheering every sketch? My *Scrooge,* Andy's *Goldilocks* were doubled in length because of the show-stopping response. I felt old, like Scrooge himself forced to revisit the past: my young self, my young friends, fearless, hilarious, untroubled by responsibility. This past *was* another country with an easier language, a lighter, simpler sense of humour. Just weeks from the precipice, the audience were telling us, tosh or not, we had wings.

It was only when we got to York and I saw my parents for the last time, that the truth sank in. Of all the cast members, I was the only one with nothing concrete to go on to. Andy had just accepted a traineeship at Granada TV. Syms, about to be ordained, already had a foot in the door of religious broadcasting. Germaine would complete her PhD and write that book. Tim Davies was about to join the Bristol Old Vic company. And Jane, Chris Mohr, Richard Harris and Ray Elmitt, would all be returning to Cambridge, for another year.

Jack Molony was in the audience. He'd said I should come to his hotel afterwards for a drink. He was staying at the Grand and I was expecting him to come and collect me from the stage door. It was one of our best performances and I was so glad Jack had seen it, and my parents too. I would introduce them to each other – it would be a moment of crossing over from the old secure world of church and faith, to the rock'n'roll of showbiz. I would say a swift 'bon voyage' with filial hand-shake and peck, then go for a drink with my agent.

My mother pointed to the note pinned up at the stage door, which I hadn't seen. Jack had phoned, so sorry, client crisis; would try and make it to Bury St Edmunds. I felt fury, akin to grief, and when my father said: 'Well Wit, this is it...' and my mother said: 'At least, we'll always know what you're doing, when we read about you in the papers...' I let them have it, with tears:

'I won't be doing anything! I've nothing lined up! All the others have things to go to! No one cares about *student actors*! And I'm not even in Equity! You need a contract to join Equity, and you have to be in Equity to get a contract! But honestly, don't worry, it's okay. Just don't expect fame and fortune. Sob! You've got to go and I really want you to. I have to do this on my own, and I will. Sorry sorry...'

I watched them walk away, side by side, not touching: my mother, child-size, setting the pace, in her cotton coat – *nothing*, not even the squealing of her son would thwart her PLAN, her launch, at forty-four, of a new Jamaican career in journalism, broadcasting, travel writing, *anything*! And I recalled her in the Easter holidays, after my grandfather had died, taking Mungo, the dog, to the vet for the last time. She had wanted him to be difficult, as he often was on walks, but today he was good as gold. Biting her lip, she walked briskly, annoyed that no one wanted him, but he obviously couldn't go with them. So stoic and for the greater good, she delivered him, signed the form, paid the fee and came home with an empty lead.

I watched them walk away. I thought they might look back, but you didn't do that in our family. Once good-byes were said, you were on your way: Ma striding ahead, Pa skipping to keep up. I watched them walk away till they disappeared.

ACT THREE
On The Road: 1966-71

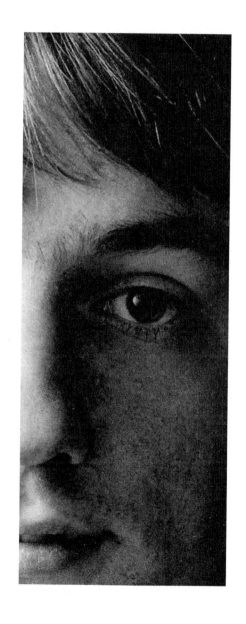

I've been a puppet, a pauper, a pirate
a poet, a pawn and a king.
I've been up and down and over and out
and I know one thing:
each time I find myself flat on my face,
I pick myself up and get back in the race.
- Frank Sinatra

*

Look at my eyes. I'm dead behind these eyes.
- Archie Rice

Scene One
'SUNNY'

Someone had been playing the song and I had it on the brain; so when you said that was your name, my heart skipped a beat. You said it the way Bobby Hebb sings it, with that smile 'so sincere, so true', as if you knew my very thoughts. We were standing in front of the coat shop window, looking at a coat which was like yours and I'd said: 'I'll need a coat like that, if it gets any colder.' (It was a sort of donkey jacket with a soft collar.) 'Did you get yours here?' I think you said 'Yes'. Then neither of us spoke. I could see beads of sweat on your nose and your eyes were gleaming. I said: 'I'm Richard. What's your name?' You said: 'Sunny'.

I told you, when we went for a beer, that I was working in City Hall, in Victoria Street, in Registration of Electors, except when I was on the street going door-to-door in the Paddington area. Did you live in the Paddington area? Because I might come knocking to find out how many families you had living in your basement; except this week – my final week! – I was in the office, licking envelopes, on the seventeenth floor. I'd finished by four o'clock but couldn't leave till five, so sat looking down on the swirling mass of match-stick people, and thinking somewhere down there is the Love of my Life, my 'sunny one so true'. I got the 52 bus, and a seat at the front on the top deck, demob-happy they used to call it, because at last I was leaving. I was going to Yorkshire on Sunday for Christmas, then getting an eighteen hour train ride and a nine hour boat to Ireland to start my career as a professional actor. Was I talking too much? I felt if I stopped you might vanish back into the crowd.

I'd got off the bus at Notting Hill Gate and would normally have taken the tube two stops, to Lancaster Gate, where I shared a ballroom at number 79, in one of those fabulous palatial blocks overlooking Hyde Park; I shared it with my ertswhile comedy partner, Colin Batty, who was now working for the Ministry of Defence and wouldn't be back till ten. So I walked along Bayswater Road feeling great. It was nippy but I wasn't cold. I even thought of taking a turn in the park, which was like our back garden; but just as I was approaching Porchester Terrace, I saw *you* coming towards me. There were crowds of people pressing on and passing by, not communicating or touching; you and I were the only ones who connected: a one-in-a-trillion chance clash of eyes, like two atoms, in the primordial universe, out of which Life sprang. On impulse, I glanced back, just as you glanced back, and I saw you smile. Then you turned and walked on. I crossed the road, zig-zagging through the traffic, nearly causing an accident, and ran along parallel to you on the Park side, intending to overtake you, cross back, and then, as in the old gag-line 'Do you believe in love at first sight, or shall I walk past again?', walk past you again. But just as I was crossing, you veered off down Queensway and I lost you in the crowd. Hordes of working people were exuding from the station; I muddled through and nearly didn't see you standing, looking in the coat-shop window. I thought: 'He doesn't need to do that; he's already bought the coat. There must be another reason.'

You finished your beer. I said: 'Would you like another?' but you had to get back and do the rice. That was your job in the house and your auntie, uncle and cousins would be waiting. But you could come back later, come to 79 Lancaster Gate for nine o'clock. 'I'll wait for you in the hall. We'll have an hour before my flatmate comes back. Or we could walk in the park. Are you Jamaican? I thought with a name like yours, you might be Jamaican. My family are Jamaican.' You said: 'It's not my name. But too many people in Mauritius are called Louis, so it makes sense to have another name.' I said maybe you were the fourteenth Louis in your family and as Louis Quatorze, you were the Sunny King. Getting up you said: 'That would be neat. See you later.'

I waited for you. I waited in the hall from 8.30 till 10, when my flatmate turned up. 'What are you doing down here?' I said 'I'm waiting for someone. We were going for a drink, but he hasn't showed up.'

The next day, at work, I asked if I could possibly go early if I'd finished. 'No problem,' said the boss, so come four o'clock, I put my coat on, my new coat, your coat, which I'd bought that morning, on the way in, from the coat-shop; streamed in the lift down seventeen floors and out into the street, onto the 52 bus, front seat, top deck, off at Notting Hill Gate, down to the tube, just got the central line as the doors were closing, went two stops to Lancaster Gate, got the lift to the street, and was up sitting in the window of the ballroom of 79, by five past five. If you were coming back from where you'd been yesterday, then you'd be passing at a similar time, between 5.45 and six o'clock. I watched every bowed, hunch-shouldered worker untouched, untouching, hurrying home, and you weren't there. I stayed watching till ten past six, and was just getting up to get a beer, when I saw you!! I shot out and down the stairs, round the corner of Leinster Gardens and onto Bayswater Road as you were disappearing into the mass. I yelled 'Sunny!' You turned. You looked puzzled. As I got my breath, you said: 'Where were you? I waited.'

I said: 'No *I* waited. Where were *you*?'

'At number 70, as you said. I even got into the hall. People didn't like me being there.'

'Oh God, did I say 70? I meant 79.'

'I thought you might have said 79, but it sounded like 70.'

'So what about now? Or do you have to do the rice?'

You said you had to go out with the family tonight, and the next night, but you were free on Saturday all day. I said: 'Let's meet, on this spot, corner of Leinster Gardens and Bayswater Road, Saturday 11 am.' We shook hands, your dark hand, my light hand, holding the moment, a little longer than was normal, like statesmen sealing a pledge.

∗

I want to write down, step by step, everything that happened on Saturday 17th December 1966.

You were waiting on the corner when I came down at eleven o'clock, and we set off walking towards town. We stopped near Marble Arch, had a coffee, then walked on down Oxford Street which was packed with Christmas shoppers. We went into Selfridges and you bought a present for your auntie and I bought one for my sister, then we continued down Regent St, swung into Carnaby Street, had a burger and chips in Leicester Square. It was looking like rain, so we slipped into the Odeon to see Cliff Richard in *Finders Keepers*. We took off our coats. I slung mine over the seat in front; you put yours across your lap. Then as the film got going – Cliff and the Shadows, accidentally defusing a bomb while gigging in a Spanish village, and facing off love (Vivienne Ventura) and pomposity (Robert Morley) – your hand touched mine under the coat; accidentally. I glanced at you, but you were watching the film, so I watched it through, taking none of it in, just feeling your slim fingers, squeezing, relaxing. When we came out, it was getting dark. We walked down Charing Cross Road to Trafalgar Square and across into the Mall and St James's Park. The ducks were settling for the night and there weren't many people around. We sat on a bench under a tree and I kissed you. Your face dark in the darkness, little beads of sweat on your nose, in spite of the cold. I said: 'It's illegal what we're doing. What if someone comes?' You said in a high voice: 'Then I'll pretend to be a woman.' Big Ben struck six. We had just four hours till Col Batty got back and he sometimes came home early. We got the tube from Westminster and were up in the ballroom by half past. I put the fire on but not the light, and we crouched over the sputtering gas jets, till we were warm. Then I helped you undress, and you helped me, and we lay on my narrow bed. If Batty came in now, we would die; it was the only thing and it would be worth it, a worthy death, which we knew was coming anyway. You were kissing my neck and the curve of my shoulder; my hands in your matted hair, my lips on your brow. We both 'died' in the same moment; we were joined, glued, in the sudden warmth and stickiness, skin to skin, like blood brothers. I looked at us in the firelight: you so black and me so white. How could anyone say this was wrong? We got dressed and I asked you to choose a record. You chose Nat King Cole *When I Fall in Love*, and I lit two cigarettes and gave you one and we sat on the sofa, your arm round me, my head on your shoulder:

> *In a restless world like this is*
> *Love is ended before it's begun*
> *And too many moonlight kisses*
> *Seem to cool in the warmth of the sun...*

When the song and the cigarettes ended, I said: 'We'd better go out; he'll be back soon.'

So we put on our coats and went out to the park. It was locked up, so we climbed over. We had all the three hundred acres to ourselves as we walked among the wintry trees. There was a hollow one, like an alcove, as if carved to the shape of two closely entwined bodies, illuminated by the moon. We nestled inside; it seemed to close around us. You said (I remember the words): '*Richard, can I tell you something? I am in love with you.*' There were tears in your eyes; I kissed them as they fell. No one knew we were there. No one known to either of us, would know we'd ever met. Our world was a separate world: our moon, our tree, our park, our time.

As we climbed out and were walking along Bayswater Road to the point where we would part, I was saying Christmas had come early this year. After months of parsimony, Santa has delivered all the presents at once: freedom from drudgery, proper work at last, adventure, opportunity, and love with wings. Put another way, hidden deep in my heart, I now had a secret burning coal to keep me warm through chilly Ireland. It might fizzle out; it might burn the house down. That was the gamble. But I would never forget this moment.

Now the dark days are done;
The bright days are here.
My Sunny one shined
So sincere...

I must have said something about not worrying if it didn't last, there would always be someone else; because you mentioned it in the letter you wrote three days later when I was in Yorkshire. I thought I'd destroyed all your letters but the other day, I found this one; nearly half a century old, it still breaks my heart:

Bayswater, W2
December 22nd 1966.
Hello dear Richard,
Since I first left you on the eve of your departure, I was feeling as if I was going to collapse but I did resist and am now feeling better. In order to keep myself at rest, I went to see the lights from Marble Arch to Piccadilly Circus. I was trying to stop myself from thinking that you were gone. This is my first love affair; that was the real reason for my upsetting on Saturday last. I do hope you understand me. It was not your departure that worried me. Something came to my mind that I was going to lose you for ever. I don't know, it was just a thought. There was something you said that really hurt me. It was your suggestion about finding a new partner if I am not satisfied with you. Nevertheless, don't bother about it. Maybe you didn't deliberately say it. I can only wish you a Merry Christmas and a Happy New Year, and enjoy yourself very much.
Bye bye
Your loving friend
Louis

*

You weren't Sunny any more. It was bleak in Ireland too. I wrote to you, we were sleeping on mattresses in a vast, unheated, unfurnished house. It tipped with rain almost every day. The one sunny day, they left me in the house and went walking in the hills, while I wrote my first professional play. Two of the actors hadn't turned up, so we'd had to change the programme and I'd said I'd write a short play, to fill the gap. The play we were meant to do would have to wait till we were in London, if we could find money and a theatre. In the meantime, we had the little Group Theatre in Cork which was attached to a pub, and it was ours to do with as we liked, for a month. We did a Christmas revue, written mostly by me and I did most of the acting, plus singing and dancing; then my little play and two other little plays. And they all went really well. The audience roared, awash with Beamish (the Guinness of southern Ireland). The critics were impressed: '*the entertainment is delicious... this comedy (my play) has agony at its roots... like a Gothic gargoyle torn from a cathedral...* ' Were you following all this? I wasn't sure how much to tell you. I didn't want to swamp you with theatricals because that wasn't your world. But what *was* your world Louis? You said you played the piano, were fluent in three languages and you liked to cook. But I'd never heard your music or talked to you in French, or tasted your rice. We'd only ever had one whole day together and nothing, I promised, would ever spoil that day, and I told you that in the letter. But it didn't solve the problem of where we went from here. I'd be coming back to England at the beginning of February. I'd want to see you and make love with you, but where could we go? You were still with your family in Moscow Road; I was staying in the Kensington flat of one of our actresses, along with several others. One morning, I rang you. It must have been your auntie who answered. I said: 'Is Sunny there?' She called: 'Louis! It's for you!' You said you were working at Barkers' in High Street Ken, and you'd be off at 5.30. I said I'd call by, but I couldn't wait till then, so I walked down the road to the store, where I saw you, in your brown overall, shifting boxes. It was like the first time we met: your face burst into smiles, *my sunny one so true, I love you...* We went for a meal. We drank wine. We talked about the future. We could get a flat together: that was obvious, but of course not just yet. I didn't know what was happening to the plays and anyway, I was acting now, trying to build a career, for which I must be free to fly wherever the theatre wind blew, whether Cork or Pitlochry or Nairobi or Hollywood. I might be away for months, so it wouldn't make sense to get a flat which I wouldn't be living in. We couldn't tie ourselves to a flat, or each other, if I wasn't going to be around. What did I mean 'or each other'? Oh God, I don't know, I wasn't ready... Nothing was ever going to be permanent. I was a member of a company that had grown together like a family. We were bringing the plays directly to the West End; to a tiny theatre called the Little Garrick in the heart of theatreland. This was to be my London premiere both as actor and writer. And we were doing the big play that we couldn't do in Cork, as well. That was all that mattered right now. I couldn't expect you to be as keen about all this as I was; it wasn't your world. I didn't even expect you to want to see the plays, and you never said you'd like to; I wasn't going to push it. The others had friends and loved ones coming to the first night; I didn't have anyone and that was fine. To have you there, on your own, watching a weird experimental neo-surrealist playlet with songs, or a 'free-wheeling political debate' about Gorky and his spat with Lenin (I played Lenin) would be distracting, embarrassing. How would I introduce you? After we'd eaten and got through a whole bottle of wine, and were walking through Holland Park, in silence, I saw coming towards us – hell! – two figures, whom I recognized from their voices, as Chris Parr, the director, and Howard Brenton, the writer of the Gorky play. They couldn't fail to see us. 'Hi Rick!' Chris would say, and I would say: 'Hi Chris, hi Howard, this is Sunny, he's from Mauritius. I'm going to fuck him in a tree.' But it was almost pitch dark. They were deep in conversation. We walked straight between them and they didn't notice. We were ghosts in a parallel universe, walking on, unseen, in silence.

It was after lock-up time, when we got to Hyde Park, but it was the only place we could go. Also it might rekindle that 'spark of nature's fire', if we could find the tree. We did find one. It was bigger; we had to crawl to get inside. It was damp and musty. Someone had used it as a toilet. But we were here now; we had to do it. I couldn't see if you were smiling. Your lips were cold.

Afterwards, we zipped up, crawled out, walked away. There was someone else in the park with a torch. We ran, got to the fence, climbed over, just as a voice shouted: 'Hey!' We jumped on a bus, going up Bayswater Road. You got off at Queensway. I went on towards Kensington.

*

I've just found two more letters at the back of a drawer: this from Lammas Avenue, Mitcham, Surrey, dated January 3rd 1968:

> Hello my dear Richard,
> I am very pleased to hear from you, as my hope of seeing you was nearly drawing to its end.
> I hope you did enjoy yourself during the past few months. As you can seen I am now living in Mitcham Surrey and am still working at Barkers in High Street Kensington. So any time you wish to meet me when you are in London, please phone me before, so that I can prepare myself. WESTERN 5432 ext 297 (Drugs Dept).
> I am now living in a family as a guest. They are very orthodox; they don't like me receiving visitors inside the house. If you wish please call upon me, so we shall decide to go somewhere else.
> I didn't expect to hear from you at all. I thought you have been fed up with me. Until then cheerio!
> With love
> Louis.

*

My letter to you was probably quite short: 'Where are you? I miss you. What are you doing? Please can we meet?' We hadn't had any communication for ten months. There didn't seem much point. I was either going to follow my star and do the work I was born to do, or be led by my heart and get arrested, gaoled, disgraced and ruined. I'd watched you walking away down Queensway, proud and cold in your soft-collared donkey-jacket and thought 'that's the last I'll see of you'. I was heading straight back into the stormy world of putting on plays, where you can't be distracted. I had to make sure I was noticed and got good reviews; I had to find a new agent and a job that came with money; I needed somewhere to live in the heart of the business where I could jump at opportunites. And I did all that. My new agent was a former soubrette, who specialized in musicals, and I *nearly* got one; almost, *almost* got another; then to earn money and keep within the whiff of the greasepaint, I did a twelve week run of tearing tickets for Brian Rix at the (big) Garrick Theatre, usurping the royal box, when it wasn't occupied, and reading the complete works of Noel Coward for inspiration and audition pieces, while Rix dropped his trousers. I was drifting away from Parr and Brenton because, despite our efforts, nothing much was happening, and there was never going to be any money. I was sleeping on the floor of 17b Ladbroke Terrace, which was home to five girls students and many more itinerant actors, one of whom's mother ran the Summer Theatre at Frinton-on-Sea, which became my gateway into Equity when I auditioned and was appointed assistant stage manager, then stage manager, then supporting actor, doing a different play each week. The wind of theatre was blowing well. I was earning £7.10s a week and doing auditions when I could get to London, the last of which led to a contract to play as cast in the winter season at the Palace Court Theatre Bournemouth. The zephyrs of Thespis were filling my sails, and with a two-month break before rehearsals and a loan from my parents, I flew to Jamaica for a holiday.

I was thinking about you for the first time in ages. I was imagining you lying with me on the beach at Montego Bay. When I went (just once) with a beach-boy in the changing-rooms, I tried to imagine it was you. When I got to Bournemouth, to play Mikey the teenage dragon in the family Christmas show *Beauty and the Beast,* I thought this was a show you should come to, and you could meet the company. It was quite a queer set-up with many a giggle from the director and his assistant (they called me 'Poof the Magic Dragon') whenever I stripped off, tanned and fit from Jamaica, to put on my spiky green costume with its stiff tail and little wings. I felt if they knew I was with you, they'd have welcomed you and I was beginning to envisage you as my rock of domesticity in this volatile profession. Gielgud had his Martin Hensler; Bogarde, his Tony Forwood. Maybe you could be my lifelong companion, amanuensis and conscience, holding me to account, keeping the home fire burning and uniting our two worlds.

We arranged to meet at Mitcham Station, 12.15, Sunday January 7th 1968. Then if all went well, I could book you a room for a couple of nights in the Semel Et Semper Guest House, where I was staying with the Beast and one of the Ugly Sisters. We'd have to be careful, flitting between rooms in the night, as others had done, and you might not be ready for all that brianrixery, and witty banter over breakfast. I would assess that, when I saw you. We had so much to assess. I hadn't seen you for ten months, and before that I hardly knew you. But I had an instinct that *you and I were meant to be*. The future could be glorious if we were sensible and brave enough. Rattling through Hants, I was thinking, Bournemouth is not for ever. With the wind under my wings, I'd surely soon be playing the National Theatre and needing to buy a house. You could cook, play the piano, organize my diary, while I brought home the bacon. If I could live publicly with you, I could also defy the stars and make fair winds blow. We would discuss this today and seriously start looking for somewhere to live. What was Mitcham like? Maybe Tooting, or further in, say Clapham or Brixton, within biking distance of the Old Vic, where the National was housed, and where you could maybe get a job in catering or front of house. We would have bikes, or a vespa and ride in together, your head on my shoulder, your arms round my waste. Then you could see plays and learn to love the world I was in. I would introduce you to Sir Laurence: 'Sir, this is Sunny, my flat-mate. Second only to theatre, he is the true love of my life.' And he would approve you with his eagle eye. Looking at Clapham as we pulled away from the Junction, I was thinking: *'Hell! I was meant to get off here!'* It was twelve! You'd be waiting, and I was rocketing on to Waterloo! It was a Sunday; fewer trains; no way of communicating. At Waterloo, I didn't even go through the gate. I just crossed to the next platform to go straight back to Clapham. Then just as I got on the train and it was moving, I thought 'Stupid! There must direct trains to Mitcham.' So I swung open the door to jump off, was dragged along, then thrown. At the gate – shit! – couldn't find my ticket. They held me up while I searched. I was missing my connection! When was the next train to Mitcham? You had go via Clapham. But I'd just *been* to Clapham. Jesus howled! I was a mess. I sat on a bench, feet splayed, staring up. I decided to let you go. It was best for you to dismiss me as a complete incompetent. I didn't even look for you when finally, two hours late, we slithered into Mitcham; just sat in a daze, going wherever the train went. It took me all day to zig-zag back to Bournemouth. The future was disappearing; ghosthood disintegrating. I was playing Guildenstern in *Hamlet*. True to the part, I had no idea what was going on. I was slipping and very soon would be discovered to be truly dead. You wrote to me; I didn't answer. You didn't need to be involved in this creeping extinction. I was just marking the lines. My heart was blank. When the run ended, I packed up, returned to London; had no work, nowhere to live. There was floor space at 17b but I had exhausted my welcome. I was running out of money. I went up for films and plays; didn't get any. I got some cleaning and gardening work and some tutoring which just about paid for a room in a basement in Shepherd's Bush which I was renting. There was offer of a job in a café theatre in Brighton, doing new plays and serving meals for a tee-shirt and scraps. I was holding out for Ariel in *The Tempest* in Regents Park, directed by the director from Bournemouth, but he'd ceased to have faith in me, as had you, and I don't blame you. So one wet April day, I went down to Brighton.

*

July '68. Paris is still smouldering. The Prague Spring is at its height. Martin Luther King and Robert Kennedy are dead. I am playing a homosexual mur-derer in the West End, ('*excellent... outstanding... magnificent...*'), having just finished a run playing a teenage gravedigger ('*mordant... sensitive... tremendous...*') in Brighton and London, and about to sign a twelve-month contract to play as cast at the Nottingam Playhouse, the third best theatre in the land. In Brighton, the actress playing my mother in the gravedigger play, has patiently eased open my hetero-floodgates and I'm going with girls now. I'm staying in a posh flat for just £2 a week, not far from Hyde Park. It's a fine evening and I'm walking through Kensington Gardens, thinking how steeply life swings! You're down, then you're up, then right down, then right up, and nothing can keep you going except ACTING THE PART, and the more wretched that person – murdering, grave-digging – the louder they applaud and the more lofty you feel.

You gave to me your all and all.
And now I feel ten feet tall...

I'm in the park now. The sun's setting. The trees are triumphantly green. There's a slight breeze. Even the hollow tree is so green, you hardly notice the hollow, which a year and a half ago, had enfolded us in the moonlight. I wasn't seeking this tree; it was seeking me, like a memory. My knees give way, as if I've stumbled on a gravestone that bears your name. You disappeared into the crowd, lost in the teeming millions. No one known to either of us, knew we'd ever met. Yet here I can touch you. I can kiss the tiny beads on your nose. I can smell your skin.

I went home. I wrote a letter. I still had your old address. I wrote on the envelope 'IF LEFT, PLEASE REDIRECT'. I wrote that I'd been thinking about you; how badly I'd treated you; couldn't get you of my mind: *You're my spark of nature's fire. You're my sweet complete desire.* I posted it and a week later, picking up mail from 17b, I found a letter from you, addressed to the Palace Court Theatre Bournemouth, and forwarded on.

This is your letter, the third and last from the back of the drawer:

> *48 Framfield Rd,*
> *Mitcham, Surrey*
> *2 July 1968*
> *Dear Richard,*
>
> *I have been looking for you but I couldn't contact you since the last time I met you. I have lost your phone no. As you see now, I am living in a flat on my own. I left the family on Thursday June 20th. I couldn't stay any longer there, otherwise they would have driven me mad.*
>
> *I hope now I would see you at my place now and then. I left Barkers' on Feb 16th. I am working locally at Lester & Cam Works in Mitcham, daily from 8am to 6pm, except Sat afternoon & Sunday.*
>
> *I hope to hear from you soon.*
> *Yours sincerely*
> *Louis*
>
> *PS. I forgive you for not writing to me. Nothing else could be done so long as I was over there. I hope you are in good health and are making your way successful on the stage. The Best of Luck from your friend who does not forget about you.*

It was odd that you didn't mention hearing from me. Then I noticed the date: 2nd July! The same date as my letter!!! After six months of no contact we had both, independently, in the same instant, been stirred to write! Whatever angel was watching over us, this was a hit for heaven. I was suddenly a believer in Goodness and Mercy as the cornerstones of the universe. When two atoms collide, then part and vanish into the swirling mass, if Love is the rule, then *they will collide again*, and stay joined for ever.

I rang you, and after the show one night, took the tube to Morden and from there it was a short walk to Framfield Road. It was already quite late and I would probably miss the last tube back, so would have to stay the night. Framfield Road is an avenue of fading, between-the-wars semis and number 48 was clearly bedsit-land. I rang the bell and an Asian man in a dressing-gown answered. I said I'd come to see Sunny. He said there was no one of that name – 'I mean Louis, Louis Armance.' He pointed me upstairs, first door on the right. I knocked. You said: 'Come in.' There was someone with you: a boy, you said, from work, who was just leaving. He had brought you two kittens, who were running around squealing. When the boy had gone, we didn't speak; I just held you. Forget the boy, the kittens, the man downstairs, this L-shaped room, and Gerry Dorsey, soon to be Engelbert

Humperdinck, on your dansette, singing *Wonderland By Night...* Stop the world, I was here. We were together. You were warm. We had the whole night.

*

All except three of the dozen or so letters I had from you, were destroyed. I remember lighting a little bonfire in the grate of the house I was living in, in Nottingham, in February 1969. But far from erasing them from the memory, the act of burning seared parts of them indelibly into the brain. The flame-licked, blackening words are still there, and I recall them like apparitions. In one you said there had been a party at work for your birthday, then you'd gone home alone. You wrote: '*Now I let you know: I have made a promise not to love anyone but you. You have always been on my mind and I will never forget you. I will wait for ever. I have patience.*' In another you wrote it was okay for me to come at the week-end and you signed off: '*I ---- you*', inviting me to fill in the blank. I didn't see you that weekend – I was rehearsing two plays, performing in two others and writing TV scripts for Kenny Everett and Germaine Greer – but you still had hope and I remember the date, February 8th, in your last letter, curling up in the flames. I'd led you to believe this date could signal a new start, and you'd said '*come any time, I'll be there: you will be welcome*', adding maybe in the spring we could go to Paris, as you had done recently with your aunt; and you signed off, happily filling in the blank (easier in French): '*Amour, mon amour, je t'aime, Louis.*'

*

You said you'd been promoted at work which meant an increase in pay, and if I was short you could cover my fare, but I'd told you, as Equity Deputy for the company, I was given a number of free rail journeys to London for meetings, so that was okay. Also, personally, I didn't like to see myself as a paid lover; acting was prostitution enough! I was travelling down to London with an actress from the company who was going to a political demonstration. When she asked what I was doing for the rest of the weekend, I said I had some personal business to attend to. Persuaded to be less coy, I told her I was involved with someone; had been for two years and was at a loss what to do. I couldn't keep it going; I couldn't break it off, and it couldn't stay as it was. She laughed: she would never indulge such an attitude in a lover, and did I want her advice? 'Rip the plaster off! Do it suddenly. It will hurt but not as much as leaving the poison to kill you both.'

I went to my meeting, got away early and came to you. The kittens had grown into stalking toms and the room stank. We smoked, we drank beer, we played music, we made love. I didn't stay the night. Returning to Nottingham, I wrote you a post card. It was brief but true. I was in love with someone else, and she wasn't the sort who would want to share me with a man. She had been playing Nina in *The Seagull* by Anton Chekhov, which is about everyone being in love with the wrong person, and how the only way out of the mess is to ENDURE. I remember taking the card to the pillar box and pausing for a second before dropping it in. It was like putting a bullet in your head, but I had to do it. Bang. Then I went home and burnt your letters.

Scene Two
JACK MOLONY

... took Andy and me out to dinner, after seeing *This Way Out* in Bury St Edmunds, in the final week of the tour. It had been a good show and Jack was buzzing with an idea for the two of us as writer/performers which he vowed would spell stardom. Even before we sat down, Andy had explained that he wouldn't be free to write or perform, having just accepted a producer traineeship with Granada, but Jack brushed that aside. 'Have you signed yet?' Andy said no. 'Then please, I beg you, listen to me, trust me.' He outlined the plan: *Knockabout Newsreaders*; BBC News turned on its head, say twice a week; surreal, satirical, five-to-ten-minute double act; nightmare in the newsroom; crazy invent-as-you-go news report, viz Andy's *Goldilocks*, or absurd veering-off-at-tangents, viz my *Scrooge*. What did we think? I said: 'Wow. Can you make it happen?' He said 'Can *you* make it happen? If you can, I can.' Andy said: 'But I'll be working for Granada.' Jack said: 'Then forget it. I'm leaving. Buy your own dinner. Hahaha! Just joking! Have a scallop!' I said: 'Does it have to be both of us?' He said: 'Tweedledum Tweedledee, the Cox Twins, you are the team. Chew on it. Plot the pilot. Get excited. Then come back to me pronto, and we'll roll.'

For the rest of the meal, we talked vaudeville, the movies. He loved my *Burton Tayloring* sketch, said he'd show it to Liz and Rich, whom he represented, or used to. He said Granada was great but Manchester wasn't London; it was like opting to do rep, as *traineeship* for the West End, when in fact, get this, it was a *dead* end, a blind alley, you could die there and who would know?

*

I had just a bag with a few essentials when I boarded the train for London. Dick Whittington had similar in his hankie on a stick, plus a cat, when he set out to trade poverty for gold-paved streets; but I was more savvy: more kudos to propel me. I had an agent on call, and a zed-bed in the kitchen of the flat of my cousin Mary, in Gray's Inn Rd, for the first few nights anyway.

I dropped the bag at the flat and went straight to see Jack. I hadn't rung him and he was busy, so I waited till I heard he was off the phone, then went in. I said I'd come, on behalf of Andy and me, to thank him for the dinner. He beamed suddenly: 'Great! Are we on? Where's Tweedle - ?' I said Andy was in Manchester, and we'd talked and decided to grow the idea of a tv satire show from the ground up, associated with his traineeship. This way we could keep control as decision-makers, not just hired hands. It might take a while, so in the meantime, yes personally, individually, I was up for anything Jack might propose, to keep me 'match-fit' as 'twere, and to earn money.

There was a pause. He looked puzzled, then curious, sizing me up: 'This afternoon, 4 pm, Peter Watkins. He made *Culloden* and *The War Game*. He's doing a feature with Paul Jones and Jean Shrimpton. How tall are you?

'Five seven.'

'She's five ten. Do you have lifts?'

Actually I did have lifts. I had them back at the flat.

'Great! Where are your photos?'

'You didn't like them. You said you'd get David Bailey – '

He was on the phone: 'Hey Gered ... ? Yep yep... Wednesday... He is the new Dudley Moore, but taller... tooth-hurtie.' Putting the phone down: 'To-day, at four.' Flicking me the casting director's card: 'Miriam Brickman, and Watkins if he's there. They'll take snaps, maybe do a test. The film is *Privilege*. The part is a male model, so walk tall, wear the suit. Then Wednesday, 2.30pm, Gered Mankowitz studios. Go "kid next door", "artful dodger", "young executive". I'm paying; don't let me down.'

Watkins wasn't there, but Shrimpton was. Six foot in heels, she seemed bored, looking down on yet another short-arse male (I'd abandoned the lifts which made me teeter like a drag queen. If they wanted me, I surmised, they could put the Shrimp in a trench.) I was unimpressed with Miriam Brickman who seemed about eighteen, but I kowtowed nonetheless until I realized of course she wasn't the legendary *grande dame* of casting, but her junior assistant. If I'd been up for a Norman Wisdom part, I'd have got it like a shot, but as Alain Delon, I was a no-no.

Gered Mankowitz also seemed absurdly young; I took him for his assistant. He was fitting me in between Hendrix and the Yardbirds, talking all the time to get me animated: his dad was Wolf the novelist and screen-writer, and no he was *not* the 'kid for two farthings' – though he *did* believe in unicorns! Dropping out of school at fifteen, he was snapped up by genius fashion-snapper Tom Blau, went to Barbados with his camera, hit the Paris *couture* scene, and before you knew it, was on tour with the Stones, and (hold that look!) shooting superstars-to-be: 'What's your playing age?' I said: 'Twenty-one'. He said (snap snap): 'I can do you fifteen to twenty-five: sexy, sultry, spooky – don't move – I do the mood.' When the proofs came in, three days later, I went over them with Jack. He'd got tickets for me and a friend to see *Strike A Light*, starring Evelyn Laye (known as Boo), who was a client and needed scripts. I took Di Lubbock, a singer and extramural Footlighter, on the fringes of the Tudor-Landor set, who I'd met up with the night before at a party at Maisie-Lou's. Di was in town seeing agents and flat-sitting for Raleigh-King who was in Morocco, and Jack said to let him know when she was next doing a gig, as he'd like to hear her. Meanwhile the photos, what did we think? I looked twelve in the polo-neck, maybe sixteen in the suit. Dreamy-eyed, slightly saucy, I couldn't look at them, however much Jack said 'fabulous, fantastico...' We left him to do the choosing. His scatter-gun style was beginning to annoy me; I didn't seem right for any of the parts he was aiming me at, and it was *my fault* when nothing hit. After *Privilege* came *Lady Frederick*, to play opposite Joan Greenwood (45), except it wasn't happening till next year; and the writing thing with Boo was a non-starter because (a) I thought she was totally wooden in *Strike a Light* and (b) she didn't think much of me either when we met after the show because (c) I was itching to get over to Raleigh-King's pad in Holland Park, where Di was *begging* me to move in and water the plants, just for a week, because Col Batty, who was off to Edinburgh with Clive James and an ad hoc Footlights B team (the cheek of it!), wanted her to come up and sing. So I'd said yes – the zed-bed in Gray's Inn Road having lost its charm – and forsaking Boo, we tubed and legged it to Zanna Rollicking's penthouse.

It was a loft, open-plan, with sloping ceilings, dormer windows and a bed wide enough for both of us to sleep in without touching. Di would be off first thing in the morning and I would ring Gray's Inn Road and go round to pick up my stuff, having first called Jack with my new Holland Park address. I could live here, solo, making movies like *Darling*, and maybe Rollicking would be indefinitely delayed (kidnapped) in Morocco and I could stretch the week into a decade.

I wrote to Jamaica:

> *I've been living, like Goldlocks, in a sumptuous pad in Holland Park, but had to move out, because the three bears came back: viz Zanna Raleigh-King, her new boyfriend and cat. They didn't know I'd been staying there...*

> *Jack Molony has plans to do a panto on the* Queen Mary *this Xmas, while it's cruising to Teneriffe. He wants a big star line-up and I'm to help with the writing...*

> *You'll see from my address, I've gone down in the world, to the lower depths of Ladbroke Grove. It's very grubby and it smells. Wormwood Scrubbs is just round the corner...*

> *Jack Molony has arranged for me to meet Barry Cawtheray who used to write for* Ready Steady Go. *He's got an idea for a Comedy Playhouse and needs help...*

Three policemen were murdered last night, just a few yards from here...

Jack Molony is getting me an interview with Hugh Burnet, the BBC satire man...

Both Di and Tudor-Landor have gone back to Cambridge and there have been times when I have been bored to death...

I had lunch at the BBC with producer Humphrey Barclay, who turned down all my scripts...

I feel I am really going through Purgatory now...

Tudor-Landor is back in town, so life is not over-dull, since she has problems galore...

Episode One of the TV comedy series went off to Frank Muir today, and Jack Molony is fixing up at least three acting interviews...

I can last out on my present money if I live on bread and water, and people pay for my lunch...

The room could be Raskolnikov's in *Crime and Punishment*. With its peeling paint, damp smell, plasterboard walls, lumpy mattress, this could be the room from which to commit the Perfect Crime. Beyond the bridge, down the wrong end of Ladbroke Grove, where prostitutes and rats are kept at arm's length from the grandeur of the Holland Park end, you could be forgiven for thinking this was as low as you could get, and the only way out for the *Ubermensch*, was up. But you'd be forgetting that no one reads Nietzsche down here. Hell has no floor; it's just a ledge you've landed on. Stubbing out the fag that has just lit the next one, I plot whom to kill: the Polish landlord who takes £3.10s a week and even charges for a blown light-bulb; the old biddy who flits in her undies across the landing – I could axe her like twigs; the boy dancer upstairs, who clumps to Tchaikovsky, listens to my phoning in the hall, wants to help, wants to talk. Once, when he was clumping, I clumped back on the ceiling with a pan, and he came down. He was upset to have upset me; had to practise for auditions; hadn't worked for a year; had to live off 'rent (know what I mean?)' It bucked him there was someone else equally on his uppers, yet keen to break free. He could help me; we could help each other. Everyone needs a friend, and a friend in need shouldn't flinch from a hug. And a smoke, did I want one? His name was Benny. Did I go to clubs? He could take me to the Spartan. Then maybe we could crawl out of this hole we were in, and share a pad, no strings; and if ever I needed relief – he squeezed my neck – or just a massage, no charge... (did I mind him doing this...?) I didn't mind. I was beyond minding. He stayed the night.

In the morning the phone rang. I'd hoped it was Jack with news, but it was Batty. Flush with Edinburgh success, he was coming to London to seek his fortune. Who was that agent I was with? We could put a double act together, and get a flat, maybe with Di and Tudor-Landor, who both now happened to be loose and looking. What about it, old mate? He had sketches and songs; I had sketches and songs. We could get Lascelles involved, and Di to do the Baez/Julie Felix stuff. He'd be at Euston by six, we could eat, then please could he crash on my floor? 'When we're rich and famous (WWR&F), we'll look back on this moment like Whittington on the turn, or Chaplin hoofing his way out of the workhouse.'

He crashed on my floor. The next day we looked for a flat and found a ballroom – nine guineas a week – overlooking Hyde Park. I gave notice to the Pole, said bye to the flitting lady and 'See you Benny,' to Benny. We took a cab to 79 Lancaster Gate, lugged the luggage up the grand staircase, to the grandest room. WWR&F, we'd buy the whole house, but for now this cavern was home: Batty's bed at one end, mine at the other; little kitchen enclosure with baby belling and sink; bathroom shared with other inmates, but clean, no smells; sprung stripped-wood floor for rehearsing and routines. Batty set up his hi-fi. I put on *Revolver* and we pranced across the floor to *Yellow Submarine* and *Taxman*. Later we walked in the Park (our back garden) and in Queensway picked up *Cooking in a Bedsitter* by Katherine Whitehorn. Batty did the meals while I poured the drinks for Di and Tudor-Landor when they came round to do the cleaning. Di had a room in a flat with Katya Benjamin who had been Hermia to my Puck in the Marlowe *Dream*. T-L was still in her uncle's hotel with her problems galore. We had a ballroom-warming ball. Lascelles came, and Andy Mayer who was in town with his girlfriend Tess, and Katya and her friend Flopsy, and all the Tudor-Landor set, except Rollicking who was away again, and Maisie-Lou who was getting married. I'd asked Jack to come and he would have adored to, but he was off to New York in the morning. I'd told him about Batty and the double act which might conceivably reawaken *Knockabout Newsreaders*, and Jack said definitely we *must talk* when he was back. When he was back, we talked. We were assembling material and fixing to do a try-out on the pub circuit next month. 'Bravissimo!' exclaimed Jack. 'Tell me when. I'll be there.' Then to earn cash, while assembling and rehearsing the act – *Arthur & Arthur* (our seldom-used second names) – and to keep us in the manner to which ballroom-occupants were accustomed, we enrolled with a problem-solving agency called *Problem?* Subscribed to by media and showbiz elite for the resolution of predicaments such as decorating, car-washing, leaf-sweeping, pan-polishing, *Problem?* deployed a pool of ex-students and resting actors with practical skills, at seven bob an hour, with a minimum of three, so you were assured at least a guinea.

Our first 'problem' was for Sean Connery. He was moving from Maple Avenue, Acton and we were to take up his carpets. We were instructed to bring tools and to 'match initiative to practical skill'. When we got to the house and rang the bell, there was no response. So instead of going back to *Problem?* with a problem, we thought 'What would James Bond do?' There was a side-gate into the garden. We vaulted it, crept round the house, testing the windows, and finding one that was on the latch, eased it open and climbed in. We had expected the house to be empty but it was fully furnished, with fitted carpets in every room: suburban, nothing flashy, family photos (but none of Connery). For the next three or four hours we shifted furniture, clawed up, wrenched up, rolled up all the carpets, and shifted the furniture back again. Then we left the way we came. Walking back along Beech Ave (*not* Maple Ave as on the note), a chilling thought began to dawn...

Batty took the rap for the Connery debacle and quit *Problem?* for a driving job with the Ministry of Defence. I was going to quit as well, but a job came up for Katherine Whitehorn: her of the cookbook which was our ballroom bible. Over the next four weeks, I became her house-boy, odd-job man, occasional painter and decorator. Her house was a tip and my indoor job was to shift piles of things onto other piles of things, and 'sweep the dust behind the door'. The outdoor job, was mostly mowing a bumpy lawn with a blunt push-mower: Sisyphean but rewarding because she never checked anything, would slip me an extra half-crown and when she had a moment, brew a pot of thick coffee and talk, while 'organizing herself', about Cambridge (she was at Newnham) and theatre, parties, people and books.

One day, I turned up and Katherine – late and rushing for a book launch – handed me two pots of paint and a brush: 'Paint the gate, then you can go; I won't be back. Any problem, ask Gavin.' And before I could say: 'But Gavin Lyall, your husband, is in the attic writing spy thrillers, and you said SHOULD NEVER BE – ' she was gone. And I would have added: '*Two* pots of paint? It's only a small gate. Extravagance! I'll hardly use half a pot and have it done within minutes.' Ah well, easy-guinea. I had it slapped on in a trice, and was just leaving when I looked at the unused pot, which said 'UNDERCOAT'. I had three choices: skedaddle, taking the pot and dumping it in a bin (she'd never notice); confess all to Gavin who I could see stomping about in the kitchen in a dressing-gown and glaring like a caged beast (I wasn't going in there!); or – opening the pot – slap the undercoat on top of the overcoat, blame the rain which was spitting, and come back tomorrow to finish the job; which I did.

Forty years on, I found myself sitting in a theatre next to La Whitehorn. She remembered me with affection, and I asked her if she ever wondered about the blotches, drips and blisters on her garden gate. She looked blank, then curious. She had trusted me to have the requisite skills. I wished I hadn't mentioned it.

*

Arthur.
Arthur.
May I join you?
Am I coming apart?
Oh please. You're in Current Affairs, not Comedy.
Only because I couldn't get into Comedy.
Why couldn't you get into Comedy?
Because the BBC has no sense of humour.
Or because you're not funny.
Funny is relative.
Says who?
My auntie. She's hilarious.
Arthur.
Arthur.
Talking of relativity –
Revel in Italy?
Everyone assumes you're my brother.
Everyone assumes you're my brother.
And that's how you got your job.
And that's how I got your job.
You couldn't get into comedy, so you came to me, your homonymous bro.
That's bosh and you know it. I got your job in the same way everyone gets a job at the BBC.
How does everyone get a job at the BBC?
Through Cambridge University.
Are you in Comedy?
I was joking. I'm done for. I'm finished. I'm coming apart.
Can I join you?
Oh please.
Oh thank you.
How's it going... in Current Affairs?
Well Don is seeing Dot, who's going with Dean, who's dating Di who's after Doug who fancies Dolly who's dallying with Dirk who dotes on Daisy...
(fade)

*

We'd booked to launch *Arthur & Arthur* in a pub and had fixed for Jack Molony to come along. WWR&F, we would remember the weary, often tetchy night sessions in the ballroom, having to tip-toe and mute the arguing, because of the neighbours. Batty's driving job began at 2 pm and he was never back before ten, and as I was often working in the mornings, the only rehearsal time we had was between 10.30pm and two. We did a practice run to the girls – Di, Tudor-Landor, Katya and her friend Flopsy – and they all applauded (except Flopsy). The whole show was twenty minutes, to be shaved down to fifteen, maybe cutting one of the songs: the dreary one which I was rather proud of, about the drudgery of work –

> *I get up every morning at eight,*
> *and go do a job that I hate,*
> *and I wait.*
> *It's not right.*
> *I walk about late in the night.*
> *I roll my cigarettes too tight*
> *as I wade*
> *through shite...*

Flopsy said if we were playing to a pub audience, they'd want a knees-up, not a reminder of their daily grind. Col said that was so patronizing! We were doing social satire; it didn't need to be funny. Katya said, in a sad way it *was* quite funny, and maybe Di should sing it. Di said she'd love to but she'd be in Canada from next week, and what was wrong with Richard's voice. T-Landor said nothing that couldn't be improved with some accompaniment. Col said we were making a feature of *a capella*, because Lascelles wasn't available having been offered a season at Nairobi Rep, and before the conversation could veer onto the ethics of playing drawing-room comedies to a white African audience, Col and I both reiterated the rationale of *Arthur and Arthur* which was to raise the plebs to our level, not stoop to conquer. But Flopsy, who had just graduated from the Central School of Speech and Drama, said we were too puerile on the one hand, too sophisticated on the other; no pleb would buy it. I tried to point out that *plebs* was a singular word and if you wanted to pluralize it, you should say *plebes*. Flopsy laughed (for the first time): that was exactly what she meant! Our niche audience was miniscule, shrinking by the minute and not to be found in pubs. 'Hang on!' interposed Katya. 'We were in a pub theatre last year, remember, doing Brenton and Grillo, and we're booked to go again.' 'That was in Ireland,' said Flops, 'they laugh differently there; which reminds me,' gathering up her coat, 'there's a meeting. Are you coming

Katch?' They wished us luck, and promised to be there in the pub on the night, as did Di and Tudor-Landor. 'Don't come if you don't want to,' said Col to Flops. 'Okay I won't,' said Flops. 'Actually, I may not be able to make it,' said Tudor-Landor. 'And I'll be in Canada, come to think of it,' said Di. They went. We shrugged, shook our heads, poured drinks, put on *Eleanor Rigby*. We were confident, pioneering, stop-at-nothing new comedians, who didn't bow to any pleb-demeaning, fucking drama-school flopsy rabbit.

*

We met Jack at the pub, had an orange juice and a coke – the fans could buy us a proper drink afterwards – and went off to prepare. I don't remember what happened next, having wiped it from my memory. We were worse than bad; we were non-existent. The audience carried on chatting and drinking as if we weren't there. We got through four sketches and a couple of songs, then bowed to no applause, no proffered drinks, not even from Jack who'd disappeared. We slid away to another pub and got paralytically depressed.

That was the end of Jack Molony. I also ducked out of *Problem?* and got a more regular job with Westminster City Council, who paid £12 a week. The office was on the seventeenth floor of City Hall in Victoria Street where I drew up and co-ordinated lists of Registered Electors, while looking down god-like, on the swirling, miniature human synthesis below; having earlier gone street-by-street in the Paddington area, knocking on doors, authenticating the demographic. If I hadn't been burdened with the *need to act*, I'd have been content, on a daily basis. The pay was okay, I had a decent flat, pleasant people to work with, and as the evenings got darker, and winter chill set in, looking through windows at families, as I walked the beat, seeing pockets of population making do, getting by, and *registering their groupings*, I felt transcendant, anonymous, otherworldy, untouchable, shadowless, like a ghost.

CHRIS PARR

One day, mid-November, I came home and the phone was ringing. A loud, male voice asked if Col Batty was there. I said he wouldn't be back till ten. Could I take a message?

'Yes!' exclaimed the voice, as if that was a great idea.

'What should I tell him?'

'Will you tell him... (pause)... that I'd like to (emphatically) *see* him before the readthrough on Monday. There's no doubt that we want him, but I *would* like to *see* him *again*.'

I said sure I would tell him, but would he know what it was about? (And what was this 'again'? When did you *see* him before? Batty never tells me anything.)

'It's about the play, in Cork, the Brenton play, *A Sky-Blue Life* January through February, with a late-night revue, in Cork.'

'You mean like last year?'

'Yes, and then London.'

'Wow.'

I said I'd heard about the Cork thing from Katya. It was brilliant apparently. (Was he seeing other people?)

'With Col on board, we'll be fully cast. It was Katya recommended him. Then I saw him in Edinburgh in revue. We'll be doing a revue.'

I said great, fantastic. (Did Katya tell you about the pub show?)

Guffaws from the phone: 'Col Batty! Dead-pan! And he writes as well! Barrel of laughs!'

(And you'll be scraping it, I tell you.) I asked him about the play.

'It's about Gorky and his spat with Lenin.'

'Is Col playing Gorky?'

'Lenin.'

(Lenin! Do you know how tall Batty is?)

'It's not a look-alike performance.'

(Lenin was five foot five. I know this because I played him, informally, on the streets of Leningrad and Moscow.)

'Will you get Col to ring me?'

(If I see him.)

'We're having the readthrough next Monday at Brenton's flat, 128 Westminster Bridge Road, 7pm. But I do want to see him beforehand. Can he come at six?'

(He works till ten. I told you that.)

'Will you tell him?'

(If I remember.)

'Thank you.'

'Thank *you*. (Thanks a bunch.) Who am I speaking to?'

'Chris Parr.'

He didn't leave a number, so how could I tell Batty? Anyway he didn't get in till midnight, having gone to a party and I was asleep by then, or pretending to be; and then off in the morning before he woke. I was deeply pissed off to be the 'agent' of good news and not the recipient, but I did tell him, a couple of days later, when I remembered, and we had a row. We were supposed to be supporting each other's ambitions, not being envious! What was there to be envious about, I scoffed. Boggy Ireland in Feb? Give me a break. He got on the phone to Katya. They had a long talk. He knew I was listening, and muttering 'Barge-pole... even with a... touch it... would I ever...'

We went for a drink. He'd told Katya to tell Chris this was definitely the kind of thing he wanted to get involved in, but he'd already called in sick once last week, for an audition (I didn't know about this) so how could he meet Chris or even make the readthrough? I said: Absolutely! They weren't paying, so why should he jeopardize a good job? Hell, he wasn't some am-dram ham; he was a worker! But listen! I had the answer. I personally had gone beyond student revue and aggro-politico plays in pubs (as I thought Batty had – but let that go). My plan – hear this – was to head north to my sister in North Yorks for Xmas, then spend Jan and Feb, zig-zagging down the country doing the reps, ie Scarborough, York, Leeds, Harrogate, Oldham, heading west to Liverpool, Manchester, Chester, crossing to Nottingham, Derby, Lincoln, Leicester, then Birmingham, Coventry, Ipswich, Colchester, weaving south to Guildford, Worthing, Bristol, Exeter, seeing shows, meeting actors and directors, being there, being willing, seizing the day, getting a job. I had cash put by and floors to crash on. It would mean cutting loose from City Hall and reconfiguring the rental of Lancaster Gate, but we could talk about that later. For now, and here's the nub, as a farewell gesture, if he wanted, I could go to the Brenton readthrough, as a shadow, you understand, as your *agent*, and take notes, read the part (badly!), seal the deal (for a percentage??), then gift-wrap the job, and leave it under your tree.

*

Howard had a room in a flat over a café at 128 Westminster Bridge Road. In the day he was working for the Ministry of Information; at night he was hitting the keys of his Remington, at his desk under a black-framed, bolted-to-the-wall bunk. There was no window in what was previously a storage room, no light except a low-wattage central bulb and an anglepoise on the desk. The ceiling, walls and floor were matt black. There were books piled high and cushions and old coffee cups. As I came in, the dank smell was yielding to the aroma of candles, being placed in jars round the room, by a tall, thin, girl in shawls, introduced as Maria. 'I rhyme with *fire*, not *fear*. Do you like the scent? It's wild fig.' The percussion of typewriter keys, signalled Howard, under the bunk, punching out final words, Chris Parr standing over him, scanning page after page through Buddy Holly glasses and rocking with laughter. Katya and Flopsy were sitting on cushions by the door; I parked myself between them. It was chilly despite the fug from fags and bodies and candles; we all kept our coats on, budging up to accommodate a stubble-cheeked, leather-coated man called Dick and a big-chinned cheery fellow, name of Ian, who passed me a lit cigarette and called me Col. 'Should I say who you actually are?' whispered Katya. 'Better be straight up,' added Flops. I heard myself saying: 'No! For tonight, I *am* Col. I'm *acting* Batty, acting Lenin. I am an alien. I am a shadow.' I had the actor's immunity to live in the skin of another and be bigger or smaller or fiercer or milder. Chris Parr would know I wasn't Batty, but he didn't know *me*. I stayed out of his eyeline. In my cloak of anonymity I could slay this script and be away across town before the Bolsheviks in their cell, got wind of an intruder.

∗

'So how did it go?' asked Batty.

'Well it's not about to spark a revolution, not yet anyway. The script was miles from being anywhere near ready. Everyone knew that and was polite or silent. Maria – rhymes with *dire* not *dear* – said, over Christmas, we should all mug up on Gorky, read his plays, and maybe think about doing one of them, or part of one of them, as a prelude to *A Sky-Blue Life*, a sort of *dawn* to the blue sky, so that the whole project had *life*, and was anchored in the real thing, not just floating. No one ran with that. Dick, in the leather coat, got up, said he had to go, great show, of course he was on board, he was an actor, he *was* Gorky, he'd be there, don't you worry. He left with Maria, he grunting, she protesting, like a married couple [which in time they would be]. Then Ian, big-chinned, said he saw no reason why this year's Cork shouldn't pop as fizzingly as last year, which was a riot if you remember. They had an audience gagging for a sequel to the outrageous *Hello Goodbye Sebastian* by Grillo, in which Howard himself had played Charly the bastard lodger, and the tanked-up Corkfolk had been so roused, they came at him afterwards, to kill him. There was no line between the actor and the character and that was marvellous. If we could rack up *Sky-Blue Life* to that kind of level, go easy on the manifesto-ing, punch harder in the arguing, draw some blood... Then Flo broke in – she wasn't Flops or Flopsy any more, she was Flo and we should go with that. Hear hear, said Ian. No no, said Katya, we go *against the flow!* We shouldn't be repeating last year, there was a new tide to swim against, and we had to hurry up and get our swim-kit together. I'm losing the plot, said Chris. The trouble is, said Flo, there *is* no plot: just noise and lecturing. Maybe Maria was right, concluded Katya, and we should be looking for something else. In the silence you could hear Brenton attacking the keys. Chris said: Thanks. You've made valid points. All I can add is that I've known and worked with Howard since we were kids, and he is a massive and growing talent. He won't stop till he's stripped this play down, like a stripping a gun, and put it back so it really fires. That will happen. Great, said Flo. We've got just a week before everything shuts down, said Ian. Happy Christmas, said Katya. Ian said he had a car and could give the girls and me a lift. Chris said: Richard, could you stay behind?'

'Why did he say that?' asked Batty.

'He wanted to know if I was there for you or for me. I said for you absolutely. There was no question of muscling in and stealing your birthright for a mess of pottage, you hairy man! I have principles for chrissake. I hadn't even identified myself and was surprised he knew my name. He laughed, then was serious, said he'd heard I wrote scripts and for the revue he was short of non-whimsical, *tough* material, with *bite*. Did I have writing of that ilk? He had a lifelong antipathy to the Catholic church and as it was Christmas, we should aim our brickbats at the bishops, subtly of course because they were also the censors! Was I up for that? Could I come up with sketches and songs with *edge*? I said sure, count me in. Then he said, about Lenin, when I was reading just now, he could sense the *cunning* of the man, and his uncompromising, ice-cold fury. He could use that. In fact, it was the decider, along with Dick's Gorky – compelling! – that he *must make this play work*. The part's yours, if you want it. Talk to Col and get back to me by tomorrow night.

'So you're going to talk to me,' said Batty.

'Sure.'

'What about the reps, the zig-zagging?'

'That was only if I didn't get a job and this is a job.'

'What's the deal? What will you earn?'

'He said it could be as much as five pounds a week from seventy percent of box office, divided nine ways: six actors, one director, stage manager and musician – the last two from Ireland. We'll all live in a big rent-free house and do our own cooking, so no one should be out of pocket. Meanwhile Maria was going to talk to her uncle, who owns the *Daily Express*, to get him to sponsor the travel.'

'Sounds like you've made your mind up.'

'Only if you've made your mind up. Have you? Made it up? Your mind? I have to tell him.'

'TO IRELAND, I...'

To Ireland I. Our separated fortune
Shall keep us both the safer. Where we are
There's daggers in men's smiles: the near in blood,
The nearer bloody.   - Donalbain

I wrote to Jamaica on the train.

I'll be at Saltburn till the 27th, then take train and boat to Ireland,
where I'll be performing in a new revue and a new play, right through
to Feb 4th. The play is by Howard Brenton; the revue, mostly by me.
That's one of the reasons I'm going to Saltburn: to write write write.
The director is Chris Parr and there are seven in the cast – all ex-
Oxbridge, except one. They originally asked Batty, but he was playing
hard to get, so they asked me instead and I said yes. He took it badly
because he really wanted it, but theatre, as I'm learning, is a dog-eats-
dog world, and we have now fallen out for ever... Katya Benjamin is in
the company, as are Flo Hopcroft and Maria Aitken, whose great-uncle
was Lord Beaverbrook. The others are Dick Durden and Ian Marter
who were both in the Oxford Dr Faustus *with Richard Burton and Eliz-*
abeth Taylor. Chris the director, and Howard the author, were at school
together in Chichester, whence one went to Oxford to read Classics
then Chinese, was sent down and became a bus conductor, and the
other, the son of a policeman turned Methodist minister, went to Cam-
bridge and now works (as a double agent [we believe]) for the Ministry
of Information...

On the train south I wrote:

I had a very nice week at Saltburn and got masses of writing done...
Thank you for the ash-tray which arrived slightly smashed but I expect
it will glue. It will go with the 50 fags E & Roy gave me, except my New
Year's Resolution is to try and give up smoking, as I tend to cough a lot
in the mornings... I got up at 6.30 today, to start my Odyssey which will
take 27 hours. I've got loads of luggage as we have to provide our own
clothes. In the play, we all have a variety of roles. It is set in Russia and
as well as Lenin, I am also playing Tolstoy and a garrulous geezer from
the lower depths called Kostylyov. Consequently I am carting Dad's big
naval coat, plus granny's hanging-out-the-washing coat and my own
coat as well. We have been told to provide bedding, but I have decided
to sleep in coats...

*

It was dark when I boarded the boat at Fishguard. A wind was whipping up and black clouds hid the sky. I hadn't booked a cabin as I hate being below decks. I was early, so I stowed my lumber and went down to the bar. There was no one there that I recognized, so I ordered myself a Beamish and sat down to flip through the latest version of *A Sky-Blue Life*, which had arrived by special delivery that morning, just as I was leaving. I'd tried to read it on the train but was so sleepy, it wasn't going in. I was beyond sleep now.

The first thing that struck me was the newly pared-down power of the writing. The diatribes and manifestoes had been compressed into small packs of explosive energy, so the lines came at you like punches in the face. Also there seemed to be no border between the actor and the character as if anyone could play anyone and be answerable afterwards, just as Howard had found last year when the audience couldn't distinguish him from the brute he had just played. But most of all, what emerged now, was the sense of history irrevocably on the turn, the great escarpments of empire cracking before the shifting groundswell of the people, inspired by a demented Tolstoy:

> 'Books? Books? I spend all my hours unwriting them… My Anna, my Natasha… I unwrite my angels. A great labour, but I'll finish it. In the end, I'll have them all. Unwritten. All the books…'

His argument is later seized on by Lenin:

> 'Kant, Hegel, Dostoyevsky? Bah! You know what I read now? Daily? Lists. Lists. Those to be shot, those to be fed. Corpses and potatoes: the true literature of revolution.'

And travelling through all the scenes is Gorky, the story-teller at the heart of his own stories, thoughtful, atheistic, fearless, humane, with his undimmed, impossible sky-blue vision. Reading the play, I felt all the traditional borders falling away: between drama and revue (these were sketches and songs in a seamless flow, delivered head-on, with no scenery); between history and the present (historic characters voicing today's arguments as if no time has passed); and between the actor and the audience, between belief and disbelief, between work and life.

We were sailing now. I was alone in the bar. No sign of the company. Had I come on the right day? Had I missed some message? Was there meant to have been a letter with the script? What would I do when we got to Cork? I didn't even know the name of the theatre or where we would be staying. I was beginning to feel sick. The one thing I'd been sure of and proud of, on the Jamaica trip, had been my heart-of-oak sea-legs. I blamed tiredness, the absence of everyone as if a trick had been played, and the Beamish which was making my head swim.

I left it half-drunk and went up on deck.

There was no one about. The wind was squally and biting cold. I blessed my father's thick naval coat which had braved the Channel on D-Day and weathered the seas to Hong Kong and back. I felt unvanquishable, and at the same time useless: Captain Ahab, without the whale; Captain Bligh without the inducement of mutiny. I looked down at the soulless, fathomless deep. If I fell, who would know? Swallowed up in a moment, would I have left any mark, made any difference to any life? (Maybe one, maybe just one...)

'Richard?'

It was Chris Parr.

'Are you feeling sick?'

'No, I'm fine.'

'Don't do it to windward, or it comes straight back in your face.'

'I'm not feeling sick.'

'You look terrible.'

'You can't see me!'

'The way you were leaning over the rail. Or were you contemplating suicide?'

'Actually I was thinking about the play, which I've just read. It's like the water down there, deep as hell and at the same time capable of leaping up and soaking you. Like the sea, it doesn't rest. You can divide it into shipping regions, but in the end there are no borders. You think you know it, but you don't know anything. Even Howard doesn't know anything, but he's always questing, risking death.'

Suddenly Chris threw up.

'Wrong side!' I yelled, too late, as the vomit flew back into both our faces: too quick to be foul, too absurd not to be funny.

When we'd cleaned up, we sat in the bar and Chris told me the situation. Ian and Dick were not coming, having made a pact with the devil, alias Richard Burton, whose *Doctor Faustus*, produced with Oxford students last year, was being filmed and they were on call. Maria, Katya and Flo didn't fancy the boat and were getting the plane to Dublin, then the train to Cork. They'd arrive tea-time tomorrow. They didn't know about Dick and Ian and that we might not be able to do *Sky-Blue Life*. I said couldn't we find two Irish actors? What about the guy who owned the theatre who was a famous actor? Jimmy Healy? said Chris. I wanted him in it anyway, at least in the revue. Would you mind him doing *Scrooge*? I sent him the script and he phoned me straight back *in the character*! You wouldn't mind? If we let you do Andy Mayer's *Goldilocks*... I said I was planning on doing that one anyway. He said: 'Then you'll be doing too much. We have to level out the cast-ing'. There was a silence. I said: 'But what about *Sky-Blue*? What do we do instead of that?' He said: 'Well Jimmy could possibly do Kostylyov the tramp, and Lenin at a pinch, but those are your parts and I don't think you could do Gorky.' I said: 'I thought anyone could play anyone.' He laughed: 'Who told you that?'

It was after midnight now. The wind had eased. Chris had booked a four-up cabin for Ian, Dick, himself and me. He said: 'Nothing is fixed. All is fluid. *Listen to the water, and you'll catch a trout,* as they say in Ireland. We should get some sleep.'

*

Cork in 1967 was a quiet, grey-faced, cathoholic little backwater, as foreign in its confessionals and booziness, as a forgotten Italian town; the only difference being the weather. The rain came down, merging day with night, in a steady film that drenched whatever might absorb, then seeped around the waterproof, down the neck, inside sleeves and up through the soles of unmended shoes. We disembarked in a soggy blur of dawn. Chris had slept; I hadn't. I admired his *sang-froid* in the face of disaster. He said most productions are like this. Out of catastrophe comes genius. You know who the Greeks say made the world? *Anangke.* Necessity! It has to be, therefore it is. We ducked into a café, Chris knew from last year. The waiter was hollow-eyed and barely awake. We ordered the full Irish with mugs of 'camp' coffee, made from an oil-like essence from a bottle and hot water from the tap. Chris ate his bangers, rashers, blood pudding and eggs with voracity, talking all the time. I wasn't to worry. Howard's agent, Rosica Colin, a middle-European terrier who, once she had seized on something, never gave up, had a plan for this play. So if it didn't happen in Cork, we would be free to fill the void with NEW PLAYS. That was the only reason to be in theatre: to do NEW PLAYS. He already had one from Grillo, a viciously funny swipe at the downfall and misogyny of the sofa-bound lower-middle-class paterfamilias – 'nice part for you!' – and there was a neat bagatelle from Andy Mayer about two old men on a beach still believing they were up for it, Beckett-like, with songs. But both were too short for a full evening, with not enough meat for the girls. What plays had I written? What plays did I want to write, quickly, out of necessity? How did I envision the three girls, projected to an extreme? Have a think. Eat up. I'll pay. D'you not want the muffin? (Eating it) Let's go.

We got to the Group Theatre at a time when he knew Jimmy Healy would be there. It was a pub, with a thirty-seater room above, not open yet, so we had to knock. Sodden with rain, we knocked and hammered, but no one came. 'This is bad,' said Chris, as we headed off, dripping, with our luggage, up winding streets, to where Jimmy lived with his mother. We knocked and hammered and hammered and knocked, but no one came. 'This is worse than bad,' said Chris, wet through. I said: 'Can we find a phone? Do you have his number?' Just then the door of the neighbour's house opened and a red-faced woman said oh poor Jimmy, did we not know? The pair of you! Look at you! She took us in to get dry and have a bracing drink. Pneumonia, he was in the rain, caught his death so nearly, thank Jesus they got him to the nuns. We called a taxi to take us to the north side of the city, to a crumbling neo-classical pile, dating back, said the driver, to the 1720s. I sensed Chris bristle as a wimpled sister with jangling keys, led us up stairs, along corridors, grieving that Cork's famed actor, so versatile in tragedy, comedy, vaudeville, operetta, would now be banished from the stage. Jimmy was sitting up in bed, at the end of a long ward, his mother beside him like the Blessed Virgin. Alert though a little husky, Jimmy was sorry but he wouldn't be able to help us in any way. However look on the bright side! We would have no interference of any kind for five weeks. The theatre was entirely ours, and we could take all the takings, bar the residuals. He expected to read in the *Examiner* that we were even more scabrous and coruscating than last year.

On emerald air-letters, I wrote to Jamaica:

> *We are having a wonderful time here in Cork… living in a huge and freezing house, where Thackeray lived when he was writing his Irish Sketches. We all have a room each, with mattresses and no furniture and we share the living-room downstairs. Chris Parr has a penchant for coal fires, but they never seem to get going. Cooking is limited to a little Belling thing, but the girls do that. We're not very good at washing up and tidying, because we're always at the theatre… We usually eat after the performance when we've got home – Katya did a very nice stew this evening – and we don't usually get to bed before 4 or 5. Consequently we don't get up till about 12 or 1… The Revue went up last Wed and it's a fantastic success so we should make some money. About a third of the material is mine and I have the most to do. A lot of the things we did in the Footlights seem to go better here, alongside sketches from some Oxford writers like Michael Palin and Terry Jones. … Iain Montague, the choreographer has taught me a tap routine and there is a lot of dancing in the closing panto-sketch which I wrote. When Katya sings my xmas carol, about the agony in the stable, everything suddenly goes very quiet… I'm also working on a pop song about a waiter…*

THREE UGLY WOMEN

There was one fine day: Sunday 8th January: bright sun, blue sky, crisp rain-washed air, a soft sheen to the landscape. As there was no Sunday performance of the revue, it was decided that the company should go walking in the hills outside Cork, leaving me alone in the house. I had at best six hours to write a 20-30-minute play, offering three plum female roles, with songs, minimal props, no décor, to make a triple bill with *Eighty-Five* by Andy Mayer and *The Downfall of Jock Throb* by John Grillo. I took my cue from the café, Chris and I had breakfasted in on the first morning. I would play the hollow-eyed, barely-awake waiter, opening the play with a fleshed-out version of the song I'd written with Batty that had gone so badly in the pub:

> *I get up every morning at eight*
> *And go do a job that I hate*
> *And I wait*
> *It's not right*
> *I walk about late in the night*
> *I roll my cigarettes too tight*

And I wait
I go white...
I got no inclination to fight
I wait like a... stalactite
Till late
In the night...
I watch the other lovers movin'
down town
The shoo-bi-do-bi-wah-wah
It gets me down
I watch the other lovers and I
watch love drown
And I frown
I go brown...

Then at the end, I reprise, *dolorosamente e cantabile*:

I get to bed at half past two
And spend the night thinking of you
I can't sleep,
I feel blue,
I think deep,
about you
I can't sleep...

And in between, the three women come in, individually, order coffee, engage in conversation, sit in silence, break into song, give a glimpse of the inadequacy of their lives outside the café, indulge in hope, see it slip away, as the lights go out and the café closes.

I typed up *Three Ugly Women* with carbon copies for when they came back from their walk, refreshed and ready for action. But as the reading progressed I felt a chill setting in. Vicious, insulting, puerile, not even funny: I knew from the silence, they were never going to like this. I was told to leave the room while Chris talked to the girls. Later I was called back in. Chris was alone. He told me what they had said. Flo had observed that there was only one good part and that was the waiter. Maria had asked if the women's parts couldn't be brought up at least to the *level* of the waiter. At the moment they just seemed to be chess pieces that didn't move. Katya said if she was a chess piece, she'd like to set her own rules; if she was ugly she'd like to be *really ugly*; if we were rats in a cage, we should be destroying each other verbally. They want you to *raise the stakes*, Chris said. Dirtier, darker, hornier. Let it bleed.

I went back to my room. They were right: I'd written the waiter, as I always wrote sketches, to give myself the best part. I now had to 'play' each of the women to the same level, plan complex chess moves, bend the rules till they broke, propelling the women to their own personal, nightmare extremes and Max-Escher-like madness. I bashed on through to the small hours, and in the morning delivered a sharper, grittier, fierier script and we went straight into rehearsal.

*

On Tuesday 24th January 1967, Jimmy Healy, in his hospital bed, read the following in the *Cork Examiner*:

> *The Group Theatre experiment for this week consists of three playlets, after which is offered a nightcap of late revue. The plays are all new and the kind of raw material just right for this workshop group. I mean the word 'raw' literally; the dialogue is deliberately undercooked; it's got a lot of silence, repetition, pause; it presumes mental speed in the player, spontaneity, pleasure in the grotesque, a penchant for caricature, nerves on wires; it also presumes a gamey audience, with above all a sense of irony...* Three Ugly Women, *by young Richard Crane, a member of the present company, deals with an awful loneliness: the outsideness of the ugly girl, her escape into myth, her darkness building against the image of beauty... The comedy, like all real comedy, has agony at its root, stubbing out the spirit in no man's land, where contact fails and the individual is an island.*

*

On our last day, as it was fine, we went on a hike. Katya and Flo had gone home the day before by plane, so it was just Maria, Chris and me. We were going to drop in on Maria's fairy godmother, the Countess of Adare, who lives at Kilgobbin Castle, about sixty miles from Cork. We hitched until we were a couple of miles from the castle and then Maria rang up and found her godmother had gone to Dublin for three days, so as it was raining and getting dark, we decided to catch the bus back.

We took the boat the next day and the train to London, having just heard that the Little Garrick Theatre, in an alley off St Martin's Lane, had offered to put on the triple bill for six performances from 14th February, then *A Sky-Blue Life* the following week. Ian and Dick were keen and available, as was Howard who had just finished the final draft, and another Oxford actor called Bob Scott, who would play Tolstoy. He would also manage the company, (and thirty years on, as Sir Bob, would go on to chair the Manchester bids for the Olympic and Commonwealth Games). Batty also belatedly came on board to play the parts Chris Parr would have played in

Ireland, making us now a company of eight, packed into the tiny forty-seater theatre, with just ten days to rehearse. I couldn't stay at Lancaster Gate, as Batty had given up the ballroom and taken a smaller room, and anyway, we agreed we had gone past the point of being able to live together. So I had taken up Maria's offer of a room in her Kensington flat, which I could have rent free for three weeks, on condition I would attend, in a Buttons-like role, when suitors called. One evening I opened the door to Crown Prince Hassan of Jordan. A small, smiley man, who was also dating the Chinese singer Tsai Chin, he offered to host Maria in his palace in Amman whenever she was free, and she said she would consider, but only if he and Tsai popped along to the Little Garrick for the first night of *Three Ugly Women*, where he could see her at her most extreme. He didn't come; in fact only two people came, so according to the rule that says you don't need to perform if the cast outnumbers the audience, we could have gone home, but as the two just happened be Tony Palmer, producer of Jonathan Miller's *Alice in Wonderland*, in which Katya had a small part, and Eric Idle, ex-Footlights, now gearing up for *Monty Python*, we went ahead, and it was good. Maria bought champagne and took cast and audience back to her flat in Phillimore Gardens, and we toasted my first play, going straight into the West End.

In the New Statesman, the following week, a round-up of new London theatre ended with this paragraph:

> At the Little Garrick, actor-author Richard Crane, has presented Three Ugly Women, *starring himself as one handsome youth; he also appears as a squashed suburban papa and as a deck-chair dotard trapped by the tide, in two other men's one-acters. 'No young man thinks that he will ever die.' Hazlitt was right of course, but they do like kicking the idea around.*

SPRING '67

The plays were mini-hits: audiences grew, response was good. Flo's agent, Beryl Seton, was impressed and I went to see her. Her forte was musicals and I did my best ever audition to her and her associate Vera Christie, smiling and swaying, their arms round each other as I sang *Surrey With A Fringe On Top* (Rogers and Hammerstein), and *Hey There Lady!* (Mayer and Lascelles), complete with hoofing. They put me up for *You're A Good Man Charlie Brown*, to play Linus, and *Robert and Elizabeth* to play Septimus, the seventh of Elizabeth Barrett's eleven siblings. At the same time Jack Molony came back into the frame, and sent me to see Jim Goddard at ABC for an ITV Playhouse and Maud Spectre and Spitfire Films, to get shot down in *The Battle Of Britain*. I didn't land any of these, though Spitfire were keen and would see me again in two years, following a delay in filming, and Goddard remembered me well enough to cast me as Jimmy the young psychopath in the series *Villains* five years later.

Playing in the evening, rehearsing in the day, fitting in auditions in the gaps, I was growing up as an actor. In Cork we had been innocents. Even though we worked round the clock and did everything – box office, publicity, set and costumes, cooking, – it was too diffuse to be 'proper' theatre. But when Bob and Dick and Ian and Batty came in fresh from filming, touring etc, with voices tuned and lines learnt, we were shocked into the adult business of putting on a full-length play in ten days. It was powerful and faulty. There were flashes of brilliance, then stubborn longueurs. It would take three years for the script to achieve its final state, at the Open Space in 1971, showing Brenton as the voice of a visceral new theatre. But I think our moment of struggle, like a Michelangelo prisoner straining to escapologize from the stone, was when the play was at its most sinewy.

And suddenly it was over and we were stripping the set, reclaiming borrowed items and hiving off to the Arts Theatre bar for farewell bubbly and nibbles pre-ordered by Maria. I knew before I even took a sip that my brain was clouding over. The switch from the seriousness of the play to the vacuity of the bar, distanced and aged me. I could hear voices, my own included, like echoes down a well, and feel arms round my shoulders, even lips on my cheek. But it was as if I'd lived a lifetime then time-travelled back, to my twenty-two-year-old self. I looked at my 'ugly women', matching their confidence to my knowledge of their fate. Maria, ambitious to her fingertips, would look back on this period as a warm-up to a glittering career in high comedy. At a time when working class drama was surging, she would row against the tide as a patrician among the plebs. Declining the offer to become Crown Princess of Jordan, she would marry Dick, divorce him, marry again, have a son, be widowed; would host her own talk show and write 'briskly and cheerfully' (*New Society*) about female acting and adventuring. Turning to directing, she would have an instant hit with the Olivier- and Tony-Award-winning *Thirty-Nine Steps* which would run in London for nine years and on Broadway for three. She had the Aitken silver spoon in her mouth and would use it to stir up success and feed others. Yes, Maria would be all right.

Katya would continue acting through the sixties into the seventies, then diverge, via motherhood, into teaching and training actors. The flat – 17b Ladbroke Terrace – that she shared with Gilly, Sally, Angie and Mandy – variously actresses, London University students and a nanny – would become a magnet for itinerant actors, singers, writers and directors, and a source of coffee and floor-space. 'Katya's flat' would become my port in a storm and occasional postal address for the two years following Cork.

Flo Hopcroft also passed through 17b. She was a good six or seven years older than the rest of us, and everyone said she would come into her own, in later years, as a character actress, but she wasn't waiting for that! She was a natural, not an intellectual performer, and considered popular TV acting as vital as the Greeks. If Euripides were writing now, he'd be crafting classic 'soap' episodes about a mother killing her children out of revenge or a stepmom hanging herself having accused her unresponding stepson of rape. Such parts Flo could play, and in a few years, famously did.

*

'Rick, are you okay? You look dead.'

'Chris, I'm fine. Thanks to you, I'm an actor on the up. I have a future.'

'Don't get hooked on the acting: abstract and brief chroniclers, not worth a hill o' beans, as someone once said to Shakespeare, or how else would he have *buckled down*? Actors, directors, audience, goddam *critics*, if we're not getting the red meat, from Brenton and Grillo and *you*, what are we left with? Dead theatre! Revivals of putrifying corpses. You can act in those and believe you have a future, and nothing will change! No apple-cart will be upset! No complacent, arms-dealing, bomb-building bastard will have the shit scared out of him! We live in the Age of Catastrophe. We could be annihilated tomorrow. So buckle down Rick! When are you writing your next play?'

We were in the cab going to Howard's flat where Chris was staying while Howard was away and where I was having to crash tonight because Maria needed the room for Jonathan, her brother, who had just landed a research job for a rising Tory MP called Thatcher; and Katya was sorry she couldn't accommodate me at 17b, without first doing Gilly, Sally, Mandy and Angie, the courtesy of asking them, and that couldn't be until tomorrow night, sorry sorry; and Batty's new room was so TINY, you couldn't swing a cat in there, even supposing pets were allowed, and anyway his girlfriend – yes he now had one! – would be kipping there unofficially, hopefully.

As we sped down Whitehall, towards the Thames, I told Chris I had no immediate thoughts about a play. The one thing I'd learnt from *The Bastard's Return*, via Footlights to the Cork experience was that you write to fill a need. Was he now telling me to create in a vacuum, on spec, with no end in view? He said: 'Look at that obscenity blocking our road. Cenotaph! You know Greek. Empty tomb. Art is the only antidote to war. As long as there is war there is a need for plays.'

Chris paid for the cab. I paid for the takeaway from the chippy on the corner. Then we went up to Howard's shared, black-painted flat and ate chips in the kitchen.

'But you're right,' said Chris, picking up from the Cenotaph. 'Theatre is a team sport. You can't do it on your own. Plays are not so much written as *wrought*, by a *wright*, as a wheel or a ship is *wrought* by a shipwright or a wheelwright. We directors and actors come aboard to give pedal-power, but it's the writer who does the blueprint and fashions his invention to be perfectly round and properly bottomed to withstand pot-holes and storms.'

Then suddenly he was asleep in his chair.

'Chris...'

His eyes flipped open, he gathered his things and trundled through into Howard's room, shutting the door. I found some cushions and space on the kitchen floor and lay awake making lists. In the morning, I was away before anyone woke, to get my gear from Maria's, convey it to Katya's; then set forth in the spring sunshine, to find food, cash, a pad and a job.

Scene Three
ENTER THE DRAGON

The Beast was staying at the Semel Et Semper Guesthouse. It was December and the only other guest was the Dragon. They breakfasted in silence at separate tables: the Beast lolling his tousled head over his porridge, as if about to fall face-first into the sullen mass; the Dragon swallowing quick spoonfuls while glancing up, seeking a reciprocal glance and permission to convey his paraphernalia across the room and introduce himself. When the glance came, it seemed more of a snarl, so he stayed put.

Afterwards he waited for the Beast in the hall, hoping they might walk into town together and when the man came down in his cuban-heeled boots, long woollen carpet-coat, floor-length knitted scarf and broad-brimmed hat, he fell into step beside him.

'I guess you're the Beast. I'm your trainee dragon. I'm only three hundred years old. I can't fly or breathe fire. I can't stop telling lies and I AM NOT A LIZARD!'

In the silence that followed, he thought: either this man is a method actor, playing the brooding Beast with a Prince locked inside him, or he's just amazingly rude.

'Why are you so tanned?' asked Vivian Mackerrell.

'Oh,' said Richard Harbord. 'That's because I've just come back from Jamaica.' He let the word hang. If Mackerrell took the bait, there was a conversation to be had. If he stayed silent, then it fitted the freeze that was setting in. It was starting to snow. The street was deserted. A bus went by.

'Were you working in Jamaica?'

'My family live there,' said Harbord. 'I had a couple of months between Frinton-on-sea and coming here.' Suddenly it clicked! 'You were on tv! *Les Miserables*! I saw you. I'd just got back. Last week.'

'Thank you.'

'In colour! I was staying with people who had colour. I made a note of your name. How do you pronounce it? Is it like the fish?'

Silence.

'Yes,' said Mackerel. 'From now on, it is, like the fish.' A pause. 'Don't you like names that one has to learn how to pronounce?'

'You mean like Main-waring, which is Mannering, and Chol-mondeley which is Chumley?'

'And Bournemouth, which is Bumf.'

'Is it really?'

'From now on, it is our destiny, to walk the streets of useless information. What's your name?'

'Harbord.'

'Pronounced Hubbard.'

'Well no,' replied the Dragon. 'It took me eight months and three trips to Equity to get the name right. I was Crane to begin with, but there's another one in Equity, so I changed it to Twidle, but no one would take Richard Twidle seriously, so I changed it to Cecil, but my mother (in Jamaica) went bananas because Cecil was not a proper family name, so I changed it to the only family name with theatre connections – my uncle Gordon was an agent, though he wasn't much use to me...'

'Hubbard Chumley-Mannering comes to Bumf!' announced Mackerel as a baby dragon entered the rehearsal room, in a tubby, tiny-winged, spiked, green costume, like a triceratops. Richard Digby Day chortled and clapped his hands. He himself had a tubby, spiky demeanour, which as director he would project onto the baby dragon to rouse laughs. He had two approaches to directing which kept Beauty, her ugly sisters, even the Beast, on their toes. He could be waspishly silly, gagging with his assistant about Butch the Beast and Poof the Magic Dragon, then, in an instant, be stressing the nightmare underpinning this horrifically modern fairy tale. We were not here to amuse, but to scare children out of their wits. Only then, when they were squealing, did we have permission to entertain. 'Digby is very good indeed,' I wrote to my parents. 'We are playing the Full Beast, which makes rehearsing a lot harder, with grunts and groans to remember, as well as words... I spend a lot of my time flat on the floor grovelling... Digby insists it's a brutal play and I find that invigorating. Twice the Beast almost tramples me to death and Beauty gets mauled and thrown about... Vivian Mackerrell who plays the Beast, and I, get on very well. He likes films, as do I, so when we're not rehearsing, we go to the pictures. Last night we saw *The Jungle Book*; the night before, a brilliant film, almost the best I've ever seen, called *Bonnie and Clyde*...'

'Nobody catches Clyde, never,' says C W Moss as the net of law tightens on the car-jacking bank robbers. Banjo music speeds them on the road, across fields, through the dustbowl. Robbing banks who have dispossessed poor farmers and their families, is easy and popular. You walk in, unmasked, with your semi-automatic, say 'We are the Barrow Gang', take the money and rattle away, firing, to the tune of *Foggy Mountain Breakdown*. It could be Keystone Kops, until someone gets hurt. Then the film hits the truth like nothing ever seen before. Death by multiple gunshot is shattering and prolonged. Such deaths are occurring in hundreds and thousands while the film is being made. Five years in, the Vietnam War is approaching its half-way mark. The My Lai massacre is just months away. Anti-war and civil rights protests will reach a peak next year with the murders of Martin Luther King and Robert Kennedy. The Land of the Free is in free fall. Free love, flower power, anarchy and drugs are the fall-out from America's longest, first televised and only losing war. And new heroes are emerging. Clyde and Bonnie are icons of the late sixties, with the pain of sex interwoven as truthfully as the shattering deaths. Clyde, the two-bit legend who can't make it, and CW, the adoring Judas who betrays him, are the modern poles of American manhood. 'Nobody catches Clyde never' says CW, because what he *is* and represents, is many times greater than what he did.

*

We were in the pub after rehearsal, buffing up our *resumes* for the programme. Viv had been a child actor, skyving off school in Nottingham to act with Leonard Rossiter in *Richard III* and Ian McKellen in *Coriolanus*. I had skipped school and run away to sea, ending up in Jamaica where I wrote his first play which was banned for obscenity. Viv had gone on to the Central School of Speech and Drama –

> ME: Did you run across Florence Hopcroft?
> VIV: Flopsy Hovercraft! Now there's a skirt! –
> ME: Did you play Hamlet?
> VIV: I play him all the time, to the top of my bent.
> ME: You could be playing it here. I'm staying on to play Guildenstern.

VIV: A true Hamlet never gets round to playing Hamlet. And Dickie Did-
dly-Dee knows that. Hence he didn't cast me, but cast me hence.

*

It was the custom for Digby Day and his assistant Michael Winter, once
rehearsals were under way, to invite new company members to dinner in
their flat. I imagined I would be going with the Beast and Jonquiline, one of
the ugly sisters, played by Alison Fisk, but Viv was not strictly speaking
'new' having worked with Digby before, and Alison cried off at the last
minute with a migraine. So I went alone. I was stupidly wearing my old
Footlights suit and tie, immediately ditching the jacket and loosening the
tie, when Digby and Michael, in jeans and sweaters, said: 'How smart! How
undragonly!' We chatted over sherry about the company, especially Viv,
who Digby said could be another Peter O'Toole. He was that rare thing: a
feral actor. You never knew what he would come up with. You expected a
roar to tear through the silken voice, but up to now, he was holding it in.
Even when mauling Beauty and trampling the wretched Dragon, you felt,
wearying of his beastliness, he was only releasing a fraction of his strength.
'How do I get him to explode?' said Digby. Uncorking a bottle, Michael said:
'You don't give him notes like "Rage, rage, go for the jugular!" because that
only makes him purr.'

Over dinner, they probed me for my ideas on theatre, my antecedents
and ambitions. They saw me as one of the Puckish/Dragonish actors
emerging in the late sixties. In fact the Dragon had originally been offered
to David Glade. Did I know David? I'd heard of him.

'He's like you,' said Digby. 'Oxbridge, revue, writes plays and songs.
Desperately wants to do Shakespeare. In fact he only declined the Dragon,
when we decided not to do *The Tempest*.'

'He did not decline it,' put in Michael. '*You* declined *him*.'

'Why should I decline a force of nature like David Glade?'

'Because, my dear, he's quite clearly heterosexual.'

'Do you have proof of that, my dear?'

'He's married with a child.'

'So was Oscar. So's Redgrave, Tony Richardson, Tony Perkins.'

'Tony Perkins is not queer!'

'Do you have poof of that my dear?'

'Were you going to do *The Tempest*?' I interrupted, through the laughter.

'Absolutely,' said Digby. 'And we absolutely, failing Glade, had you pen-
cilled in for Ariel. I know Guildenstern doesn't compare, but we are throwing in Marcellus and Reynaldo, who's usually cut. So be a good Dragon, and
when I do *Tempest* next year – *please please* give me a nudge!'

'I certainly shall,' I replied.

*

And I was a good Dragon: too good when it came to it. Trying to stir the Beast to raise his game, I found I was pushing it, inventing new business, rehearsing winks to the audience, which Digby expressly vetoed. Even on the first night, when you'd have thought the adrenalin would at last fire up the Beast, Mackerrell stayed grounded. So what could a dragon do, but slip the winks back in, to roars of laughter? The Beast responded with a baring of teeth but not much more. He seemed bored, as if acting on the stage was a chore to be got through. He was born to amuse, *as himself*, day and night. Doing it formally, to a paying audience, was the price one had to pay, to gain a warmer, drink-buying audience, in the bar afterwards.

His reviews were lukewarm. His Beast-turned-Prince was 'impressive' and 'convincing' but the Dragon stole the show, thus skewing it, away from Theatre of Cruelty, to more lovable Christmas fare. Matinees were full; evening audiences dwindled. Chris Parr, Beryl Seton, Flopsy Hopcroft, Katya Benjamin and all the Gillies and Angies and Sallies from 17b, came and feted the little Dragon, while Mackerrell's pub crowd thinned.

ALONE AT SEMEL ET SEMPER...

...I could look back on my first year as a proper actor. Jump-starting in Cork, after months of stalling, I had driven straight into the heart of London, convincing critics I could act and write as well as anyone. I was on the ladder, going up. In Beryl and Vera, I now had agents to guide me, without bullshit, and even though plum jobs were *just* slipping from my grasp, it was felt if I broke out of my 'minimalist' corner, and stuck a thumb in the pie of popular yet mould-breaking, *avant garde* yet money-making theatre of today, very soon my thumb would pluck the plumpest plum... So how, after a year was it working? Pretty well, I'd say. I was earning a living as an actor, and trying to write well-made plays. Having got a taste of the West End at the Little Garrick, I'd stuck around after *Sky-Blue*, going to matinees of everything from *The Rivals* with Ralph Richardson, and *Oliver!* with Ron Moody, to *America Hurrah, Your Own Thing* and *Mrs Wilson's Diary*, then clocking in at the Big Garrick to tear tickets for the Brian Rix Theatre of Laughter, which enabled occasional disbursements to 17b where I was crashing on Katya's floor; only temporarily of course, just as Rix and the lowering of trousers in British theatre was only temporary. I was a *moral actor* for fucksake, writing sophisticated comedies which, when discovered, would herald the return of Wit to the West End. But in the meantime, said Katya, you should talk to Sally and quickly. Her mother is casting for the summer season at Frinton and she has Equity cards. It's how I got mine. But you'll have to change your name.

You can't have Equity members with the same name and there were two other Richard Cranes. One was American who featured in war films of the 1940s; not a member of British Equity, as I learnt when I called at the Equity office in Harley Street, the next day.

'So I'm okay!'

'Well, no. Just last week, another one popped in. You might know his face; makes tv commercials. What name would you like to change to?'

'My mother's maiden name is Twidle. So, Twidle,' said Richard Twidle.

Testing the name on the girls at 17b drew guffaws. 'What producer would cast a Twiddle-twoddle-twiddly-twat?' said Sally Ducrow, whose mother Joan Shore, had just auditioned me for Frinton Summer Theatre and offered me acting/assistant stage manager plus Equity Card. If you could answer the question 'Do you have your own tennis whites and dinner jacket?' with a yes and a yes, you were laughing, and so was Joan whose laugh was a sprinkler, with her tongue out, like blowing a fart.

Having discussed the name with his agents, who agreed it might be an impediment to serious casting, Richard Twiddle-Twoddle returned to

Harley St, and came out as Richard Cecil. It was a distant family name, going back to William Cecil, Lord Burghley, advisor to Elizabeth I.

The response from Jamaica was a cable: *PLEASE CONSULT PARENTS BEFORE CHANGING NAME.*

Then came the letter:

> *Last night I had one of my ghastly nightmares about you... I woke at 3 am and wandered round the verandah... The thing is I just HATE the name Cecil... There was a loathsome child in my kindergarten called Cecil Ward, who would say his name in such a spluttery way... Ever since you decided to make your career as an actor/writer, I have dreamed of a time when (back in England once more) I shall come to your first nights and read all your books and see your tv plays and be able to say 'this is my son' but how could I even remotely claim any connection with a Cecil? ...*

Richard Cecil wrote back:

> *I've just written TWENTY LETTERS to rep companies about work for after Frinton under my new name... But don't get me wrong. I am terribly pleased you care about what I call myself but it has to be my choice... It's really a very eminent and dignified name and lots of famous people have been perfectly happy with it: eg Henry Cecil, William Cecil, Cecil B de Mille, Cecil Beaton, David Cecil Lloyd-George, actor Jonathan Cecil and Cecil Cullingford (my school chaplain)... It's origin of course is Latin and it means 'blinded'...*

FRINTON

'Harwich for the Continent, Frinton for the *In*continent' is a flippancy considered unfair and (not completely) unfunny by the elders of Frinton-on-Sea, whose lavatory practice is as closely managed as their bursts of laughter. The town lies mid-way between meek Holland-on-Sea and mild Walton-on-the-Naze, with the brash lights of Clacton just five miles down the coast. The railway encloses the town like a moat, the only way in being across the gated draw-bridge of the level crossing. There are no pubs in Frinton, no clubs (except the Tennis, Golf and War Memorial Clubs), no 'amusements', no fish and chip shops and no picnicking on the greensward. The Summer Theatre, in the utility-design Women's Institute Hall, is the sole evening attraction, with every seat sold for every performance of the eight-week season. As a nursery for new actors, the theatre boasts among its alumni, Vanessa Redgrave (too tall for a theatre with a high stage and low procenium), John Osborne (too loud, too rude -

he was expelled from the Tennis Club), Julie Christie, Jane Asher, David Suchet, Timothy West, Anthony Sher. Casting favoured dynasties and 1967 was a bumper year: Sibyl Ewbank, playing female lead character, with the same *hauteur* as her aunt Thorndike; Tamara Ustinov, daughter of Peter, playing female juve character; Colin Skipp, male juve, known to listeners of the Home Service, as Tony, son of Jack and Peggy Archer (a role he would go on to play for forty-six years); Sally Ducrow and Peter Ducrow, (female juve and male character), daughter and brother-in-law to Joan the Artistic Director, herself wife of the co-founder and General Manager, Sam Hoar.

Sam Hoar's first act was to promote ASM Richard Cecil, to Company Stage Manager when the CSM they had engaged, cried off. They wouldn't replace Cecil, just upgrade Nina Thorndike (daughter of Daniel, great-niece of Sibyl) from student observer to working stage hand – she didn't need to be paid. Cecil's wage would increase from £7-10s, to £9 per week, and even though he had no practical experience of stage management, he *had* coxed a Cambridge boat, with all the organizing and steering that that involved, and he had, so he said, between acting jobs, painted and decorated for discerning clients. This would surely suffice to keep the weekly changes rolling, as flats were repapered with differently patterned wallpaper, and doors and French window repositioned and rehung. It would be a baptism of fire but young Cecil would cope, content to bottle his frustration by accepting supporting roles in *Doctor in Love, French Without Tears, Barefoot in the Park* and *Watch it Sailor!* He would however to forfeit the curtain call, since as 'officer-in-charge, he would have to be pulling the damn thing.

I swam every day, organized line-runs in the beach-hut, pinned up the cooking rota for company suppers, made sure the final dress rehearsal was concluded just the audience were coming in; then the next morning set up for the next read-through, and when not needed for acting, get repapering and rehanging. This whirlwind of work kept the raging envy at bay, poured out privately in letters:

> *18th July: The plays are dreadful and the standard of acing low with the exception of Tammy Ustinov. She has a brittle, transparent quality that forces you to reconsider the awfulness of the plays, whenever she comes on stage...*

> *1st Aug: At last a proper part! I am to be Able Seaman Carnoustie Bligh (Scottish!) and Tammy is Daphne Pink in* Watch It Sailor! *They are the best parts in the play, and the best we've had all season. We should have some fun!*

> *25th Aug: I've been offered a job at Bournemouth Rep, in December... I shall start by playing the Dragon in* Beauty *and the Beast* over Xmas,

then something in Hamlet, *and more parts to follow, taking me well into 1968...*

12th Sept: Frinton is over... It has actually been the best kind of training ... The last night of Watch It Sailor! *was amazing, especially when Tammy and I got a round of applause on our stage kiss...*

20th Sept: Returning to London, the first thing I did was consult Equity about my name... I thought it best to stick to an undisputed family name... so after lots of dashing to and fro, I sloughed off Cecil and metamorphed into Harbord...

25th Sept: I need to do something special in the two months before Bournemouth... I'd love to come to Jamaica but can't afford the fare. Could you loan me the money (£200?), which I would repay in instalments...

28th Sept: The return air fare to Jamaica is £217 which means I will need a little more £o££y, say £240... I'd like to go to Bath to stay with Granny and to Saltburn to see Elizabeth and Roy, and to FIND MY PASSPORT...

3rd Oct: I came to Bath today... Granny is out with her bridge-playing gang and I'm home making plans... Leave for London Mon 9th; Saltburn Wed 11th; return to London Mon 16th; and on Wednesday 18th Oct...

...FLY TO JAMAICA!!!

They got to Palisadoes Airport in plenty of time. Bee was as excited as she was, though of course he wouldn't show it. Her own fever of anticipation, akin to childbirth, she kept battened down, which only increased the pressure, till she was finding it hard to breathe. The previous year, Haile Selassie, King of Kings and Lion of Judah, had landed at this very airport, to such as riot of expectation, they'd had to abandon the welcoming ceremony. Today with a welcoming party of just two, there would be no civil disturbance, though the private explosion of joy in her heart, surely exceeded that expressed by any Rastafarian multitude. The tide was turning. Richard Harbord was coming home. The moment he wrote saying he had a job starting in December and wanted to spend the two intervening months with them in Jamaica, and if they lent him the money, he would *change his name*; the moment she read the letter, she felt everything was suddenly going to be all right. The homesickness that had dogged her for more than a year, would fade into a bad dream. The screeching of crickets, the ceaseless rhythmic pounding of pans, the slowness of officialdom, the gullibility of the people, the stupidity of her maid and the exhausting heat that made her want to sleep in the afternoons, though she never could, with so much to worry about, so many letters and *lists* – all these things suddenly, without lessening in any way, turned into aspects of the country, to be embraced and enjoyed, now her son was coming home! Being parted was so wrong. At the height of the row over his name he had written: 'I'm sick of this whole thing... I was absolutely staggered by the general family reaction. I felt kicked out... Anyway don't mention it in your letters as it's really a technical matter and it makes me so angry.' To which she had replied: 'You said not to mention your name business, but I must just say, please never feel you are "kicked out"... I thought you would have realized that you are, and always have been, and always will be, my favourite – but don't tell the girls that! And it's missing seeing you from time to time or being able to phone you, that makes life out here quite intolerable for me...'

And now the plane was coming in. They watched the great bird gliding in across the water and touching down on the runway. Very soon, they would be sharing all the family news: how Bee's hip had eased, and the tests had come through on the blood he had been coughing up and it wasn't cancer after all, just a broken vessel! And Judith had stopped her habitual rudeness, and suddenly seemed *kind;* they had been on a mother-daughter shopping spree and the boyfriend whom Judith had presumed she would object to on account of his colour, in fact had flaunted his negritude in her face like a red rag, had been introduced and was so charming she felt she should warn him about the tantrums and summary disposal of his prede-cessors, but she let it go. Judith, or *Jude* as she must now call her, like Ja-maica, was changing. She had passed her first-year exams and was now heading into her middle stretch at UCWI, as Chairperson of This and Lead-ing Light of That. And Monica, miserable and bullied in her boarding school – they hadn't realized how barbaric some of the practices were (no running weater, cleaning teeth in slops, the under-bed steel-band of urine-filled 'chimmies') – after suffering inverse racialism as a lone white girl among blacks, brave Monnie was now hailed the most popular girl in the dorm, because her famous British actor-brother was coming to visit.

And now she could see him, crossing the tarmac in the fading light. He would have news of Elizabeth: was she expecting her third? And Granny in Bath with her bridge-playing friends, was she now at last content in her widowhood?

Driving over the mountains, through lush groves, in the dark, round vertiginous switch-blade bends, she was wondering, if she shouldn't have insisted that Richard sit in the front, but Bee had wanted to say the Office and would go green if he did that in the back, so she allowed her son to pile himself and his hand-luggage onto back seat of the new Vauxhall Estate. Of course he could have driven the beast himself – he had his licence – but he was dog-tired after the flight, so she had said he should just fall asleep in the back, having finished his cigarette, and not talk too much because she wouldn't be able to hear. She herself wasn't tired. She liked driving, and very soon (she wanted to tell everyone, but not yet!) she would be *getting her own car.* She had seen it and fallen for it – a little red, two-seater MG – just right for zipping, like a person of importance, round the 'dangerous curves' to San San and Blue Hole, her actor-son at her side, as guests of this reception or that cocktail party, on the Lord Ronald Graham Estate, for whom she would shortly (hush-hush till it's confirmed!) be employed as Estate Manager. She had met Tony Gason and his wife Dee at just such a party, and had been struck by the cordiality and relaxed Englishness of the Gasons, who would soon be taking over the management of the letting of the luxury houses on the Estate, and had need of a no-nonsense, preferably ex-pat, local person to organize staffing and welcome the rich and famous to their temporary piece of paradise. 'I'll do it' she had said, half-joking, but he took her seriously, and before she knew it, they were clinching the deal with a clink of gin. But it couldn't start till the new year and she shouldn't bruit it about just in case the dead fist of Jamaican nationalism refused the permit.

She put him in Jude's room, lined with posters of Marcus Garvey. In the morning, over codfish and johnny cakes, served by Clare the maid (if she turned up – she was twenty-two, the same age as Richard and already had four children, all by different fathers, and was syphoning off half her wages to the televangelist Oral Roberts, when she could much more profitably come to Christchurch for nothing!) They would discuss over breakfast her seven-week plan, which would include a short stay in Kingston – Jude wanted him to spend some time with her on campus, discovering Jamaican theatre, meeting her friends, even going on marches. At the same time, she was sure the lure of cocktail parties at San San and swimming at Blue Hole, would be a consummation not to be dished. And he would definitely, she felt, want to go with Bee and herself up into Maroon country to the tin-shack churches that were part of Bee's cure, while at the same time not missing out on the exuberance of a lodge service at Christchurch which was the beating heart of Port Antonio. And there would be quiet days at home, when they could talk, and go walking, through the market, down to the port and out onto the promontory where Errol Flynn used to live. This was Richard's holiday and hers; and also a period of preparation for both of them: he for his first full-acting professional contract; she for the first paying job since her wartime ARP days! And if he wanted – and how would he not! – there was the possibility of just the two of them, spending a few last days of sand, sea and sun, at Montego Bay.

Was it her or was it him? Would it ease as the days, then the weeks, flew by, this feeling, quite irrational, that she didn't really know him? There was hardly a moment, however close they were, when he didn't seem like a stranger. It was natural to start with, because they hadn't seen each other for so long, but one would have expected that kind of strangeness to have ebbed away as they conversed, shared meals and chores, went on trips. And they did all that perfectly. He was gracious, appreciative, sensitive to the ups and downs of Rectory life, knew when to join in and when to stand back, was clearly enjoying her company. They watched TV together, particularly *Peyton Place*, which was becoming an obsession. He helped her purchase the MG, even test drove it for her and became her chauffeur to parties which he clearly relished. He was a hit with all her friends and a great spur in the broadening of her social horizons. Tony Gason, in particular, was much taken with his candour and intelligence, sharing the same English sense of humour. Just having him there, definitely raised her status, and drew people into her circle. But he was not her son. He was *acting* her son. He was a kind of imposter. It was the same feeling she had had when they first deposited him, aged seven, at The Old Ride. He was a changeling. He wasn't hers. She didn't deserve him and she knew, one day, he would abandon her, just as she had abandoned him. She knew all this but couldn't speak about it to anyone. The horror of it – as if her son had died and been replaced – was eating into her brain till she couldn't sleep. One night she got up and went down to the kitchen and found she was crying. 'What's matter Mum?' he said softly, standing in the doorway. She said: 'I don't know. I expect it's just because I'm so happy you're here.' He gave her a hug and kissed the top of her head, then left her to her stupidity.

One Sunday evening, mid-way through his stay, they decided, instead of occupying the Rectory pew at evensong, to go upstairs onto the balcony. It was cooler up here, with seats for two hundred or more, always empty, she didn't know why, when downstairs was regularly packed to overflowing. Leaning on the rail at the front, they had a God's-eye-view of the service as it progressed, the multi-coloured jubilation of swaying and clapping and 'answering back' - Hallujah! Yes Lord! Tell it Father! Amen! This was Bee in his element, bearded, revered, in his white robes, like a prophet. Far away, down below, he didn't need a 'rector's wife' as he had done back home. Amen and Hallelujah were not her style; so she had come up to the balcony, with her son, to look down on the rejoicing, like an alien, in wonder and some envy.

'These are the best seats in the house,' whispered Richard, in his theatre language. 'Why does no one else come up here?'

The answer came when darkness fell, like a curtain, as it does in the tropics. First one, then another, then ten, then a hundred – bats! – came swooping. There was no way out from the squeaking and clicking, like evil laughter, multiplied a thousand times; the diving and zooming, aiming straight at them and just at the last second deflecting, like spitfires, then wheeling round and jetting straight back. They couldn't move. They were trapped. No one down below had any inkling what was happening. They crouched, covering their heads, trying not to scream. And that did it. You can't *act* being someone's unfamiliar son, you can't *agonize* over the true feelings of your rejected offspring, when being assailed by bats! It was dangerous and ridiculous in equal measure. Bowed, on their knees, as if squirming in prayer, they tried not to shriek with laughter.

He went to Kingston but didn't stay over. Jude was busy. He didn't seem to mind. Monica came home for a long week-end, so they didn't need to trek half way across the island to visit the school. But they did get to Montego Bay, for three days at the end of his stay, returning on his birthday. This was to be his 'present' – he didn't want *things*, which would clutter up his luggage. Sun, sea and sand were what he craved, then a party at the Gasons' at San San on the return journey. These last days would be the best. He was relaxed and tanned, looking four or five years younger than his approaching twenty-three years and she was utterly happy and at ease with his company, and with the island, and was even mentioning to Bee that they might consider a second four-year term when the current one expired in 1970.

They stayed in the diocesan accommodation at Mo Bay, not far from Doctor's Cave beach which they walked to each morning, to spend long, easy hours, swimming, reading, picnicking and dozing.

On the second day, she noticed something that should have disturbed her, but somehow it didn't. It didn't even set her imagination racing as it would have done in the period of his stay 'before the bats'. Also it helped to have had a conversation at a recent party, with Boyd Lewis, their friendly Canadian bank manager, a 'confirmed bachelor', as he put it, who had remarked that Richard was a fine-looking young man and should have no trouble finding a wife, if that was his inclination. And she remember, with regard to 'inclination', ten years ago, when Richard was leaving The Old Ride and she and Bee had decided it was time to acquaint him with the realities of the birds and bees – she would do the 'birds'; Bee could do the 'bees'! – she remembered, after Bizzy-Bee had buzzed off having been assured by his son that he *did* know about these things so there was no need etc; she remembered walking with Wit, just the two of them, and him telling her about the Persian boy who had been expelled for doing things which he had had to tell Mrs Flynn about, because other younger boys were becoming involved, and she had admired the adult way Witty had approached this problem and dealt with it so responsibly. He understood the 'inclination' and that it shouldn't be indulged, or if it was, then it should be practised discreetly, without harming others, or 'frightening the horses' as Boyd would say.

Being a private beach, Doctor's Cave offered an exclusivity, like a club, not found on English beaches. It was always pleasantly crowded with people one could chat to, if one wished, or just smile at and say hello. They had got to know a young family, in the way one does on holiday, enjoying the present moment, without reference to past or future. Richard, she noticed, had an aptitude for this kind of friendly interaction: something Bee had in abundance, but Richard seemed to be taking it to another level. He could communicate with just a look, glancing over his sun-glasses in response to someone who was doing the same, and evincing an instant smile. There was a boy, Chinese-looking, about his own age, lying on his front in the sun a few feet away, and wagging his sunglasses as if that was the new language, and Richard she noticed was grinning and wagging back. They had had their picnic lunch and she was resting, trying to concentrate on *Peyton Place*, the original 1950s novel which had spawned the TV series. She was learning how the story had grown from its original source and how layer by layer, libidinous secrets were being uncovered, often with tragic consequences, in a small conservative gossipy New England town. Blink, and this might be their own Anglican parish life, harbouring scandals that could be only dreamed of.

'I'm going for a swim,' said Richard, jumping up suddenly. She noticed the Chinese-looking boy was already splashing out in the blue water as Richard ran down to join him. She sank back with the book, then pulling her hat over her face, let it drop and dozed off.

When she woke, it had clouded over. Neither Richard nor his towel nor the Chinese-looking boy were anywhere to be seen. Any moment, a tropical storm would crash down, just for a few moments, as if to wash away her suspicions, and all would be fine again. She was just gathering up her things, to take shelter, when Richard appeared.

'Where did you go?'

'I took a shower.'

'I was beginning to worry – '

'And talking of showers, it's going to tip down any minute.'

They hurried to the shelter of the bar as big drops began to fall.

On the drive back to Port Antonio, they stopped off at San San, at the Gasons. Tony had said he would host a party for Richard's birthday, and even if he had forgotten, they decided to turn up anyway. He had forgotten, and to castigate them for not reminding him, he ordered them to come inside and keep him company for at least an hour, and because his special talent was mixing work with pleasure (like mixing a good cocktail!), he and Nan, he proposed, might seize this opportunity, Dee being away, to run over a few points about the job, due to start, permit permitting, on Jan 1st; while Birthday Boy fixed the drinks. With his springy, combed hair, greying at the edges, his ruddy face and pipe, Tony G had a Jack Hawkins look about him, like a military man off duty, with a fondness for stories of derring-do and double whiskies. Richard would be driving, so Nan was persuaded to allow herself more than her usual ration of gin fizz, as they swiftly totted figures and assimilated lists. She was confident that Richard, behind the bar, would be responsible and know his limits, as he knew the discretionary limits to whatever his inclinations might be. She was getting a touch tipsy and happily so. She felt layer by layer of secrets could be peeled away both from Tony, who was also now slurring his words, and from Richard who was glowing and bronzed and at his best, following his adventure on the beach. She wasn't going to probe, or peel away the layers, knowing that, as with onions, if you go on peeling, in the end, there is only disappointment.

They drove back in the dark. He was driving like a Jamaican, grinding the gears, taking corners at full throttle. If they crashed now and were both killed, at least they would die happy. But she wasn't ready to go yet; her new life was just beginning. Richard had helped to unlock the cell door, whether of monastery or prison, and the light was streaming in. She felt Jamaicanized at last, and at the same time blessed with the kind of Englishness that had once helped civilize a savage world. And the exhilaration that came with this feeling was akin to the machismo of Richard's driving. They swerved on the wrong side, past Frenchman's Cove. Keeling over or not, what did it matter? Everything, after so many fizzy gins, was in God's hands.

The day before he was to due to fly away, they stayed over at the Diocesan house in Kingston. She rose, as she always did, at 6 am, and while the house still slept, took out an air letter and began:

> *My dear Richard, I decided to write to you even before you leave us, to say thank you for coming to see us. I only hope as the months go by, whilst you are paying off the air fare...* [she would hold him to this debt, as a lifeline, if nothing else]... *you will never once regret having to part with so much. I'm afraid we haven't been able to show you as much of the island as we should have, being restricted by time and money, but really it's all much the same: hot, beautiful and relaxing (God's gifts); dirty, shoddy and frustrating (man's contribution). But I believe it may have been more to see us, and our friends, that you came, and I hope you are going back feeling happy....*

XMAS '67

I sorted the carbon copies of my letters. A pattern was emerging, a kind of destiny, which I'd imagined was the product of hard slog and luck; but now seeing the journey panning out and *going somewhere*, who was to say there wasn't a Higher Power calling the shots? It made me think of my father, for whom vocation was everything. God's plan, however obscure, would always turn out well, if one trusted it without question. It had brought the family, via Yorkshire and two parishes in Birmingham, to the working paradise of Jamaica. It had even brought Wit across the ocean and back into the fold, which in turn brought cheer to Nan and the girls. It was all planned and it was good.

I would get just two days off over Christmas, then be back in Bournemouth on Boxing Day. I could choose to stick around with the Beast and Jonquiline, or I could take up Angie's offer and go to her family in Southampton. When she and Katya and the Sallies and the Gillies had come down to see the show, she'd suggested I get the bus on Christmas Eve, and she and her parents could drive me back on the 26th and see the matinee – she liked to see friends in plays at least twice! If I wanted to go to midnight mass, there was a church nearby and she would accompany me, as a curious heathen. It seemed planned. So I said yes. We had fun. I took communion. We ate turkey, pulled crackers, wore paper hats, opened presents, the parents tacitly assuming I was the boyfriend, though putting me, for form's sake, in the spare room which was fine by me. We watched Harry Secombe and Ken Dodd on tv, then the Beatles' *Magical Mystery Tour,* which we all thought was terrible.

On Christmas night, I had a dream. It was the final performance of *Beauty and the Beast.* The audience, at the end of a dwindling run, was pitifully small. The Beast was giving his world-weary performance and the Dragon was playing for laughs. Suddenly, Mackerrell crossed the stage and seized the luckless lizard by the neck, causing him to yelp and the costume-fastenings to pop. This had not been rehearsed, nor had the howl of rage let out by the Beast, as he throttled his prey, halting the action for several seconds. Eventually, the Dragon freed himself, said 'That was a surprise!' and together they clawed the play back onto its track. But a line had been crossed. The audience were silent when the curtain fell.

*

Was it a dream or did it actually happen? I remembered the two of us, walking back to Semel Et Semper. Neither of us spoke. The Beast had downed several pints after the show, but his stride did not falter. The Dragon, keeping up, having had just one beer, kept slipping on the pavement. It was snowing again, softly, absorbing all sound. I glanced aside at the striding figure in his carpet-coat, long scarf, broad hat. Mackerrell was a leader of fashion with no followers. His clothes, taste in music, attitude to acting, were designed to provoke, but not be copied. He was ahead of his time and a throw-back to former times. Once, during the run, he invited me up to his room for a spliff. 'I'm going to take you to another planet,' exhaled the Beast. 'I know what you are; indeed *what you are not.* You and I, we're kidding people we exist. If they ever find out we're only acting, then *the cloud-capp'd towers, the gorgeous palaces, shall dissolve* etc. I could play that part.'

'Then you should,' said the Dragon. 'Digby's doing it in Regent's Park. I'm playing Ariel. He said so, if I give him a nudge. You should too. Give him more than a nudge. Throttle him as you did me.'

But Vivian Mackerrell would never play any leading role, except one, and even then someone else would play him. There would be a film of his life, or just a very small portion of it. The Greatest Actor Who Never Lived would be a career-defining role for Richard E Grant, and Mackerrell, as Withnail, would dine out on his success, drinking the 'finest wines available to humanity' until throat cancer got him. It's wrong to say he had no followers. He had an audience of many. Of followers, he had three: Bruce Robinson, his flatmate from Central who made the film; Colin Bacon, who wrote the biography and saw him through the voiceless, still boozing final days; and unsung, unknown, once-upon-a-time, semel-et-semper, Old Mother Hubbard Chumley-Mannering von Bumf, alias the Dragon, alias I.

CRUSADERS

Beryl rang the stage door and left a message to call her urgently tonight on her home number. We were into the second week of *Hamlet* and had already, with good national coverage, raised the status of the Palace Court Bournemouth, from provincial rep to serious regional classical theatre, to vie with Birmingham and Nottingham. Peter Egan's Hamlet was 'contemporary, unadorned, energetic, superb...' When he seized me, as Guildenstern, and stuffed the recorder in my mouth saying 'Will you play upon this pipe?' I truly felt he was going to choke me. With Harry Waters (nephew of music hall stars Elsie and Doris) as Rosencrantz, coming to the rotten court from outside, we weren't sure if we were meant to be a comedy duo, or juvenile spies, working for a noxious regime. When we put the question to Digby, he chortled and said both. We were innocent idiots, wrong-footed at every step, and in the end, along with everyone else, we would be dead.

I rang Beryl in the interval. She said: 'Can you come up to London to-morrow? Miriam Brickman is casting a film and wants to see you. You'll be playing seventeen. The director is Lindsay Anderson. Go to her office for 10 o'clock. That should get you back easily in time for your performance. The working title is *Crusaders*.'

Of course I should have told the stage manager but he would have said: 'Let me have a word with Dig'. And Dig would have said: 'Absolutely not! My dear, look at the state of the trains. Have they ever been on time? I'm so sorry but we do have a contract with the audience. If any actor misses an entrance, the whole enterprise turns awry. I'm amazed you were even considering it!'

But I did tell Alison (formerly Jonquiline) who since Mackerrell had gone, was now my walking and drinking companion and co-creators of sub-plots. She said: 'Go. It's a film. It's Lindsay Anderson. Are you nuts? If you're late, I'll stand in for you.' Egan apart, she was the best actor in the company and would go on to great things at Stratford and beyond. She was playing Felicity, attendant to the Queen, who is in love with Horatio. ('Absent thee from Felicity awhile,' snaps the dying Hamlet.) 'But wait,' I said. 'Who will play Ho?' As well as Marcellus, Reynaldo and Guildenstern, I was also playing the Chinese guard in the duel scene, who when bidden 'Look to the Queen there Ho!' catches the poisoned consort as she falls. 'I can do that one as well,' said the amazing Alison.

I skipped breakfast, got an early train to Waterloo and was at the Brick-man offices by 9.45. On the train, I realized I knew nothing about this film, escept the title: *Crusaders*. Either it was about the Christian youth organization I had briefly been a member of at Leatherhead, where you clapped and sang choruses such as: 'I'm H,A,P,P,Y! I'm H,A,P,P,Y! I know I am, I'm sure I am...etc.' Or it was a historical epic like *Knights of the Teutonic Order*. I hoped it would be the latter and having seen Lindsay Anderson's *This Sporting Life*, that it would break the mould of epic films, and be a classic for the modern audience.

The Brickman offices were much as they had been a year and a half ago, when I'd failed to measure up to Jean Shrimpton. More experienced now and bolder, I went straight through the lobby into the inner sanctum where previously I'd mistaken the young assistant for the great casting director herself. I wouldn't be doing that again! A pleasant-looking blond boy about my age was waiting while a fearsome secretary riffled through his *resume*. Having been one myself, I knew how to deal with dragons! 'Is this where one waits for Miriam Brickman?' I blurted. She turned as if to incinerate my head with a single breath: 'I *am* Miriam Brickman!'

Back in the lobby, another young actor was waiting. He must have been there when I came in but I hadn't noticed. He said his name was Richard Warwick, but I wasn't in the mood to talk. He was vastly amused that I'd walked straight in. 'That's the way to get cast. She'll remember you.' But I knew it was bad form to get pally with the competition. He said he'd come early. He was in rehearsal for a telly. Would I mind if he went in next? I said: 'But I'm next on the list. What if she thinks you're me?' 'Then you'll get the part, lucky sod!' he laughed. He had a natural manner. He was dangerously close to my own style. I could have liked him. But casting is like gladiators; you have to be ready to kill your friend.

I said: 'What do you know about this film?'

'Only that it's something to do with Rudyard Kipling,' said Warwick. 'Lindsay doesn't want you to know too much. He likes innocence in actors. He always cites Ingrid Bergman in *Casablanca*. She never knew, till they shot the scene, if she was going to get on that plane.'

'Do you know him? Have you worked with him?'

'No but I know someone who has.'

At that point, the door opened and the blond boy came out. I knew I knew him. It was David Glade.

'What school did you go to Richard?' asked Miriam Brickman, after Warwick had gone (remarkably quickly) and I'd re-entered the sanctum and sat down. She was thumbing through a *resume* which seemed far too long to be mine, but then maybe Beryl had fleshed it out a bit. The thought that I'd done more of significance than I'd imagined, gave me confidence.

'I didn't,' I said. 'I went to Cambridge.'

She looked up with the puzzlement Germaine Greer used to give idiots who dared to cross her. 'So you went straight from birth to university?'

'Oh no!' I retorted. 'I thought you meant *drama* school! I went to St John's Leatherhead. It's a minor public school in Surrey, mostly for sons of the clergy.'

I couldn't see where this was going. I'd been sitting in the lobby, feeling marginally pissed off that Warwick had gone in front me. So he was rehearsing for a telly? *I* had to get back to Bournemouth for a performance! I had a contract with my audience, which if broken would turn the whole pithy enterprise awry!

'Tell me about St John's Leatherhead.'

Was she trying to appease me, knowing I'd come all this way to no purpose, Glade and Warwick being far gallanter material than I? Or was she just rubbing my nose in the mistake I'd made about school, probing the idiosyncrasies of the dullest period of my life? Well, I gave it to her, the full barbarity of fagging, toilet-seat-warming and 'wappering' – sticking a de-bagged new boy in a bin, and blacking his face and genitals; and dorms with fifty beds in, where House Prefects' Beatings were staged, like executions; and the corps, and Field Marshal Viscount Montgomery of Alamein, who was wrong-footed then white-knuckled with rage when we mutinied. I had no idea what this had to do with Richard Coeur de Lion, or indeed Rudyard Kipling, but I went on talking and she was riveted. After ten minutes or so, she said: 'Richard, I'm not going to say "we'll let you know" because I'm telling you: *I want you to see Lindsay.* We'll arrange it. I'll talk to your agent.'

All the way back to Bournemouth on the train, I was hearing her words: *I want you to see Lindsay.* 'He likes innocence in actors,' Warwick had said, so I'd make a point of *not enquiring* what the film was about. My career truly was being planned by a Higher Power, for whom La Brickman and Mr Anderson were angels not to be struggled with. In films, I'd been told, you don't pump the adrenalin as you do on stage. You let it flow. Your face flops. You let the camera caress you. You don't assume anything. You ride a cloud to reach the stars.

I was back at Semel Et Semper by three, well in time for a natter or a nap before the 7.30 performance, but Alison wasn't there. I knocked on Egan's door – he now had Mackerrell's room – but he wasn't there either. I was suddenly dog-tired, so went and crashed in my room and was out like a light with my boots on. When I woke it was dark. Somewhere a phone was ringing. In my dream, I got up, put on collar and tie and my suit, because later in the day there would a press conference and I would be doing interviews; then I went out into the early dawn to where the car with my driver in his peaked cap was waiting to whizz me on trafficless early morning roads to the location, where the make-up team would be poised to muddy me up and I'd climb into my chain mail, sling on the blood-stained tabard and clank off to be hoisted onto my whinneying steed.

I looked at the clock: 4.15. What day was it? Thursday. The matinee!! *Fuck!!!* I'd forgotten the fucking matinee!!! I was off the bed, out of the house, pulling on coat, and down to bus stop as a bus was pulling away. I ran, leapt on. *I knew there was a matinee!* I could have gone straight to the theatre from the station and been just in time. I had broken contract, betrayed my fellow actors, and the bus wasn't moving! Snow was dancing down like Christmas. I got off and skidded the last mile into town. At the stage door, I could hear pandemonium in the theatre, Harry Waters as Osric screaming: 'A hit! A very palpable hit!' I ran up to the dressing-room, threw on my guard's gear and was on stage just in time to catch the poisoned queen as she fell.

Then a strange thing happened.

The noise in the theatre, the tension in the actors, my own race to get here, my relief at being on stage at last, if only for the final moments; the whole chaos of feelings: rowdy audience, angry actors, my own weariness and Hamlet's merging into a deathly sleep: 'Absent thee from... draw breath in pain... the election lights on ... the rest...is silence...'

I must have blacked out, because the next thing I knew, I was being helped to my feet for the curtain call. It was obvious I was ill, which explained my absence, except no one seemed to believe me. In the break between shows, Michael Colefax, the stage manager, took me to one side. He looked at me, waiting for an explanation. I should have said: 'Okay. I went to London. I didn't tell anyone because this was MY CHANCE to blast myself out of the mediocrity of provincial theatre, into the starry heaven of film.' I fact I muttered: 'Sorry... I blanked... couldn't focus... it's chronic... kind of migraine, allied to *petit mal*... The only cure is *acting*. I'm only alive when I'm not being myself. That's why I forced myself to get here. And I'm better now, thanks to dear old Doctor Theatre, and thanks to you for being concerned.'

He was unconvinced. It would be written in the show report, that I had missed the schools' matinee and that Alison had had to go on with a book, and suffer jeering and ridicule. I was lucky Digby wasn't in. I should go and see him tomorrow, to pre-empt his response, which would be caustic to say the least.

No one spoke to me in the break or at any time through the evening performance. I had hoped Alison would at least ask me how the interview had gone, but she had apparently been wounded to the point of tears by the barrage of chanting 'Learn your lines! Learn your lines...!' whenever she came back on with the book. I so wanted to thank her and prepare to say good-bye because at the end of the week, I would be quitting theatre for ever. Whatever Digby might say – in the end he said nothing, just froze me out – whatever he or anyone might think, I could shrug it off, easy. *I want you to see Lindsay*, Miriam had said, and even though Beryl, when I told her, warned me not to count my chickens, I disregarded the caution. I had them numbered, every one of them, tweeting in their shells, ready to break free and fly, like whooping cranes.

IF (ONLY)...

I shook the sand of Bournemouth from my boots and went up to the smoke. I was intending to stay a few nights at 17b, then when I'd *seen Lindsay* and the film had moved up, notch by notch, to the point where Beryl just had to fine-tune the contract, I would find a place of my own. Somewhere like Rollicking's pad in Holland Park, where I'd stayed when I first came to London, would be ideal for starters, or another ballroom. From Waterloo, I rang the flat and Gilly (or Sally or was it Mandy?) answered: No, Angie was away and Katya was no longer living there. Did I not know that? She, or Tammy, who had taken Katya's room, should have told me, they'd had a House Meeting and decided: sorry, no more peripatetic dossers! Honestly, no offence, but it had all got too much, tripping over the grizzly and the unwashed in the living-room every morning, and having to queue for one's own bathroom! In future, only those in a sexual relationship with an *official inmate* would be permitted to to stay. So unless you can penetrate the crinkly sheets of the Ice Queen (ie chum up with Angie), everyone else being spoken for, including Tammy who was now seriously involved with Chris Parr...

I put the phone down. Gosh. I hadn't been in touch with Chris since before Christmas, when he'd returned my latest 'frivolous boulevard jaunt' that was of no interest to him. (Whatever happened to the author of *Scrooge* and *Three Ugly Women*?) And if he was now seriously involved with Tammy, well that was two friendships down the drain. I took a deep breath. It was two o'clock and snowing. I had to find shelter by nightfall, or freeze. Lugging my bags, I took the tube to Notting Hill Gate and was ringing the bell of 17b Ladbroke Terrace, by 2.45. If Angie answered, I knew I could persuade her to pretend we had formed an involvement over Christmas, and for one night at least, I might sleep, if not in a discreet corner of her ample bed, then on the floor, I didn't mind. Mandy (or Gilly, or was it Sally?) answered down the intercom:

'Hello?'

'Hi, it's Richard. Sorry. Is Angie in yet?'

'She was. She came back, got changed, then she went out. He came for her in his powder-blue Bentley.'

'Who came for her in his powder-blue Bentley?'

'Her new beau. We were watching goggle-eyed from the window as she sped away. She's a dark one. We never knew. Did you know?'

'Did I know what for chrissake?'

'Fagin. Her sugar-daddy. Star of *Oliver!* We're having to revise our opinion of the Ice Queen.'

I walked away. If Angie was dating Ron Moody, I too would have to 're-view the situation'. There was nothing I could imagine of the *femme fatale* about her, and Moody, for all his craft and cunning, was an unlikely lothario. But puzzling the loss of another friend down a gilded drain, does not find you a bed.

I think I'd better think it out again! Hey!

I found a card in a newsagent offering a room – 'reasonably spacious, lower-ground floor, with shared kitchen and bathroom, ideally situated on the border of Holland Park and Shepherd's Bush' – and without even phoning, went straight to 22 Royal Crescent W11. A short man in his forties, with a pencil moustache, wire-framed glasses and thinning hair, reminiscent of Dr Crippen, eased open the basement door. Ushering me inside, he began his monologue:

This is the room if you want to take it. As you see, it's large – large-ish. Bed, table, chairs, large-ish wardrobe. Oh and the rent. The rent will be four pounds and two weeks in advance. The drawers. I ought to point out that I keep my shoes in this drawer, and this drawer I use for my dirty washing, and the third drawer, the third drawer, the third draw-er… is broken. But you could put your things… er… in this … bin. The rent is four guineas. I have sublet it before and I do insist on no visitors after eleven. I mean I can't have all your friends coming round, so as I said, absolutely no guests after 9.30, because I have to use this room to go to the bathroom, which is through here, or rather was. There is a

bath, but as you'll see, it isn't, it isn't, it isn't...attached to anything. The chap who was here before, he was from Bombay, in the West Indies, and he left without paying three weeks rent in advance, which I would have to ask you for: three fives, three fives... eighteen guineas, in cash...

When I came to write up the speech and perform it, I made the tenant tall, silent and black, and gave Denis Grebe, as I renamed him, a stammer which got worse the more he entangled himself in the impracticalities of the room and the inflating rent. For now though, I was just grateful to have found, in one afternoon, a temporary home that I could move into straight-away – he didn't seem to want references, just cash on the nail – with the bonus of a resident character straight out of Pinter or Patrick Hamilton, that I could study and later play.

He left me to unpack. I didn't see him till the following morning. There wasn't a phone in the flat, so from the call-box on the corner, I rang Zanna Raleigh-King, whose flat from which she had ejected me a year and a half ago, was just across and down the road. I was thinking I might meet her and patch up the festering wound with a drink and so reclaim a rung on the social ladder. Newly confident being now independent housing-wise, and on the threshold of a film career, I was nonetheless massively relieved when it wasn't Rollicking but Di Lubbock who answered. She was thrilled I'd rung. Where had I been? Where can we meet? She was once again plant-watering for Zanna who was away, and I could have stayed there, except the Bears might walk back in any time, and no one wanted a repeat of the Goldilocks caper. We agreed to meet *right now* for a pasta at Presto in Notting Hill Gate. I raced to get there to bag a table but Di was there first, jumping up as soon as I came in and hugging me. She was looking beautiful with her long, loose, pre-Raphaelite hair and silken voice, inviting unconditional agreement with whatever she might say. Were we both, she wondered, on the cusp of success: me, with *Crusaders* which surely *must* happen, because she and I believed it would and what you truly believe *will be* (but shouldn't I be helping fate along with a few phone-calls?); and herself with her singing: she was getting regular cabaret bookings as well as currently, socially, seeing a lot of Chris Jagger, brother of Mick, whose mother – get this! – kept calling her, instructing her to take care of her boys! We ate pasta, drank wine, had a gelato and a capuccino, then popped on the spur to the Gaumont, to see *Camelot,* with Richard Harris and Vanessa Redgrave. You pursue your dream only to see it brought down by the people you trusted most. It was a tragedy for our time, which we knew we could rise above, because of the glorious songs.

I walked her back to Zanna's flat and tried to kiss her, but she turned away, giving me a mouthful of hair, a short giggle, then a finger pressed to my lips, and a 'not yet'.

How to handle a woman...?
I hadn't a clue.

*

I needed a phone. I couldn't keep going to the call-box on the corner to ring Beryl – 'Any news from Miriam? When do I see Lindsay? Digby Day said to give him a nudge; did he call?' – and I had to have a hot-line to *Problem?* for jobs. Four in a week would just cover the rent of Royal Crescent. Five would allow me to eat. Then signing on at the Actors' Labour Exchange in Chadwick Street (good for gossip and news of work) could double that and allow pudding. Also I had to keep putting by at least two pounds a week to offset the 'national debt' to my parents. So the next morning I went back to 17b. I'd given their number to both Beryl and *Problem?* on the assumption I would be staying there and needed to check they didn't mind me dropping by to pick up messages. Angie made coffee. In the flush of her Moody liaison, she was happy to oblige on the messages, and I could even have crashed on her floor if she hadn't already promised it to Col Batty from tomorrow. He was finding his niche as a children's entertainer, and having completed a short season at Butlins and a run of gigs in the west country, featuring daredevil disaster-prone Colonel Batty, was coming to London with scripts.

I said: 'What about Moody?'

'What about him?'

'Won't he mind someone sleeping in your room?'

'It's not that kind of relationship,' laughed the Ice Queen.

Did she mean Batty or Moody? Did I care, beyond a twinge of jealousy and a need to know more, about the latter at any rate?

'I was usheretting at the Aldwych,' she obliged, 'for the World Theatre Season. It was the Berliner Ensemble doing *The Resistible Rise of Arturo Ui* , about the emergence of Hitler set among the vegetable trade in Chicago in the thirties. I was walking up Kingsway towards High Holborn and thinking how much stronger the play would have been with more humour and songs, when a man fell into step beside me. I remembered him from the theatre, having made the mistake of greeting him as I tore his ticket, convinced we were acquainted, when in fact he was just a famous actor I'd seen in something, but couldn't remember what.

'"How did you like the play?" he began.

'"It was great. How did you like it?"

'"I felt it needed less *sturm* more wit, less *drang*, more song; Littlewood could do it, with a score by Bart."

'Clang! The penny dropped! I was walked with Fagin! Agreeing with him too, and thinking how much better and funnier and more horrible and rotten to the core, he would have been as the Cabbage King.

'"Do usherettes get meal-breaks? Are you hungry? Have you had dinner?"

'He took me to the Ivy. We had lobster bisque, *oeufs en cocotte* with steak tartar and zabaglione to follow; then he took me to where his powder-blue Bentley was valet-parked, with its stereophonic radio and electric windows, and sped me home by midnight.

'And yes there has been a message, in fact two.'

I rang Beryl. Did I object to commercials? There were a couple she could put me up for: Milk of Magnesia and Cococola. But no news from *Crusaders*, which generally in this business, she sighed, meant *bad* news. But there were exceptions, so I should keep my pecker up.

The second message was from *Problem?* Was I free this afternoon? Sylvia Syms needed a gardener.

Miss Syms lived at the bottom of a leafy lane in north London. Like me, she was 'resting' so had decided it was time to 'do something about the garden'. But first it had to be cleared. She was dressed in gum boots, rough jeans and a sweater and I thought at first she was going to help me, and I imagined, as we hacked at the jungle and scythed the brush, she would let slip anecdotes about acting with Cliff Richard in *Expresso Bongo* and Dirk Bogarde in *Victim*. But just as I was mentioning what I did, had done, hoped to do, the phone rang and she was away for the rest of the morning. I hacked on alone. When I came back the next day, she was dressed as befitted the leading screen-star of her day, in high heels, pencil skirt, busty blouse, blond hair swept back in a French roll. She had a casting. They'd sent the script. It was sub-James Bond and unactable. But she'd always been told: never say no (unless it's porn) or you'll regret it, especially as now, after a gilded decade, her career seemed to have stalled. *Ice Cold in Alex, Woman in the Dressing-Gown, Conspiracy of Hearts, The Punch And Judy Man*, these were all in the past. She loved acting but not all the hoo-ha of film. Did she look her age? She hoped so. As a mother of two with a house and garden, she was looking for more mature and *interesting* roles. A car came, and she was gone. I slashed and stacked and burned till it was dark, hoping she might come back and we could talk. I even dug over the beds and tidied the shed. Then I left: a good job well done, but I felt deflated all the same. It was agreed I should come back just one more time and I did. 'But you've finished,' she smiled. 'I'll pay you of course and you can go early. But please have a glass of something first.'

The next morning I rang Beryl and told her what Sylvia had said over the beaujolais: (1) find a director - for her it had been Herbert Wilcox - who truly believes in your talent and will always encourage and admonish you; (2) go hammer and tongs for the parts you would die for, as Dirk had done with *Victim*, because he was passionate about changing the law on homosexuality; (3) never say no, never apologize or look back; (4) keep fit, keep cheerful, keep believing in rainbows; and (4) don't get too good at gardening!

But all that was just ballast for what she happened to say, as an afterthought, as I was leaving:

'What was that film you were up for?'

'*Crusaders*.'

'What do you know of it?'

'I think it's about the Crusades.'

'I've heard it's about a school. And it's not called *Crusaders* any more. It's called *If...* You should make some enquiries.'

I sensed Beryl was wearying of me flogging this nag. The Milk of Magnesia commercial was what mattered. Would I go to the Max River Studios in Great Newport Street tomorrow? I said yes yes yes but couldn't she just ring Miriam? Couldn't she just *shift her fat arse and wring Miriam's fucking neck! 'I want you to see Lindsay. We'll arrange it.'* She'd said that. Make her act on it. It's not a tabard and chain-mail epic. It's about a *school, today*; exactly like the one I'd nattered on to her about: not the Knights of St John, but St John's School Leatherhead, in all its hidebound mediocrity, out of which a trio of disaffected leavers stage a mutiny and kill everyone! That was the gist of what Sylvia said. That's what I'm destined to star in. It's my career!

> *If... you can dream and not make dreams your master...*
> *if... you can meet with Triumph and Disaster...*

As I walked home, I was trying to cram Kipling's dictum into the mindset of the actor, with particular reference to this film, but of course it wasn't going to fit. The title was ironic. That was the message of the film. There were no moral rules in this rotten universe, with its gung-ho cruelty and ingrained class prejudice. It was all acting, bitching, lying, betraying. Camelot, for all its glorious songs, ends in napalm and assassination.

*

I feel sick as a dog, in a crowded lift going nowhere, then a hand from heaven reaches down with the bottle, and a choir sings 'New Milk of Magnesia...' in multiple harmony. As the lift ascends, the pain recedes and

I'm right as rain by the time we reach our level. A week later, I'm sitting at an elegant alfresco table sipping Cococola, draped by three leggy models, outside Buckingham Palace during the Changing of the Guard; then suddenly we're all dancing and prancing down Portobello Road, donning and doffing historic military uniforms.

I got £12 for each job, which I salted away against the National Debt which now stood at £170.

I wrote home:

> I'm still set on being a film star, but so many other opportunities keep popping up. The Peanuts musical, You're A Good Man Charlie Brown, which I auditioned for last year, before it was postponed, has now resurfaced, to run in the West End at the Fortune Theatre and they've asked to see me again. Then there's Stoke-on-Trent, Canterbury, Windsor, Lincoln, Pitlochry and Westcliff-on-Sea, plus interviews at ATV, BBC and a Persil commercial...

I didn't get any of them. I'd go in, do my pieces – Cuthbert from *Boy With A Cart* for straight, Davies from *The Caretaker* for character, then for singing: 'C'est Moi C'est Moi', from *Camelot* or 'On the Street Where You Live' from *My Fair Lady*. *Peanuts* called me back twice and I walked on air for a couple of days, then slowly – no news, bad news – deflated, like a farting balloon. Just two commercials in eight weeks was nothing to write home about. I was getting too good (as Sylvia had warned) at not only gardening, but cleaning, dusting, serving champagne, driving typewriters to Watford and hoovering and emptying pedal bins for the Regenerative Cellular Therapy Centre; then retreating into a cupboard when clients came by, so as not to be glimpsed by Marlene Dietrich, Somerset Maugham, Gloria Swanson and Charlie Chaplin, who had come for their thousand-pound injection of a cocktail of living cells from the organs – spleen, bladder, lungs – of unborn sheep. They would come in aged eighty or seventy or sixty and go out aged seventy or sixty or fifty, having first passed a urine sample which it was my job to package, and despatch to a lab in Switzerland for analysis. The Centre was operated by 'Doctor' Peter Stephan, a lithe thirty-year-old (formerly forty), who with his late father, the pioneering cellular regenerative surgeon Dr Ernest Stephan, had developed and personally tested the serum. Unseen in the cupboard until W H Auden, Dr Adenauer and Pope Pius had gone by, then emptying their swabs from the pedal-bins, and packaging and carrying their piss to the post office, I wondered about taking up Stephan's offer of a free jab, and coming out aged thirteen, fit to play Linus or the Artful Dodger or one of the younger parts in *If...* Then driving back from Watford having offloaded five hundred Olivettis and timing it to hit grid-locked Marylebone Rd at five o'clock – I was paid by the hour – I thought: WHY AM I DOING THIS? WHEN DID I LAST SEE MY OWN TYPEWRITER? HAVE I TAKEN A WRONG TURNING? WILL I EVER GET BACK ONTO THE ROAD WHERE I BELONG? Then later that night, pouring champagne at a fashion show, watching PVC mini-skirts, high-heeling down the catwalk, and keeping my head down because Suzy Menkes, formerly editor of *Varsity* now fashion editor of the *Evening Standard*, was wafting towards me, and I'm sure I saw Sue Ayling...

> *If you can keep your head (down) when all about you...*
> *If you can trust yourself when all men (and women) doubt you...*
> *If you can wait (and wait and wait) and not be tired by waiting...*

But I was, so tired, and Kipling was no help. The addressee in his poem, for all his callowness, is the foundation on which the future will be built. He had nothing to say to me. Forget Triumph and Disaster, my besetting impostors were Indifference and *Envy*. I'd watch other, sleaker runners streaking ahead: Tammy and Maria heading for Hampstead and the West End; Katya and Flopsy up for long-haul contracts at Worcester and Bristol; Di just signing a TV deal for two of her songs; Batty blooming as a solo artist in his new children's niche, and Chris Parr now anchored into mainstream theatre on a trainee director's bursary at the Nottingham Playhouse.

I went round to 17b – no messages, no mail – and found it packed to the gun'ls. Obviously the ban on peripatetic dossers wasn't holding. Batty was in Angie's room, Parr with Tammy, various boyfriends and friends of boyfriends of Gilly, Milly-Molly-Mandy and Sally in the kitchen and bathroom, on the phone and answering the door to a man with a trunkful of orchids for Tammy from her father who had just come back into her life with a fabulous plant of each of the twenty-one birthdays he'd missed.

Grillo was asleep on the sofa in the living-room and another man I didn't know was sitting on a bean bag. 'Hello,' he said softly. He wore cheese-cloth and crushed velvet, had a sad smile and sleepy eyes under a peruque of tumbling locks. 'Rick!' exploded Chris, coming in with coffee. 'Meet Noel Greig! He's about to start a café theatre in Brighton. You should talk to him.'

Over coffee, Noel explained how he and two friends from university, Ruth Marks and Jenny Harris, had found an old building down by the sea in Brighton, which they'd rented and were converting into what would become the Arts Lab of the south coast. Combining café with cinema, disco, music venue and art gallery, the Brighton Combination would be a meeting place for writers, actors, music-makers and artists, and at its heart would be a *theatre*.   They were to open in May with Grillo's *Hello Goodbye Sebastian* – did I know it? (Yes I'd seen it) – then do new plays, improvised or specially written, and become the hub of a politico-dramatic revolution! No one would get paid – only whores do cash! Free food, free bedding, no stars, no agents! Flo Hopcroft and Tim Davies were already signed for *Sebastian*, with David Glade to play the lead.

'David Glade?'

'If he's free. He's up for the Lindsay Anderson film everyone's talking about. If he gets that, we're fucked.'

BETTY'S HOUSE

Betty Tadman and Michael Church were moving into a house in Chadwell Street, Islington, a five-storey late Georgian terrace property, behind Sadler's Wells. Rented from the New River Company, for twelve pounds a week, the house was unfurnished, and though structurally sound, much neglected and down-at heel. In the 1820s when most of the area was built, this had been an elegant estate much sought-after by the gentry, but with the coming of the railways and noxious smoke billowing over from King's Cross, bringing lung disease and early death, the elite had moved away, and the riff-raff, poor clerks and petty criminals, had swept in, with their rickety children, scrawny horses and dogs. This depression had persisted, with fluctuations, for over a century until now, in the late sixties, with diesel replacing steam and the Clean Air Act cleaning the air, new colonies from the rising media aristocracy were beginning to snap up the terraces with their fixed low rents, and redefine Islington as the with-it place to be. The post-war, baby-boom zeitgeist had descended and Michael Church and Betty Tadman, as media critic and iconoclastic artist, were among its absolute beginners.

The house was a shell, hardly touched in over a century. They wanted to preserve its historic integrity while at the same time rendering it efficient as a work-place and comfortable as a home. Michael needed his office; Betty needed her studio; they both needed the embrace of a domestic nest, and a steady income from subletting. Being a designer herself and a teacher of design, Betty wanted personally to oversee the project which would reflect her preference for the Dickensian period. She would have loved to have Michael working alongside, but he was no handyman. What she wanted was a keen and competent builder/plasterer/decorator/gardener, with artistic leanings, who would give wing to her dreams and do the donkey work. It was suggested she rang *Problem?*

The doorbell was unchanged since Boz first called on Phiz, at a similar house, in the next street, to discuss his *Sketches*. I pulled it and heard it jangle. Foot-steps on uncarpeted stairs preceded the unchaining and opening of the door by a sparkling-eyed woman, with long straight brown hair, and a warm, smoker's laugh. She wore a home-knitted cardigan over vintage clothes, with beads and rings, which accentuated fingers, gnarled with needlework. She led me upstairs past walls she had already begun papering with brown sheets – 'Parcel paper! Don't you love it?' – into the kitchen on the second floor, still with the original black range, and a blackened kettle which she filled from a juddering tap over a chipped sink.

'Tea or coffee?'

'Coffee please.'

'Do you like cats?'

'I love cats.'

'DOWN MINNIE!' A massive red tom was swiped off the table and leapt sullenly onto a cushioned rocker. 'We didn't know she was male till after the naming ceremony. Nor did we know she'd be so huge, did we Minnie, you sulky puss?' She lit a cigarette and coughed, spooning nescafe into two mugs and adding the boiled water:

'Black or white? We're out of milk.'

'Black please.'

'Don't tell me you're an actor.'

'I'm an actor.'

'I thought so.'

She outlined the plan: fill in cracks in the walls, then line them with lining-paper. Did I like brown? Lining paper is brown, and brown is the colour of the period of this house. There will be posters and pictures: old, less old and very old, on the walls and they go better against brown. Mr Turveydrop – had I read *Bleak House*? – might have practised his deportment here. Mr Brownlow – had I seen the musical? Isn't it *ghastly!* – might have brought Oliver here after the pick-pocketing experience. Uriah Heep and Mr Mikawber etc etc... Am I paying you by the hour?'

She led me through the house, from bottom to top, listing what was to be done. The basement and ground floor were to be let to a young couple with two chihuahuas which she hoped mass-murderer Minnie might mistake for rats! They had just two weeks to wallpaper, carpet and furnish, in tenant-proof, William IV style, getting bargains from Chapel Market; then upstairs to the first floor which would be early Victorian – did I see what they were doing: 'advancing up the decades as we ascend'? – with a baby grand for Michael (he could have been – could *still* be – a concert pianist), a double-bed with screen and in the bow window, Michael's rosewood desk; then up to the second floor with kitchen at the back leading into a dining-room which would double as Betty's studio, already active with Hockneyesque portraits and studies of shattered antiquities, the originals – arms, legs, torsos, buttocks and busts – piled like a battlefield on the floor –

gifts from our buccaneer-friend Alfred, explained Betty; did I do shelving? – the walls to be draped in arts-and-crafts fabrics, degraded by paint. And finally up to the attic and a single room for 'staff' or guests – I could crash here when working late: just shift the sewing patterns, fabrics, treadle machine, peg dolls – 'I buy them naked and costume them for selling'; next to the Beardsleyesque bathroom with prints and posters, mahogany toilet and central free-standing bath with feet.

'That's the plan. You're impressed! Let's shop and as we go, tell me what you do as an actor, how long you will be with us, where in the world we can come and see you *act*.'

We bought brown lining-paper, a papering table, polyfilla, scraper, paste and brush; then from the market, after bargaining, an authentic 1830s mirror for the basement, a short library ladder which could stand in for a step-ladder and swathes of leafy William Morris for 'my' room. We could start right away! I said actually I couldn't stay late, not tonight. I had an audition in the morning.

'Who for?'

'Worcester Rep.'

'Is that what you want to do?'

'If I don't get the film that I'm up for.'

'What film?'

Then I told her about *If...*

I sat bolt upright in bed in the pitch dark. *She mistook him for me!* He went in first because he had a telly, and I let him! She had my own rather measly CV in front of her and she obviously didn't bother to match him up to my photo; whereas when *I* went in, she had *his* much longer, more impressive achievements to thumb through, page after page, which she didn't need to look at closely because suddenly I was saying precisely what she wanted to hear: how I'd been to the very same school she was casting for, was naïve enough not to have the slightest clue about the film which was what Lindsay loved: the innocence of the actor! I, Richard Warwick, was perfect for the part. *'I want you to see Lindsay. I'll talk to your agent.'* I felt sick. I felt winded in the stomach by the Fist of God. I felt like jumping up *now* – it was 2 am – throwing on clothes, running to the callbox and ringing Beryl at home: 'There was a mistake! The part's mine! She thought Warwick was me! She thought I was Warwick! You've got to put her right!' But just as I was throwing back the bedclothes and putting the light on, there was a creak of a door, and Moldy Warp in his grey woolly dressing-gown and slippers, peeped round: 'Is it convenient...? I'm so sorry... Am I interrupting...?' As he padded across the room to the toilet, I fell back. I felt dead, worse than dead, I felt rotten, crumbling. I wasn't there. I was empty space. Of course, Warwick, as me, would have been to see Lindsay, and with that CV and Miriam herself (erroneously) gunning for him, would be cast on the spot. And David Glade would be cast (and Noel Greig would be fucked). It was done. I was finished. There was a flush and the unbespectacled mole padded back: 'Are you all right? Do you want to talk? I do enjoy having you here.' And squeaking the door shut, he slipped back into his hole. I sank into the pillow. I had an audition in the morning. I was sick of posturing as an actor, pretending to pretend, spouting chunks from plays I was never going to be in. *Boy With A Cart* was such a prissy play anyway, and *The Caretaker* was so far from showing me as *me* – I only did it for the laughs which never came. Was it time to crash out? Gardening, driving, wallpapering, was that my destiny? I could ring Beryl to tell them I was sick, sick to death? I could kill myself and who would notice? Denis Grebe would find me expiring and lean over, to deliver his halitosic kiss. I gagged. I had a job to do. Now! Before the words were lost! *'This is the room if you want to take it...'* Write the speech. Get it down. 'Whatever happened to the author of *Scrooge* and *Three Ugly Women*?' Chris Parr had bemoaned. He was *here*, in his shitty shared basement, at two in the morning, scribbling down – no – *typing* – scrolling paper in the typewriter and clack-clacking the opening speech of the play that would later be his ticket to Edinburgh and the Festival, and Scottish TV, and the Highlands and Islands, and the Lindsay Kemp Mime Troupe and Miriam Margolyes (again), Wully the Bull and Bette Davis. It would be his passport (in four chapters' time – don't skip!) to the adventuring-packed, work-bulging, wonderland summer of 1971. But for now...

*

'I don't know this play,' said John Hole of Worcester, when I'd finished the audition. 'Who wrote it?'

'Richard Crane,' said Richard Harbord.

*

I was called back to Betty and Michael's to start the work. There were less than two weeks before the chihuahuas moved in and just a month to complete everything, before Betty left for Hong Kong.

'Why are you going to Hong Kong?' I asked as she poured coffee.

'It's a long story that can't be told. Are you free to keep coming?'

I said sure. I didn't have any prospect of work, at least until the autumn, unless Digby Day, forsaken by Glade, relented and offered me Ariel in the Park. Worcester was a cert, my best ever audition but that wouldn't be till

October and it was only a rep, and I'd done two reps. So I'd probably say no, as I definitely would to Brighton, if also foresaken by Glade, they came begging me to do the Grillo. I was a professional for Chrissake! (Slapping paste on paper) I would *never* do *anything* (climbing and hanging it) – for cheese-cloth and rice-cakes! – (and smoothing it down, then smoothing it across, and down and across, all the way down, all the way, and across, both ways).

'Oh well done!' she exclaimed.

'Is it straight?'

'Straight enough.'

'It's very brown.'

Then over lunch, while Michael played a Beethoven sonata upstairs, we would read his latest article in *The Teacher*, and do the crossword.

'Oh well done!' I'd cry as she solved what I'd solved but kept quiet about, not wanting to impugn her intelligence. We were piecing things together, following clues, inventing answers, furnishing and peopling the house with living art. I would arrive every morning at nine o'clock prompt, and running up the front steps, swing open the door – they'd given me a key – like stepping into a life-size Victorian doll's house. Remove the frontage and imagine the rooms laid out floor by floor – living-room, dining-room, bedroom, second bedroom, bathroom, kitchen ... – all then trangressed, scored through and destabilized to admit sculpture, music, antiquities, books. We were playing cards over tea on the terrace, following an afternoon turfing and rolling the new lawn, slashing through it with crazy paving, when I challenged the primacy of Dickens. 'Isn't he just dabbling in poverty and scooping up cash from his tearful readers? All those cardboard villains and soupy-eyed children: isn't it just two-dimensional penny-dreadful pap, dressed in flouncy language? 'Of course!' she laughed, with a crackling drag on her Peter Stuyvesant. 'That's why everyone loves him, the same way they love London! It's the backcloth against which you can paint a moustache on the Queen, and give Oliver a twist of spiky green hair. "One must have a heart of stone, to read the death of Little Nell without laughing," said Oscar Wilde. Isn't that why we're here, to prick the bubble and get slum-dwellers rocking with anger?' Somewhere, on the rough side of Islington, there lived two artful lads, called John Joseph Lydon and John Simon Ritchie. Only ten at this time, she would meet them six years on, as art students at Kingsway. They had a raw, angry talent and a snarling sense of humour which fitted the rising punk mood of the 70s. One day Betty, walking on Hampstead Heath would hear her name called: 'Hey Bet! You coming to my gig tonight!' It was Ritchie sitting on a wall, hollow-eyed and hopeful. 'Me and Lydon got a band.' She couldn't go; she had a night class, and so missed the debut of Sid Vicious with the Sex Pistols. Johnnie Rotten and Sid were as much her creation as Malcolm Maclaren's. Strip the gloss off Dickens, and you'll find

Vicious and Rotten are the true progeny of Fagin. Douse them in happy endings, and their spores hang in the air, and we inhale them and become either fascists or punks.

*

'Have you ever built a wall?' said Betty. I said yes. (And I had, at school, in the Field Club, instructed by Tick Turner, mixed sand and cement, laid brick upon brick, for the housing of chemistry's neutron tank.) We were in the garden, surveying the trellis that formed a flimsy boundary with the real world. 'There would have been a six foot brick wall here to protect Mrs Jellyby from prying eyes,' explained Betty. 'Can you come Wednesday?'

When I arrived on the Wednesday, there'd been a delivery of a ton of old Georgian bricks, plus sand and cement which we set about mixing in a wheel-barrow. 'Is it one sand to four cement or one cement to four sand? I never know,' said Betty. 'The former,' I averred. 'I mean the latter. One or the other. Odds on, fifty fifty.' I mixed one to four, or four to one, either way, and we finished it in two days. I stayed over on the second day, for dinner and wine, to celebrate the Great Wall, which as night fell, must surely be visible from the moon. I found it hard to sleep under the drapery of the 'staff' bedroom, dreaming of my brickwork tumbling to the blast of critical trumpeting like Jericho. But when I looked out of the window in the morning, it was still standing.

As I was leaving, the new tenants of the ground floor and basement were arriving with their chihuahuas. Former students of Betty's, Quintin Carroway and Juniper Scroggs also brought a pair of rabbits. 'Is this dinner?' said Betty. Quintin roared and Juniper sobbed. They were a gift from her sister who had been nanny to Julian Lennon till John and Cynthia split, leaving the rabbits on the doorstep. They were called Bonnie and Clyde and it was all right, said Quintin, they were neutered so, as with their namesakes, there would be no children. 'Please cuddle them,' said Juniper.

Michael picking up Bonnie and feeling her belly, said: 'I think she's pregnant.'

*

It was party time. Betty was leaving tomorrow for Hong Kong, though oddly, I'd seen no sign of packing. But I had felt a frostiness between her and Michael and putting two and two together, I made at least three. I'd been there when buccaneer-friend Alfred had popped round a week earlier, after leaving his job teaching army kids at the British school in Cyprus. Hauling in another trunkful of hoovered-up Ozymandias body-parts for Betty to immortalize on canvas, he sank onto the bed, gently mocking the foreign policy that puts troops and their entourages in faraway places, just to give ex-prep-school masters *and their wives* an inflated income. Instilling Britishness into British children is all you have to do, and your *wife* doesn't have to do anything, except prove to them, by her presence, that you're not queer. And she doesn't even have to stay. Just one visit, preferably at the beginning, is enough. Then she can take the money and run.

Michael left the room at that point and I carried on unpacking and stacking the thighs and loins and torsos. In the silence that followed, I said: 'Alfred, where did you find all these?' He laughed as if I'd said something hilariously stupid: 'I didn't find any of them! They found me! They were about to be bulldozed and broken up to make rubble for the driveways of luxury villas.'

I was away for the next couple of days. Something I'd eaten kept me up all night being sick. Denis Grebe peeped in as I was vomiting. 'Are you not well?' When I told him to FUCK OFF, he melted away and I later found a note in his microscopic hand saying if I could not be civil, he would have to ask me to leave. I took this as my cue to get writing the rest of *The Tenant*, which seemed to come in great spurts of bile, as if my gut was writing it. I finished a rough draft and was going to show it to Beryl, who I knew wasn't a writer's agent but she knew people who knew people. I dropped in at 17b on the way to town and there was a letter for me postmarked Brighton which I pocketed unopened, and a phone message from Betty. The wall had fallen down. They were having a party tomorrow. Would I come *now* and rebuild? I could stay over and help prepare and do the drinks. And bring your girlfriend. Angie, who took the message, said Betty sounded exotic! Could she come as the GF? Moody was away in the US promoting *Oliver!* and they were cooling off anyway. He'd tried to put his hand up her skirt and she had firmly removed it, twisting his fingers in the process. She was ready for a party. She longed to see the house. Should she come early and help? I said I'll ring you and kissed her, and was away to the tube.

The garden was a catastrophe as if a bomb had hit it. 'We made the wrong mix,' said Betty lighting a cigarette. 'Too much cement, too little sand. Or vice versa. Let's have coffee.' We worked at it all day, still not sure if we'd got the mix right. It looked far too sloppy to me, but I wasn't going to argue. We had it done by nightfall, and once again the Great Wall assumed its majesty in the moonlight. It was quite like old times, except Michael didn't join us, and there was no sign of Alfred. I slept like a log in the staff/guest room and in the morning we began preparing the party. Quintin Calloway and Juniper Scroggs offered to help but Betty dismissed them. Bonnie, had had her bunnies, and there was drowning to be done. We were ready by five. Guests were coming at seven. I went into the garden to practise Flute's speech from *A Midsummer Night's Dream*. We were going to make the wall the focal point of the party. I would come forward and embrace our shrouded creation:

> *O wall, full often hast thou heard my moans,*
> *For parting my fair Pyramus and me!*
> *My cherry lips have often kiss'd thy stones,*
> *Thy stones with lime and hair knit up in thee.*

Then Betty would whip off the covering, and everyone would gasp – but not touch! It's already fallen down once!

I needed a crap, a sudden rush of diarrhoea about to flood my pants. I ran up to the bathroom on the top floor and burst in. I should have knocked, but I was desperate.

Betty was standing naked in the bath covered in soap:

'GET OUT!'

Actaeon surprising Diana in the pool, could not have been more stunned, as antlers burst from his brow and he was dismembered by his dogs. The shock of her shriek had stopped the flow, as if my bowels had turned to stone. Was she voicing the truth? Was that how I should take it? 'Why are you still here? Do you have no life of your own? If you want to act, why don't you *act*? Are you a parasite or just a loser? We have our own problems which are none of your business. We can't go on supporting you.'

It was starting to rain and I was glad. We wouldn't have to do the wall. The party would be indoors. When Angie arrived, I would tell her I wasn't well. She could stay if she wanted to. I would have my shit and then go.

On the way home, on my own, I opened the letter from Brighton. Noel Greig was offering me the part of Sebastian, the teenage gravedigger who wants to be a hairdresser. There would be one week's rehearsal and one week's playing, no cash, but I'd be fed and given a bed (well, a mattress). Would I let him know by return? The job starts on Monday.

Scene Four
THE BRIGHTON LINE

Y ou come in past a jumble of old crescents and terraces piled anyhow into the hillside, then suddenly swing round the final bend against an escarpment of chalk, into the cavern of the station. NEW CHAPTER STARTS HERE, you decide as you cross the concourse into a blaze of sun. You can't see it yet, but you can smell the freshness of the sea: *thalassa thalassa*, as your sandals slap the pavement, all the way down Queen's Road into West Street, as the mighty salty main hoves into view; the word 'hove' reminding you there are two towns here, united in acrimony, like a Donald McGill couple: he, springy and priapic; she, frigid and fierce. The difference, you were told, can be seen in the two statues of Queen Victoria. In Hove, she is majestic, at the head of Grand Avenue, the mighty black widow, engorged on her dead husband, gazing out over the waves which she rules and always will. In Brighton, in the Old Steine, shut out from the Royal Pavilion, head sunk into her shoulders, she looks wrecked after a bad night, festooned, as often as not, in toilet rolls with a traffic cone on her head.

Just yards from the sea, you veer east as instructed, under an arch bearing the sign EVA PETULENGRO, CLAIRVOYANT TO THE STARS, and enter a modest brick-built one-storey Victorian schoolhouse. Inside there are rough tables and chairs and a counter, behind which Jenny, blond and curly, and Ruth, straight and dark, are tossing salad and filling rolls. 'Go straight on through,' smiles Jenny. 'They're waiting for you,' advises Ruth. 'You're not late. We were early,' murmurs Noel with his sleepy eyes, as you enter the windowless, black-painted empty space that was once a schoolroom. He introduces Tim and Flo.

'We know each other.'

You get a hand-shake from Tim and a hug from Flo. You haven't seen Tim since *This Way Out*, two years ago. He looks rougher and villainous, with his piercing black eyes and stubbled, undershot jaw. You saw Flo when she came with Katya and the gang to see you in Bournemouth, but you haven't talked to her properly since *Three Ugly Women*, which you don't think she enjoyed. She looks fatter now and older and grumpier, in a perversely friendly way. The atmosphere is tense and Noel keeps apologizing. It's not like Frinton or Bournemouth or even Cork. Maybe it's knowing it's sunny outside and people are on holiday, or the fact that you all have misgivings about working for no money, but can't voice them without betraying the revolution for which workers are risking their lives in Paris, and for which Martin Luther King has just died.

'Eric Dury,' says Noel, 'whom you don't know, I'm afraid can't be here till tomorrow. He'll be playing the old man. He's eighteen and still at colllege, but he does do a fine line in wheezy old geezers!'

'I thought Grillo was playing the old man,' says Tim.

'So did he,' smiles Noel. 'He so wanted to be part of this, but suddenly he's not free. So!' he slaps his script. 'Now Richard's here, shall we read, if you can put up with me standing in?'

'I could read the Old Man,' offers a husky voice in the shadows. You hadn't noticed the figure, hunched over a script, lit by a lamp which he adjusts so you can now see a curve to his lip which spells mischief and the gleam in one eye, set at variance with the other, as if he's watching you while at the same time scanning the script.

'Paul, you're on the book,' says Noel. 'You said you didn't want to act.'

'I could be persuaded,' says Paul.

*

Tim has a 1948 Sunbeam Talbot, silver, with flappers and running-boards. We pile in: Flo, Paul, Tim at the wheel, and me. After a day of forlorn fantasies in the sepulchre of the Combination, we head off whooping like the Barrow Gang, eastward along the coast, away from the declining sun. It was stifling in the black box, with only half an hour for a late lunch, eating the leftovers in the café, *in character*, insists Noel. But Charly and Sebastian's mum, says Flo, would have gagged on falafel and lentil salad; can't we have chips? Noel smiles without answering. This is going as he intended. Theatre is compression: confinement, cyclical argument, unease, the smell of death. We are rats in a cage. The audience come hungry to watch us savaging one another.

Out of Brighton through Peacehaven, crossing the Greenwich meridian into an unknown tomorrow; out of Newhaven, on to Seaford and East Dene, then swinging south along a rough road, then a track, then a rutted greensward to the sudden cut-off at Beachy Head. The sun is sinking as we spill out, turning the white cliffs red. This is where it ends for the desperate. It's waiting, a sheer drop, should rehearsing a gallows-humour play for no money, become too much. It was Tim's idea to come. He's done this play before, and for one moment I'm imagining, after the tension of Noel's 'methody' approach which was depressing everyone, he's planning to end it all, and take us and the car with him. But when we stop and get out and look down and go cold, it's clear to me why we've come.

Theatre is a precipice. On false step and you're dead. Or you might just fly.

HELLO GOODBYE SEBASTIAN

...is a comedy about death. An old man is sitting by the grave of his wife which is about to be filled in by Sebastian the grave-digger. The Old Man persuades him his wife is not dead but will rise again like Jesus. Sebastian seizes any chance to stop digging; he would rather be a hairdresser, and will be, just as he will escape his mother's clutches and get married; in fact he is secretly married already, just as he is secretly a trained and acclaimed lady's barber. His life is on a roll. Power and fame are his for the asking. The Old Man need not worry. Sebastian will never fill in any grave ever again. At home, the next morning, the newly confident married lady's barber confronts his mother and Charly the lodger with his fantasy-come-true. Very soon he will be free of the graveyard and also this repressive home life and the sordid presence of Charly who can't work due to his cough, and is shagging Sebastian's mum in lieu of rent. But reality seeps in; the fantasy fades.

Mum, tiring of Charly's lust and her son's absurd dreams, rejects them both. Sebastian, cast out, returns to the graveyard, deflates and rejects the Old Man and fills in the grave.

I came across the text of *Hello Goodbye Sebastian* in an old issue of *Gambit*, the International Theatre Review, that I was about to take to the dump. I stopped everything and reread it. Forty-eight years on from playing what turned out to be my best role to date, I found I was speaking the words from memory, timing the gags, playing the pathos. Sebastian is Billy Liar at his most mendacious, pre-Monty Python in his absurd rambles, and at the end hard as nails. In the *Gambit* issue, *Sebastian* is preceded by *Breath*, Samuel Beckett's shortest play, which at the time we dismissed as what it was, a small pile of rubbish: a breathing in, a pause, a breathing out, the end. Originally commissioned by Kenneth Tynan as the opener for *Oh Calcutta!*, but withdrawn by the author when a stage direction was tampered with – 'Faint light on stage littered with miscellaneous rubbish', becoming 'Faint light on stage littered with miscellaneous rubbish *including naked people*' – it now stands, in the *Gambit* issue as the overture to three plays of the late 60s, pitting the human spirit – the breath – against institutional desolation. *The People Show* offers foetuses waiting to be fished out of the cesspool of non-existence; *Social Service* by A F Cotterell poeticises the rotting of a tramp in a hostel; and *Hello Goodbye Sebastian* takes Beckett's thirty-second void and fills it with an hour's worth of impossible dreams.

'They give birth astride a grave, the light gleams an instant, then it's night once more,' says Pozzo in *Waiting For Godot.*

'I do listen, sometimes. I listen to see if they're still breathing. They do make mistakes. Sometimes, not often. Least I don't think it's often,' says Sebastian.

Initially we were to rehearse one week, then play one week, but as the Combination programme – jazz nights, poetry nights, new wave films, discos – was adapting day by day, and as the play hour by hour was coming to chilling life like breath from the grave, it was decided, before even one ticket was sold, to extend to a second week. We'll fill, said Noel. We're new, we are the future!

He gave us Thursday morning off, so we could go to London to sign on at the actors' Labour Exchange in Chadwick Street. The deal Tim and Flo had worked out with Noel was that the Combo would refund our train fares and the cost of one meal. And so it was, the first Thursday morning, slaying both these birds with a ticket on the Brighton Belle, we found ourselves boarding the plush-seated, brass-fitted Pullman, and eating kippers, just seats away from Laurence Olivier, whom we ventured to congratulate on the success of his campaign to have this threatened item retained on the breakfast menu. I wrote home:

Sebastian *is going marvellously. We open on Tuesday and run for two weeks. It's a huge part I'm playing and is me through and through... My mother (Flo Hopcroft) is really, brilliantly horrible to me. She and the lodger (Tim Davies) get married and throw me out, so I go back to the graveyard and become a thug... John Grillo is coming tomorrow and will stay till we open. All 17b will be there on the Saturday, and Betty and Michael are coming on the Friday... Tomorrow we are rehearsing the grave scenes in a real graveyard... It has rained almost every day and the sea does not look inviting, though the other night, Tim drove us all down to Rottingdean. It was an improvization and everyone swam in the nude, except me: I kept my shorts on, as Sebastian would... The Combination is amazing. They show films and as it's a club, there is a chance to see underground films by people like Andy Warhol... I went on the pier the other day with my 'mother' to watch Richard Attenborough who was directing a film on it. John Gielgud, John Mills and Ralph Richardson were there too.*

Noel was right. We filled. Extra seats had to be squeezed in, to accommodate Jim Haynes from the London Arts Lab, the lady from *The Stage*, John Grillo himself and Chris Parr. We were all on edge and there was a *frisson* backstage, just a knuckle's width from fisticuffs. Flo had made the mistake of saying 'good luck' to Eric Dury. He was the outsider whom Noel had insisted should not be spoken to, for dramaturgical reasons. Then Paul let the rumour go round that once again all the café takings had been stolen so there would be no cash for the party at 2 Montpelier Road, the two-up-two-down town house where everyone and his girlfriend were staying wall-to-wall. Noel's only note before the show was a sad smile and a softly spoken: 'You're all crap. All I beg is you deploy your resentment into becoming fab crap.'

I wrote home:

Boy do I understand frustrations and uncertain futures. I am feeling very tired and morose today for various reasons... Sebastian *finished on Saturday after extending to four weeks, and we've been booked to do two weeks at the London Arts Lab, in Drury Lane. I should be feeling great about that. It's the best performance of my career, tho that's not saying much. And we did a thing on Sussex University tv and were far and away the best thing, but that's not saying much either. I suppose I'm just exhausted. We did a couple of late night cabarets which were a knock-out, and in the day we're rehearsing* The Rasputin Show, *with Chris Parr directing and a large cast including Katya, John Grillo, Tim Davies, Paul Brooke and Ian Marter, who was in* A Sky-Blue Life *last year and Ian's girlfriend Katie... I wrote twenty letters the other day and have two auditions coming up if they give me the time off. I didn't get Regent's Park... If I don't get a job by the end of July, I will take an ordinary job. I am not going to stay on the dole. I feel sick every time I go to the Labour Exchange. I went today which is probably why I am feeling morose and exhausted... Most of last week we didn't get to bed before five... David Lascelles, who'd been acting in Kenya, was here playing for the revue and Flo, David and I are planning to set up as a cabaret threesome. It will be nearly all singing. Flo has an amazing jazzy voice like Nina Simone...*

FLO

I look at her face turned towards me on the pillow. In the dim light, she is like a child; no trace of the lines that in the daylight drag her face down into a form of grumpiness. Her lips, slightly open, absolved of distaste, are now soft and kissable, but I don't want to wake her. Her nose, so erect by day, sniffing out any whiff of bullshit, has a squeezableness that is hard to resist. Her eyes are hardly closed, the lids with reddish lashes, not quite elastic enough to veil the popping eyes, which seem to be watching even in sleep. I used to fear her and still do. She has a brow that can fell you, which she uses to terrifying effect on stage, but I can ride that now. I can indulge the fear, and be excited by it, both on stage and off. I never imagined, back in Cork, that we would ever come close. Of the Three Ugly Women, she was the one who seemed least happy with the part, but I was wrong about that, as she told me on Saturday night as we were walking home after the show. Until *Sebastian*, it had been the most painful part she'd ever played. It got right to the heart of her, and she would have cried if Maria and Katya had not been crying already. So she opted to be harsh. In the year since then, she'd had a good run of work, but nothing to challenge her and the harshness had become set; she had put on weight and felt older. She was twenty-nine with a playing age of forty, not that she minded, as long as the parts kept coming. She just wanted more depth, more height, more range, more passion. She was a diva in need of a leading role or she would die. Medea, Cleopatra, Lady Macbeth, she was ready, especially if stripped of royalty, she could play them on the street, with real hunger and deep love. Sebastian's Mum came close. The lines were merciless. Her heart had hardened till finally it broke, when '*you*' – she stopped suddenly, grabbing my head by the hair with both hands – 'when *you* – bloody brilliant – dared – to look at me – and say "bitch" – in that tiny voice – "you *bitch*". How could I turn you out then? But I did.'

We stopped to look at the sea. It was a clear night full of stars. We walked down to the water's edge. 'Come on,' she said suddenly, stepping out of her dress and all her clothes. 'Like Rottingdean. Only this time, be your-self; no shorts.'

I look at her body, half covered by the sheet, unashamed in its fullness, like a Rubens goddess. We had come in from the beach dripping wet in sodden clothes. The house, yesterday packed wall-to-wall with actors and friends of actors, was empty, Tim, Paul, Eric and Noel having got the last train to London as it was Sunday tomorrow. The *Rasputin* crowd wouldn't be back in till Monday and Ruth, whose house this was and who had the only single room, with curtains and a proper bed, was away for three days at a family event. It hadn't occurred to me, till the door clicked shut and we were standing in the hallway breathless and soaked looking at each other, what this emptiness might portend.

'And so to bed,' I said, heading for the boys' dorm.

'Aren't you going to dry yourself first?'

'Sure, if I can find a towel.'

'Ruth has towels.'

We went up to Ruth's room, with its double bed, sheets, floral curtains and fluffy towels.

'Won't she mind?'

'We are a commune. We share. Property is thefty. Love is free. Give us a kiss.'

I made fish lips. She did too. It was all a joke. We'd take the towels and get dry, then crash out in separate rooms. We were grown-up. We were friends, respectful of each other. We were tired. We were alone. Her pertly pointy fish-lips were touching mine till the laughing broke out and the real kissing began. Between the giggles, as we collapsed on the bed, I tried to tell her this probably wasn't my inclination. 'Let's work on the "probably"', she said, rolling me over and unpeeling the wet clothes. She was a careful and patient teacher. She said the part of a man's body she liked best was the 'haunch', that area of thigh rising up to the waist-line, the secret muscular strength of the upper leg, normally encased in pants. With fingertips and lips she traced the subtle borders between haunch and flank and loin and groin. This was her territory which she'd longed to explore ever since Cork, when she saw me at the dress rehearsal gambolling across the stage en-cased only in pants. She sang softly as she worked:

> *I put a spell on you*
> *Cos you're mine..*
> *I can't stand it*
> *The way you always*
> *Running around*
> *I just can't stand it*

The way you always
Putting me down
I put a spell on you
I put a spell on you...

The way Nina Simone sings it, it's a song of fragility, a last resort to use witchcraft because she will die if she loses him. I didn't know at the time, because she hadn't told anyone (only Noel), that it was *she* who would be leaving, and it was this that had spurred her to a galop astride my steaming flanks. She called me Dick, I called her Flopsy, which drove her giggling across the salty terrain. 'Flopsy-Flopsy-Flopsy-Flop... Keep it up, keep it up... siflopsiflopsiflopsiflop... si... floooow.... Go with it... sorry... too soon... too late... is that it...?'

I'm watching. Lamplight giving way to sunrise. We never did shut the curtains. This is our third night. We spent the whole of Sunday together. We watched Sylvia Pankhurst being heckled on the Palace Pier: '*The men of our country are being sacrificed in vain to the blunders of boobies...*' We could have been in the crowd, lacerating Miss Redgrave and earning money as extras, if we hadn't been performing. Then we had fish, chips, peas and tea at Bardsley's in Baker Street, where, for your delectation, the *patron* will do 'cheeky chappie' impressions of Max Miller. Then we just caught the matinee of *The Charge of the Light Brigade* at the Regent, same argument on a smaller scale – booby blunder, vain sacrifice – as *Oh What A Lovely War!*, also featuring Vanessa Redgrave. Then we drank beers and whiskies at the Star and Garter, where Pinkie (my part) meets Ida (Flo's) in *Brighton Rock* and tips the plot into tragedy. When we got back to Montpelier Road, Paul was there, with his sly lip and wall eye, which could see round prevarication. He knew we'd been in Ruth's room. He knew Ruth, having been at University with her and Noel, and had just spoken to her and she was cool, as long as we didn't rumple the sheets and leave pork scratchings in the bedding. She'd be back from the *bar mitzvah* on Tuesday.

That night was slow and long and lovely. I did ask at one point if we shouldn't be taking precautions. She said that was all taken care of. So we carried on. We didn't bother to get up till lunchtime. And even then we just ate from the fridge and went back to bed. Paul was at the Combo, working with Grillo (Rasputin), Ian Marter (the Tsar) and Katie Heyland (the Tsarista). I wasn't called till tomorrow.

It was then that she told me she was leaving.

We walked into Hove. She wouldn't tell me the details. She didn't want people to know because it was a kind of betrayal. When she told Noel, he was characteristically, mildly, furious. She didn't tell him what the job was, just that she couldn't after all play the Dowager Empress in *Rasputin* or do

Sebastian at the Arts Lab. We would have gone to a tea dance on the West Pier but Richard Attenborough was still filming. We swam from the shingly beach, had a meal and a drink and went back to the house, just as the Rasputins were moving in. The boys' dorm was now full and spilling out into the hall. The smaller girls' room, previously Flo's on her own, was now equally crammed. There were even mattresses in the kitchen. Flo and I could have Ruth's room for one more night.

She's waking now. The sun is streaming in. She slips out of bed and pads off to the bathroom. No one else is up yet. She talks to me through the door. She has a train to catch and a new life starting. It's not what she wants to do, but she'll be paid. She'll be famous. She has a meeting this afternoon and starts rehearsing on Monday.

Paul is in the kitchen in his silk dressing-gown making breakfast. The milk is off but there are eggs. Flo has coffee and a piece of toast. Paul calls her a taxi. No one can keep anything from anyone at the Combo. 'Good luck with the Dick Emery Show!' Paul shouts as she steps into the cab, and all of us gathered on the door-step chorus:

'Ooh you are awful! But we like you!!!'

THE RASPUTIN SHOW

John Grillo found the play, gave it to Chris who showed it to Noel, Ruth and Jenny. It had a cast of twenty-five and could be played by fourteen actors.

There was no way such an epic, with riot scenes, mixed media and a jazz band, was going to fit into the tiny black room.

'That's why we're doing it,' said Noel.

'It's the policy of the Combination to have no policy,' said Ruth.

'We don't apply for money,' said Jenny; 'it just falls into our lap. For our children's season on the beach, we went to Apple Corps, the Beatles' company, who said "Great idea! How much do you want?"'

'When we moved into the building,' said Ruth, 'it was a complete tip, but we knew it was what people wanted, so we made it a communal activity for students to come and knock down walls and paint the floor and the chairs.'

'Paul Lundberg,' said Noel, 'a brilliant local artist, did the mural for free and he is now our stage manager, because our stage manager, also called Paul in now acting.'

'We all do everything,' said Jenny. 'We couldn't function if we had a hierarchy.'

'You have a milk-shake in the cafe,' said Ruth, 'and Rasputin is wiping the table.'

'You go for a crap,' said Noel, 'and the Empress of Russia is cleaning the toilet. Which is absolutely true to the play and why we're doing it. Wherever you look today – Paris, Czechoslovakia, Grosvenor Square, Memphis – ruling elites are being overturned, people of peace killed and violence in the name of liberation erupting. You saw it in Russia starting in 1916: the peacemonger assassinated, the oppressed masses crying "Freedom!", the mighty plucked from their seats and made to clean toilets.'

We had three weeks' rehearsal, two of them while *Sebastian* was still playing. The cast, unpaid, though travel and subsistence were found and Equity contracts would follow if the play toured or went to London, were assembled from Combination regulars and the Oxbridge network that came and went through 17b. Grillo was the prime mover, having discovered the Israeli playwright Michael Almaz, newly arrived in London after stirring trouble in Tel Aviv with subversive plays. Ian Marter, who would go on to be Tom Baker's side-kick in *Dr Who*, came with his wife-to-be Katie Heyland to play imperial love-birds Nicky and Allix. David Carson (formerly Collins, alumnus of Leatherhead and Cambridge), David Lascelles (doing the music), John Dodgson (ex-Oxford and distant nephew of Lewis Carroll), Andrew Grant, Giles Block and Nicole Holdaway, joined Tim, Paul and me to complete the cast, with radical class warrior Pam Brighton from Bradford replacing Flo as the Dowager Empress.

I wrote home:

> *I dyed six shirts black for* The Rasputin Show *today...*
> *I play half a dozen parts including Prince Felix Yussupov...*
> *I'm really hoping this will be my last month on the dole...*
> *I seem to be having a lot of auditions these days...*

Rasputin opens on Tuesday. We are sold out for the entire run...
Beryl has got me an audition for a musical called Hair...
I had an audition for Nottingham Playhouse which went brilliantly...
Two people from the New Arts Theatre came to Rasputin *last night...*
I'm writing a short play about two girls and a psychopath...
I haven't forgotten the National Debt; I just haven't any money...
I play the Tsarevich (13) who suffers from haemophilia...
We all line up at the end, but instead of bowing, we get shot.

*

It was never going to be as good as it was in the black hole of the Combination, filled to bursting every night. The West End plushness of the New Arts where we transferred for a two week run – the same venue where *Waiting For Godot* had been trashed by the critics – would be a challenge we felt we could meet, presuming the critics had learnt their lesson. And it did go well. So when, after the first night party and a late dinner in Chinatown, we piled into Tim's Sunbeam to catch the first editions as they came out of Fleet Street, we were stunned to read: *total lack of wit... farcical send-up... shovelled onto the stage... undergraduate romp inadequately prepared... ineffably silly and dull... a very noisy evening... forced, feeble and painfully unwitty... Of the numerous illegitimate offspring of* Oh What A Lovely War!, The Rasputin Show *seems the most pointless...*

It was Sunday before the mood changed but by then it was too late. There would be no future beyond a pre-booked week in Cambridge which we assumed would now be cancelled. But as with *Godot*, and Pinter's *The Birthday Party*, it was the Sunday reviewers who would take time to assess the impact of the play, and give it a fair hearing.

Ronald Bryden in the Observer:

> *It's the nearest I've seen in the modern theatre to genuine melodrama... Both belief and disbelief, laughter and horror accommodate themselves within the play's convention... In Keystone Kop slow-motion, Rasputin's assassins tip-toe in to view their work, tugging grotesque false moustaches. Satisfied they retire to drink mimed toasts, leaving Yussupov to be savaged by the uncannily risen corpse... The killing of the Tsar and his family is handled even better. Seating themselves graciously for that last photograph at Tsarkoye Selo, they fall into the attitudes of waxworks. Guns rattle, red lightning flashes. The waxworks collapse open-mouthed and staring, like a heap of stiff dolls. The greatest of Europe's empires crumbles before your eyes into a crude pier-end peep-show of European rubbish.*

And Harold Hobson (Sunday Times)...

> The Rasputin Show *reminds one of the shock caused to the cultivated by the early films of Chaplin, those slapstick, slung-together, unfinished manifestations of genius which were dismissed as rough, raucous and very very common by people of good taste...* The Rasputin Show *too, is crude pop-art stuff; the late 20th century equivalent of the custard pie. Its dialogue is as simplified as old subtitles; it abounds in false beards; it is tinglingly, stunningly alive... John Grillo uses the freedoms of burlesque to do what in straight playing would be impossible: to get us to believe that Rasputin is at once a sexually-obsessed swindler, and a man who can perform miracles... Richard Harbord as Prince Yussupov and Paul Brooke as a portly minister, are outstanding... The show lasts two and a half hours and (a rare thing for me) I would not have it a minute shorter.*

SUMMER OF '68

Things were happening thick and fast, prospects soaring, love-life unleashed, it's hard to assemble the summer of '68 in any order. I remember the decline and collapse of civilization at Montpelier Road: mould in the milk, mice in the trash and rancour in the stinky six-mattressed boys' dorm, spilling out into the hall. I remember missing Flo and trying to bed down with Nicole in the hall and people walking over us; in outdoor shoes because of the state of the bathroom, where the cistern lurched away from the wall when you pulled the chain, so generally you left it unpulled and the bowl filling up with unflushed shit. I remember a standoff with Ruth who had taken to locking her room, while we rats devoured each other. I remember Noel, uncharacteristically losing his rag and hammering on her door, and Jenny weighing in by phone from her own under-occupied three-bedroom family home in Hove, that she'd slogged for a year to enable jobless actors to have jobs, and people with a social conscience to be thankful to have any kind of roof over their head; and if these thesps continued to be uppity, then she would pull the plug on the West End, which was such *anathema* to the Combo's founding ethos, it was making her want to shift the whole thing to a really needy location, such as Deptford.

I remember going to London: a last trip on the Brighton Belle, and sighting, not Olivier, but Dora Bryan, who was not bothered that kippers were no longer on the menu. I remember auditioning for Lincoln Rep and discussing *The Tenant* with the director Philip Hedley. I wanted to act in a theatre that did new plays, eg mine. He said he couldn't offer anything immediately but I should send him the play and come and see him in Lincoln. I remember auditioning for *Hair* and being asked to strip, as if for a school medical. I moved into a room, with no windows, in a communal flat in Clanricarde Gardens, where I finished a short play about two girls with physical problems – one is pregnant, one has no arms – in a park as it gets dark. They encounter a man who wants to help them, out of love for humanity. If they resist he will have to kill them. I gave the script to Chris who showed it to Jim Haynes, one of the exiled American counter-culture pioneers, who were igniting the Fringe. Jim had co-founded the Traverse Theatre in Edinburgh and was now running the Drury Lane Arts Lab, where we were scheduled to play *Hello Goodbye Sebastian* for two weeks; Grillo playing the Old Man, Katie Heyland playing Mum.

Jim read *Girl With No Arms*, and said Chris should direct it, in a double bill for the second week of the *Sebastian* run. Paul Brooke would play the man, Nicole and Katya would be the girls and I would book-end the play, as I had done in *Three Ugly Women*, as the singing park attendant. As long as we were working, it was okay, but recreationally, this was a sticky period. I hadn't realized that the moment with Nicole, being trodden on under the stairs of 2 Montpelier Road, was expected to lead to something. When I went round to 17b, where she was staying with Katya, and I'd heard she was in a mess, Katya turned me away. I learnt later that Nicole had downed pills and a bottle of vodka and as I walked away, pissed off and self-righteous, was being induced to vomit up all feeling for me.

> MAN (from Girl With No Arms): *I really couldn't understand what she was fussing about. So I knelt down and shook her. And the more I shook her the more she cried. It was very dark; I could hardly see her. She was huddled on the ground. I couldn't understand why she was so afraid. It was dry inside the tree although the ground was damp. I could feel bits of fungus sticking out of the wood. I had to hit her to stop her crying. I didn't want to hurt her. I wanted   to talk to her. The last thing I wanted was to hurt my precious girl...*

✳

I didn't get *Hair* which I'd felt, like *If...* was mine and in the bag - good money, shock potential, in the eye of the zeitgeist etc - but what the hell. I was offered Westcliff-on-Sea, playing juve character for the season, but I'd been there, done that at Frinton, so turned it down. Then just as we were opening *Rasputin* at the Arts, Beryl phoned to say Nottingham were offering a year's contract, to ASM and play as cast, starting next week. 'I know, I know,' she said, 'how could I even *think* you'd do ASMing? But theatre's a funny business. Sometimes you have to go one step back to go three steps forward.' She said I'd start with *King John*, playing the Archbishop of Canterbury and a French Lord, rehearsing in London, so it wouldn't matter if I was acting in the evening. Except, as I pointed out, I would be in Cambridge the following week and obviously couldn't commute. Also there was a new Tsar, Roger Gartland, to be rehearsed in, as Ian Marter would be off in the Tardis with Tom Baker. How many scenes was the Archbishop in anyway? Was the French Lord a pivotal role? I looked them up in my Shakespeare and found neither had any lines. Was this some kind of joke? Stuart Burge, the director, had told Beryl, if I was uncertain, I should come and have a talk. He lived just round the corner from Clanricarde Gardens. We'd got on well at the audition. I'd done the speech from *The Tenant,* emphasizing the stammer, not realizing till he spoke, that he also had a speech impediment. He wanted to know about the play the speech came from, and the Combination and *The Rasputin Show*. Could I arrange tickets for him at the Arts? So I did, and wished I hadn't; it was a poor house and not our best show, and he didn't stay at the end. So I was ready to decline everything when I knocked at his door, and he led me into his kitchen, and at first didn't hear him saying *Rasputin* was *just the sort of show he was wanting to do at Nottingham*. He was taking over from John Neville who had built the Playhouse up to be the third most talked about company in the country. He would start with two classics: *King John* which he was directing and *School For Scandal* which Jonathan Miller would direct. His aim was to treat the plays as newly written discoveries, hot off the typewriter. Then having eased the audience in, he would shock them with a really new piece, an epic, he chuckled, to knock spots off the establishment. *The Ruling Class* was by an unknown writer called Peter Barnes. Christopher Plummer would play the lead. What did I think? Was I up for it? I said it all sounded very exciting, but why (I should have added) couldn't I play the Dauphin in *King John*, or even the child Prince Arthur who gets killed? I was playing a convincing thirteen-year-old as the Tsarevich (who also gets killed). I would have been playing seventeen in *If...* but for a cock-up. I didn't say any of this, just sat mute, till Stuart, very kindly, said he realized it must be a shock, after coming through the hothouse of the Combination and in one leap, playing a major part in London to considerable acclaim; it must be a downer, to be offered only an acting/ASM position playing minor roles, but he wanted to be able to build actors from the ground up. There would be no shortage of work. In addition to the repertoire – and I would be in all the plays, either acting or ASM-ing – there would be schools' work, special Sunday night shows, try-outs of new plays and a cart at the Goose Fair, Nottingham's annual gala, for which the Playhouse would perform political cabaret in the style of a mystery play.

Was I up for that? He would be asking Chris Parr, who'd had a director's traineeship at Nottingham under Neville, to direct the Goose Fair show. Was I on board? It would be okay to miss rehearsals during the Cambridge week. Come to the White House Hotel, Earl's Court Square 10.30am Monday and all week, then missing the next week, come to the Playhouse for 10am 29th August? The fixed acting/ASM wage is £12 a week.

SANGYANG WITI

The first person I saw when I walked into the Arts Theatre Cambridge was Di Lubbock. She was working on a temporary basis as Personal Assistant to Commander Blackwood, the theatre manager, and playing cabaret gigs in pubs in the evenings. She was renting a little rose-trellised cottage on the river. I should come and have tea. Better still, tomorrow, Zanna Raleigh-King, Estelle Tudor-Landor and a boy (well a man – he was a former child actor) called William Pennell Rock, were coming down in his Lincoln Convertible. We should have lunch then go punting.

That night, after the show, there was a party in the Circle Bar. Di sang and we danced. She asked where I was staying. I said we were all in a flat next to the Footlights Club, but it was like Waterloo Station with friends and everyone coming and going. She whispered in my ear: 'Come and stay at my place.' As we were calling a taxi, I told Tim if I didn't come back, someone else could have my bed. 'Let us know where you're going,' said Chris. But we'd gone, holding hands and giggling. When we got to the cottage, she lit candles and put on the new Beatles' single and we sang along to it, dancing, kissing, then falling out of our clothes, into bed:

> Hey Jude, don't be afraid...
> You were made to go out and get her
> The minute you let her under your skin
> Then you begin
> To make it better...

*

William Pennell Rock was a graduate student at King's reading philosophy. He had previously studied at Yale, Harvard and the Sorbonne. He had just come back from Bali researching Oracular Art, specifically Sangyang Witi, the Balinese god of inspiration, that actors pray to, to drain them of ego and allow the Muse to take possession. Over lunch at the Eagle, then punting us all upriver to Grantchester, then in the open-top Lincoln cruising the fenland by-ways and stopping for cream teas under cloudless skies, Pennell Rock was talking keenly, wittily, about what makes an actor. He was one as a child, till he got bored with learning lines, and being obliged to be a public person both onstage and off, never losing himself completely inside the role, never becoming the ghost that houses the muse that makes the play. He had seen *The Rasputin Show* in London, and was coming again tonight. There was something primordial and frighteningly modern both in our acting that transcended conventional theatre, and in the subject of assassination, which was coming to be the hallmark of 1968. When people of grace and healing are destroyed and the pillars of peace are brought down; when Robert Kennedy says it's time to 'tame the savageness of man and make gentle the life of this world', and is then killed; when Martin Luther King says he has been to the mountaintop and seen the Promised Land and is then gunned down, war becomes the only option. Rasputin was a peacemonger. 'Make love not war' was his mantra but the Tsar would not listen. Rasputin had the power to stop the blood, both in the bruising of the Tsarevich and in the broken heart of Russia. The Tsar was God's annointed but God was vengeful, and not always right. Remember the weak! Rasputin shouts to Him. Crucifixion is not the answer! Hundreds of thousands of corpses of young Russians strung out on barbed wire, will not save our country! If I die at the hand of peasants, you, Tsar of all the Russias, will have nothing to fear. But if I am murdered by princes, then the blood will never be washed from their hands; brother will kill brother, till there are no men of nobility left in the land, and you, your beloved Allix and all your children will be killed by the Russian people, just two years from my death.

They dropped me at the stage door a good hour before the show. It had been an idyllic day, following a beautiful night. My years at Jesus, my time with the Marlowe and the Footlights, had raced by at such a pace, I'd never imagined indulging the beauty of the landscape, trailing a hand in the water as the punt glided under the willows, and listening to a philosophy that seemed tailor-made for this moment. Sangyang Witi, my namesake and my god, would go with me on stage tonight. I would yield to his genius and be lifted into giving my finest performance. Then on Sunday after the sunniest, loveliest week of my life, Di would see me to the train, put a finger to my lip and vanish like a dream – we would never meet again – and I would surrender to the topsy-turvy law of the theatre, that sends you up the ladder to national acclaim, then straight down the snake into acting/ASM-ing in a provincial theatre; from steadily acquired mastery of your art, to apprenticeship at a stroke, sitting unknown, in a row of beginners fresh from drama school, in the ballroom of the White House Hotel, watching Barry Foster (King John), T P McKenna (the Bastard), Moira Redmond (Constance), and a nose-in-the-air, stage-school kiddy-actor, who you wouldn't mourn when he was killed (Prince Arthur [my part!]). I had worried about rushing into taking a backward step and spending months regretting it, but Pennell

Rock had convinced me that planning, reasoning, expecting things in the theatre was a mug's game. The Muse knows best. Let her lead.

Signing in at the stage door, I thought I was early and would have time to immerse myself in contemplation of Sangyang Witi, before the company breezed in, but they were all there already. I felt a chill in the air as if something had happened. I asked Katya 'What's going on?' She said: 'It's Roger. He was rushed into hospital last night. Chris will be playing the Tsar from now on. We've been rehearsing with him all day. You should have been told but no one knew where you were.'

It was actually our best performance. We were all on edge. All thoughts of the Muse and Sangyang Witi, went out of my head and I just acted the part. We were not a happy company. Chris, since Cork, had grown to loathe performing, and his discomfort showed through as a fatal weakness of the Tsar. At the end, when he carried me on in his arms for the final photo – the Tsarevich was bleeding inwardly and couldn't walk – I could feel his heartbeat slowing, as if relieved that soon, instead of being photographed, which he hated, we would be shot and it would be over; until tomorrow.

Scene Five
NOTTINGHAM

I step into the light and the roar goes up. The solo call dates from Billy's time as a dancer. In his day there were flowers, a reaching up to the gods and a deep choreographed bow. With us it's step in, quick bow, step out, join the line. There are seven actors, and one nude artiste, to be got through. I come on fourth after Gorgeous Gladys (now clothed) and the two actors who only appear in the last scene; then comes Kika, my sister; then old David, our grandad; then Kathleen, our gin-sodden, singalong mum; and lastly Denis Quilley, the finest actor I ever knew.

As I bow, do I know this is the apex of my time here? I arrived in August; I will leave in July. It's now February, the mid-point, but I don't know this yet. There's *The Hostage* coming up; I could play the captured English soldier. And *King Lear* in the autumn; I could be Edmund, or the Fool. Or I could stay with *The Entertainer*, do the tour, go into town. This seems to be the pattern here. The show does well, it travels and gets known, and this one is a hit: all due to Billy Chappell. His long fingers, balancing his slim cigarette, have a magic touch. After forty years of ballet, revue and only recently straight plays, he has crafted 'an unclassifiable classic'. Is it music hall merged with kitchen sink? A star vehicle in collision with a

Shakespearean tragedy? Or just 'rattling good entertainment that rivets the attention and bites with irony' (The Stage)?

However you look at it, the reviewers seem to be saying that Quilley is more human than Olivier who created the part ten years ago, and that this production with its 'distinctive and satisfying quality' has taken Stuart Burge's phenomenal first season at the Playhouse to dizzying new heights.

I join the line. Kika's next. They love her (so do I). She smiles as she grips my hand, then Kathleen Michael bows like a seasoned pro. I once asked her how you get noticed in a large company, when there are new actors coming in all the time; how do you avoid the 'school for scandal' of the green room and not end up dead behind the eyes? She said there are three sure ways to keep the passion burning: act, act again, act better. And so I have done. I have been a mute archbishop, a sedan-chair-carrier, a consumptive servant who takes an age to get his lines out because of mucus and bleeding, a crumbling lord, a silhouette of Jack the Ripper, a rescued miner in a mining disaster, a golly who transforms into a Jamaican pickney-boy, and Donalbain. I've stage-managed a schools' tour; done get-ins and get-outs; been primper of wigs and provider of fags to Madame Arkadina (Fenella Fielding); had to learn the whole of the King in *King John* when Mr Foster was unwell, only for him to recover (shit); and the whole of Konstantin in *The Seagull*, when Mr Eyre had the snuffles, ditto (ditto). I have done my apprenticeship. I have earned my promotion out of the shadows into the light.

*

It all began on Monday 12th August, 10.20 am, as I crossed Earl's Court Square and skipped briskly up the steps of the White House Hotel. I was a West End actor, in the final week of *The Rasputin Show*, now about to rehearse *The Life and Death of King John*, which would be Stuart Burge's inaugural production at Nottingham. I had accepted 'play as cast', even 'acting ASM', presuming a rapid ascent through the ranks, towards featured, even starring roles, and had already negotiated a week's leave of absence to accommodate the run of *Rasputin* in Cambridge. *John* would rehearse the first week in London, then decamp, minus me, to Nottingham, whither I would hasten on Sunday 25th, to report at the Playhouse for stage management duty, 26th 9 am.

I cross the lobby towards the throng of noise in the ballroom: actors with trained voices hailing one another, drinking coffee or tea, choosing bourbons or digestives. There are faces I half know and names I catch in the medley of conversations: Barry Foster, stocky with spun-gold hair and pale eyes, who will play the King; T P KcKenna (the Bastard), warmly Irish with a resounding laugh, greeting Moira Redmond (Constance), stately and amused. 'After you,' I bow to a kindly tallish actor at the coffee urn, whom someone has greeted as David Dodimead. 'I think I saw you,' I mention, 'in *Hamlet* at the Old Vic, some years ago. We were introduced by my teacher who knew you, Geoffrey Bernau.' 'Why, bless your sweet memory,' smiles Dodimead, doddering off, as I am led by Ken the stage manager to a group of youngsters stationed, like servants, behind the chairs which they have previously set out in a broad circle. I am introduced to John, Joan, Jean, Francis, Ben and Evadne. They have been here since 9.30. Was I not telephoned last night that I should have been here then also? 'I was on stage,' I reply. No one says: 'Wow! Where? What in? Why are you here? Why is a West End actor taking a deliberate step down...?' And I don't reply: *'Because I'm a ghost who can't exist without acting, even mute roles...* and because Nottingham is the finest regional theatre north of Stratford, and I will clamber over all you eager turks to reach the stars if it kills me.'

There's a tall, stocky boy with dark curly hair and a square face heading towards me. 'You must be Dicky Hardboard,' he grins. 'I saw you being brilliant in the West End. I'm Nick Clay.'

The room is hushed, as if his name has stunned everyone. We all sit. Stuart is talking: '*Commodity*, or self-interest, is at the core of this play, and what makes it so modern. People act for their own advantage and dress up their action to dazzle the ones who in the end will suffer. So our stage will resemble a hall of mirrors revolving to fairground music, and the costumes are all silk with silver and gold trimmings. The only plain figure, in brown leather, is the Bastard. He comes from nowhere, is caught up in and plays along with the "commodity" frenzy, assesses the carnage and his own prospects of kingship, then steps aside. He's a fiction, not mentioned in history, and as modern as Jimmy Porter. This play could have been written yesterday and we will do it as if it were.'

The readthrough gets under way. As the French Messenger, Nick has a total of eighteen lines. I have not a word. But that's fine: starting from rock bottom, the only way is up. '*Mad world! Mad kings! Mad composition!*' protests T P's Bastard, with a dash of Irish.

> '*Commodity, the bias if the world...*
> *This bawd, this broker, this all-changing word...*
> *Since kings break faith upon commodity*
> *Gain be my lord for I will worship thee!*'

But he doesn't. In the end, self-interest is not enough, just as acting, if you're good at it, is more than 'strutting and fretting'. Not many thesps are smart enough to make it from petitioner to *practitioner*, but Nick Clay will be one. Mature in his muscled skin, heroic in a square-faced, broken-nosed way, he is cool about ASM-ing; will make tea, buy props, sweep the stage, hang lamps; always just keen enough, but never too keen. Men are drawn to him; women love him. Stripped, he has a hairless, alabaster torso, which he wears with a boxer's ease. He could be the white younger brother of his namesake Cassius, now free of his slave name and fighting beyond boxing against oppression and war. Will Nick similarly raise his game and transcend acting? His special friends are his RADA mates Hayward Morse and Cherith Mellor who have been launched, straight from drama school, as instant rising stars, playing the Dauphin in *John* and Lady Teazle in *School for Scandal*. 'Don't you feel just a twinge of envy,' I say to him, 'seeing them in the limelight while you're still shifting flats?' He just smiles as if to say: 'Natürlich, Rickety Sideboard: when the eye can't hit what the hand can't see, go sting like a butterfly, float like a bee.'

*

I wrote home:

> *I have just crowned King John. I am the deaf-mute Archbishop, and a* sourd-muet *French Lord. The production is dazzling. The set is all silver and with silver and gold swords and banners and with everything revolving and reflecting light, it looks like we're on fire. We go up on Sept 24th, then* School for Scandal *opens the following week, directed by Jonathan Miller. Being a doctor he wants all of us, right down to the lowliest servant (me) to have a disease. Rowley, the butler, who has to carry a full tray of filled glasses across the stage, and back again, has Parkinson's. Lady Sneerwell, under her powdered beehive, had a second balding, pox-pitted wig. The style is Hogarth, rather than Gainsborough. The stage gets noisy with extroverts not listening to one another. When someone is speaking at length, those addressed, are going 'yes yes yes yes yes...' like nodding puppets. Jonathan insists there are no small parts. With just two lines (seventeen words), as Lady Sneerwell's servant, I've been granted a heavy head-cold, bordering on emphysema, with a rope of cochinealed chewing-gum spirit-gummed to my nostril, and every precious word wrung out of snot-filled lungs.*

The reviews hailed the '*anti-romantic, blackly humourous... stripping away of layers of varnish and chocolate-box prettiness... the shock of showing Georgian gentry living in flea-ridden squalor...*' What they didn't see was the brilliance of Miller in rehearsal. If he sat at all it was like a coiled spring, which would twang and he would be up on the stage with a new thought, a new attitude, playing cartoon versions of characters, out of which the actor could then extract a performance. This was rehearsing as jazz, and we were the lucky audience. Though ground-breaking in performance, it was never going to be as funny, as spontaneous as this.

THE RULING CLASS

The most exciting thing that can happen to a dramatic critic (wrote Harold Hobson) *is when he is suddenly and unexpectedly faced with the explosive blaze of an entirely new talent of a very high order. This happens very rarely. In twenty years of reviewing plays it has happened to me for example, only four times. The first was the original production at the Arts Theatre in 1955, of Samuel Beckett's* Waiting for Godot; *the second, John Osborne's* Look Back in Anger *at the Royal Court a year later. The third was Harold Pinter's* The Birthday Party *at the Lyric Hammersmith in 1958; and the fourth, Peter Barnes's* The Ruling Class *at the Nottingham Playhouse, directed by Stuart Burge, in the autumn of 1968.*

When it first landed on Stuart's desk, *The Ruling Class* was six hours long with a cast of twenty-five, and multiple sets. After the extravagance of John Neville, Stuart wasn't expected to blow a whole year's budget on the first three productions, and it's a measure of his skill that he could get the play approved and the script edited down to half its length. Casting Christopher Plummer, a respected classical actor, as the lead, was what probably swung it, plus the *dramatis personae* – an earl, a bishop, a QC, a toastmaster – which made it sound like William Douglas Home. The fan was whirring, cooling any misgivings, unaware of the glittering shit heading towards it.

We were gathered in the rehearsal room for the readthrough, waiting for the 14th Earl of Gurney to make his entrance. A call had been made to the hotel where Mr Plummer was staying and we were assured that he was, at that moment, just finishing his cornflakes. He was not known to be a method actor, yet this attitude, serene and godlike, sounded very like the character he was about to play. The 14th Earl was a paranoid schizophrenic with his own sense of timing. We took a coffee break while the Deputy Stage Manager was sent in a taxi to the hotel to escort the star, who was known to be critical of the acting industry following an 'awful, gooey' film musical he had made two years earlier, retitled *The Sound of Mucus*. The DSM came back alone, having just missed Mr Plummer, who having finished his cornflakes, and a second cup of tea, had ordered a taxi to take him to the station, whence he had caught the next train to London.

Maybe he just didn't like the play and I agreed with him. I wrote to Jamaica: 'It is an awful show, very boring and pretentious... A few visual effects come over well, but the rest is a long yawn...' Reading the text again, half a century later, I still can't understand how it won West End awards, Oscar nominations when filmed, pride of place in the Hobson canon. The characters are cartoons, pitching cliches to the gallery; the text relying on borrowed snatches of song-and-dance and cod psychiatry. The bonkers Earl who flabbergasts his crusty relatives and gets away with murder, makes his impression by spouting lists: *I am the Creator... Khoda, Yahweh, Shangri-Ti and El, the First Immovable Mover... Lord of Hosts, King of Kings... the One True God, the God of Love, the Naz!* It reads like a schoolboy sketch, stretched out till it's threadbare, but you'd never know that from the production. All the stops were pulled out to make a horrific last swipe at an imperial system that was refusing to die. But take away the sound and fury, and in my lonely view, it was the the same dead duck as the film *If...*, the message of which seemed to be: if your house is resting on rotten pillars from a bygone age, you should just pull it down on your own head. I wrote home:

> *Derek Godfrey, who stepped in to play the lead instead of Plummer, is a very likeable actor, the last you would ever cast as the Earl, which makes him perfect... I play the manifestation of his inner thought, in the form of Jack the Ripper, in silhouette: just a pose, and you can feel the audience go silent as I raise my knife. Later I play First Lord in the House of Lords who makes a speech about flogging. There are three of us and twenty-eight dummy lords, wheeled on, on two giant trucks swathed in cobwebs. For make-up, we use cotton wool in the mouth and up the nose, plasticene for eye-brows and cheek-bones stuck on with spirit gum, and fuller's earth mixed into a flaky mud-pack and spread all over the face, and shoe-whitening in the hair. As it is impossible to speak with all that on, our lines have been pre-recorded and we mime to them!*

REBELLION

I was beginning to stagnate. We were four plays in, *Close the Coalhouse Door*, inserted, on its way down from Geordie-land, for a pre-London run. I had joined John, Joan, Jean, Nick, Francis and Evadne, as miners and their wives, at the pit-head and in the pub, and between singing anti-capitalist songs and drinking Newcastle Brown, we ad-libbed our frustrations. With evening shows, matinees and two schools' tours, we were doing twelve shows a week and working up to a fifteen hour day, including Sundays. This meant I hadn't been able to be in the Goose Fair show which Chris Parr had come up to direct. He had been staying in my flat, which I shared with a Old Catholic deacon, a friend of a friend of Betty and Michael's; the Old Catholics being the remnants of a sect from the 19th century who parted from Rome over papal infallibility, taking with them a love of dressing up (so the deacon demonstrated) in elaborate copes and chasubles. I had hoped to spend time with Chris and maybe work on something we could offer for a Sunday night, but being so busy, I hardly saw him, and when I did, he wasn't in a mood to talk, being pissed off with the zero attention he was getting from the Playhouse.

On the night of the final performance of *Coalhouse*, things came to a head. The stage hands, spurred on by the politics of the play, had been agitating for better rates and who-does-what clarification, following a dispute over the shifting of a book-case in *Scandal*. As a container of props (books) was the book-case itself a prop? In which case, shifting it was the business of the stage management. Or was it scenery, in which case only separately unionized stage hands could touch it? With four plays in repertoire, and get-ins and get-outs jostling to fit the schedule, we all had to get down and shift book-cases willy-nilly. This was grossly unfair, we contended, for us ASMs, who had performing to do as well, including costume changes and 'sooting up' for the re-enaction of the famous rescue from the 'thin seam'. One of our number, John Manford, a big-fisted actor, who had been called to audition for the next James Bond, but been barred from going, led a walk-out of both branches of the backstage staff including Joan, Jean, Nick, Ben, Evadne and me. Mutinous, we went up straight to the bar to join the company: they were actors, we were actors, and even though we had been supping Newky Brown all evening, we felt entitled to have another as a farewell to departing colleagues. When Ken the Stage Manager squared up to John, reminding him of his contract, John's fist lashed out. There was a brawl and Ken with a bust lip phoned Stuart, who came round, said nothing, just watched as we bolshevists reprised our anthem:

> as soon as this pub closes,
> as soon as this pub closes,
> as soon as this pub clo-o-o-o-oses,
> the revo-lution starts...

and slurping our whiskey chasers, went back to strike the set.

The next day, we were summoned to Stuart's office, all of us plus Ken. Behind the desk, flanking Stuart, were George Rowbottom, the general manager and the company secretary Amanda Wilkins. I should have mugged up on Stuart's background, to understand the steel in his little frame which along with a skittish charm and a difficulty sometimes forming words (so you had to listen with extra care), had got him, as Peter Barnes later wrote of him, to be 'one of the greatest English stage directors':

> With his crumpled neck-scarf and tousled hair, he always looked like a bemused gnome who had turned vagueness into a higher art form. It was partly an act, of course. Behind the air of blinking bewilderment lurked an incisive, laser-tooled mind.

He trained as a civil engineer but gave that up to play the boy in Olivier's *Henry V* at the Old Vic. His audition piece was *You Are Old Father William*, which he did standing on his head. He spent the war with the Army Intelligence Corps, on top of a mountain in Sicily. And at Nottingham, in his first season, he led a company of two hundred or more actors, through a repertoire of fourteen plays, six of which transferred or were recreated in London. He was as visionary as Diaghilev, as unyielding as Bligh. When all his acting ASMs came before him in a mass, protesting overwork and exhaustion, and threatened a walk-out, he had Amanda bring in a pile of actors' letters with photographs – so high, she could hardly see where she was going! There were enough, this week alone, standing by to replace each one of us, ten times over. He understood the complaint but was not going to allow it to cast a shadow over the season. Were we not being paid extra for every performance over the eight, almost doubling our weekly wage? 'If you think this is hard, walk out now, the door is open.'

*

I once played the triangle in the Leatherhead school orchestra. I had to wait seventy-five bars before coming in with my ting-aling. I was told it was a first step towards fuller participation in the adventure of making music. The terror of missing or mis-timing my moment, was worse than any stage-fright, and after one concert, I gave up. The same dread was now beginning to overwhelm me at Nottingham. I was getting paranoid about cues, and heard my precious lines coming out, mis-pitched, in a tinkle or a bark. I watched the other actors, especially the young ones, Hayward and Cherith, commanding the stage with richly toned voices and practised moves. And the new actors coming in for *The Seagull, Whoopsadaisy* (a comedy by Keith Waterhouse and Willis Hall), and for *Macbeth, The Entertainer* and the two plays in the Christmas season – Barrie Rutter, Sheila Ballantine, Kika Markham, Peter Eyre – had a freshness and a vigour that made me feel old, unnoticed.

I decided to see Stuart. He said his door was always open, though he usually wasn't there, and he wasn't when I went. So I left a note and two scripts with Amanda. 'He's away,' she said, cocking her head to one side, as if welcoming a diversion. 'For three days, didn't you know? Pre-production. The film. *Julius Caesar* which he is directing with Chuck Heston and Johnny Gielgud. How can I help?' I explained these were plays I had written to accompany *The Tenant*. 'What's *The Tenant*?' I told her it was the short play that grew out of the speech I did for my audition. 'I was there!' she enthused. 'I remember it!' This was great. I went on: 'These plays all have a Jamaican theme – it's where my home is – and as a trilogy would be amazingly economical to produce.' I wanted to say after the extravagance of the opening season, surely Stuart would be looking for something cheap and at the same time topical and controversial. But I couldn't get a word in. She was bowled over by Jamaica. Did I grow up there? Could I do the accent? I wanted to ask her to remind Stuart that he'd promised to promote me to playing real parts, instead of walk-ons. He was bringing in all these eager new actors and I felt I was being side-lined. But Amanda was gabbing on about a brilliant part in one of the Christmas plays that required an actor with a Jamaican accent and she didn't know of any in the company who could do one. Could I do one? If I could, then the part of the Golliwog in *The Forest of Change* by Merula Salaman, who was mine for the asking!

RUDE CIRCUMFERENCE

But if you fondly pass our proffer'd offer,
Tis not the roundure of your old-fac'd walls
Can hide you from our messengers of war
Though all these English and their discipline
Were HARBOR'D in their rude circumference...

We were into the final week of *King John* and discipline was slipping. When David Dodimead as the King of France, in warlike fury before the walls of Angiers, declaimed these lines, on the word HARBOR'D he would fix his eyes on me, in full tinfoil armour, challenging me to giggle. In the bar afterwards, we got talking. He knew I was dissatisfied, with my progress in the company and also my accommodation. The Old Catholic Deacon had lost his fascination and was now plain weird, and the rent – four pounds – was more than I could afford, if I was ever going to repay the 'national debt' to my parents. Doddy said he couldn't help with 'progress in the company' but he did have a small spare room in his flat which he could sublet for £2, if I could get hold of a bed. I said I'd happily sleep on the floor for £2. He said there was his bed as well which was large enough for two, but dear heart that I was, he would never presume... I said: 'Fine. Let me check it out.' It was walking distance from the playhouse, first floor, nice view across the park, a clean bare spare room with a one-bar electric fire. I said I was used to a chilly bedroom having been brought up in Victorian vicarages, and could I take up his offer from next week? We sealed the deal with a whiskey and chatted on, till it was too late to go back to the deacon, so I agreed, just this once, to snuggle up with him in the big bed. He said once was all he expected. He never liked, at his age – 49 – to propose, as he feared rejection, and also, in his experience the first time was always the best time, and if not repeated, would become a cherishable memory. The next morning I left him cherishing the memory and went back to the deacon and told him I was leaving. He said was it the copes and chasubles because he was tiring of them too. He was thinking of having them cleaned and returned to the clerical outfitters. I said no not at all. It was just that someone in the company had a room going and it was cheaper. He said how much cheaper, because he could match whatever it was. I said no it wasn't that. He said what was it? Are you fucking him? I said yes, but just the once. In lieu of a deposit. Which reminds me, can you return me the £10 against breakages? He said but you broke my heart. I said oh please.

I bought a bed, a pillow, sheets and blankets from the Salvation Army, got boxes for my things and a rail from the playhouse wardrobe for my wardrobe. Doddy was as good as his word. We lived like two monks in our cells till the New Year when he went to London with *The Ruling Class*.

*

My mother wrote:

> I had another of my dreadful nightmares about you last night. I hardly ever get them these days, but this was very real, so I have decided to write to you in the early hours of this Sunday morning...

> Rumour has it that Daddy and I are parting company simply because he has gone off to a clergy conference and for a few days' holiday at Mo Bay en route. Some people don't seem to realize that I neither can nor want to attend a clergy conference! However it's quite fun to see what can be made of a perfectly innocent situation...

> I really do love this work and Daddy is happier here than he has ever been...

> Jude is appearing on TV in a programme for students where she is giving advice on choosing a career. She is still at JBC in the daytime, earning £10 per week. Then she is earning £2.10s pw coaching some child. And she is playing the lead part in a play at the Barn Theatre...

> Here is the moment to tell you the way things are working in my mind about the future, though for the present please keep what I have to say strictly to yourself...

> My interests are moving farther and farther away from the Rectory side of things. Also I have earned about £750 in my first year and there seems every likelihood that this will increase very considerably...

> So the net result is that I have put down a deposit on a lot of land in San San. It all happened very suddenly, when Tony was taking me round all the houses and lots that are for sale, and I just knew I had to live here. I put the matter to Daddy when I got home and he rather nervously agreed...

> The site is £1,750, though I shall get about £70 back as Tony is waiving the commission. If we can build a house for about £8,000 we could sell it for anything up to £20,000. But I would want to live in it. My idea – and I have talked Daddy into it – is for us to live there and for him to have a church office, and leave his work behind him each day. I should have my own office in what would be built as a maid's room...

> I have now paid the deposit, and the land should be officially ours by the end of this year. It is so exciting. Lot 166 is just slightly over one acre and has the most glorious view over Alligator Head. It's a very sloping site, so it would be a split-level house, which can be most attractive, or a cantilevered house...

We went to see J's play at the Barn last night and she was excellent in a very difficult part. She has talent, so it could be that we shall have two famous offspring in the acting world...

What on earth do you think of all this? Tell me. It would mean committing ourselves to Jamaica for at least 10 years, possibly for life...

I feel sure you will be in a position to visit us regularly and we'd have a lovely house, with San San beach and a prime piece of real estate to leave to you all when we cease existence...

I'm sending you a crate of grapefruit for Christmas to share with who-ever it is you're living with at the moment... Love from your ever devoted but somewhat crazy Mum.

THE SEAGULL

I got Nick to do my props and slipped through the pass door, up to a front seat in the circle. The only other presence in the auditorium was Jonathan at his director's table in the stalls, with the DSM and the lighting designer. If questioned I would say that it was more important for me, as Peter Eyre's cover, to see the play from beginning to end, than to be fussing over Kika's flowers and Fenella's wigs and fags. But I also wanted to be alone in an empty theatre, watching a comedy drained of all laughs, about a playwright who fails. From the first moment, when Cherith, as Masha, is asked 'Why do you always wear black?' a chill sets in, like the mist from the lake. Dr Dorn calls it romantic, but we all know it's much more heart-tearing and wretched. Everyone is in love with the wrong person, but can't let on; so they pour it into their art, whether as actor or writer, unaware that all hope will be dampened by the lake and darkened by the coming storm. A new generation should be making its mark, but the weight of expectations falling short and love ripening into jealousy, mean any winged hopes will be shot down as soon as they fly. When people leave with emotional debts unpaid, the worst is thought of them. 'Absence makes the heart grow vicious' is Jonathan's note. The comedy he says is in reacting against the genteel approach and making the relationships coarser. These characters are misfits and they don't know it, and we ache for their not knowing it. Where *The School for Scandal* was Hogarthian, this *Seagull* is Munch. There's a scream in it that can't be heard. One feels this superbly, alone in an empty theatre. No one else will ever see the production in this way. Once the seats are filled there will be warmth, shared laughter, some tears, drinks in the interval, the release of applause and exit in a crowd. The reviews will praise *'the country estate beautifully evoked with gauzes and projected images... a delicate study of human disappointment... surpassing anything in London'*. There will be amusement at the outrage in the local press at the rumour that freshly slaughtered seagulls are being despatched from Norfolk for enhanced realism. The casting of Miss Fielding (not known to be a serious actress) as the 'serious actress', will be talked of as a brilliant irony. Sir Laurence will come and see the play, and offer Jonathan associate directorship at the National Theatre. But only *I* will have seen the play stripped to its bones: the absolute loneliness of having, after all the dreaming, to make do with second-best (at best) both in love-life and career; the bleakness of Konstantin's symbolist drama of a long-dead world, set against the vanity of acting and living only for the present; Nina's high hopes for success on the stage and as the lover of Trigorin, the famous writer, brought down but not dashed, because 'I know now... the most important thing... isn't fame or glory... but the ability to *endure*'; and Konstantin's terrible and silent choice at the end, when there are 'no cranes in the meadows and no cock-chafers in the lime-trees', between desolation and (undramatic, offstage, beyond lonely, hardly spoken of) a gun to the head. You won't feel it or hear the bang.

GETTING POLITICAL

My mother wrote:

The purpose of this letter is to let you know that we have been most unhappily obliged to change our plans completely. I am feeling too sad and deflated to go into it all deeply but the main reason is political... There are strong indications that the island is in for a difficult time, which would point to there being no place for the English to stake their all. So a dream is ended... It reflects such a sadness on the situation in Jamaica, and it also means we shall virtually have to sever connections with Jude, as she is very much involved. She now regards herself as a West Indian, not English any more. I saw her yesterday and she looked so changed. Her nails were bitten, she looked dirty and a mess, and she has come out in ulcers on her legs... I just hope she will be able to finish her course, but as the government are firing nearly all the lecturers, it is questionable... She has decided to let politics be her field and I do sympathize with her desire to put the world to rights. There are very terrible aspects of life in Jamaica: the rich far too rich and the poor far too poor... Oh how I wish I could talk to you, instead of trying to write! And please don't let through to ANYONE what is behind all this, if in fact you can see yourself... Need I say the hardest part for me will be

the loss of my job when we leave in 1970... At least Monica and I will; Daddy may stay on to complete another three year period... What you will make of all this, I can't imagine. I am writing it before breakfast and must now prepare for a very busy day ahead... I am feeling quite physically ill and am not wanting you to write back and say you are sure it is all for the best etc... I am very tired... Well, think of your darling mum in her confused state out of which she will no doubt emerge triumphant...The one thing for me which will compensate for the whole sad set-up is that I shall now be able to watch your career more closely.
Love as always, Mum.

Me tek aff big gollyhead n' Kika, Peter, Nicky n' all say kiss-mi-rass, weh di playhaas git dis picky-picky-head Jamrock acta-bwoy? I was black, I was Jamaican, we were kids: Peter (Eyre) as the Fox, Nick as Tom the little boy whose toys come to life, Kika as Dolly, me as Golly. The play was *The Forest of Change*: Kika with jointed, porcelain limbs and big blinking eyes, me stuffed and bendy with no joints or fingers and a big black, white-eyed, red-grinning head, skipping and bounding into the forest where we transform, like falling in love, into white girl and black boy. But before I could dare to dream this might be real, we were back in the nursery as dumb dolls again. It was lovely little play, the only one by Merula Salaman, alias Lady Guinness. Would Sir Alec, we wondered, pop along to see it? Would Sir Larry whom we met when he came to see *The Seagull*, drop by to assess the sheen of my face- and body-paint, applied to the standard set by his 'outsize, elaborate, overwhelming' Othello, though *I* did it quicker, coming in for just one hour before the show – not having to extend to legs and torso? We played mornings and matinees, full with noisy kids, who would crowd the stage door afterwards, and while Kika and Peter and Nick were signing programmes, I would slip away, white again, like Sir Larry, unseen, in his office glasses and raincoat. ('Is your friend in the theatre also?' asked a fan once, of Edward Woodward as he and Sir stepped out into Waterloo Road. 'No no no no...' muttered the Greatest Actor of the Twentieth Century.) I couldn't do Golly nowadays of course, but we were innocent then and for me living *was* acting and I wanted to act black. My parents having to repatriate too soon meant the romance of being 'raised in Jamaica', as it said in the programme, would fizzle out with their dream. I also had to show I had gone the distance while they were away and would be steady enough, in both work and life, to support them in their troubles. Having them at ocean's length while I was roughing it, suited me, and if they *were* coming home in 1970, then the heat was on. 'Act, act again, act better', was not enough. I had to get political.

The Equity Deputy was the shop steward of the company, and with the transfer of *The Ruling Class* to London, the post was becoming vacant. I thought Kika would go for it, but she said I would be more suited being 'less of a firebrand'. I was elected unanimously. I could now get paid trips to London for meetings and by the by, pop in on Andy Mayer at his Granada office in the West End. For a while I had been submitting ideas for a comedy programme called *Nice Time*, which Andy and John Birt were producing, starring Kenny Everett and Germaine Greer. I had been getting £10 a minute of playing time for such items as 'playing billiards with eggs', 'hen-hurling olympics', 'sword-swallowers swallowing the cutlery in a restaurant'. Now I was being offered a resident script-writer job at £30 per week, including supervising the filmed sequences. I went to see Stuart and told him I might have to take it, if, to put it crudely, I didn't start getting better parts and more pay. A lesser man might have retorted: 'But you're playing a lead in the Christmas play. What more do you want, you uppity golliwog?' Instead, fixing me with his cloudy eyes (he would soon be on sick leave for a cataract operation), he said: 'Don't do anything. Leave it with me.' The next day, I had a letter from George Rowbottom, the General Manager, saying my salary was to be increased to £12 per week and that I would be relieved forthwith of stage management duties. I went straight round to the general office to say sorry this wasn't enough, but George was busy and Stuart wasn't in. 'Can I check the spelling of your name?' said Amanda, fingers poised above the keys. 'Is it BOARD as in BLOCKBOARD, or BORED as in BORED TO TEARS, or just BORD as in BORD.' I said: 'You know how to spell it Amanda. What are you typing?' She said: 'It's the cast list for *The Entertainer*. You're to play Frank.'

THE ENTERTAINER

I step into the light and feel love flooding down. Joan is operating the spot. Tonight after drinks in the bar and a short walk through the frosty park, we'll crouch over her gas fire, play some music and go to bed. Joan is lovely, loyal and good, but not *quite good enough*; just as Frank, son of Archie in the play, is a good part, but only as a pointer to better parts to come. 'And you made the most of it,' says Joan. 'Have you read the Guardian review?'

> *Denis Quilley... is magnificent, embodying perfectly the character's status as broken-down comic and symbol of our times... and there is good support work from Kika Markham and Richard Harbord.*

There you have it. Get used to it, the two names conjoined: Richard and Kika, Markham and Harbord, Burton and Taylor. I made a joke of it in the green room and she gave me one of her 'warning looks' which always turn me to jelly. She wants me to go on the march next week and sell the *Socialist Worker*. Only then will she take me seriously. I tried to tell her the other day, in the bar, after *The Seagull*: 'I *am* serious, I'm in love with you. I can't help it. It's like the play. I'm absolutely shredded with love and the more you look at me with those eyes, the deeper in it goes, like poison; it's sickening. I might have to shoot myself.'

I walk back from Joan's, across the park, in the early hours, to the smart flat I now share with Kathleen and two others: Jon Whatson and Murray Head, who have come up to do a community show called *Lace*, about the Nottingham lace industry. The misplaced 'h' tells you all you need to know about Jon Whatson, and about Murray you need only picture the face of the swinging sixties: Keith Moon or Terence Stamp. I suppose the thinking was 'put an old-style thesp to do the writing and the acting, alongside a groovy young rocker to do the music and the singing, and you crack both audiences: old fogies and kids'. Well it wasn't working; they weren't speaking. You could cut through the air of this plushly furnished, deep-pile-carpeted flat, with a pearl-handled knife. Notes on pink bond in JW's loopy hand, requesting said knife, plus fork, spoon and all china and utensils be washed, dried, *put away,* and not left festering till dawn!!!; and no music or raucousness *please* after 10pm, nor any caterwauling dolly-birds occupying the bathroom in the morning!!! And for the milkman there was always a neat note on the door-step: 'Dear Ernie (apologies to the incomparable Benny Hill!!!), just two pints of pasteurized please today thank you!!' I don't know why Murray came to Nottingham. He'd been acting since the age of seven, had a featured role in *The Family Way* with Hayley and John Mills and had just signed a recording contract. He would leave Nottingham as soon as *Lace* was done, to be in *Hair* in the West End, then shoot to fame, topping the charts as Judas in *Jesus Christ Superstar*, and starring with Peter Finch and Glenda Jackson in *Sunday Bloody Sunday*. That was a part I could have played, caught in a tug of love between a man and a woman, and maybe Murray got a whiff of my style because I was in fact playing it through the period we shared the flat, though with more comedy, stemming from the winding up of our resident Malvolio. On the night JW locked us out for 'hell-raising', we rewrote the milk note – 36 PINTS PLEASE. WE'RE HAVING A MILK PARTY!!! - then giggled off and kipped at Joan's.

THE ADVENTURES OF DONALBAIN

Sheila B, known as She, came to Nottingham to play opposite Barry Foster, in *Whoopsadaisy* and *Macbeth*. She had recently starred as Fay McMahon, the murdering nurse, in *Loot* by Joe Orton, so casting her in the Waterhouse/Hall play, about sleazy neigbours in the suburbs, was seen as a smart move. Few however understood that Fay McMahon is the comedy cousin of Lady Macbeth, or that She was already an accomplished Shakespearean, (having played the Shrew, Adriana in *Comedy of Errors* and Lady M herself), so was as well able to 'unsex herself and fill her breasts with gall', as she was to murder sick people for their money. It was seen as one of Stuart's quirks of casting that the Scottish Queen should be played by one who could get laughs even in the 'give me the daggers' scene. Barry and She were playing the worst kind of murderers, hell-bent but incompetent, like Orton characters trapped out of their depth in blood (*'Who would have thought the old man to have had so much blood in him?'*). This Lady M, like the black widow nurse, would be a force of nature, but wrong-headed and unintelligent, dwindling into an obsessive/compulsive housewife going mad over stains.

Riding high in her career, She could now seek to match the thrill of acting, with some offstage diversion. With no ties herself, and so free of the shame of the married yet 'playing away' leading actors, she could assess, without bother, the juvenile talent. Square-faced, boxer-bodied Nick (First Murderer) was setting hearts racing, but seemed to be settling in with Cherith (Second Witch); Barrie Rutter (the Porter), a sporty, Hull-born comedian, who led footballing warm-ups - 'the most physically exciting actor to have hit the stage since Albert Finney' said the Times of his performance in the National Youth Theatre's The Apprentices, for which he had had all his teeth out, so as not to be diverted by dental appointments; Barrie the Porter was too 'gym'; Peter Eyre (Banquo) was too slim; David Allister (Malcolm) too prim, and John Manford (Menteith) too grim. So it was down to Donalbain. Slight of body, light of voice, he seemed under-age, till she ascertained he had spent three years at university, then two as an actor, which must make him at least twenty-three. 'What's in it for Donalbain?' she asks him, during a break. 'What's his role in the murder? Why does he instantly run to Ireland, thus incriminating himself?' 'Well,' says the Don. 'He's a complex character. The Spare not the Heir, he's the Princess Margaret of the House of Duncan, likes parties and fast cars, has just had a blazing row with his father, over refusing to join the military. So when he finds himself in "the second chamber" and the King is killed, it's obvious: Blame the Bain! Of course he didn't do it, but he could have done; he wanted it done and it was done, so he runs. But that's not all. Being just a spoilt kid, he's confused in his sexuality. At dinner with the Thanes, he's sitting next to the Thane-ess who asks him about his mother and he tells her she died when he was a baby. That's funny, says She, my own child died as a baby. (I plucked my nipple from his boneless gums and dashed his brains out!)

*

Sex romps like Tom Jones and Entertaining Mr Sloane were sliding down zeitgeist towards Carry on Camping and Confessions of a Window-Cleaner. We were mid-way on that scale for a couple of weeks after Macbeth had opened. She had her own dressing-room which she had to share with Kathleen and Fenella who were not in the Scottish play, but it was never totally private. I couldn't accommodate her at my flat without provoking the whaspishness of JW. And She herself was renting a room in Stuart's family house while one of his daughters was away; so there was no way I could be smuggled in.

Until one evening. In the break Lady M has between the banquet and the sleep-walking, She peeped into my dressing-room and beckoned me into hers. Stuart had left with the family that morning for London and wouldn't be back till the following day. Did I want to come over? 'Oh phooey,' I sighed. 'I've got family in tonight and they're taking me to dinner.' Unce Arch, Auntie Joan and all the cousins from Ashby had booked a table for ten. I couldn't really get out of it. I think she thought I was making an excuse, and anyway she had to change. I tried to catch her after we'd come down, but by the time I'd showered, she'd gone and my cousins were waiting at the stage door. It was a good meal, and a free one, so I ate it with relish. They'd all loved the show - was it meant to be so funny? - were not sure about the Macbeths but impressed by the Macduffs. 'They're sitting over there,' I observed, nodding to Kika and TP, who were deep in conversation at another table. Throughout the meal, in a fog of wine, I kept glancing across, trying to decipher their relationship. They had been the love-tangled Nina and Trigorin in *The Seagull*, where rejected by him, she had had his baby which had died; now in *Macbeth*, she and all her babes had been slaughtered to punish the husband who had abandoned her. Closely arguing, Kika's eyes fixed on his, they seemed to have a catalogue of issues to interrogate, not just related to the plays. I had learnt from Chekhov how love past its season can mutate into bitterness, which was making me gag on the *coq au vin*. I was going to feign weariness and slip away before the dessert, but the cousins had so many questions: how did the blood spurt from my mouth so realistically when I was skewered? Was Birnam Wood meant to look like decorated trellis work? Was I really wearing pyjamas and gum boots in the battle? It was nearly midnight before we'd finished and I'd waved them off back to Ashby-de-la-Zouch. I could return to my flat and have a laugh with Murray, persuading myself that Kika should know I was serious and *able to endure*. Or I could follow my feet. It was raining and I was running in the direction of Stuart's house. If there was no light on, I would definitely have to presume she'd gone to bed. She was a leading actress and who was I, knocking her up, or wanting to? I'd slope off, relieved. But to do that I had to know the house was dark, that I was capable of turning away, that honour ranked higher than hopeless lust, and it did, it was, the house, when I got there, was dark, almost totally. Just the teeniest glimmer of light on the second floor. It was so late and so wet. The whole street was dead to the world, and to prove how dead, how sodden, I raised the knocker. I thought the wet would mufle it, but it rang out like a gong. A brighter light went on. Then another. She was coming down. I could hear foot-steps. I was soaking, too drunk to be terrified, too sober not to be pepped up for what was coming. Would she be the sleazy, come-to-bed *Whoopsadaisy* neighbour, or Lady Macbeth, steeped in blood in her night robe? Then suddenly there she was, in a kimono, in the doorway, drawing me in, unpeeling my dripping coat and laughing - 'You need a drink!' - and opening and closing cupboard doors looking for bottles - 'Stuart said I should treat the house as my home - like Goldilocks in the House of the Bears. *Voila!* Would you care for a Martini Rosso? Too sweet? A Noilly Prat? Too dry? Then it has to be a Cinzano, "fragrant, full-bodied, extremely versatile", just right.' We clinked, drained the glasses. A pause. 'Let's go to bed.' We went up to the second floor, to Baby Bear's bed, but that was too narrow, so leaving clothes and kimono, went down a floor to the master bedroom. 'It's okay if we leave no trace,' she said, laying out a towel and pulling me onto it: 'Just do what comes naturally - FIE UPON IT! FIE! COME FILL ME CROWN TO TOE TOP FULL...'

When I woke it was daylight. The bed was a mess. She wasn't there. I could hear voices downstairs: too loud from She as if she wanted me to hear, and a weary friendly stumbly response – from Stuart!!! FUCK!!! I leapt out of bed, tried to straighten it, hide the stains - *what's done cannot be undone...* - into the ensuite, where I thought I'd left my clothes, but they were in Baby Bear's room, and Stuart and She were coming up the stairs! Stuart was saying he'd come home early without the family, to catch an hour's shut-eye before a meeting. I was done for and She knew it. She was heading for the little room and hoping he might follow, giving me time to jump out of the window, except there wasn't a window! She absolutely had to show him a telegram begging her to play Lady Middleton in a new TV version of *Sense and Sensibility*, which would mean having to decline Betty Dullfeet in *Arturo Ui* - Stuart are you there?   But he'd diverged into his bedroom, and not noticing the bed, was heading straight for the ensuite! The door-knob was turning. Then it stopped! Has he seen me, nude and wedged against the toilet behind the door: a blur, twice fogged through the tear-drop glass, and his cataracts? He was walking away, downstairs, saying to She, in the tone of a king signing a death warrant: 'I'll put coffee on.' And I'm out of the room like a bullet up the stairs, to find my clothes, tossed anywhere, can't find a sock, dragging on jeans and jacket, one shoe off, one shoe on, down the stairs, past the talking in the kitchen, about Brecht, Blakemore, Betty D, not me Or were they waiting till I'd gone?

DENIS QUILLEY

*M*acbeth, *The Entertainer* and *The Resistible Rise of Arturo Ui* were all given stature by the presence of Denis Quilley. When Barry Foster left the company, Denis stepped in as the troubled thane, and lifted the production from the 'banality of evil' into a terrible dilemma for the audience. With his craggy face and Tommy-Cooperish grin, this most versatile performer – song-and-dance, TV cop, tragical-comical-operatical – could channel all his talents into making you feel for him whatever horrors he had committed. This also made his fellow-actors raise their game. Sheila B as Lady M, was now lethal, not hectoring; truly mad, not just obsessed. Malcolm and Donalbain, who had been so prone to creasing up, they had to play the 'To Ireland I...' scene back-to-back, were now fleeing for their lives. The 'screavy leans' from the garden centre, ceased to get laughs and, without change of pace or light, became a tank regiment advancing. I was switched from Cream-Faced Loon to Liar-and-Slave, bringing news of the advancing wood, and when Denis threatened to hang me alive, it was as if he himself were to be strung up. This Macbeth was a soldier, in a country on a war footing. He had to become king by whatever means, because only an army-man could martial the strength of Scotland against the invader. Duncan was too old, Malcolm too green, and Macduff and Banquo, too civilized and familial. Even the witches, under Denis's interrogation, became more political, less haggish, especially the third one, played by acting-ASM Penelope Wilton, who hails him 'King hereafter', meaning Best and Rightful Commander-in-Chief. She made the seriousness of this line over-ride the 'ambition' in Macbeth, triggering the doubt in the Daggers Scene, and making the thane human. This was Penny's first job after leaving Drama Centre. Within a year she would be playing Cordelia, then Isabella in *Measure for Measure*, Masha in *The Seagull*, Beatrice in *Much Ado*, Hester Collier in *The Deep Blue Sea*, winning Critics' Circle, Evening Standard and Olivier Awards, an OBE and, ultimately, a Dameship.

Arturo Ui, directed by Michael Blakemore, came down from Glasgow, stayed seven weeks in rep, with recastings, then moved on to London. Leonard Rossiter was torrential as the resistible Hitler-figure who corners the cauliflower market in Chicago. Spit and sweat sprang from him; he could get through three suits in an evening - you didn't want to be too near! Described by Simon Callow as '*a kind of psychopathic robot-moron*', he is wheeled on at the end on a scaff tower, declaiming the list of cities now in his thrall, and you wonder how we ever allowed this crazed idiot to control us. The final speech, written just months after Hitler's downfall, carries a dire warning:

> This was the thing that nearly had us mastered;
> Don't yet rejoice in his defeat, you men!
> Although the world stood up and stopped the bastard,
> The bitch that bore him is on heat again.

*

Just days after I left Nottingham, I went to the opening night of *Arturo* in the West End. This was Blakemore's third version, after Glasgow and Nottingham and I felt it lacked something. I had played various parts including the Court Physician who gives false evidence in favour of Ui then exits blowing bubble-gum. On a good night I could get the bubble to splat back in my face just as I was leaving and it usually got a round. The new actor just exited: no gum, no splat, no round. But that wasn't it. And it wasn't Rossiter, who was as terrifying as ever. Nor was it Blakemore's production which was no less razor-sharp. It was the absence of Quilley. Playing Roma, based on Ernst Roehm, Hitler's closest ally who is betrayed and assassinated, Denis humanized him till, in spite of his actions and beliefs, when he is killed, you grieve. The new actor had all the power, but was as cartoonish as Ui, with no flesh behind the mask. Puzzling the difference I realized afterwards it came down to one line. Shot in the face, Quilley had screamed 'I'M GOING BLIND!' as he fell, as if sight was life. The new actor kept the original scripted line – 'I MUST HAVE BEEN BLIND!' – as if reasoning the cause of death while dying and expressing anguish not pain.

I step into the light. It's the final moment of *The Entertainer*. We've been in rep for four months with good houses all the way. It's been serious fun, like an elite company within the company, but lately there has been a cloud. On the back of our success, Billy Chappell was offered another production and proposed *Love and a Bottle*, a Restoration comedy he'd done in Dublin three years before. His line is that the late 1660s are a model for the late 1960s, and next week we open with the Swinging London version of Farquar's play. With added songs in the style of Leslie Bricusse (lyrics by Billy) and costumes – velvet suits, cuban heels, bleached wigs – (designed by Billy), and the script spruced up (by Billy) to be 'permissive, selfish, corrupt, riotous and very lively', the whole show will stand or fall on Billy's invention. My part, the crafty servant Brush, has been cut in half to become a double act with a twin called Comb, played by John Joyce, and we have some perky little numbers, but it's hard to raise a laugh. The truth has sunk in: there is zero humour in this twee little tale of mistaken identity, sexual innuendo and transvestism, and the more you puff up the love and dandy up the bottle, the emptier the whole thing gets. But Billy is a trouper. Once upon a time, he danced in the steps of Nijinsky, recreating *Le Spectre de la Rose* and *L'Apres-midi d'un Faune*. In his pink jeans and loose cheese-cloth, smoking his 'coffin-nails', he can deflect the full force of actors' despair – scripts flung down to cries of 'What *is* this CRAP!' We will open on Tuesday. It will dazzle with prettiness. If Nottingham isn't ready to herald the Glam Rock era, then fuck it (says Billy). The sad thing is he's not now pressing to take *The Entertainer* into town. There may be a fill-in fortnight at the Theatre Royal Windsor, which Denis could do before going to the National. But I won't be free, being stuck with *Love and a Bottle* and the final show of the season, *The Hostage*, in which I shall be blacking up again as 'Princess Grace', the gay black sailor. Then I'll leave. There's nothing for me next season – I've been offered a 'lord' in *King Lear,* and a nameless drunk in *Playboy of the Western World.* Fair enough; I get the message. If I'm not camp or black – stereotypes not yet considered incorrect and disallowed – it's back to living scenery and 'being lucky to have a job at all'. Frank was a sop. I could cut capers with Archie, pull the rug from under my righteous sister and sing along with my drunken mum, but when I come on at the end of Act II with the news that Mick, my soldier brother, has been killed, and all I can blurt is: *'The bastards! The rotten bastards! Those bloody wogs, they've murdered him...',* and the audience goes numb and the play turns dark and all hope disappears, they forget it was me doing the acting that brought the house down. 'Ah! Vengeance!' I could have cried with all the passion of Hamlet, and been up for casting as the next Dane. Billy saw that, when I first erupted with the news, and said so; not articulating the words, but pausing stunned and letting his fag burn down, uninhaled, till the ash fell.

*

It should at least have seen me cast as Leslie Williams, the Engish squaddie taken hostage by the IRA and then killed. But that went to Nick. With his perfect body and calm head, his was a Billy-Budd-like sacrifice that struck to the heart. He wasn't *portraying* the death, he *was* the death, from which his *life* as an actor then took wing. Easy to work with, good to look at, fun to be with, he would be summoned by Olivier to join Denis, Penny Wilton, Jonathan Miller and Michael Blakemore at the National through to the seventies; thence to Broadway and epic films.

*

You see this face, this face can split open with warmth and humanity. It can sing and tell the worst unfunniest stories in the world to a great mob of dead, drab erks and it doesn't matter. It doesn't matter because – look at my eyes. I'm dead behind these eyes. I'm dead, just like the whole shoddy lot out there. It doesn't matter because I don't feel a thing, and neither do they. We're just as dead as each other...

It was Denis's skill to make you believe, though his world was collapsing, and he was dead behind the eyes, he could still keep his pecker up, a trouper to the end from his boater to his taps; you felt as long as the big man with the face of Henry Cooper and the nimbleness of Gene Kelly, could keep hoofing and singing his song, even after the set – just gauze after all – had flown away, leaving only the bare back wall; as long as Archie was still singing and tapping and entertaining, then why should you or anyone...

...care?
Why should I let it get me?
Why shouldn't I
Sit down and try
To let it pass over me...

*

I saw Denis on stage three times after he left Nottingham: in *Hamlet* with Albert Finney, in *Sweeney Todd* at Drury Lane and in *Long Day's Journey Into Night*, with Olivier. The *Hamlet*, in the new National Theatre had to be performed in working lights as the computer system had failed. This meant Denis, as the Ghost, in 'hideous, ambiguous night', had to appear in broad daylight. Everything suddenly depended on the acting: Finney turning his soliloquies into direct dialogues with the audience, and Quilley, twinning the Ghost with Claudius, using just body and voice to give us the warrior and the pragmatist, the dead and the living: two sides of one conflicted man. A singing barber who slits throats and has his patients turned into meat pies, you would think beyond entertainment, but Quilley, even in the vastness of Drury Lane, made Sweeney as intimately human as his Macbeth, his heart torn by what he was *having to do*. *Long Day's Journey,* about a theatrical family falling apart through drink and drugs, with Olivier leading, in his penultimate stage role, seemed like the Rice family transplanted into American classic theatre: Quilley as Jamie the elder son, the 'Frank' of the Tyrone family, grown older and cynical, a drunk like his dad. Was this how Frank and Archie would have ended? I preferred not to think of any kind of ending. Plays may end but actors live on. Olivier survived his fatal diseases, hoofing on into his eighties, gaining a peerage, an auditorium and theatre awards in his name, and playing Lear on tv, claiming the part 'is easy: he's like all of us really, just a stupid old fart.' When he died, when Stuart died and then Denis, self-confessed stupid old farts all, it was like the light going out, dream over, family gone, jobless again, but still hoping.

*

F ebruary 2001. I'm watching the BAFTA awards on TV. There's a serious moment when we remember those who died the previous year. Bookended by Alec Guinness and John Gielgud, the parade includes icons of films such as Hedy Lamarr, Loretta Young, Jason Robards, Lila Kedrova; then suddenly, filling the screen, in his prime as Lancelot in the film *Excalibur*, there's Nick. Nicholas Clay. He had bowel cancer. He was fifty-three.

ACT FOUR

Free Fall, Free Flight: 1969-72

Backward I look upon my life
To see onse waste of storm and strife!
One wrack of sorrows, hopes and pain,
Vanishing - to rise again!
- Branwell Bronte

*

Yowza yowza yowza!
Round and around and around we go…
and on and on and on and on…
When will it stop?
When will it end?
- MC in 'They Shoot Horses Don't They?'

Scene One
THE BLOODY CHILD

The walls are black. The bed is a black, metal-edged shelf to crack your head against. Underneath is a small table, painted black, with my typewriter on it, and a metal chair that folds. I thought I might get Howard's room which is black but with windows and three times the size – we gathered there two years ago to read *A Sky-Blue Life* before going to Cork; but there's a pecking order at 128 Westminster Bridge Road and my predecessor in the black hole, a skinny doctoral student called Kurt, with hunched shoulders (from crouching under the bed-frame) has already slipped into the larger room with his girlfriend whom he is now shagging, as if claiming territory. I'd be happy in the tomb-room if Howard were still in residence, hoping some of his genius might seep under the door to my advantage; but he's out on the road now with Portable Theatre, doing *Christie in Love*, directed by David Hare, about a man who strangled eight women and buried them under the floorboards. He won't be coming back. His garret days are over. Within a year he will be the undisputed dramatic firebrand of the left, married and moving into the house in Camberwell where, forty-seven years later, he still lives with his wife Jane.

Flo was in town. She was playing Sister Laura, in *Abelard and Eloise* in the West End. I went to see her and, without warning, called round afterwards. She screamed, burst into tears, then kissed me, my eyes, my nose, my whole face, like a starving animal. If she was acting, it was way over the top, provoking 'there-she-goes-again' eye-rolling from the other nuns in the dressing-room. We went for a drink. 'Single malt, make it a double!' she commanded, within earshot of Keith Michell and Diana Rigg, and when (tiring) I said 'Shall I see you home?' she retorted: 'Absolutely not! Let *me* see *you* home! Show me the garret, where you're writing your masterpiece, my Rimbaud, my little Chatterton!' We took a taxi, she said she'd pay, but shit, she'd left her purse in her dressing-room! Acting all the way, she was biting my ear, saying she'd pay with her cunt, as I acted being loaded, no sweat, I was signing on, just got my dole. Up in the flat, through the kitchen, where Kurt and flatmates Preston and Gerard were frying eggs while watching *Psycho* on tv, I led her into the den and she stripped to the lacerating shower-scene strings, cracked her head on the bed – fuck! – clambered onto it, unpeeling me, loving the haunches and shrieking, as I speared her to the heart. Then, when we were damp and going cold, as if the show were suddenly over, in the black, she said:

'Last summer, after Brighton, after *Dick Emery*, I went to stay with friends in Greece. I wasn't going to tell you. I didn't think we were going to meet again. But you ought to know, just for the record. I had an abortion.'

The latest bombshell (wrote my mother) *is the result of Daddy's X-ray... It showed an arthritic condition with aseptic necrosis, which means the ball-and-socket joint has fused into the hip joint, at an awkward angle; hence the great pain and swelling in the groin, and his inability to go upstairs in any other way than ONE-PLONK-ONE-PLONK... An operation to insert a metal cap on the femur is essential and our obvious thought is to have it done in the UK... So to cut a long (and to me, very sad) story short, we are now working towards a final return, possibly in August...*

Yes (I wrote back) *I'm miserable too. I've been out of work a fortnight and so far had only one interview, to play the lead in an Italian film set in Brussels, called* Tulips of Haarlem. *I play a socially repressed boy who is made a fool of and never achieves anything, so it should be right up my street, but so far I've haven't heard... Actually social repression was far from the case last Saturday, when I went to the Ashby wedding... The reception was the best bit because there was SO MUCH FOOD... It was a lovely sunny day, and it all took place in a marquee on the tennis court...Then when the 500 had dwindled to about 400, we all went off to Repton School for an open-air swim which was blissful. Then we had supper in the marquee and Uncle Arch made a funny speech, after which we groovy youngsters grooved away to Newton Solney to a groovy discotheque where we grooved till the small hours... The next day was spent in the saddle riding the range and in the evening we all watched a repeat of* Nice Time *and saw RICHARD HARBORD flit by on the screen in fancy letters.*

I can't see her in the dark but I know she's not sleeping. I could strangle her and bury her under the floorboards for what she did. I want to tell her I'd rather not see her any more, not because she isn't fun – having her here two or three nights a week has raised my status in the flat, and the boys all get on with her; she even cooks. But it's the apparition in the night, the Bloody Child that rises from the cauldron when we switch the light off. *Be bloody*

bold and resolute! Laugh to scorn the power of man! But I can't do that. I can only write it and act it. Take a leaf from Howard's book. Make theatre what it is: no pleasant escape from the dreary round, but the razor's edge that cuts life from death. All those Frintonish, Rix-type comedies I'd been penning, so proud of, and sending to Chris Parr who had given up responding, even *Three Ugly Women* and *The Tenant*, which were just sketches after all, didn't *hold up the mirror*: just clever-clever vehicles for an unsatisfied actor. I had to find my Christie, my Archie Rice, even my 14th Earl of Gurney, who would stop the public in their tracks, as I had just been screeched to a halt by a casual, *memento-mori*. Snuffing out one's own child for professional reasons, or because you 'didn't think you'd meet again', must be the defining crime of the decade; then to have it assumed, *as the father*, that it's not really your business and when told of it, you'd shrug it off, even smile with a kind of pride in your balls, is when acting fades, and you taste real life. My ghost-baby has grown up with me year by year in his lonely other universe. He might have been adopted or raised by Flo's mother or even Flo herself in her motherly moments; or more likely, gone into care and fostering, children's homes, borstals, gangs and prison. Twenty or so years on, when I was working in Bedford Gaol, I would look at the stream of kids coming in for their first adult incarceration, all following the same track through neglect into crime; and wonder which one is my boy.

THE HOMECOMING

I had a seven-page, closely written, letter from Jude, dated July '69, but I didn't receive it till August:

> *Dearest R*
>
> *I've started a thousand letters to you and none has yet found its way to the mailbox. However this one* will *get to you, being personally carried by Mother on the Northern Lights, leaving Oracabessa 13th August, arriving Port of London 24th ... I am in one hell of a fix at the moment, though Ma and Pa know nothing about it. They think Don Lilley is just a friend who can pull strings with the Ministry of Labour and get me a work permit... I do have a superfab job with Texaco in Trinidad, and everyone's telling me to take it, but I know it would so dry me up inside I'd never finish MY NOVEL... The only reason I would go would be to break completely with Don and I physically cannot do that...He's getting divorced anyway but it's taking an age and God knows what M & D will say when it all comes out in the Gleaner. They love him as a fantastically generous host and friend – last week we all watched him*

playing polo for Jamaica. He looked so princely in his tight white pants on his glistening steed!... I'm expecting him to come breezing in any moment if he can get away from his WIFE... In my darkest moments, I wonder if he's cooling, and deciding to make do with his current hell; come which or high water, I WILL MARRY HIM, I promise you... And now let me fill you in on the family:

1.) Daddy: By the time you read this, you will have seen him and had quite a shock. The leg-business is much more serious than any of us thought, because he's such a stoic: calm in the face of unbearable bantering from Mummy, and stubborn as a mule with the pain. But the main thing is his amazing spiritual state. He can rise above anything, even the crushing disappointment of having to leave the best job he has ever had, because of politics (and me!) and his leg.

2.) Mummy. What can I say? She is oh so tired, never stops or sleeps, running on thyroid alone. She will drive you up the wall with her great expectations, and sweetheart, you have so much to live up to! I'm a perfect bitch for saying this, but I'm sick to the teeth of the canonizing of St Richard. Monnie and I are of the opinion that it will be the best tonic if you can tarnish your halo just a little, show her your feet of clay, throw a tantrum, as we do, even a little one. You're so perfect in her eyes, could you please fail in something, for all our sakes? ...

3) Monica: This is the first time I've witnessed adolescence in the family and you'll be amazed how she's grown up... You may find her a little hostile to you at first because of the canonizing, but just let her know you're human like the rest of us and she'll be your friend for life. Of all of us she's the one who will be happiest back in UK. She survived three years of boarding school and will now be a free person, going to grammar school in Bath and living with Granny who is so much more livable-with than our darling Ma...

Must stop, having tons of letters to write, things to do like washing hair etc, before Donny comes – (WHERE IS HE???)... Whenever I'm on edge, feeling dumped and ready to scream, I remember The Island by A A Milne that we all had to learn – I still know it (TO BE READ WITH EXPRESSION AS WE WERE TAUGHT!):

> If I had a ship
> I'd sail my ship
> through eastern seas
> down to the beach
> where the slow waves thunder
> the green curls over

and the white falls under
boom boom boom...
and I'd say to myself
as I looked so lazily out at the sea:
there's nobody else in the world
and the world
was made
for me.

*

'This is where I come on,' I whispered to Angie, high up at the back of the Saville Theatre, at the start of the trial scene in *Arturo Ui*. In a flash of panic, I saw the action freeze, because I wasn't appearing. The linch-pin had been removed and I saw the whole Heath-Robinson creation teeter. Except it didn't of course. Angie's sideways glance confirmed I was never that important. 'There are enough actors to replace you ten times over,' Stuart had said. And there the boy was, the imposter in my costume, with my lines, my moves. No Quilley, no Nottingham swank, no ME, made this *Ui* a pale copy, just functioning. Even Rossiter seemed mechanical, a tiny trapped creature, to be studied not feared.

In the interval I told Angie that my parents and sister were coming home in a fortnight. They had the option of a room in a clergy house for the first few days, during which my father would be seeing his specialist in Harley Street; they would then decamp to my grandmother in Bath where Monica would be going to school. But the clergy house, for my mother, was emphatically the last resort. She had grown to hate all things clergy, having made a new life for herself in Jamaican real estate, so cruelly snatched away. She would much prefer a taste of my 'bohemian style', with rugs on the wall, exotic cushions and joss-sticks. But there was none of that, I sighed, at Westminster Bridge Road. What to do?

'We can offer rugs and cushions,' obliged Angie, 'and we could buy some joss-sticks.' She had left 17b, and was now renting the top room at Betty's. She and Michael were both away for a month in Hong Kong, hosted by Alfred, whom Betty had finally married, in name only, for the perks. As they were leaving, Betty had told Angie that, in exchange for feeding Minnie and doing a little light dusting, she should treat the house as her own, hold parties, have people to stay, as long as everything was back to rights when they returned.

'So yes,' said Angie. 'I could cable Betty, as a courtesy, but I know she won't mind. And there are plenty of beds, if you include the chaise longue and the cushions. And you and I could share,' she added, without even a blush.

After the show, we went round to see Sheila, Kathleen, Cherith and other mates, for hugs and a drink; then caught the bus to Islington. Angie asked what I was writing. I knew she never asked idle questions; there was always a 'because…' then an offer of help or a connection. I said, inspired by Brenton's aura in the sepulchre, I was working on an idea, so shocking, it would wipe the smirk off the face of British theatre. *Because*, she broke in, there was a new general manager at the Hampstead Theatre Club whom Katya knew, called Bernie James, who was actively seeking the next New Talent. Together she and K could fast-track my script to the top of the pile on his desk. I said hang on, I haven't written it yet and anyway I'm kind of obliged to give Chris Parr first refusal. He's been the first to refuse quite a lot of my scripts lately; so maybe you're right, he's gone off me and I don't blame him. There are so many fish to fry, and I've been sending him sprats. Where is he anyway? Bradford, said Angie. Didn't you know? He's been made Fellow in Theatre at the new University. We all think it's a backward step, probably calculated to offset being embraced by the Ustinovs. You must know about him and Tammy. She took over Katya's room at 17b, while I was still there, and Chris kept staying over. Then one morning they called us into the kitchen – Gilly, Sally, Mandy and me – and announced they were getting married! So yes, he has fish to fry; he's in a pickle, no question, and he hardly sees Tammy – she's at Chichester being brilliant with Alastair Sim in *The Magistrate* – while he's at Bradford doing agit-prop with mechanical engineers. They say Peter, Tammy's dad, is terrified of his future son-in-law, being a new-wave director with only scorn for the West End and the 'well-made play'.

By night and uninhabited, Chadwell Street was a wonderland. Cluttered with antiquities, subverted with modern daubings, it was hard to imagine the empty shell, just eighteen months ago, that Betty and I had drunk coffee and done crosswords in, between lining the walls and stripping doors and floors. Betty's plan to climb the decades of the nineteenth century, from Byron to Beardsley, as one moved up the house, had bloomed into a jumble of classical, medieval, oriental, gothic and *art nouveau* styles, blended in with living plants, marble body-parts and Betty's interventions. The brown lining paper, never painted, helped age the new hangings; the 'Ming' vase, side-lit on the half-way landing, gave the lie to its newness – thrown and glazed by Alfred himself, as a 'fake' wedding gift for Betty. The house was as old as a film set, as real as Bohemia. I imagined my parents and sister, sleepy from their voyage, entering the dreamworld: my father, for whom Dickens was second only to Bunyan as a guide, saying: 'Coo Wit! What a Havishamish den! What old curiosity!' as Angie and I assist him – one-plonk, one-plonk – up the wooden hill to Bedfordshire; and Monnie, moody, cautious, in teenage limbo, taking in weirdness with a shrug; and my mother, *so tired,* feeling the weight of all this *play-acting* coming over her like a drug, and finding it not unpleasant, even soothing: her son had a girlfriend; they had a house and possessions; they were welcoming and considerate. If the house wasn't theirs, if she wasn't a *real* girlfriend, if in the morning they turned out to be cold-hearted and cruel, that didn't matter in this 'acting' world. 'Time Present', as it might say in the playscript, was the sedative. And Angie, come to think of it, was refreshingly mature, with a streak of no-nonsense. Only one worry still niggled which she knew would stop her sleeping. Why had Richard never mentioned her?

Because if he did, the spell would break and she would become the Ice Queen again. I once joked with Angie that ice was cool. To have a cool haven after the sweatshop of theatre was the actor's dream. Here the mask might slip. Here 'he' could become 'me'. To check the beds was the reason why I'd come tonight; to check the stairs for a dad with a bad leg was the excuse, and we'd done that; the candle was guttering; the 'acting' girlfriend, having sustained the role for so long, was melting into the real thing. Within the coolness, her heart was a burning coal and I was warming to it. Angie was my hearth, my inglenook to get lost in. Only she could banish the fog breathed over me by the witchy woman we called Aunt Neurasthenia. In the narrow comfort of the lumpy little Chadwell Street bed, I told her this blurriness had nothing to do with anything. I'd had bouts of it since childhood, and in a perverse way, I welcomed it as a protection against the infestations of death. Even though Flo had gone north – out her her nun's habit into the blousiness of *Coronation Street* – the room still stank of our murdered Child. I knew if I told all to Angie, she'd be so cooling, the curse would lift, but I needed to keep it wrapped. The knowledge that a life I'd helped create had been snuffed out, was growing inside me like a play. If I moved from Westminster Bridge Road, I might lose it. I'd also got used to having the Old Vic on my doorstep. Seeing everything in the National's repertoire from *Love for Love* and *A Flea in Her Ear* to *Dance of Death* and *The Merchant of Venice*, was nurturing the 'babe' in my brain me till it kicked. 'You look gaunt,' said Angie as we left the theatre after seeing *The Merchant.* Didn't I like it, this collision of Jonathan Miller and Laurence Olivier which was sending out such sparks? Hailed as the theatrical event of the year, this *Merchant* so humanized Shylock that even Olivier's money-lender teeth seemed natural, and his howl at losing his child who herself (by shifting her love scene to the end and making it forlorn) appeared equally lost, had struck me dumb. 'You should move,' repeated Angie, on the steps of 128 and not coming up. 'Aunt Neurasthenia is a horrid landlady.'

We stood in silence, then I said: 'I'll see you home.' We got the tube to Angel, walked to Chadwell Street, stood on the step. We weren't a couple; never wished to be. Free as birds. As cranes, she suggested, who stay loyal for life, in spite of huge distances? I didn't know that, I replied. Or penguins she added. I was getting cold.

CRIPPEN

He called her Wifie; she called him Hub. He was forty-eight; she was twenty-seven. He was five foot four; she was two inches taller. She liked to arrive at Munyon's at least ten minutes before him, so she could open the post and sort the orders on his desk; so that when he came in, so quietly she hardly noticed, she was ready to take dictation, do the typing, make the tea; then accompany him to the post office, and later, the park, where if it was fine, they would eat the sandwiches she had prepared; after which they would take a taxi to a hotel, checking in as Mr and Mrs, though of course they weren't married! He had a wife who would sometimes come to the office and start upsetting things. She was a singer with a high-piched sing-song voice, that could turn into a shriek, if you ever failed to greet her as Miss Elmore, *not* Mrs Crippen!

But in the hotel, when they shut the door, Hub and Wifey as they were born to be, felt all the horribleness melt away. There was a song they had heard a boy singing in the street; it wasn't popular yet, which made it all the more personal. Hub would hum it, as he undressed, looking across at her and smiling, his teeth gleaming like piano keys, though she knew they were false, but then so were most of her own! And she would join in, as she folded her skirt and blouse neatly, her voice pure as a choirboy's:

> *If I were the only girl in the world*
> *And you were the only boy,*
> *Nothing else would matter in the world today*
> *We would go on loving in the same old way*
> *A Garden of Eden just made for two*
> *With nothing to mar our joy...*

Wrapped in his arms which were so much more muscular than you'd imagine, and looking deep into his sky-blue eyes, no longer swollen under his spectacles, she knew heaven for an instant. He was the doctor; she trusted him. He could examine, explore and adore every part of her; take her to pieces and scatter her; then make her whole. As he filled her with his love, she vowed she would go to the ends of the earth with him, if only to keep gazing into the pools of his eyes.

*

I'm in the Chamber of Horrors, looking up at the little man in the dock, with his droopy moustache and gold-rimmed spectacles. He is staring straight ahead, eyes bulging in disbelief. What is he doing here, among the psychopaths? Christie, Haigh, Jack the Ripper, they were monsters: necrophiles, sex fiends, multiple killers. But Crippen, what did he do? He fell in love; that was all. If this were a Greek tragedy, you could say he was cursed by Aphrodite. His love led him to do things no human should ever do. But you wouldn't fear him on a dark night. You would look to him for comfort and healing hands. Why had no one written a serious play about him? The story is a classic blend of Sophocles and Shakespeare: the man who 'loved not wisely, but too well', tries to use his skill to free him and his love, makes a series of fatal errors, but so believes in his own cleverness he thinks he's got away with it. Till... enter Nemesis! Inspector Dew! Alarmed the little doctor escapes, disguised, with his Ethel, dressed as a boy. They cross to Canada, are about to step ashore into happiness ever after, when newly invented WIRELESS TELEGRAPHY traps them in its toils. Drama is all around: music hall, melodrama, mystery, horror, the chase, cross-dressing, new technology, banner headlines, a mass audience following every step of the story. But what caught me in the waxwork stare, was how a man, for whom love and the protection of his beloved transcended everything, could cut his wife into little pieces, then make elementary mistakes, digging himself deeper and deeper into his own guilt, yet continuing to shield Ethel and in the end die for her.

The more I ran through the story, lying in the dark in my black room, the more obvious it became: *the mistakes made the man*, compounded by the shifting plates of the modern era. The Edwardians were done. The days of empire were numbered. Zeppelins, gas attacks, tanks, were on the horizon, heralding the slaughter of millions. The Music Hall was beginning a long decline from its great height, towards its last gasp in *The Entertainer*. The masses were on the rise, into the cinemas, onto the phone, into the readership of tabloids. New inventions were changing the world and making it ever more difficult to get away with murder. And to make a play that released Crippen from the Chamber of Horrors, I had to argue that *there was no murder*. Sir Edwin Marshall Hall, the leading defence lawyer of his day, if he had defended Crippen, claimed he would have argued that Crippen had bought the hyoscine *to reduce his wife's libido*, but mistook the dosage! Then when disposing of the butchered remains under the cellar floor, he slaked them in *ordinary* lime, not *quick*lime, which did not destroy but *preserved* the evidence! Inspector Dew relates how, when confronted with the fact of the recovered human organs, Crippen's face filled with blood, till it was beetroot red, then visibly drained away, till it was white as death.

I knew that feeling.

Chris Parr was in town. He rang me: 'Rick! Let me buy you a pint!' We met at the Royal Court. He wanted to tell me about Bradford: 'Forget the Open University, *Bradford* is Wilson's educational flagship. If you can't stand the white heat of the technological revolution, then stick to your dreaming spires! Oxbridge is yesterday; Bradford is tomorrow. And the genius of it is the new Gulbenkian Fellowship in Theatre. Can you imagine theatre uncoupled from literature, and yoked to science and sociology, engineering, colour chemistry? There are no arts courses, no Mods and Greats, no BAs of any kind! Even for Mod Lang you get a BSc. And all I have to do is make theatre. That's the brief. No facilities, no equipment, no pros arch and plushy seats; only ideas, and people, and energy, and *plays*. I need plays, new plays. Can you write me one Rick? There are those who say the playwright is dead; the actor just makes it up. But that's like saying you can have butter without bread, and revolution without Marx. You can, but it ends in anarchy which is what some goons want. So before they get their jackboots in the door, I want you to come up – we can pay the fare at least and I'll buy you a curry, how about that? – I want you to meet the group and get ideas. It'll be good for you Rick. You're vegetating here. London's the end of the line, not the beginning. Don't go to Hampstead. You'll get fucked.'

How did he know I was talking to Hampstead? Why did he presume I would want to uncouple myself from literature? Was he coming to me just because he couldn't get Howard or Hare? I should have told him a flat no, but in all my almost three-year career, I'd made a point of never saying no to anyone. Things pan out. You go with the flow. But this didn't mean I had to jump. Even when he said he'd like to start with a revival of *Three Ugly Women* which he had exactly the cast for, I didn't do more than pucker my brow; even when he said I could direct it myself, and we could do it in a real café, with real people at real tables, I may have smiled, but I didn't nod. In fact I hardly said anything. I was feeling shattered and sore, having been up most of the night, being fucked by Bernie – 'Mr James', as I stupidly called him when I walked into his office at the Hampstead Theatre Club. He spun round in his chair, stubbing out a cheroot as he swivelled. I said I was an actor and a writer, friend of Katya Benjamin who said I should come and see him.

'Ah Katya! How is she?'

I said she's fine. She's been in a couple of plays that I wrote.

'You're a writer?'

'I just said so.'

'We don't do plays that have been done. We do new plays.'

'That's what she said I should talk to you about: my new play.'

'Have we read it?'

'I haven't written it.'

He looked at me quizzically: 'What's it about, your play?'

'It's a docudrama in five acts exonerating Dr Crippen, who was a lover with a fatal flaw like Othello and should never have been associated with psychopaths like Christie. I went to see him in the Chamber of Horrors - '

'Whoa! Whoa!' cried Bernie. 'Hold it there! Hold the light bulb! *Christie in Love*, by Brenton. We want to bring it it in, but it's way too short - '

'I thought you didn't do plays that had been done,' I said, quick as a flash.

'*Touché!* I like this boy!' He was grinning, reaching in to squeeze my thighs with both hands. 'If we can make yours a one-acter, thirty mins max, and a barrel of laughs, we might go with it for a curtain raiser. *Grand Guignol,* not a whitewash. Horror horror horror, to offset the starkness of the Brenton. Who's your agent?'

'I don't have a writing agent. Who would you suggest?'

'Rosica Colin.'

'She's Brenton's. She's fierce.'

'She's a tiger. She might eat you, but she won't spit you out. She's loyal to the point of losing you jobs. But first she will want to read the play.'

The little man in the dock with the droopy moustache and bulging eyes, had been let down again. I wanted to tell him, in the fake world of theatre – which he *must* know about! – you have to leap at your chances even if it means junking your principles, shrinking your most serious project, to a 'barrel of laughs'. Attention was the aim. Once you'd got that, and some acclaim, then you could bend people to your message, but to start with it was only one step on from being a tart.

'Do you want to see a play?' said Bernie. '*The Death and Resurrection of Mr Roche*, it opens tonight and we're not full. I'm seeing it. We could eat first.'

I had beer and spaghetti; he had steak and wine. We talking about casting, as if *Crippen* were already written and accepted. I said did he know Tammy Ustinov? She was coming into town with *The Magistrate*; but it was a limited run, so she should be free to play Ethel. And Flo, Florence Hopcroft, was a dead ringer for Miss Elmore. She could sing badly very well! And for Crippen, well that was my part in maybe twenty years. In the meantime, what about persuading Stuart Burge? Brilliant! said Bernie, ordering me another beer. He'd seen him long ago, acting the ultimate non-actor. You could love him to death. He could cut you up and bury you and *almost* get away with it.

I don't remember much about *Mr Roche*, except that it was directed by Richard Eyre and we talked to him in the interval. I said I remembered him acting in *Expresso Bongo* at Cambridge, but he didn't remember me.

Afterwards Bernie said: Come home with me. He said John, his housemate, was away making a movie and they had this agreement: what the eye don't see, the heart don't etc. He was smiling all the way and it was easy to smile back.

WALKING TO EALING

I looked at the map and worked it out. You could walk in open parks almost all the way from Westminster Bridge Road to the King Edward Memorial Hospital Ealing. My diary was blank except for the show I had to be back for in the evening, so I thought if I started early and proceeded at a regular, thoughtful pace – I had plenty to think about – I could cover the eight or so miles by lunchtime. Over the bridge, crossing Parliament Square, I'd head into St James's Park, over the Mall into Green Park, under Admiralty Arch, into Hyde Park and on through Kensington Gardens, Holland Park, Shepherd's Bush Green; then hop on a bus up the Uxbridge Rd, all the way to Ealing Common, then cross Ealing Green, on the far side of which stood the King Edward Memorial Hospital, where my father has just been fitted with a new hip.

I set off early, just as the sun was coming up, crossing the bridge *than which earth has not anything to show more fair*, towards the sleepy Mother of Parliaments. I had a pile of questions to address as I walked, the most immediate being Pa. Who was he? Why was I wary of him? We'd had the one-to-ones on Aquinas and the Proofs of God, but we've never discussed *my* beliefs. I've served him at the altar, received the Sacrament from his hands, but always with the shadow of God hanging over us. My mother told me how even on the boat coming over he was still praying for a miracle to relieve him of the operation. All that carpentry, sawing through the bone, hammering in the prosthesis, was devil's work, not God's and he did feel a whole lot more mobile on the voyage, playing quoits, even deck tennis, but the moment they disembarked, had to cross London and face all the stairs in Wit's lumber-filled house, it was clear the miracle was being withdrawn. The pain, the fear of falling and knocking into things, the shame of misinterpreting God's Grace, and now having to be tortured for it. This was a test akin to Job's and he must learn to *endure*. We could discuss that endurance. Chekhov speaks of it: Endure and work! We might talk about our work, our vocations, the similarities, performance, singing, robing, having to hold your audience. He wrote sermons, I wrote plays. I had one lined up at one of London's finest theatres. I hadn't written it yet and had been told *not to start* by Rosica, my new terrier-like Romanian literary agent. To secure a commission, I should *write nothing* till the deal was signed, though actually I *had* started. I'd been sending drafts to Bernie James, which I knew was wrong, because he wasn't responding. I was alone, in my bubble, writing writing, with no end in view.

'*Take your protein pills and put your helmet on...*'

Somewhere, *Space Oddity* is pulsing from a car radio. I feel empty-headed, not subject to human law. Men are walking on the moon; I am walking on the earth: living men on a dead moon; a dead man on the living earth. I can carry on as long as I carry on acting, and I *am* acting. Out of a dozen auditions, I've landed a bunch of possibilities and one reality for now, in the West End. It wasn't what I'd hoped and I didn't want anyone coming to see it. It was as much as I could do to drag myself every afternoon across the river, stopping first at the National Gallery to stand before one painting - a crucifixion, an allegory of hell, a massacre - to brace me for the shame.

> *WHY THIS FALL FROM GRACE AT THE ARTS?*
> *It was here that* Waiting For Godot *was first performed, and* The Care-taker *and* The Iceman Cometh. *The Arts launched Joe Orton with En-tertaining Mr Sloane *and more recently produced a superb* Man and Superman *and a memorable* Hedda Gabler *[not to mention* The Rasputin Show*]... All this makes it baffling why a disaster like* The Slapstick Angels *should have occurred... All the essential theatrical ingredients were lacking. Even judged on the level of pantomime, it was inferior. As is usual with bad plays, it was laced with lines such as* '*Something's afoot, but what is it?' In fact nothing was afoot but hectic inconsequence and a plot even the author seemed to have grown weary of after a couple of scenes...* - Evening Standard

I sat down on a bench under a tree in St James's Park. In those questionnaires where they ask what was the best kiss of your life, I'd say it was on this bench, 17th December 1966. When they ask when were you happiest... what would your superpower be... who would you most like to apologize to...

> *Sunny One so true,*
> *where are you...?*

I walked on past the ducks, through the park, over the Mall. Like Christian, his face set for the Celestial City, I was beginning to feel burdened by enfeebling ghosts.

Ahead was the Arch, commemorating Waterloo, flanked by monuments to the Dead of two World Wars; the nude soldier, head bowed, weight thrown onto one hip, hand resting on sword, seeming to say: 'Think lasciviously of me if you dare. I died for my country. What did you do?'

I crossed into Hyde Park. The sky was clouding over. I shouldn't have come this way. The park was thick with memories I thought I'd burnt. The aim of this walk was to ponder my options for when *Angels* finally crashed. Of eight plates spinning, which to keep, which to let go?

(1) Offer to stay on with Unicorn (resident company at the Arts), doing 'theatre for young people' – (*smash!*)

(2) *Crippen* at Hampstead, if Bernie James's lust for my *work* can match ditto *per mio cazzo* – (*plate wobbling!*)

(3/4) two films, I'd been up for: *Tulips of Haarlem* – no response; *Battle of Britain* – starry epic, no response, but filming delayed to secure Olivier as Sir Hugh Dowding, so worth hoping (*one crash, one wobble*);

(5) Worcester Rep, following audition of a year ago, offer of summer season next year, including possible Sunday night reading of *The Tenant* and would I consider writing a musical? (*Yes yes, keep it spinning!*)

(6) *Billy West's Own*, Andy's Mayer's surreal TV sketch show for Granada, set to challenge BBC's new clumsily titled *Monty Python's Flying Circus*; writer/performers to come to Manchester to brainstorm ideas, including Tim Davies, Andy himself, Paul McDowell of the *Temperance Seven*, Hilary Pritchard of *The Avengers*, and ex-*Corrie* Co-Producer Bill Podmore – (*really artful, extended spinning required here!*)

(7) play perky servant in *The Provoked Wife* at Nuffield Theatre Lancaster; would normally let it crash, being out of town, minor part, minimal money etc – but hold on for two reasons: (a) being up north could dovetail into *Billy West* plans and (b) sited in war-torn University, tabloids headlining STUDENT STORM! OCCUPATION AND RIOTING! DEAN HANGED IN EFFIGY! THEATRE UNDER SIEGE FOR DENYING STUDENT ACCESS! RUBBING NOSE IN ROYAL SHIT! CHANCELLOR HRH PRINCESS ALEXANDRA TO BRAVE GALA PERFORMANCE OF *THE PROVOKED WIFE*! (*See crashfest of crockery! See fan-hit shit fly!*)

(8) Bradford and Chris. Surely - sorry Chris - moved on from all that (*smash!*)

*

The Serpentine coils like a lake of steel along the border between Hyde Park and Kensington Gardens. Monochrome under spitting clouds, it sucks you towards it. If I can reach the bridge, swap the randomness of the Park for the orderliness of the Gardens; if I can savour the coffee and toast I know they serve in the Orangery, then catch a bus to Ealing Common, I should still have time to cross Common and Green and be at the hospital by twelve.

But the Orangery is closed. It's tipping with rain. I hurry on to Notting Hill Gate just missing a bus. I turn off into Holland Park. My shoes are waterlogged, my pack-a-mack running with rain on the outside, sweat on the inside. At Shepherd's Bush I just miss another bus, so hail a cab. The driver hasn't heard of the King Edward Memorial Hospital and has to look it up. 'It's a cottage hospital built in the 19th century,' I inform him, 'then vamped up in the twenties, out of nostalgia for the Edwardians.' Demolished in the 1980s, I'm now imagining the memory.

We pull up outside a smoke-blackened, Gothic-revivalist fortress with leaded widows and battlements. I get out, pay the cab, pull the bell, hear it jangle, hear the clump of steel-tipped shoes on tiles, the screech of seldom-used hinges opening.

'Yes?' says a wraith-like nurse, eyeing me fiercely.

'I've come to see my father, Rev Robert Bartlett Crane.'

'Oh,' she looks shocked. 'Haven't you heard? There was an accident.'

As she leads me along corridors with peeling walls, up cracked-lino stairs, through wards blocked with trolleys, she tells me how my father, following his operation, had been visited by an angel, who said 'You are forgiven. God loves you. Take up your bed and walk'. So rejoicing, half-sleeping, he slipped out of bed onto the floor, 'fracturing the prosthesis, which will have to be replaced, in a second operation. He is now heavily sedated. You won't be able to converse. Oh and your mother is here.'

She's sitting by the bed. 'They rang me in Bath. I got here in three hours. He won't wake in time for lunch and he can't eat it anyway. We'll stay for a few moments, then go to the Wimpy across the road.'

Did she say that then? Or am I merging the memories, joining one hospital with another? Twenty-six years on – no time at all in the scheme of things – she was sitting by a similar bed, in a larger, simpler ward in a different hospital, the day before he died. I came in, having run from the station. She was sitting, holding his hand, older, tinier, her hair cut short. 'He won't wake. He's peaceful. Are you hungry? We'll stay a few moments...' There wasn't a chair, so I knelt; as he had knelt by my Laxton bed when I was dying, and the prayer had been heard. There was no prayer this time. I looked at him, white-bearded, breathing heavily. Was he peaceful? I kissed him on the forehead. His eyes flipped open, staring up at the cracked ceiling. Would it open and the clouds part and choirs of angels descend? Or had it all been a fantasy? He seemed to be struggling. I said: 'Daddy, it's all right... it's all going to be all right.' 'Don't worry him,' said my mother. I squeezed his hand. His eyes turned to me, as if what I had said was true. His lips parted, so dry, the skin tore just wide enough to say: 'Wit...'

THINGS FALL APART

Over lunch in the Wimpy, my mother told me the news. Monnie was being difficult, not going to the Abbey with Gran on Sunday, and Gran herself digging in with rules. No one was *ever* to change the TV channel! To get ITV, one had to get the man in, which meant a call-out fee, so don't expect *Coronation Street*, or even whatever that show is your meant to be doing at Granada. No one wold be watching anything. I hadn't seen their wretched little L-shaped room, in Clergy House. No alcohol, no smoking, no TV of any channel! Jude would explode! Had I heard from her? Did I know she was heading home, in tatters? The University in lockdown, Jude herself a target. And Don Lilley - you know he dumped her? Here's the letter. Read it and weep!

*

She was home in time for Christmas, on a turning tide. Dad, walking, on crutches, had taken a locum in Brixton, with a vicarage to live in, newly built like Kingstanding. Jude and I shared the spare room, talking as we used to through the night: Dennis, the true love she was so lucky to be free of; Jamaica, just *being there* as Union Vice-President, in the eye of the storm. Always though, with rebellion, it was rum and ganja that won out. The kids lost the will and sloped off to the bar. Same in Lancaster I said: all over when we got there. No siege of the theatre. No deans hanged in effigy. The gala passing without incident. I was presented to HRH who was bored stiff you could tell, so I pre-empted her question with one of my own; then chatted on till she said loftily: 'Would you care for some champagne? It's over there! (Just feck orf.)'

On New Year's Eve, I said: 'So what has Jude Crane got planned for the seventies?'

'Simple,' she said. 'Get the means and the man to get as far away as possible. Australia! What about you?'

*

Me? Plates, five, still spinning. (1) *Battle of Britain*. It came back. I was recalled. (See ekw under DASHED HOPES.) (2) *Crippen*. Bernie was right. Rosica was loyal to the point of losing you jobs. She wanted equivalence with Brenton, even though I was a newby. In the end, she took both scripts away: *Christie* going on at the Court and winning awards; *Crippen* slinking, unperformed, back into his box. (3) *Billy West's Own*, the premise of which was that Billy was late (was he dead?), so we do our own unregulated show without him. *Luck, Bullshit and Talent* was my title but I missed the brainstorming. I flooded them with scripts: good, goodish, bad, worse, worse than worse: it didn't matter. We had ENERGY and YOUTH. *Monty Python* was highbrow. We were the Scrawl on the Wall. Superstars in the making, we turned up for the pilot, ready to dazzle with shit. I'd offered Belle Elmore's rude song from *Crippen* as a closer, and suggested Flo – now a name in *Corrie* – should sing it as a guest. I met her in the canteen and showed her the lyric. She rad it: 'What's it about?'

'It's a metaphor,' I explained. 'Her husband has an *udgie-wudgie-budgie all forlorn…* It's all there in the words: *I held him in my hand and let him go; he couldn't stand!* So she opts for the laundry-boy next door who has a…'

'Perfectly enormous cockatoo.'

'Absolutely.'

In the end it wasn't included. A bad sign I thought, as we entered the airless, oddly-shaped studio. We were to perform to a bank of cameras with the live audience facing away and watching us on monitors. Cameramen can't react, even if they've a mind to. Between takes, they could be heard muttering 'What the fuck was that about?' And the audience laughter, at a distance, sounded canned, as if anything, ie nothing, was uproariously funny. When it was over, in the bar, we were saying 'We are the pioneers of 1970s comedy. One day they'll discover us, as they did Beckett.' But Granada didn't agree. Producer Bill Podmore was replaced by John Birt, the new broom who would soon be sweeping through the industry. Orders were given for all obscurity (all the jokes) and half the cast to be cut. *Billy West's Own*, a zero-sell title, became *The Billy West Show*. The pilot would be rewritten, reshot and transmitted as a one-off. And that would be it. With a gun to his head, Birt forced Andy to write to me:

I've been studying the tape of the dry-run in some detail, and in doing so I've confirmed a nagging feeling which had been in my mind for some weeks. It's this: for some reason… the comic presence that makes Richard Harbord so funny on the stage and in cabaret, does not survive the process of television… I hate writing this letter which seems so pompous and horrid… I'm not at all happy about losing you… but I can't see that there is any alternative. I hope you will agree…

HAPPY DAYS

When the letter came, I was two plays into a four-month season at the Swan Theatre Worcester. It was the happiest of happy companies, and all happy companies being happy in the same way, I don't need to expand on it. It would be like opening an album of old holiday snaps and expecting you to be excited. Look there's Marcia, high-kicking with the Mecs in Irma La Douce! And here's Anna! She was pregnant and continued acting right up to when her waters broke! And dear Richard Carrington, dressing-room Scrabble champion, who went on to find radio fame as the Vicar of Ambridge. So let the happy Swan sail by. No need to recall pasting over the chasm of despond at being the first of many hundreds to be purged by Birt. No need to enlarge on the happy fun with box-office submanager Trish in the moonlight, or the flash of fame when it became known that my great-great-grandfather had been Mayor of the city, and his grandfather-in-law, Dr John Wall, had founded Worcester Porcelain. Spinning priceless plates was a family skill, and when the prettiest smashed, there were instantly three more saucers on sticks, in the triple triumph that closed the season – Wanted One Body, Come Blow Your Horn and the satirical revue Dead Centre of the Midlands, with lead actor Harbord, outplaying Brian Rix, Edward Elgar and Elvis, and hailed a 'comic genius'.

But let the Swan paddle by, leaving just the ripple of a final diary entry:

Saturday 29th August 1970

Last night after the show, I drove the van to the Malvern Hills, Peter P beside me, Janet H giving directions. Janet C, Marlene, Marcia and others singing raucously in the back. Trish there also. Parked at base of the Iron Age Fort and climbed to the Castle. Drank cider, ate crisps, sang sea shanties, made love with Trish. Took charge with Peter P to find out where we were. Eventually found the van. Pacified a curious cop. Ate chocolate cake, drove back singing, and all had coffee at Janet H's until about 3.30. Drove everyone home eventually. Dropped them off one by one, till only Trish and I left. Parked van at theatre and walked home. Trish stayed the night. The most ecstatic, wonderful night – probably because we knew it was the last... Trish had to get up early. Went back to sleep. Up at 12. Matinee at 3. A good show. Evening performance terrific. No drinks afterwards. Some of company going straight on to Plymouth for the tour. Walked home with Trish – her home. Drank beer and lay on the floor listening to Everly Brothers: 'So sad...' Walked home about 1am. Went round to say good-bye to Carrington and perhaps a farewell backgammon, but his lights were out. Didn't want to wake him. He has been my best friend while up here. We've done many a good double act together: Harold and Wilfred in Spring and Port Wine, Regan and Goneril in the revue, Blundell and Mickleby in Wanted One Body, etc etc. I'll miss him. I always say I'll be back at Xmas, but who knows?

Scene Two
BRADFORD

Something from the bottom of the job pile was stirring, beginning to creep into the blood. The hard slog of London, the happy days of rep, were obscuring a plain truth. When you're dead behind the eyes, no amount of acting and being applauded will revive you as a human, beyond the traffic of the play. Bradford was the heart-beat of the corpse I'd been ghosting in, and after so long being denied, was now about start   pounding. Come back with me to Sunday 12th October 1969.

I'd been to an afternoon showing of *Anne of a Thousand Days* with Angie. She'd wanted to see *Easy Rider* or *Kes*, but T P McKenna and Denis Quilley were in this one, so we went. It was a mistake. They hardly featured at all and Richard Burton, as Henry VIII, wasn't really trying. If this was a lesson in how to dispose of a woman who had come to dominate your life, it was depressing. I felt Angie was taking it personally. She'd had a stand-off with Betty and was taking this as her cue to break with Chadwell Street. As we crossed Westminster Bridge, she was debating, *either* to run home to her parents in Southampton, *or* hunker down with me in the tomb-room - she might brighten it! Even though her room at 17B had been the largest, she was adept at confining herself to small spaces. If I wanted the 'bliss of solitude' as all writers did, she could always nip downstairs for a coffee in the Square Pigeon, which flat-mates Kurt, Preston and Gerard had established and were now making a going concern. She might offer her waitressing services, why not?

Angie, I said, I'm really tired. You should go home.

As soon as I got in I rang Chris Parr. He had said come up to Bradford, see the new Brenton Trilogy and meet the three beautiful women you're going to transform into ugly ones when you direct your play while I do your new one. I'd said hang on a minute Chris! (a) I haven't agreed to do any plays in Bradford, certainly not a new one and (b) I can't just drop everything and come up; I do happen to be acting in the West End for fuck's sake! Except I wasn't, and he must have known. *Angels* was such a flop, we were closing on Saturday and cancelling half the performances which meant I would be free Monday, Tuesday, Wednesday, which were the days of the Brenton plays. So I rang him and said okay I was coming up. He said: 'Catch the 8.10 tonight, gets in at eleven! I'll meet you!'

On the train, I wrote to Angie. I'd been incredibly selfish and mean and she was such a stoic. I was forfeiting my cool haven, and was in danger of being dashed on the rocks of unfulfilment. There had been not a peep from Bernie James about *Crippen,* and Billy West had gone quiet, as if the idea of basing a TV comedy show around someone who doesn't turn up, had persuaded everyone to stay away. I don't remember what I wrote to Angie, except it was long, but I have her reply which runs to six pages. I must have styled myself as a pig.

> *You're quite wrong you know* (she wrote). *I'm very fond of pigs... Don't think for a moment that you've 'used' me, because if I ever suspected it, I'd have left long ago... Let me answer your four points, in proper debating manner: 1) that we'd been friends for years. True, though not particularly deep friends; 2) that we made love one night, and the situation became 'complex'. Did it? Wasn't it much more complex before? Men and women rarely have platonic friendships when they're our age and I didn't feel your friend at all when you came back from Nottingham. I saw you preferred Betty... Love-making is such an unreliable activity - but to wake up beside someone you're fond of, is always wonderful. 3) That you're unreliable and don't belong to people... Richard, I've never belonged to anyone, not even Col Batty (did you know about him? [No I did not!!!]), who I know had another woman at the same time as me. 4) That I need constant affection and true love. The very thought of either scares me to death... Do you know Richard, if we lived together for a week, I'd be bored by Thursday... I'm fond of you, as a talker, a walker, an adviser, a confidant, a friend, a lover and all kinds of aspects I can't think of at 1 am... But I know you're a nomad. Each time I see you, I almost expect it to be the last... All I can say is that I'm at the office every day, if you want to get in touch... I'm so glad I came home. Wasn't it beautiful yesterday? Autumn is a season that doesn't affect London much... I'm too tired to write more. I'm very very glad that you wrote.*
> *Love to you, dear pig, Angie xxx*

Boomtown Bradford sits in three bowls, three culverted valleys, filled with fog. Ancient cottage industries of wool spinning and cloth weaving had caught the flame of industry and in just a few decades, raised the little town to become Wool Capital of the World. Other dark satanic milltowns lacked Bradford's bowl-trap of sulphur and soot from more than two hundred chimneys, sucking in migrant labour mostly from Ireland, but also Germans and Jews, and limiting life expectancy to just eighteen years. But hell has its upside! Out of the cauldron came Salt and Ripley, business moguls who saw profit to be got from better housing, education and longer lives for their workers; and philanthropists Behrens and Moser who put the city on the map as the place to invest in. New confidence brought organized labour led by orators and reformers from W H Drew and William Leach to J B Priestley and Denis Healey; and artists, actors, directors, musicians, from Delius, Hockney and Lindsay Kemp to Bill Gaskill, Rodney Bewes, Kiki Dee and Billie Whitelaw. Yet these all left, coughing the smog from their lungs and heading for fairer climes. Why was I now sliding into the soot-black, fog-thick maw of Bradford Station?

Chris was standing in the lamplight, duffle-hooded like Death in Bergman's *The Seventh Seal:* a flash from his lighter, and a glow from his fag, as he spotted me and came towards me.

*

'You know what I've learnt Rick, since I came here?' says he, striding up the cobbles of Great Horton Road.

'What have you learnt Chris?' says I, keeping up, two paces to his one.

'That I'm not in theatre; I'm a pig-farmer! I raise a farrow of perky playlets, sired by Brenton, Grillo and yourself, if you'll do it, and a couple of other geniuses I've got my eye on – to keep you on your trotters! – then I fatten them up through the year, and truck them to market on the Edinburgh Fringe, where they get slaughtered! Ha!'

'I don't follow you Chris.'

'Hog, sow, swine, crashing boar – when did pigs ever get a good press? Becket, Pinter, even Chekhov and Euripides, they all took the knocks before joining the canon. You could be up there, I mean that, if you don't mind a couple of critical black eyes. Forget London.'

'But Chris, you've just directed Howard's *Revenge* at the Royal Court. That didn't get slaughtered. Why are you hiding away here, when you're just beginning to get noticed? Isn't it true that anyone who's any good in Bradford, always leaves? Why are you sucking us all into this pea-souper?'

'Rick, I'm hungry. Let me treat you to a curry.'

*

The Taj Mahal was set back, up an alley. It seemed to be open round the clock, serving a limited range of curries, mostly minced beef (keema), in clarified butter (ghee), to be scooped up with traditional flat bread (chapatis). Three students were already seated round a candle-lit table, half way through their meal. 'These three,' said Chris, 'are Brenton's muses. He came up last term, had a curry, then went home and wrote three short plays which Greg, Phil and Michele will premiere tomorrow night.'

'Wha!' barked Phil.

'Gug gug gug,' chomped Greg.

'Hello Brian,' cooed Michele.

'They're quoting from the plays,' explained Chris.

'I Gum Gum.'

'I Goo Goo.'

'He Goo Goo.'

'He Gum Gum.'

'Who you?' said Michele.

'I'm Richard,' I said.

'He's a writer,' said Chris. 'He's very talented. He's come to see how we work. Then he'll write three plays to put in the mix with the Brentons, to take to Edinburgh. Isn't that right Rick?'

'Up to a point Chris.'

Chris roared: 'That's from *Scoop* by Evelyn Waugh! You never say no to Lord Copper. You say "Up to a point".'

'So he's not going to write any plays,' said Michele.

'Unless we offer him a drink,' said Phil.

'Up to a pint!' said Greg, fishing out a bottle from his bag.

We ordered keema and chapatis, and talked about the *urgency* and *conquest of disgust*, in making plays: how Howard, on the train to Bradford, racing against the clock, had been typing up *Heads, Gum and Goo* and *The Education of Skinny Spew* till his fingers bled; and how Brenda, Chris's Yorkshire-housewife secretary, then had to bash out the scripts onto stencils, stabbing FUCK, PISS, CUNT, her nose wrinkling, eyes averted, as if the keys were smeared with shit!

The dark room went darker. A tall figure in greatcoat and hat was in the doorway.

'Hi David,' said Chris.

'Can't stop,' said David, handing him a package.

'Is this the one?' said Chris. 'Your first play! Rick meet David Edgar. He's just written his first play.'

'What's it about?' I said.

'It advocates the banning of the rugby tour to South Africa.'

'Haven't they banned that already?' said Phil.

'Not yet,' said David. 'So can we expedite this Chris? Can we make history? Can we talk? Not tomorrow obviously.'

'Will you be there,' said Chris, 'for the Brenton plays?'

'Not to speak to,' said David.

'David,' said Greg, 'as well as being University correspondent for the *Telegraph and Argus*, also reviews plays. He won't even nod to you when he's wearing his critic's hat?'

'Will he review his own play?' enquired Michele.

'Not if it's crap!' laughed Phil.

David, his middle finger nudging his specs up to the bridge of his nose, said: 'Let's talk in a week.'

I've just had coffee with Greg. He is now seventy, still gangly with ashen hair, and chomping his consonants, as he talks hard politics with the softness of a friend. I asked for his memories of Chris. There was a pause. Never known to search for words, Greg was taking his time to assess the complexity of Chris.

'I was Chair of the Drama Group, before Chris came. There was a Fellow in Music who seemed to be interested only in Delius and Vaughan Williams. This was quite out of tune with the technological theme-song that 'Red' Ted Edwards the VC, and Harold Wilson the Chancellor, wanted sung. So they pressured Gulbenkian to fund a Fellow in Theatre. I was on the selection committee and the moment Chris walked in, I knew there was no point seeing anyone else. He didn't *want* the job, *he knew he had to have it*. He saw theatre, springing from engineering and sociology, as essential to human development. Telling stories and playing them out, was what nurtured the mind, as food fed the body. It didn't need to be taught, because it was naturally within everyone; but it did need to be set free. The embrace of tradition - polite comedies, revered classics - was now being being prised apart by the Attlee generation. Chris's excitement at being *alive in this dawn* and *young in this very heaven*, gave him an energy that many, even liberal, entrepreneurs couldn't take, and he always reacted badly. Putting the boot in was his style, but he needed a 'good cop' (like yourself, said Greg) to pre-apply the soft soap. It was the same with Brenton and Edgar who had the flexibility Chris lacked, until they went on to higher things, and the cultural mood changed from "fire in the belly of the sixties revolutionaries" into the "fitful, liberal flicker of the sedate seventies". I suppose the best summing up of Chris,' went on Greg, 'is that he was *brutally honest*. I never met a more honest person and it came at you with brute force. If you rebuffed it, he didn't fight you; he set his jaw and stomped away leaving a trail of bewildered enemies. He was on a mission and the clock was ticking. In the end the new-play bandwagon went racing on without him, and he would say he was well shot of it. I hear he went into television. I love him, still do.'

*

'Rick,' said Chris as we walked up the path to the never-locked back door of 279 Great Horton Road. 'You can have the bed downstairs, to fend off the burglars.'

'Are you expecting burglars Chris?'

'Only if they're desperate. We don't even have a kettle! I sublet from Fitch, who manages the Bradford Festival. His room is like a boudoir, apparently. I'm not allowed in; I'm in the attic. Do you need to write? Howard writes at this table. He'll be staying here tomorrow night, which means you'll *either* have to kip on the floor or share the bed – like Laurel and Hardy, ha! – sitting up in bed with your hats on! Alternatively, here's an idea – can you take it in or are you knackered?'

'I can take it in Chris.'

'John Carbery directs plays at Bingley College. We do an actors' exchange. He's dress rehearsing *Oh What A Lovely War!* tomorrow night. You could go – I can't – to see the actors, some of whom could be in the plays you haven't written yet. Then Howard could have the bed and you could see *his* plays on Tuesday, because you're not having to leave till Wednesday, is that right?'

'Will John Carbery put me up?'

Chris had gone. I checked the room. The 'bed' was a mattress, with pissstains and loose stuffing. There was a poster for the Bradford Festival 1968 on the wall.

'Yes he will,' said Chris, coming in with blanket, sheet and pillow. 'JC is the friendliest fellow I know.'

It was two o'clock. I slept till nine. Chris wasn't up, so I went for a walk. There was a transport café just a few yards down the road. David Edgar was in the window, tucking into a full English. I could have joined him but he was reading. I could have reminded him we'd met at the Taj last night, but he'd hardly noticed me. I could have joked: 'That's because I'm a ghost, which is Shakespearean for actor.'

'*Shadow* actually,' he might have replied. '*If we shadows have offended...*'

'That's Puck. I played him.'

'Did you offend? Is it not the duty of the actor to offend?'

'No I don't think I did, and I'm not sure it's the business of theatre to be offensive.'

'Then I must be in the wrong job! Offenders are what we crave. Richard III, Captain Hook, Arturo Ui: how much more *vital* is it to be hissed and booed! Or have twenty centuries of theatre got it wrong?'

I imagined a pause. I didn't know he was an actor.

If he'd looked up, I'd have gone in, ordered what he'd had and over mouthfuls of waffle, egg, sausage and coffee, discovered, despite his stature and resonant tone, how mercurial he was - playwright, performer, journalist, lecturer, politician; how domestically cavalier and professionally meticulous, almost puritanical, he was; how aloofness could slide, on a whim, into jocularity; how knowledge was for sharing and gossip for ignoring. He could have been a Cicero or a Founding Father. He seemed to be a generation older than the rest of us, though he was still only twenty-one.

∗

Oh Valiant Hearts, I Vow To Thee My Country: we used to sing these every Remembrance Sunday, in honour of the Glorious Dead, and I used to wonder where the glory was in being disembowelled or having your head blown off. I'd watched *Oh What A Lovely War* being filmed on Brighton Pier, then seen it in the cinema, with its star-studded cast, and been impressed and disturbed; but not emotionally wiped out as I was sitting alone in the tiny theatre at Bingley College. The actors were students, the same age as the kid soldiers who were dying in their tens of thousands. The innocence of the old songs, set against the flashed-up figures of those killed, said it all, without the need for gunfire and gore. Earlier I'd watched a runthrough of the Brenton plays in Bradford. Phil, Greg and Michele, tightly orchestrated by Chris, had delivered Howard's battery of words, with childlike vigour. Innocence again, and I understood now why Chris had come here and how *I* might benefit from working with rough talent, untroubled by ambition. Alone in the dark of Bingley, John Carbery and his lighting man just a few seats away, I could contemplate hell: the entertainment that masked the void; the jaunty marching to wave upon wave of gassing and slaughter. And later, in JC's flat, in his bed – 'Don't worry, there'll be a bolster between us!' – I couldn't help thinking of old shell-shocked Carneggie, our French teacher who hanged himself; and the presence of JC, happy to talk through the night, just a sand-bag away.

∗

I hadn't told Beryl I was away, so in the morning I asked JC if I could ring her. I also wanted to tell her frankly that I didn't any longer need to be put up for rubbish jobs like *Angels*, or impossibilities like *Tulips of Haarlem* and *The Battle of Britain*. The truth was I now knew what I wanted to do with my career. It was what I had talked to JC about over the bolster, into the small hours, till he fell asleep. The Brenton plays had been the catalyst; *Lovely War* the decider. Whether in Bradford or Bingley or Cork or Timbuktu, I wanted to use my talent as writer and performer, to change the world just a fraction; by offending sensitivities, help pluck the pompous from their thrones and emancipate the oppressed. Beryl would understand having started as a soubrette, in life and on stage, serving the mighty in the hope of a Cinderella transformation, then waking up one day to discover her true talent, which was to promote talent in others. All this I was ready now to lay out before her, but she didn't let me speak:

'WHERE THE HELL HAVE YOU BEEN? THEY'RE RECALLING YOU FOR *BATTLE OF BRITAIN*. CAN YOU GET TO MAUDE SPECTOR'S FOR 4.30 THIS AFTERNOON?'

*

JC drove me to Bradford station. He said he'd ring Chris and explain why I couldn't stay. As the train came in, he delved in his bag, and brought out the book I'd earlier expressed an interest in, having noticed it on his shelf. I'd read most of Daphne DuMaurier but never heard of *The Infernal World of Branwell Bronte*. I mentioned that I too had been raised in a Yorkshire Parsonage, had three strong-willed sisters, and frequently felt on the brink of an 'infernal world'.

'Then this is for you,' JC smiled, leaning in as the train doors slammed.

I tried reading, but couldn't concentrate. I was churning inside, as the train pounded down the Pennines, like a troop train plunging with all aboard into war. I was a raw recruit, swept along on a tide of songs, like Uncle Mo in the Ypres salient – '*those years were the happiest of my life, because of the comradeship and self-sacrifice...*' I was a young pilot, geared up, goggled and helmeted, running with my comrades to get up in a crate and tangle with the Luftwaffe! I was just one of the 'few' over half of whom would go down blazing, flesh blackening, screams unheard.

I got to Maude Spector's on the dot of 4.30. I knew the part was mine and I had no choice but to take it. It would mean missing the risk of being slaughtered in the front line of Chris's Bradford Revolution. But hell! Was not a far more lucrative risk on offer to me here!

HOPES DASHED

Branwell Bronte wrote more – stories, novels, epic poems, dramas, letters, journals – than all his sisters put together. The 'brilliant versatile genius of the family', who despatched his work, unsolicited, to publishers, magazines and personally to William Wordsworth, then waited confident for responses that never came; this slightly-built boy, with flame-red hair and dark desires who entranced his sisters with tales of morbid longing and love denied, then got them all writing; this entertainer who could deliver monologues and ballads to the railway lads and canal-diggers in the Black Bull, then kneel in prayer with his widowed father, in the bedroom they shared, looking out over the gravestones and wondering how the young dead could be grateful for the sickness that killed them, and whether hope of heaven would ever compensate; this wasted genius, weighed down with debt, and pursued by scandal, who fell through the trapdoor into an infernal world of envy, desperation, drink and drugs which killed him at thirty-one...

'Let that be a lesson to you,' said JC.

We were walking, duffled-up, through the snow that was carpeting the cobbled streets of Haworth, up to the Parsonage. Having learnt not to wait for sluggish responses – Maude Spector, Hampstead, Granada TV – I had returned to Bradford, to direct *Three Ugly Women* and deliver a second play, bashed out Brenton-style mostly on the train, about a cocky boy who thinks he has everything – talent, money, good looks, popularity – only to be brought down by three smart girls. Without changing a word, the Ugly Women were morphing into the Bronte sisters, and the Cocky Boy into Branwell, giving both plays a pedigree to live up to, and promising a longer, deeper play to come. As rehearsals progressed, I told Chris to watch out: *I liked directing*, and one day soon, might take his job. He said no *I* should watch out: one day soon, he might *want* me to take it! He had proposed to Yorkshire Arts that they should fund a pilot repertory season in Bradford and Halifax, to run through the autumn. He would be looking for someone to step in at the University as temporary Fellow, and run the shows up till Christmas. In the meantime, he was demanding another short play to complete the trilogy, and then a full-length Bronte play with songs, for which I should begin the research *now*. Did I have to go back to London on Sunday? Get the steam train to Haworth. Set your face to the Heights! The Parsonage will be closed but JC knows the man with the key. He was at the show last night, but couldn't stay.

Branwell took a job as ticket clerk on a track similar to the Worth Valley Railway which today runs steam trains from Keighley to Haworth. The day after the last performance of my plays, I decided to do as bidden by Chris and go the full Bronte: steam locomotion, the Black Bull pub, the hilly cobbled street up to the church and graveyard, where under cold stone lie three of the four unquiet *genii* of the Parsonage. Then having ghosted room to room through their time-warped home, which being closed today, JC would fix for me to explore on my own, I would set my face across the windswept moor, like Mr Lockwood, for Wuthering Heights.

'Branwell!' said JC who having met me off the train and walked with me up the hill, was now buying me lunch in the Black Bull. 'Where did he go wrong?'

'Maybe he was trying too hard,' I offered. 'Maybe he was just too over-the-top, writing simultaneously with both hands, doing painting, poetry, performing, maybe standing on this very table! I really warm to him. I could play him.'

'Are you ambitious?'

'You tell me. You were there last night. Why did you rush off at the end? Wasn't it great, the reaction? What did you think?'

'I thought,' he finished his mouthful, 'that you were trying too hard. The first play had a strength, a kind of eeriness which was quite affecting. You'd done it before; it had maturity.'

'And the second one? *Nigel the Sexual Athlete*, what did you think of it?'

'I thought...' JC was thinking   .

'Actually I don't really care what you thought. The audience loved it. That's the main thing.'

I thought Chris made a decent job of it, but it left a bad taste, *because* of the audience reaction. The best lines were from the girls when they were virtually lynching the poor boy. I'm sure you didn't intend it, but you seemed to be urging the mob to go out and beat up a homosexual.'

'That absolutely was not my intention! Though I'm not sure a writer has to *have* an intention. He provokes. Isn't that the aim? He gets into his ene-my's skin, and gets your hackles up.'

'Absolutely! And you did the opposite! It's a fine line, when you're playing an argument, between inhabiting the cause of a queer-basher or a mass murderer and being so good at it you become popular; and having to convince as the good person who may be just a bit boring. Where are our sympathies meant to lie? Certainly not with the boy. People like Nigel get murdered, even though the law's changed, and it always starts with mockery.'

'Wow, that's some criticism.'

'Take it professionally. You're just starting out on a long road with many pot-holes.' He smiled, finished his beer. 'Sup up. I'll see you into the Parson-age, then I have to go.'

THE BOG BURST

I am the ghost of Branwell Bronte, coming out of the Black Bull with my friend John Brown the grave-digger. Beyond dazed, I am floating. Beyond unrecognized for my work, and dismissed as an artist, I am *erased,* like the 'pillar' in the picture I painted of my sisters, which people say used to be me, but I blanked it out. I am standing in the snow with John, before two rows of tall rectangular windows which are the shuttered eyes of my home. I am depressed beyond envy. I have been judged in the cruellest way by the friendliest of fellows who now bids me good-bye: 'Call by later; I'm at home' – and walks away. I am a ghoul, shaking off snow in a dingy hallway. I can hear my voice telling the curator: no need to explain. I know this is the table where we sat to write rpoems. And here is the couch on which Emily sat, refusing to die. And this, I know, is the bedroom I shared with Papa, who is now kneeling by the bed, with the Genii Tallii, Emii and Annii standing over him, and John Brown in the doorway. One by one they fade away, till only John is there. He bends down to kiss me – Oh John, I am dying – then it all goes blank.

I am the ghost of the boy who was raised in a Yorkshire parsonage and had three strong-willed sisters. There's a studio photo of the four of us, from the 1950s that mimics the Bronte painting. Except the brother is there: not a pillar, more a guardian angel, standing over Elizabeth, upright and commanding as Charlotte; Jude, wayward but reined in, just for the duration of this picture, as Emily; and baby Monnie as Anne. I'm looking at the picture now, drawn to Monnie/Anne, the sister I wished had been a boy. When Jude and I were jiving on the upper deck of the *Ascania*, Mon was itching with eczema and having her head shaved and bandaged. She never married a priest, as Elizabeth did, generating her own vicarage-born dynasty; she didn't, like Jude, raise hell in Jamaica, then run with husband and child to the end of the earth. She married Dave from Thames Water, pioneered early years education in England and Sweden, helped our parents, one then the other, through the fog of dementia, arranged the funerals and the transporting of the ashes for burial in Laxton churchyard, where once a year she still goes to remember and be at peace.

*

Anne Bronte, says Samantha Ellis in *Take Courage: Anne Bronte and the Art of Life* (2017), was the George Harrison of the Brontes. Dazzled by brighter stars, Emily (Lennon) and Charlotte (McCartney), you have to blink as you reread Anne's books and poems to see *she* is the defiant one, optimistic against the odds, ahead of her time, the gentlest and yet most feminist of the sisters. *Here Comes The Sun* and *Something (in the way she moves)* are her themes songs. She says bondage to an abusive husband, however cruel, does not have to be the end. The only power to be deferred to – ungently – is Death, who will come for you just as your second novel is topping the charts. The God of Thunder who splits the heavens and tears open the earth, can be explained away as 'weather', but still has to be respected. You saw this when you were four, out walking on the moor with Branwell and Emily, and the BOG BURST happened! Suddenly the earth wobbled like jelly under your feet, and you ran for shelter as the moor exploded. You enquired what caused it. Was it God unsheathing his sword in wrath, as Papa claimed from the pulpit? Or was it a deluge of rain after a dry summer, seeping through the upper blanket of peat and down through the cracks in the parched lower layers, to the hard shale beneath, where it could not drain away, so must turn and struggle upwards, with a terrible strength, shaking the moor like a rug, then bursting through in seven-foot high torrents of sludge, toppling bridges, uprooting trees, flooding roads and fields with the peat-black shit of the earth (as you so vividly described it, before your letters were bowdlerized by Charlotte)?

I come out of the Parsonage onto the snow-covered moor. No blizzard, no wind, it looks peaceful, innocent. I want to crunch the virgin-white veil, as far as the waterfall, then on to Top Withens. There's still an hour or more of light; it's only two miles. The curator, like the misery he is, advises against it. I tell him the Brontes did it in worse weather than this! He says the moor was less bleak then. There were more people, more farms: Low, Middle and Top Withens, Ponden Hall and a dozen more, before the land was cleared for the reservoirs. But my hood is up. I'm away into the snow, ankle-deep – it's easy – though on reflection, I'll probably only make it to the waterfall. Top Withens, people say, is a disappointment anyway, with none of the 'grotesque carvings' and 'crumbling griffins and shameless little boys' that Mr Lockwood admired over the frontage of Wuthering Heights. Banks of heavy grey clouds are blocking the light and fresh flakes are falling. In the event, I don't even make it to the waterfall which is surely frozen anyway. As the snow tumbles down and the wind whips up, I turn and head back, bent forward into the blizzard. It's dark now. No lights ahead, only thickly swirling, blinding snow. JC was right. I'm a fool and a chancer. I played for easy laughs. I stoked prejudice and hatred. I sent a boy with my own inclinations to the wolves and I'm paying for it now. Nature is God, and God is in a rage, *unless you dare to disbelieve*. And that's where Branwell and I part company and I side with Anne. There are causes and effects. You *can* change the world by resetting the causes. But don't delay because Death is already swinging his scythe. You have life. You have breath. You're not lost. You are redeemable. And I'm rambling. I plod on. I'm walking on stumps. One-plonk, one-plunge. I struggle to get up. My squinting eyes search the tumbling black for a pulse of light. Car headlights pass. I'm coming to a road. Another car lights a sign, then it's gone. BINGLEY! I've crossed Bingley Moor! I've made it to Bingley!

'Call by later,' said JC. 'I'm at home.'

*

There's a light in his window. I've no idea what time it is. I bang the door with my fist. I try to throw snow at the upstairs window. 'John! JC! John Carbery! Open up!' If it wasn't iced over, I would shin up the drainpipe, and like Catherine Linton, smash the glass - *'Let me in! I'm come home! I lost my way on the moor!'* I sink down against the door. I'm frozen to the bone. I've wasted my life. Here he'll find my stupid corpse in the morning.

There's a movement behind me. The door is being unlocked and eased open. Falling inwards, I'm caught by strong arms and dragged inside. 'My God... you're frozen...' He's hauling me step by step up the stairs. 'Let's get you thawed out...' He has a fire in his room. He sits me beside it. I'm shivering. 'Don't speak...' He folds me in blanket, goes to pour me a brandy: 'Drink this, slowly slowly...' I thaw and get warm. He helps me undress, drapes my clothes round the fire to dry, then lifts me, guides me to the bed, lies me down, warm under the covers, no bolster this time, and slips in beside me, flesh to flesh in the dark.

BUMBO

*T*he Battle of Britain was a nono, but Beryl had got me two days on another B of B, *The Breaking of Bumbo*, a post-swinging-sixties sex romp with political undertones, about a guardsman (Richard Warwick) and a dolly bird (Joanna Lumley). I was to play a skinhead, with swastika tattoos, jumping over a wall at the head of my snarling army, shouting 'FUCK THE KNOBS!' and surprising the love-birds as they canoodle in the hot tub. I did get to talk to Joanna who had worked with Sylvia Syms who I'd swept leaves for, but Richard Warwick, who had stolen my part in *If...*, shied away.

When JC came to town, we met up and he took me to his club: a plain door with an entry-phone, strictly members only, up dingy stairs to a crimson-walled, dimly lit bar, like the club scene in *Victim*: single men, wary, anonymous, casting glances, talking in code, as if the law had never changed. With my shaved head, I was a curiosity, not altogether welcome, till it was explained that I was an actor, which distanced me even more. We decided to go to Mandy's. I told JC I nearly went there once, with the Tudor-Landor set from Cambridge. It was founded by Mandy Rice-Davies, from the profits from her book about the Bog Burst that brought down the Macmillan government: Profumo, Christine Keeler, Lord Astor (who denied everything – 'Well he would, wouldn't he?') and the new unfettered sexuality, lighting up London.

The club, in Henrietta Street, just off Covent Garden, was a million miles from the grim bar we'd just come from. This was Mandy leading the baby-boomers down her 'one long, slippery descent into respectability': gay, not queer; all classes all races: Italian waiters, Chinese hairdressers, Bowie-boys, Jagger-fans. Heads turned as I entered, bald, with JC, down the steps to the dance floor. I saw Danny La Rue in cahoots with his entourage, and I thought I saw Richard Warwick, and would have gone to him and said: 'No sweat about you stealing my part in *If....* you bugger. I'll forgive you if you dance with me.' But I was spoken for, dancing with JC, to Anne Bronte's mood-music:

> *My sweet lord*
> *Hm, my lord*
> *Hm, my lord*
> *I really want to know you*
> *Really want to go with you*
> *Really want to show you lord*
> *That it won't take long, my lord (alleluya...)*

*

My father, mobile again, had secured the job of Area Secretary for the United Society for the Propagation of the Gospel (USPG), in the Diocese of Southwark, and the house that went with it: 2a Templar Street, on the corner of Myatt's Fields which divided Camberwell from Brixton. The house was a two-storey, detatched property, part-pebble-dash, cottage-style, with a small garden, panelled hall-way and three fair-sized bedrooms, one of which, forsaking the tomb-room, I had landed in, coming back from Bradford, to be shared with Jude whenever she dropped by. Having gone in as a dish-washer for Westby's the West End catering firm, she was shooting through the ranks and in a year would be Deputy Manager. She was dating a colleague Michael Maxwell, whose father was head barman at the National Theatre, and whose grandmother ran the actors' canteen at the Old Vic. Monnie was still in Bath with Gran, in her final year at school, so her bedroom in Templar Street was technically available, but Jude and I preferred the twin beds in the bigger room, having so much to talk about. I'd finished the film and was now playing Stanislavsky at the Royal Court in a dramatization of Chekhov's letters, for schools, directed by Pam Brighton who, since playing the Empress Mother in *The Rasputin Show*, had given up acting and, along with most new directors at the Court, was desperately depressed. Twice the size since I last saw her, she would arrive lank-haired, with mask-of-tragedy mouth, in the same flouncy kaftan, and flop, head in hands, barking 'FUCKING *SHIT* RICHARD!!' to my every move, my every word. So I switched to automatic, ghosting through the bile, playing Stanislavsky as a zombie, and fucking off, not stopping to mingle misery in the bar; then two or three times a week, going to Mandy's where I was now a member, following JC's return to Bingley, and dancing with whoever and going home with him, or to some toilet; then in the small hours, if it wasn't raining, usually walking home to Templar Street.

My mother was up.

'What's the matter Mum? Couldn't you sleep?'

'There were three phone calls for you. One from Chris Parr who said he's expecting you on Monday but hasn't yet had the script. Another from someone who said his name was JC. He said you must come and stay with him in Bingley. He sounded nice. Then the third one...'

'Who was the third one?'

'I don't know. He was extremely rude. I don't know what you've been getting up to, but you really *must not* use our phone for these sorts of call.'

And there was a letter from Worcester, offering me the summer season starting in May.

Whatever it was I was getting up to, it was not the worst of my mother's worries. Elizabeth and Roy had been to stay, and I had dropped by to have dinner with them before getting the late train to Bradford to work with Greg, Phil and Michele on the third play of my trilogy, which hadn't been written yet. I had offered to cook the spaghetti bolognaise and was just conveying it into the drawing-room, to be eaten on laps, because the dining-table was stacked with USPG papers that my mother was filing, when the phone rang and I went to answer it, putting my spaghetti on my seat. When I came back to tell them it was Andy Mayer ringing with the news that we now had a studio date for the pilot of *Billy West's Own* (21st May), which magically filled the gap between *Spring and Port Wine* and *Irma La Douce* which I'd be acting in at Worcester; when I came back in ready to celebrate – we might even open a bottle of wine! – I found the atmosphere thick with horror: Elizabeth red-faced, my mother ashen, biting her lip, Dad and Roy wishing they were miles away. 'What happened?' I said. 'Was it something I cooked?' and forgetting where I'd put my plate, sat smack in the bolognaise: classic slapstick that should have been funny! But it was viewed as proof of what Elizabeth had just said: that there was *no love* in this household, no sitting round a table *being a family;* always *work* and *crisis,* in place of *nurturing* and *parental care.* She had *never* been considered as a daughter, just an *impediment* to be shifted out of home into *nursing,* and then *abandoned* when they fled the country. *She* would *never* treat *her* children in that way. They were *precious* to her, above everything. My mother relayed all this to me in whispers in the kitchen as we cleared up. Then I went upstairs to change my trousers and left to get my train.

∗

I had crabs. I'd been itching, thinking it was eczema or athlete's crotch, but when I examined the infected area, I saw them: tiny microscopic mites with legs, embedded in the skin. Up in Bradford, I mentioned it to Chris who instructed me, to BOIL MY PANTS and shave off EVERY HAIR ON MY BODY, down to the last follicle, then smear myself all over in CRAB POISON, available from the chemist, only to be washed off AFTER THREE DAYS. Count it a blessing! Now you will *have* to put yourself in PURDAH in the downstairs room for three days, and FINISH WRITING THE PLAY.

DEATH ON THE MOOR

K ing Conrad: His Life and Times would be a comedy with songs about an ex-king, ex-queen and ex-prince, awaiting execution, by a revolutionary regime which would turn out to be even more fascist than they were. The trio who had inspired Brenton would be my muses for *Conrad*, and I promised, smeared in poison, to have it drafted in three days. But nothing came; I didn't do it. Haunted by JC's critique of the second play, I revisited it, rewrote it, but it still wasn't working. The gay boy was still an object of derision, fit for lynching. I wanted to talk to JC. Would it work if the boy was *actually murdered*? Might that turn the tide of sympathy? But I didn't know how to do it. The girls were too much fun; I couldn't turn them into killers. But when I phoned him, he wasn't there. I phoned again; still no answer. It got to the point when I knew I had to speak to him or give up on the whole trilogy, which would collapse if the centre play wasn't right. But he was never in. When, after three days, it came to bath-time and soaping off the holocaust of the creepy-crawlies, and I was cleansed and packed and about to leave, I told Chris I was so near to finishing, almost done, but it was too raw, too rough, it would spoil if I showed him. I'd finish it, I promised, in London and get the script to him in time for rehearsal in two weeks. Back at Templar Street, when my mother said JC had called, I'd already done the rewrite, including the death, and I felt it worked. So I didn't ring him back. I didn't want to be distracted from finishing the third play, which was now coming along fine. I took both scripts up with me on the train back to Bradford, intending to read through *Conrad* with Chris over breakfast, so he'd have time to develop his directorial ideas before the readthrough in the evening. But when I suggested it, he didn't reply. He seemed to resent my presence, as if delivering the script so late, made me unprofessional. I was about to pre-empt whatever he had to say by reminding him: 'Chris, this is how we work, on the edge! Risk, you always said, is the oxygen of theatre!' He said:

'You knew him.'

'Who?'

'Carbery, JC. You got on with him.'

'Absolutely. The friendliest of fellows. He phoned me just the other day.'
'What did you know about him?'
'What's this about?'
'He's been murdered.'

Chris was continuing: 'Apparently he picked up some kid, some bovver-boy who he thought, against appearances, might be queer. But he'd picked the wrong skinhead. Someone walking a dog found a body.'

*

No one knew I'd ever been with him. He was as secretive as I was.

I said to Chris: I need to go for a walk.

I wanted grey skies but the sun was high. I wanted open, empty spaces but I seemed to be walking into town.

A murder wasn't something I could afford to be caught in. How would it help anyway? I hadn't seen him for several weeks. Whatever we had was long over.

People I'd never met were smiling. Someone even said: Cheer up pal! It might never happen.

It wasn't like St Peter, denying the other JC. We had no formal connection, except at Mandy's, and even there, I'd only been his 'guest'. I never signed my real name.

Walking past the University, I saw Phil and Michele coming towards me. Before they could stop me and talk cheerfully about the new script, I veered off down a side-street.

I felt huge and clumsy, encased in a sandwich-board: 'KEEP AWAY! I AM A LIAR! I DIDN'T KILL HIM! I NEVER KNEW HIM!'

I needed a piss.

I told him even then: Don't count on me. I don't have ties to anyone. Footloose and fancy-free, that's me. And he laughed: That's what I like about you!

I'm standing in the stall. There's a guy next to me. He knows I'm not me but I could be (imagine): same height, same build, looks younger (but my playing age); shaven head, clip-on braces, bovver boots (I'm acting); and the same down there, when he looks. I zip up.

You always kill the one you love. I do anyway, I'm sorry.

He said: Richard, that is sweet, sub-Wildean crap. You're not brave. You're Judas. Your weapon is the kiss.

*

They Shoot Horses Don't They? was showing at the Odeon. I went in. It was just beginning: the hopeful and the desperate gathering to register for the Greatest Dance Marathon on Earth! The grand and the greedy assembling to lay bets on which couple will dance on to the end, to win the prize. They must keep going for an hour, then rest for ten minutes, then dance for an hour, then rest for ten minutes, and so on and so on, for days, then weeks, then months, till they drop. To quicken the drama, there are occasional 'derbies', when the tempo flips to gallop and the dancers become racers, screamed at by the crowd as they haul each other round and around the track to the finish, knowing the last three pairs must be eliminated. The band plays on, the punters roar, the desperate hopefuls stumble, get up again: all for the prize which only one pair can win – minus expenses (they weren't told this): weeks of bills, which will all but wipe out the prize. Herbert Hoover's words – *freedom is the open window through which pours the sunlight of human dignity* – fade out behind the closed doors of the arena, and the cell-like dorms and shower-rooms where you learn to snatch a ten-minute kip, a quick fuck, or a wash. This is the new generation, born into the collapse of capitalism. The punters are waiting. They may back you and throw you dollars.

> *Yowza yowza yowza!* (yells Rocky the MC) *Round and around and around we go... and on and on and on and on... When will it stop? When will it end? Only when the last two starry-eyed dancers, stagger and sway, stumble and swoon, across the sea of defeat and despair to victory...*

I've just seen the film again, four decades on, and I know why it stunned me. It was the *shape* of the film, the power of the moment: actors trapped in one time-span, one dance-hall, spiralling through eliminations down to one final singularity, which in the end is a void. And we learn this through the fragments of flashback that break up the forward plunge of the film, overtaking it, to become *flash-forwards* to the chilling finale. And the wheel keeps turning. The yowza yowza yowza goes on. With Gig Young as the MC, you know it's not going to end. The film, appearing in the 1970 golden age of cinema – *Midnight Cowboy, Easy Rider, Butch Cassidy* – was garlanded with awards and nominations, but it was Young who got the Oscar. On paper he is a bastard, exploiting the desparate, free to seduce and extort. He mouths the platitudes of the depression era – prosperity for all is just around the corner – but he says it with a weary brio as if he knows we're all going to hell, just some faster than others. He could be a pantomime villain, but he plays it, as Quilley played Sweeney Todd, with only sixty percent of his strength. You know if he pulled out all the stops, he'd bring the house down, but he's not going to do that. He is a professional. He will carry on.

SUBSTITUTE FELLOW

My parents, my sisters, my grandmother and my Auntie Maureen were all coming to Worcester for the last night of *Spring and Port Wine*, after which I was heading straight off to spearhead the new comedy wave at Granada, before returning to Worcester for the rest of the season. Hope was springing. Summer was coming. Rising from the ashes of *Billy West*, I would enjoy success as Mr Mickleby in *Wanted One Body*. I was out of the alley and back on the high road, seeing Angie again, and also Trish, our slim, horse-loving, assistant box office manager. And on the wider front, Worcester, the heart-beat of Conservative England, would have its MP, the Rt Hon Peter Walker, back in government, after the victory in the June election of 'Selsdon Man', a sailor and conductor, admired by my parents; who themselves were secure again, Pa promoting the Propagators of the Gospel in the Diocese of Southwark, Ma free to go people-spotting. She wrote:

> ... *Today Mon & I have been to Iain MacLeod's memorial service...We saw so many people. Jeremy Thorpe looks so lonely. Ted Heath is a most imposing figure and looks every inch the PM. Harold W looks very ordinary indeed. Harold Macmillan read the lesson in a very old voice & he leans heavily on his stick. Anthony Barber look rather anxious about his new job. The Arch of Canterbury has aged a lot & the Bp of London* [my godfather's predecessor] *looks lugubrious, though he preached a fine eulogy. The MacLeod family were a most interesting clan – Mrs is very lame. The Abbey was packed but M & I got there early & got good seats. Afterwards we had lunch & collected M's glasses & I bought my brown lace-up shoes.*

*

After Worcester, I went straight up to Bradford. My perky playlets weren't going to Edinburgh after all – I wouldn't have been free anyway – but to the NUS drama Festival in January where they were less likely to get slaughtered. I had more work to do on the second and third plays, following the first showing of *Conrad*, which had been critically clobbered by David Edgar. My heart hadn't been in it anyway, what with the murder, the crabs (which came back), trouble resurfacing at home (E not communicating, J vanishing with her guy to Wales for the summer, and M in a froth about what to do, where to live, who to date, when she went to Tottenham Tech in the autumn to study hairdressing). For now though, all energy was to be directed to Chris's Yorkshire Arts/Gulbenkian-funded pilot season for the Bradford and Halifax Theatre Company. I would play a small linch-pin part (Lucius) in *Julius Caesar*, adapt *The Causasian Chalk Circle* for primary schools which Phil Emanuel would direct, then stand in for Chris as Fellow in Theatre at the University, hosting visiting companies, attending Arts Advisory meetings, directing *Lysistrata* and then *Toad of Toad Hall* for Christmas: all to be wrapped up by 10th December when I would whizz to Worcester, to rehearse the panto version of the summer revue at the Swan.

*

Looking back, I'm amazed at the trust Chris put in me. The Fellowship in Theatre, the job he *had to have*, he was loaning to me, to do with as *he* would, and put my own stamp on. He wouldn't interfere; he had enough on his plate, navigating and troubleshooting the unpredictables of his new company. I told him I'd never organized anything beyond cooking rotas at Cork, and Equity meetings at Nottingham, and I'd only ever directed one short play - my own - originally directed by him. Now I would run the office, chair meetings, promote and host visiting companies, and direct two large-cast plays with complex technical requirements and music. He must have seen something in me I wasn't yet aware of: a shift from blowing in the wind, to wanting to make my own storms. There was no template for the Fellowship, just the simplest of briefs: to create and deliver theatre in the university and the region. Chris was doing the region; I was to do the university. And as long as we both kept our shows on the road, the authorities would shine on us and give us money.

Lysistrata was my choice. We needed a play with a wealth of female parts, an anti-war stance and sex as the driving force. The Vietnam War was blundering on. Frustration at the do-nothing Heath government was intensifying. Women, with *The Female Eunuch* as their text, were wielding chastity as a weapon. It was a world Aristophanes knew well and I didn't need to modernize the costumes and set, only the language and the accents. The cities of Greece became the countries of Europe each personified by a different woman: Athens as Britain, Sparta as Germany, Megara as France etc. Without bending the text, I wanted to show the Peloponnesian War as a microcosm of World War One, and there were moments I hoped when the hilarity of the sex jokes would be pierced by shafts of horror, just as the jolly songs in *Oh What A Lovely War!* were shot down by the casualty figures. But it didn't work like that. In performance, the raunchiness over-rode everything. The pity of war stood no chance against prick-teasing nudes and engorged foam-rubber phalluses. JC would have hated it.

Toad of Toad Hall was Chris's choice: too infantile I protested for a student audience. Where was the politics, the sex? Poop poop, said Chris, there is no sex on the river bank: this is England! Politics though, runs thick on every page. Kenneth Graham, who wrote *Wind in the Willows* was a fascist; A A Milne, who wrote the play, was bourgeois to his finger-tips. A clever director can turn all that on its head. Who are the weasels, stoats and ferrets if not the homeless and jobless, alcoholics, psychotics, that toffs like Toad and his chums want swept away. So when they squat in Toad Hall and get violently evicted by the Tory-voting bastards, where do our sympathies lie? Who are we voting to avenge?

In the end though, again, it didn't quite follow that tack, probably because of the casting. David Edgar as Toad, David Cowling, President of the Union, as Ratty, student journalist and pillar of the left Ken Westgate as Badger, and chubby charming Rob Holleyhead as Mole - all having a ball playing against their professed politics - were never going to be hated. I had borrowed Jonathan Miller's take on *Alice in Wonderland*, making everyone people, not animals. There was no hiding behind masks. Bare-faced, any suppressed conservatism in the actors, could be outrageously released. It was Christmastime after all, and the show had to end with the full cast - fascists, bourgeoisie, squatters and psychotics - letting rip with streamers and balloons.

I left the last night party about 2 am, knowing I had to get a train to Worcester in the morning. There were no taxis, so I walked the two miles to the big house I was sharing with members of the Bradford and Halifax company. I was drunk, less with booze, more with the knowledge that I had turned a huge corner in my career. No longer the Jane Fonda figure from *Shoot Horses*, hopeful against hope, dancing on and on to someone else's tune, for a phantom reward; I was the MC, in the driving-seat, peddling the big lie, and only now, on the bed, in the dark, in my little room, aware that knowing I had the power to end it all, was what kept me going!

Scene Three
EDINBURGH

The Other Pool Synod Hall is located on two floors of a five-storey Regency terrace house half-way up Hanover Street. Hurrying up to Princes Street in your lunch break, you would pass it by, were it not for the stocky street arab, with fez and Nasser moustache, barking from the steps: 'NEW LUNCH-HOUR THEATRE! EAT HOT TATTIES! SEE HOT NEW PLAYS!' You're curious. He catches you: 'Hey, you wanna see Donkey have sex with my wife? You wanna see Churchill, Roosevelt, Stalin and de Gaulle watch Big Dick the Donkey shag Aisha the Big Cunt? NEW LUNCH-HOUR THEATRE! *THE PORT SAID PERFORANCE* BY MICHAEL ALMAZ! STEP THIS WAY!'

You're in. It's about to start. You just have time to purchase a tatty, a tassie and a ticket, as the crush sweeps you down, past the mural of the many-legged Jabberwocky, all the way down into the dark of the theatre, seating thirty or so at tables, with jalousie hangings and the smell of candles and incense. The play is crude, as you would expect: a pantomime donkey and a belly-dancer being auditioned, as entertainment for the troops, by the leaders of the free world (and Stalin), plus comedy guest star Tee-Hee Lawrence. It's a junk-show that defies scrutiny, the latest in a chain of new lunchtime plays, shown at the Pool since February. At the end, Ali the street arab, steps forward to announce that next week's play will be *The Tenant*, by Richard Crane.

✳

When I heard Chris was putting plays together for Bradford and Halifax, I decided to send him *Crippen* and *The Tenant*. Hampstead was a dead duck and the Swan at Worcester wasn't singing as I'd hoped. Chris read the scripts overnight, and phoned me to say why he couldn't do either. He already had a music hall/melodrama slotted in to close the season, which would rule out *Crippen* (why hadn't I sent it sooner?); and *The Tenant* wasn't radical enough for the short-play slot he'd been thinking of, which now wasn't happening, because Yorkshire audiences wanted only thrillers and comedies (both of which *The Tenant* was!). But he had passed it on to Phil Emanuel who was planning to launch a lunch-hour theatre in Edinburgh in the new year. *Crippen* we could discuss later. Dramaturgically it needed to decide what it was: a forensic re-examination to exonerate a wronged man; or full-on, late-night horror. 'Having fallen between the two, which stool should you clamber back onto Rick? In my view, the latter; then if it's really well done, it will also be the former. *The Tenant*: don't touch it. It's a gem.'

But first he wanted an *amuse-bouche*, to preface a tough feature David Edgar was writing for the Bradford Arts Festival in March. *Acid* would be Edgar's take on the Charles Manson murders of the previous year. Set in a well-off but lefty household on the Isle of Wight, during a Rock Festival, it would feature the murders of Jack, Margaret and their daughter Jill: good-time Labour voters who would have their complacency shredded by a trio of hippies who break in with knives. Not spaced-out psychopaths, as the title might suggest, Mike, Max and Patti are rational kids on a mission to kill. They believe the revolution must happen and it will be violent, starting with a class war to be triggered by random assassinations. Jack and Margaret have been mouthing a similar argument from an academic platform, not realizing that they, as bourgeois intellectuals, are first in line for extermination. They are eager to debate; the killers are eager to kill. As fear, then panic, then hysteria set in, they beg for Jill at least to be spared. But even she must be sacrificed. We are not asked to take sides. The crisis is presented and left for us to argue over. Like *Lovely War* and *Shoot Horses*, it is deeply offensive and unsettling and stays with you like a foul smell.

I wrote *Oil (or there's a lot of it about)* as a companion piece. Looked at again after forty-five years, it's a masterpiece of nonsense. Like an old

Greek, I seemed to have written a satyr play to offset the tragedy of *Acid*.
Three young flat-mates, Pearl (studious), Beryl (restless) and Ruby
(libidinous) have their power struggle arrested by the intrusion of two
strangers, Cuddles and Lofty, who start ripping up the cushions in search of
something unspecified. There is no political debate, no breaking and
entering, no violence to humans. Lines like 'the door was open... I walked
straight in...' are repeated without challenge. There is a car crash
(unconnected), a nose bleed, a murdered goldfish and Conway Twitty's *It's
Only Make-Believe*, as the theme song. I remember writing it almost in one
sitting, with the song on my dansette, playing with the dreamed-up selves
of assorted Bradford actors. Four in particular loomed large. Edgar himself
(six foot three) and Alan Bridger (six foot five) played Cuddles and Lofty as
an apologetic teddy-boy and his slow-thinking side-kick. Sally Dalglish (six
foot) and Sue Myerscough (five foot ten) would bring mental fragility and
closeted intellectualism to these and a string of plays.

Chris directed *Acid*, I directed *Oil*, in the university as part of the Drama
Group programme, then in the region as highlights of the Bradford Arts
Festival. Later, when Chris was assembling plays for Edinburgh, I assumed
the two would go up in tandem, but in the end only *Acid* went, because, as
he explained, there couldn't be two Crane plays in the Bradford programme,
and *Crippen* was a better sell.

> Tonight we bring you murder
> mutilation blood and lust
> for man is always man and cannot
> but return to dust...
> You are the jury, you and
> you alone must now decide
> how and why and when and whether
> Cora Crippen died.
> Watch the prisoner,
> watch his eyes;
> watch however
> hard he tries
> to veil the truth
> with perjured lies!
> He lives by you alone
> or dies!

The audience is the jury. The trial is end-of-the-pier entertainment, the
plot poking through the cracks like pop-up Shakespeare: star-crossed

lovers in flight - she disguised as a boy, he hounded by Nemesis and the march of technology. The little doctor - Moley (Rob Holleyhead) from *Toad of Toad Hall* - is an underground man, soft-spoken and driven to murder by his foghorn spouse, but still plodding and digging (in the cellar to hide the remains). Sally Dalglish, with her height, strange eyes, and operatic range, plays Cora, both the wrecker-ball wife, and the eviscerated wraith who comes to warn her killer 'BEWARE WIRELESS TELEGRAPHY!' Ethel (Michele Ryan), known as Not-Very-Well-Thank-You (her response to 'How do you do?') is the ingenue who knows more than you think she knows, but is kept mum by her lover, thus escaping the long arm of Inspector Dew (Ken Westgate - Badger from *Toad*) and the duff-you-up fists of Sergeant Mitchell (John Stratton - one of the engorged-phallus boys from *Lysistrata*) who also play, variously, Cockney rats in the Crippens' house, knockabout barristers in the trial, Marconi and his assistant, racing to get wireless telegraphy invented before Crippen lands in Canada, and Saints Peter and Paul welcoming the executed little doctor into an eternity of terrible singing from his everlasting wife.

I came up for *The Tenant*, meaning to stay for two weeks, then straight back to London where I had prospects of paid work. Bradford had been a tonic, and the Pool, with its emphasis on new plays and new audience, was an offshoot of Bradford, but it was unpaid, and I had to live. If Chris Parr were directing, maybe London venues might come, but he'd chosen to champion *The Port Said Performance*, which would go on to the Royal Court. Though miffed, I wasn't crushed, having a (secret) megabucks bonanza coming up at Worcester. *Tom Brown's Schooldays* the musical, book and lyrics by me, music by John Toll, the Swan's musical director, had been proposed by John Hole, the artistic director, after the success of the Christmas Revue, and we were working on getting script and score done by Easter, to go into production as the Swan's Big Summer Show. West End, then Broadway, were lining up as dreams for the new Crane-Toll combo. Then I got this from Hole:

> *Bad news, I'm afraid. We're going to have to postpone... impossible to cast in term-time... even your acting schools will be immersed in exams... Secondly it does seem that the appeal will be primarily to a very young audience. I myself had always thought it had the wider appeal of say an* Oliver!, *but... the universality of* Oliver! *is that it's the story of a child in an adult's world.* Tom Brown *(you see I'm coming round to your shorter title!), however well written (and I think it is) is always the story of a child in a child's world... My thought at present is*

that the show might work...as a secondary Christmas show... and I will definitely explore...

Added to all that, my mother was about to have a hysterectomy. The womb which had borne me, twenty-seven years ago, was worn out and being removed and I wanted to be around. I had just done a BBC schools' telly - *So You Want To Be A Car Mechanic?* - and there was the prospect of more similar, to keep me in London. I tried explaining this to Phil on the phone. 'No problem,' he laughed. 'WE ARE DOING YOUR PLAY, and if you're not up to being in it, we'll just have to cast Jeremy Irons. As for the Tenant himself, next week, there's a totally Caribbean play at the Traverse. T-Bone Wilson, Oscar James, Stefan Kalipha, are all free in the day - if we can get to them, before Lindsay Kemp who's doing *Woyzeck* late-night, and also looking for people! You don't know how EXCITING it is up here. Come now!'

I stepped into the Pool and straight into a crisis. The actor playing Captain Rosehip in *The Port Said Performance* had decided it was so disgusting he couldn't go through with it. He was something of a 'method' actor and disgust being the emotion that underpins the character, Chris and Phil weren't too bothered. The Captain has been deputed to arrange the performance with the donkey for the Leaders of the Free World (and Stalin) to assess its suitability for the victorious troops. Typically, he has no sense of humour, which makes comedy of his every action. So when the actor walked out, it was assumed to be just a quirk. Then the note was found: *'I'm sorry I can't do this. I'm a Christian.'* At which point, Richard Harbord walked in.

They sat me down, gave me a coffee.

'Rick,' said Chris, 'has never said no to a challenge.'

'We've got two days to plot you in,' said John Cumming, lighting designer and co-founder of the Pool.

'We're putting a gun to your head,' said Phil, as the street arab (and Stalin).

'As you will be putting a gun to mine to make *me* "perform",' said the backend of the donkey.

'That is so *not* the way to do it!' exclaimed Aisha. 'Let me talk to him.'

In her padding, she looked monstrous, so I was shocked in the dressing-room, when it all came off, to see a slim-legged, peachy-soft *gamine*, who looked fifteen, though as she said when I asked her if she was old enough to be shagging on stage, she was in fact twenty-six and married ('but don't let that stop you'). She helped me with the lines, going over them and over them - I was also FDR and Tee-Hee Lawrence - and steering me, as Rosehip, towards Captain Mainwaring from *Dad's Army* which Chris, Phil and Cumming said caught the character exactly.

After the first lunchtime, Aisha, unpeeling her grossness, said 'Let's go to the movies.'

Catch 22 was the latest in a stream of new hero-debunking comedies. From *Dr Strangelove* to *A Clockwork Orange*, these were a way of laughing at the news and heating up the cold war. The big boys could keep roaring like rutting elephant seals, mutually assuring their own destruction, then pulling back, and in proxy wars, beating up the little guys like Hungary and Laos. In the old 'modernist' days, you could dream of rising from the ashes with new philosophies and artforms to ensure no more war. Valiant hearts had laid down their lives in supreme sacrifice, so a new Eden could bloom. But when 'blooming Eden' invaded Suez, and Russia invaded Hungary, and America invaded everywhere, people like Heller, Kubrik, Altman and Nichols weighed in, up to their clapper-boards in blood,.

✳

As we came away from the cinema, the sun was still high. She had an hour before she needed to get the train home to Glasgow, so we took a detour down the steps into Princes Street Gardens.

'Will he meet you, your husband?'

'God no. We're hardly speaking. Ever since I discovered he preferred boys. He's a fucking liar. The film said it all. We're pigs in shit; that's why we piss about acting, till one comes along who's above it all; says he loves you, will lift you out of acting and make your life real. So do you marry him? Of course you do, and to start with it's just too sexy to be true, till gradually, day by day, moment to moment, you realise, it *isn't* true, it's all play, and it's getting cold, like in the film, when the wounded boy says "I'm cold" and Yossarian, holding him, says "it's all right, you'll be all right"; till he gingerly unpeels the shirt and a whole sickload of half-digested sludge comes flooding out, and the boy is still saying "I'm cold... I'm cold". Where are you staying?'

I told her I had a room in Guthrie Street, in the old town, sublet from Roz Birks, David Edgar's girlfriend. She was doing a doctorate in political science, coming back in two weeks, which was fine by me because I definitely wasn't staying longer than a fortnight. It was nice here, seductive even, but I couldn't afford to get stuck in the sticks. The main chances, we all knew, were down south, so you had to *be* there. And I didn't actually go with the 'pissing about acting' argument. Acting *was* my life, and if I was pissing about, it was just because I hadn't yet found my niche.

We were sitting on the grass under a tree. The sun was sinking. 'Every boy needs a niche,' she agreed, 'for slotting into;' then kissing me: 'I can help you find one.'

No one passing by seemed to notice two actors having sex in the gloaming in Princes Street Gardens. When we'd finished, she said: 'Ach! Missed the train. I'll have to stay over with you.'

Out of the geometry of the New Town, we cut across to the higgledy-piggledy of Auld Reekie. Guthrie Street had seen whore-hunting, witch-whipping; Burke and Hare dragging bodies up the slippery setts; child-murderer George Robertson, howling, as he carried the corpse of his son. 'This is it,' I said, looking up at the tenement untouched since John Knox's time. 'We're at the top. Six floors.' It was as I'd imagined old Carneggie my French teacher climbing his last climb. Is suicide painless? Does it bring on many changes? Roz's room is a bare-boarded, curtainless attic with washstand, chamber-pot, cold tap on the landing and a big brass bed. There are no lamp-shades or moral standards. We can do as we like here: sleep a bit, love a bit, talk a bit, cuddle a bit. How many times? I was keeping a tally. By morning, including Princes Street Gardens, I'd clocked *seven ejaculations*, which though not a world record, was a personal best, and remains so.

HIGH DRAMAS

LETHAL PASSION OF THE TENANT

Richard Crane's The Tenant *is a duologue that begins sedately enough and midway bursts into a lethal passion. But the characters, a mild little bespectacled gas-meter reader and a Negro who has dropped in, have on their minds, at least at first, no more than the tenancy of the basement flat. The man in occupation is played by Richard Harbord, as everybody's idea of a harmless clerk; he has advertised a room to let, and Oscar James as the Negro is his first caller... It transpires that he has not read the advertisement and that in fact he has a better title to the flat than the sitting tenant...Oscar James's authority highlights the other's shifty untrustworthiness. His sudden access to power surges up like that of a well-built car, and subsides only beyond the curtain.*

- The Scotsman

Ruth Tarko was in. She had come to see Oscar but he already had representation, so she took me to lunch instead. I should have told her I also had a London agent and would be heading down south as soon as *The Tenant* was over; but the lunch was free and the old mantra 'never say no to anything' was raising its hungry head. And she had loved *The Tenant*, loved the writing - who was the author? - loved the way right from the start, the physical difference between me and Oscar had provoked an audible ripple that bubbled up into laughter, then back down to a ripple, before a word had been spoken. She was new to agenting, she said, still uncluttered by doubt. Fancy-free, vagabond actors were her bag. Was I such a one? She had seen me in *Port Said*, flitting between widely divergent roles, and now this one, so unsettling, because you feared for him as well as hating him. Thank you, I said, and I'm the author as well. Having different names helps, especially if someone is okay on the acting but dubious on the script, or vice versa. Was I free, she got to the point, tomorrow for an interview? I'd have to come to Glasgow. There was a part in the final two episodes of *High Living* - had I heard of it? TV soap about a family relocated to a high-rise? I said sure, there was an actor at the Pool who'd been in it, said it was terrible. Ruth laughed, a head-thrown-back laugh you had to join in with, as if 'terrible' were just the ticket, and there was no way you wouldn't be on the train tomorrow, straight after the show. I could stay over at her place - she ran a nursing home as well as the agency and there were spare beds for vagabonds. But hang on hang on, I couldn't do that, I told her, because tomorrow was the first night of *Woyzeck* at the Traverse and apparently I was in it. What time, she asked. Ten-thirty, late night, but the call is 8pm for notes. I'd told Lindsay - that's Lindsay Kemp - I was only in it for one week and he should try and retrieve the guy I was replacing - what was his name? - and he'd said sure Ziggie Stardust is just pining to get back into my pants! Well that was the deal I told him last night after the chaos of the dress rehearsal - typical Kemp everyone said, mainly because the script had been abandoned because Lindsay hadn't learnt it - he didn't do *lines* for fucksake! He was *a silent artiste* reinventing the *genre* with his first talkie!

Ruth was flipping her diary. Seems I'm coming to that tomorrow. We can get the six-ten.

She wasn't on the six-ten and I was relieved. I'd wasted a train fare. I'd got to Scottish TV in good time then sat around for half an hour. When the director called me in, all he said was 'Can you play guitar?' (I said yes) and 'How's your Glasgow?' (I said fine), then the phone rang and he was arguing. I should have walked out, but his assistant was gluing me to my seat with her eyes, as if I were catch of the day. Call over, he stood up, shook my hand: 'Welcome to *High Living*. Give him the scripts Morag.'

As the train rattled through Kirkintilloch, Cumbernauld, Falkirk, I skimmed the part: a failed rock star and Celtic fan who terrorises lassies in the lift, then sings and plays inappropriately at a ceilidh. Never say no, but I might have to. I'd never touched a guitar and to do Glasgow in Glasgow was to trigger kibbles of shite. As I was reading, I was rewriting. What if he's *really* an outsider? What if it's *Birmingham City* not Celtic, and his guitar has been *vandalised*, so he can only play it *badly*, which is why he gets mad in the lift, and how he gobsmacks the gillies at the ceilidh, singing

> bheir me o, horo van o
> bheir me o, horo van ee
> bheir me o, o horo ho
> sad am I, without thee...

in a brummie accent?

When I rang Ruth the next day, to say I wasn't doing it, she was full of apologies. Her husband Wally was sick, 'and I mean *sick*, as a scottie, after a *Glasgow Belongs To Me* reunion. So I missed *Woyzek*. How did it go?' I told her it was a triumph and I'd agreed to stay on the extra week. 'That's great', she said, 'because *High Living* is in studio August 3rd to 13th, so, hang on, that's one more week, I'll put you up.' I said: Can I ask you something? Can I rewrite the script? She laughed, her full-throat, head-thrown-back laugh: 'Oh please! It needs it! Do what you like; they don't do retakes.' So I did it in brummie. I ditched the guitar. I sang 'bheir me o...' like Elvis unaccompanied, and no one batted an eyelid. You didn't rehearse, you just went straight in and unless you yelled 'SHIT! I'VE FUCKING DRIED!' it went out as it was. It was a challenge to make your mark in the story, because these, after ten years, were the final two episodes: people were emigrating to Canada, or being crushed by trucks. Added to that, half the studio were not speaking to the other half. The rift that had been widening for a decade was now unbridgeable. The director's wife who played the lead - I only noticed this when I watched the episode - was in close-up *reacting* for the whole of the great declamation of her rival, even though she was hardly in the scene. It was my first foray into soap, and the fifteen minutes of fame it engendered, actually saved me from hypothermia, as you shall see...

It went into studio just as *The Tenant* was closing and for a week I was commuting to Glasgow then back to Edinburgh, late night, to be mucked about by Lindsay and made to drink his piss - just water from a squirter to start with, then on the Wednesday, the real thing because he'd downed too many lagers. I'd always been told: *never drink before the show*, because while *you* may feel fabulous, all the audience sees is a sad drunk. And I told him, in the dressing-room, when he came in glowing, I just yelled at him: HE WAS RUINING THE SHOW! HE WAS EVEN DRINKING IN THE WINGS! I WAS A PRO! I HAD STANDARDS! HE HAD TO PROMISE HE WOULD NEVER DRINK AGAIN OR I'D BE OFF AND I MEANT IT! I'D LEAD A WALK-OUT, EVEN IF IT MEANT CLOSING THE SHOW! BECAUSE NO ONE HERE WAS PREPARED TO PUT UP WITH THE EMBARRASSMENT!

There was silence. No one moved. Then he said, quietly, soberly: 'So piss off, you cunt. Fuck off back to your Other Pool Wee-Free Synod *matinee entertainment*. We are not actors here; we are hedonists to the hilt. We are terribly into intoxication. It frees the spirit. It loosens your pretty arse, you script-based, shit-faced, fucked-up little thesp. Have you not heard of Dionysus?'

I cleaned my face, hung up my costume (for the last time); put my street-clothes on and my PVC mack, packed my make-up - unused because Lindsay himself paints your face with his paints: blank white base; eye-brows and side-burns, straight slashes of black; black holes, black chasms for the lips and eyes - and walked out, never to return. The day before, I'd given all my STV earnings to a fellow actor who was selling his Vespa. I needed to be independent and see something of Scotland. I had the key, a full tank and my freedom, ready to go, but I hadn't yet ridden it. I'd never ridden a Vespa or any motorized bike. So it suited my mood, to kickstart and rearing up like a bronco, roar wobbledy-wobbledy up the setts by the Castle, onto Lothian Road, out of the city, into the night.

*

Once there was a poor boy with no mother and no father. Everything was dead and there wasn't a soul left on earth. And the boy went out and searched day and night. But since there was no one left on earth, he wanted to go to heaven, and indeed the moon looked down kindly on him, but when he got up to the moon, it was just a piece of rotten wood. So he set off for the sun, and when he got there it was only a withered sunflower, and when he got to the stars they were only gold-en gnats that a shrike had stuck to a blackthorn bush, and when the boy wanted to go back down to earth, it was just an upside-down piss-pot and the boy was all alone. Then he sat down and cried and he's still sitting there to this day, all alone.

I couldn't get the speech of the grandmother out of my head. I'd done with *Woyzeck*, destroyed it, because I knew they'd never replace me by tomorrow. I'd imagined I'd be racing, free at last, along the highway, hair streaming in the moonlight (I had no helmet), but it was only *dead wood, a withered sunflower* and *gnats* that came to mind as I phut-phutted west - was I on the right road? My plan was precise: head west for the hills, get to Oban by morning, book into a b&b, have breakfast and a kip, then catch the ferry to Mull, scoot across the island, hail a boat and pass a peaceful day in the solitude of Iona. But I was already going wrong. The Lothian - *loathian* - Road was diverting me. The bike was sluggish. I was tired. It was pitch dark and beginning to rain. I could feel drops finding a path down my neck under the PVC, and trickling off the end of the mack onto my jeans. A heavy-goods truck barrelled past so close I skidded into the kerb. I was going to have to stop. My plan had been to restore myself, as Columba and his monks had done on Iona back in Celtic times: find a beach in a cove, secluded, out of time, swim free in the sun-kissed waves of the Gulf Stream. But it wasn't going to work. If I ever got there, I'd have to turn right around and head back. I wasn't called for *High Living* till Friday, so I'd need to be at Ruth's, in a vagabond bed, Thursday evening, ready to go. I'd have to phone her, but when? It was already Thursday one o'clock, and what would I say? I'd imagined, when I flounced out of the Traverse, I'd ride through the night, on the wings of fury, but I was dropping with tiredness. Another truck blasting past made me veer off left towards the Forth, and suddenly there it was: shadowy in the dark, defiant in the rain, the mighty affirmation of industry in the face of nature, magnetizing me downwards. My mother had been born here. The shadowy galumphing piers had been her strength. However slight her frame, however short her slimmed-down name (Nan), the NOWELL, the CHAMBLERLAIN and the HARBORD of her christening, would carry her across any surge of fate: even hysterectomy. As I parked the bike and looked up at the mighty girders, I knew where I should be: on a train, racing south to be at her bedside when she woke: the fruit of the womb she was losing, now grown-up. Tomorrow, I vowed, I would ride back to Edinburgh, get the next train down to London.

But first I needed shelter. Where to look? Behind me I could hear the creak of a swinging sign: the Hawes Inn, a name I recalled from *Kidnapped* by R L Stevenson. Davie Balfour would have heard that creak, as he went in with his uncle, prior to being to be stowed, unconscious, aboard the *Covenant*. But all the lights were out. Uncle Ebenezer, Captain Hoseason and Ransome the cabin boy, must all be abed. But I rang the bell anyway then hammered on the door - I was drenched, exhausted, nearly dead from cold - and went on hammering till a light came on, and I heard the yanking back of bolts and a key turning.

A year or so before, I had been with my mother to see her favourite actress Bette Davis in a film called *Whatever Happened To Baby Jane?* Bette, said my mother, was the epitome of style and a force of beauty, who had challenged the tyranny of the studios and won two Oscars. In this film she would play a child star grown up, now caring for her crippled sister, played by Joan Crawford. But instead of style, beauty and the challenge to tyranny, what we saw now was a monster: a child grown hideous, a face collapsed, eyes bloodshot and sagging, and a mouth like a black-rimmed, cackling, bottomless pit. This was the foulest performance by any actress I had ever seen, the kind of hell-hole Lindsay Kemp was adept at sucking you into. However far you phut-phutted out of his orbit, he-she would always be there to confront you, hammering on any door.

'Wha' d'ye want?' said the smoked-wrecked, Scottish Baby Jane, peering round the still-chained door of the Hawes Inn.

'A bed for the night, if you have one, ma'am.'

'Nae vacancies. D'ye nae ken wh' o'clock it is?"

I stuck my foot in the door: 'Please. I'm toired. I'm nearly doying with cowld.'

In my despair, as sometimes happened, it was coming out in brummie.

'Whissht,' her face cracked. 'Do ah ken ye? Or are ye jest famous? What was it ye were in? What did ah see ye in?'

I said: 'Possibly you saw me in *High Living* last week...'

And that did it. I was in, but there was no bed yet. I had to talk, over a dram, and another one, and a third, about how it was all going to end: who was emigrating to Canada, who was being killed by a truck, what would happen to the unflappable, newly widowed Mrs Crombie. I made a pretence of not being able to spill the beans so she must promise not to tell. It was tragic, shocking, the only way; it was Life. And Mrs Crombie would be honoured with a soap all of her own. (I would be in that one too.) 'And now,' I said, as a clock struck three. 'You need yair bed,' she interposed and softening from Baby Jane into Janet from *Dr Finlay's Casebook*, she filled a stone hot-water-bottle and led me to a little room in the roof, promising porridge and eggs and tattie scones in the morning.

*

The more determined you are to leave, the more certain it is you will come back. Those body-parts in the cellar, will always smell up your dreams. There is no happy-ever-after for the one who sticks a knife in his friend. Such whisky-fuelled truths were fuddling my brain as I chain-smoked in the attic room. I must have slept about an hour, because suddenly the sun was beaming in through the window and there were voices on the stairs. Ransome, Hoseason and Ebenezer were up and about, having breakfast. I decided to wait till they'd gone, then realizing I'd slept in my clothes, took them off, had a wash, put them on again and went down to breakfast. My saviour from last night, was now the busy landlady, ladling the last of the porridge, regretting no tattie scones. I checked out at mid-day. The bridge, rust-red and sturdy in the sunlight, seemed to be saying: Don't rush away. So I took a tour round the village, stopping at the tiny six hundred year-old Priory Church where my grandfather had been priest and my mother, with her monumental names, had been baptised. Then I sped back to Edinburgh. I'd forgotten that Roz Birks, David Edgar's girlfriend, was coming back and I'd have to get out of Guthrie Street. I got there just in time to clean up and pack and ring Phil who said sure I could stay at his place, if I didn't mind sharing with Viv Stanshall of the Bonzo Dog Doodah Band who was doing a gig this weekend. I said I'd be in Glasgow late Sunday and Monday, back Tuesday (the Traverse didn't play Mondays) so that was fine; would he be in if I came round now in a taxi? I was out just as Roz was coming in - neat timing - and round at Phil's spacious, multi-occupied flat in the Meadows in time for tea. Before I could tell him, I'd walked out of *Woyzeck*, he said he was coming tonight, so I'd better live up to the Scotsman review which had singled me out as the best thing to hit Lindsay's company since Bowie. Had I seen it? No I hadn't? Did he have a copy? No he didn't. Would I be stupid enough to harm myself even more than Lindsay by not turning up, thus creating a scandal that might lead to legal action? The more determined you are to leave, the more certain it is you'll come back. I came back.

No one commented when I walked into the dressing-room, stripped, got white-faced, daubed the black tapering streaks for eye-brows and side-burns, black holes for eyes, black chasm for mouth. Lindsay, nice as pie, checked me - 'smile for your darling' - even ruffled my hair, placed the top-per and tapped it as if to say 'silly thespian tit'. Then we went on stage to do breathing, dance moves, vocals, reverse bowing - with Lindsay you *un*-bowed, starting down and slowly growing, reaching out and up, miming: NEVER SUBMIT TO ANY BASTARD CRIT! Had anyone read the Scotsman? The Traverse normally pasted them up in the foyer, even the bad ones, and when I asked Poppy Front of House, had they been in, she said no, and when Phil didn't come as he'd said he would, the penny dropped. He'd been in last night and heard about the walk-out, so did what he does: invent, distort, cajole, have a laugh - 'oh and by the way, Jack Ronder's *The Free Ranger*, we're doing it, battery chickens, Miriam Margolyes, Alex Norton and you, type casting! Double bill with *The Tenant*, first week of the Fest, with *Port Said* to follow. Wanna do it? Say Cluck!'

*

The Doctor is on the roof with a cat. Woyzeck is below, seeking a cure for neurasthenia. The Doctor, like David watching Bathsheba in the pool, her knickers on the line, is distracted from marking the critical distance beyond which the cat, when thrown, will not land naturally on its feet. Woyzeck, a soldier in a world gone mad, wants only to be convinced that Marie, the love of his life and mother of his son, is not in a sexual relationship with the Drum Major. The Doctor throws the cat; Woyzeck catches it; it bites him. Point diverted, not proved. The doctor prescribes peas for the pulse, and pulse for the peas. There are muscles in the ears unused that must be trained. Eat pulse, drink pee, waggle the ears, be free. Woyzeck is cowed by the Doctor, loving with Marie, noisy and rude with the drinkers in the inn, broken up and racked with suspicion when alone. He blows with the wind that is whirling across Europe as the New Napoleonic World Order is washed away, in the blood of Waterloo. Now might is right, the loudest wins and everything is permitted. Only a knife in the heart can arrest the deceit.

Let her have it Franz! *Woyzeck* is not an unfinished play, just a montage of scenes, like genes on a chromosome: a time-bomb, undiscovered for forty years, unperformed for seventy. Georg Buchner, a doctor from a family of doctors, the rebel who ran away and could only waggle his ears, three generations before Dostoyevsky, a century before Stravinsky, Eisenstein and Munch, died at twenty-four, unsung, leaving just two expressionist plays and a thread of scenes, all of which, at some point, as an actor, I was in.

BETTE AND THE BULL

I had three spare days between the end of *High Living* and rehearsals for the Festival, so I scooted down to London, stopping at Saltburn for a vicarage lunch with Elizabeth, Roy, Nicholas, Rosalind and Felicity, then straight on down, non-stop to London to be at her bedside when my mother woke. Freed at last of the trapping of motherood, she could now take a job, as she had done in Jamaica, and not worry (too much) about us sibs and our schemes: Elizabeth having babies, Jude wanting to marry Mike, Mon partying at Tottenham Tech, and me in a tumble of far-away plays, about to break into film. 'There are two,' Ruth had said, 'that I'm putting you up for, the first one starting the week after next. You'll have an interview for that one this afternoon at four. The director of the second, is coming tomorrow to the double bill. *The Duna Bull* is about farming, so he'll appreciate battery hens, in particular your ability, and Miriam's, and Alex's, (exploding with laughter) to be stuck in a tea-chest, waggging only your heads!!!' Ruth, I said, there's just a couple of snags. I'm committed to *The Port Said Performance*, week after next, and the Bradford group are doing my *Crippen*, next week and I'll need to see it in. She said *Madame Sin* didn't start till the following Tuesday, so *Crippen* was fine (would I get her a ticket?), and for *Port Said*, she already had a replacement in mind, a hugely promising young actor just out of drama school called Ian Charleson. There was going to be recasting anyway - hadn't I heard? - with Miriam stepping in as Aisha, instead of whatshername, who was pregnant and having to quit.

*

David Greene, feet on the desk, wore high-heeled cowboy boots and a stetson.

'How tall are you?' was all he asked.

'Five foot ten,' I replied. (I'd been warned to be tall, so was wearing three inch lifts.)

'The part is the naval policeman who arrests Robert Wagner - he's six foot two; you'll be on a box - then drives Gordon Jackson in a motor-boat round the bay. Could you do that?'

I said sure.

'You'll be needed for two weeks. It's all on location at Tobermory, Isle of Mull. Do you have any questions?'

'Who's Madame Sin?

'She's the villain, wants to rule, then destroy the world.'

'I mean who's playing her?'

'Bette Davis.'

*

Alan Dobie, Denholm Elliott, Dudley Sutton, Roy Kinnear and Gordon Jackson were just some of the actors I was holed up with for two weeks in the Isle of Mull Hotel. Robert Wagner was the James Bond figure, inveigled by global menace Madame Sin into hijacking a Polaris submarine for a third-world tyrant. With the stature of a Kennedy, and divorced from, and soon to remarry Natalie Wood, who would later die in a suspicious boating accident, Bob (as we called him) was chummy with all strata of actor, including me; tossing fivers at the barman (but not buying us drinks), and demanding fair combat at the ping-pong table which, being who he was, he always won, but only just. He was dating Tina Sinatra who was with him all through, but having no role in the film, was at an even looser end than I was, so we spent a lot of time together,. Every night there'd be a phone call, which I answered for her once.:

'This is Frank. (Wha-hay!) Can I speak to my daughter?'

I wrote home: 'I just spoke to Frank Sinatra! But I haven't met Bette yet.'

The next evening, I was having dinner with Alan, Denholm, Dudley, Roy and Gordon, when she came in. She looked tired, a little lost, but disguising it with the film-star hauteur she could never completely lose. Her face, hoisted every morning by make-up, had slithered down through the day to its Baby Jane worst. Her famous eyes were at their bloodiest. She had lost the don't-care sluttishness that had become her acting trademark, and was much too thin.

'Did you,' her voice cracked, 'have a good day's filming?'

'Yes Miss Davis,' we chorussed like schoolboys.

Actually it was far from a good day; it was chaotic. We'd done the scene where I had to clap a hand on Bob's shoulder and say sternly: 'You're under arrest!' But I'd forgotten my lifts. Suddenly I was a full eight inches shorter than my prey, and however many boxes they put me on, it still failed to convince. In the end, David Greene, himself in high-heeled boots, sent Bob's stand-in, to be costumed and to play the part for me. That left me only one scene, the motor-boat ride round the harbour, which, not being insured, I wasn't allowed to drive. 'Do I even need to be on it?' I asked, keen to get back to my Scrabble game with Roy Kinnear. 'Just get aboard,' said Greene. 'You're the radio operator.' But there wasn't a radio, so as we swirled around the bay, as Lindsay would have done, I mimed it, forgetting that film is a naturalistic medium, so that if you ever watch the scene, you'll see a figure with a hand to his face, as if picking his nose. But of course you won't see it. Coming out the following year, *Madame Sin* went straight back in again. I saw it just once in the early hours on tv, and I understand now why Bette was so uncomfortable when we met her, It was the worst film she'd ever made and it was probably her decision that it should never be released.

One beautiful day, when once again only Bette, Denholm and Bob were called, I took Alan Dobie on my pillion across the island to Fionnphort, where we hailed a boat to Iona. He was a serious, intelligent actor, now marking time on a pot-boiler and, so he said, enjoying the break. We had plenty to talk about: Yorkshire - he was from Barnsley; the Old Vic School, where he studied under Glen Byam Shaw and George Devine ('You have to go to drama school, because at least you're acting all the time instead of just looking around'); the Royal Court in its glory days with Arden and Wesker ('it's the *writing* that makes a play; if you're a writer, then *write*, don't mess about acting!'); and Prince Andrey in the BBC's *War and Peace* which would be his next major role. We walked in silence round the abbey, dating back to the sixth century, then wandered, listening to the gulls and the waves till we found a beach in a cove where I thought we might swim. But Alan was lost in thought; so we just sat on a rock, in contemplation of the universe, as the sun sank and it grew cool.

We got back too late for dinner, so had bar food and a bottle of wine which we shared with Bob, Denholm and Tina. I felt happy, though slightly dissatisfied and superfluous, hearing talk of the day's filming, in which I no longer had a part.

*

A year later I was watching Alan again, lying wounded among the corpses on the battlefield of Austerlitz, looking up at the sky:

> How quiet, calm and solemn it all is! So different from the noise, the screaming, the fighting. The way the clouds creep across the infinity of sky! How did I never see this before? How happy I am to be seeing it at last! All else is vanity; all is false except this infinite sky. Nothing else exists, nothing except this, this silence, peace...

*

The road from Oban to Cape Wrath is just under two hundred miles, across the most mountainous landscape in Britain. Laurence Henson, director of *The Duna Bull*, would have sent a car, but I assured him, doing Edinburgh to London and back, plus the trip to Mull, was proof of my proficiency as a long-distance easy-rider. It was a blissful day, clouds creeping across the infinity of sky, as I phut-phutted up hills and scootered down dales, the warm breeze in my hair, a new film on my mind. *Madame Sin* had been big and I was tiny within it. *The Duna Bull* was tiny but I was the linch-pin, if not the lead. I would arrive independent, having crossed the heartland of Scotland, as Robert the Bruce had done, in the saddle, chasing the wind. I'd read somewhere that riding, helmetless, at speed, exposed to the elements, was as heady as any drug! Up hill, down dale, alone on the road, except for a few cars who didn't know, being behind glass, the exalted state they were missing: I was flying to the sun, a star in my own firmament! And that was when the clutch-cable snapped. Phut, and it was dead. Like severing an aorta. I hadn't even reached Fort Augustus, the crossing place from the Grampians into the Highlands: still some hundred miles to go along winding mountain roads, to Tongue where the company were staying. Would I get there before six tomorrow morning when the call was? And I had lines to learn, and a cast and crew to be relaxed with and get to know. How long would it take to push a Vespa, heavy and stubborn, up hill, then free-wheel down dale, for a hundred miles? I cursed my fate and the actor who'd sold me a bum bike. Better to die, and be picked clean by eagles, than succumb to praying to a God who must be killing himself laughing. But I did pray: Oh God, send me a motor-cycle repair shop, and I will eat your flesh and drink your blood, if that's what turns you on. And I looked up and through the mist of tears, I saw, on the horizon, a church. Aha. Prayer answered, a little too literal, but I could at least phone and maybe Laurence would send a car. Then as I drew nearer, I saw a sign, not JESUS SAVES, but (this is true, I swear!) *MOTOR CYCLE REPAIRS!!!* Yea Lord! I believe! The world was made in six days! The sun circles the earth! Alleluia! I pushed the bike to the door. The ex-church was a wonderland of Triumphs and Harley Davidsons. A little man came out from under a machine. Clutch cable? Ach, as guid as fexed, wee laddie! Almost sobbing, I paid him twice what he asked, and scooted off across the treeless wastes of Sutherland, getting to Tongue in time to have supper with Laurence and Juliet Cadzow my co-star, before turning in early, learning lines, saying prayers, and crashing instantly like a log.

*

Charlie Johnson doesn't enter the film until a third of the way through. He is a desk-bound official from the Ministry of Agriculture, despatched to the island of Duna, to investigate the disappearance of a bull. Duna lies way out in the Atlantic, beyond the Outer Hebrides, and sustains a small cattle-breeding community. The beauty and brains of the island is Helen (played by Juliet) who teaches in the school and is loved by Calum, a beefy but surly cowherd. When the islanders' only bull falls off a cliff, breaks a leg and has to be shot (and eaten) they send a message to the ministry requesting a replacement. Before such an expense can be met, Charlie Johnson must investigate and, to save costs, recommend, not an actual bull, but artificial insemination. Johnson arrives, seasick and awkward, to be ridiculed by the islanders who flatly refuse the offer of insemination. But Helen has taken a shine to the official, and when the tabloids seize on the story of an isolated community facing down a heartless bureaucracy and threatening to scandalize the government, Johnson (who has taken a shine to Helen) argues successfully for a shaggy-fringed, longhorn highlander, called Wully, to be delivered to the island, insisting that he himself should transport it. Braving wind and weather, man and bull make it across the sea, to find - oh no! - there is no landing on Duna. Undeterred, Charlie pushes Wully overboard, not knowing if he can swim. The islanders and Helen watch anxiously from the shore, as bovine nostrils bob in the water, and the great shaggy beast rises up from the waves, then skips off to the meadow to meet his happy harem. Charlie and Helen exchange a look and a laugh which confirm that they too have romantic matters to pursue, and so the credits roll.

*

I've just seen *The Duna Bull* again and one thing is certain: this is Juliet's film. Coming from a cattle-breeding family, she radiates 'the good earth' like a Hardy heroine. She was raised on the Isle of Luing in the Firth of Lorn, which her father and bis brothers had bought in the 1940s. Here they crossed Shorthorn with Highland to create the Luing, a fast-growing breed that could forage in all weathers so didn't need indoor wintering. As Helen in *The Duna Bull*, with her knowledge of cattle and island life, Juliet was a handy adviser for Laurence and a fair challenge to me. Not since applauding a bull 'footing' a cow with Trevor Beeton at Laxton, when I was six, had I had any contact with cattle, and watching the film again, it was obvious I was acting. 'You're not Brian Rix', said Laurence on the first day, when I made a meal of jumping off the boat and wading ashore in my socks, carrying my wellies to keep them dry; whereas Juliet hardly acted at all, which I suppose is what you learn at drama school, *not* to act. She had just graduated from the Royal Scottish Academy, and gone straight into playing Meg in *The Birthday Party* at the Lyceum. We had an instant rapport which added an extra layer of comedy not evident in the script, but she easily won out in the what-to-do-with-your-face-on-screen stakes, keeping hers loose and still, whereas mine was all over the place. It got better as we went along and you can tell, watching the film, which bits were shot first and which came later. Just thirty minutes long, *The Duna Bull* became a minor classic, shown at festivals and as promotion for the Scottish Tourist Board, coming somewhere between *Whisky Galore* for its Gaelic charm, and *The Wicker Man*, made two years later (in which Juliet once again played a woman of the land, this time pagan and murderous). By the end, I was wishing I could have rewritten some of my scenes. There was more to be had in the lead-up to pushing Wully overboard and seeing him sink - this was done with a dummy bull, in reality a sofa with a rug on it - and I'd have liked to have had more to say to Juliet at the end, instead of just laughing at the heifers dancing round Wully like dizzy girls. Dobie had said: 'If you want to write, write. Don't mess about acting,' and I began doing just that, as the fortnight wore on, in my room, after supper, writing a short, Pinterish comedy - *Decent Things* - about a mismatched honeymoon couple on their wedding night, which Juliet and I would play at the Pool, the following year.

But first I had to get back down south. I'd come up originally for just two weeks and I'd stayed for fifteen. I'd acted in two films, three lunchtime plays, one of which I'd written, plus a late-show for the festival; I'd survived the roller-coaster of *Woyzek* and indulged the brief froth of a slippery soap. I was a proven easy-rider on the thespian scene. I now needed to apply all that chutzpah and derring-do genius where it mattered. I was ballooning with ideas.

I rang Chris.

Scene Four
THE BRADFORD REVOLUTION

I stopped over at Bradford on my way down to London. Chris was excited. He had a trio of plays on his mind which he said should form the guts of the beast he was rearing for next year's Edinburgh. One wasn't even written yet; one (he believed) was written but not yet performed, and one, though it had been written *and* performed in a big way, was actually just beginning its journey.

But we were getting ahead of ourselves. First there was curry to be eaten and a summing up to be done. As we dunked our chapatis and scooped our keema, we reflected on how far Bradford had come in just two years, and the key factor was Edinburgh. Back in 1970, Bradford had hardly been out of Bradford, let alone over any cultural or national border. 'Make theatre in the university, the city and the region', was the brief for the Fellowship, and Chris felt he had fulfilled that with the Bradford and other local Festivals, the Bradford and Halifax season, collaborations with Bingley, Bretton Hall and Bradford Art College etc. It was now time to hit Edinburgh with a cargo of squealers: entirely new plays by new writers, risky even on the Fringe which back then was still hosting mainly revivals of classics, recent hits and student revues. But in 1970 a Bradford ball had been set rolling: a cannon ball as it turned out, that would presage havoc in '71 and *hecatombs* of havoc in '72 with the imagined quake of Chris's trident of 'gutsy' plays.

'Which are...?' I enquired.

'More cucumber raitta (pronounced "writer")!' barked Chris. 'Raitta for a writer! More Bombay duck? Which is a fish! Ha!'

'You were telling me about the three plays that are on your mind,' I ventured. 'And I'm not sure the "squealers" reference is still relevant. We weren't slaughtered this year, or even last year.'

'Horses,' said Chris. 'Theatres now have "stables" of new writers: not the angry young colts of the fifties, but their kid brothers! *Anything may happen, no predictions are possible.*'

He was quoting the strapline for the '71 programme. Between the Traverse, where later he would be Artistic Director, and the Pool, founded on his principles by his former student Phil Emanuel, he was forging a path straight to the heart of a new audience. Behold today's human monsters, he was telling them. Look them in the eye, get under their skin: Lieutenant Calley in Brian Waddington's *Callousness and Dessert*, on the My Lai Massacre; Charles Manson, in David Edgar's *Acid*, reimagining the Hollywood killings. Then add in the imperative to relive history as news, in

Michael Almaz's *Inquisition* about fifteenth century Spain and the application of absolute cruelty to ensure happiness, and then the late-night *Crippen* - *'brilliantly harmonised into one continuous act by Crane...not for the squeamish'* (Scotsman).

'Too right,'I smiled.

'But you weren't there,' said Chris.

'I was there for the first night. Someone fainted. Someone puked.'

'We had casualties every night. It was a triumph! Then the debates in the bar; you should have been there. Crippen, Calley, Manson, Torquemada, where do you draw the line with murderers? Do we have to be moral? Can we twist things for entertainment? What if we end up applauding Hitler? In my view, and Howard's, and David's and I hope yours, we should get as near to the very edge as we can, with our heroes, before toppling them over. Rick, what do you think? You saw *Scott?'*

SCOTT OF THE ANTARCTIC

...or What God Didn't See by Howard Brenton, was performed on ice at the Silver Blades Rink as the high point of the Bradford Arts Festival, March 1971. It featured David Edgar as God, in a wheelchair; Tim Davies as the Devil, on a motorbike; David Cowling (Ratty from *Toad* and former President of the Union) as Scott, with his chums Evans, Bowers, Oates and Wilson, on tennis rackets, pulling sledges, falling over, getting up again, falling over etc. In contrast, the Bradford Ice Skating Club performed exhibition skating to Vaughan Williams's *Sinfonia Antarctica,* and to counter Scott and his team's gung-ho British pluck, an anti-Scott ghost figure (Roland Miller from *The People Show*), frost-bitten, in rags, clutching a teddy bear, haunted the performance, on the ice and in the audience. I was in Bradford at the time, and in two minds about seeing *Scott.* I wanted it to be brilliant, because I wanted to be in it, but as I wasn't, I didn't want to be just a punter, cheering it on. I'd read the first few scenes, which were terrific and had offered to play the empire-obsessed George V, in a double act with long tall Sally Dalglish as Queen Mary; but Chris wanted an older actor. (Why? The man was new on the throne, forty-something and immature; I could do that!) So I was less than happy, walking in with crowds of schoolkids and local worthies; finding Roland Miller's interventions distracting, and the dialogue laboured, being repeated three times, in different directions, through loud-hailers; and wishing Chris wouldn't stomp round the audience, snatching crisp-packets from kids and yelling WATCH THE FUCKING SHOW!

He called it a 'glorious failure'. The glory was in the concept, which like the expedition, went on to acquire mythic status. The failure was in the script. It was published by Methuen in *Plays For Public Places*. Re-reading it, I wondered at the shortness of it, how it fizzles out in the second half. If I'd been Chris, I'd have sat down with Howard and asked where was Scott: where's the man? You set him up as the tool that God will use to secure the last unclaimed land-mass on earth for the British Empire. But then all we get from Our Hero and his struggle, is upper-class schoolboy tosh. And why no Amundsen? If the flag matters more than anything, then the discovery of the Norwegian flag already in place, should be a body-blow to the British Empire. This could be the moment when knockabout satire turns to tragedy in an instant, and the long march home, with each of the team falling over and *not* getting up again, could be effortlessy poignant.

Chris knew there was power in the play to be released, and his plan now was to revisit it, in an acoustic-friendly venue, on roller-skates, with Howard given time to re-imagine Scott as a Promethean figure, harnessed to his sleigh by the greed of a Higher Power, only to be pipped at the pole by a Nobody With No Empire, and in death, with his dead comrades, devoured by fame-hungry future pioneers like Edmund Hillary and Neil Armstrong; all that would have blast, and as the first of the three salvoes from Chris's '72 bazooka, would blow the lid off the Festival.

So what was the second play?

TOM BROWN

We were walking up Great Horton Road.

'This *Tom Brown's Schooldays* you were adapting? Is it finished?'

'Oh that. It was Worcester. For the Swan. Yes it's finished, in the sense of "dead". It's a dead duck.'

'It may not be dead. It may not be a duck.'

'What do you mean Chris?'

'All this talk of upper-class schoolboy tosh set me thinking. We need a Christmas show and quickly.'

'Chris, it's about Elgar and fagging. It would never work in Bradford. It was too posh even for Worcester.'

'Subvert it.'

'What do you mean Chris?'

I gave him the script. I went back down to London. He phoned me:

'Rick! We can do this! I've mentioned it to David who I know, having played God, now wants to release his inner Flashman. And Milton wants to work with you - Milton Reame-James, who was brought up in Birmingham (like you) and likes to row against the tide (like you) - did you know his real name is Harry Farmer, but he wanted to posh himself up, just as posh people (like you) were dumping their double-barrels and renaming themselves Harry Farmer.'

'I know Milton Chris. He did the music for *Crippen*.'

'And the young-uns Brown and East - '

'Chris they have to be boys of school age. That's where it all foundered at Worcester. There are no girls in the story.'

'Oh yes there are!'

'Oh no there aren't!'

'This is the panto version! All the young-uns will be principal boys, ie girls; and we have a mod lang drag-artist professor to play Matron, caught in a love duo with Cock of the School Big Brooke. It's a wizzo wheeze Rick! It's a corker! Can you rewrite the whole thing by next week?

*

Out of the tin trunk of scripts going back fifty years, I extract a roneo-ed copy of *Tom Brown* and start to read. After all that time, no cell in your body is as it was then, so it's like discovering a lost early work by Lionel Bart or Jay Lerner. As I flip the flimsy pages, I'm thinking: by George, he's got it! Juvenile, because he is, but he knows where he's coming from, how to build a two-act play, how a song advances the action, where laughter erupts and tears flow. With hardly a nod to the original, he has shredded Thomas Hughes's out-of-copyright school story, and creamed it with lashings of Bunter and Molesworth, while still honouring the notion that bullying will always be biffed by solidarity. It also references, as do Bart and Lerner, classic film adaptations, where characters, shorn of verbiage, can be inhabited by actors: in this case the 1951 film starring John Howard Davies, who grew up to be producer of *Monty Python's Flying Circus, The Goodies* and *Fawlty Towers*, all of which, stemming from the Footlights, were inspirations for *Tom Brown*. We should have invited him to see it.

I spoke to Chris the other day, now seventy-four and living in Belfast, and we talked about *Tom Brown*, which he said was his busiest, happiest Bradford production. We did five performances opening on 8th December 1971. He let me do most of the directing while he managed the company, and also played the ineffectual Latin master, Mr Birchwell, victim of Flashman's withering wit, and Brown and East's tricks. Brown was Jackie Newbold, a blonde mechanical engineer at a time when girls didn't do engineering. Her easy charm and tough stance with the boys, played well for Brown in his stand-off with Flashman and the toadies, and led to a serious post-show affair with David once he'd shed the caddishness and returned to his big-hearted socialist self. Chris thought it was Flashey and Harry East (Valda Dagnall) who were in cahoots, but I assured him that couldn't be and I had photographic proof. In the tin trunk, with the script was an old snap of Valda in my dungarees smoking my pipe (just an affectation) and me topless in her maxi skirt. She had just graduated in Mod Lang at Bradford and was now in teacher training with acting at Bretton Hall. I'd written her a monologue, a lament for lost love called *Man With A Tooth Missing*, for a slot in the previous Bradford-in-Edinburgh programme, which I hadn't seen, being away filming in the highlands. So when I came up for *Tom Brown*, she gave me a personal performance, on the mattress on the floor of her Bradford pad, and someone took the photo.

It was the busiest, happiest time. *Tom Brown* was my first main-slot, full-length play, planted in the conventional, bone-meal of Worcester, then dug up and thrust into the steamy horse-dung of Bradford. Milton, soon to join the glam rock band Cockney Rebel, composed a sporty school song, a torch song for Matron, a rock'n'roll roasting song for Brown, Flashey and the toadies, and a rousing, ironic *Good-bye Flashey Good-bye,* as the arch-cad humps his trunk down the stairs, following his expulsion.

Why were critics not invited? Maybe we were too busy and too happy, to do a press release. Maybe, as every performance was sold out, it wasn't seen as necesssary. Or maybe, after the drubbing he got for *Scott,* Chris decided to delay full exposure till the proven triple-juggernaut circus came to Edinburgh. Whatever the reason, one doughty critic sneaked in and wrote:

> *TRIUMPH FOR TOM BROWN...the slickest, cleverest show Bradford has seen this year... so ingeniously staged, so infectiously portrayed... I hope Messrs Crane and Parr will not keep their next production to themselves.*

THE END

The next production was *The End,* David Edgar's anti-nuclear polemic which would complete the Edinburgh trilogy, and Chris had said I should come and talk about being in it, and also take a weekend with him in Edinburgh, to suss out venues for the Festival. I'd actually just been in Glasgow, playing in *A Place of Her Own,* the sequel to *High Living,* with Miriam, Juliet and Alex Norton, but had not had time to cross to Auld Reekie where I needed to chat to Phil about *Decent Things,* the short play I was writing for Juliet and me, while filming *The Duna Bull,* which incidentally, Juliet said, was having a showing in Edinburgh, and the director Laurence Henson was hoping we'd be there. So after a quiet Christmas at Templar Street, and no castings in the offing (had Beryl given up on me?), I found myself scooting out of London up the A5, towards Rugby, thinking if Dr Arnold or Matron needed recasting for Edinburgh, I could play either - or *both* (they didn't clash); and with snow beginning to fall as I hit the Peak District, I was surmising, if it was true that David Cowling (Scott) had been offered a job with the Labour Party, they surely wouldn't give him time off to go claiming an icebound wilderness for the Empire. I would talk to Chris (chugging on through a blizzard towards Huddersfield) about my access to Uncle Arthur's Antarctic archive and my affinity with the title role, if Howard could beef it up a bit.

I parked the bike at Chris's, slept in the downstairs room and in the morning we caught the train to Edinburgh. This was paid for by Bradford, so we could stay in a hotel, take taxis, have meals and drinks. Chris had done a budget, which though three times last year's, 'will have to be nodded through, because *the objective of theatre is to initiate change, the culmina-*

tion of which is not the aesthetic phenomenon, but the shock of real life (Augusto Boal).

Murrayfield Ice Rink was first on the list. Instead of ice, in the summer, the hard surface would suit roller-skates, and be easier for the tennis rackets, wheelchair and motorbike. There would be banks of bleachers within the rink so the playing space would be smaller, and the acoustic clearer. I didn't know about *The End*, but I thought the Rink would be perfect for both *Scott* and *Tom Brown* - especially the rugger match - but Chris wasn't letting himself get enthused, as he explained as we walked away: the Main Festival had provisionally bagged the rink for a double bill of school plays based on the Bible: a mystery play about the Creation, and a new short musical about Joseph and his coat. What! Bible stories, school plays! Not what an international festival should be bothering with, we opined in unison!

Next on the list was a Catholic Church hall, in Lauriston Street, adjoining a functioning church, through which one had to enter, to be ushered by a nun towards a line of confessionals, against the wall. I'd dipped my hand in the stoop of water as we came in, to cool my forehead. 'Angels' piss!' muttered Chris. 'Remind me not to shake hands with you.' Then he vanished as if sucked into a confessional for blasphemy. 'This way,' said the nun, guiding us through a door in the wall and flicking the lights on. I saw a vaulted, Victorian, empty space, with a stage at one end and porticos down either side, as big as the Great Hall at Bradford.

'We'd hardly need to change anything,' I observed, 'at least not for *Tom Brown*.'

'We might need to change everything,' retorted Chris. 'Whatever gets put on here, has to be checked by the brothers for moral turpitude. God in a wheelchair, gender-bending at Rugby, can you imagine the tonsured men in skirts bowing to that!'

'But last year,' I pointed out, 'the Cambridge ADC did *Ghosts* by Ibsen, which is rotten with turpitude. Can we factor in some syphilis? The brothers might go for that.'

'It wouldn't work here,' said Chris. 'It stinks of God.'

As we walked away up West Port towards the Royal Mile and the third and final venue, I asked Chris why the visceral aversion to Catholics? What about the art, the music, the poetry, the cathedrals?

'What about' he broke in, 'the obscene wealth, the banning of condoms, the snatching of babies from "fallen women", the pontificating that suffering is good for you - "grovel now, glory later!" - all the art yes, for salivating sadists! The crucifying, skinning alive, boiling and barbecuing - they love that! The cannibalism of the mass; the peddling of pardons through confession, so long as you titillate the priest with your sexy sins then go flagellate yourself. And the worst thing which they always cover up, the worst sin is the law that sexless "fathers" must bottle their lust so it leaks out in abuse of children. Yes it's visceral. Anathema! Don't get me started.'

*

The Edinburgh Wireworks, just off the Royal Mile, had been unoccupied for a decade. It was as if the wire-workers had walked out suddenly leaving everything as it was: industrial tools, benches, worktops, machinery, swathed in cobwebs and dust, as if Miss Haversham might enter down the iron steps from one of the landings, in grease-encrusted overalls. A lofty, constructivist interior, with levels linked by criss-crossing metal stairs, long abandoned and dangerous: the venue itself *was* the drama. Did we *need* the plays? More practically, how do we clean it up, make it safe? How does this heavily particularized location become a snowscape, a rugger pitch, a post-nuclear desert?

Chris's replied:

'Bradford has the most progressive engineering courses in the country. Never underestimate our techno pioneers. My job as Fellow is to exploit *all* resources, to make *new theatre*, not only costumes and wigs, but scaffolding, gang-planks! Don't fret about the words. They'll rattle through, on time, like a train crossing the Forth Bridge. Such science! So many rivets! RIVETING THEATRE! Churchill, out of office, wrote *A History of the English-Speaking Peoples* and won the Nobel Prize. Wilson, our Chancellor, in a similar situation, will be looking to generate the WHITE HEAT of his Technological Revolution and win a NEW PRIZE, for *riveting* Arts and Music to Science and Technology. I've already had a nod from PVC Mackinley, who thinks I'm the bee's knees, and an unmistakable wink from VC "Red Ted" Edwards, who knows I'm Cock of the Rock, and I believe we're only one puff of a pipe away from Harold himself commanding the Uni to stump up. You know what he said to me when we met: 'Mr Parr, if I hadn't been Prime Minister, I'd have been an architect, not one who builds tower blocks, but one who reclaims the abandoned palaces of our industrial past and returns them to the public for entertainment or sport.'

*

I don't have a script for *The End* and it's not in print. David has one somewhere, in some trunk, but he seems to be not of a mind to disinter it. I have an old betamax recording of my part in it, but I'm wary of converting it into a seeable form. Let it be what it was: a one-brief-thermo-nuclear moment, remembered 'with advantages' by the few who saw it or were in it. I was both. The betamax has stored my performance as the Face On The

Screen, fading up on monitors round the hall, coaxing volunteers to come forward and 'play the game'. There's a global crisis: a spy-plane shot down, a peace treaty violated, unverifiable missile installation etc - and the audience member, led onto the stage by dolly-birds, to a fruit-machine-size computer, has to key in a response: call a conference, impose sanctions, send a gunboat... Then as clouds gather and gulfs widen, the crises escalate, the responses harden. What if oil states revolt? What if rogue regimes go nuclear? Do you jaw-jaw, talk to terror, appease? Or USE YOUR ARSENAL? DEMONSTRATE ITS POWER! SET UP MARKETS ACROSS THE WORLD? If *you* don't sell, others will. Play the game! Play to win! Press the button...

I have to stop there. The post has come. A script-size jiffy-bag has flopped through the letter-box. The sender is David Edgar. He is the consummate professional. If someone asks for a script and he has one, he will send it.

*

I'd forgotten the scale of the writing; that it's actually three plays in one. He wrote it when he was twenty-three (same age as Buchner when he wrote *Woyzeck*) and you might expect this roneo'd copy bashed out on stencils forty-six years ago, to be an 'early work'. But then I remember him saying that, as a writer, he wanted to do his 'middle period' first and leave the early work till later. *The End* is not the beginning or the middle. It stands alone. It has a cast of twenty-five, plus however many in the audience, who become protesters, anti-protesters and observers packed into a school hall 'somewhere between Aldermaston and London'. They join in political songs and watch vignettes of the spat between CND and the Committee of 100, Bertrand Russell and Canon Collins slugging it out in the ring, and the fight-fight-fight-again of Gaitskell's pro-nuclear wing, against Benn's pacifist core. Argument is everywhere, even fathoms down in the Polaris submarine, where the American commander and the English doctor argue the absurdity of the arms race. And in the audience, volunteers are called to be hawks or doves in multiple-choice responses to crises. Some of the speeches are verbatim, some are instant ripostes - crowd ad-libbing is encouraged - and some are fashioned into song lyrics. Though heavyweight, often lumbering, the play swings its own weight: in the verbal duelling in the schoolroom; in the claustrophobic sub, where the crew smoke dope and extol the beauty of the bomb; and in the Cold War Game, where the vox-pop answers, are fed into the computer which will decide, irreversibly, which of two final scenes will be played. I saw the show on two nights. On the first night, the computer determined a 'de-escalation' ending, and the audience left shocked but relieved that civilization could carry on, at least for the time being. On the second night, when the audience was more cynical, the result was war.

> *The four-minute countdown starts.*
> *Someone tries to organize people into sleeping bags.*
> *Some put them over their heads,*
> *Some get in a foetal position to cushion the blast.*
> *Someone calls for a prayer meeting.*
> *The singer sings softly; some join in.*
> *Someone suggests occupying the regional seats of government.*
> *Someone becomes hysterical.*
> *After two minutes,*
> *BLACKOUT.*
> *Panic. Pandemonium.*
> *Action continues in darkness.*
> *The countdown ends:*
> *five, four, three, two, one…*
> *A very long pause.*
> *Lights up.*
> *The company are frozen into the positions they occupied*
> *at the end of the countdown.*
> *They stay quite still until the audience are gone.*

ALAN BRIDGER

I put the bike in the guard's van. Alan Bridger was on the train - all six foot five of him, coiled like a serpent on the damask upholstery of a first-class compartment. Swishing the door open I said: 'May I see your ticket please?'

'Craney!' His legs swung to the floor. 'Come on in! Let's travel.'

'I don't have a first-class ticket.'

'You have a first-class *brain*. That's your ticket. Tickety-boo!'

I tossed my bag onto the rack and sat down opposite him as the train started. Chris, David and I had had dinner with him and his girlfriend Snooks, in their bedsit the night before, after the post-show wind-down. He was serving prime rump steak.

'Where did you get this?' asked Chris.

'Mr Morrison's,' replied Bridger.

'Did you pay for it?' enquired David.

'Oh crumbs you fellers! I forgot!' exclaimed Bridger.

'So we are,' Chris considered, 'literally receiving stolen goods.'

'The only theft is property,' said Snooks.

Her real name was Sue Ashton, but playing Snooks, one of the young'uns in *Tom Brown*, she found the name had stuck. Bridger had been Speed, one of the toadies, and in the offstage canoodling between toadies and young-uns, Bridger and Snooks, like Flashey and Brown, had become an enduring item. It was good to see him happy. He was a most useful actor, getting laughs even in small roles. He had been a horny soldier in *Lysistrata*, a gangly rabbit in *Toad*, a dozy burglar in *Oil*, one of the falling-over, getting-up-again sledge-pullers in *Scott*, and Flashey's cane-carrier in *Tom Brown*. His height and spindliness were natural assets to be exploited both for comedy on stage and as a free-loading anarchist. We tried to warn him: one day the law will catch up with you, but in the end it was *he* who caught up with himself. I met him again, some twenty years after leaving Bradford, and he had morphed from artful dodger into respected legal aid lawyer, and pillar of church and community.

'Of course the ending was rigged,' he was saying about *The End* as we rocketed south.. When it's not war, everyone goes away thinking "Oh well that's all right then". But when it's war, then it's theatre. People are so stunned, they don't even clap. It has to be rigged! Rigging is what theatre does! Let's go to lunch! Quick!'

We grabbed our bags and were out in the corridor just as the inspector was approaching. We got to the dining-car, stowed the bags, took a table for two -

'Don't we have to be first-class to sit here?' I wondered.

'Do we? I don't know,' said Bridger, suddenly choking, grasping me and demanding water.

'I'll come back,' said the inspector, moving on down the carriage.

'So,' said Bridger scanning the menu, 'mulligatawny, then rack of lamb, with two veg, plum crumble for afters, and is it wine or beer, me old mate?' We rattled along, talking theatre, discussing Edinburgh, what was it like, he'd never been, Chris had talked about the Wireworks, doing *Scott not* on ice, *Tom Brown* and *The End*, would this be the making of old Craney as the new Bertolt Bart, and seriously what were the chances for a Lofty going pro? I said nothing was funded yet, it was all crumble in the sky, but if any-one could put in his thumb and find a plum, it was surely Bridger. 'Was it a fact, when you moved in with Snooks and needed sheets, you nicked a set, and when they didn't fit, you complained and Mr Snelgrove, or Mrs Marshal, was so shamed to have disconvenienced so lofty a client, she threw in a set of bath towels?'

'Oh fuck!' said Bridger as we were pulling into Leicester. 'We're on the wrong train! Get the bags!'

We were off the train, just as the inspector was reappearing in the dining car.

'What about the bike?'

We were running up the platform to the guard's van, dragging the bike off, even as the doors were slamming. I showed my ticket at the barrier.

Bridger made out he was having trouble with the bike and the man let us through.

'So where now?' I said.

'Staines,' said Bridger. 'Can you take me? It's where my old lady lives.'

*

Michael Rudman, Director of the Traverse, after seeing *The Tenant*, had asked to read what I wrote next and I was already at work on a modern-day *Oresteia*. I also had the honeymoon comedy for the Pool to fine-tune, plus a Christmas show for Bradford and the Bronte play simmering. And I had a new bespoke living/work place to set up: an attic room I was renting in a house in Knatchbull Road Brixton, with access to the roof, where I could lie out and think then go in and write. So why was I digressing by fifty or more miles in the clutches of Spiderboy? The answer was simple. He was now embedded in my work. The physicality, speech patterns and serpentine attitude were sliding in between the lines, and casting him in parts I'd normally save for myself. The Harbord roles, as in *The Tenant* and *Decent Things*, even Branwell and the boy who murders his mother in the Traverse play, were being rolled out, spaghettified into absolute Bridger. Here was Orestes, grown to excess, now riding home to confront his guilt-racked mother, whose denial of him and horror at his pleading, will lead to her murder. The thought of carnage was so vivid, I decided, when we got to 'Old Lady Bridger's abode', that I should follow him in, to ensure all was okay, but when we got there, I'd hardly stopped before he was off with his bags, and hugging me lankily, bounding up to the door which opened as he approached, and snapped shut behind him.

It was dark now, with rain clouds, as I headed for the ring-road. The phut-phutting was irregular and I ignored it, willing the old nag not to pack up on me, but she did. She dragged to a halt. I kick-kick-started and flooded her, but she wouldn't go. It wasn't fuel - I had plenty - so it must have been sheer old age, and death. She was dead and I went on flogging her, as rain pattered down. I pushed her about a mile, then finding a patch of waste land, dumped the old dear, and went looking for a bus.

When I got home, my new home, there was no one in, so I left a note for my landlord, an actor called John Gulliver, to say thanks for the cheese and beer - he said I could raid the fridge - and went up to the attic and onto the roof. I sat on a wet lounger, ate the cheese, drank the beer, and lay back looking up at a charcoal sky, no stars, convincing myself I was on a roll.

BRIXTON

I had two months between *The End* and going to Edinburgh for *Decent Things*. To pay the rent I got a job in the typing pool of the Royal Dental Hospital in Leicester Square. I was the only man in a room full of Janes, Jeans, Joans and Junes, in serried ranks, clackety-clacking letters about teeth, and taking tea-breaks. At five pm they all rose, retrieved coats, hats and hand-bags, and said 'good night' as if that was it. For me, it was just the start of the working day. I'd be home by six, with coffee and snack, a cup of tea, fags, matches and ashtray, at my desk in the attic, pacing, rnting writing, till three, up at seven, shave, shower and shit, and off on the bike to be at the dentists' for 8.30.

Plays on the slate:

1: THE BLOOD STREAM, a modern Oresteia.
2: THUNDER, a play of the Brontes.
3: MUTINY ON THE BOUNTY, a mammoth extravaganza.

I'd watched *Brief Encounter* on TV with my mother. The wife of a dull middle-class husband meets a romantic hero in a waiting room. Over a number of Thursdays, they go to the pictures, go rowing, almost have sex, till social pressure sends. them back to their spouses. No convention is broken. The hypocrisy continues. But what if there's a murder? Set the play in the blitz, and the lovers can mourn the husband's death as bomb damage. The only witness to the truth is the wife's young daughter, who is cowed into silence. When the wife finds she is pregnant, she has the baby adopted. Twenty years on, in the comfort of her suburban home, nursing her awful secret, she is visiting by a delivery-boy, who has brought her a gift. He seems troubled; she takes pity on him. There's something familiar about his face, the way he smiles, which gives her the creeps. He finds a gun in a drawer, says he'll shoot himself if she doesn't let him stay. She says it's her husband's weapon from the war; it isn't loaded. Gradually, horribly, she realizes who the boy is. The link is the daughter, whose mission has been to reclaim her discarded brother. He was in prison when she found him, having been raised in children's homes, gangs and borstals. She tells him the truth of his parents and stepfather and gives him their address to go to on his release. The double murder when it happens is more accident than design, provoked by his mother's reluctance to let him stay, and the stepfather's drunkenness. That's the end of Act Two. Each act is performed in the theatrical style of the day. Act One is Cowardesque, backed by Glenn Miller and Tommy Handley. Act Two is in early 60s Pinterland: domestic stasis set on edge by the menacing stranger. I'd been here with *The Tenant*, so wrote the second act first, then built the other two around it. For Act Three the model was to be Genet, with a nod to *Woyzeck*: the outsider driven to murder and insanity. With Acts One and Two falling into place almost too easily, I spent night after night searching and not finding the key to Act Three. After a month, I put my stack of foolscap on a shelf to marinate and turned to...

Thunder, for which the Greek is *Bronte*: it came at me in a storm. I had the books - *Jane Eyre, Wuthering Heights, The Tenant of Wildfell Hall*, plus Daphne Dumaurier's *The Infernal World of Branwell Bronte*. At first it was going to be Branwell's play, hailing him, like Milton's Satan, as the Bringer of Light, flung to hell by his own presumption, his angel siblings in attendance.

But I couldn't make it work. The sisters were not for pushing aside. Whatever he fired up in the them, went on to blaze down the literary canon, while his own spark burnt out. In my play, they would be a wrestling, four-headed force, like plaited snakes, bonded in one whole, with distinct competing voices. Their 'wrack of sorrow, hopes and pain' was there to be plundered, for a show they all might have have written, as they had the An-gria and Gondal sagas in tiny booklets as children. I wasn't going to put any of this in order just yet. The complete picture would emerge when I'd lined up the pieces, some theirs, some mine, which I'd then stack in a rough edit on the shelf, with *The Blood Stream,* and turn to...

THE BOUNTY

I'd seen Charles Laughton as Bligh and Marlon Brando as Christian in two films about the *Bounty* mutiny, three decades apart. Reading Nordhoff and Hall's *Mutiny on the Bounty*, I had relived the adventure through a midshipman, accused of mutiny, who had faced execution on his return. I'd built a model of the ship from a self-assembly kit, using match-sticks for cannons and cotton-thread for the rigging. I had learnt that the *Bounty* had been commissioned in 1787, to transport breadfruit saplings from Tahiti to Jamaica as food for slaves; that the crew had mutinied on the return journey, setting the captain and his followers adrift in an open boat; that the boat and all those in it had survived an epic journey, and on his return to England the captain had set about exacting revenge; that the leading mutineers, escaping the ship sent to arrest them, had found a bolt-hole on Pitcairn Island where they turned savage and killed each other. Such salty adventures ran in the sap of my family tree, from Uncle Arthur and his brothers who between them had rounded the Horn five times, to Grandpa

Twidle who had slithered down the deck of his ship into the sea off Jutland, to my father who had ferried troops to death and glory on D-Day and then sailed to Hong Kong. I was ready now to start plotting my own nautical extravaganza, that over the next fourteen years, would have three epic outings. I spent a weekend in the Reading Room of the British Museum, going through Bligh's journals, contemporary comment (Paine, Rousseau, Burke), and the mystery surrounding Christian. I read that Bligh, sailing with Cook, had learnt that dancing and a diet of sauerkraut and lemon concentrate, were better for health and discipline, than ship's biscuit and the lash. I read in *The Wake of the Bounty* by C S Wilkinson, how Christian, a former schoolfellow of Wordsworth, years after the mutiny, had returned to England, an ancient-looking mariner, to be introduced to the poet's friend Coleridge, who was just then looking for the subject for a new 'rime'. Thus, at a stroke, top-class, copyright-free lyrics were available, along with shanties and ballads. The show had everything going for it. There hadn't yet been, as far as I knew, a balanced telling of the story. Clark Gable's Christian had been no match for Laughton. Trevor Howard's Bligh had been out of his depth with Brando. I thought if a script could ramp up the two protagonists to the level of Laughton and Brando, the ship itself a microcosm of the revolutions (French, American, Industrial) that were occurring at that time; if the romantic dream of South Sea innocence could be matched with the savagery of the Maritime Articles of War, what a success we might have! The sea, the lash, duty vs passion, the dashing of hope and the perversion of a dream, were all summed up in the poem I wrote to set the tragedy rolling.

(A man has been accused of stealing a cheese. The truth is the cheese was offloaded before sailing and carried the Mr Bligh's house for his family. Mr Bligh cannot be seen to have transgressed, so the sailor must be flogged, even though it shatters Bligh's dream of a punishment-free voyage.)

> *The lash came whistling down and struck*
> *his back and breath flew out.*
> *A crimson welt was drawn across*
> *and blood began to spout.*
>
> *The Bosun flexed his gleaming arm*
> *and down it came again.*
> *A second welt criss-crossed the first*
> *and shook the grating frame.*
>
> *The man sank down, then braced himself.*
> *The bosun struck once more.*
> *A shout, a welt, a spout of red*
> *and down came number four.*

And Mr Bligh he bit his lip
as five and six were given.
His high intention hung in shreds
as down came number seven.

His bold resolve spreadeagled hung
as eight came down and nine.
The back was torn from neck to waist;
all raw the open spine.

But Mr Christian's eye were bright,
no rational thinker he.
The passion in the lash was like
the passion in the sea.

Then ten, eleven, lastly twelve
interminable did seem
The man sank down, all black his face
and black the Bounty's dream.

CHRIS RESIGNS

'HE BALANCED HIS BUDGET. Do I want that on my tomb-stone?'

'But Chris, you ran up a deficit. They were never going to bankroll Edinburgh on top of that.'

'Capitalism, Rick, is founded on debt. Only plutocrats make a profit. To bring them down, you pump up the debt bubble till it bursts.'

'But McKinley, Red Ted, even Harold, are they the enemy? I thought the aim was to do shows.'

'You're right, and they *are* the enemy. Deficit - *fuck* - there is no such thing! The word is *subsidy,* non-returnable: investment in talent that defines the future. So what's to do? Walk away, stick to acting? That's a mug's game Rick. Imagine if Shakespeare had stuck to acting! You should be running this show! I've resigned, on one condition, that *you go for the job.* It's yours for the asking. You'll be continuing the journey you and I started. Only difference is *you'll* be doing the driving, and starting a tradition - hear this! - of *re-employing the previous Fellow to do shows!* I'll be a bridge for you into professional *subsidized* theatre, and you'll be a bridge for me back to Bradford. Because Rudman - didn't he tell you? - has asked me to direct *The Blood Stream* at the Traverse. If that's your wish. Then I'll come and direct your Bronte blockbuster. If that's what you want? *Do* you want? Is it a deal? Are we on? Will you apply?

A pause.

'Chris, you impose these conditions, after you've resigned, without ever talking to me.'

'Because I was hoping you wouldn't need to *think* about applying.'

'I didn't even know you'd resigned!'

'My resigning is not the issue! It's you, seizing what's yours for the asking. Don't blink! Tergiversation! The only snag in your otherwise venturesome tapestry. And the acting. Don't say you're acting. Are you acting?'

BAD BAD

James Leo Herlihy wrote *Midnight Cowboy* about a country boy who comes to town to earn a living as a gigolo, but it's not as easy as he dreamed. He meets a sickly con man with a limp, who offers to hustle for him and the two form a bond which grows closer as their fortunes spiral downwards, ending in flight and death. Ever blurring the line between acting and life, Herlihy later recalled the duo, in a short play called *Bad Bad Jo-Jo*, about two boys who visit a reclusive writer Kayo Hathaway, creator of a series of 'gory, camp melodramas', about an ape-like innocent-looking giant in an Uncle Sam hat, led on a chain by a little white-haired old lady with tiny eye-glasses and sensible shoes, whose joint hobby is murdering people. One of the boys, Frank, purports to be a fan and has come to interview Kayo, about his personal philosophy: 'You get what you give'. He introduces his creepy friend Dennis and together they impersonate Jo-Jo the giant and his psychotic mother, and in a stroboscopic nightmare sequence, backed by newsreel projections of a policeman clubbing a peace marcher, soldiers burning a Vietnamese village, Nixon waving and smiling, Allen Ginsberg praying, they hack the head off the writer and fuck his neck. Sex and savagery in Warhol's and Nixon's America, was the strapline for Jo-Jo, coming to London as a lunchtime try-out at the Act Inn in King's Road; set to be the trendiest thing, and the first in a trio of West-End-bound horrors, with TV star David Hedison, muscular and moody (the spit of Herlihy himself), as Kayo, and the comedy duo of Conrad Asquith (6 foot 5) and Richard Harbord (5 foot 6), last seen together as the two secretaries in *The Slapstick Angels* at the Arts, playing Frank and Dennis.

My memory of the show is fogged up, deliberately. *Jo-Jo* was even worse than *Angels*, but we didn't know that at the start. Lacking guidance from the director, I based my performance on the Act Inn's publicity officer whose name was Pete. He had bird's-nest hair and a smile carved into his pumpkin face which kept grinning at me through the readthrough. We chatted in the break while the others sat brooding. He knew I was a writer, and in return for my help with the press release, bought me dinner and we went to see *A Clockwork Orange* - mild, compared with *Bad Bad Jo-Jo*, which could be the making of me, said Pete. If I would come back to his flat, we could discuss a publicity blast for Richard Harbord, starting with Limelight in the *The Stage*. I have it in front of me, the oval photo of a rising-star actor, glancing off to the left, slightly wary but up for it, above a column in italics that begins:

> *RICHARD HARBORD, who has received particularly good notices for his performance in* Bad Bad Jo-Jo *at the Act Inn...*

I don't remember these notices. I only recall tiny audiences, mostly my friends - the Tudor-Landors and Raleigh-Kings, Angie and the 17b diaspora, Betty and Michael, even Ma and Jude and Mon (but not Pa). Mostly they were sickened, but we live in a sickening world, I explained, where innocents are slaughtered and you get your centre-spread in *The Stage* through shagging Pete the Publicist. Then in the morning, still smiling, he makes you eggs on muffins then walks with you to rehearsal. It was nice. He was a friend. He made me famous for a week. Then as the show slowly sank from bad-bad to worse-worse, he began backing off, still smiling, not minding when I told him I couldn't sleep over, because the Bradford Fellowship was now advertised, and *The Blood Stream* needed looking at, and the Staines Police were onto me about paying a huge amount for disposal of the abandoned vespa, and I had the part in *Decent Things* to learn before getting the train to Edinburgh the day after *Bad Bad Jo-Jo* finally closed.

On the last Thursday, after the show, Pete popped his smiley head round the dressing-room door and said: 'I've got tickets for *Godspell*. For the matinee. We can make it if we run.' We got there just as Jeremy Irons was singing *'Pre-e-e-e-pare ye the way of the Lord...'* It was the first time, apart from pantomime, I'd ever seen actors in a conventional theatre performing among the audience, and the first time, I'd ever heard the story of Christ retold as entertainment. There were two Jesuses currently in town, one a superstar - operatic, spectacular - and one a clown, as here, with red nose and baggy pants, and happy-hippy followers, acting out parables and facing down hypocrites. The message was love in its day-by-day simplicity. God was not going to save the people; only a godlike fearless fool could do that, but not before suffering crucifixion on an electric fence. *Godspell* would be the making of a little group of new stars: Irons himself, Julie Covington, Marti Webb, Gay Soper and most of all, David Essex. Harold Hobson, in the *Sunday Times*, compared his Jesus with the Christs of El Greco and Rubens, and linked his performance with Olivier's in *Long Day's Journey into Night*, as the two finest in London.

In the interval of *Godspell*, the audience is invited onto the stage to 'have communion' with the actors. Pete stayed seated; I went up, like a neophyte, to chat with Jesus. Did I tell him I too was a rising star, and had also once been singled out by Hobson? Did I tell him my Pa was a Padre and would love this show, just as he would hate *Bad Bad Jo-Jo*, but one needed both ends of the spectrum, didn't one, to tread the tightrope of theatre? Or did I prophesy, to Mr Essex, that one day, he and I would embark on a stormy six-year voyage, with Paradise as its aim and Mutiny at its core? Or did I just say 'Wow...' and did he just, with his glittering eye, say 'Rock on...'?

I had to get home afterwards, and quickly. I told Pete I wasn't well, and it was true. I was in a fever of ideas, top of which was...

THE APPLICATION

Applying for the Fellowship and writing *Mutiny* were two sides of one coin. If I tossed it, I knew, whichever side it came down, I would do both. To apply, I needed to have a flagship show with wind in its sails to power me through such flotsam as the deficit. To write and direct the show I needed to know my vessel and be captain of it. As with Edgar's *The End*, the Great Hall would be the setting - the ship itself - with scaff towers for masts and able-seamen shinning up them to man follow-spots which would lurch and sway as the ship set sail and ran into storms. The opening number would preview the story, as a work song, as the crew prepared to sail:

> *You've heard of Captian Bligh*
> *and his good ship the Bounty*
> *and Mister Fletcher Christian*
> *from Cumberland County.*
> *They sailed the seven seas*
> *on a perilous route.*
> *The reason for the voyage was*
> *Bre-ead-fruit...*

The audience come aboard as passengers for the outward voyage, go ashore on Tahiti for a 'six month' interval, then re-embark for the return, the mutiny, the long-boat voyage, the search for and capture of a few of the mutineers, and the hangings.

Planning a pitch for the Fellowship, structuring the 'voyage' of the show, were conjoined efforts to be worked on now. I knew what I wanted and had to make happen. The Fellowship was the vessel for my career, with *Mutiny* its sea-lane. Like a navigator, I drafted and typed up the Application through the night, read it through in the morning, and posted it en route to the Act Inn for the show. They hadn't told me the last three Jojos were cancelled, so I went home and slept. I never saw Pete again; can't remember his face, only the grin, the great ear-to-ear slash as if someone had taken a razor to his cheeks, the last relic of Herlihy's no-hope world, disappearing into the ether.

THE ACCIDENT

I paid the Staines police to dump the vespa and bought a new one: a bright orange, latest model, 750cc bucking bronco, to be paid for in instalments, from the regular income I'd soon be getting from the Fellowship (mine for the asking!), boosted by the London Weekend fee - more than anything I'd ever earned - for the guest lead which I'd just been offered in *Villains*. Beginning 17th June - just one episode - it would neatly fill the gap between *Decent Things* premiering at the Pool and reprising in the Festival. Thus the summer was sorted, the bank was flush and I could test-run the bike, all the way to Edinburgh to premiere *DTs*, and also talk to Laurence Henson about *The Leader* - a book he had the rights for, about an office-clerk, born to lead a fascist revolution ('you were born to play him' said Laurence with a trace of irony).

I'd break the journey in Middlesbrough, overnighting with Chris who was doing a new play there with a young writer called Robert Holman, and would break off to do a day's pre-production on *The Blood Stream*, now scheduled to open at the Traverse, 2nd October. I was stepping on the gas of both life and work, keeping options open, but also doing things properly: slapping on L-plates, booking to take a test, buying a helmet, gauntlets, leather jacket and boots: a 'wild one' on a scooter, a mod in rocker's clothing. Ambivalence, dodgeability! Theatre is the fool. Gay or grim, actor/writer, keep 'em guessing, keep the humours, not in balance, but see-sawing: from classical Cambridge to techno Bradford, Tick Turner/Mr Ludo, Laughton and Brando. Tell truth to power, proclaim porkies; love your enemy, kill your friend. Don't take it seriously; it's only life.

*

I'd just come off the A1 on the road to Middlesbrough. I wasn't expecting to have to slow down on this minor road, with a closed lane due to works, and a traffic light out of nowhere. I must have opened the throttle instead of jamming on the brake because the next thing I knew, I was head-butting a truck, and crashing my front wheel against metal. The truck was unaware and we continued, slower now, and there was a warm flow of liquid from the rim of the helmet. I didn't stop, even though I was having to steer at an oblique angle. People I passed looked shocked and I couldn't tell them it's only blood, my helmet saved me, otherwise it would have been brains as well!

We were to meet in a pub. I was half an hour late but that didn't warrant the horror on Chris's face. I thought the blood had dried but the suddenness of taking the helmet off, must have restarted it. And I was choking now. Pity mixed with horror, can turn the taps on full. The face contorts, the more you're blubbing that it's nothing. I hadn't noticed the boy sitting beside Chris, concern in his dark eyes. This is Robert, said Chris, he's a genius but out of a different bag from yours. He was brought up in the Yorkshire countryside. So was I, I retorted. I watched chickens being killed. I watched a bull footing a cow. We ought to get that cut seen to, said Robert, summoning the waitress, and as he and she took me away to be cleaned up, Chris followed, continuing on the subject of Robert: he writes about ordinary people, in ordinary situations, no murders, no battles, just humans being human, slowing down, in the shadows, as the light changes through the day and through the seasons. He's just twenty, but he writes like someone who has seen the whole of life pass by. He is the embodiment of the notion that theatre, of all the arts, is nearest to farming. He wants to write a play with pigs.

Later, over a beer, Chris was saying about *The Blood Stream*: Act Three is your chance to invent. Be yourself! Act One is Noel Coward. Act Two is Pinter. Act Three will be Crane: your own voice, your own cry. It could be quiet like death; it could be a continuing gad-fly probe, like a life sentence. There's a boy who has killed his mother which is the worst thing any man in any era can do. Aeschylus has him pursued by Furies. Sartre calls them flies. There's poison in the air, brought on by the murder, and fogging up his brain. When you came into the restaurant covered in blood and not knowing it, then when you struggled not to break down out of exhaustion and having to face people, I thought that could be the key: your head stuck in a helmet, bleeding internally. Are you sane or mad? Are you alive or dead? Acts One and Two are in the bag and in my view and Rudman's, are as powerful and funny and clever as anything there's ever been at the Traverse. Act Three has got to top that. And there's just one more thing (are you with me?): we want Tammy to play Electra, the sister who channelled the murder. She's hungry for a good part and will only appear in Act Three, so needs a meaty role, to sink her teeth into - ha! She should be the equal of the boy, and we want Charlie Bolton for that. Do you know him? He has a face like a skull. He's just played Derek Bentley, in the Craig and Bentley drama. Did you see it? He was stunning, as the retarded lad who says 'Let him have it Chris' and gets hanged for it.

DECENT THINGS

Richard Crane's new play threatens to be one of those hackneyed comic sketches about a honeymoon couple, awkwardly preparing for bed. Fortunately it develops into something more sensitive and intelligent...

John Cumming's production has the benefit of an excellent performance by Richard Harbord as the bridegroom...

Juliet Cadzow plays the bride in a gauche and hearty manner... but her change of mood towards the end, when she becomes tenderly melancholy, is very effective...

The most impressive thing about Decent Things *was the uncanny skill used by the author, to bridge the gap between the roaring farce of the first three-quarters and the intensely moving 'message' of the end of this brilliant piece of work...*

To experience at first hand the work of a young playwright who can compose with such deftness of touch and who displays such all-round mastery of his medium is both encouraging and exciting...

The play ends with a gleam of hope and mutual understanding... a superbly written short comedy.

'Why,' said Poppy from box office who I was staying with, 'are you hiding yourself away in Bradford of all places? *The Blood Stream,* everyone's saying, will be the cleverest thing to hit the Traverse in years. *Decent Things* at the Pool has got everyone talking. You should be concentrating on those, if you're serious, and writing new stuff, instead of running for cover into academia. What is it Tynan has on his desk, that quote: *Rouse tempers, goad and lacerate, raise whirlwinds?* That's your forte, not pontificating and marking essays.'

I tried to tell her that Bradford Fellowship carried no academic responsibilities. But she had a point and I couldn't argue. I'd never been poised on such a daunting threshold, more a ledge on a top floor, like the sill of the window of the flat we were looking out of, high up above Buccleuch St. I'd been staying here rent-free, on a mattress on Poppy's floor, and last night, after seeing Billy Connolly and Juliet in *The Great Northern Welly Boot Show,* we had joined our mattresses together and snuggled up. Then in the morning, over breakfast with Steph, Poppy's Hungarian flatmate, we discussed my career options. Steph had come over as a refugee from Budapest in '56. Wiry and taciturn, she was still having nightmares, having woken one morning, aged eight, to see the two students they'd been sheltering, hanging from a tree.

VILLAINS

Jimmy is the creepy kid who cleans Chas's V8 car, while singing along to Nat King Cole *When I Fall In Love*. Chas disappeared six months ago, and Rene, his wife, is going spare. Chas has loads of money from the caper his mates were banged up for, though he got away. But he and the swag vanished after two strangers came to visit him in the garage, and Rene has mounting debts on top of doubts. Maybe Jimmy knows something. Roy, a chancer, who works behind the bar in Chas and Rene's old pub, says he can help find Chas, and the money. Someone was bleeding Chas. Maybe Roy can bleed the bleeders. There's a gravel pit where villains who grass, have ended up, and under that gravel is now the likeliest place for Chas to be. But where's the money? Roy visits the garage and makes Jimmy open the boot of the V8. There's a sawn off shot-gun in there, and the spare tyre, when Roy slashes it, is found to be stuffed with cash. He takes it to Rene, says he'll take her away from all this, but she's not going. And nor is Roy, because Jimmy is at the window with the shot-gun.

It took all afternoon to shoot the scene. There was a stunt man in Roy's clothes, wired up with exploding pellets. When I pulled the trigger, he leapt over the sofa in spurts of gore. I was given another gun - the blood-gun - to shoot Rene with, who was in the armchair yelling 'No no no!' I pulled the trigger, and she jerked up and down, spattered with blood as in *Bonnie and Clyde*. The whole sequence when I saw the episode, lasted less than a split-second. I then went back to the garage where make-up was waiting with my tears in a little bowl, which she smeared on my eyes, not the classic single tear coursing unimpeded down a cheek, but a soggy mess on a sodden face, as I sat there, by the car, hugging the gun. I've just seen the episode again on DVD. TV plays in the 70s, especially cop dramas, were peopled with hard-smoking, gravel-voiced males and their big-haired, high-hemmed wives and girlfriends. Scenes were dialogue-heavy, spoken in actor-voices, and as lengthy as scenes in a stage play. Jimmy stands out, as a non-smoking, pas-sive-seeming youth with few words, because he's creepy and 'knows some-thing' - just 'Eh?' and 'I dunno, do I?' with a sly grin and suspicious eyes be-hind wire-frame glasses. Caroline Blakiston played Rene, married to Russell Hunter who I knew from the Edinburgh Fringe. They came to the Traverse to the opening night of *The Blood Stream*, to see Charlie Bolton playing 'me', killing Diane Fletcher playing 'Caroline', in a *deja vu* of the scene from *Villains*.

The interview for Bradford came on the one day when I wasn't called. I would get the train up, do the interview then go straight back home. I was going to wing it; I wasn't prepared, beyond knowing that if I took the job (which I might not), I'd simply carry on where Chris left off, creating mammoth extravaganzas in extraordinary places - Bradford Cathedral, St George's Hall, even the Silver Blades Ice Rink - alongside pocket-sized plays, experimental *and* conventional, a lot of which would be written *by me* and I'd act in some of them too. I'd go in strong, on the assumption that *they* needed *me,* more than *I* needed *them.* As to budget, I was aware there was a deficit, and I'd be responsible but only insofar as money did not defer to art, and *subsidy* was sought, not loans. All this was coursing through my head as the train left King's Cross. Deep down I was annoyed, to have my first significant TV performance interrupted by a formality. In a sense, it wasn't me, but Jimmy going for the interview, and I saw myself entering with a sly grin and suspicious eyes. The other candidates I expected would be affable with planned answers. I would stand out, passive-seeming and creepy, but murderous behind the mask. Bradford, I knew, would have student reps on the panel: at a guess, Ken Westgate (Badger from *Toad,* Inspector Dew from *Crippen*) and Jackie Newbold (Tom Brown). They'd know I was playing a game and would play along, if they wanted me. But as the Pennines loomed and gritty northern towns crowded in, I felt the chilled blood draining. Acting was not enough, and I was wishing I'd prepared an argument. As I stepped off the train at Bradford and began walking up the hill, I was thinking of turning round. If I wasn't serious about this job, why was here? Up to now, coming to Bradford, I'd been cushioned by Chris. I was now on my own, and this was underlined in bold, when I entered the room and there in front, as in a dream, were Jackie Newbold, Ken Westgate, PVC McKinlay and Gordon Doble, the professor who had played Matron in *Tom Brown.* But there was no spark of recognition. They were acting as strangers, which threw me. The sly grin froze. The suspicious eyes became rabbit's eyes caught in the headlights. The whole ghost thing which I hadn't experienced since schooldays, descended on me like a fog, till I could only see shadows, only hear minimalized voices. I was in there for half an hour. I was speaking, but it wasn't me; yet they seemed to be *acting* as if it made sense. 'And what shows in the coming year, can we expect from you Mr Crane?' growled Badger. 'That depends,' I said. 'On what?' chirped Tom Brown. 'On whether we offer him the job!' guffawed Matron. And that was it. I stood up, and as I left the room, they were still giggling.

I knew I hadn't got it. The other candidates, who I didn't talk to, looked far more clued-in: the sort who might use the opportunity to do a doctorate on the alternative dramaturgies of Brecht, Beckett and Bond. And I was relieved. Poppy was right. I should be done with universities. I was a pro of the first water with all my chances before me. Chris would be disappointed but I would tell him I was free now to write a whizz of an Act Three, just as soon as *Villains* was in the can. We were in studio tomorrow. I had a V8 to polish, people to kill, tears to shed; and directors and producers to hobnob with at the wrap party.

THE OFFER

When the letter came, I tossed a coin. It came down tails, which meant refusal. I phoned Laurence to check what was the progress with *The Leader*. He said it was ninety-nine percent certain not to be happening, sorry. Then just as I'd put the phone down, David Edgar rang. 'Just an exclamation and two questions. Congratulations on the Fellowship! I have a similar one at Leeds, and I'd like to live in Bradford. Chris's house at 279 Great Horton Road will be available. If I say you can have the attic, and you promise not to complain about the state of the sink following my dinner parties, would you be prepared to share? And secondly, if you *are* doing *Mutiny On The Bounty* as a panto, I've checked my schedule and I'm available to do my Bligh.'

I posted my acceptance letter, then went up to my room in the roof of Knatchbull Road, and took down from the shelf, the Brixton scripts: *Mutiny On The Bounty, Thunder* and *The Blood Stream*. If David was to play Bligh, *Mutiny* had be as original and brilliant as *Tom Brown*. If I was to go biking on the moors, the first place to visit would be Haworth, to breathe truth into the Bronte play. *The Blood Stream* would take its turn. I wouldn't be attending rehearsals as it was slap in the middle of term. But I knew what I had to do, and it would be done just as soon as the Bradford programme was in place. And I had thoughts about *Decent Things*. I would go up to the Festival for just the week of performances at the Pool. I'd stay in John Cumming's flat which was quieter than Phil's, and less prone to discussion about my career than Poppy's, though I might occasionally 'pop over'. Revisiting the *Decent Things* script, I was thinking about directing it, as an opening production at Bradford, with Bridger as Basil, and Snooks, who could do a good posh, as Ga-Ga. It would go well with a short play of David's about Marilyn Monroe and Rosa Luxemburg, called *Conversation in Paradise*. I made contact with Brenda, secretary to the Fellows in Theatre and Music, and she put me in touch with the new Music Fellow, Chris Mitchell, who asked me to send him lyrics for the *Mutiny* songs. In a week, I felt I had grown up a decade, though I still had a few juvenile issues to put to bed. Trish from Worcester was in town, so we spent a night in a sleeping-bag on my roof, under the stars. Then Flo, wouldn't you know it, breezed by and we did the same. Then the night my episode of *Villains* was on, I watched it with Angie at Betty and Michael's and stopped over. Things were getting out of kilter, so I rang Pete, but he wasn't in.

FESTIVAL '72

L uing is a small island in the Firth of Lorn, west of Argyll, a few miles south of Oban. Juliet's family own it and it's here that they breed their famously hardy Luing cattle. 'Why not come for a couple of days,' said Juliet, 'you and John, and we could go over the script before reopening at the Pool?' I booked a sleeper, put the bike in the guard's van, bunked up and slept all the way to Waverley. Arriving in the early hours, when only the all-night Festival revellers were on the street, I pootled to John Cumming's flat, woke him and we had breakfast. Then we set off in his car, heading west and were on Luing by lunchtime. We didn't do much rehearsing, just a double-time run - it was the sort of show, we felt, that needed its freshness preserved. Better to walk the hills and ruminate with the cattle. The lines were sure to be hard-wired into our craniums. Every seat as sold anyway. We just had to let it flow. When it all fell to pieces at the first performance, I accepted it was my fault for not *demanding* more rehearsal. Some lines towards the end were similar to some near the beginning, and we got confused, cutting two thirds, then scrabbling to get back, popping in lines as we thought of them, reinventing the ebbing and flowing of the wedding night, and somehow getting it all in. Over lunch afterwards with Ruth, we apologized for the catastrophe, and she was amazed, she'd noticed changes, but thought it was deliberate, really edgy, the upside-downness of the struggle, spontaneity *in extremis*, like acting with Lindsay Kemp!

*

Paul Brooke, who I hadn't seen since the Combination, was at the Ice Rink with the Young Vic, playing God in a mystery play, and one of the brothers in *Joseph And His Amazing Technicolor Dreamcoat.* This was the hot ticket for the main Festival, and Paul fixed comps for the first night, for me, Juliet and John. As we walked into the venue, with its shafts of light, subdued music and mass of people like sheep being ushered across the expanse onto gargantuan bleachers, I thought: This could have been us! *Tom Brown, The End* and *Scott*, in this space, would have been sensational! I felt the Young Vic had capitulated. Playing up to the pimms-sipping, nice-night-out brigade was a dereliction of theatre's duty. The first half, with Paul in his Heaven, beaming down bluff authority, and creating the whole thing, was sweet enough, like son et lumiere for Bible-readers. John pointed to Ian

Charleson in the ensemble, being clear-voiced and nimble. He had taken over from me, last summer, as Captain Rosehip and Tee-Hee Lawrence when I was away filming on Mull, and they'd said he was a bit boring; so it was irksome to see him now being a fixture in a national company on the Main Festival while I was still grubbing about on the Fringe. In the interval, Juliet questioned, with her farm-girl shrug, whether an *English* private school kids' show, should be headlining the Festival, and wondered if we should stay. Then the music struck up. Instantly, this was untrodden territory. Rice and Lloyd-Webber had already gatecrashed the West End with their New Testament supershow; now in a piece written earlier, this Old Testament gem, in all its story-telling Jewishness, was breezing in, just forty minutes long and not a moment wasted. Envy and scorn flew to the winds on the upswing. Did one have to stalk the moral high-ground in theatre? This was rock'n'roll joy! Even when Pharaoh/Elvis's mike didn't work, he just carried on, in his silver-suit, hallucinating about lean and fat cows, inaudible in the frenzy. And transcending the glitz, succumbing to, escaping from, outwitting and in the end pardoning his funky brothers, was Gary Bond as Joseph. *Close every door to me, hide all the world from me, bar all the windows and shut out the light...* Shirtless, cast in a pit, sold to slavers, seduced and lied about by Potiphar's wife and thrown into gaol, you just knew he'd sing his way out of it with flying colours, as dazzling when denuded as in his amazing coat. Afterwards, Paul said 'come backstage to the party' and we met Ian and Gary and Gary's friend Jeremy, and a jubilant Andrew and Tim, and wily Frank the director. I wondered, to Tim the lyricist, why the author of Genesis had thought to slip the story of Onan, who spilled his seed on the ground, between the early chapters about Joseph. Was there a gay agenda here? Andrew the composer chipped in with a laugh that I should talk to Gary about that! Later, after Juliet and John had gone and I noticed Ian and Jeremy in cahoots about something, and Gary on his own at the bar, I went up to him. I told him I was an actor and writer and he should come and see me at the Pool lunchtime, final performance tomorrow; sold out but I was sure we could squeeze him and Jeremy in. He said Jeremy was going back to London tonight, but maybe Ian would come. Ian, hearing his name, glanced across with the look of injured purity that would become his trademark as an actor, then turned back, pointedly, to Jeremy. The air was suddenly stiff with a chill. 'Do you have transport?' said Gary. 'I don't like hailing taxis.' I told him I had a vespa. 'I'm at the North British,' said Gary.

As we sped along Princes Street, his chin on my shoulder, his hands on my thighs, I was remembering him in the cell, following the alleged rape of Potiphar's wife. Vulnerable yet defiant, needing love, but on his terms, he was Joseph, and if required, I was ready to be his comforter. *Do what you want with me; hate me and laugh at me...* Was he really so passive? Where did the actor meet the man?' Don't go,' he whispered as he dismounted at the hotel. I parked the bike and followed him in. 'Kirstie! How was your evening?' he enquired of the girl at the desk, as he took his key. 'Oh, this is Mr Harbord. He's just come to pick up some scripts,' and to me: 'Come on up'.

As soon as the lift closed it was *go-go-go-Joseph*! Mrs Potiphar's hottest-kissing dream come true. Then a lady got in and we were two gents, po-faced. Then she got out and we were animals again, all teeth and tongues and grinding groins! Was this fun? Was it a fight? Whatever happened to passivity? I thought maybe in his room we could relax and talk. How had he got to where he was? What was it like having the whole weight of the show on his shoulders? How would he advise a young actor-writer on the cusp of success, yet about to disappear into the white heat of a new technological university? But the moment the door closed, the light was off, and we were grappling, gagging, tonguing and tearing, stripping and struggling. Why the fury? Why no light? Why deny me the vision of the Apolline torso I'd had a preview of on stage... but we were crashing in the dark, like footing farmyard bulls; sweaty, shitty-fingered, he was thwacking, driving some bargain, not yet hard, like suckling on a limp teat, gobbledy-gobbledy at the blow-hole. It wasn't fun, it was tiresome: no way, I could have quipped, *to stiffen the sinew, summon up the blood.* But out of respect for his stardom, I helped him help me to a spurt, far too soon, not soon enough, I was whacked, a bit pissed... I felt him slacken. The race was over, the room ripe with sweat. We could have slept in each other's arms. But the bed was empty. I found a switch and flipped the light on. He was at the basin, rinsing his hopeless cock as if it had done something. 'You should get dressed,' he said, slipping into his silk robe. 'Sure,' I replied. I felt slimy, in need of a shower, but he was handing me my pants, my shirt, my jeans, looking down on me, as I put them on. 'Are you okay?' He was smiling, as if everything had gone to plan, and in a sense it had. My spilt seed like Onan's, was a kind of blasphemy and I was lucky not to be struck dead by God. Joseph meanwhile was now robed and clean. But I wasn't just going to leave. My hand on the door-knob, I turned, as you do in films. 'Gary...' He came up to me and sealed my mouth with a kiss, and I felt him begin to grind. But it was too late. I was dressed. I had a show in the morning. I was staying at John's and didn't have a key. He relaxed, took a long look with his penetrating eyes; judging me, acquitting me, with a sad smile: it hadn't worked, no matter, no one knew. He opened the door, a firm hand on my shoulder, pushing me through.

I didn't wait for the lift. I ran down four flights, crossed the hall, avoiding Kirstie's curiosity - 'Did you manage to collect your scripts Mr Hardboard?'

- kick-started and sped away, as the tarmac shook and the whole edifice shuddered and crashed down behind me. A ravine opening in Princes Street, I cleared, as it widened, sucking down a generation. Sodom was in flames and I was out of it, in the nick of time, with conditions. Don't look back. Any dream will not do. Pursue, harness and ride your own fiery-footed dream! Let the white-hot foundry be the next stage of your pilgrimage! Ride on ride on! Time flies! Nothing lasts! In the blink of an eye, you will be old! Don't linger! Look back and be turned to salt! Look back in twenty years and see the golden boys, the gods you envied, toppled like corn! We are such stuff, merely players, walking shadows. The curtain falls. The party's over. Who picks up the tab? You got away. They didn't. They're all ghosts now. You read the obits: Achilles and his Myrmidons; Gary, Jeremy, Ian and the rest, all long dead from AIDS.

ACT FIVE
Making It: 1972-74

Art is not a mirror held up to reality,
but a hammer for shaping it.
- Bertolt Brecht

*

Work is more fun than fun
- Noel Coward

Scene One
JOBS FOR THE BOYS?

I've lived in several attics, but 279 is the tops. The stairs come up into the centre of the room that spans the building, dividing it, one side for sleeping, the other for working. Two mattresses, a bank of pillows and a duvet, cover the floor on the sleeping side, under a ceiling that begins at the height of the house and slopes steeply to floor level. A slab of timber laid across two stacks of drawers forms the desk on the working side, with typewriter flanked by filing trays and a rack of reference books within reach. There's a narrow divan under the eaves, that can be cleared of papers, if Chris or anyone is coming to stay and the downstairs room is occupied; and a row of hooks and a shelf the length of the back wall are crowded with clothes, boots, leather jacket, helmet, gauntlets, flat cap and my trade-mark dungarees. On the far side of the desk is the dansette, stacked with tone-setting LPs: Glenn Miller and Vera Lynn for *Blood Stream* Act One; Perry Como for Act Two; Janis Joplin and the Grateful Dead for Act Three - to be revised for when Parr comes up next week. The heat is rising, stoked by the clackety-clack from the room below, where my fellow Fellow and house-mate, in his own sleep-work arrangement, is meeting multiple deadlines. Come 9.30 he will will call up, to see if I'm game for 'a last half' at the Crown, but I will have to decline, *having just cracked Act Three!!!* The Kindly Ones are not Furies, but the siren words of a prison visitor, who may or may not be the boy's sister. Laws of logic have broken down. Are we in the future or the past? Is she comforting the murderer, or *giving him permission to assassinate their mother?* We're in a crack of time here, and it's driving him (and me) mad.

In the morning the phone rings, and I bound down two flights, to the wall-phone in the kitchen, to find, as often as not, that it's David's mother - would I be so kind as to...? - which I do, just as he, as often as not, when I'm out, comes bounding down, to find it's *my* mother - would he be so kind etc... Hell! This is getting out of hand! What if, I suggest, we invest in an 'answering service'? What if, suggests David, we cut out the middle man; let the mothers talk to each other?

But today it's Brenda. Am I coming in, because it's Arts Advisory tomorrow and 'you still haven't done your schedule, you bad lad? And there's that *Javelin* editorial you need to respond to...'

Out the back, through the wild garden to the shed and the bike; kick-start and whizz down Great Horton Road to the Uni; park, lock, salute the porters - they are your friends; they have keys! - ping the lift, up seventeen floors, ping-ping, speed along to the last office on the left and -

Morning Brenda!

Afternoon Richard! Chris P wants you to phone him and Chris M - Hello. Richard!, sings the Fellow in Music, from his adjoining office - wants to play you some tunes.

Brenda Hiscocks is fiftyish, amply built, with a chuckle that belies the tight rein she keeps on her frisky Fellows. Hot-flushing, she types and tippexes, retypes and roneos, swaying like a Rockette to the rhythm of the duplicator; then stacks, collates, assembles and staples the piles of clean scripts. In an age when secretaries are typically dolly-birds, you will never get Brenda to hop onto your knee and 'take a letter'. She sits, pencil poised, then racing across the page, doubling back, erasing, as I stall, start again, trying orally to respond to that editorial in the student newspaper:

> ## JOBS FOR THE BOYS
> *For those of you who don't know, Richard Crane has just commenced his post as Fellow in Theatre... The previous Fellow was Chris Parr... Chris concentrated almost totally on new plays written by close friends... Chris lived in a large house up Great Horton Road... When he resigned, the Fellowship... went to a little-known, bit-part actor, name of Richard Crane, close friend of Chris Parr, and frequent inhabitant of a large house up Great Horton Road... All but one of the shows so far planned for this term, have been written by Richard Crane or David Edgar... For those of you who don't know, David Edgar was a reporter on the Telegraph and Argus who covered mainly University affairs... and just happens to live in a large house up Great Horton Road... It is reported that a number of people were sick, after the last offerings of both Mr Edgar and Mr Crane... Still, not to worry, David Edgar is not exactly one of the starving poor; rather he is the handsomely salaried Fellow in Creative Writing at Leeds University... So what is the end result?... The University is losing out because Richard Crane is flagrantly flouting his brief... The students are losing out, subjected as they are to poor plays written almost exclusively by two people of little talent, who just happen to be very close friends. Aspiring writers are losing out, unless of course they can crawl hard enough to become 'one of the boys'... and that means we are losing out on what could be a lot of very interesting new drama... On the other hand, a certain two people who just happen to live in a large house up Great Horton Road, appear to be making a considerable amount on top of their already quite considerable salaries... Next time these two feather their own financial nests, and their own egos off your backs, don't vomit in the toilets, do it somewhere else...*

Some welcome huh? Or just a crack of the whip to get me started. Chris and David had already replied: seizing the chance (Chris) to set in print his record of innovatory drama, from some dozen new writers, many of whom (yes) had stayed at 279, which in its slimness (being one of three vertical slices of a mansion once owned by a Victorian plutocrat) was in fact quite a modest abode; ... scant thanks to the Student Union, whose organ *Javelin* was, for consistently failing to fund productions, specifically the Crane-Edgar-Brenton trilogy that should have taken Edinburgh by storm.

Sadness was the tone of David's riposte: that sour grapes should so sicken the young *Javelin* writer (who had applied for the Fellowship and been rejected), that FACTS should be flushed away in his bile. FACTS are the wellspring of the journalist's creed. Published UNTRUTHS, whether through laziness or malice, are poison in the well, both little distortions such as mis-naming the sponsor of Edgar's Fellowship (Leeds *Poly*, not University), and whoppers such as the source of funding for his plays - just four commissioned by Bradford (through Parr, not Crane), out of twenty so far, of varying lengths, initiated by thirteen professional managements, blah-bi-di-blah, take that, biff, thwack you pillock...

What could I add? On Brenda's advice, I peg my response to the schedule to be presented to Arts Advisory tomorrow. The autumn is already programmed through Chairman's action. It's the spring that now has to be sorted and costed, and I decide to list all, October to April. No shame! Crane and Edgar, denied their Edinburgh triumphs, will launch the season with two nearly-new short plays: *A Conversation in Paradise*, featuring Rosa Luxemburg and Marilyn Monroe, and *Decent Things* featuring Bridger and Snooks. The Christmas extravaganza will be *Mutiny on the Bounty*, by Crane and Mitchell, directed by Crane, starring Edgar as Bligh. The Easter extravanganza will be an opera on a Biblical theme (yet to be decided), staged in Bradford Cathedral (yet to be confirmed), music by Mitchell, words by Crane, directed by Parr, possibly featuring Edgar in a leading role. And if that sounds like 'jobs for the boys', hear this! The Fellows are committed to maximizing the workforce: upwards of forty student actors to be sought; fifty choir and instrumentalists; thirty or more technicians, engineers, scaff erectors, light and sound designers, riggers and operators; ten to twenty stage management, costumes and props supervisors, stitchers and patchers; add front of house, box office, ushers and publicists, and you have an army Mr de Mille would be proud of! And that's just the big shows. In-between come experiments, pot-boilers, joint shows with local innovators like John Bull Puncture Repair Kit, Welfare State, Mr Spooner's Magic Theatre; plus happenings, readings and visiting professional companies. With no building to sustain, we can subvert existing venues: then with the best of the best, cross borders, storm festivals. How to syphon all that into budgetspeak, was Brenda's and my challenge: by the last internal post, to have it typed and despatched to Arts Advisors, with a salvo of bullet-points aimed at *Javelin*, and hitting home.

CRIPPEN IN SHEFFIELD

I'm riding south to see a matinee. I have to be back in the evening to host a visiting company. Sheffield will be the first time I have seen a play of mine that I've had nothing to do with; so I'm excited and rather nervous. The director, Caroline Smith, said the first night was a riot, but they haven't sent me any reviews. She said the running time was two hours, plus an interval which is troubling. In Edinburgh the show ran for just ninety minutes, straight through - there's no natural break. So what has been added? The virtue of the piece is that it's a fire-cracker; extended business, extra songs, would dry it out. But, as she said, it was a riot and the hottest ticket. So I'm open to any shocks; it's a nice day; the road is clear; I'm cruising to success. Last night I came through the Baptism of Fire that is the Fellow's Address to Freshers, and the day before I survived the Baptism of Ice, when Arts Advisory scrutinized my programme and its budget. Confirmed and costed, we were now set fair, through to Easter, and this triumph, and the need for the manpower to effect it, is what you have to proclaim the next night to the Freshers. You wait in the wings while the Union Entertainments Officer, a stocky Welshman called Aneurin Hall, introduces you with a snort, as the new 'Fellowe in Theartah' - knowing you're already arraigned in *Javelin* as a jobs-for-the boys, Oxbridge toff - and you bound on to a hail of flour-bombs.

I park at the Crucible. There's time for a snack in the cafe, keeping my head down. I don't want to meet people, either before the show or after. It's like visiting your child who you nurtured till he could walk, then sent away to school where he may have turned against you. You still love him, the memory of him, when he was your personal creation. But will he know you? Will you like him? What will you say to him? Will it matter?

*

I'm riding north out of Sheffield in the gathering dusk. I saw Caroline and the cast briefly, after the show. The matinee audience had been in stitches and they loved the singalongs. Did I mind the extra numbers? She should have warned me but they were springing up so naturally in rehearsal. Whenever the dialogue hinted at a music hall song, they just slipped one in. Instant flesh on the bones! Instant reduction of gruesomeness which let's face it, is a niche market not familiar to the Crucible. Happiness is the key to good theatre, she seemed to be saying, and never, in her career, had there been a happier production! The songs were the show. It was wall-to-wall mirth. Everyone went away feeling reconfirmed in their opinions, having had a jolly good knees-up. Nothing intrinsically wrong with that, but it wasn't my play. As Penistone Crag hove glumly into view, I felt a theatre law emerging: the happier a show is in the making, the flabbier it will be in performance, and the soggier will be the audience's reimmersion in comfy values.

*

I was back in time to host Incubus, the visiting company who were not happy with the arrangements. The Union Ents Office had fouled up the room booking, and I hadn't helped, putting their little show - Kafka's *Metamorphosis* - into the vastness of the Great Hall. All could have been resolved, three days before, when Aneurin 'Great' Hall, received a call from a Mr Jagger saying the 'Stones' were coming to do do a 'No Satisfaction' FREE GIG in the Uni.

'No chance boyo,' quoth the Welshman. 'The Great Hall is booked. Visiting drama. Could be shifted to the Small Hall, but not without say-so of the Fellowe in Theartah, and he's an elusive little bugger. You'll just have to give us more notice in future - what d'you say your name was? Because you can't', pontificated the Pontypoolian, 'always get...what you want..."

'But you can try,' said Mick sadly.

THE BLOOD STREAM

When I took the Fellowship, it was understood, as it had been with Chris, that there would be four months in the year when I could take time out to further my career. If I were organizing the group going, say, to Edinburgh in the summer holiday, I could even slip away mid-term, as long as cover arrangements were made. So when Chris Parr required me at the Traverse, for the start of *Blood Stream* rehearsals, I fixed for Noel Greig, formerly of the Combination, to stand in for two weeks and direct *The Erpingham Camp*: a trusty pot-boiler, made proof against *Javelin* prods, by the casting of the Ents Officer himself as the Camp Commander: a stroke of genius on my part, which marked the turning of the tide in relations with the Union, and the launch of an impressive acting career for Nye Hall.

It also marked an upswing in Noel's career as a political theatre-maker. He had chopped off his tumbling locks, as if coming out as gay had obliged him to look brutish. I hardly recognized him at the station, till his face crinkled into laughter, provoking a hug and a lip-to-lip kiss, as we mounted the bike and sped up to the Uni. It was the first night of the Edgar/Crane double bill, and over a pre-show drink, we had a chat about *Erpingham*. I didn't want to dictate to him, but if he could lean more towards *The Bacchae*, on which the play was loosely based, and less towards *Carry on Camping*... Then the bell went and we joined David for *Conversation in Paradise*. I was with the *Decent Things* cast in the interval so missed the discussion about failure of ideals being the key to good drama: how Rosa Luxemburg's pacifist socialism died with her when she was executed in 1919; how Marilyn Monroe's potential as a political actor (she was the original casting for the Jane Fonda role in *They Shoot Horses Don't They?*) finally fizzled out when she took the pills.

✳

When Snooks, short and dumpy, enters the honeymoon suite followed by Bridger, all gangling limbs, before either says a word, the ripple has begun, that will continue through the show, occasionally breaking into guffaws, till the painful silence at the end. I thought Juliet and I had cracked it, but we were pros; we knew the tricks. Bridger and Snooks had only their physicality and the social force-field that had them manoeuvring round each other like repelling magnets. This was a masterclass in natural acting, The situation was all, stoked by something electric in their relationship. Snooks was the love of Bridger's life (he still says this); she wasn't sure if he was hers, but he might be, if he would only *back off* occasionally! We took the play to the NUS Drama Festival in January, then toured it, with the hits of the Dramfest, till clearly it was only the play holding Bridger and Snooks together. When it finished, they were finished, and Bridger, after two more iconic performances with Bradford, took his sadness on alone into a short, hard-worked, under-rewarded acting career.

✳

I made three trips for *The Blood Stream*: for the start of rehearsals, for the opening night, then for the final performance; each trip seeming to highlight a different act of the play. To start with, it was the 1940s pastiche of Act One, with Glenn Miller, ITMA and Vera Lynn as backing, which the actors all fell into with gusto. Strictly within the clipped vowels of the period, the heroic cad (Guy Slater), the despised pacifist (Roland Oliver) and the plucky, love-torn wife (Diane Fletcher), formed a lethal triangle, retelling the *Agamemnon* as a *noir* tragedy, set in the blitz.

When I came up for the first night, it was Act Two that stole the show. Clytemnestra, now in her fifties, respectably suburban, nursing a terrible secret, while sustaining an alcoholic, ex-hero husband, is confronted in her living-room, *some sunny day,* by 'a pathetic waif' played by Charles Bolton. Fresh from being hanged as the 'mentally substandard' Derek Bentley in the TV play based on the Craig and Bentley case, Charlie Bolton with his sunken eyes and deathly pallor, shifts the play into the present era. He has come to reclaim, not to kill, but recognition confirms the rejection by his mother and the gun (her husband's) is fired. The critics wrote:

> '*What gives* The Blood Stream *stature is Richard Crane's insight into the Orestes character; the fact that Charles Bolton can find in him, and therefore project, such a sense of sweetness, warped beyond redemption...*'

> '*Bolton plays this discarded child of a wartime affair with a crumpled innocence that is appealing and in some ways alarming. The play suggests that he symbolizes a generation that is not responsible for its behaviour...*'

> '*The central part of Crane's new play, is so cleverly written that the first and last acts are almost superfluous. It has mystery, suspense and retribution - all the elements of a first-rate thriller... Crane has compressed almost everything he has to say into that half-hour, creating a modern revenge tragedy...*'

> '*The Blood Stream is a neat, effective play but seems to represent a transitional phase for the playwright, from minor to major work...*'

> '*Perhaps I missed something, but the last act could have been dropped with no noticeable ill effect...*'

His head was swimming. He was in prison; that much he knew. But she wanted to set him free. Doing time, do you do it in the past or the future? As long as you're inside, the tense moment continues. But she wanted him to set himself free and start living. Was he real or a ghost? He was born, then discarded. He was the abortion that lived. Beware the Bloody Child! She seemed to be saying he could challenge his fate. He could redeem the love that had created him in the first place; or the hate, the pain... She was smiling. The sky darkened. Was she just a do-gooder with love to spare? Or had she a bloodier purpose? His head was in a whirl. He wanted to be happy, but at what price? He wanted to belong, but not as a secret eating away at the heart of the one who should love him. How close was love to murderous hate? How easily did mother's milk curdle into poison? He knew the answer and was paying the price. He had done the deed, in his head, the blood spattering his memory. He had killed his life-source and was being hounded into madness by the cohorts of the Kindly Ones. *She made me do it*, said the brother of the sister. Whose side was she on? Whose good was she doing? The father's, the mother's or her own? He knew the answer. She had goaded him into killing, so that *she* could be set free. The smile, the sweet voice, had persuaded him into killing, so that *she* could be revenged. She had loved her father for all his weakness and the brother, in her name, had killed both the killers. The do-gooder prison-visitor had driven him into killing the killer of her father, who was his father too. Except he wasn't! She wasn't there. Had he dreamt her? In prison you dream of a family, a mother. You dream, within the dream, that you escaped the mother's shriek of shock, twisting like a knife, into mocking revelation. Learn this! And never be free of the horror! He had not killed the killer of his father. He had killed his father! The cuckolding war-hero was his father; it couldn't be otherwise. And now they were dead. All over in two cracks of a gun, irreversable.

*

When I came up for the last night, the surprise was Act Three. One critic had praised my 'juggling with time' as I 'illuminate recollections' but not many had noticed this. Act Three, they thought, at the opening night, was just filling in the gaps, psychologizing the horrors, and I'd discussed with Chris either reframing the act, nightmare-style, or instituting savage cuts. In the end he did both, so that finally the play was advancing act by act: from traditional past, to everyday present, to out-of-time, out-of-mind future, with the cuts replaced by gaping holes like wounds that would never heal. Chris hadn't told me what he'd done and was as nervous as I was dissatisfied, coming back in for the last part. Act One had run like a train: the laughs assured, the acting slick, the agony that had once rattled the cut-glass vowels, hardly evident. Act Two as well, had run so smoothly, you felt murdering your mother was not so terrible after all. How would Act Three look now? On the page it was pedestrian, filling the pauses of Two, speaking the unspoken from One, till all you could feel as observers of the mess, was mild *schadenfreude*. At least *we* wouldn't have done that!

But now the wounds were opening. Language, dialogue have no function when you've killed, except to keep you existing. The flipside to entertainment is boredom and this is boredom, not the dreary kind, born of laziness, but the gaping negativity you find in Chekhov. 'I'm *bored, bored bored*,' says Masha. But at least she says it. In my play, it's unspoken. The audience is taken to the brink of wasted energy. There is no redemption, as there is in Aeschylus; just an awful continuing.

It had taken the three-week run, to get the balance of the play right, due to Chris driving the actors to the edge, and to Charlie's and Tammy's willingness to be stretched beyond the dimensions of acting. So the starry first-nighters, the professional invitees including London managements who could have backed the play, all the lordlings and ladyettes that have to be seen to be impressed by your bankability, never saw the perfect show. Maybe only a couple of hundred could claim to have had their worlds shaken by *The Blood Stream*.

Amongst whom was Tammy's Dad. He arrived at the last minute, unannounced. A fanfare for the Emperor Nero, Hercule Poirot, and Captain Vere, would have turned too many heads. Instead, smaller than you'd imagine, and able to curl into a ball of anonymity, the Oscar-Golden-Globe-Tony-winning Knight-to-be, slipped into the middle row, and stayed put during the interval. Was he moved? Was he impressed? Over dinner afterwards, it was all stories: of Kubrik, Olivier, his schoolmates Anthony Wedgwood Benn and Donald Swann, and the adventures of his Russian and Ethiopian forebears. Then just as I was wondering if he had actually clocked me as a fellow playwright, he slipped me the napkin he'd been doodling on, and here it is forty-six years later! Captioned '*SAN RICARDO CRANI by Signorelli*' it shows a haloed, floppy-haired, bespectacled cherub with still-juvenile wings and the nascent, bequeathable Renaissance curl of a Ustinovian upper lip.

MUTINY ON THE BOUNTY

Almost as soon as Bligh had come home to tell his story, the myth-makers were onto it. MUTINY ON THE HIGH SEAS! PIRATICAL SEIZURE! MURDER IN PARADISE! Headlines and dust-jackets, extracts and synopses, are the stuff of a scrapbook of Bountyana, assembled with scholarly glee by Donald A Maxton in his book *The Mutiny on HMS Bounty: a Guide to Nonfiction, Fiction, Poetry, Films, Articles and Music* (McFarland & Co 2008). As a contributor - eight complete scripts, from which came three epic productions over a fourteen year period - I am included by Maxton, in a list of *Bounty* hunter-gatherers, from Byron, R M Ballantyne and Jack London, to directors and screenwriters Lewis Milestone, Robert Bolt, David Lean and actors Laughton, Gable, Brando, Errol Flynn, Anthony Hopkins and Mrs Vining (see below). One of the first play-versions was an 'aquatic melo-drama' adapted by Douglas William Jerrold, from Byron's four-canto poem *The Island* or *Christian and His Comrades,* which filled Sadlers Wells and then Covent Garden, on and off, between 1823 and '31. The hero was neither Bligh nor Christian, but an invented midshipman, named Torquil, who, after mutiny, tempest, fire and slaughter, finds love and happiness in the South Seas. In the show, he is played, as a travesty role, by the above-mentioned Mrs Vining, 'with great spirit' said the Literary Gazette, 'though would not the character have been more interesting in the hand of a male performer?' There was no such query when I cast Jackie Newbold as the Torquil equivalent in *Mutiny on the Bounty: a Seafaring Show* in Bradford University Great Hall, December 1972; in fact we sailed with not one but six ladies in pantaloons, as midshipmen and cabin-boys; plus guest appearances from Captain Cook - was Bligh's temper the cause of Cook's death on Hawaii? - as an admonitory ghost; Johnson and Boswell, vigorously arguing freedom and responsibility as they tramp the Highlands; and George III, bloated and bonkers, appearing, in the nick of time, in a sedan-chair to pardon the condemned mutineers. I wanted the play to be Christmas entertainment, with the ability to flip on cue from vaudeville to tragedy. Thus, just as Christian and the men are singing good-bye to their loved ones, promising to write and (after its invention) phone, a shot rings out. Enough fun with words! Enough dalliance with savages! Christian's lover drops dead. Bligh blames the bus'un, but his musket is smoking. Like Byron, Brando, Laughton and Mrs Vining, I was taking liberties with history for the sake of the show. In later versions, I would be subtler with the causes of the mutiny, and all contemporizing - the shipping forecast as they set sail, Cook's Australian accent, quotes from Elvis and Frank Ifield - would be quietly excised. Re-reading the later scripts, you see a straightening of the narrative, a psychologizing of the protagonists: Bligh, bi-polar, prone to rage and depression, tunnel-visioned over mission-accomplishing and discipline; Christian, romantic, libertarian, known to Wordsworth and Coleridge, follower of Wilberforce and Thomas Paine: fellow-mariners who could inspire with their difference, or under provocation, split apart. You can admire the research and the rebalancing of the story, as you do with Hopkins and Mel Gibson in the Robert Bolt film, but it's Laughton's Bastard Bligh and Brando's foppish Christian, in the two previous films, that create the myth, however wrong. So with my own three-production, eight-script, fourteen-year saga, it's still the rough-hewn bravado of the Bradford version that entertains: compressed into nineteen evening rehearsals, an all-night tech, and a dress rehearsal finishing as the audience are coming aboard; the whole gelling into a mix that you dream will explode into foot-stomping, hand-hurting acclaim, as it did on the last night.

> *Crane and Mitchell* (said The Stage) *have fashioned a superb Christmas musical extravaganza... bursting at the seams with bright ideas, witty lines and bouncy songs... which would do credit to a full-blown West End production.*

*

At the post-show party, hosted by David and me at 279, I had to go down the the cellar for some bottles. How far had we come! How many leagues, against all the odds, had we sailed! No more 'jobs for the boys', I had put my marker on the Fellowship, and claimed a place in theatre history. Since the Sadler's Wells adaptation of Byron's poem, as Donald Maxton notes, there had been no stage version of the mutiny on the *Bounty*. This was a first and it had wings. But I wasn't thinking of the future. In the pause, in the cellar, against the noise of the party, slightly seasick with tiredness, I was remembering lying back, being carried along under the stars, on the *Ascania* in '61, after seeing *Night of the Hunter*, back-to-front, on the flapping, deck-spanning screen. And now, decades on, a ghost song comes to mind, which I wrote as an interlude, set to music by David Essex, but in the end cut. Here it is in public for the first time:

One night long ago the tropics,
An hour before sunrise,
I was ordered out to the jib-boom,
To set the flying jib-guys,
And I turned when the worked was finished,
My head, by the skys'l stay,
And gazed at the sails in wonder
As over the boom I lay.
Up from the shimmering water
,Poised on the tiny craft,
A billowing canvas pyramid rose
To a soft breeze aft.
Lower, top, to'gallant, royal
Skys'ls high,
Still as marble, silent
In the still night sky.

*

I'm in a car going south. David is driving. Chris, Howard Brenton and a writer called Snoo Wilson are in the back. They came up to see the last night of *Mutiny* and now we're all heading down to London pre-Christmas; except I'll be heading straight back again in two days, to wrap up the production and prepare *Decent Things* and David's *Tedderella* (about Edward Heath's dream of attending the Common Market Ball), for the NUS Drama Festival in Durham, opening January 1st. Then it's up to Edinburgh to rehearse my alternative Nativity play at the Pool, which, while there, I'll be expanding into an extravaganza for Chris P to direct, in March in Bradford Cathedral.

I'm still fragile from the success of last night's show, so it's annoying to hear Chris, Howard and Snoo picking holes in it. I can feel David bristling as well, as Chris assesses his portrayal of a trio of Christmas-show bastards, concluding that his Bligh lacked the punch of his Flashman and the arrogance of his Toad; Snoo noting that when you're playing your third villain in a row, you need extra fierce direction, maybe more than an author/director can give; Howard adding that the boy playing Christian, though dashing enough, was no match for David's 'bastard' tendency. That was no 'boy', laughs Chris; that was David's successor as University correspondent on the *Telegraph and Argus*! So maybe, says Howard, they were just too chummy; and maybe, continues Chris, giving the game away in that long explanatory, and in his view superfluous, opening number, took the sting out of the coming conflict. *Was* there an opening number, wonders Snoo, because he couldn't hear a thing due to distortions and general hubbub, prompting Howard's comment that the technical shortcomings of the Bradford group, after his experience of *Scott*, should by now have been got on top of. More sex, more blood, more death, concludes Snoo, author of *Pignight* and *Blow-job*, (who, thirteen years on, would be brought in by the West End producers of *Mutiny!*, to rewrite parts of *my script*, after I'd been excluded from rehearsals for objecting to the unauthorized mangling of my words and eviscerating of my characters). But it was a good start, says Chris. It was a lot of fun, says Howard. You don't have to be so FUCKING PATRONIZING! I yell. IF YOU WANT TO CRITICISE, GO WRITE FOR THE FUCKING YORKSHIRE POST! In the silence that follows, I'm remembering something Chris said last night. We'd cleared up from the party. It was 4 am at a guess. Howard and Snoo were asleep in the downstairs room. Chris was on the couch in the eaves of my attic. 'Rick,' he said, 'are you awake? Can I float something? About the cathedral show. Chris Mitchell would like it to be music-led, and I agree. He said he wants to do an oratorio based on the Psalms of David. Could you write something around that? I know you're wanting to expand your Nativity play but I'm not sure that would wash in the runup to Easter, and I can't think of two more diverse venues than the Pool and Bradford Cathedral! They'd have to be totally different shows, so the slate's clean and we might as well go with Chris's music-led thing. Are you up for that? You've had a tough first term. This would take some of the weight off. Just a thought, but it needs action. You and I and Chris need to go and talk to the Provost who I'm told is a crusty old stick who objects to everything, ha! Rick? Are you asleep?'

BLEAK MIDWINTER

The Angel Gabriel made a complete cock-up of the Nativity. It had all started so well. The birth of a beautiful baby boy, a little Prince of Peace, would bring joy to a troubled world. A virgin mother, full of grace, would open a channel of intercession for the oppressed and be blessed of all generations.

And yet, no sooner had Gabriel appeared to the Virgin, than he felt sickened by doubt. He hadn't expected her to be so afraid. He also had never imagined how a 'seed' could be 'quickened' in the sealed uterus of a girl just entering puberty. When he told her she was lucky to be God's chosen Virgin, and He loved her so much, He wanted her to have His Baby, it sounded coarse, as if lust was at the heart of it; and when she replied, with innocent finality, that she couldn't have a baby because she wasn't yet married, his reply was cruel: *'The Holy Ghost shall come upon you! The Power of the Highest shall overshadow you! The Thing that shall be born of you, shall be called the Son of God!'* In that instant she seemed to lose her childhood and become a woman, a veiled wife, a unvoiced accepter of whatever intrusion might be laid upon her. 'Be it according to thy word,' she said glumly when it was all over, and, having told her to tell no one - this was God's little secret (how sordid did that sound!) - he departed.

As an angel, he had absolute trust in God's handling of His Incarnation. It would be immaculate, magnificent! He should have conveyed that to the girl, but somehow, her fear as she opened herself to receive the Seed; the clinical nature of what should have been an act of love; the smear of blood which he should have hailed as a symbol of God's passion; all conspired to make him doubt, or at least convince him he was being tested. Once out and away, he could only watch and hope that she would imbibe and indeed boost his own flagging belief, and above all, keep the secret. But she didn't; she told her boyfriend: 'Joe, please believe me. I was visited by an angel who said I would bear a child...' But he was disgusted, and straightaway set off to tell her parents she was soiled goods; there would be no marriage deal. So Gabriel had to act. They might have the Thing aborted or the girl cast out and the child sold for adoption! He had to fly down and stop the boy in his tracks: 'Stay with her you idiot! Marry her! Don't tell anyone! Take her away, out of reach of the gossips of Nazareth, till the baby is born. God will provide.'

And it came to pass, that a decree went out from Caesar Augustus that all the world should be enrolled. The parents of the virgin were presumably on the list, but Mary herself with Joe, being unlisted, would have to travel to Bethlehem. Was this God preparing the way, Gabriel dared to wonder, for the proclamation of a new King, the Heir to David, who would liberate through peace and rule through love? As the couple set off with their donkey for Bethlehem, so trusting of God, they did not even book a room; as the Holy Family, as he now called them, joined the Davidite traffic jamming the road into the little town, Gabriel, his faith emboldened, went off to check - not intervene! - that the Star in the East, presaging an imminent theophany, had been spotted by Wise Men, who were even now travelling westward.

So he wasn't aware of the chaos in Bethlehem: the travellers spilling onto the streets, all accommodation taken; the only place to rest being the caves under the town. When he found them, he was horrified. The girl was in labour. As a virgin, she was going to be torn in half by the birth! The boy was on his knees, terrified and cursing God. Gabriel would have to transgress the 'no intervention' rule and pull out all the stops. Shepherds! They delivered lambs and this was the Lamb of God. Yet how to persuade them? Away through a crack in time, he summoned Michael and the Host and Raphael and the Choir, who were standing by to hail the Nativity with panoply and song. He had to tell them, in the first instance, since there had been as yet no nod from God, to limit the show to the shepherds. Amaze them, dazzle them, then let me make my announcement and lead them into the caves.

Meanwhile, the Wise Men had come to the capital, saying 'Where is he that is born King of the Jews?' 'There is only one King of the Jews', came the reply 'and that is Herod, called the Great, for having kept the peace in Judea for forty years. He is our Prince of Peace. He is the Saviour of Israel. But he has moods, he can be cruel, he's not well. Don't upset him.'

But the Wise Men had no idea of the politics of the Middle East. When Herod heard they were seeking the new King of the Jews, he said: 'Go, follow your star, find the baby and return, so that I may come and worship him also?'

So they came to the cave, deposited their gifts, and would have returned to Herod, had not Gabriel intervened: 'Take a detour! Don't go to Herod! He will kill the baby!' And so the Wise Men climbed onto their camels and teetered off eastward out of the story. The end.

Not yet!

Herod, when he saw that he was mocked of the Wise Men, went forth and slew all the children that were in Bethlehem, from two years old and under. Gabriel had to spirit the Holy Family out of town, like thieves in the nigh. 'Lully, lullay...' sang a nameless mother of Bethlehem, to silence her child. But the baby woke and was killed.

*

Ever since I'd sung the carol at The Old Ride, I'd wondered how a story of such horror and despair, could be refashioned into glad tidings. Who hushed up the massacre? Why was *Lully lullay* so rarely sung? How could the slaughtered babies (who were all Jewish) be celebrated as Christian martyrs? The story stank; so I wrote a play.

The script I have is a rewrite from a later production. The message is sombre and guaranteed to dampen any decent person's Christmas. But it wasn't originally so bleak. The reviews of the premiere at the Pool describe a much zestier satire, with an edge of anarchy and circus: angels on trapezes; God enthroned on top of the fire exit; Satan flitting among the audience, serving lunch, spreading rumours. In the later script, the set is fixed like an altar-piece: God and the angels above in glory; Mary and Joseph confined beneath in a letter-box-shaped stable, so low they can only crouch. The reviews talk of a happy ending with mulled wine and mince pies glossing over any unpleasantness (don't mention the massacre!). The script ends with the screams of mothers drowning out *Ding Dong Merrily*.

The one thing the script and the reviews have in common is the desolation of the stable.

> *The story of Mary and Joseph* (wrote David Leigh in *The Scotsman*) *has a curious appeal to agnostic dramatists. Once one stops taking the business about Holy Ghosts and Messiahs literally, the plight of this hapless couple is rich human material... Richard Crane takes this to an uneasily logical conclusion. Mary... is having a hard time with Joseph, mysterious visitors notwithstanding. Their personal relationship reaches its nadir, when miles from home, penniless and without a roof over their heads, Mary gives birth in the straw to a child they both know is fathered by someone else...'*

My plan had been to do a chamber-version at the Pool, then expand it for the Cathedral. Chris and Chris would come in on it, to rock the church to its roots, with the host and choir of Heaven, the storm-troopers of Herod, and multiple Madonnas holding slaughtered babes. But several factors stood in the way: (1) It would be March going on April, and you don't do Nativity plays at Easter. (2) For all the trapeze-work, the focus was on the stable. The earth scenes were the cake; the heaven scenes, the icing. If you reversed these, all you'd have in the vastness of the Cathedral, would be epic-scale blasphemy. (3) 'Carrying on' in faith is at the core of the play. Like Vladimir and Estragon, Mary and Joseph are faced with huge questions they will never understand. If it's all mockery and catastrophe, what is the play except a nullifidian manifesto? I hadn't yet read *Brothers Karamazov*, but I knew that to gain faith, first you must lose it. That's what my father would say, and my grandfather, and my godfather, and my brother-in-law, and various uncles. Did I want to risk losing all family support and write myself off as a spiritual corpse? And finally (4) the Chrisses had already made it clear they'd rather do a music-led oratorio on the Psalms. If I wanted to concoct a libretto (measly word!) as the basis for the show, I had just weeks to get it done. So after a couple of nights discussing the whole thing with Poppy, and not sleeping, I opened my Bible - 1 Samuel 16 - and began reading about David.

HARBORD'S LAST STAND

While I was in Edinburgh I had a meal with Ruth Tarko, who said Douglas Moodie, who had directed me in *A Place of Her Own*, wanted me to play a weird kid in a little horror story called *The Great Uncles* for Scottish TV. It was a sort of *Psycho*, a two-hander, with me as Anthony Perkins, and an eminent old actor called Alan Webb playing my great uncle. Filming would be in February; I checked the diary. Roland Oliver, fresh from *The Blood Stream*, was even now guest-directing *Tedderella* to open the NUS Drama Festival in Durham on January 1st (coinciding with Britain's entry into the European Economic Community), with *Decent Things* following later in the week: both virtually in the bag, with *Ted* coming back to Bradford at the beginning of term, and *DTs*, if successful, playing odd gigs around the country. The big thing was *David King of the Jews*, which I was now writing round the clock, merging Old and New Testament stories with a modern parable of my own. If I could hand it to the Chrisses by end of Jan, I'd could surely use a short diversion in Glasgow, while they perused and composed, before falling into writer/producer role; maybe also playing a cameo. But I also wanted, as director, to tuck in an actor-led production, mid to late Jan, to stretch the talents of some of the girls in the Bradford group, who weren't getting enough chances. If the Brontes were waiting in the wings to do *Thunder*, as planned, to be the inaugural show for the new Ilkley Festival in April, then go to Edinburgh in August, I'd need well-tested female talent for the sisters, and Sue Myerscough, Verity Stoakes, Jenny Roebuck, Fiona Taylor, Jane Hackwood and Elaine Smith, were all up for it and ready. I chose *The Killing of Sister George* by Frank Marcus, with plum female roles for Sue, Verity and Elaine, while finding nice parts for Fiona, Jenny and Jane in *David*. Chris P couldn't see why I was airing a play that had already inhaled months of oxygen in the West End, when there were new writers such as Robert Holman, suffocating in their garrets. But I didn't want to prove a play; I was testing actors, and they rose to it, trashing the theatre law that happy rehearsals make slack shows. Sue (said the review) was '*bustling, raucous and immensely impressive*' as Sister George, with

Verity and Elaine *'providing exactly the right sort of counterpoint... in this marvellous production, rich in female talent... If you're one of those people who looks down on University drama because it involves students, go see this and get your preconceptions smashed!'*

*

Who was Alan Webb?

He was born in 1906. Early photos of him make him look old even in his teens, with his gnome-like features and high domed forehead like Gielgud or Coward, with both of whom he acted, several times, in the twenties and thirties. He had hooded, piercing eyes (if you could see them) and a wide mouth with no visible teeth, which when opened to speak, hitched up into a sneer, even if he was just saying 'This is the room where you will sleep tonight' not knowing I have come to kill him. In films he was cast in put-upon or sinister, reptilian roles, when Peter Lorre and later, Donald Pleasence, were not available. He was the coward in heroic fims (*The Cruel Sea*) and the wicked one who gets his comeuppance in family films (*Challenge to Lassie*). He had his vile jellies popped as Gloucester to Scofield's Lear, and was the gullible Dudard who accepts people are becoming pachyderms in *Rhinoceros* with Olivier, directed by Welles. So much we could have talked about! Did he ever yearn to play the lead? Did he regret missing out on world fame and big money? Why did he turn down playing the first Doctor Who, letting it go to William Hartnell? Was it pride in his art, because Gielgud and Coward would never have stooped to playing a time lord? If so why did he go on to do bit-parts in *Whack-O, Dixon of Dock Green* and *The Alma Cogan Show*? Was he satisfied with his long career? Or was it job-to-job drudgery, powered by envy and the dread of ever having to be himself? Who was the real Alan Webb? Was he a joker, or had someone slit his cheeks with a razor? Was he a shadow of himself? Was he dead behind the eyes?

I would meet him again two years later, at the National, in *Happy Days* and *John Gabriel Borkmann,* but by then he was frail and not up for talking. He probably still thought of me as the boy who was always late, didn't know his lines and, instead of chatting, would dash off in breaks to phone his 'secretary'. Was I really so hectic? Was it a mistake to go awol from the Uni, just as my most mammoth extravaganza was getting under way? Choir, orchestra and most of the cast were in place: a hundred bodies in all! I'd delivered a mild version of the script, to appease the Provost, and now needed to ramp it up, away from Chris M's liturgical mellifluence, towards the lynch-mob rumpus argued for by Chris P. I was staying with Greg Philo, now lecturing in politics at Glasgow University. We would talk into the night about the message inherent in *David King of Jews* - the title itself having Christian overtones: more C S Lewis than Karl Marx! - alongside the rationale of a show called *Yesterday's Revolution* about the betrayal of the Labour movement by Ramsay Macdonald and later Gaitskell and Wilson, which Greg was putting together to run with whatever Bradford would be taking to Edinburgh in the summer. I wasn't sure about impugning Wilson who was notoriously touchy about being impugned, and could have the Edinburgh plug pulled. Greg, for his part, was curious about a chance being missed, in the Cathedral show, to expose the dark side of Christianity. Nationalism, belligerence, escalation of savagery, redeemed by sacrifice: was that not a ground-plan for bourgeois religious attitudes? Where was the sadism and genocide endemic in the Bible, but politely covered up, or made pretty, by the church? I said it's right there in the script, or will be when I've finished it. I'm feeding through re-writes to Brenda every day, to type up for the Chrisses. I can imagine Parr going YES! and Mitchell going NO!!!, and me when I get back going maybe-maybe-maybe, and the Provost, not yet having signed a formal agreement, yet seeing posters around town, and his photo in the paper, going fuck...

'Mr Harbord,' says Mr Moodie, when once again I am almost an hour late, having overslept and taken the wrong bus; 'you may or may not be blonde and preferred by gentlemen, but you are no Marilyn Monroe. Mr Webb and I have run out of curses to hurl at you. Now get into bed.' We're rehearsing the scene where I wake up and slip naked out of the four-poster, to find my clothes have been taken and the bedroom door is locked. 'You can wear your pants,' sighs Douglas, lighting another coffin-nail, and inhaling. 'But make sure they're clean.' He has the same attitude and vocabulary as Billy Chappell who directed me in *The Entertainer* at Nottingham; but whereas that production was the highlight of a highly-lit season, *The Great-Uncles* is pap: a sad swan-song for Richard Harbord, whose career stops here. You can google IMDB and read his three screen credits: *The Duna Bull*, *Villains* and *Late Night Theatre: The Great Uncles*. Actually when I saw it, in Bradford, with a group of the *David* cast, it wasn't so bad, and I wished I hadn't given Dougie and Alan such a bad time. There was no wrap party and I didn't even say good-bye. If I'd known this was Harbord's last stand, we might have celebrated just a little. It's a poor summary in IMDb, omitting *The Breaking of Bumbo* and *Madame Sin*, and no mention of course of the six-year stage career. But that's showbiz: a fleeting wisp of glory, then oblivion. Who's heard of Mrs Vining? Who remembers Alan Webb?

It was always going to be tricky having an *alterum-nomen alter-ego*. Crane and Harbord, as well as muddling bank accounts and tax, had been tussling over my soul for five years and Harbord was losing. He still hoped a star part like *The Leader* would turn up, but that was a fantasy. Acting was now subsidiary to writing, and when the writer at Bradford was called upon to act, he would side-step Harbord and trawling the Yellow Pages, be credited as Trellis Fencing or, more grandly, Scaffolding Erectors. He even called Equity from time to time, to enquire if the other Richard Crane, who had pipped him at the post in 1967, was prepared to leave the union and return his name.

Skip ahead to one night in early spring 1975. I'm at my desk in my study in the three-storey Edwardian terrace house in Clapham that I bought on moving back to London, after leaving Bradford. I haven't yet put the curtains up, so anyone passing in the street may see the posters pasted on the walls, advertising plays by Richard Crane - *Crippen, The Blood Stream, David King of the Jews, Mutiny...* A shadowy figure passes the window, a glint in his round-framed glasses as he catches my eye, then stops at the door. It's annoying to be interrupted. I'm trying to write a play about the Emperor Nero and his dream of ruling the world through art. The door-bell jangles. I get up with a sigh; it's not recommended to open doors after dark, but he's seen me. He rings again, just as I unchain, unlock, open the door.

In the light of the street-lamp, I see a man, my own height, my own build, my own age. He has long straight hair like mine, and round gold-framed glasses on a square-shaped head, like mine, like mine.

He says: 'Are you Richard Crane?'

I say: 'Why?'

'I've come to return something.'

I let him in. If there's trouble, I can shout for Bridger who is renting the front upstairs room and researching a play about the IRA.

'I saw your posters on the wall,' says the stranger. 'I pass your window every day.'

'Would you like a drink?' I say, in spite of myself. He's unsettling me, hovering in the hall, inspecting my curiosities.

'That's the Rugby School clock,' I explain; 'from my play *Tom Brown*. It's not stone; it's polysteirene. And that is the skull of a bull that I found in the hills above Glasgow. There was a complete skeleton, but I couldn't fit it in my bag! I like to think it was a bull, though it doesn't have horns. I call it Duna, after a film I was in.'

'Do you have a brandy?'

He comes into the study and follows me through the double doors into my bedroom where the drinks are.

'I don't like to have drinks in the room where I'm working. But it's the end of a busy day. So brandy it is...'

He's sitting on the bed, which is in fact two single beds pushed together filling the room. I pour two brandies, and hand one to him. He doesn't rise, so I sit beside him.

'You haven't told me your name.'

'Can't you guess?'

'Rumplestiltskin?'

He's swilling the brandy in his glass: 'Cheers.'

We drink.

'I'm Richard Crane.'

The brandy incinerates me. There's a mirror behind him, but it's not a reflection I'm staring into. I'm staring at me. His face is my face. His eyes behind the glasses are my eyes, unblinking. His slightly crooked smile is exactly like mine, as with my voice, he explains: 'I had a message from Equity. I haven't acted for three years. I only ever did commercials, then the work dried up, so I went into advertising. They said you wanted your name back, so I've come to return it. Thanks for the drink.'

I tell him I don't do much acting now either, but I thank him anyway. I'm feeling giddy. I close my eyes. When I open them, he's gone. I hear the front door click.

In the morning I ring Equity. 'Yes,' says the girl. 'Richard Crane is no longer a member. The name is available.'

DAVID KING OF THE JEWS

*O*nce there was a Farmer who built a farm. On the farm, there were
cattle, pigs, horses, sheep, a Cat and a Dog. They were all vegetari-
ans and lived in peace. The Cat and the Dog were companions for the
Farmer and had no specific function on the farm.

*One day, out of boredom, the Cat and the Dog desecrated the Great
Tree which stood in the farmyard. In anger the Farmer threw them off
the farm, retired to his room, depressed and disillusioned, and handed
over control of the farm to hired Shepherds.*

*The Cat and the Dog grew up in the wild, developed a taste for meat,
grew into Lions and Wolves, raided the farm and destroyed all the animals except the Sheep who were strictly guarded by the Shepherds.*

*The policy of the Shepherds was to enclose the Sheep in a strong fold,
to allow no contact with the world outside, and to prepare the flock as
an elite body, chosen and beloved by the Farmer.*

*This policy failed. The flock was attacked and all but wiped out, when
up rose the Youngest of the Shepherds and answered the challenge of
the Champion of the Wolves and killed him. Overnight, he became the
hero of the flock, but also a victim of the jealousy of the Chief Shepherd,
who forced him out.*

In exile, the Youngest Shepherd, moved among the Wolves and Lions, and discovered that they had originally been dogs and cats and that all animals were equal in the eyes of the Farmer. He proposed a peaceful meeting for the Wolves and Sheep (the Lions, being cats, went off on their own) to put an end to the feud, and to save the farm. The Shepherds refused to accept his plan, and the Wolves lost patience and devoured the flock.

The Youngest Shepherd saved a few Sheep from the slaughter, and in bitterness and anger, worked on them and trained them up to be Super-Sheep, carnivorous and of giant proportions.

The Wolves also developed with equal ferocity, until finally the two sides confronted each other with monstrous power-houses of destructive energy, sufficient to wipe out all creation.

At the critical moment, the Farmer returned, and asked what had become of his peaceful farm. The flock disowned him and took him for an impostor. The Wolves were amused by him. Together the Sheep and Wolves baited and attacked him, and unleashed on him all the energy they had built up against each other, and finally tore him to pieces.

Justifying their action, and sated with blood, the Super-Sheep and Super-Wolves established a fragile peace. Only the Youngest Shepherd saw the full horror of the killing, but he was now of no consequence, being old and close to death.

*

Unlike Orwell's farm which is an allegory and remains a farm throughout the story, my farm is a myth, arising out of sheep and other animal references in the Psalms and Isaiah, and invented to colour the human story of David, Saul, the Israelites and the Philistines. It weaves in an out of the play as the tribal credo, sometimes invoked to rally the troops, sometimes acted out to mask the horrors. It also lifts the story out of the comfort of ancient times, into the conflicts of today: from the sling-shots against tanks, of the Israel/Palestine wars, to the Cold War escalations of the 60s and 70s. There is no certainty in the faith that sustains the two armies. Only David, being naive, truly believes in the Farmer, and defeats Goliath and wins the kingship, through belief in himself as the chosen leader of the chosen people. But he is prey to human frailties (pride and lust), and the emotions of others (envy, fear, revenge), until with age, family trauma and the madness of Mutually Assured Destruction, he acquires despair along with wisdom. The script I have must be an early one because it omits David's final test. In old age, he has to prove he has the balls to continue as King. So the sexily named Abishag the Shunamite is introduced into his bed. For the seed in the ground to grow, the King's seed must also floourish. But he fails, and so he dies. I think we kept this scene out of the script, for fear of the Provost's disapproval; he could hardly object to a crucifixion in a church, but sex was beyond the pale. In fact we needn't have worried. I have several abiding memories of *David King of the Jews*. The first is coming into the cathedral when Chris M was rehearsing the music. Fiona Taylor, known as Effie, as Michal, Saul's daughter and David's wife, is singing Chris's hauntingly erotic setting of *When I Arose and Opened for my Beloved*, from the Song of Songs. She is standing on the chancel step. Her voice is effortlessly playing with the acoustic and softening the stonework, making the ancient most modern. An elderly priest in a cassock comes out of the vestry and is walking down a side-aisle. He stops and listens, then sits down in a pew and doesn't move, even when the songs ends. He wrote to us after the show, after we'd settled the bill and cleared everything from the Cathedral:

> *Dear Richard and Chris*
> *Thank you for your very kindly letter, and generous cheque... I must say that whatever my considerable apprehensions were in the early stages, I slowly warmed to the whole thing and ended by enjoying and being greatly moved by the final result. You both deserve many con-gratulations for the persistence and patient care with which you car-ried it through. The final clear-up on the Saturday evening was a marellous cooperative effort on its own...*

Other letters were less flattering:

> *Dear Mr Crane*
> *I will try and explain what I felt, after seeing* David King of the Jews *at the Cathedral last Friday; which was a deep and disturbing revulsion to the violence throughout the performance... I felt the play was anti-semitic and would prove in certain circumstances a powerful incitement to religious hatred. I know (or think I know) that there is much violence in the Bible, but I have a vague idea that there is beauty there and good sentiment also, none of which came over to me... The ending of the play in particular shocked and frightened me quite literally. The crucified figure was undoubtedly that of Jesus Christ and the audience were presented with the spectacle of this cruel act as a finale. If your intention in producing this play was a gesture against violence, then I would say it has failed abysmally...*

I replied:

> ... *I'm sorry the play upset you and that you saw it as anti-semitic. It was anti-nationalistic certainly; anti- any nation, be it Jewish, British, German, American... which sets itself up as racially superior. By sending me David Holbrook's article about the current trend for violence, you seem to be equating my play with films such as* A Clockwork Orange, *where violence is used as an easy answer to any problem and not seen as immoral... We have received a great deal of reaction from teachers, students, clergy etc, the gist of which was that they found the play disturbing, thought-provoking and a powerful statement against bigotry and violence...*

I could have sent her the reviews:

> *In all its centuries, Bradford Cathedral has probably never seen anything like it...* David King of the Jews *lacked nothing in ambition or enthusiasm from the University drama group, orchestra and chorus... Dramatically gripping throughout... a thought-provoking comment on nationalism as a religious duty... The standard of production and timing was superb and the acting impressive,.... As a theatrical production with costume, lights and music, it was a triumph... The combination of Crane and Mitchell has not been long in existence, but on its showing so far, it promises a great deal of excitement in the future.*

When you've worked so intensely on something so huge in so short a time for just three performances, and it's over and you've done the clear-up, had the party, paid the bills, answered the letters etc; when you wake and it's so quiet, you find you're *either* in the grip of acute post-natal depression (and the baby is dead!); *or* it's a new day, job done, dream fading, future beckoning, because you're now onto the next thing. But flashpoints remain, fragmentary and piecemeal, like the script as you remember it. Rereading it, even the milder version, I'm amazed how daring it is. It starts with a bleat, then an answering bleat, then more and more till the cathedral is filled with bleating. We are at the point of annihilation of the sheep by the wolves/of Israel by the Philistines. The Chief Shepherds have been captured and had their tongues torn out. Goliath, Nye Hall on twelve-inch *cothurnoi* making him seven feet tall, throws down his challenge. David played by clean-cut first-year student Pete Brent, springs up and shoots him dead with a gun. Then we're straight into the Bathsheba story told, buffoon-style, as a play within a play, with Jane Hackwood bobbing shoulder-high down the aisle in a swimsuit in a tin bath - is she representing Israel, wrested from Uriah (Saul) by the psalm-singing David? Or is this just an interlude between atrocities? There is heightened language, crude verse; formal argument in iambics on obedience and rebellion, between Saul and David, and David and Jonathan; comedy horror with the Witch of Endor; then out of the din of battle, come soaring anthems, and a full orchestral requiem (*How Are The Mighty Fallen!*). It's impressionist, like the battle: now ominous, now fired up, now raucous, now lyrical. No one knows who will win, only that tens and hundreds of thousands will die.

It's at this point that a tall, thin figure descends from the pulpit, to confront the tribes. The Supersheep say he's a fake - too young, too thin, too frail to be the Farmer. The wolves mock him for a simpleton who is asking to be ripped to pieces. Gradually the two sides come together to destroy the Farmer. You can imagine he is taking their aggression on himself and so bringing about peace; or you can see it as just one more eruption of violence ending in a fragile calm that won't last. However you take it, the moment of the assault, the stripping of the robe, the hammering of the nails and the roar of triumph as the cross is raised above the crowd and slotted into place, mirrors the nihilism of the Biblical Crucifixion: the being forsaken by God, the darkening of the world, the complete failure of redemption. I had a letter from a priest, deeply moved by the production, but asking 'What about the resurrection?' For answer I could only recall, at the end of the final show, the elongated figure of Bridger hanging on the cross, and a group of ladies standing before him, gazing up in awe like the Marys of the *Stabat Mater*. If there were to be a resurrection, it would be so ordinary, you'd hardly notice: just a gardener, passion play over, clearing the garden; or a stranger accompanying two friends home to dinner; or the El Greco figure of Bridger looking down on the ladies and silently urging them to fuck off, so he can go home.

THUNDER

S cripts get restless when unperformed and *Thunder* had been rumbling in my drawer for over a year. All the other shows since October - *Blood Stream, Mutiny, Bleak Midwinter, David* - had been developing scriptwise right up to the wire. *Thunder* by contrast had been fully formed since Brixton days, having had a two-year gestation, going back to 1970 when I got lost on the moor. I'd originally hoped Chris Parr would direct it, but he'd just done *David* and was now busy at the Royal Court, and that was fine by me. *Thunder* was my baby and the more I worked on it, the more I didn't want anyone else touching it. I wanted to be the complete *auteur* like Bergman, or Peter Ustinov. To unleash the imagination, to deliver the bog burst, and make a mammoth extravaganza out of just a room and six actors, was my signature promise to the Brontes and myself. I'd even done the music, having offered it to, and taken it away from, both Milton and Chris M, because tunes just came into my head for the Bronte poems and I felt they couldn't be bettered. I sat down at the piano with Effie, who would play Emily, and she notated the music, starting with *Cold in the Earth...* from Emily's poem *Remembrance*, as the three sisters, emerge rising from the dead and singing *a capella*, grouped as in Branwell's painting. Then through the pillar (where he had painted himself out), Branwell, Top Genius and Hope of the Family, bursts into life with a requiem for his doomed hero:

Backward I look upon my life

To see one waste of storm and strife!
One wrack of sorrows, hopes and pain
Vanishing to rise again!
That life has moved through evening where
Continual shadows veiled my sphere,
From youth's horizon upward rolled
To life's meridian - dark and cold!
All dark without! All fire within!
Can Hell have mightier hold on Sin!

I knew I would have to keep Branwell in check. I'd written plays before with three women and one man and the challenge was always to keep from crafting a plum role for myself with the girls as just backing. But I soon learnt the best way was not to rein the boy in, but to loosen up on the sisters. They lived in their heads, on the moor, in their books, in battles and romances; trapped 'between stairs' as governesses; needing and sustaining each other and their father; aware of doomed love, and death just a blood-stained napkin away. There are plays within the books, and protagonists eager to fight, love and die. Papa Bronte is the book-ends. Refashioning his name (Prunty) into the Greek for 'thunder', and rising unbelievably from log cabin in County Down to Cambridge University, he filled the parsonage with books, and his children with a thirst for knowledge. And he outlived them all. He would be played by Nye Hall, who, having taken one small step, from Union Ents Officer to Erpingham Camp Commander, then a giant leap to Goliath, was now a pillar of the Drama Group. But should he, as Papa, put aside his Welsh and go the full Ulster? I said sure and the children should do the same, as they all supposedly had Irish accents, and we tried a few scenes, only to be blasted by a caterwauling of competing Ian Paisleys. Matching person to *persona* was key to the casting. So we stayed Welsh for Papa and 'Yorkshire Parsonage' for the rest. Gill Baraclough would be Anne: a Keighley girl, untried in theatre, but eager to *'walk where her nature would be leading...'*. Elaine Smith, sociologist and future delegate to the Church of England Synod, would be Charlotte. Effie, singer, pianist and musical director, would be Emily; which left Bridger to be Mr Nicholls. And for Branwell, Blob.

Brian Wyvill, known as Blob, came to Bradford in 1971 to do a PhD in Computer Science. He'd been in Edinburgh that year with Bristol University, and hearing of Bradford's reputation, had crashed one of Chris Parr's rehearsals and been shouted at. Unbowed, as soon as he got to Bradford, he joined the Group. A mountaineer in his spare time, as well as scaff-climbing skills, he brought a reckless energy to the team and a talent for hanging on. He had a birdlike face, stretched taut by the sun and a grin that demanded laughter. There was no flesh on his bones, just gristle and elastic. He had never yet gone off the rails or had to contemplate failure. Was he ready to take on Branwell?

We had four weeks' rehearsal. There was money from Ilkley, whose inaugural Literature Festival we would be headlining. We would then play the Bradford Library Theatre with funding from the University, the Union and Yorkshire Arts. Then it was off to Edinburgh under the auspices of NUS Drama, to play eighteen performances at the YWCA theatre. Because of exams, there would be no other Drama Group production in the term, apart from Greg Philo's *Yesterday's Revolution*, which would join *Thunder* in the Edinburgh programme, along with two lunchtime shows, and a late-night review, called *Examination in Progress*, after the sign on the door of the Great Hall prohibiting entry. We were back on track, going to Edinburgh with a clutch of shows headed by my best-laid play to date, from the viewpoint of which I could now look beyond Bradford, to the uplands of the profession, as Parr had done, and Edgar was doing. On the advice of both, I moved to a new agent.'Try Serena Rampton,' said Chris. 'She saw *The Blood Stream* and I talked to her about *Crippen* and *David*. Give her a bell.'

We had a good meeting. Serena was a rising-star agent, in kaftans and rings. All she asked was total loyalty. You have it, I replied, too quickly, as she pinned me with her eyes as if to say 'I'll hold you to that!' She would see *Thunder* in Ilkley and get managements up to Edinburgh. The National, now in transition from Olivier and Tynan, to Peter Hall and Professor John Russell Brown from Birmingham (had I heard of him?), would be up at the Festival spotting talent; she'd alert them. In the meantime, what was I writing and who for? Mike Ockrent, the new director of the Traverse, should be lobbied for a commission to follow *The Blood Stream*. I had done my *Oresteia*. What about a *Medea*?

Thunder had its gala opening at the King's Hall Ilkley on Friday 27th April 1973. We had a few problems. The van with all the gear had broken down on the moor, and when we got to the venue, we found they'd delivered the wrong scaff for the rig - cast-iron, instead of alloy - lying unshiftable across the acting area. We lost an hour, while I pleaded with Scaffolding Erectors of Heckmondwike, to take the stuff away and bring alloy as requested. This meant we didn't have time to do the light-plot, which was complex and exact, the basis of the set being the room in the Parsonage, out of which stories explode in an extravagance of cues. In the end the acting had to come first, and I instructed Fred Shipley, the washed-out lighting guy, just to improvise - go jazz! I looked across at him, over the heads of the packed house once we were up, playing the cues like a keyboard: thunderclaps out of nowhere, strobe lights on a clear morning, and the snow when it came, falling *upwards*! He slumped, head in hands. I wanted to rush over and shake him: Freddie! You are the blues! Just this once, you've hit the jazzpot! Even Serena who came early and sat at the back, said the paradox of the lighting was shockingly perverse, as if ordered by a cruel God, and it was only the absolute naturalness of the acting that countered it. I said that was exactly my aim at Bradford: to use the energy of the actors in its raw state, so it didn't matter that Papa was Welsh and little Auntie Branwell was six foot five. There were layers within layers, like tearing through cobwebs, from the actor to the character, to characters created and inhabited by characters, all seamless, all fluid. Thus Effie becomes Emily who becomes Cathy who tells the housekeeper: 'Nelly I *am* Heathcliff!' Elaine becomes Charlotte who becomes Jane who transforms the inadequate Nicholls/Bridger into the gothic, tormented Rochester, bonded heart-to-heart with an unbreakable string. And Anne slides into Helen from *Wildfell Hall,* returning to redeem her wrecked husband played by Branwell, just as the fictions dissolve and we're back in Haworth, facing sickness and a land-slide of deaths. I had thought that Anne/Helen's religiosity, praying for Branwell's soul on the brink, would be too pious for a modern audience. But Gill just played the lines, driving adventurer/libertine Blob/Branwell, to cry out: *Death is coming! It is coming now! And if only I could believe there is nothing after!*

'It was asking a lot of student actors,' said the *Times Educational Supplement*; 'but what professionals could have done the thing better?'

Well, there was a company doing it, better or not. Anne Stallybrass, Robert Powell, Angela Down, Vicky Ireland were playing the Brontes in *Glasstown*, a first play by Australian writer Noel Robinson: opening in Cambridge the same week we opened in Ilkley; playing Leeds the same week we were playing in Bradford; then just as we were setting off to take Edinburgh by storm, reviews were coming in of the play's debut in the West End. THIS WAS *THE THIRD TIME* A SHOW OF MINE WITH LEGS HAD BEEN KNEE-CAPPED!!! In 1971, just as *Crippen* was opening in Edinburgh, Ned Sherrin and Caryl Brahms were staging their sparkly musical romp about the little doctor. In 1972, just as *Tom Brown* was gearing up for post-Bradford fame, the 'lavish and literate' Keith Chegwin/Simon Le Bon musical was premiering at the Cambridge Theatre. THEY'VE STOLEN RICHARD'S THUNDER *AGAIN!* lamented the *Telegraph and Argus*, lacerating Stallybrass, Powell and co with a scathing review:

> *Like the wind, the Brontes cannot be bottled, only felt... As a play, this Bronte revelation, was opaque... Charlotte, all outwardly school-ma'am... shocked into writing novels by her unrequited love for her professor... Branwell, half demented, half buffoon, shocked into drugs, by ditto ditto for Mrs Robinson... Emily, icicle cold (what travesty*

here!)... Anne, quiet and nervous as a church mouse... Not one sweet breeze from the countrysde was allowed to enter... If you don't FEEL that, you will never even start to KNOW the Brontes.

If any of the triple whammies had been good, I'd have been devastated. As it was, I was too busy to be more than mildly pissed off. Some mingey God had it in for me for keeping on writing critically acclaimed shows which for some reason never got beyond Fringe or University. But was fame what I craved? Well yes it was, if only to have cash in the bank and not to have to work so fucking hard! I was doing plays that tore strips off your Sherrins and Chegwins, and should have buried Frith Banbury, director of *Glasstown* which bowed at the Westminster Theatre, home of Moral Re-Armament for chrissake! The play apparently began with a prayer meeting (God!), the *'excess of good taste'*, wrote The Times, *'encapsulated in the wiping up of Branwell's vomit with a pocket handkerchief!'* How was it, I grumbled to Serena down the phone, that the writers of these shows could leap to fame with one bound, while I had to keep bashing out play after play? How come you're so prolific, people were asking, when it was obvious: my plays don't earn. They're exquisite minnows, when what I want is a shark.

✳

As a child, I collected Nelson Classics, those little dark blue volumes, fake-leather-bound with gilt lettering on the spine. I still have a shelf of them in my glass-fronted book-case: John Bunyan, Jane Austen, Harrison Ainsworth, the Brontes... The faint mustiness that greets you, when you inhale the close-printed pages, is a time's arrow straight back to my ice-blue bedroom in the vicarage at Balsall Heath: my father in his study, my three sisters at their desks or the kitchen table or the piano, and me, crouched on the floor over the gas fire, reading *Wuthering Heights*. I have the book beside me now: the first and most thumbed of my Nelsons, but still intact, which, prompted by a recent damning reappraisal in the Guardian, marking Emily's bicentenary, that endorses F R Leavis's exclusion of this 'blast of contrariness' from his canon; wanting to reaffirm Emily as the Most Thrilling Writer I've Ever Read, I've just reread, the whole thing.

It holds, and more than that, like the best of novels, it grows with time. The advantage of having narrators within narrators, is you can step into the story at different levels. Untouched, at first reading, by the shocks of true love, family strife and avoidable death, you can go with Mr Lockwood, for whom everything is new and hopeful, horrifying and redeemable. Later when you've tasted some of life's bitter fruit, you can suffer with Cathy and her terrible choice between Linton, love for whom is like the foliage in the woods, changeable with time, and Heathcliff whose love is essential and *necessary*, as the eternal rocks beneath; when you've had to make the choice between convenience and danger, being a teacher or an actor, loving briefly and brilliantly or securely and for life, you can feel for Heathcliff's rejection: how the heart, aided by an unforgiving climate, can be twisted into cruelty. Only time and the grave and the snow may heal; and when you know that, you can be Nelly Dean, telling the story; vamping it into melodrama, then seasoning it with homely wisdom. But what distinguishes Emily from her sisters, and makes her unclassifiable for Leavis, and '*a hot mess*' and '*a wilfully retro... screechy melodramatist*' for Kathryn Hughes in the *Guardian*, is her anonymity. Charlotte and Anne are self-portrayed in their heroines; Emily could be anyone. Reports we have of her, from disgruntled pupils in Brussels to Charlotte's post-mortem enshrinement of her sister as a '*child of nature...wild and knotty as a root of heath...*' are nothing like Cathy or Isabella or Nelly. We know as much about the private Emily, as we do about Shakespeare, which makes her fair game for interpreting in any medium, in any age.

THE ALLY PALLY

The People's Palace for Entertainment and Recreation in North London, was destroyed by fire just days after it opened in 1873. Fire again engulfed it in 1980, but not before its magnificent stages and studios had been bestridden by Charlie Chaplin, Max Miller, Gracie Fields, Pink Floyd and our own Bridger and Effie - Snooks had gone. *Decent Things* was now a mini-classic and this was the second of two gigs prior to opening in Edinburgh as a lunchtime show. The house was full, the response was great, we had free after-show drinks; so why was Bridger unhappy? He felt he was 'acting', because though he liked and respected Effie, he wasn't in love with her, nor she with him. So what? I retorted. You're being paid, you were good. And you extinguished the sputter of last week's squib! Was that still the damper? The Old Fire Station in Oxford, which had ceased putting out fires in 1971, was a challenge and we overcame it. As a new centre for theatre, dance, music and visual art, this was Oxford roughing it like a red-brick. But it still smelt of privilege - a whiff I hadn't smelt since leaving Cambridge seven years earlier. We were welcomed by two students: Jon Plowman (future producer of *Ab Fab, The Thick of It, The Vicar of Dibley, Little Britain*) and Sandy Nairne (future Director of the National Portrait Gallery and Chair of the Fabric Advisory Committee at St Paul's Cathedral). I was to stay with Plowman, the others with Nairne. They were go-getters I could tell; useful for a leg-up, if we performed on their level. I was in the

Footlights y'know. Germaine, Clive James... And I knew Prince Richard of Gloucester, slightly. Great, said Nairne. Anything you want, said Plowman, just ask and we'll come running. Then they ran - so busy! Where's the wardrobe? said Bridger. Where's the bed? said Effie. How do we make this barn look like a honeymoon suite? Does anyone know we're here? Have any tickets been sold? In the end, we found a mattress and an old cupboard for the wardrobe. Plowman and Nairne and a few chums showed up just in time for the performance. They laughed uproariously at what was mockery at their own expense: upper-class idiots in a pickle! Then quick drinks and off to our crashpads for the night: me with Plowman to Univ. I would stay on his couch in his oak-panelled study, and maybe we could talk *Gesamtkunstwerk* and *Zeitgeist* over a chaser, but he had a meeting, so crazy! Anything you want, just yell. Ciao.

MRS MERCE

The rule 'no sex please' between staff and students, supported by my own rule 'never during production' was holding up well. If asked, I would say I had a girlfriend in London who understood I was wedded to the work. But the 'moratorium' had to end sometime. Directing *Sister George*, with its all-lesbian cast, I could allow girl-on-girl banter to grow to a *rapport* then bloom to a *frisson* with prospect of *liaison* - in French because Mrs Mercy Croft, the BBC producer and killer-off of Sister George, was *en verite*, a first-year mod lang student, fluent in *double entendre* and needy too. More Birkin than Bardot, and quirkier, larkier than Corale Browne in the film, my Merce was a spring blossom on bike-trips to the moors, then a load of singing and laughing fun, *dans mon grenier d'amour*.

I had a fortnight between publicising *Thunder* in Edinburgh and being back in Bradford to rehearse, so took up Merce's offer to bike over to St Nazaire, where she was on secondment for her 'sandwich' course. I would take three days getting down from Scotland, stopping at 279, then a long hop to Shaftesbury Dorset where Roy and Elizabeth now lived: divert to Bath, stay over with Gran, then speed down to Plymouth, catch the ferry to St Malo, cross Brittany and be singing under canvas with Merce by sundown. It would be a chance to clear the head before plunging into Edinburgh. Like the *Bounty,* I was sailing into uncharted seas. Was that why I'd opted for the widest Channel crossing - five times Dover/Calais - to be where the Bligh and Christian had sailed, and the Ascania after them, into the maelstrom of the Atlantic? In a year, I'd be reading *Zen and the Art of Motorcycle Maintenance*: a career-travel-guide, that would become my bible. I didn't know the word yet, but this trip out of Scotland, down

England and across France, would be a *chautauqua*, or period of personal enquiry, best achieved not through drugs but speeding *en plein air* on a motorbike.

It was easy as far as Shaftesbury and I was looking forward, as prep for *Thunder*, to a literary conversation in a parsonage setting, but just as I was turning into the cobbled streets of Hardy's Shaston, I skidded and fell off, tearing the flesh off my middle finger and cutting it to the bone. I pushed on to the Rectory, where Elizabeth cleaned the wound, then drove me to the cottage hospital, to have it stitched. Before I could argue, she rang Gran to say I was staying an extra night in Shaftesbury, so wouldn't make it to Bath. But I left anyway the next morning, after Roy had shown me the neck of Brittany, on the map: no swan's neck, more a bull's, which would take half a day to cross. Arriving in Plymouth, I tried to get an earlier ferry but they were all delayed. The weather was foul. I was sick on the boat, from something I'd eaten, not the sea! - and crossing Brittany through the night, in the rain, crushed by trucks, took seven hours. Some break! Some *chautauqua*! I had no means of communicating with Merce who stayed up waiting, till 4 am thinking I was dead.

FRINGE FIRST

I got back to Bradford on 23rd July to terrible news. Blob, away climbing in Sweden with a friend (also called Brian), had been killed in a car crash. They'd been driving through the night, taking turns at the wheel, and Blob falling asleep, had wrapped the car round a tree. The other Brian, asleep on the back seat was unharmed. My first thought was crudely practical. We had a week to find and rehearse a new Branwell. I could ask Greg, or Pete Brent, or I could do it myself. We already had one other cast change to assimilate. Elaine had said she wouldn't be free for Edinburgh, so I had sprung Sue Myerscough from her sandwich course, to step in as Charlotte. As the anchorage of the play, she would need time to 'shrink' from her own height to Charlotte's diminutive frame, and to explore her cloistered passions. One tends to take Charlotte for granted, since she outlived her siblings, achieved fame in her lifetime and managed to find a husband. She has also been derided for her obsessive love for her Belgian professor, and for so caring for her dead sisters' reputations that she edited out anything devilish in their work and enshrined them as saints. All this makes her a complex challenge to the actor who may focus on the thwarted love, brought to book by the need to care; or on the need to care made bearable by the invention of a thwarted love that triumphs.

Then Blob walked in. It was the other Brian who had been driving. He wasn't going to talk about it. Again, Bronte-style, practicality won through. Blob has said climbing and theatre are both life-and-death games. You can 'die' or cause others to 'die' on stage, through a missed cue or blanking out, just as you can literally die on a mountain through misjudgment. *Thunder* was now real. Actors were merging with characters who were merging with their own created characters. Sue who had previously played the soap-star June Buckridge who had created Sister George, now merged herself into Charlotte, who bloomed into Jane. There were no tears allowed because this wasn't 'acting'; the Third Rule of Theatre being that the less the actor cries, the more the audience will be moved. I once saw a production of *Hamlet* where Laertes was so overcome with sobbing, each mangled word of his short speech, had the audience sighing and looking at their watches. When death comes as relentlessly as it did for the Brontes, you become as stoic as the rocks beneath. And we achieved that in Edinburgh.

The Scotsman Fringe First is an award for Most Enterprising New Production. As many or as few as are deemed worthy are presented by a famous person each week of the Festival. There is no 'winner takes all', no cash prize or competition where you have to beat down your colleagues. This is a plateau of excellence where all the winners stand equal. There's something absurd about treating artists as horses to be bet on (or shot). We're more typically like beavers, beavering away at our dams, or moles 'scratching and scrooging' in the dark, only occasionally coming up to be dazzled in the light. The Fringe Firsts were first awarded in 1973, with *Thunder* standing equal with Mike Ockrent from the Traverse, Hector Macmillan from the Pool, Tadeusz Kantor with *Lovelies and Dowdies*, and Russell Hunter as *Jock*. Rumour had it that the first famous presenter of the Fringe Firsts was to be Princess Margaret, who was at Holyrood for a few days, but there was a mix-up with the timing and when she failed to appear, Allen Wright, head critic at the *Scotsman*, stepped in, better informed about drama but, as he admitted, less glamorous.

NATIONAL INTEREST

The note said: 'Richard - John Russell Brown from the National Theatre, will meet you for a drink before *Thunder* tonight, between 6 and 6.30pm.' We met in the bar of the George Hotel where he was staying. I spotted him at once, as he rose to greet me. He was tall, fiftyish, assured yet cautious, professorially inquisitive, yet instantly friendly, with silvery, slightly unkempt, patrician curls and the ability to smile and frown at the same time, as if agreement and disagreement were just a wafer apart, and what you saw was not going to be what you got but something much more surprising. He had seen *Thunder* the night before, which he thought was *super,* far truer to the Brontes, than *Glasstown* which he had seen in London and thought was *awful;* the twin adjectives *super* and *awful,* spoken with the same italic stress, and betraying the binary judgment of the butcher's boy who left school at fifteen, loved end-of-the-pier shows; read, watched, directed, wrote books about, and taught Shakespeare from its roots as popular entertainment, having, like Papa Bronte, pulled himself up by his straps, to get to university, then climb the academic ladder to the top. But I didn't know anything of his background at that point. I just saw the newly installed literary lieutenant to Peter Hall, brought in as heir to Kenneth Tynan. If a title was required, then he was the 'resident researcher and critic in search of plays that surprise me'. What he loved, what was *super* about *Thunder,* was its innocence. The technicals were crude; the acting was raw; there was a kind of tussle between man and machine that an audience loves. They even cheered when there was a mishap and the actors over-rode it; then later he heard sobbing. But most pleasingly, the anchorage that held the play steady, was the poetry of the text, both the Brontes' own and mine. Could he read it and show it to Peter? Not that he'd recommend it for production at the National; that would be to destroy it! But there was thinking to be done about new writers to be got on board, especially ones who can stretch time beyond the norm. Heavens, and I haven't even bought you a drink! I have tickets for *Lovelies and Dowdies* at the Poor House. Now there's a new poetry, and it's all in Polish! Do you have to go back to your show tonight? Does the director *have* to keep a tight rein on his actors? Will you have lunch with me on Friday?

I should have gone with him to the Poor House. This was Kantor! I'd heard of him the year before at the Poor House with *The Water Hen.* Richard Demarco, founder of the Traverse and firebrand of the Scottish arts scene, had prised open the iron curtain to release the artist and chronicler of his times, out of Poland to a stripped-out cellar in Edinburgh. All the conventions of director- and designer-led theatre that JRB abhorred (so why was he working for the National?) would be swept away by Kantor, who, ever present, and keeping a tight rein on his performers, would move among them, long-faced and hunched, beating out time like a conductor. I should have gone that night, but I had to be at *Thunder,* not so much to 'beat out the time' but because Mrs Merce was jetting over from St Nazaire for just one night to see *Thunder, Yesterday's Rev,* and the Revue. She was coming with Blob's and Bridger's girlfriends and we were going to have a party at the company flat. But then, what do you know? They'd told us the wrong day! It was *tomorrow* they were coming, when we *weren't performing* - it was our one day off and I'd promised to take a pootle with Poppy to Cramond Island - so Merce would hardly see me. Were things falling apart? There was friction between the two main shows, the *Yes Revs* accusing the *Thunderees* of backsliding. Capitalist expats, amdrams and the National Fucking Theatre, were queuing to clap the Brontes, while the Revs were out on the street leafleting. Nye Hall, who was in both shows, was just about keeping the peace, but with three more bodies to be accommodated tomorrow, in a four bedroom flat already sleeping twenty-five, *detente* would strain. Not the moment to tell them what I'd just heard from John Milligan, adminstrator of the Fringe and manager of the Club, that there was a cabaret slot for us at one o'clock tomorrow night, special request from a personage he wasn't allowed to identify. We were 'commanded', he said, to do twenty minutes of the best from our shows. Great, I said, we're not performing tomorrow, but does it have to so late? Cryptically, he replied: PM doesn't do pm, and rang off; then rang back. 'Forgot to say: the directors want to co-opt you onto the Board. Come to the Carlton, lunch Friday, then the AGM Sunday when you'll be ratified. You can't refuse.'

I rang the George and left a message for JRB to say I couldn't do lunch Friday. Becoming a director of the Fringe, I felt, was more important than being dallied with by someone, however nice, who said my work, however *super*, was not robust enough for the NT. Then I called a meeting of the whole company at the flat after the Revue. We were still having the party, with or without the girls, so it was difficult being heard. I said: Who's up for a cabaret, one o'clock tomorrow night at the Fringe Club? It's a chance to big up audiences for the shows that aren't filling. We'll need to rehearse in the day. It's voluntary and we were specially asked for by an unidentified Famous Person who might just be Princess Margaret.' Aw fuck gob shite... Through the chorus of retching, I went on to project how we could subvert the event with marxist irony, but they knew I was a royalist, class traitor, tory-fucker, which made me mad. How do you argue that as a playwright you must *hold no views*, let the characters speak, let the audience judge? Ambivalence is all. Ask Shakespeare.

I went for a walk. I wandered up the Mound to the Royal Mile and the Fringe Club. They would be open till three. In a corner of the bar, surrounded by young Americans, I spotted a woman I knew. I hadn't seen Joan White since 1968 when she was Mrs Candour in Jonathan Miller's *School for Scandal* at Nottingham. I bought a whiskey and joined them. 'Mr Richard Harbord,' said Joan, 'Mr Rickety Sideboard, as we used to call him, is a prime example of the prudence and perspicacity, you'll need to acquire, my darlings, if you're to become more than jobbing superstars!' These were her students from Seattle, doing James Bridie's *Tobias and the Angel*, followed by *Vaudeville USA!!!* at the Viewforth Centre. She introduced them one by one, sitting me next to a tall, afro-headed boy, with protruding teeth like Freddie Mercury. His name was Anton; he was nineteen. He was an actor and a singer, playing the Archangel Raphael, except I wasn't to know that if I was coming to the show: it's only revealed at the end. So you've spoiled it, I shrugged. Not if you're smart, he retorted. It's in the title! I said unfortunately I might not make it, having a full programme to see to. Was this his first trip out of the States? Was he enjoying Edinburgh? He replied yes*sir*; except he didn't understand Scottish and would I show him the city? I said I had a bike and could take him for an easy-ride in the morning. Come here to the Fringe Club. I'll pick you up at ten.

OYSTERS AND SNAILS

W hen you're riding a tiger, if you lean one way, soon you'll need to lean the other way, and I'd been leaning of late, as Olivier put it to Tony Curtis in *Spartacus*, towards the oysters of Poppy and Mrs Merce and away from snails. So I called Poppy in the morning: she was fine about not pootling; she was busy anyway (and I knew she had another boyfriend). Then Blob told me Merce and the girls wouldn't be arriving till the afternoon, which was all pretty pointless, as they wouldn't see any shows and would be off first thing in the morning; as would I, I pointed out, having had a message from JRB, saying: if not lunch, then breakfast. Come to the George, Friday, 8am.

I was at the Fringe Club, ten to ten. Anton was waiting. He jumped on. 'First I'll show you Arthur's Seat,' I shouted against the wind. 'Seat's fine!' he shouted, as we sped past Holyrood and up towards the crags. 'Should I lean when you lean? Can I hug you? This is wild!' He felt huge on my back, swinging almost horizontal to one side, then the other. 'Hey steady! You'll have us over!' It was a typical, monochrome Edinburgh day and I should have been on top of it: Fringe First, fab reviews, *super* interest from the NT, Fringe directorship etc; but with the boy, so big, so strange, clinging on, I felt freakish and uncomfortable. He might be saying *Memento Mori*, and sure, the angles he was leaning at, could send us flying over the crag. 'DON'T LEAN FOR FUCK'S SAKE!' He went silent. He was nervous. We should talk. Then if it didn't work, I'd just deliver him back to the Viewforth and be ready for Merce when she came. We got to the top and I was about to say: 'Bugger! I forgot! I have a meeting...' when he stood up, astride the bike, transfixed by the view: 'Wow! This is ripping! Isn't that what you say?' I said: 'No one has said "ripping" for at least thirty years.' 'But that's my era,' he grinned. 'I'm a traditionalist. Judy Garland, Doris Day. Don't you love them? How long can we stay here?'

There's a scene in *Spartacus,* just after the bath-house scene, when Crassus (Olivier) leads the slave-boy Antoninus (Tony Curtis) into the bedroom to fuck him. But first the boy must be humbled by '*the might, the majesty, the terror of Rome... bestriding the world like a colossus...*' The hooded eyes, razor lips, clipped vowels of Olivier match the cityscape below: eternal, irresistible. Crassus has got his boy, and will defeat and destroy Spartacus. But when he turns, Antoninus has gone.

'Have you seen *Spartacus*?' I asked Anton, as we stood on the crag, overlooking the city, in all its moody grandeur. He was silent and I half expected him, like his near namesake, to have disappeared, but he was still there, close enough to touch. 'It's my favourite epic,' I went on, 'because it features the three stars who are my role models for acting - Laughton, Ustinov and Olivier - but mostly because it's classical, not Christian. It reminds you that Jesus wasn't the only one to be crucified. Did you know when Crassus asks Spartacus to identify himself and all the slaves say "I am Spartacus!" he has them all crucified down the length of the Appian Way?' I could feel Anton beside me, his fingers close to mine, as if to say 'Jesus is my friend and you're demeaning him.' So I cut to the chase: 'There's a scene in the bath-house, where Crassus discusses with his slave-boy, why it's good to eat oysters but bad to eat snails. What do you think that means? The censor thought it was code for "do you prefer girls or boys?" so he cut the scene. It was only a few years ago, but you still had to be cryptic, which was actually good for writing. You had to work on your metaphors. You couldn't say "Are you queer?" You had to say "Do you play backgammon?" or "Are you a friend of Dorothy?" meaning Judy Garland; which you are, aren't you, being a traditionalist? Anton?'

We were on the edge of a sheer drop. He was holding my hand, gripping it. Suddenly, he said: 'Richard, if you were to die now, would you be content?' Then he jumped: straight up, and fell back laughing.

I was in awe, not love: wonderment, fascination at beauty so troubled. Lying on the grass, he told me, just a year ago, he had tried to kill himself. He had been an altar-boy, filled with the love of Jesus. He used to dream he was the Beloved Disciple, grieving for the naked body on the cross, climbing up to extract the nails, letting the still-warm corpse fall on his shoulder as he lowered Him. He knew the only way to revive His Saviour, was to take the Flesh in his mouth and drink the Seed. When he confessed the wickedness of this dream to the priest, he was told to come to the vestry after dark. Don't put the light on, said the priest. This sin is so grievous, angels would weep and devils cheer, if they could see. Shut the door, turn the key.

I dropped him off at the Viewforth. He asked if I would come and see his show tonight. They were doing *Tobias* at seven, but not the Vaudeville. I said could I bring my girlfriend who was up just for the day? He seemed surprised and amused. 'My taste includes both snails and oysters,' I lisped in my best Olivier, then put-phutted away.

*

I was going to take a walk with Merce when she arrived and tell her we couldn't afford to get serious. She would be away for a year and shouldn't hold back, if fancied by a Frenchman. I, for my part, could only do my job if I had no ties. Short flings, no strings; that was the deal. But she got in first.

She said: 'Look, I'm going to be away for a year. Can we agree to be free?' We sealed the deal with a sing-song in the boys' dorm, while the others were at lunch, then went haggis-hunting at Jenner's. Then at 6.45, with Blob, Bridger and their girlfriends, we took our seats at the Viewforth for *Tobias and the Angel*. It was awful. We were the only people there apart from Joan, and some members of the company, whose laughter only encouraged the bad acting to get worse. The exception was Anton. As the stranger who befriends Tobias on his way to reclaim a debt for his father who has been blinded by sparrow-shit, Anton had a presence that transcended the awfulness. We knew he was an angel from his stature and quiet voice, bidding his good-for-nothing companion, hear the song of the trees and the symphony of the river. Afterwards I told Merce, I would have to go with Joan and the company for a drink and I'd see her later at the party. She and the rest went back to the flat, while I exuded to Joan the actor's response to a disaster: 'What can I say? Unbelievable! Sparrow-shit is not the word!' - and headed off with the company towards the Fringe Club, picking up the bike on the way and offering anyone - Anton! - a lift. 'Do you need a drink,' I yelled as we bounced along the Royal Mile, 'or would you rather go for a ride?' We went for a ride, out of town, into the dusk, heading for Cramond Island which lies at the juncture of the river Almond and the Firth of Forth. We could listen, in the moonlight, to the symphony of the river as it merged with the sea. It was low tide when we got there and we rode across the causeway. The moon was up and the stars were out. Let's swim, I said. There's no one around. So we stripped and splashed about. Stay close, I advised. But he was already carving a passage through the water, heading for Norway! He came back laughing. We reclaimed our clothes. Don't dress yet, I said. Let's lie under the stars. But he was searching for something: My purse! It's gone! My passport! My money! We scrabbled about, naked, like rootling animals, around the bike, down the beach to where the water was quietly rising. 'It's a judgment,' he was crying. 'You brought this on! Fuck! How will I get home?' 'Is this it?' I said, 'where you left it, you twat? Is this another judgment? Is everything okay and hunky-dory now, you hunk? Or shall we just go home?' I gave him the purse. He was choking with relief, like a child, and hugging me, so tight we fell over, locked together, all passion, all need, trapped for nineteen years in his screwed-up soul, erupting and searching: his eyes, his lips, those teeth, his tongue. As in the altar-boy dream, he was agob on the flesh willing the seed to spring. Gielgud has said, in letters to friends, how he liked to unpeel a willing friend and 'take a drink'. The boy drank his fill.

We lay, side by side, looking up into black clouds. The moon and all the stars had gone. Heavy drops were beginning to fall, and cooling water, as if from a spring, was lapping at our feet. Relief ran cold. I had a meeting with

JRB in the morning which could decide my future; then lunch with the Fringe Board when I would be co-opted as a director. The tide was turning! We were on an island linked to the mainland by a causeway, which flooded at high tide; hence the water swamping our legs and rising! It was coming in! After the panic with the purse, this second panic was farcical. We snatched our clothes: I grabbed some of his; he seized some of mine. Quick-swapping, half-dressed, still wet, we mounted the bike, kick-started - come on, *start!* - kick-kick-started, mounted, roared, splashed away, Anton hallooing like a cowboy, me yelling - DON'T LEAN! - through the surge, wheel-deep, then dragging the bike, the final yards, onto dry land.

It was after two when I got back to the flat. The boys' wall-to-wall dorm was sweaty with couples. Merce was awake, alone on my mattress. I dumped my wet clothes, and stepping over the bodies, slipped in and sank straight to sleep in her arms.

BREAKFAST AT THE GEORGE

'You look tired,' said JRB. 'Have you been up all night writing?'
'We had a party. I'm fine.'
'What are you currently working on?'
'It's called *Secrets*. It's for the Traverse.'
'Are you allowed to tell? The secret.'
'I don't know yet.'
'Who's directing it?'
'Well it was to be Mike Ockrent, but he's passed it on to Chris Parr, because Chris knows my unwritten work better than anyone.'
'Have some coffee.'
'Black please.'
'Eggs? Hash browns?'
'Can I have porridge? Then scrambled egg, toast and marmalade.'
The waiter took the order. I wasn't ready to talk about a play I hadn't started, but JRB persisted:
'Where do we begin? Is it the person, or the place? Who's the main character? Or is it an ensemble, like *Thunder*? I'm interested in first ideas: where a writer's ideas spring from. Before it's finished, before it's polished.'
'It's a about a writer who never polishes or finishes anything,' I began, off the top of my head, 'because if she did, it would be the end. She's a calculated mess. Everything she touches, fails: her marriage, her efforts to reclaim her son, her house improvements, her novel...' He was smiling with frowning eyes, so genial, I felt I could say anything without thinking, letting the force of the unimagined end product drive the flow. '...We never know,

and nor does she, if she's in the real world, or trapped in the story of her main character, which is herself as she'd like to be. There's the dream, and there's reality. The secret of the play is the interchange between the two...' I was hoping he might have a tape-recorder under the table, because this was flowing as it never would if I was just sitting at my desk. 'Her house,' I continued, 'which isn't legally hers, is full of half-completed projects and badly hung artworks: a metaphor for her life, like the novel she hasn't finished and the "husband" she never got round to marrying, and then lost. She is left with their son who is equally aimless and incompetent. They row continually but never resolve, even when the "husband" turns up to say he's sold the house to demolishers, which he hasn't in fact, it's only a plan, because he also can't complete things. Their only hope is to unite in their common deflated lives, and this lifts them for a moment and they plan to go for a country walk; but small niggles about what to wear, where to go etc, delay the setting out till the sun has gone in and the projected walk comes to nothing. The woman see herself as a latter-day Medea, but she can't even get around to killing her child, except in fantasy (or is it for real?). She stabs him in the face with an old jagged, unfinished artwork which fell off the wall, then drags the corpse into the kitchen just as the "husband" returns, because, having walked out in a rage, he couldn't start his car.'

Porridge arrived, along with kippers for JRB. We ate for a moment in silence. Then he began:

'They say plays about people who consistently fail, will probably fail as plays, because the writer isn't bold enough to put a bomb under at least one of them. But that's not always the case. *Hamlet* can be stretched to four rivetingly long hours, because the Prince can't get his act together. And look at Chekhov and Beckett. I suppose what I'm saying is you're setting yourself a daunting task. Failure is like boredom in the theatre. If you can make it work, pushing the audience to the limit of their patience, then you are truly a dauntless writer.' Delicately filleting his fish, he concluded: 'Pinter can do it, as can a young writer I've been reading, called Robert Holman. But can Crane?'

I was too busy working through the meal to respond - moving from porridge to omelette (I'd ordered scrambled), with bacon, hash browns and 'neeps' (which I *hadn't* ordered). But a free meal for an actor is not to be picked at, and JRB was continuing with a monologue about power struggles at the National, up in which I could only rustle marginal interest, so had no cause to suspend mouthfuls. Times were critical, JRB didn't mind saying, with the crossover from Cavalier Olivier to Puritan Hall, creating a wobbliness that increased with every day of the tandem period, Larry still nominally steering from the front, but PH doing all the pedalling; appeasing the old guard but with the smile of an assassin. Who will exit through one door; who will appear through another? Who will fall, who will rise? A pertinent comparison would be *Richard III*, except Larry is no longer playing the part. Am I boring you? Tynan, he went on, has exited left, leaving his shoes for me to tip-toe around in. Then there's the ugly-sister duo of Miller and Blakemore, incandescent about PH being appointed over their heads, without consultation even with Olivier. But this is the *realpolitik* of the 1970s, and Peter's time, in my albeit biased view, has come. I can think of no one else who, at this time of cuts and clashes, could turn the Sword of Damocles into his own weapon. Managing the transfer of an actor-led, leaky-roofed, pre-fab-officed company, into the occupiers of a triple-stage, concrete, unfinished national monument, is a Coclean task, and Peter, adept at stirring up enemies, is equally equipped with the means to see them off. I'm ambivalent, as you'll spot. I have no answers, only questions, and I don't even ask those; that's for the writers and the actors. As a dramaturg, I'm a match-maker, a bawd if you like, whose job is to pair the client with the whore. It's not a happy lot, but who wants to be happy? We're living in the most thrilling period of theatre since Shakespeare: the Lord Chamberlain gone, along with all those prohibitive social laws; new theatres, new companies, new writers writing for tough new actors like Finney and Hopkins. What an age to be creative in! Though I'm personally his polar opposite, I carry Tynan's flame, seeking writers who can match intellectual flair with provocative entertainment, and I've a hunch you could be one of them.

I was onto the marmalade now and the coffee, alert now, replete, sitting back and asking questions. When was the new building going to open? What sort of policy was envisaged? Writer-led, actor-led, director-led, or a mish-mash? He liked the mish-mash, but with writers at the core, because where would we be without the bedrock of the Greeks. Had I read Aristophanes' *The Wasps*? Take a look. It could have been written yesterday. If the NT is to thrive between government and the unions, shouldn't we be addressing the strife in our own language: rooted in Greek and retold in the arena of television and civil unrest?

He had to go and for the first time lifting his frown, but not smiling, he replaced his napkin, and leaving his card on the table, said: 'Peter takes over as sole director November 1st. Let him get feet under desk, then we'll meet, we three. But do call me when you've looked at the Aristophanes. I'd like your thoughts.'

Scene Two
A VISITOR

The phone is ringing. David bounds down the stairs. Let it not be the mothers! Let it be America and news! The rosiest apple now rotting at the core! Is Tricky Dickie, re-elected by the biggest landslide in history now teetering on impeachment? He brokered peace in the Middle East, he signed the nuclear deal with Brezhnev, he ended the draft and the Vietnam War and took a call from the Moon. So whence the whiff in the air? What's the smell behind questions about a break-in at the Watergate? Is drama about to steal a march on news? Or can the two march on together?

'Hi,' says an American voice, soft-spoken, unfamiliar.

'Hi,' says David. 'What's new?'

'What's new, Dickie old man - why are you doing that voice? - is I'm spare for two days. Can I stay?'

'Er, who is this?'

'It's Anton!'

*

Billy Liar is a Yorkshire story, about a boy who wants to liberate himself from his humdrum home and create his own destiny as a London-based script-writer. Even though he doesn't make it, the play itself succeeded in bringing a new generation of actors - Albert Finney, Tom Courtenay, Julie Christie - into the limelight; and as a 'youthquake' show, could neatly tick the box, for our Freshers' Week opener: so many Billies for the first time, forsaking humdrum homes for the asperations of studenthood. So when Blob proposed directing it, and asked me to play Billy, I accepted on the spot. To write, to direct and to *act*, was my brief; and to stir theatre, which is to stir trouble. The Fellow, like the Fool, comes in as the show is rolling, speaks truth, peddles fibs, and leaves before it ends; he is the spanner which tightens nuts and also rucks up the works. With *Billy*, we'd be starting the year with a hit, and could use it - because most of our actors would still be away - to inaugurate a collaboration with the Bradford Civic Theatre, England's premier amateur company, founded, and still presided over, by J B Priestley, and home in the forties and fifties, to Esme Church's Northern Theatre School, which had produced actors like Robert Stephens, Billie Whitelaw, Bernard Hepton and directors Bill Gaskill and Tony Richardson. Ever short of older actors, at a stroke we could also have a real dad for Billy's dad, a real gran for his gran. Chuffin eck! This could be a winner!

The phone is ringing. David bounds down the stairs. Let it be his agent, or the Bush Theatre! The commission - his first for a London company - was all but in the bag and he now had a TITLE, which was not only driving the plot, the structure, the characters and the *style*, but was also a TRIPLE PUN which he's immensely proud of and tickled by! *Dick Deterred* neatly referenced Shakespeare's trickiest villain, while prefiguring the eventual comeuppance of the President, and flavouring the whole with a gangster faecality. But it depended on Nixon falling.

'Hello David.'

'Aha, Mrs Crane!'

'Is Richard there? I have to speak to him.'

David pauses. He could say: 'Yes, but I daren't disturb him. He's currently in bed with a six-foot, Afro-American dancer (male). I'm as worried about him as you are.'

Instead he said curtly: 'I'll tell him you rang.'

I'd met him at the airport. I couldn't use the bike because he said he had luggage, so I borrowed the Union van. I told Brenda I'd be out of action for two days and could she firm up the visiting companies, advertise auditions for the Christmas show *Pied Piper* and get copying scripts. If Chris Parr rang, could she tell him I was still working on final tweaks for *Secrets* and he'd have it within the week, and could she drop a note to John Russell Brown, to say I'd be in London 23rd October for the start of *Secrets* rehearsals which might be a good time to meet.

Bombing along to Leeds-Bradford in the van, I felt justified, skyving for a couple of days, having worked flat out all summer except for the time in France with Merce. That had been something I could shout about and be admired for in a macho way, whereas going to meet Anton was kind of secretive and weird, as if I were breaking the law, (which I actually still was, as he was under twenty-one). I even contemplated turning round, leaving him stranded, not answering phone calls, feeling feeble, stuck in the attic, not able to write. So I drove on, got to the airport just as the plane was landing, just in time to watch him descend to the tarmac, waving to me and smiling. His hair was close cropped; he had smart new clothes, and matching luggage. He'd grown even taller, in just two weeks.

'How ripping to see you, old bean!' He hugged me like a bear. 'Top-hole, whizzo, whizz-bang! You see! I'm learning your words!'

'I'm learning words as well,' I chipped in, as we walked to the van. 'I'm in a play, which I have to be word perfect in tomorrow night. I'll have to park you in front of the telly like a theatre widow, I'm so sorry.'

'No sweat,' he retorted.

'And tonight,' I continued, 'I have to do the door for a show I'm co-producing with a group from the Art College, a mad show about pizzas, naked athletes and nuns.

'Can I come to that one?' said Anton.

Full of news and intentions, he was talking all the way. He would finish college, then *not* go into acting, but into the *army* - yes sir! Now the war was over and there was no more draft, he'd be with professionals, real men! They'd do drugs and have sex, as soldiers did, but now, for the first time, it would be for *peace*, not war. Why should laws have to change? Why should Dorothy's friends, as you call us, have to be liberated? The adventure was in operating under cover, not protesting! He was friends again with Jesus. No church, no priest, could spoil the dream. He was blessed with *permission* to suck on the flesh and drink the seed, so long as *he told no one* except those he truly loved, such as me. He was so in love, not only with me, but with himself. And with Jesus, amen.

*

I slipped into my Mother Superior habit and high heels, and setting my piggy-bank on the prie-dieu, took the money. Audience were invited to remove their shoes and crunch through scattered cornflakes to candle-lit tables, past Ken Westgate, posing nude, as the Discobolus, flexing his bulky limbs, to hurl his pizza, and Nye Hall, as Marlene in top hat and fish-nets, singing *Coughing Up Blood Again,* as chapatis were tossed and whirled hand-to-hand, from pan to plate to table. The show was effortlessly brilliant and horrible at the same time: more installation, being an Art College piece, than drama; hardly arty, plenty farty.

We went straight home. Anton rolled a spliff. I put on Glenn Miller, adjusting the dansette so the record played and replayed, from *Elmer's Tune* and *Chattanooga Choo-choo* to *In The Mood* and *Blue Evening*, over and over, till dawn. David and his new girlfriend Sue came in at two, but we were asleep by then. Breakfast was strange, like being kids, said Anton later, sleeping over without telling our parents, thinking they'd be away, but not having to explain because *they* hadn't explained that they weren't in fact going away till Wednesday.

I took him to Haworth. He'd never read the Brontes, and knew nothing of their lives, but had adored the classic films of *Jane Eyre* and *Wuthering Heights*. Welles and Olivier were his gods and he could picture them striding, cloaks billowing, up the cobbled streets and through the graveyard. The grimness, the harshness, fired him up, stopped him talking, made him laugh and weep, as we climbed through moorland mist to the waterfall; had sex among the harebells and lunch at the Black Bull. Then I drove him home, sat him in the downstairs room with the telly, and went off to rehearse. I was suddenly, momentarily, intensely fulfilled. I was *acting* again - essential for a writer, even more for a director. I was bridging the void between amateur and pro, challenging Chris P to excoriate - why aren't you doing *new plays*? - and JRB not to frown; I was getting commissions and a reputation for delivery in the nick of time, plus diversity of style, not to be pigeon-holed or predicted. And tonight and tommorrow night, out of the blue, and then off again into it for ever, I had an archangel, mad, bad and dangerous, to come home to: all the past, all the future compressed into the nucleus of the present, to the point of fission.

When I came in at 10.30, he was sitting at the kitchen table with David. I was tired, beyond politics. They were polarized on Nixon. Anton, the traditionalist, believer in God and saluter of the flag, was a cheer-leader for the President, for peace breaking out and the world coming right, just as he hit adulthood. Why lose this huge relief for a little burglary? David was nodding, jotting notes, occasionally pushing his specs up the bridge of his nose and interjecting: 'But you're black, you're gay, you're an artist. Are you happy? Are you free? Are you kidding me?' And Anton answering yes even to the last, because kidding is the price you pay for carrying on. That's acting, that's what we do, till we're dead and in the arms of Jesus. You don't believe that, so you piously impeach the elected leader, provoking chaos and fear. And David scribbling, in his rapid shorthand; he's a pastmaster of inhabiting the skin of his political opposite and this was quality raw hide!

As I write this, he is acting, aged seventy, in his own show, playing his older and younger selves, at loggerheads over his generation's legacy. Like Balzac, to quote *The Guardian,* he is the 'secretary for our times', weathering storms and doldrums, while managing to be both inside and outside the argument.

∗

I'm awake. It's three o'clock. I'm looking up at a swollen moon through a cracked sky-light. The boy is beside me, untouchable. He came up an hour ago, thinking I was asleep, slipped out of his clothes, into bed, and was out like a light. I'd left them at midnight: two tall men at the kitchen table, discussing statecraft and world peace, as I shuffled off to bed. This was *my* argument, *my* adversary, but I'd just come in from a shambolic dress rehearsal, thinking of cancelling tomorrow's first night, but it was sold out. Then to be faced with a debate I would normally have relished, and maybe used as grist for a show that addressed a crisis, Edgar-style, full-on instead hiding in myth. Admiration, as I lay there, was mouldering into envy. I was a fraudulent actor, dead behind the eyes, but hoofing on, because that was all I knew; whereas David, a slattern domestically, was professional to his finger-tips; doing the myth to perfection in *Dick Deterred,* and the full-on direct action with the 'living newspaper' company he wrote for, The General Will. One thing was certain: Anton had to go, not only away, tomorrow, on the mid-day plane, but out of mind, out of memory. I looked at him, uncovered, the moon casting a sheen on his race-horse limbs, the little curls on his chest, rising and falling. His eyes were lightly closed. He wasn't asleep. His lips were moving, softly as I kissed them, releasing the gleam of smiling teeth. He'd be off in the morning, into the infinite universe, and I'd be driving back to work. That was the way of things, no sweat, no tears. He seemed to sense this as I curled into him, inhaling his pungent smell, like sweet poison.

A phone is ringing. The alarm didn't go! Hey hey, he says. It's ten past ten! We roll apart - *shit!* Like when the tide came in at Cramond - dragging on pants and clothes - purse! Where's my purse? Tumble downstairs with bags. 'RING YOUR MOTHER!' comes a cry from David's room. Snatch an apple, a banana, out to the van. Keys, *keys*!? I go back for them. 'Can we talk?' says David, coming down in his dressing-gown. 'Later!' I'm up to the attic, overturning bed, books - found them! Tumble down, out to van. He's panicking! Get in, get in! Shit, bugger bugger! I'm flooding the engine. We left the fucking lights on! He's howling. Get a taxi! Get David's car! Get David to drive us! *We're missing the plane!* Get out and push! I shout. What do you mean *push*? he's screeching. *I'm not pushing to the fucking airport.* It's how you bump start, you bumfuck! I yell. Christ! he hollers, pushing. Sorry Lord sorry! Do not judge me! I slam into second, we roll, he lets go, chuggerchugger! Jump in! He jumps in. We *will* make it! Thank Christ! Love you Jesus! Hosanna! Foot to the floor, we crash gears, cut corners, like the car chase in *Bullitt.* We get there in just *twenty minutes!* He jumps out, grabs his bags. We might just have time to play the last scene from *Casablanca*? But he's away. He's running. The plane is on the tarmac. He glances back. Here's looking at you kid...

BILLY

BARBARA: *What a nice room! What a beautiful cocktail cabinet!*
BILLY: *I made it.*
BARBARA: *How clever of you sweet. I didn't know you could do wood-work.*
BILLY: *Oh yes, I made all the furniture. And the garage.*

That was when the set fell down. Quick as a flash I said: 'I didn't build the wall!' and that brought the house down on top of the set. Up till then, we'd been, at best, tolerated. There'd been short, polite laughs, respectful applause at the end of each scene. We were almost dull. If we'd been up on the stage, framed in the proscenium, we'd have heard snores, I'm sure of it; but Blob had decided, prompted by me, to play on the floor where rows of chairs normally were: close the balcony, shut off the stage, play to just the banked seating. It was a risk because it meant breaching the 'fourth wall', and allowing a less humdrum audience to see the whites of our eyes, as they pelted us with flour bombs. But this intake of freshers was different: Heathite new conservatives, pro-business, anti-anarchist, keen to learn, slow to pelt. And so it was, till the flat fell down. On cue, releasing a deluge, audience and actors became one. Polite kids became stage-hands, integral to the show. Was this what JRB meant when he applauds in his book *Free Shakespeare* 'the basic dramatic excitement... the aspiration of an Elizabethan style of spontaneity...'? Or was it just theatre at its natural best?

JUDE

I rang Ma. It was about Jude. Would I please *talk her out of this madness!* She was doing so well at Westby's, having gone in as a ticket-tearer and rocketed almost instantly to the top of the top West End catering firm. It's the *awful* Michael, she's sure. You'd have thought, having a father who's a bar manager and a grandmother who runs a theatre canteen, he'd be encouraging of her career, but it's obvious, he hates his family as much as he hates us and just wants to get Jude and his *dreadful self* as far away from us as possible. We've accepted - not happily, but at least it lends a modicum of respectability - the idea of their getting married *in a registry office*, but *Australia!* Migrating to *Australia,* the very next week!!! This is killing me, I don't mind telling you! Only the other day, she was hosting the Queen Mother and Princess Margaret, at Drury Lane. She's earning a good salary. She has a future and she's throwing it all away! You've got to talk to her. Will you talk to her?

I said I'd talk to her, when I had a moment, but I hadn't a moment, and anyway what could I say beyond: 'Go for it, girl! Marry, travel, see the world! There's more to life than curtseying!'

SECRETS IN BELFAST

I was sitting in the canteen of the National Theatre offices in Aquinas Street, within whispering distance of the curious little black-haired old lady behind the counter.

'You're not Richard?' she enquired. 'You look just like her. '

'Like who?'

'You could be twins. Are you twins?'

'Are you Rose? Are you Michael's grandmother?'

'She's taking him to Australia. Isn't it wonderful?'

'My mother doesn't think so. She wants me to talk to her.'

'Would you like some tea?'

JRB came in with Peter Hall and John Gielgud. He shot me a glance that said: 'Don't expect to be introduced', as they moved to a table distant enough for private conversation, near enough to be heard.

'Because' said John G, 'he's *boring*, it's a *boring* part and I don't want to look *boring*. I've played him - how many times?'

'Five,' smiled Peter, his mind on other things.

'Four, I think,' said JRB.

'I've been divinely oriental in a turban and pointy shoes. I've been a wily old boffin with an *endless* beard and glasses. And for Brook, he had me in some raggedy hermity sackcloth with sandals. But grey or black and an *average* beard, if I have to have that, then I'll have to, I'm not the director - oh God did you see the *Caesar* at the Aldwych? Odious! Ghastly! All in black leather pants!'

'Johnny, I'll never put you in black leather pants,' laughed Peter, his mind on casting.

'But I do, I do love the cloak idea, William Blakeish, so huge it embraces the whole world, and the staff like a ship's mast. Sixteen feet high, I could grow to that! Don't listen to a *thing* I'm saying, I'm an old romantic! But why does Ariel have to be sexless? Marianne Faithfull, humbly I say, would be *catastrophic*. If he has to be female, then Penelope Wilton or Kika Markham. But I'd always prefer a boy, and a young one, a rebel spirit. What about Courtenay - how old is he? - if we have to go *nouvelle vague?*'

Peter's mind snapped to attention, but as ever it didn't show. The smile masked a mind flipping keenly through the pages of Spotlight, the actors' directory. *Chutzpah* (pronounced 'hootzpah'), I'd read was Peter's favourite word, and mine too! I had the pluck of Puck and the *chutzpah* of Hotspur! I'd played Billy Liar and (nearly) Ariel. Look no further than the boy, out to catch your eye, at the next table but three. If I was coming here as a writer and, as I'd heard, in the current climate, the NT was having to tighten its belt, I could take two jobs as one. A writer and an actor, equally spaced, like Ustinov, I could help crew this rocky ship at a bargain price! Your tricky spirit! Your dainty Ariel! *Merrily merrily shall I live now, under the blossom that hangs on the bough!*

JRB brought his tea to my table: 'How's *Secrets,* the casting? Have you found your Maud?'

I told him yes. A falling star, a real catch. But she hasn't signed yet.

'When do you start rehearsing?'

'Tomorrow at ten. We're right up to the wire. But that's always the way with Chris.'

'Richard,' JRB leant forward, frowning. 'I've a wheeze for casting, if your Maud fails to sign. But there would be strings attached: shiny, gold-plated strings, but still strings. May I elaborate?'

He explained he'd had dinner with Peter Brook and his wife Natasha Parry - had I heard of her? Cordelia to Welles's Lear, Lady Capulet in Zeffirelli's *Romeo* the film! He had told her about *Secrets,* about Maud and she was intrigued. More than that, *Brook* was intrigued, and urged her to find out more: was the script available? JRB had said it was, but in his view - might he say this? - it did need some *pruning* (which he could help me with). It was all very well having people waffling on inconsequentially, but in his view, on a first reading - which was how the audience would experience it - my potentially *super* script, breached the line between creative boredom and tiresomeness. Could this be, he wondered, why we were having problems with casting. *It didn't read well.* A dramaturg might see the play within, but to the untrained eye... Okay okay, I murmured, feeling cornered. *Because,* continued JRB, prior to dining with the Brooks, he'd had lunch with Howard Gibbins who ran the Bush in Shepherd's Bush. Did I know it? I said only in that the writer I shared a house with, was about to do a play there. Then hear this, he went on, Howard has offered me a slot in June, to direct the play of my choice, and that choice, if you're agreeable and the play is available - *and shorter!* - would be *Secrets,* no question! With Natasha in the role, it could be just the London exposure you need, before (PH willing) you come aboard the NT. Of course Chris is the director for Belfast and Edinburgh. And Natasha might be persuaded (PB inveigling) to step in, if your star fails to rise; ready to reprise in June for me at the Bush. Just thoughts to think on. Oh and prior to meeting Howard, he'd bumped into Peggy Ramsay, you must know of her, Orton's agent (as was), and Bolt's, and Ayckbourn's, Priestley's, Ionesco's, you name them. He said he'd happened to mention Crane - she knew the name and the plays! *Thunder! The Blood Stream!* Did he have respresentation? Could I get her the scripts? I already have an agent, I reminded him. She put you onto me. Of course, he nodded. And Peggy would never poach a client, but if one were to disengage oneself, *in advance,* in his view, she'd scoop me up.

*

I stayed over with my parents. There was no mention of Jude, apart from a joke from my father about deportation, the Queen Mother and elephants, or rather, *kangaroos* in the room! (What *are* you talking about? said Mother.) I felt ghostlier than ever. Peter Hall could wear his smiling mask while his mind raced through casting options. My mask was a death-mask, my mind a blank. It was true, the play was unreadable. Chris had offered it to a dozen leading actresses who had all turned it down. Only the last - Elaine someone? - had leapt at it, said it was the part she was born for, had dreamed of it her whole life. She was American, she'd been in films, styling herself as a 'young' Bette Davies, with the stature of Cyd Charisse. Was she famous? I'd never heard of her, nor had Chris, but we were desperate. She hadn't worked for a year, not since fleeing Hollywood, following the collapse of her marriage which had left her with the burden of a growing child and no money (just like Maud in the play). But it was wrong to say she hadn't acted. She was acting *all the time,* the despair, the expectation! The *gratitude* to Chris, whether he cast her or no, for restoring her faith, not in herself - that never failed! - but in *acting,* in the audience, and 'whatever god is playing poker with my existence!'

I rang Chris. I had a thought. Natasha Parry - Mrs Peter Brook! She was gunning for the role! JRB had mentioned it and if I agreed to him directing the play at the Bush... Stop there! said Chris. We *are* cast. And even if we weren't, has she read it, Miss Parry? How do you know she won't react like all the others? I said no she hasn't read it, but John Russell Brown, with your say-so - John Russell FUCK!!! exploded Chris. I carried on: He knows it needs pruning, and can explain to her, and Peter. Peter who? said Chris. How many *Peters* are you working with? Rick! It's a mausoleum, creaming off talent and leeching money from regional theatres! But it's your choice, if you want to be *buried in concrete.* Because if you're pissing about with Peters, I'm out of it. If you don't trust me to do what I always do with your fucking plays, which is *make them happen,* then we'll cancel. I've a play of Robert's I can do. He went silent. I could hear him breathing. But she hasn't signed, I said. Elaine, she hasn't signed. And do you know why? he said. Because she couldn't find her 'signing pen'! He ended the call with a horrible, hooting laugh. I went to bed. I didn't sleep. There were elephants in my head. Let the show go on, let disaster happen, or pull the plug, lose Chris? Trust to JRB and his 'pruning', trust to PH and his *chutzpah*, hidden behind the mask? Or stay honest and rough-hewn and invisible at Bradford? I had the *fellowship* of the liveliest student drama group in the country. As a director of the Edinburgh Fringe, I was in the engine room of new theatre. My plays were getting published. I had an agent who believed in me. Should I now dump Serena and queue up to join Ramsay with her *super* boy-writers? Hell would have no fury like Serena scorned. 'I'll hold you to that,' she'd said when I vowed total loyalty. I was stuck in the ugliness and nastiness of theatre, alone in the spare room listening to my parents arguing: Ma urging Pa to take a stand with Jude, and him saying prayer was the way, trust the Lord etc - just as they must often have heard Jude and me, like twins in the twin beds, talking through the night. Now the other bed was empty, and my parents were so tired, knowing she was lost to them, but still bickering.

I was dreaming. I was seven. I was leading Jude (4¼) down the slope to Kingstanding Road. She was pulling away, eager to skip along to school. It was foggy. I let her go. She ran on, into the road. I couldn't see the bus smashing into her, mangling her into the tarmac. It didn't stop. I waited, then turned around, came home. I said nothing. They presumed she was safely at school. I prayed to God to extend this present moment for eternity, so no one would ever know.

Secrets is made by Elaine Ives-Cameron's performance...She has one chilling soliloquy when, sitting on the stairs of the empty house, we watch madness grow in her. Rarely have I seen an actress so look and act the part. She was a smouldering volcano, a woman so ravaged by misery and pent-up hatred, that she believes, like Medea, she is destined to kill her son.   - BBC Belfast

Crane is a young writer who is both romantic and prudent. He enjoys heightened verbiage but knows enough to create valid reasons for its use... He is a writer worth watching.   - Guardian

It is the kind of play Pinter might have written, and some of its most effective moments recall the shock tactics of The Birthday Party.   - Glasgow Herald

In the Old Library, Queen's University, Elaine Ives-Cameron, Christopher Hancock and Charles Bolton... talk and talk and talk. Suddenly there is unexpected violent action, then just as suddenly an even more unexpected denouement... It is the kind of play that can keep you talking long after you have seen it. And no doubt anyone who wants to talk to the author can do so when he gives the Guinness Lecture tomorrow afternoon.   - Belfast Telegraph

On the morning of my lecture, I heard a thump in the distance; it was a car going up outside the lecture hall. On the assumption bombs didn't strike the same street twice, at least not on the same day, a fair-sized crowd turned up, and the event became more of a conversation than a lecture. The subject I'd chosen was theatre in the front line, something I'd never experienced except in plays: Euripides using myth to expose the horrors of civil war; *Troilus and Cressida* exemplifying cynicism and betrayal as a conflict drags on; *Oh What a Lovely War!* melding casualty figures with vaudeville, etc. I'd never written a 'war play'. I'd never, till now, been greeted off a plane by soldiers ready to shoot. Theatre, which on the mainland presented take-or-leave issues to the complacent, had a different role here. *Secrets* might not be *Hecuba* or *Mother Courage*, but it showed a family so long divided, its dialogue could only be worn-out and repetitive. Ancient hatreds and tribal solidarities were locked in historical rancour, which was stunting the next generation, the only emotions surviving being fantasy and intolerance. Theatre, we agreed, could release warmer feelings, thought-provoking in peace-time, essential as food and clothing here. Or as Elaine later put it in her *Scotsman* interview :

> *The people of Northern Ireland are starved of theatre and it's sad that more actors are not prepared to risk a visit... We played to packed houses, and were turning people away... The arts become far more important in times of stress.*

Was this fear of the war zone, why so many 'known' actresses had declined the part? And why JRB, so keen to see if his call for 'judicious pruning' had been heeded (it hadn't), at the last moment, couldn't come? I so wanted him there! Just reading the script missed all the subtleties of performance, the ambience of the library, the creaking of shelves, the smell of old books riddled with words, not read for decades, but still hoping forlornly to impart wisdom, like Maud with her never completed projects, her failed life that went on failing: like character, like actor. Elaine *was* Maud. A known actress would be wrong! Restless, romantic, she was a single mother of a son she had wanted to bring up in a rural community in the mountains but had never got round to it. There was an unwashed smell about her, mixed with bleach from occasional, unfinished extreme cleaning, and tippex. She had a long lost lover whom she feared, on dark nights, would be dead, if she did not TYPE HIM BACK TO LIFE, then listen, as it dawned, for the clang of the door-bell, which never came, but would tomorrow! She acted to live, and I was tempted to tell her it was the same with me, but that would have breached the buffer between author and actor, that says don't get too pally. You are a lion; she is a tiger. Even when in neighbouring cages in a zoo, you dream of different continents. She wrote to me afterwards, like a mother to a son, wary of overstepping the mark, but eager to express a cascade of gratitude for the part that had defined her career and her life. She was now getting sizeable roles in films, in America and on the Continent, but nothing would ever top the magnificence of Maud.

THE UGLY DUCKLING

A ll hell was breaking loose in Bradford, while I was away. We'd been in danger of respectability, winning the Edinburgh Fringe First, and kudos from the Arts Council, as the 'most active student drama group', and *The Stage* as 'one of the powerhouses of student drama'. It was time to break the mould, and the man to do that was Tim Wiley. Tim had been a student of JRB's at Birmingham, and recommended by him to ruffle feathers, while I was away. He was a director, journalist, media critic and gay activist. The play he wanted to produce at the University, then tour to local primary schools, was *The Ugly Duckling* by Gordon Wilson. A modern, left-wing response to Hans Anderson, it targeted the hopelessness of working class life, in a similar way to *Billy Liar*, but with swearing and violence. Tim's approach was to abandon the script (did the author mind?) and turn the actors loose on sub-textual frustrations, through improvising and workshops. The result was a mixed bag of blasphemies and juvenilia unfettered by text, that amused a tanked-up student audience, but risked revulsion in schools; most of which let it pass. Kids had probably heard worse at home, and teachers, glad to have classes off their hands for a couple of hours, nodded it through with little comment. One teacher however, offended by a blast of over-ripe expletion, summoned the head who stopped the play in its tracks and sent the company packing. I received a letter of complaint and responded with apology, and that would have been that, if a child had not told a parent, who happened to mention it to a Councillor, who let it slip to a reporter on the Yorkshire Post, who wrote a piece that was picked by Yorkshire TV, who rolled it out on the news to the horror of the whole of Yorkshire. The opprobrium gushed on over the Christmas holiday and dribbled into the spring, long after the company had disbanded and Tim had gone back to writing obituaries for the *Guardian*. I found it tiresome having to do the *mea culpa*, in print, or in the post, once or twice a week, especially when the *culpa* wasn't *mea*, and if it had been, and if the show had been any good, I'd have defended it to the hilt. To be reminded, from time to time, that political theatre, by its nature, is obliged to cause offence, is refreshing, as long as it hits home and makes a difference, which unfortunately *The Ugly Duckling* didn't, because it was crap.

SECRETS IN LONDON

Up until I came to Bradford as Fellow, I used to paste all my archive matter - cuttings, correspondence, photos, programmes - in large albums to be stored in a tin trunk, not unlike the ammo box my parents locked their love letters in, but more aesthetically presented. Each page of each album was designed as a collage of a moment or season from my life, with symbols - floral, classical, mystical - highlighting the main attraction (usually me). I have fifteen of these albums, showing some four hundred moments or seasons of activity from the mid-forties to the late sixties, all beautifully displayed and mummified like pressed flowers. I've never shown them to anyone, for fear of yawns being suppressed and eyes glazing over. But as soon as I got to Bradford, with its commotion and pace, I had to put away solipsism and live in the moment. If I had things to be kept, I would drop them in a drawer, which when full would be tipped into a box and stashed in a loft till I moved, then shifted to another loft and so on, loft to loft, till all is now piled floor-to-ceiling in a storage unit.

A box file marked 'SECRETS (scripts)' fell open. It contained two roneo'd versions of the play and a bundle of fungus-infested stencils, crushed and stuck together, with ridges of correcting fluid like scabs over wounds. One script, much scribbled over, once white, now sepia, had on the title page, a contact address, for RICHARD CRANE, Fellow in Theatre, University of Bradford, % SERENA RAMPTON ASSOCIATES etc. It ran to sixty-four closely typed pages. The second script, on pink paper, still blushing and clean, had a contact address for RICHARD CRANE, Resident Dramatist, National Theatre, % MARGARET RAMSAY LTD, 14a Goodwin's Court, St Martin's Lane, London WC2. In larger type with wider margins, it ran to just fifty-three pages. A re-reading of both, comparing cuts and changes, confirmed JRB's fear. Script One was a mess, too cluttered with stage directions, author's meanderings and repeated dialogue. The untrained eye would quickly tire. Script Two, stripped of excrescence, had a sinewy strength, significant moments, irony and gag-lines clearly signalled. It read like a well-made, actable play that might sit well in the West End. But it was Script One that got the reviews, was felt to be life-changing and necessary. Script Two, at the Bush, was *'solid and workmanlike... composed out of stock ingredients, suggesting nothing much has happened in the theatre since* Gaslight... *well supported by the soft-pedalling direction of John Russell Brown...the acting, superb, the direction intelligent and the designs exactly* right...' If it hadn't been for Belfast, I could have been satisfied with this as a first step towards what JRB called 'visibility' as a playwright and London recognition. But all through rehearsals, I was thinking: Why is JRB just sitting there? Why isn't he leaping up and demonstrating, like Jonathan Miller? Why isn't he barking at the actors, pushing them beyond their capabilities, like Chris Parr? Natasha *'jerkily nervous and pilled up to the eyeballs...'* was *playing* being Blanche Dubois or Miss Haversham, and getting no direction, beyond JRB's comments on the *meaning* of the script. 'When she puts the light on, it signifies... When the shelves collapse, it symbolizes...' I wasn't usually invited to concur, and when I was, I said she puts the light on *because it's dark*; the shelves collapse *because they weren't put up properly*. The result was unrestrained high melodrama from Natasha, prompting similar over-the-top performances from the other actors. *The Stage* reviewer said: '*One yearns for a little calm and a lot bigger theatre... The whole thing is out of proportion,*' adding that it was all right for the audience not to be sure about what they were seeing, but the author at least, must know. No one in Belfast questioned the author's knowledge, because Maud *was* the author. Elaine, with her straight-up Giacometti spine and billiard-ball eyes, was the sole creator of her world. She imagined and murdered her ingrate son, played by skull-faced Charlie Bolton; she invented the return of Jack (Christopher Hancock), drawn into her web like Brad in *The Rocky Horror Show*. There was no make-up, just raw faces in the sallow light of the library. Chris maintained only clowns and whores wore make-up; so when Elaine rouges and lip-sticks up to greet Jack, clown/whore is what she becomes in our eyes. I suppose JRB, standing back, letting it happen, was simply putting his *Free Shakespeare* into practice, as was noted in the reviews. '*The real interest,*' said Harold Hobson, '*is in John Russell Brown's direction... It will be interesting to see what he does with better stuff.*'

There was a birdlike figure in a turban at the first night, sitting at the back, her eyes hooded and fixed on the action like a hawk. The theatre held just sixty, a third of whom were critics, filling the front two rows, heads down, scribbling in note-books. Serena was there, in her kaftan and beads, just a few seats away from the turbaned figure. The set and performances were much too big for the tiny space. '*For an hour and a half'*, said *The Stage*, '*the audience is treated to a whirlwind of drama and pathos... one is left fascinated and gasping.*'

'It doesn't perform as well as it reads,' said Serena afterwards, over a drink. 'I might not encourage London managements to see it, but I will send them the script,' adding: 'if you want me to.'

'Sure I want you to.'

'But I need to know something first.' She leant forward. 'When you originally came to see me, I asked you for total loyalty. Do I still have that?'

'Of course.'

She looked suddenly awkward, in her rings and exotic robe, like someone who had come to a fancy-dress party to find everyone in jeans. For the first time, I noticed how fat she was, and why her clothes were always voluminous and shapeless. By way of changing the subject, I said:

'That person in the turban, sitting a few seats away from you, who you kept glancing at, who was she?'

Serena laughed, a short bark of a laugh, as if stabbed:

'That was Peggy Ramsay.'

LEAVING SERENA

When I rang Serena to arrange to collect my scripts, she said: 'They'll be ready for you at five.' I was doing what JRB had said I should do: free myself up, then talk to Peggy.' She had intimated to him that she *might* take me on, but NOT if I already had representation! She had read both scripts of *Secrets*, had HATED the production! (JRB smiled and frowned), wanted to WARN me about Hall and the yawning MAN-TRAP of the National; be given DATES for *The King* - my upcoming Edinburgh production - insisting that I CHANGE THE TITLE because Cregan, her client, had written a play - not a good one - with EXACTLY the same name on EXACTLY the same theme!

It was spitting rain as I walked up the steps to Serena's office. Chris had warned me that changing agents was like getting a divorce. Broken promises, guilt, venom, threats, depression: I could go through all that, or just walk away covered in shit. I wasn't handling it well. I had rung her and said I hadn't yet gone to another agent but was intending to, I was so sorry, I wanted to thank her, but I had to think of my career - WELL FUCK YOU!!! yelled Serena and rang off. I later heard from her assistant, that this was happening all the time now. She'd discover a new talent, work her arse off getting productions off the ground, shows running and earning money, only to be ambushed by big-time hyenas like Ramsay, snatching the meat from her very jaws.

I knocked and went in. She was on the phone, talking sharply and stabbing figures onto a pad. I sat down by a black rubbish bag, indicating that I could wait; I wanted at least, to say a proper thank you. She saw me and waved violently, pointing to the rubbish bag and then the door. I twigged. Okay. We don't need to part as friends. I don't need to stick around, just to be be beaten up verbally. So these are my scripts, on their way to the bin, huh? That's fine. I'll be off. Thanks a bundle!

It was tipping with rain when I came out. I couldn't find a taxi. The bag was stuffed with scripts and beginning to tear. Setting off at a run, I slung it over my shoulder and it burst shedding all the many copies of my plays onto the pavement and into the gutter. A wind was whipping up. Some of the scripts were loose pages and were now flying down the street. As I was scrabbling after them, a group of Hare Krishnas, in saffron robes with little bells and drums, came dancing towards me. These kind people will help me, I thought. High thinking, simple living, must also include, helping a fellow creature in trouble. But they just dancing on over the dancing papers, soaked and joyous, as if to say 'Abandon your vanities! Cast your follies to the wind!'

But that was the last thing I was going to do.

Scene Three
THE PIED PIPER

The townsfolk of Hamelin - the prettiest town in Brunswick - are rehearsing a dance display for the Mayor and Corporation, that will celebrate four centuries of municipal niceness. Anyone may join in, because Hamelin is a 'family' town and open to visitors (as long as they are clean). But a smell is breaking through the deodorized bunting. There are creatures in the crowd with whiskers and tails and before you know it, the rehearsal is in tatters. RATS are dancing, prancing, squeaking and shrieking, and are only dispersed when bleach cannons are turned on them by orders of the Mayor. His left-leaning daughter Heidi, is outraged. It's time the Corporation accepted there is an *underclass* in this town, denied representation, and forced to degrade themselves selling liquor and drugs! Admonished by her father - he should never have agreed to her reading sociology - she stomps out, only to be set upon by rat-boys. They bring her to the speakeasy where Alphonso, Godfather to all the Rodents, resides. She protests she was campaigning for justice in Hamelin, but has now been totally PUT OFF by the rats' depravity and *smell*. Alphonso assures her she *will* be returned to her father - piece by piece, till a ransom of 1000 guilders is paid! Imprisoned in a tower, Heidi is called up to by Bert, the dissident son of Alphonso. He shares her desire for justice in Hamelin, and knows of a Pied Piper whose music can charm both rats and children and may lead to a rapprochement. He just needs to make a call. Meanwhile the Mayor and Corporation are having to go ahead with the Quatercentenary Celebrations. Three things the Mayor needs: a purging of the rats, a 'clean' superstar to headline the Family Festival, and his daughter returned to him. But when Heidi (on crutches, having broken her leg, escaping from the tower) reappears with the answer to the Mayor's three wishes, the consternation of the Corporation is quelled by a rat-a-tat-tat! *What was that?... 'Come in!' the Mayor cried... And in did come the strangest figure! His queer long coat from heel to head, was half of yellow and half of red?* 'Are you the Pied Piper?' says Heidi. 'No love, I'm his manager,' says the wily Piper look-alike. Delight soon turns to concern then horror, as Heidi witnesses the deal being done by the Manager and the Mayor. The town will pay a thousand guilders for the rats to be charmed into following the Piper, and drowned in the river. Bert, emerging from the shadows, has an ideological row with Heidi. This 'charming of the rats' is surely the solution they dreamed of (he didn't hear the word 'drowned') being *drowned* out - cut to the concert - by the Piper's prolonged intro. Rats abseil from the balcony, swing in over the audience. Climactic, Alice-Cooper-like, PIED is revealed. Frenzied, the Rats are led out to the river, to be drowned and washed away. Heidi hobbles after Bert with a life-jacket, which he refuses. 'I'll give it to him,' says Alphonso, in the darkness, slyly. End of Act One.

*

This was my fourth Bradford Christmas extravaganza and the first without David Edgar playing the lead. I wanted him as the Mayor of Hamelin, who reneges on the deal with the Piper and stands to lose a whole generation of children including his own daughter. But I sensed he'd had his fill of playing right-wing bastards, and was up to his eyes anyway, dramatizing Nixon his own tricky dealer, not only in *Dick Deterred* to open in March at the Bush, but also in a TV documentary featuring edited highlights from the tapes, which he was now trawling through transcripts of, in his room, down the stairs, on the kitchen table, discarded sheaves in box files, going down even to the cellar. He was racing, as if on horse-back, against the chuck-wagon of history, which would lead inexorably to Nixon's resignation, but no one knew this yet. Would the drama get there first - as it would have to, opening in March - and be seen as prophecy? Or would he have got it all wrong?

*

Clean-cut *Kinder* in *lederhosen* are the chorus for Act Two. Hamelin, purged of vermin is celebrating. Pied's Manager interrupts with demand for payment. The Mayor and Corporation deny owing him anything, and with mockery, send him packing. Heidi pleads for justice. A compromise is reached. Pied will sing for his supper tonight at the Gala Ball. And maybe there'll be a whip-round. Now Heidi is in a hurry. To find Bert, get him to the ball and break the prejudice against him, she needs magical powers. She sets off through the forest, with a trifle as payment for her Granny (a witch) who is boiling her a Frock, the wearer of which will be granted three wishes. Through the trees, she sees a figure in a high-viz life-jacket whom she presumes is Bert. 'Don't come any closer,' says the figure. 'What's happened to your voice my darling?' says Heidi. The Figure explains he caught a chill in the river, when, saved by the life-jacket, he witnessed the drowning of (choke!) his father, his family and faithful *consigliori*. Heidi is overjoyed. 'Wait here till I return. I have to take the longer route to Granny's cottage (the shorter being too dangerous).' Alone, Alphonso is revealed! *Okay so I done him wrong!/ I took my son's Mae West/ But I'm no angel, I'm just a bum/ And I did it for the best...* He takes the short-cut. Granny dipping the Frock in the pot sings of its powers, with the coda: *But should a stranger capture me/ And cast me headlong in the pot,/ I should emerge in an hour or three/ The fairest flower of the blooming lot!* Alphonso, entering, seizes, strips and dunks Granny in the pot. Heidi, bursting in, is set upon and bound. More than a hostage, she will now be a HUMAN SHIELD for the invasion of rats from out of town, led by Alphonso, to re-RATIFY Hamelin! Meanwhile Bert - having, *stout as Julius Caesar/ braved the waves of the rolling Weser!* - has encountered Pied and his Manager, planning to wreak revenge on Hamelin by leading the children to be ENTOMBED ALIVE in Koppelberg Hill. Cut to the Gala Ball, the sanitized pageant, the entrance of Pied, now a weeny-bopper superstar, and Bert, disguised in the Frock, intervening too late, wasting two of the Frock's wishes, as he pursues Pied and the skipping children. Heidi, lame, can't keep up. Bert tries the restrain her. The children enter the mountain. The mountainside slowly descends as they realize, screaming - too late! - that they are trapped inside for ever!

*

But wait! Does Bert not have one Frock-Wish left? If he wishes hard enough, maybe the safety curtain, under which Heidi, half-in, half-out, is writhing, will rise again and we can have our finale, with encores. Christmas is coming! The god of pantos is in his heaven! We've tech- , dress-rehearsed and played four sold-out performances with not one power cut! The show is a hit! The party is at Blob's, but I don't stay, because I have to be in Bracknell in the morning.

XMAS '73

I'd rewritten *Bleak Midwinter* for John Cumming, now Director of the new South Hill Park Arts Centre in Bracknell, for his inaugural production. This version was darker and bleaker, in tune with the times. There were power cuts through rehearsals and we decided, even though Cumming had designed a moody lighting, to do the whole thing by candlelight. Bethlehem is cut off from Heaven which itself is powerless. God, taking a leaf from Brenton's deity in *Scott*, is demented and confused as to the identity of Gabriel, whom he mistakes for his beloved Lucifer. Since the Bringer of Light was expelled, light in heaven can only be generated by earthly worship and that is now at its lowest ebb. But what God presumes, even when His Mind is unhinged, *must come to be*, and Gabriel, preparing to fly down and announce to a virgin that she will conceive and bear a child, is racked with foul thoughts of sex and death. Suddenly the Gospel makes sense, in the same way that cock-up and blunder in politics, are given rationality in history! Mary's terror at a stranger breaking in to implant the

Seed in her womb; Joseph, refusing to believe her story, being forced to toe the line; the catastrophic accommodation crisis in Bethlehem; shepherds bedazzled into midwifing a virgo intacta, in a cowshed, and laying the baby in a trough; the proclamation by angels of the birth of a King to rival Herod, unaware of his paranoia; Wise Men diverted from giving the babe's location, and having to be hustled out of town; the systematic, door-to-door, slaughter of all babies in Bethlehem, save only one; Mary and Joseph and the Child (whose nativity caused the massacre!) having to flee for their lives. How, with all this, did Christmas ever come to be 'happy'?

*

My mother persuaded my father to persuade the Diocese to sell Templar Street and buy a larger, more presentable, suburban semi in Shortlands, in the Borough of Bromley; and it was thither I scooted from Bracknell on Christmas Eve to spend two days with them in the new house. 'Wit,' said my father, as Monnie, now studying Beauty Culture at Tottenham Tech, was trimming my hair and laying slices of cucumber on my eyes, 'how about coming with me to midnight at Southwark Cathedral?' As Area Secretary for the United Society for the Propagation of the Gospel in the Diocese of Southwark, he could claim the Cathedral as his church, and tonight would be officiating, alongside the Dean and chaplains, with his old Cambridge buddy, Bishop Mervyn Stockwood. The alternative was to stay with Mum and Mon, honing a strategy for pressuring Jude, who would be here tomorrow, into forsaking Michael and Australia, and returning to Westby's, or *anywhere away from the dreadful influence of that man!* I chose to go to Southwark. I wanted to balance the raw shock of *Bleak Midwinter*, and the bile it was engendering after its opening in Bracknell, with memories of happier times: the music, the liturgy, the carols, the communion; and the star presence of Bishop Mervyn. Processing behind the choir, in full cope and mitre, he was every inch the flamboyant, 'turbulent priest', who wore jeans under his cassock and preferred a bow tie to neck-bands. The political opposite of my godfather, now Bishop of London, though similarly effective in style and influence, Stockwood had promoted John Robinson, author of the heretical *Honest To God*, to Bishop of Woolwich; advocated homosexual law reform; hated committees, loved good wine. I wanted to hear him preach. I was soon to direct *Hamlet*. Walking distance from the Globe, this had been Shakespeare's church, and Stockwood cherished the connection. On this spot, Shakespeare had knelt after his brother Edmund, a young actor, had died and was buried here. There was a statue of Will, reclining, head on his arm, exhausted with grief and thinking about death. I was alone, a ghost among ghosts, in a crowd of revellers, lulled into silence, as a boy chorister sang *Lully lullay, thou little tiny child...* as I had done years ago. I felt tears prick my eyes. Something rotten in the Christmas story was being brought to the surface. *Ah woe is me, poor child for thee...* And now Mervyn, mitreless, copeless, was ascending the pulpit. His text was not from the Bible but a quote from the Jewish writer and Auschwitz survivor, Elie Wiesel: THE OPPOSITE OF LOVE IS NOT HATE; IT IS INDIFFERENCE. His theme was Bethlehem, not then, but now. It was political, as you'd expect. Bishop Mervyn was the spokesman in the House of Lords for Palestinian refugees, and he used Palestine as an example of the plight of refugees everywhere. Mary and Joseph today would be just two among tens of thousands fleeing the terror. Persecution, displacement, flight were signs of an uncaring world and this had to change. Christmas was a time for 'vomiting up the truth': the unpleasantness that follows our over-indulgence and neglect of the starving... He was telling it straight with a crowd-shocking inflection and the revellers were quelled. His voice was a fine-tuned baritone - he liked the sound of it - playing the vaulted acoustic without amplification, as Shakespeare would have done - *List, list, O list...* - as the Ghost of Hamlet's father which they say the Bard played. And now I'm drifting. It's been a long day; I'm getting drowsy, remembering the only *Hamlet* Ghost that ever really got to me. Most actors play it with full military bombast, overwhelming the young prince with *HORRIBLE, MOST HORRIBLE!!!* Only Paul Scofield in the Zeffirelli film with Mel Gibson, compels you to listen. There's no thunder-crack and lightning, just an old grey man hardly visible against the stonework. He is so *hurt* by what was done, the pain of it is conveyed to the very heart of the listener, urgent, demanding revenge through love. I could play this ghost, except as director I'm going to need to stand back, to ensure rhythm, controlled energy, thought versus action, giving substance to shadows. Also I'll have to be winding down *Spring Awakening*, the joint production with the Civic which I'll have directed, back-to-back with *Hamlet*. These ghost-laden plays are tangling in my brain. 'We can do anything,' says Moritz Stiefel in the last scene of *Spring Awakening*, in the graveyard, his head under his arm. '*We're beyond sadness and joy... We can see the actor's face through the mask.*' He is serene in his loneliness. He can vomit up the truth for the benefit of the living. His revelation is of the meanness of human life, the ridiculousness of suffering. Blowing your brains out becomes mandatory, when you know this truth, even though no one will ever listen. In *Hamlet*, the meanness, the ridiculousness, is a hugger-mugger killing, a most foul drip-drip of poison in the King's ear, which must be exposed or the world will rot. We're out of time in this church. I won't see the film with Scofield's Ghost till 1990, but things conflate when you're remembering. I'm looking back forty-five years, and four hundred back to Shakespeare, as in sonorous tones, the Bishop concludes with a story from Elie Wiesel: how, in the camp, they were paraded in the night frost, to watch the hangings. The men were strangled quickly, but the boy was too light for the rope; they could see him struggling. It took him thirty minutes to die. A man standing behind Wiesel said: 'God, where is God?' Wiesel heard a voice in his head saying: *Where is God? He is here. He is hanging on the gallows.*

And now we're moving slowly in line up the aisle to receive the Eucharist. I haven't tasted the wafer and the sip of wine, for a year. I'm a fraud among frauds. I shouldn't be inching forward with this crowd. We weren't called forward by an evangelist. No one is shouting alleluya. We're just doing this because not to do so would prick the bubble of Christmas and the fizz would die. And I'm thinking Mervyn in his sermon has already done this effectively; that's why we're shuffling. I'm passing him kneeling at his prie-dieu, eyes open, half shielded by his fingers, not praying but watching. He has the eyes of Scofield, full of hurt at my doubt. Here is the friend of my father who can compel you with a look to rethink your life. He is the servant of the living Christ, who bears His cross, and on Good Friday, will ritually haul it up the aisle. Do not collude in the death of Christ by turning back or passing by. Denounce the murderers of the hanging child or count yourself one of them. Total commitment to Christ is all that's required! And I'm moving on now to the altar rail and kneeling. The Dean is passing down the line with the wafers - *take, eat, this is my body...* - and my father is following with the blood.

NEW YEAR'S EVE

Fred Shipley was waiting at 279. He was sitting at the kitchen table with his model for the set of *Spring Awakening*. I'd forgotten we'd fixed to meet, 3pm New Year's Eve, and I certainly wasn't expecting a finished model before I'd even formulated my ideas. My head was full of *Hamlet*. *Spring Awakening* was first off the blocks in the coming term, but that was just a directing job. We were using the published text, with all admin and technical work, in the hands of the Civic. Whereas *Hamlet* was totally mine. If it flopped, I'd flop. If it flew, I'd be in the clouds. And JRB was coming to see it. I'd mentioned, I wanted to direct it according to *Free Shakespeare* principles, ie *not* direct, let the Bard be heard, let the actors lead, and he'd nodded, tapping his lip and saying 'super'. But the more I read the play, and the more I envisaged it wowing a Bradford audience, the more I wanted to impose *my view*, that the whole thing is a jumble in Hamlet's brain, a modern, out-of-joint, time-warp tangle, impossible to unravel as events race by. Would JRB go for this? Or would he shake his silvery locks and say 'awful'? It was a challenge, which I hoped we'd both rise to, as a first step towards a cut-down text for the *Hamlet* I'd heard Peter Hall had in mind for Albert Finney to lead as the opener for the new theatre, before HM the Queen who famously only liked short shows.

'The door was open. I walked straight in,' said Fred.

'That was David. He probably just nipped out,' said I, 'though we don't always shut the door. That's the thing about Yorkshire. You can leave your door open and you'll never be burgled.'

'We were burgled,' said Fred. 'My mother lost all her jewellery!' He laughed as if this was the funniest thing. Then the air chilled. It was getting dark and no one was putting the light on. The model on the table, demanding to be looked at, was making me depressed. In the semi-dark, it looked like a cowpat with a metallic mesh hanging over it. I wanted to go to bed. It was only four o'clock but I could sleep for an hour then force my mind to turn to *Spring Awakening*. But I could only do this, if I set my own pace, wasn't pressured, in JRB's words, by 'the designer usurping the divine right of the director'.

I said: 'Can you explain?'

'Okay,' he nodded. He looked nervous but determined. And I remembered I *had* talked to him, briefly, last term, during a break in rehearsals for *Pied Piper* which he was helping on. He said he'd read *Spring Awakening*, and the tensions in it were right up his street. I'd said: And what is your street Fred? He'd laughed and said: They expect me to go into farming, but I want to do stage design. Art and its relation to technology, is my 'street', as instanced in scenography, which has to be both harmonious and workable. And I'd said (I remembered now): Go think about it over the holidays, and come and see me first thing when I get back.

'So go on,' I said. 'What's it about?'

The phone rang.

'Oh fuck, sorry.'

'Are you going to answer it?'

'It'll ring off.'

'It's still ringing.'

I answered it.

'Aha!' exclaimed JRB.

'Just got in, sorry.'

'Is this a good moment?'

'Not really.'

'Okay. I've talked to Peter. He's rehearsing *The Tempest*, but that's only one of the many plates he's spinning! He's thinking ahead all the time, and right now all the stars are in alignment, for opening April '75. No promises, just *possibilities*. He wants to meet, two weeks Friday, the 18th.'

'Let me get the diary.' I shot upstairs, came back, flipped the pages. 'I'll be rehearsing, though not till the evening.'

'It's a breakfast meeting.'

'And I'm rehearsing the night before.'

'When's the first train in the morning?'

I flipped through the timetable at the back of my diary.

'There's one gets in 7.15. It leaves Bradford 10.27. Takes nine hours.'

'Or you could skip rehearsal. Get them learning their lines. Is it *Hamlet?* '

'*Spring Awakening.*'

'I don't believe it! Bill Bryden's doing that one for us, in May.'

'Oh no! Oh fuck! Sorry but this always happens to me. I think I'm doing something original; then everyone does it. Don't come and see it. My heart won't be in it.'

'I'll come to *Hamlet* - even though we're likely to be doing that one as well! Though not for the opening. Albert's not available till '76. So the door is wide open for *Wasps*, which I know Peter wants to talk about. Have you had ideas?'

A pause. That's when I noticed Fred had gone, leaving the model.

'So!' said JRB. 'Shall we see you on the 18th?'

'Do I come to Aquinas St?'

'The Savoy Hotel. Meet me there 7.30. We can chat, then join Peter for breakfast at eight.'

'Done. Great.'

'And just a tip. Avoid the kippers. Too fiddly. You'll need to concentrate.'

∗

It was snowing now, heavily: thick flakes dancing in the dark. He must have walked off into the silence like Captain Oates. I carried the model up to the attic. When I put the light on, nothing happened; either we hadn't paid the bill or it was another power cut. I put the model on my desk, then sat and looked at it by torchlight, the metallic mesh throwing spiky shadows on the cowpat. Was this what Fred meant by it being 'right up his street': the angular steel of adult repression obfuscating the shit-cake of adolescence? Second year civ eng would make him nineteen or twenty, though the blandness of his skin with scarcely a whisker and the rash of acne on his forehead when he drew aside the lank hair from his pallid eyes, made him look fourteen at the most. He could be Moritz from the play, caught in the headlights of puberty then crushed in the mash-up of failed exams, impossible dreams, confused sexuality and suicide. I should phone him but his number was in the office. First thing tomorrow then, even though the university would be closed - I had my keys - I'd go up and call him. I'm so sorry. You shouldn't have gone. Your design is super. It absolutely answers the the problem of the play being a sequence of scenes in different places. Going symbolic - the earthiness of youth threatened by the metallurgy of authority - tells the essence of each scene far better that realistic drawing-rooms, schoolrooms, the river bank, the graveyard, even if we could afford them! Let's fix to meet again, Thursday 6pm, my office, and this time I'll be prepared, I promise.

I heard David coming in. He called up to me. Was I home? Was I working? Was I in a meeting - ha ha? (We used a coded language. To be asleep was to be 'working'. To be working was to be 'having sex'. To be having sex was to be 'in a meeting'. To be in a meeting was to be 'sleeping'.)

'I'm having sex!' I yelled. 'Just finishing. Coming down.'

He was lighting candles and the fire, still in his coat flecked with snow as were his glasses, slipping down his nose, and the bags he instructed me to unpack: meat and veg, curry powder, packet sauce, naan bread, yoghurt, cucumber, cheese, apple strudels, packet custard, cigarettes, whiskey, port and beer (twelve bottles).

'How much do I owe you?'

'Nothing. If you wash up. Have you seen the sink? It was over there .'

It was stacked to invisibility with plates and pans from previous meals, going back, some of it, to last term. That was our practice. You leave things till you need them. Then you wash them - *I* wash them - with extra vim because they're encrusted like ancient artifacts, and you're racing against his cooking, so do the pans first. It was all in the wrong order, and not how I'd be brought up, but this, as he pointed out, was Bohemia, not Bromley. They do things differently there.

'Who else is coming?'

'Just us.'

'Not Sue.'

'She's with her husband.' He struck a match, igniting the gas under the pan, like a fireball, then his cigarette. 'New Year's Eve seems to be a time for retrenchment and guilt. I may have to join you in the moratorium on lechery. How's it going?'

'Pretty miserably thanks. '

'Great. Open a beer.'

We drank a toast.

'To 1974!'

'To the three-day week!'

'May it bring on the revolution!'

'May it bring opportunities for writers.'

As we ate and drank, I told him about the National, how the stars were in alignment; how I was to meet Peter Hall; how JRB was to do the London premiere of *Secrets* at the Bush. Then you must, he broke in, come to *Dick Deterred* in March, to see the little place in action. They were almost cast, with Greg Floy as Dick, Duke of Gloucester, later President of the United States and John Grillo as Clarence, aka Eugene McCarthy. And *you* must come, I said, to the opening of the Olivier Theatre on the South Bank, April 23rd next year, to see *The Wasps* which JRB said PH wanted me to think about adapting as a satire on a Labour Government and its relations with the unions, assuming there *is* a Labour Goverment to satirise, and the NT isn't brought to its knees by those very unions. Ah yes, says David, isn't that always the gamble with theatre? Ah yes, I agree, for what if Nixon doesn't fall? What if Watergate peters out? How then fares your *Dick*? Then, he's fucked, laughs David. But I don't think he will be. All the stars, as you say, are in alignement, for me anyway, if not for you. Are you sure you're not barking up the wrong tree with the National? What do you mean, I protest. I mean I saw *Pied Piper*, and in my opinion, he pauses, finishing his mouthful, takes a gulp: in my estimation, even though I wasn't in it, *Pied Piper* was the finest of the four fine Crane Christmas shows. You're a very good writer, that goes without saying, but what I hadn't understood (munch munch, gulp, gulp) was that you are, in my own and the general estimation, a very *very* good director; which points in this increasingly (helping himself to more naan bread, more beer) *polarizing* industry, to a professional path that you'd do well to tread *more specifically* even than the-soon-to-be so gridlocked writing path. Because that's where (dipping into the raitta [pronounced 'writer']) in my own and the general view, you shine. The National is a fabulous temptation that could be a trap - I'm not saying it is! - but if you angle, (scooping the ghee, chewing the chunks) indeed *wangle* - your director-potential alongside the writing, that's where, in my comradely view as a fellow Fellow, (wiping the plate with the last of the naan and slurping it) you could gain clout as well as kudos...

Others have called him a 'patronizing, pompous prick' and to his credit, no stranger to self-mockery, he reclaims the soubriquet in *Trying It On,* his current solo show, turning the laugh to his advantage. Back then, as '73 was tipping into '74, a PPP he certainly was, but to me he was also an oracle, an incentive, the yardstick I knew I would always fall short of. I watched him dining and opining, and through the beery haze, reflected *this is how he does it!* He sets the agenda; you follow. He knows where he's heading and he's well on his way. Even rebellions in theatre companies, even fallings out with directors, even lukewarm reviews and betrayals will not stop him, because his schedule is more arduous, his research deeper and more thorough, and his plays wordier, longer and more 'of the moment' than anyone else's. We were house-mates for two years. I was Wise to his Morecambe, feeding him the lines to which he would get the laugh. Forty years on, we met again at a funeral in Brighton. I drove him to the station, where the drop-off is now at the rear instead of the front.

ME: I'm having to take you up the back as we say in Brighton.

HIM: That was always my fear!

SAVOY BREAKFAST

It was still dark when I rode up to the Savoy, dismounted, took off my helmet and went in, like a suppliant knight to meet the King at his table. I'd left the cast learning lines and taken the train the night before, putting the bike in the guard's van. On the journey I reflected on what David had said about directing, having never previously given it thought. I was an accidental director, as I had been as a writer. Now crossing London, to get to Bromley for the night, I reflected on my service to the three goddesses of theatre, and while it was Acting (Aphrodite) who took the applause, and Writing (Athene), the Wise One, who owned the copright, was it not Artemis, the director, the hunter, who hit the mark and drew blood? *She* carries the can, in the practical sense, because she *gets the thing on*. She cracks the whip, cries havoc, and has the private, unsung, satisfaction, when it works, standing back on the first night, thinking *I made this happen.*

My mother was still up when I got to Bromley. Since Christmas, her mood had swung from clouds of despond to cautious hope and blue skies, fuelled by the imminence of Jude's wedding, now fixed to take place in Bromley Parish Church on Saturday 9th March. They'd been shopping for dresses; drawing up and sending out invitations and fielding replies; and having Max, and more importantly, *his parents*, over for dinner. Steve and Dana were clearly from a different class, but in a sense that made it easier. There was no jockeying, as there can be with social equals, just laughter and generosity. How bravely, the Maxwells had pulled themselves out of poverty into catering, and a wealth, with jewellery and a home in Spain, undreamt of by any clergyman!

JRB was in the lounge of the Savoy, with a pot of tea. Peter would be in the dining-room at ten to eight, so we had just twenty minutes. If I wanted the toilet I should go now. I said it was okay, I'd already been. Then excuse me, said he, won't be a moment. He came back in less than a moment. His nervousness he explained, was more akin to excitement, because now we could *believe* that the building blocks were falling, tentatively, into place. He'd had assurance from Peter Stephens, the National's General Manager, that a Thames Television Resident Dramatist's Bursary, would be attainable. If it started in September, it would lock in comfortably to the (more than) putative opening of the Olivier on Shakespeare's 411th Birthday, for which we should be thinking, not about Shakespeare - Hall's National, though fed on the legacy of the classics, would be contemporary - but about *Aristophanes*, reinvented as living newspaper, with the wasp-sting of the very strife that was besetting British industry.

*

Peter Hall, said Kenneth Tynan, 'seems to be made not of flesh and blood, but of some resilient, gelatinous substance, like a jellyfish'; and you could add 'without the venom, which he does not need'. It's said he never fired anyone, just dimmed the light, till it was so dark you had to leave; or if your status was higher and he needed your good report, was so admiring, so sweet, only sycophants would touch you. And if he wanted you out of his life, never to return, he might offer you one of his bespoke cigarillos and, brow puckered with regret, even light it for you.

We went in. He saw us crossing the floor and rose to greet us: 'Richard, I've been longing to meet you! John, thanks so much for fixing this!' His eyes vanished in smiles; I was the sunshine of his life. At the same time, as JRB had hinted, there was a schedule ticking. He got straight to the point.

'I read your two plays.'

'Er,' I could have said, 'I've written twelve. Which two in particular?'

'I liked *Secrets* more than *Thunder*, which reads - no disrespect - like theatrical *son et lumiere*. Tourism stuff! Whereas *Secrets* is a bombshell. So glad John's doing it with Natasha. What would you say makes a good play?'

'Well first,' I ventured, 'it should *challenge* its audience; *provoke* them into action, and at the same time *illuminate* the crevices of today's world.'

'No no!' laughed Peter. 'Absolutely no!'

'But *you* wrote those words,' I might have retorted. 'Scrambled egg please,' I said to the waiter. Peter ordered kidneys; JRB, against his own advice on unfilleted fish, opted for Arbroath smokies.

'Do you truly believe,' said Peter leaning in to me, 'that the *audience* is your first concern? Do they come to be put on the spot by you, to be recruited to your cause, and have their crevices illuminated?' JRB laughed uproariously. 'Or do you just create your very best and present it, no excuses?'

I sensed a trap.

'As I writer,' I said, 'I do offer my very best. But I need to know my audience, as do the people who are funding me.'

'I think we're veering off the question,' smiled Peter. 'Can I put it another way? Where does theatre begin?'

'As a writer,' put in JRB, 'we might expect you to say "with the writer", with the argument, the idea, the dialogue, which the director then fixes and the actor delivers.'

'Is that your view,' said Peter, 'or is there something deeper going on?'

I was ready with my answer.

'It begins with the *need*. In my view, the best plays are responding to an urgency. It could be just the fact of a deadline, an opening night that is fixed, or it could be a revolution or an injustice, where the theatre can speak louder than rational debate because it cuts to the heart. But the key to it all is teamwork. I don't believe the writer is a separate item. I don't believe anyone in the theatre is unconnected with anyone else. Everyone contributes.'

'Is it a democracy?' wondered Peter.

'Well no, but it's not a dictatorship either.'

'What about my job at the National? Do I have to refer everything to everyone or can I insist on driving my own programme, bringing in *my* writers, *my* actors? Or as a writer, seeking a job, would it be unwise to comment?'

'He's not just a writer,' interposed JRB. 'He also directs and acts.'

Peter cocked his head, fixing me with his little eyes. I knew he too was a multi-plate-spinner. As well as directing plays and running the National, he was about to present a television arts programme, was editing a couple of films, producing operas at Glyndebourne, and as a self-confessed awful actor, but needing to keep his hand in, nipping off to join Maximilian Schell in Germany to play bit-parts in films.

'I'm looking at you,' he said, 'as a writer; that's why you're here. It's writers the National has been short of till now and John is backing you as a new front-runner. Pinter, *was* an actor, *is* a director, but for us it's his writing alone that we're looking to. His latest has just landed on my desk - I read it this morning. It effortlessly underscores what I've been trying to articulate. *No Man's Land,* and it's exactly that: the unknown stretch between two known sides.'

'*Terra incognita,*' observed JRB.

'No one knows what the fuck it's about,' Peter laughed, 'not even the actors, and the audience won't have a clue. The Board have said it's a nonstarter.'

I said: 'Does that mean you won't be doing it?'

'It's the very reason we *will* be doing it! Harold has written the most incendiary play I've ever read; it's a minefield. John agrees. Not unlike your *Secrets.* We both got a similar whiff of cordite when we read that one, the genius of which is that in the end *it fails to explode.* Hugely promising, if Natasha and John can pull it off!'

'*Deo volente,*' said JRB, seeming to be find refuge in Latin.

'Whereas *Thunder,*' added Peter, 'illuminating though it was, seemed sob-stuff to me. Plenty waterworks, no fireworks.'

Food came. We ate for a moment in silence. I wanted to tell him *Thunder* wasn't mine, it was 'of the Brontes', in the way that *Oh What A Lovely War,* was the squaddies' and the war poets' and if it taught you something about sex, drugs and death, then that was drama enough. And I wanted to say *Secrets does* explode at the end, depending on whether you believe the myth or the life. In Belfast, backed by real bombs and gunfire, the myth blew their minds. The anticlimax of reality at the very end, was like what they wake up to every day, the chill of sameness, continued living under threat, knowing nothing will change.

'Are you, when it comes down to it, a propagandist?' Peter asked. 'Aristophanes always had a section in his plays called "Author's Message". Do you have a message?'

I said yes. A pause. He waited. I began:

'*When priests are more in word than matter,/ When brewers mar their malt with water...*'

'I like that!' he laughed. 'The Fool. '

'This is how I see theatre.'

'*Then shall the realm of Albion/ Come to great confusion...*'

'Absolutely!' I agreed. 'It's the threat of that kind of confusion, provoked by theatre, that makes me want to work at the National. When you don't stick to your hierarchies, when you break out of your little boxes, when you're not satisfied with what has been ordained for you, that's when it gets truly messy and transformational. The challenge, managerially, is how do you contain all that confusion within the building. How do you keep Pentheus and Dionysus under the same roof? But that, you'll say, is not the business of the writer. He's there to set the fireworks; you then light the blue paper. He is the Fool in every sense. Trickery, prat-falls, inconvenient truth: his language, because it's childish, can break hearts and raise the dead. How else do Holy Fools work miracles? Economists, politicians, can't do this, only playwrights, if they're innocent and fool enough.'

This dialogue is not word for word, but a re-assemblage. It came with a genial urgency in flashes which I lodged in mental snapshots. I didn't prepare for the meeting or debrief on it afterwards, so the whole is a blur. But single out the moments and they have the sort of shock that comes upon you at funerals when time, after racing by, stands still and you're among ghosts. JRB lived to his nineties. I spoke at his funeral in the old Saxon church, next to his home in a Tudor hunting lodge near Battle. I stayed over with him once, when we were reading through my version of *The Wasps*, which by then we knew would never happen because the South Bank opening was so delayed. It was a kind of requiem, like his funeral, a noble work cut short, a long life, unfulfilled. How different from Peter Hall: '*the single most influential force in modern theatre... the crusading titan of post-war British culture*': a pirate who boarded the ship of state, then fought the state without let-up, on behalf of his comrades; a charmer and job-juggler of dark skill and voracious energy, who married four wives and raised six children, all of whom recently I watched as they paraded hand in hand down the aisle in Westminster Abbey, applauded by a thousand actors, writers, directors, designers, at his memorial. Whatever people said of him, for those he was true to, he was truer than true; and foxier than foxy to the grumpy and faint-hearted.

'Richard, what age are you?' he said as we shook hands after breakfast that wintry morning. I told him I was twenty-nine. 'Exactly the age I was,' he smiled, 'when I founded the RSC!'

FRANK WEDEKIND

...was twenty-nine when he wrote *Spring Awakening: a Children's Tragedy*. It was never going to be performed in the morally re-armed, newly unified Germany. When Max Reinhardt premiered it, after fifteen years in the drawer, key scenes had to be cut, and the child's distorted view of authority, seen in the nick-names of the teachers - Rev Littlecock, Dr Shitface, Professor Twatt - rendered respectful, by giving them normal names. Trotsky, after seeing the show, found it 'aesthetically unacceptable' that the generation gap should be narrowed by having adults play the children. I believe my 1974 Bradford production, was the first to have the kids played by real teenagers (first-year students) and the adults by actors from the conservative tradition of the Civic Playhouse. I discouraged the two generations from mixing - no buying rounds in the bar, no chit-chat in the green room! - and so promoted distrust, which fed effectively into the show. Previous productions, had had grown-ups such as Lotte Lenya and Peter Lorre playing the children, and the National production that followed fast on mine and the recent Broadway musical version, saw a similar up-aging. If the kids 'know the score', and have to act as if they don't; if, as in the musical, they are played as streetwise punks, and adult opposition is reduced to just two actors, and the Man in the Mask, the *deus ex machina*, originally played by Wedekind himself, who dismisses the martyred ghost and tells Melchior to 'choose life'; if he is CUT, as he is in the musical, if you bridge the gulf, and laugh away the pain, you have commercial entertainment, but no void.

As I sat in the darkness of the Playhouse auditorium, going cue-to-cue with Fred Shipley, my head bunged with flu, my throat scoured raw by hacking (swigging benylin from the bottle); as I watched girders of light shaft onto the soft, steeply tilted 'pat' through the scaff 'crown of thorns', the actors, for now just marking their lines, finding light, finding shadow; as it was all coming to be, the show I thought I could walk through as foothills to *Hamlet*, had turned out to be an Alpine wonder all of its own. I was thinking, as I rasped, let me not die now! My desire is pure: to change lives through theatre and to gell my rules into just two: that the actor match the character - not *learning* to be, but being *originally* in essence that person before even being cast; and (2) that *nothing*, however close to the sexual edge the play gets, should ever tip the director, love his darlings as he might, into lecherous thoughts. As I sat in the dark, beside Fred with his gimlet eyes and slender sliding fingers on the board, I reflected how, all through rehearsals, even in the group masturbation scene, my *piccolo* (Wedekind's word) had not stirred. Even when Hans and Ernst were kissing under the trees, I hadn't envied their innocence, hadn't imagined the warmth of soft lips on mine. And when little Wendla, was whipped, at her own request, then raped by Melchior, I hadn't leapt up and cried STOP!!! I was concerned, at arm's length. The love I felt ran deep. These kids were my creations to whom I had promised, as the Man in Mask promises Melchior:

Come with me and expand your horizon.
Come with me and see everything the world has to offer...
Give me your trust and I will give you knowledge.

*

From the *Telegraph and Argus*, 5th February 1974:

Whispers from the wings had informed us that the play at the Civic Playhouse last night might set off a roar of moral indignation... The truth is that although it has had a history of condemnation... Spring Awakening... *is life-enhancing, liberating in ideals... as fresh and relevant now as on the day it was written... The play, set in a small German town with its repressive school, its spiritually deadening reformatory... highlights the crimes of teachers and parents who build a barrier against their offsprings' self-knowledge. Richard Crane's superb production underscores the spiritual and sexual prison through the setting's use of scaffolding and a bare circular ramp... It is greatly to the credit of the Playhouse and the University Drama Group, that they make Wedekind's plea for sexual honesty, so clear and moving.*

THE SCRABBLE CHAMP

Of all the clean-cut fresher intake of '73, John Lamb was the cleanest. Son of a WW2 torpedo bomber, with a yacht on the Isle of Wight, he was cast as one of the masturbators in *Spring Awakening*. Jacking off, he laughed along gamely with the rest, but I could tell he was suffering. He'd left school at seventeen, with twelve O-levels and three As, done a year as a teacher, then gone to Bradford not Oxbridge, because he wanted, like Orwell, to immerse himself in how the other nine-tenths lived. But did not the cavalry twills, hush puppies and cravat, give the game away? Well, yes. Was he unsure of himself? Definitely. Would he commit murder? Probably not. But if he had to, for instance, if he were cast as Hamlet? Well only in a fair fight. But seriously, he'd never yet taken on a lead role. At the same time, it wasn't every day you got offered the greatest part. Hell! The dilemma! He was a thinker, a scrabble-player; croquet was his sport. He liked sailing with the wind, at the same time, digging his heels in. Soliloquies! The very thought gave him the willies. I said: We'll cut them, the soliloquillies. Or merge them with other speeches so they look like disjointed dialogue. We can do that: out of joint - that's the theme - something rotten. I'm confused, he said. That's why I cast you, I rejoined. Ambivalent, shitting yourself: that is the *essence* of Hamlet. He's the ultimate, privileged, over-sensitive student actor, faced with a horror only *he* can sort. By acting! So *do* the play. He laughed his princely laugh. I don't know, he said, I've read the play, seen Olivier's film. He's an old head on young shoulders. If you cast young shoulders, the duelling works, but not the *ennui*. If vice versa, then versy vicer. Let's play scrabble Mr C. If you win, I'll do it. If I win - and bear in mind I was the regional junior champion! - I'll seriously think about whether to suffer or take up arms.

The board was out, the game afoot, and not going my way. Sad little three-letter words were all I mustered. Lamb was in fits, setting time limits, pouring me whiskies. Then suddenly - whoa! - what's this on my rack? Jumbled, like a crackable code, I had an X, an O, two I's, a C, a blank and a Q. What to make of it? Normally, one would use the blank for a U, to enable the Q, but on the extreme down left, one space beneath the top triple-word, Lamb had laid down a U to make URGH, locking on to the G of my feeble GOB. If I laid the Q on the triple-word, accepted the U, then laid an I, then the X on the double letter, then the O, the blank for a T, the other I and finally the C, I would have (*drum roll*) QUIXOTIC!!! which would bring me a score of... $10 + 1 + (8 \times 2) + 1 + 0 + 1 + 3 = 33 \times 3$ for the triple word = 99! Not so, says Lamb. Your C has landed on a second triple-word, making your total a modest TWO HUNDRED AND NINETY SEVEN!!!!! Modest because - alas poor Dickie - QUIXOTIC is pie in the sky, disallowed.

'What do you mean?' says I, trembling.

'It's an adjective derived from a proper noun and so capitalized. Shakespearean, Pinteresque, would you demean those with a lower case?'

'But surely,' I protest, '*quixotic* is part of the language, like *hoover* and *galvanize*.'

'Are you asking me to challenge?' snorts Lamb, reaching for the OED, 'because if I do and you're wrong as you will be, the rules state, you lose all you would have gained.'

'All I set out to gain,' I mumble, close to weeping, 'was your pledge to play the Dane, but I see now, your iffiness is not the character's but your own, and you'd be better placed, playing Horatio (which you will describe, when I ask you, decades later, for your reflections, as "one of the most boring roles in Shakespeare... All Horatios must sympathise with Tom Stoppard's replacement theatre critic in *The Real Inspector Hound*: '*Sometimes I dream of revolution, a bloody coup d'etat by the second rank; troupes of actors, slaughtered by their understudies... stand-ins of the world stand up!*'")'

We didn't finish the game. The point had been made. He would swap parts with Pete Brent, who after his punchy footballer performance as David in the Cathedral, would bring a keepy-uppy/shinpad modernity to Hamlet instead of wishy-washy intellectualism.

(After Lamb had gone, I checked 'quixotic' in the OED and it *did* have a small q. There was also no mention of 'urgh'.)

SOMETHING ROTTEN

I gave the cast three days off, to learn lines and be word-perfect for when we met again on Monday. There was still a week to go, and the show, honed down to ninety minutes, was in fighting shape. Having Brent play the Dane, was like dropping a First Division player into a crap team of cheats on a sludged-up playing-field. Hugger-mugger haste was the tone of the play: blurring of life and death, the 'ghost within', real life deferred and ending in a bloodbath. The poster image was a grinning skull.

Thoughts raced on the train going south, bike in the van. *Things rotten to the core make the best theatre.* They fall apart, moulder and generate new life. *Hamlet, Spring Awakening, Pied Piper, Bleak Midwinter, Secrets* are rotten/resurrectional plays. *Dick Deterred* too. This is where theatre scores every time over politics, because politics, being the art of the possible, can only follow, whereas theatre, driven by *im*possibility, leads by making an art of it.

I'd told David I hoped to make it to the Bush, Saturday evening. My sister was getting married in the morning and after all the hoo-ha, I might be looking for an excuse to get away. He said *Dick* wouldn't be best pleased to be viewed as an *excuse*, but sure, he'd put a ticket by. I said actually could he make it two, as I'd been looking for an excuse (another one!) to mend fences with Chris, out with whom had we not both recently fallen, over other people directing our work. He said sure, he'd make it two.

I had half an hour to think ahead on *Hamlet* for Monday, half an hour to think about Chris and his block about JRB and the NT, then an hour to write my speech. As Pa was taking the service, I would lead Jude up the aisle, then at the reception she wanted me to make me people laugh, or she would cry. I said laughter and tears are so close, she'd probably do both, and I heard her laugh, then cry. I should have said: Darling, do you really want to go through with this? We're supposed to be the same, free spirits, happy wanderers; I'd never box myself in. But she'd rung off.

I have photos of the wedding: me in my black velvet suit and kipper tie, Jude on my arm, in white with a frilled hem and page-boy hair, about to enter the church. In the mass photo with umbrellas, everyone, from Gran in her costume, getting cosy with Rose from the National canteen in her fur, to Ma, trim as a teenager and Pa in his cassock, and Steve and Dana, all bronzed from Spain, and Mon as bridesmaid, and Elizabeth and her three children mixing with other people's children; all are jubilant, in spite of the rain. This was a happy day and it got happier. Roars of laughter are all I remember from the reception. I'd stayed off the booze as everyone else laid into it, giving me a clear head for the speech. My theme was Jude TAKING CHARGE. Wherever she went, however humbly she started, within days she's TAKEN CHARGE, rising to the top at school (head girl), University (Vice-President of the Union), Westby's (managing director) and now - Australia beware! (Laughter [but not from Mum]). When it came to the toast, I prefaced it with an extra wedding vow to be honoured: that they should VOW TO RETURN. They looked at each other and Mike said SURE THING and everyone applauded. In the end it was the only vow that survived. Eighteen months into the marriage, I had a call from Jude. She was on the run with her baby. She had just produced *Thunder* in Perth with an amateur group, then gone into labour. In the same ward of the hospital was a girlfriend of Max's having a miscarriage. Like Helen in *The Tenant of Wildfell Hall*, she took up her child and fled. She enrolled at university, took a doctorate, married again, had two more children, moved to Tasmania, combined farming and family with a professorship in Rural Health, which allowed her an annual trip to Europe and the UK. I last saw her in September 2018, when she came to Brighton, hairless from six months of chemo- and radiotherapy, still in charge, still my twin.

*

Chris was waiting at the Bush. We didn't have time for a drink. We went straight into the show. The tiny theatre was bursting at the seams. The reviews had said things like *'brilliant parody... devastating humour... teems with cleverness, anger and spirit... the plot fits so closely that it hurts...'* You felt the heat of a hit show: six actors playing twenty-three roles, spilling out from a stage no bigger than a small room. But the main thing was the closeness of the fit, the grinding pain as Edgar shrank Shakespeare into the confinement of Watergate. This was no ordinary play, holding the mirror up to nature, but a true story playing out, in iambic pentameters, as if racing against the unfolding reality, and finally, inching ahead to a conclusion that hadn't yet happened. It packed the same punch as *Arturo Ui*, but with the extra sting of drawing the audience into the plot as soon as they entered the theatre. Casual conversations were recorded and played back to listeners in the interval. Likewise at the end, the audience leaving, heard their voices recorded reacting to the recordings. As with *Ui*, written in 1941, which ran the rise of the cauliflower king against the actual rise of Hitler, *Dick Deterred*, running parallel to unconcluded events, also carried a dire warning. Edgar, prefiguring the fall of Nixon, has the line *'It's definitely all over now'*; upon which from the coffin, the tape-strangled corpse of Dick, rises growling *'Wanna bet?'*

This was the theatre we should be doing, and the Bush was the space for it. I'd come to check it out for *Secrets*, scheduled for JRB's production in July, and the more I loved the space for its closeness and bonding of actor and audience, the more I knew we were doing the wrong play. It had meant something in Belfast, exposing a tumbling into hell as the troubles blundered on, but here in London, with a declared 'hands-off' director and a script shorn of excrescences (Chris was appalled at the pruned version), the play would look staid. He said I should withdraw it, but how could I, if I wanted to go to the National? But you *don't* want to, said Chris. It's a swamp; they're sucking you in, just as they're sucking the funding out of theatres like the Bush. Look who they're getting in the company: Gielgud, Richardson, Ashcroft - they're old! If you go there, you'll be fossilized and you're not even thirty! You've only had the Fellowship for two years. You're on a roll. They're giving you money! Then he said something truly ridiculous. He said Jones and Palin, his old mates from Oxford, were making a film with the Monty Pythons about King Arthur and the Holy Grail. He knew I was always being clobbered by copycats, doing inferior but better financed imitations of my own shows. Why shouldn't I now pip the Pythons at the post and do an Arthurian extravaganza, which would - he could swear from my previous plays - be both comical *and* tragical, whereas the

Pythons, from the evidence of their TV work, would be just silly. If I would write it *now*, try it out in Bradford, then take it to Edinburgh, and if he, Chris, were to direct it - *for was he not the best director of my work!?* - he swore he could get me back where I belonged as a writer. Why the fuck was I doing *Hamlet*? The words rang in my head all the way back on the train. What a betrayal! What a waste of energy! Telling JRB I was doing a *Free Shakespeare* production, when I was slashing like a vandal. I was abusing him and perverting my actors. I should be doing the play that had landed on my desk before Christmas, about drugs and teenage gangs, called *Downers*, by Roy Kift. It would have counter-balanced *Spring Awakening*, which had been weighted towards the Civic, being performed in their theatre. This could have been the 1970s response to Wedekind, again using Civic actors for the adults, but this time weighted towards the kids at the University. Why hadn't I thought of this, instead of pissing about with a known text. The University kids who had thrown flour-bombs at Tom Brown and gone ironically berserk for rock-star Pied, wouldn't care a toss if I filleted a soliloquy, or gunned down Polonius instead of skewering him in the arras. But I didn't show any of this. I went to the Monday rehearsal relieved that it was on track with all lines learnt. We were a well-oiled machine. The cut text rocketed through. Pete Brent, an athletic, slightly dim Hamlet, was like a line cutting obliquely through the symmetry of the play: a long-distance pace-setter when everyone else was sprinting. John Lamb was a noble and, as he predicted, boring, Horatio. Mrs Merce was Rosencrantz, with a boy we called Superfresher, because as a fresher, he joined everything, as Guildenstern. Ken Westgate and his new wife Kate were the King and Queen, eager to scotch criticism of their speedy nuptials. And Blob was the ghost, with his fleshless face and skull-grin as if the murder was a cruel joke, to be deleted. JRB came to the final performance. The audience was full to bursting. The actors, so sure of the show and the speed to take it at, played the comedy to the hilt. Never had *To be or not to be* got so many laughs, Ophelia cutting into each line with '*Good my Lord... My lord... I have remembrances... my honoured lord...*'

The party was to be at 279. David was away. I had to see JRB off to his train, so wouldn't be along till later. I gave Ken and Kate the keys (though the door was never locked) and cash to get booze, and spuds to roast on the fire. JRB had intended to take me for a meal, but I sensed he didn't want to discuss the show, so didn't press it. Walking to the station, all he talked about was the escalating nightmare of the National. The building was months behind schedule. Peter was tearing his hair, what was left of it. There could be no move, let alone a royal opening, till well into the second half of next year. And that wasn't all. *The Tempest*, after a *super* first night, was descending into farce. Gielgud, tired and retreating into aloofness, was becoming what Peter and he himelf most dreaded - boring! And Michael Feast who played Ariel had gone missing with depression and his understudy who was no 'dainty sprite' and couldn't sing, hadn't rehearsed the flying scene and, plummeting, was nearly killed. The reviews, though respectful, had been eclipsed by a lacerating assault from Harold Hobson. Why do we do it? sighed JRB. At least here in Bradford, you can fail catastrophically and the world won't notice. Have they offered you a third year? I said they had and I'd turned it down. But what did he mean by 'fail catastrophically'? Was he referring to tonight? No no no, he lied. He meant notionally speaking. Falling flat on one's face can be good for one's physiognomy, as long as it isn't plastered all over the papers! No what I was saying - we were at the station, hurrying now, because the train was due - what I was implying was there's not a lot of point being Resident Dramatist of an outfit whose back is against the wall. What would you say to postponing? For a year? Maybe two? Stay on at Bradford, then come to us when we're ready. Will you think about it? I said: John, I'm writing the *The Wasps*. It's current: about what's happening in politics and the arts *at this moment*. I want it to be my final show at Bradford, as a practice for the National. And just so you know, being part of a streamlined, superbly functioning enterprise isn't where I want to be. If your back is against the wall, I want to be there too, even if they're throwing daggers. He said: Fine. Okay. But we are dependant, as you know, on the Thames TV bursary and, for political reasons, they might not play ball. And secondly, if we're not expanding the company, there'll be next to nothing for you to do. No new plays by new writers, nothing on the scale of *Wasps* or your Christmas shows, only very minor, probably outsourced, experimental work. You'd be better off staying at Bradford. But we'll see, let's see shall we?... (he was on the train, leaning out, as it pulled away) ... put hands in pockets, walk around a bit, cogitate, and then see... shall we see...?

AFTER THE PLAY

I deliberately didn't go to the party till it was nearly over. I had thinking to do. The triumph of *Spring Awakening* was draining away under JRB's less than super verdict on *Hamlet*. I knew what he thought of it: puerile, playing for laughs, no debate, no shape and worst of all, no freedom for the text to speak. I shouldn't be going to the National. Chris, David and now JRB were all saying forget it, stay at Bradford. And I hadn't in fact turned down the Bradford offer. I just didn't want to start going downhill with productions. Up to now, every show (I felt) had been better than the one before, till *Hamlet*, which in fact, looking back, in its irreverence and in the way the players and the gravediggers, played as savage clowns, subverted the text, was proto-punk, anti-establishment in the way Chris said the NT would never be. But it was less than *Spring Awakening,* which had been greater than *Pied* which had been greater, being more subversive, than *Thunder,* which had been neater and sharper than *David,* which had been more ambitious, more enormous even than *Mutiny.* And the very fact that I was now taking even a moment to look back, meant it must be time to move on.

I stopped by at the University. Everything was dark, except for my office high up where I saw a light on. I wanted to ring Jude but couldn't do that with the party at 279. I hadn't spoken to her since the wedding and she was leaving tomorrow. My last image of her after the reception, had been a brave face hiding tears, just as years ago she would try not to cry when I left for school. I put my helmet on, then took it off, to kiss her for the last time. She laughed, then for an instant, burst into tears; then corrected herself. She wasn't going to let any doubt spoil the day, any fear impede her desire for a new life as far away as possible. I wanted a private last talk and could do this from the Uni. But who was up there in my office?

I'd forgotten Fred Shipley had offered to do the door, which meant he would have a bagful of cash and ticket stubs. Normally this would be handed to me after the performance, but I'd nipped off with JRB. He must have got the porters to unlock my door, and gone up there with the bag. But why was he still there?

'Why are you still here?' I asked him.

'I thought... you might come up.'

'Did you want something?'

He didn't answer.

'Are you pissed off that I didn't ask you to design *Hamlet*? I would have done, except it didn't need designing, and to be frank, I didn't want a designer's ideas getting in the way. You should read the book by the guy from the National who was here today. He says conceptual designers such as they have at the RSC, can completely muzzle Shakespeare. The actors have to be allowed to speak without negotiating the scenery. Not that you're a conceptual designer in any way - even if I knew what that was! All we needed for this show was blocks in an L-shape: the "sterile promontory" jutting out into the audience as in Japanese Kabuki theatre. Did you like it? I actually didn't. It was too restrictive. In fact for the first time since I came to Bradford, I was pretty disappointed generally. Why are you staring at me?'

'I love you.'

Did he actually say it? I didn't see his lips move. He has a face like a young sheep with no muscles in it, just a circular chewing motion when he eats, as I recall, from a lunch we had, to talk through the staging of *Spring Awakening*: how his sloping, earth-filled island rostrum, could be a table at the top for the teacher to stand behind, or lain on head-downward by the two boys in the orchard scene. He flicked the light off and came towards me. His eyes in the darkness were like stars in the curtain of hair. His lips were cold.

'Let's go to the party,' I said.

I'd left the bike in the car-park. I kick-started. He hopped on behind. Normally pillion-riders keep their hands to themselves, but he locked his arms like a tourniquet round my waist, as if any moment he might fall. We bumped along the cobbled back lane then stopped - 'Freddie, you can let me go' - and jumped off. I parked the bike in its little shed and we waded through the long grass to the back door. A blast of noise showed the party in its final throes: empty bottles and cans on the surfaces, floor and up the stairs to David's room. 'You're not to go in here!' I said fiercely to Pete Brent embracing his Ophelia, who till tonight I'd imagined was Blob's girlfriend. Blob himself was in the front room, in commiseration with Mrs Merce. John Lamb was playing Scrabble with Superfresher - and losing! Ken and Kate had long gone, as had Laertes, a dread-locked post-graduate in Yugoslav Studies, who had been rock-star Pied last term, and Melchior in *Spring Awakening*. Fred started to clear up. I helped him, draining any not-quite-empty bottle. There were some potatoes like lumps of coal gone cold from the fire which had gone out. People sensed, with the clearing up that it was time to slope off, till only Fred and I were left.

Leave all this, I said.

I led him upstairs. I said what music do you like? He chose Nat King Cole. Oh God. Oh fuck. I shouldn't be doing this. He was like a child, curling up in my arms. I didn't even undress. He was cold as a corpse. I unbuttoned him, kissed his belly, his chest, drew the curtain from his eyes which were the only signs of life. 'Is this what you want?,' I said, helping him. He stirred and sighed. I was like a doctor in a porn film, curing him of a need, which if it couldn't be shared, should be abandoned. I knew that. But he was naked now and I was with him for the duration, the long-drawn-out physical trial, which must end in some joy, if not for me, then for him. But there was no cry, just a gasp like a stricken animal, and a streak of seed like marrow from the bone. We lay listening to Nat King Cole's last words. This had been a mistake, which I'd want to erase from my memory, but couldn't.

> That's why, darling, it's incredible
> That someone so unforgettable
> Thinks that I am
> Unforgettable, too....

When I woke, in the pitch dark, the song had ended. He'd gone.

Scene Four

THE LAST BATTLE

... but before this foray, we happily had had an Austerlitz, when Brad-ford University presented at Lauriston Hall, Richard Crane's The Quest, *directed by Chris Parr, with music by Chris Mitchell.* The Quest, *in that it is about the Arthurian legend, recalls a play by John Arden, recently produced by the Royal Shakespeare Company. In emotion, in accessibility of language, in clarity of idea and in theatrical effective-ness, it is a far richer experience than the Arden play. It is bound to be one of the very biggest things of the Festival.*

- Harold Hobson, Sunday Times, 18.8.74

*

I took three weeks over Easter, alone, undisturbed, in 279. David was in America. No one knew I was back. I stocked up for a siege - tins of meat and beans, eggs, biscuits, coffee, beer, cigarettes - lowered the blinds, locked the door. I wouldn't emerge till I had a cycle of mystery plays ready to go and a rehearsal script of the Edinburgh play. The *Mysteries*, originally for Lent, were more than a month late, but as I'd said to John Cumming, who would now produce them on carts outside Holy Trinity Bracknell on Easter Monday, haste and rough edges were the stuff of this genre, and these plays

- each just ten to fifteen minutes long - would be so edgy, so rough! If I did one per day for six days, then revised, retyped and posted them on the seventh, he would have just a week to get them together. As in mediaeval times, I would take a sideways look at stories from the Bible, like Bruegel paintings: the Nativity as background to a sheep-stealing incident; a who-does-what dispute on Golgotha with unionized crucifixionists... I told him, if he trusted me and I fulfilled his trust, he could come up to design the lighting for the show I hadn't yet written for Edinburgh. I was right on the cliff edge, but not (yet) panicking. It was just that doing the *Mysteries* right now would mean cutting down to *two weeks - just fourteen round- he-clock days and nights* - my essaying the ascent of the highest summit of my writing career. The six playlets would be the foothills. Fun to do, they loosened my fingers on the keys. I had them completed, typed onto stencils and express posted with a day to spare.

A letter from JRB, 23rd January 1974

Dear Richard,

I was glad that you could meet Peter Hall at the Savoy and that we agreed that we would go ahead to find a way for you to be associated with the National both as a dramatist to work on documentary projects and on your own work, and also as an occasional assistant to a director...

I am enclosing a copy of the guidelines from the Thames Television playwright's scheme. Mr Anthony John of Thames Television has said that it would be adapted to fit the particular requirements of the National Theatre...

I would like to move ahead and make out an application... to be sent together with four copies of a sample play or plays. I think that we should send them Thunder *and also* Secrets, *the former being particularly relevant to the kind of association that we have in mind for you in the Cottesloe Theatre.*

I would be glad if you would think this matter over, obviously keeping it under your hat until we have had a response from Thames Television... I think we should indicate that we would hope for a rather closer association, than is outlined in the guidelines, in view of your experience as an actor and director...

Yes but what about *The Wasps*? You pressured me to do it, and now's the latest I can get down and write it. I want to do a try-out in Bradford, then take it to Edinburgh to have it road-tested for the opening of the Olivier which I still have to believe will be April next year. You haven't said it's *not* happening and you know that the subject is like today's news, ie delay will make it irrelevant. But I want to do it! And I have a chance to give it a rigorous testing such as Stopppard did with *Rosencrantz And Guildenstern Are Dead* in Edinburgh before speeding to the National. Surely, if Olivier himself could sign off as actor-manager with his Glasgow shop steward in *The Party*, then a fiercely left-on-left comedy, rooted in the classics, could surely grace the royal opening? Featuring her favourite Prime Minister, it might even amuse the Queen. (Apparently, she and Wilson play memory games at their weekly meetings.) It's a winner for sure. All the stars are in alignment.

The phone was ringing.

FORETASTE OF CRANE'S FORMIDABLE TALENT
The Festival has provided a foretaste of a formidable new theatre tal-ent. Richard Crane who goes to the National Theatre as a resident writer, has devised two entertainments for Bradford University stu-dents which are not only original, they are cunningly crafted to exploit youthful talent and high spirits.

- John Barber, Daily Telegraph, 26.8.74

It was Chris. He'd been reading Tennyson. From *Guinevere* in *Idylls of the King*, this speech of Arthur, when it's all up for him bar the slaughter: the collapse of the Round Table, the betrayal, the approaching horror and utter loneliness. We could build a whole play round this one speech. Was that not my forte? *The Tenant, Thunder*, did they not each spring from one stand-alone monologue? Here surely was the key! Could he read it to me? Then could he urge me to crack on? He could come up next week and we could suss out St George's Hall. Surely built for jousts! Rip out the seats, put in bleachers! Whence it's a mere hop to Edinburgh and Lauriston Hall. Had I talked to the priests? Could I soft soap them in advance of him coming to put the boot in! This one had legs, with boots on, ha! Galahad in jack-boots! Had I read *Gawaine and the Green Knight*? *Sithen the sege... the borgh brit-tened and brent to brondes...* Could be right up my alliterative alley! How was it going? Or was I still faffing about with *The Wasps*?

The stage is like a football field, with platforms in the positions of the goposts. One has to swivel one's neck like - to change the game - the umpire on Centre Court, but the spectacle is worth swivelling for.
- Harold Hobson, Sunday Times

The Quest... was first of all, a dashing spectacle. Knights sent each other flying from wooden horses, while the arrival of Guinevere was a thrilling parade through an audience ranged along each side of a long hall. - John Barber, Daily Telegraph

The stage area is a long strip in which rival parties become sporting contestants. ('Come on Arthur!' the woman behind me shouted, as if cheering on Rangers.)... Brecht always wanted a theatre that resembled the sporting events: well here it is.
- Michael Billington, Guardian

*

I was the first of all the kings who drew
The knighthood-errant of this realm and all
The realms together under me their head
In that fair order of my Table Round,
A glorious company, the flower of men,
To serve as model for the mighty world...
To cleanse the basic animal in man,
To teach high thought and amiable words
And courtliness and the desire of fame,
And love of truth and all that makes a man,
And all these throve before I took a wife
Believing: Lo my helpmate, one to feel
My purpose and rejoicing in my joy!
Then came your shameful sin with Lancelot;
The came the sin of Tristram with Lynette;
Then others following these my mightiest knights
... So that this life of mine
I do not care to lose, but rather think
How sad it were for Arthur should he live
And sit once more within his lonely hall
And miss the wonted number of my knights
And miss to hear high talk of noble deeds...

*

Thirty-seven years on, I'm in the Gold Room Eastbourne, directing a rivival of *The Quest* with a youth group for the 2012 Cultural Olympics. We're tight on funds, so are using 'found objects': shopping trolleys for the horses, a trampolene for the Round Table, a paper crown for Arthur's crown. The cast are also 'found', ranging from Eastbourne College, through trainee builders and electricians, to rough kids off the street. The exception is Arthur. He is a serious boy, about to go to drama school. He doesn't mix with the others, can turn in on himself, then suddenly explode. It's like directing dynamite. We're having our first runthrough. Arthur has summoned knights and ladies from across the land. The Round Table has flourished, been rocked by scandal and is now breaking apart. Lancelot, in his madness, has just killed Gawaine, the loyalist of the knights. The two sides are poised, in a deadly hush, for the final fight. I told Arthur to take the Tennyson speech slowly, right round the circumference of the stage (this production was in the round), threading like a ghost through the waiting figures, all armed to the teeth. The speech grows from an indictment of Guinevere into a requiem for a lost dream. I couldn't hear him at first. The exhaustion of failure seemed to be killing him from within. The hall went silent. We were picking up every choked-up word, confirming the rule that fits actor to character. He was crushed with grief; his knees seemed to give way. But slowly, harshly, he got through to the staggered ending. Now he would have to lead his troops into battle, brother fighting brother, sister killing sister, but not before his one last appeal was lost in the din of war.

I told the cast to take a break. I noticed Arthur hadn't moved. I went over to tell him just to bottle that performance. But he hardly stirred. His face was ashen. I'd only once seen a face so drained, on a newsreel of a freedom-fighter being dragged to execution. He was frozen, beyond sobbing. He wanted to go home. The next day I called him. His mother said he was unable to speak or stand. We had to recast.

THE SOUNDS OF WORDS

I didn't go out for fifteen days. I let the writing rule. I might wake at three, work for four hours, have a meal, then sleep till I woke, write a scene, write a song. Such wealth I had to draw on! So many intertwining stories, such language! Malory's rough-hewn *Morte d'Arthur*, *Gawaine and the Green Knight* with its alliterative gymnastics, even my old *Knights of the Round Table*, retold by Enid Blyton for children of all ages. But it was Tennyson I plundered most. Theatre is a jackdaw. You borrow, you purloin, then claim it as your own. That's where acting scores and where the whole thing can fall down if it looks like you've just nicked things. Stuffed with so many gems, I was beginning to feel queasy. I was three days in and it was looking like a gorgeous, spangly medley with no plot. I went back to the drawing-board. I forced myself to stake out a narrative.

The key was the word, the sounds of words, the entertainment, class structure and weaponising of words. *The touchstone of the play, the standard by which moral value must be judged... is fineness of speech...* (Hobson). *Arthur wants to create a kingdom based on moderation and justice; but its outward symbol is less the Round Table than his determination that everyone speak in verse.* (Billington). *This brilliant idea had the audience revelling in puns, internal rhymes, and every kind of verbal trick.* (Barber). *The sad glory of Arthur is that he set a standard no society could maintain... Some men and women can reach a Tennysonian nobility. Some with effort can manage pantomime rhymes... It is not without reason that Mordred speaks up for those with no capacity for rhyme or metre: not surprising that one ends with slain bodies and murdered hopes.* (Hobson).

I finished the script, had it packed up and posted. Chris rang back by return. The versification was terrific, the pageantry dynamic, but the play lacked a heart. We needed a scene in Act One, after the wedding: Arthur, Lancelot and Guinevere on the subject of purity - Who is the whitest knight? Who has a skeleton in the cupboard? - interrupted by Mordred wanting to know why, even though hopeless at verse, he is being given special treatment. Then we need another scene for balance in Act Two, when the two men are fighting over the Queen like stags. We should hear the crash of antlers, the broken verse, the spill of blood on the page, with her voice, the proto-feminist, closing the scene, as she shames them both. We have the spectacle, the operatics; let's now see the secrets that pull it all down.

A letter from JRB, 10th March 1974.

> *Dear Richard*
> *The application to Thames Television has gone in on your behalf. Here's wishing it well. Peter Hall and I have talked over the kind of arrangement that we look forward to establishing with you following the Savoy breakfast talk. The financial situation for the immediate future is such that it is very difficult to give a firm round-the-year undertaking, unless we have the Thames bursary... The decision will be made on May 7th. We very much hope you will be able to delay giving*

your notice until that time. If the bursary does not come through, then
we will have to think again...
Yours ever
John

∗

I wrote the two scenes to put heart into the show and packed them off to Chris. He came up for auditions and to talk to Chris M. Then the three of us went and stood in the body of St George's Hall, imagining it as a sporting arena and listening to Mitchell's coronation anthem on the organ. Casting was complex in that many of our best actors said they wouldn't be free for Edinburgh. Unspoken was the thought that if we died a death in Bradford, or if the budget was pulled, we wouldn't *need* to go to Edinburgh. It would do me no good, on my road to the National, to be hobbled by bad reviews. But none of that was uttered. We had a scintillating script, quitessentially English music from Chris M, a thousand-seat concert hall that dated from the Pre-Raphaelites. And we had actors keen to act, fitting the chivalric characters like gauntlets: croquet and scrabble champ John Lamb as Arthur; a rock of a lad called Pete Clegg as Kay, Arthur's brother; and as Lancelot, a barrel-breasted baritone with flowing auburn locks, named Paul Nesbitt-Larking, who rides in singing: *I have no blemish, I have no blot; blister or blain, bile have I not...* and pushing the horse, disguised as his squire, Alison Viney (Wendla from *Spring Awakening*) as Elaine *'an astonishing triumph of control as she moves from farcical pathos to martyrdom ...'* (Owen Dudley Edwards, Irish Times). And as Lynette, Effie T (Princess Michal, Emily Bronte); as Merlin, Arnie K (King Saul, Pied's manager); as Mordred, Blob W (Branwell, First Gravedigger); as Bellicent, Mordred's mother, Jackie N (Tom Brown, Heidi); as Isolde, Gill B (Anne Bronte); as Gawaine, Derek O (Moritz, Bert Rat); as the Green Knight, Nye H (Goliath, Papa Bronte); as Galahad, Pete B (King David, Hamlet); as Leonora (Mrs Merce, now back from France and dating Paul Nesbitt-Larking); as Gareth, Mick D (the Ugly Duckling and Ernst from *Spring Awakening*). And as Guinevere, the Queen...

∗

It's a blur, the memory. We're down in the cellar of 279 at the after-party for *Downers*. We'd been flirty friends since *David*, when she played the Witch of Endor. Then in *Pied*, she was Heidi's Granny, another witch, who by being tipped into the transformational pot, emerges virginal. She had the solemnity to play Guinevere the spotless bride; a streak of mischief to tease the straight-backed boys, then a hunger for the sex she was not getting from

Arthur but knew, with witchy skills, she could unleash from Lancelot. At the readthrough I felt she was overplaying it and said so, earning a stricture (meant to be jokey) from Chris, that any authorial comment should be channelled through the director. I took this as a slight, which led to a damper on the reading. In my 'author's preamble' - the first and last time, said Chris jovially, that they would hear directly from the author, who for most of the rehearsal period, would be away questing fame with Sir John and Sir Ralph! - I had stressed the formality of the blocking - my job! expostulated Chris - and the strict rhythm of the text in a court where sloppy speech was an offence; I had noted the dominance of the Perilous Chair, like a throne at the head of the Table, not to be sat in except by *the Purest, Most Beautiful, Sublime Knight in All the World;* I had pointed to the emergence of Mordred the Bastard, like a worm eating into the Table, and Galahad in white appearing as the rot is setting in. I made it sound as if I was backing Galahad, and the more I denied this and tried to build up Mordred, the more false I seemed and the more distanced and isolated I felt from this team, that I'd nurtured over two years. I was dousing their flair and the consequence was a script, I had the highest hopes for, coming over as flat, rather pompous and in the end nihilistic. The only shreds of humour that broke through came from Mick Diver, playing Gareth. He was the gangly boy in his first year who had survived playing the title role in *The Ugly Duckling*, by stretching his popping eyes and doing Jagger-pouts with his rubbery lips. Gareth has the final lines in the play. I watched him, the sole survivor, the last sane voice before silence returns, still trying to conjure a last laugh and failing.

Then we all went to the final performance of *Downers* in the Great Hall. This was the play by Roy Kift, about drugs and the urban jungle, that had landed on my desk, and I knew we had to do, from our social perspective and to redeem the ugly smell still lingering from *The Duckling*. It would also be a chance to attract a director who might take over from me as Fellow. JRB had again recommended a former student, Patrick Barlow, who agreed he would be a perfect fit for the job, were he not now planning to launch his own National Theatre, not of Britain, but of Brent, doing two-hander versions of *Zulu!*, *The Messiah* and *The Complete Guide to Sex*.

> *It is midnight, Hampstead Heath London. Three young men are waiting. Stamping their feet to keep warm in the November wind. They finish the dregs of a bottle of whiskey. They are waiting for Martin. When he comes, they will beat him up and steal his wallet... There is a sound and somebody walking towards them. Alone. Martin. Silent, they slide into the bushes and wait...*

I should have been outraged when Mick, as Martin, is stopped, beaten up, almost killed. But I was numb to the play's *'power, conviction and above all, humanity'* (*Telegraph and Argus*). I couldn't see any hope for a society that allowed its young to be so wild. This was Mordred's world, without the distancing of myth. But the answer was not the Grail, or the shining-eyed Jesus-freak in *Downers*, who challenges the muggers. To know there is no answer, no future, was bleakly comforting, and Guinevere, sitting next to me, leaning into me and taking my hand, seemed to agree. Live now, with what's left. Forget tomorrow. Come to the party. I took her on the back of my bike to the *Downers* last-night bash at 279. Chris and Pat were both staying there and I needed to talk to them, but through the din, someone said they'd both gone to London and I was suddenly, massively, relieved and tired, as if falling through the floor, into the cellar, where I was now, with the Bitch Queen of History. We'd come down to get more bottles, and leaning over to avoid cracking our heads on the ceiling, I kissed her neck, and as she turned, her lips, and she responded, then burst into laughter, just as Mick was coming down with a note from next door: 'WILL YOU PLEASE CUT YOUR NOISE DOWN... I AM JUST ABOUT FED UP WITH YOUR ORGIE EVERY WEEKEND. ARE YOU ALL SEX MAD? We left the bottles and when we'd managed to shuffle most of the orgiasts out, including Mick, and only a hard core remained, she came up with me to the attic.

✱

A year later, after I'd left Bradford, she wrote to me about the child: little trivia, sweet descriptions, and I began thinking what if... I remember her perfume, mixed with coal dust from the cellar. She was newly married and happy, with a surfeit of love to be given free. I remember visualizing, out of the myriad tiny tadpoles, spilled on the sheet, one who *'stout as Julius Caesar... swam and swam right over the dam...'* But the calendar didn't bear it out. She was only beginning to be pregnant when we got to Edinburgh, and that was months away.

THE THAMES PLAYWRIGHT SCHEME

Final adjudication - Tuesday 7 May 1974
Board Room, 4th Floor, Euston Rd
TIMETABLE
10.30. Panel assembles
10.45. National Theatre
Prof John Russell Brown with
RICHARD CRANE
author of Thunder
11.15. Open Space Theatre
Charles Marowitz with
HOWARD BARKER
author of Previous Convictions
11.45. Northcott Theatre
Clive Barker with
ROY KIFT
author of Downers
12.15. Birmingham Repertory Theatre
Michael Simpson with
DAVID EDGAR
author of Death Story
12.45. LUNCHEON
2.30. Bristol Old Vic
David Horlock with
IAN TAYLOR
Author of Kelly's Winder
3.00. Royal Shakespeare Company
Ronald Bryden with SNOO WILSON
author of Quilp

I entered the room to a roar of laughter. JRB, like a kindly uncle at my side, seemed amused at the joke. I could only assume someone had farted as we came in. Whatever it was, it was a bad start. I was on my own, excluded from the biggest cracker of the day. Centre at the table was an ageing actress called Renee. I knew her from *Carry On* films, but she was also a writer and had worked on *Repulsion* with Roman Polanski. She seemed to be in charge, straightening her face, which then creased once more into a ripple of pops. 'Sorry sorry... We were just...' I glanced at JRB, who almost winked as if to say: keep to the high ground, you're winning. He wasn't going to speak unless I gave him the nod, and I didn't have to, not once. The questions were mostly stupid. 'Would you ever consider cutting your favourite line?' asked Renee. 'Of course,' I replied, 'but I'd store it for future use.' (Laughter.) 'Do you think a writer should be discouraged from directing his own work?' asked Anthony John, the administrator of the scheme, with the hangdog look of a man with no surname. 'That depends on the writer,' I said. 'Coward liked to direct his own, and star in them too. Berkoff is also the best director of his own work. ('Berkoff? Who he?' enquired Renee coyly.) 'But discouraging *good* writers,' I went on, 'from doing *anything*, in my experience, is a non-starter. If anyone discourages *me*, and I know this is what I want and *have* to do, then that makes me even *more* determined.' I saw JRB wanting to insert: 'which is Peter Hall's philosophy exactly!' So I added: 'which is Peter Hall's philosophy exactly!' 'Bravo!' exclaimed Renee. 'Well said,' said Anthony John, cracking a smile. 'And so,' I was rolling! 'When people I'm working with try to *discourage* me from going to the National, because it's *established* and as a small fish in a pool full of dolphins I might well be swamped (chuckles), I just remind them I am one of those *positive* writers who likes to say YES. I feel the theatre is like a wave. If you buck against it, you might drown. But if you ride it, if you let it carry you and you're on top of it, then there truly is nothing more thrilling, more likely to produce your best work! That's not to say I'm not wary of being taken *for* a ride. I just will never say no to an opportunity to have a stab at what I know I do best, even though discouraging winds may blow me... off the map... and maroon me...' I was petering out. Renee was looking at me with some pity. Anthony John was furrowing his brow. Then the third member of the panel, who hadn't yet spoken, said: 'Tell me something Richard. The National is not going to open on schedule; we all know that. It's likely you'll be stuck at the Old Vic for the whole of your residency, playing no part in the expansion planned for the move to the South Bank. What would you say if we postponed offering you the bursary, till it was clear how it might actually be to your own and the theatre's advantage?'

The question stuck with me all the way home. I'd replied pretentiously with a reference to Goethe and 'commitment'. If you commit yourself absolutely to your dream, then Fate is also committed to supporting you. You create the wave that will carry you to success, wherever that may lead. But they were tiring of me by then, having decided (I could tell) to pass me by for at least a year; and eager to move on to the next interview: Charles Marowitz of the Open Space and his candidate Howard Barker. Barker was the playwright who would carve his own furrow *against* the wave, saying NO, not YES. For him, drama was a chipping away at solidarity (which equals complacency and *musicals)*, till it cracks. His plays *Claw* and

Stripwell would be directed in London by Chris Parr, within a year, and would establish this writer as the *refusenik* of his generation, adhering to no trend, reactionary or revolutionary.

I'd arranged to meet David Edgar and Roy Kift at Euston, as also Snoo Wilson, who was workshopping a play with the Art College that week. We would all be staying at 279 Great Horton Road: four of the six Thames TV bursary candidates, hanging on the same phone at the same address for the same news. What had been highlighted as a jobs-for-the-boys scandal in *Javelin*, two years before - the inhabiting of a certain large house in Bradford being key to playwriting success - was now confirmed as *truth*: that this old Yorkshire town, was home to the foundry where white-hot new theatre-writing was being hammered out. But you wouldn't have known that from the conversations in the train and later round the table at 279. We'd got in take-away curries and beer with cake to follow, and the talk was raucous and gossipy, about actors - Wilson, Nixon, Mao, these were the true thesps, performing in high winds on the head of a pin before impaling themselves on it; agents - Peggy Ramsay in her Dickensian *bordello*, with her stocking tops showing, laying into her 'boys' - Ayckbourn, Hampton, Bond and Bolt, for succeeding when they should have failed; directors - Chris Parr, pilloried for his head-banging and eating habits - just as he blew in from *King* rehearsal - 'We've turned a corner Rick! Terrific jousting scene! Blob nearly got killed!'

The phone rang. It was for David. He took it in silence, then crossed the room to go to bed. Turning on his exit, and glancing over his specs, he said quietly: 'Why the long faces? I am the Thames TV Resident Dramatist at the Birmingham Rep. I bid you good night.'

When he'd gone, we had more beer, then I went with Chris upstairs to talk about tomorrow, before he bedded down on the single mattress. I heard the phone ring and raced downstairs. It was for Snoo. He sounded happy, so it was assumed, being a contrarian, he'd failed, and we were not wrong. Yuk, he gagged, those RSC grapes were truly sour! He'd been a fool even to reach for them. Then just as he put the phone down, it rang for Roy. Oh wow, said the Thames TV Dramatist for Exeter. That's fabulous. That's brill. He chatted on, while Snoo made finger-down-the-throat noises, then flung open the door and threw up for real. Sorry Rico, said Roy, I won't be applying for your Fellowship after all.

When they'd both gone into the downstairs front room for the night, I sat and contemplated the sink. If the phone didn't ring by midnight, I'd start clearing up. I wasn't going to bed. JRB had said he'd ring me whatever the result, but it might not be till late as he had to go to a preview of the National's *Spring Awakening*. I could have gone with him, and thus learnt my fate earlier, but I knew I'd hate the play. My production was still too fresh to allow comparison with a conventional version. It would kill me if it was good, and if I didn't get the bursary, I'd be double dead. I was dead now. Sleepless among snores, I was a skivvy ghost, clearing bottles, scraping pots, sweeping the floor, swabbing the table. I was thinking I might cut loose from the phone and go walkabout across town. I was just putting my jacket on, when the thing shrieked.

'Hello?'

'Hello?'

'Hello John.'

'Is this too late?'

'No no. How was the show? *Spring Awakening.*'

'I can't tell you...'

'What?'

'How *awful* it was. It was ghastly, embarrassing. When an actor plays innocence for laughs, it's like a flasher at a funeral. I wish I'd seen your version, with youngsters playing the youngsters.'

'*I* wish you'd seen it.'

'I wish we'd shelved ours and got *you* to do it. It would have been something for you to do,' he sighed. 'You can't just be doing *The Wasps,* especially if it's no longer new. Is it going to Edinburgh? Or are you still faffing about with King Arthur?'

'I'm still faffing. John, what's the news?'

'Peter wants Jonathan to read it, Jonathan Miller. Do you have a script?'

'Of what?'

'*The Wasps.*'

'I haven't started it.'

'Or Blakemore. Would you be happy with that?'

'I'd happier to know about the bursary.'

'Oh, you got it. I thought I said. There was never any doubt. Renee fell in love with you. She wants to play Maud in *Secrets,* but I told her it was on offer to Natasha, who will be stunning! We've still got the boy to firm up and the man to be replaced. Did you know we'd cast a soak?!! When are you next in town?'

*

I went to bed and slept like a log till Chris woke me. When I told him I'd got the bursary, he said he'd guessed it already. Institutions like the National had clout and Hall had tentacles in so many pies. But he was genuinely, sweetly pleased, because I was pleased, and because, with no NT move in the offing, I'd have little to do except write. He'd been offered a season of lunchtime plays at the Royal Court and I could certainly have one of those, and direct it too. Then after the Barker plays - at the Open Space and the

Court - he'd be taking over as Artistic Director at the Traverse (not yet confirmed, but it was nods and winks that counted and these were coming at a dizzying rate!) He'd already put in a list of writers to be commissioned and I was up there with the best; with a strict clause in the contract to have the script on his desk as soon as his feet were under it, or rather *on* it, leaning back, head on hands, grinning at the ceiling! This is going to be an *annus mirabillimus* Rick! Go to the National, take the money, but from day one make it clear, *you are not their poodle*. Creep in politely, with a clean sheet, and they might not even piss on you. But arrive with a clutch of commissions in your bag and they'll treat you like Pinter! I wasn't going to argue. I wasn't going to tell him that acting and directing would be drafted into my National contract, as outriders to the writing, with an extra thousand pounds assured plus performance fees. No I wouldn't be a poodle, more a three-headed guard-dog at the gate of the new Cottesloe Theatre, through which *only new plays might enter;* and it was to find this haven and believe it might one day be the heart-beat of the new building, that JRB and I, after the Thames interview and a light lunch, had crossed under Waterloo Bridge and, donning hard-hats, entered the shell of National. Could this monument to delay, this Stonehenge of a millstone round the neck of British theatre, be the new metaphor for our time? Windowless, concrete corridors to get lost in, occasionally opening into a Soviet-style arena for adoration of the leader, or show-trials: this was as far as you could get from the backstage, greasepaint-smelling tawdriness which I loved, and as close as you dared to the death and burial of theatre. Dionysus/Christ, incarcerated/crucified, presumed beaten and dead, leaves the way clear for reason and dictatorship. The antonym of 'raffish' (Jonathan Miller's epithet for our lived-in, loved-in world of work): this building, by walling in passion and foolery, recruiting managers instead of actors, unknowingly compresses art to the point of explosion with plays like *The Bacchae* and *Spring Awakening*. These wouldn't happen in 'raffish' theatres, or if they did, they'd be parodies. Without concrete to beat your head against, you're in clover as a writer, giving the people 'what they want'. The play I would write here, would be set in the monkish cell of a dressing-room deep in the ground, where actors are waiting for the delayed, delayed, delayed grand opening of a National Temple to Art. My special subject in Roman History at school had been Nero: his folly, his fall. Young, bearded, adored, the last of the Julio-Claudians had turned the empire on its head, exchanging military triumphs for conquests in drama, singing and sport. Egocentric, ruthless, depressive, he cleared Rome by fire to build a citywide fun palace, and used Christians for the lighting. But the Golden House never opened. The military who will always in the end get the funding, installed a general as Emperor. 'What an artist I die!' cried Nero, falling on his sword, as the boots of the legions were tramping into Rome. Of course *Nero and the Golden House* (Traverse 1976) would be much more than a parable of the National and Hall who, young, bearded, ruthless etc, would come through hell, to become 'the titan of postwar British theatre'. My task would be to honour my complex boss with a mix of emotions, and have him absent but 'waited for'. I would take a leaf from Howard Barker's book: chip away at the concrete; see what happens when it falls.

We were lost. Temporary lighting, on loose wiring, threw shadows on what you might expect to be doorways. Walls were set at obtuse angles and there were stairs leading to blocked landings. Time was flying; I had a train to catch. 'I'm so sorry,' said JRB. 'I thought I knew the terrain...' Then a frail old man with his arm in a sling, appeared round a corner. 'No point asking him,' I murmured. But JRB was already shaking the man's good hand, the left one. Two years on, I'd have recognized the stiff jaw and steely glasses from *Marathon Man*, expecting a blade to shoot from the cuff, to slit JRB's throat. But this monochrome, patched-up creature was so far from the Olivier I'd worshipped, from Henry V and Richard III to Tyrone in *Long Day's Journey*, and Tagg in *The Party*. It was as if the concrete had crushed him.

'Sir,' said JRB, 'may I introduce Richard Crane, a young writer, we're hoping to work with?'

'Why only hoping?' said Sir Larry, his eyes flashing like steel. Then to me: 'Dear boy, why do you write?'

'Because I have to, I want to, I love doing it.'

'You know what they asked Peter and me the other day?'

'What did they ask you?'

'The same. Why do we do it? You know what Peter said?'

'Er... to challenge, provoke and illuminate?'

'Spot on!'

'And what did you say?'

'I said what you said. Then they said why do you have to, why do you want to, why do you love doing it? And to that there is only one answer.'

(*I step into the light, and the roar goes up...*)

*

The applause. He never denied it. When he should have died from a muscle-wasting disease, following cancer and thrombosis, it was the applause kept him going. Having been given just weeks to live in 1974, he went on, acting at full stretch - *Marathon Man*, Zeus in *Clash of the Titans*, Lord Hood in *The Bounty*, *Brideshead Revisited* and King Lear himself - for a further twelve years, defying his doctors with 'a curious and startling immortality' (Dr J Miller).

And applause, well-earned, was now coming to me. The buzz around *The King* - the extravagance of the subject, the daring of the staging, the expectation of a show to cap even *David*, *Thunder*, *Pied Piper* and *Spring Awakening*; the sense of a Grand Finale, of further garlanding in Edinburgh, and my upcoming elevation onto a National plinth - all that, fired up with the keenness of cast and orchestra, many of whom, having said they wouldn't be free for Edinburgh, were now reconsidering, plus Chrises P and M seeming to walk in step and laugh in the same language, assured me the show was in good hands, and I could slip away for a week.

*

Mr Crane is going to the National Theatre on a bursary from Thames Television. I would myself have commended him to Peter Hall, were it not obvious that no such commendation is necessary. It is clear that Mr Crane has the large imagination, the sense of spectacle, the feeling for new form, and the respect for civilised expression that the great stage resources of the new National Theatre will both want and be uniquely able to satisfy. In fact if the Olivier Theatre were to open with The Quest, *I, at least, should shed no tears.*

- Harold Hobson, Sunday Times

EXPECTATIONS

The rhythm of the train was like applause, driving me on. I had permission from Sir Laurence to indulge it, for a moment. My work was done and I could bask in the rattle of appreciation, and the great career strides I was making on several fronts. For starters, I'd be stopping off in Birmingham to attend a matinee of *Thunder* at the Crescent Theatre, the leading amdram company of the Midlands. They would be the first to do the play after the Edinburgh premiere and I was keen to see how it looked, without my guidance. They'd written with a query about the length of some of the speeches and could they make some cuts and I'd instructed Serena to say: Absolutely not! The text soon to be published by Heinemann was sacrosanct. English audiences, I had argued, must learn to endure long speeches, as the Irish did. That was before JRB had ordered the 'slashing and burning' (Chris's words) of *Secrets* for the Bush. London punters, he had insisted, weren't yet ready for the meanderings that had set the Irish on a roar. But I wasn't to fret, I'd done good work: just enjoy the pleasure of interviews and *passive attendance* at rehearsals. True we hadn't yet cast the boy, but agents were sending in the cream of young talent to be auditioned tomorrow morning. Then Natasha would come in, to be joined by Edward Judd, replacing the jettisoned 'soak'. Judd was the star of gritty 60s films like *The World Ten Times Over* and *The Human Jungle*; now in decline as an actor which was spot on for Jack. Natasha, could play with him like a cat with an old rat. I'd said why not go for Charlie Bolton as the boy, but JRB had said he didn't want anyone harking back to the Chris Parr production. However fabulous that was, this was a fresh start, having been whittled and buffed up to its new sleek self, 'which incidentally,' he added, 'Peter Brook thinks is "skilled", which is Brookese for "super". What's this I hear about you *buying a house*?'

It was true. My mother had said she and Pa would help with the deposit, and Uncle Arch would do the conveyancing. She'd started looking, south of the river, so as to be bikeable to the National and also to Shortlands. She'd lined up an estate agent with properties to inspect while I was down for *Secrets*, for which incidentally, should *she* buy the tickets or would *I* be treating my parents (just asking)? And what was this about the mother being based on herself? She wasn't sure if she'd want to see that! But she would, very much, like to meet John Russell Brown - and Sir Laurence Olivier if he was available! She'd understood that I'd be unable to stay at home for the rehearsal period, because of distances involved, but could I please tell her where I *would* be staying?

I'd be staying with Betty. I'd rung her and she'd said of course, any time. But you do know Angie is still here and there's only one spare room; I thought you'd split. I said one doesn't split from Angie. She's a friend for life, and I could have added that to have her cool haven to sail in and out of in these choppy waters, was my absolute dream. You could say she was my rock, except a rock is something you splinter on or that weighs you down and that was never the case with Angie. So I rang her at her work, and she said fine, and the more I thought about it, as the train rattled south, the more fine it felt to me too. At a turning point in life, when you're about to step into a blinding light, you need a cool hand on your brow and soothing arms to sink into; then at breakfast, to come down to Betty in her vintage robe still puzzling over a crossword, and Michael playing Schubert on the baby grand.

And as we pulled into New Street Station, I was thinking this was like coming home from school for the holidays. However much they bulldozed the terraces and replaced them with motorways, Birmingham would always have a homing pull. Whenever a chapter was ending, I would be drawn into the force-field of the long-faced accent and the tiger-coloured buses. And as with the closing days of The Old Ride and Cambridge, the Bradford chapter was now rushing to its end in a flurry of praise, so it was fitting I should stop here. Also they were choosing my successor at the University, so it was politic to be away, knowing the appointment was ninety percent sewn up, but shouldn't look like a fix. The panel knew what was needed to ensure continuity, and even though Pat Barlow and Roy Kift were no longer free, Chris's man, Tom Wilkinson, had been subtly talked up to the top of the short-list. A farmer's boy from West Yorkshire, who had turned to acting at Kent University, then gone on to RADA, Tom had an energy, as Chris observed in his reference, that was rooted in the peaty soil of his beginnings and went way beyond acting. He was that rarity among theatre artists: a purveyor of real emotion that drew you to admire the villain, and forgive even the murderer. He had an easy rapport with colleagues, a good ear for what makes a play work and a natural affinity with current times that enabled him to translate public dilemmas into entertainment.

The Crescent Theatre was walking distance from the station. They didn't know I was coming. I would leave a note at the stage door, then go round to the front as the audience were streaming in. I could already feel applause welling up and the satisfaction of sitting at the back unrecognized, as it warmed me with its glow.

She sent them the wrong script! I was sitting at the back thinking *what is this lumbering crap*? Interminable chunks lifted wholesale from *Shirley, The Tenant of Wildfell Hall* and Branwell's ramblings, were interrupted only by embarrassingly long extracts, sung and danced to, from the Community Song Book. It wasn't until half-way through the first act, that the truth sank in. When I originally joined Serena, she had been curious to know how I assembled my material; what kind of block did I chip away at to reveal the living drama. So I'd sent her my first draft which was basically uncut Bronte text, so she could see the authenticity and my skill at dissecting it. Here now, on the stage, to a mercifully small audience, was the fullblown horror of untreated raw material, which I'd instructed must *absolutely not* be cut. I should have slipped away at the interval - no one knew I was there - but the cast were so skilled at just getting through the verbiage, I felt I had to come clean, and it did have a kind of epic quality, that made you want to hug them for learning so much and delivering it without complaint. I even spotted certain passages that could do well to be re-included if I hadn't just returned the galley-proofs to Heinemann. There was a ripple of applause at the end, and I was the last to stop clapping. I even shouted 'Bravo!' Then I went round to introduce myself, to congratulate and explain.

*

I'm alone in Angie's bed, dog tired, but I can't sleep. When I got to Chadwell Street around ten o'clock, Betty said Angie had gone, she didn't know where, so it was okay for me to have the room. When I pressed her for some detail, all I got was an imitation of Angie's sniffy-nosed look I'd often seen when she was so angry she couldn't speak. At least I assumed it was anger, heated emotion never being part of Angie's repertoire. Feelings just froze, till they melted and drained away. I took my bag up to the room, thinking there might be a note, and remembering her once saying, as if it expained everything 'Betty hates the sight of me'; yet they went on being friends. So the reason was obviously me turning up out of the blue like a tomcat who'd then be off again into the night.

There's a faint smell of her on the pillow, the trace of someone who can embrace you, at the same time affirming this is not going to last. *Angie*, the song from the Stones' *Goat's Head Soup*, topped the charts just a year ago... just forty-five years ago, and the lyrics still hurt. *Angie, A-a-a-angie, where will it lead us from here... Angie, you're beautiful, but ain't it time we said good-bye...* We met up again in 2014 at a lunch at Brunstane, her castle home outside Edinburgh. She was in her late sixties now, married to George Kerevan, soon to be Westminster MP for East Lothian. Her cancer was in remission. Two years later, it had all returned, along with a heart attack, but you'd never know it from her Facebook postings. Her stoicism, as strong as her castle walls, made it seem like someone else defying the prognoses, continuing to entertain friends. *Angie, Angie, ain't it good to be alive?* As I write this, on the day of her funeral, I'm reading her last posting:

> *I had lots of visitors today. Patsy, Gerald, Mayam, Martin, all visited from Manchester and Liverpool. Mary dropped in from Bergen. Carol and Lynne, my kind neighbours came round with toffee popcorn and a lovely plant. Just hope I don't wake up one morning...*

*

The plan was this. I'd stay a week in London, attending *Secrets* rehearsals, doing interviews etc; looking for, choosing and setting in motion the purchase of a house south of the river; going to Bermans & Nathans the costumiers, to select tabards, chain-mail, bodices, wimples for *The King*, then to Bapty's the armourers, to find longswords, shortswords, axes, maces, poignards, flails, all to be red-starred to Bradford, and picked up from the station in the Union van, by me, after my return, in time for fight arranging in the gym and dress rehearsal in St George's Hall. I'd then stay for the run of performances, then *drive down* to London in a rented five-tonner, to return weapons and costumes (to be rehired for Edinburgh), the plan dove-tailing into Ma's brainwave, as Treasurer of the Bermondsey Medical Mission, to bag the best of a house clearance bequest in Reading, that included a three piece suite, dining table and chairs, beds and bedding, cupboards, cabinets and their contents, and a whole library of rare books, which I could have for my new abode, for fifty pounds total.

Did it all work out? Not really but we got there. I didn't stay on at Betty's. I said my mother was ill: her racing thyroid impelling her to organize my happiness and my life. Yet it was comfortable at Shortlands. I could sleep, I was fed, my laundry was done. And it was good to be forced to get fixed up for living in London. We looked at only one house. Situated between Clapham and Wandsworth Commons, this 1890s terrace property was going for just over twelve thousand, hadn't been renovated in all its years, was dark and Dickensian, on three and a half floors, with cellar, loft, a small garden, outside toilet. I could create a home here from scratch. I could let the three bedrooms and have the ground floor double room for my bedroom and study. There was no need to look elsewhere. We made an offer which was accepted.

Almost immediately, doubts set in. I'd be tied to a debt - through mortgage and parental loan - of TWELVE THOUSAND POUNDS! Over three times my salary from the National, and that was only for *one year*. From the first moment the residency had been broached, JRB had insisted I shouldn't count my chickens, but I truly believed, in the random world of theatre, you should drive your fate to suit your dreams. 'What's this I hear about you *buying a house?*' said JRB more than once, and I could have said: Sure! And you've got to help. It's not enough to be going to the National for a year, when it's in stasis and new writing is on hold. I have to get launched *now*! *Secrets* at the Bush must become PLAY OF THE YEAR, transferring to a neat little West End theatre - the Duchess or the Criterion - and running for a decade! We have a real star in Natasha, and Edward Judd is ready for a major comeback, and Karl Howman - was it *fate* he turned up just as we were despairing at the 'cream of young talent' the agents were *not* sending? - he's a cert for Best Newcomer, replacing the sullenness of Charlie Bolton, with an innocence which is endearing, till you realize there's nothing behind it. So could you *work these actors* John (I wanted to say) and not just sit there in rehearsal letting it run, with hardly a comment, then at the end, instead of notes, *philosophizing* about the symbolism of Maud's picture-hanging skills, invoking author's intent, then nodding wisely when I speak?

When I went for an interview with Bill Hardcastle on *The World At One*, I was ready with stories to make the show hot news, but hotter 'smoking gun' news was beginning to issue from Washington, and I was kept waiting nearly an hour. When it seemed the programme was over and I was about to slip uninterviewed away, I was met through the glass by the glare of the great man, now informed of my presence. Beckoning me into the studio, he sat me down and we chatted about new drama, the National, Belfast, Euripides, why do mothers kill their children, can reality be fabricated out of *stuff dreams are made on*. This was good! I was on a roll, just hoping the tape was running. Then he said: 'Hold it there. Let's record.'

*

JRB had said he and I, after rehearsals each day, should go 'slumming' in the West End. If it was true I'd 'burnt my chickens' before my own and the National's destinies were intertwined, then I should not flinch from learning, without prejudice, what the punters were flocking to. If I was game, he could get tickets.

First up was the first part of *The Norman Conquests*, Alan Ayckbourn's trilogy about the amorous exploits of an assistant librarian (Tom Courtenay), set concurrently in different areas of one house. I wanted to use the opportunity of asking JRB, when he was going to start directing, but we were rushing, and then in the interval and later, walking to the station, there was so much to discuss about the Ayckbourn play: for instance, the funniest moment, when the action had to stop for a good minute because the audience were so paralytic with laughter; prompted by nothing Ayckbourn had written, just a simple mismatch of positioning: the image of Michael Gambon, the easily embarrassed nextdoor neighbour, seated at the dining table, pretending his low chair was on the same level as everyone else's. What did JRB as a words man think of a non-verbal, unplanned *still moment* usurping the comedy? His response - he loved this kind of argument - was yes he was a words man, but he also believed in the actor shaping the drama, and the seat-level moment wasn't, in all probablility, unplanned. Ayckbourn was a master trickster, and if this was a pre-planned trick, it was top drawer. I could then have gone on to say couldn't we find a similar moment in *Secrets*, couldn't he help the actors find it, because the play - early days but it was worrying - was coming over rather flat and *un*directed. But my train was in; I had to run.

The next night, we went - because wasn't Maud in *Secrets* just the *awfullest* imitator of Agatha Christie? - to *The Mousetrap*. I had several opportunities, over our dinner before the show, and in the interval, to voice my concern about JRB's directing, but I flunked it, gabbing on about having seen this play sixteen years earlier, when I, my parents and three sisters had gone to London for a week, to do the sights and see plays. The first play had been *The Party* by Jane Arden, starring Charles Laughton, with Albert Finney (the main reason we went) in his first London role. The second was

The Mousetrap, six years old even then and with many of the original cast. Aged thirteen and an ardent Christie fan, I'd found it riveting and inspirational, and I enjoyed now recalling how it had informed *The Bastard's Return* (my first play).

On the third night, I told JRB I wasn't free. Natasha had asked me to escort her to dinner with her friend Paola Welles. Peter, then in Paris, had suggested it and I saw it as a chance to find out what she was feeling about the show so far, and if together we could get JRB to do some directing! In the taxi to Paola's house, I managed to say: 'Natasha, you might have noticed...' but she cut me off with a laugh: 'It's such a *relief*, I can't tell you Richard, to play it through uninterrupted. You've written a terrifying tight-rope, and I'm up there crossing Niagara like the Great Blondin! One false step, one break of concentration, and I plunge! John's wisdom, his *placidity*, the *permission* he gives his actors, I love, as I love your play.' Then she turned to talking about Paola and her worries, everyone's worries, about Orson. All he seemed to want to do now was go on chat shows and do food commercials.

'Will he be there tonight?' I asked glibly.

'Quite possibly,' said Natasha.

But he wasn't. The only other guests were Bruce Myers, one of Peter's actors, and his girlfriend Helen Mirren, who was in a deep sulk all evening.

On the fourth night after rehearsal, after another uninterrupted run-through, JRB asked me if I'd like to see *Oh! Calcutta!* I said sure, so off we went. This was the nude revue Kenneth Tynan, JRB's predecessor at the National, had put together in 1969, which would play over a thousand performances on Broadway and nearly four thousand in London. It was curious of JRB to want to see it, in that the style and subject were as far from his patch, as he was personally from Tynan. As I sat there watching the sketches - by Sam Shepard, John Lennon, Edna O'Brien, Jules Feiffer (there had even been one by Beckett but he withdrew it) - as I watched the actors getting their laughs, indulging the saucy bits, casting a cosy light on the misogyny and the violence; after JRB had slipped away ('this is *awful!*'), an impossible desire crossed my mind. I wished for time to turn back, so I could have come to the National under Olivier and Tynan, when Quilley was there, Jonathan Miller and Michael Blakemore, Penny Wilton and Nick Clay. Oh for real crises about plays, not buildings! Oh for a mentor I didn't have to defer to, sitting beside him, suffering the cold tits and shrivelled cocks, till he couldn't take any more! Tynan, for all his waspishness and cruelty, had flair and *ideas*. He would know me for one who had burst onto the Cambridge revue scene, as he had at Oxford. I could have taken his idea to *intellectualize* the nude revue, get in modern poetic writers, including Lennon and Beckett and *me*, with Pinter directing. '*Be light, stinging,* insolent and melancholy,' Tynan advises in his diaries. 'There is no reason,' says Irving Wardle in the *Times* review of *Oh! Calcutta!*, 'why the public treatment of sex should not take in lyricism and personal emotion, along with a harvest of bawdy jokes'. And I could have done all that and more. I could have written for this 'ghastly, ill-written, juvenile, attention-seeking' show (Wardle) and turned it on its head; shown the dark side of liberation, pushed the audience to the edge.

I came way thinking at least I've got a two-pronged stab at immortality. If Natasha can't quite pull off her solo high-wire act, then *The King*, with Chris P and Chris M at the helm, will surely deliver. *Secrets* was over for now till I returned for the first preview. Tomorrow, I was due at Bermans & Nathans for the costumes and Baptys for the weapons; then I'd catch fast train to Bradford.

EXIT THE KING

C hris met me at the station. 'We've lost Chris.'
'What?'
'I sacked the orchestra and he walked.'
'You did *what*?!!'
'I said he should do the whole thing on the organ, but he wasn't having that.'
'What was wrong with the orchestra?'
'They were drowning the singers. A cacophony of farts, not even laughable! Whereas if he did it all just on the organ as we're going to have to in Edinburgh, because most of the orchestra can't come - thank Christ! - if he puts everything on the organ, not just the anthem, but *everything*, it'll be English Hymnal to the core, with blasts of J S Bach, which is *what you've written*! But he won't have that. He stomped off. They all fucking stomped off.'

I was lost for words. I glanced at him, as we walked, his eyes like fire behind the thick-framed glasses. I said: 'But Chris, there's still a week to go. Remember *David* in the cathedral. You had the same problem then. Orchestras work at a different rate. They don't learn their lines, but they do learn to read them; and they were brilliant in the end in the cathedral, you said so. Except for Marjorie Sidebottom. Remember her, first violinist? She needed three chairs for sitting on, then in the middle of the dress rehearsal, she got up, packed her things and walked out, because she had to catch her last bus!'

'St George's,' continued Chris, as if I hadn't spoken, 'has the finest organ north of Watford. I don't have your diplomatic skills Rick. I just told him to *fucking use it*! If you'd been here, you could have explained this is *not an opera*; it's *a play with music*. The songs are a device like the verse. That's why when everything's going to pot in Act Two, you've written *no songs*, except deliberately low-key *echoes of songs*, until the battle when it's not music, it's *a wall of sound* like a thunderstorm. Imagine that on the organ! But Chris won't see it. He'd rather pull the whole thing down, than lose his orchestra, which even if they were the Halle, would be wrong, don't you see? And there's something else you don't know, which you're not going to be happy about. Tom didn't get the Fellowship. He was pipped by the surprise wild card on the short list, who apparently will be turning up tonight to watch rehearsal. Only *you* can put a stop to that extremely *bad idea*; though if she's anything like she was in the interview, she won't take any shit, even from you.'

'She?'

'But there may not even be a rehearsal. If Mitchell isn't there and willing to go solo on the organ, I'll have to say we're cancelling.'

*

...I suggested to one or two of the cast afterwards, that Crane was in fact a splendid teacher... At first the Bradfordians didn't like it. Teaching is a dirty word nowadays. Crane was a great man, they assured me, the 'Kissinger of directors' who never lost his temper or failed to compose a dispute, the supple diplomat with strength and assurance...

- Owen Dudley Edwards, Irish Times

*

Chris Mitchell and his wife Fran lived in a semi on a leafy avenue on the edge of town. I scooted straight there, leaving Chris P at 279 with my bags. I had no idea what I'd say; I just knew 'supple diplomat with strength and assurance' was not in my armoury. The best way out, I thought as I phut-phutted into suburbia, under louring clouds, would be to crash into a brick wall, but there were no such walls, only box hedges and trelliswork. The clouds burst as I parked the bike, walked up the path through tipping rain, rang the bell, ding-dong - it was bucketing down now - and again, *ding-dong-ding-dong-ding-dong...*

Fran answered, through the chained door.

'I'm sorry Richard, he won't see you.'

'Please, can I come in? I'm getting soaked.'

'He won't listen. He's had enough. He's depressed.'

'*He's* depressed! For fuck's sake!'

I put my foot in the door before she could shut it. I wasn't wearing a helmet or anything waterproof. Rain was matting my hair and cascading down my face.

'Take your foot away.'

'Let me in.'

'I can't let you in unless you take your foot away. I can't unchain the door.'

I took my foot away. The door snapped shut.

'OPEN THE DOOR! FRAN! WILL YOU OPEN THIS FUCKING DOOR!!'

She opened the door. I tumbled in. I was incapable of speech. The rain on my face felt like tears but I'd gone beyond that. Fury at being shut out, then being made to seem like an emotional mess, when I should be riding high, with two shows set to garner national acclaim, only to have it all pulled down by colleagues who couldn't work together! Vanity, was it all vanity? A 'cacophony of farts'? How could I argue for Mitchell to shelve his pride, when it was all in the end for *my* name on *my* show? Necessity, wasn't she the loopy spinster aunt of dramatic invention, never the mother? The pain of 'birthing a play', the need to act and to watch acting, being as vital to humans as eating and breathing, all tosh when you think about it? Just a week ago, I'd written an article for the *Telegraph & Argus*, refuting the argument of a councillor demanding subsidy for his matchbox collection, if public money was to be showered on bolshevik twaddle like *Downers*. If I could give it all up now, if there was a bus I could fall under... but I was saddled with it. Condemned to life!

Fran sat me on her sofa as we listened in silence to a moaning sound, like a trapped animal, coming from upstairs. 'It's Chris on his synth,' explained Fran. 'It's his way of grieving.' She went to make me a cup of tea. Did I want sugar? Sure I did. And a tissue to blow my nose, dreams dissolved in sweet tea and a quick exit, still drenched, into sheets of rain.

*

I parked at the Uni and went up in the lift to tell Brenda to get a message to the Successor not to come to rehearsal this evening, but she was on the phone, talking in soothing, persuasive tones (to Mitchell - fuck!); so I left a note. Hurrying back to the lift, I passed a woman in the corridor, with shades like black saucers, high hair, high-heeled boots, who seemed to want to ask something, but I shot past, I was in a hurry. I had to get to the van to get to the station to get the costumes and the weapons which had been red-starred, awaiting collection. I was trusting Goethe - holding his feet to the fire - that with passion and commitment you can bend fate to your will, and clattering over the cobbles to the loading bay, I was bending it, bending it!

I'd forgotten I'd rung Brenda to ask Sir Percival and Sir Bors to meet me there to help with the lifting and they were waiting, doing lines.

- *We should like to register a complaint.*
- *Our disgust at what's going on.*
- *As Champions of the Grail, it is our duty to affirm...*
- *That we are appalled by the filthy practices of this court.*
- *We are stunned and shocked by your turpitude.*

We got the skips from the station, and the two Pure Knights trollied them to the gym, while I returned the van. The sun which had flashed like a vision of the Grail, had gone in again and I was sweating with doubt. I just wanted to go home, pack a bag, scoot off, get the next train to London. I'd done with this farce. Then I heard laughter and music. I was so set for disappointment, I wasn't sure I could take this. Opening the door, I peaked in. Sudden silence: all heads turned. Then before anyone could cheer, Chris M at his synth, played a mean cord, then lapsed into the moaning, moody strains I'd heard earlier at his house.

'Listen to this Rick,' said Parr, 'to be played subliminally *on the organ*, under the Tennyson speech, and crescendo-ing through the build-up to the battle, then crashing in like *Zadok the Priest* when the fight begins.'

'And there are vocals,' put in Mitchell. 'Just as everyone in the anthem sings major-key harmonies, here they all have to sustain whatever note they can think of, as long as it's *harsh*.'

He laughed, Parr laughed; then quietly, out of earshot, whispered: 'Well done with the diplomacy Dr Kissinger. You get the Peace Prize.' I wanted to say honestly it was Fran who fixed it, then Brenda who sealed it. But John Howard, the fight director, was calling everyone to come and get to know their weapons, including me.

'Oh yes,' said Chris, 'I meant to tell you, we lost an actor, whats-his-name playing Tristram. The part is yours! This could be your big break Mr Harbord!'

*

Sir Tristram, equipped in full costume, stood aside from the great swirl of battle, surveying the slaughter with what looked like a pleasing blend of irony and compassion. He might have been taken for the spirit of Fringe theatre, or a cop on a stake-out, depending on the sublimity or otherwise of your metaphors... I had seen the pre-festival showing of Richard Crane's The Quest, *and Richard Harbord, as Sir Tristram, had given the most mature performance of the show... 'It is bad luck for you,' I said sympathetically [to Richard Harbord], 'that so impressive a man as Crane is going to the National Theatre in London. I suppose you must be feeling pretty depressed about it. 'He looked at me like a father reluctantly deciding that his son was old enough to know the facts of life. 'I suppose,' he said, 'I ought to tell you that I* am *Richard Crane.'*   - Owen Dudley Edwards, Irish Times

She entered, like the Angel of Mons, to turn the battle. Undeterred by any note I might have left for Brenda, attended on either flank by the Chairman and Vice-Chairman of Arts Advisory, the Successor stepped in, high-haired, high-heeled, in a fur-trimmed blue velvet suit, like Elizabeth Taylor. We were gobsmacked, verging on outraged: how anyone less suited to the rough house of the Bradford Fellowship could have been given my job! I was too stunned to step forward to greet her, as she walked among us, talking easily, meeting the Chrises and laughing in a rich warm voice, till the Chairman and Vice Chairman spotted me, introduced me and I shook the proffered hand. 'You ran past me in the corridor this afternoon,' she said kindly. 'Can we talk, when you're less rushed?' As she turned to go, I noticed how flame-red her hair was in the late sun slanting through the window, and how her eyes, viewing everything darkly through her shades, seemed to see more through being themselves unseen. And I noticed something else that suddenly made me want to hug her. Her stack boots which gave her an extra three inches of height - she was really quite *petite* - hadn't been accounted for when turning up her hems, and showed an untrousered ankle-gap, like a chink in her armour.

*

I felt good again. I felt ecstatic and overwhelmingly sad. It was the last week of the last term of my Fellowship at Bradford. I was concluding the most productive two years of my career, and looking ahead to new writer/actor/director opportunities offered by the National. I had the promise of three writing commissions from Chris Parr, and doors opening into television through the Thames TV connection. I had a play opening the week after next in London, and a mammoth spectacular, tech- and dress-rehearsing over the next four days and opening on Wednesday in a thousand-seater hall. Simultaneously, I was setting up, promoting, recasting the show for Edinburgh, and dreaming up a revue to be its late-night companion. I had an eye to the details of moves, cues, harmonies, steps, thrusts and parries, as actor/singer/fighter/dancer in the show, and as Director on the Board of the Edinburgh Fringe, a view of the exploding nationwide dramatic scene. I was buying a house in London and furnishing it lock, stock and library, from a house in Reading, with Sir Gareth (Mick Diver) agreeing to help with the lifting. I was enjoying a blazing summer with time for tennis with Effie Taylor and Scrabble with John Lamb. I had the love of uncomplicated, ships-in-the-night friends, with dreams of permanence, but not yet. I had surely earned this elevation. What could possibly bring me down?

＊

Bradford Telegraph & Argus
KING ARTHUR UPSTAGES RICHARD AGAIN
Don't mention coincidence to playwright Richard Crane. Right now it's the dirtiest word in his vocabulary. In fact he rather suspects the Laws of Chance were enacted against him personally. It seems that whenever he comes up with an idea for a play, someone else hits on the same notion at the same time. You may remember that his musical version of Tom Brown's Schooldays *clashed with a West End version and a TV serial; that his play* Crippen *was paralleled by a musical on the same theme and* Thunder, *his highly successful play about the Brontes, coincided with a West End production, also about the Brontes which added insult to injury by transferring to Leeds Grand just as Richard's play was staged at Bradford's Library Theatre. And now it's happening again. Richard has a new show based on the life and legend of King Arthur, entitled simply* The King, *which is about to be presented at St George's Hall. And guess what... a new musical play has just opened in London by David Cregan, about King Arthur and his knights, and most depressing of all, it's also called* The King. *Lightning is not supposed to strike in the same place twice, but for Richard it keeps striking again, and again...and again.*

＊

Barnsley, 1st July 1974
Dear Mr Crane
Having endured Wednesday's matinee performance of The King, *I must strongly object to your pre-show blurb's reference to a musical spectacular. Musically, it was a non-starter and the use of the word 'spectacular' would be more appropriately associated with 'flop'. To invite a school party to see such an abysmal performance was unfair to the youngsters - financially and aesthetically - and does a disservice to the theatre and education. What do you think will be the response when next I want pupils to visit a theatre? One pupil commented that there was more jingle in my bunch of keys than in the whole show. 'Not all that bad' was the kindest comment offered. Specific complaints: the*

organ was far too loud, making it impossible for us to hear the dialogue and lyrics; some of the cast sounded to be wearing clogs; too much of the dialogue was gabbled; and often the action was too 'busy' and noisy. I agree with the pupils. The speech and movement lacked the control expected in a production such as yours. We came away feeling bitterly disappointed.

Yours sincerely,

R Sykes

Head of English.

*

Dear Mr Sykes,

Thank you for your letter about The King.

I'm sorry you felt your trip was wasted... We have had some comments that the visibility at St George's was at times difficult and that the singing now and then was out of sync with the organ. We could not do much with the former because of the geography of the hall... the latter improved as the play went on. Other reactions to the play have been very complimentary, indeed ecstatic... In general, I try not to defend my plays. I realise they are not going to go down well with everyone. My policy at Bradford has always been ambitious: never do anything by halves. The risks therefore are very great... and coordination of all the elements... requires a degree of dedication and tactical skill, which does not always bear fruit at the first performance... A number of teachers who saw the play on the Wednesday afternoon, came back again later in the week and remarked on the general improvement. One of them said it was the most exciting theatre he had seen...

*

BRADFORD'S 'THE KING'

The legend of King Arthur and the Knights of the Round Table has fascinated poets, painters, authors and playwrights for centuries, so much so that there would appear to be little more dramatic mileage left in the subject, apart from the sort of total debunking David Cregan's The King *has tried so unsuccessfully at the Shaw in London. Yet with his latest play (also called* The King*), Richard Crane, has succeeded in fashioning a witty and spectacular work, that is both entertaining and refreshingly different from almost all previous interpretations.*

- The Stage

*

I was exhausted. *The King* had been good, but not good enough, and was proving a nightmare to recast. The curse of coincidence - and always being pipped by a show critically judged to be inferior - was draining my energy. The notion that second or transferred productions were never as good as the first, was corroborated when *Secrets* attracted mediocre reviews, extolling JRB's direction and hoping he might find better material in future. Moving from Serena to Peggy Ramsay, which should have kick-started a new journey, felt dirty and underhand - what did I have to bring to Peggy anyway, except a 'mediocre' play and an unrecastable 'flop'? I would see her when I came to London, to return costumes and weapons, and also collect furniture from Reading and take it to storage; and in the evening maybe see *Secrets* again before it closed; and the next day clock in at the National and suggest maybe they *should* postpone for a year., because no one, not even JRB, had come up with anything for me to *do*. And sometime as well I had to extract my scripts from Serena then then tell Peggy I was free for commissions as I probably *wouldn't* be going to Edinburgh; except hadn't Chris fixed for me to meet a lighting guy called Hugh Wooldridge who might light *The King* in Edinburgh, John Cumming having backed off, and also direct the revue I hadn't written yet?

I've found an old journal, just a few random entries, in a long, thin, half-used, hard-backed ledger originally belonging to my great-aunts. Recorded in real time, it contrasts the build-ups to *Secrets* and *The King*, and the highs and lows of the last days at Bradford:

> *Saturday 1st June:*
> *Excellent dinner party last night. Good food, good company, good con-versations, good arguments... 'S' shrieked a lot about smashing reactionary cripples and OAPs if they didn't rally to the flag. She was very pissed and collapsed later and had to be carried off to bed. Then 'D'... collapsed ditto and I was left entertaining the guests - I, who wasn't meant to have been invited in the first place...*

> *Wed 5th June:*
> *Rehearsal for* Secrets, *most depressing. Must keep away from this one. JRB's directing...awful, embarrassing...Train to Bradford with Chris... Talked about the joys of doing theatre in Bradford. Student theatre is so much more exciting because unpredictable, innocent. At rehearsal actors must work and laugh... Mick is a nice lad... John Lamb is good...*

Monday 10th June:
Head-ache. Very tired. Nothing has changed. After two years, theatre is still a vagrant, poor relation. We are still putting the desks back and confronting the Karate Club over double bookings... I love Mick. It's a sickness. If it happens, I'll give up smoking...

Tuesday 11th June:
Good crazy day. I am Sir Tristram. Quick breakfast, then into the office to fill out Trellis Fencing's particulars [he will revert to Equity actor Richard Harbord in Edinburgh]. *Very obliging of him to step in..... Went to pick up the horses and the Table - they are fine. Got the measurements for the scaff off Sir Percival. Good rehearsdls... Alone in the office, Mr Fencing declared himself to Mr Diver who was flattered but said no.*

Saturday 15th June:
I am going to write something out of my system. Write till my brain clears or I fall asleep... So what did I do today? I went to see Mick. Took my heart in my hands and knocked on his door. We talked a lot about sporting jokes for the revue. That was the pretext I went round on. Of the 'other', there is no chancel. Hated expression which I normally reject, but this is final.

Sunday 16th June:
Love is like flu. Hurt pride is all it is. Akin to being winded... Went for a walk in the park. Didn't think, just breathed... Told Mrs Merce I can't make her party on Wed. As I said to Chris, it was a one-night stand that lasted 18 months. Am I growing up at last?

Tuesday 18th June:
Started today by mending the toilet. Successful morning at the office. Seating for Edinburgh will cost £400... Excellent rehearsal though the horses are failing. They need new wheeels... We did the battle twice tonight and I was utterly fucked. My blood pressure rose when the techs tried to no-chance me... I am listening to lovely Julie Dawn on Night Ride. *Gran's birthday - 80 today. I sent her 20 roses.*

Then the burglaries began.

Bradford had always been a neighbourly place. You seldom needed to lock your door. We would often leave ours open all day in hot weather. One evening after a sticky dress rehearsal in St George's, we came back to 279 and Chris wanted to watch *Wimbledon: Match of the Day*. We settled into the downstairs front room, and Chris leant forward to switch on the telly., but there was only a stump. We'd been burgled! David had been typing upstairs all evening and hadn't heard a thing. As nothing else had been taken, and there was still a lingering belief that 'property is theft' and the fuzz were the enemy, we let it go, no sweat. A few days later, we came back and my attic had been raided. My dansette and all my LPs had been taken (except *Kenny Ball and his Jazzmen*); also my leather jacket, my dungarees and my boots. (I was, paradoxically, miffed that all my final draft scripts - of immense value to me - neatly and in full view, had not been touched.) This time we did call the police, who advised us to lock the door in future, which, still believing in the basic honesty of Bradford, we failed to do. Two nights later, I came in to find the whole house turned upside-down, drawers emptied, cupboards trashed, but nothing of substance gone that we could see. What was left to take anyway? David and I had a conference whereat it was resolved (a) that perhaps we should start bolting the stable door, even after the horses had themselves bolted... and (b) it was now time, with heavy hearts made lighter by the absence of stuff, to travel on.

Driving in the van with Mick down to London, I quizzed him about the course he was studying at Bradford. He was in the first-year of the first intake of *Human Purposes and Communications*. The youngest brainchild of Vice Chancellor 'Red' Ted, HPC had been launched, deliberately, with a blank sheet: no rationale, no syllabus, no learning outcomes, no reading list; the first task of the first intake being to define what the course was. Mick's airing of his scribblings on the blank sheet kept us jigging down the motorway, stopping at Scratchwood for a snack, where we filtered the discussion down to current economics, which was Mick's special interest. Boom and bust, recession, stagflation: what were we in for in the mid-seventies? Would inflation peak at twenty percent or go through the roof? How does a trickster ride it out? How to intellectualise despair? How to get laughs, at the point of drowning? Sketch shows, even nude sketch shows were yesterday's *divertissements*. 'Immersive': the word wasn't yet in theatre parlance, but the revue show coming into focus at Scratchwood, the holiday cruise out of debt into dreamland, would become *literally* immersive when the ship sank and the audience with it. I was already juggling lyrics, borrowing shanties from *Mutiny*, thinking up a Brechtian happy ending so the audience could get out alive; and casting Mick as the spiv/stowaway and symbolic death figure Albert Ross (Albatross).

EDINBURGH'S BRADFORD

... Mr Crane has also written the company's late-night show, a hilarious satire on the economic state of the country, represented by a holiday cruise aboard the SS Spanish Castle, bound for Utopia. The Entertainments Officers deprive the passengers of their money, their food, their liquor, all in the name of fun; the crew who live on bread and water, are constantly threatening to pull out the plug; the captain is nowhere to be seen. A sinister figure in oilskins sells black market copies of the Financial Times *and* The Economist *to gullible passengers who believe they can make instant fortunes. It is all extremely funny and, a rare thing in satire, good-tempered. Directed with skill by Hugh Wooldridge, it achieves the unusual target of getting most of the audience to join in.* - B A Young, Financial Times

*

But like the passengers aboard the cruise ship, we were sailing into dreamland. Edinburgh was off because people's hearts weren't in it. We'd survived St George's but with, in all probability, *lesser* recastings (if we could get them), and no Mitchell and only partial Parr - he had to be in London prepping the Howard Barker plays - the effort of dragging it all together again - costumes, weapons, publicity, budgetting, travel, accommodation - was it a labour too far?

Mick helped me return the costumes and weapons and advised taking a raincheck when I was about to cancel the re-ordering. He came with me to Reading to pick up the furniture and the books, and Mother came too. She treated him like a worker, offering him tea when we got home and a tip which he accepted. Then we lodged all the stuff in a storage unit in Bromley, and I took him to see the Clapham house. There were damp patches on the walls that I hadn't noticed before, the roof appeared to be leaking and there were puddles in the cellar. He said I should get a full survey done and renegotiate the price. I said we'd already exchanged contracts, so nothing could be altered. How long, he enquired, had the house been uninhabited? I said ages, I didn't know. That was its attraction. It hadn't been messed with. Presumably we'd had a Search? Absolutely! All okay. No motorways planned, no history of subsidence; though Uncle Arch, my solicitor, had discovered to his surprise what the property had gone for, just a dozen years before. I'd guessed ten, maybe nine? Did I mean thousand? No, hundred. It had sold for just *nine hundred pounds!!!* But Mick was moving on now to how I'd be apportioning the rooms. I said I'd let the three bedrooms, to offset the mortgage. He could have one if he needed to be in London after graduation? Or he could share mine, on an easy-come-easy-go basis, if he followed me. He followed me, down to the big double downstairs which would be my study and bedroom. 'Up to you,' I added. 'I'm nuts about you, as you know. Can't hide my feelings.' He was leaning against the sliding door that divided the room. 'I'll let you know,' he pouted, acting, as he always did. Or was it genuine? You never knew. This was what made him a heart-stopper in life and so natural on stage. Whereas others had to be coaxed out of funny voices and extreme gestures, Mick fell into a role as if born to it, then afterwards slid out of it into another, so missed the flak (*Ugly Duckling*), and the praise (*Spring Awakening*). Later, in the spare room at Shortlands, looking across at him sleeping in the other bed, I was thinking this is the end. In the morning he'll be away to Ipswich, his home, which is all I will ever know of him. His background, his future are blank, like the Fool in *Lear*. His eyes loosely closed, and his lips loosely open, he is the true 'fool in theatre', with no existence behind the mask. Of all the Bradford actors, though the least ambitious, he was the one with the most promising future if he bothered to go for it, and it was only the thought of him as Gareth, the trickiest of the knights and in the end the most loyal, or as Albert Ross - now you see him, now you don't - around whom the late-night revue would be built; it was only the joy of seeing him unnerving the audience, getting laughs and then gasps, that got me thinking maybe... wondering at the crossroads, which untravelled path to follow... muddling the need to do Edinburgh, with the need for Mick.

PEGGY

Goodwin's Court is next on the left after Little St Martin's Lane where in 1967, at the Little Garrick, my first play had its little West End premiere. As I'm turning into the quaint Dickensian alley with its gas-lamps and leaded, bow-fronted windows, I'm telling myself I have now come full circle. The apprenticeship is complete. I've done my time learning the craft and getting noticed; now the real work starts, the grown-up work of the practitioner master-playwright. The brass plaque says 'MARGARET RAMSAY LTD - PLAY AGENTS'. I ring the bell. I wait. I know what I'm going to say. I've learnt my words and practised making them sound spontaneous. I'm about to ring the bell again when a friendly voice answers: 'Hello Richard, Peggy's expecting you.' The door opens and as I climb the narrow stairs, past posters of plays by Ayckbourn, Bond, Ionesco, Orton... all the words I was so sure of, begin to disappear. A door opens and a cheerful young woman ushers me into a little room, crowded with assistants at desks clacking typewriters, or up ladders alphabetically-ordering scripts, with names daubed down the spine - BRENTON, BOLT, CHURCHILL, CREGAN... 'Make space for CRANE,' smiles a kindly American-accented voice. 'I'm Tom,' he says. 'This is Madeleine. This is Vanessa...' 'Hi Tom, hi Madeleine, hi Vanessa...' I shake their hands. 'Go up one more floor,' says Madeleine, clackety-clacking again. Vanessa, down from the ladder, says 'Tea? Milk and sugar? I'll bring it up to you.' 'Just milk, please,' and as I go through the door and start up the final stairs to the attic, I feel a perspex armour thickening around me, legs like jelly carrying me. 'Come on in dear,' says Peggy, as I'm about to knock. JRB has said: 'Don't be scared of her. She's ferocious but only as a mother defending her young, and you're one of her newly-fledged ones. She will die for you; though it may not seem so, when you see her, and she's lying on her ottoman in a turban, with her shoes kicked off and her stocking tops showing, on the phone to a client saying his play *stinks*, he should abandon it!'

She was sitting at her desk, her hair neatly waved, her eyes keen but kind. She had the script of *The King* in her hand, and before I could even sit down or say hello, she said 'The title must change. I told Cregan to change it but he wouldn't. It's a *terrible* title and his is a *terrible* play. He should have changed the whole play as well as the title! *The King*! What king? It could be any king. *Exit the King*. Now there's a play. Except the title gives it away. I told him, Ionesco, you can't have him announcing he's exiting at the beginning. A play has to have somewhere to go, don't you agree? Rise first then fall, build your dreams then watch in horror as they collapse as your King does. Yours is a *much better play*. Your best! You sent me *all your plays!* How could I read *all your plays?* I read the first one, about the women, and the Bronte one, and the Bush one. You write like a woman. Has anyone told you that? You have an urgency, yet *urgent* your Bush play was *not*, was it dear? It made *sense*, which is the last thing a play should do! But that happens with second productions. You shouldn't allow it, not on a London stage where the critics will destroy you, or worse, praise the director who quite clearly did *fuck all* on this one.'

'That's why,' I ventured, 'I don't actually want to take *The King* to Edinburgh.'

'Then don't take it.'

'It could only be lesser than the Bradford version.'

There was a pause. She flipped off her specs and held the script close to her face: 'What's the purpose? Where are they going? What's the *action*? What's it *about*?'

'It's about a quest.'

'Then say it dear. In the title.'

The tea came in and she carried on talking. She agreed *The King* could never go to Edinburgh. They'd think it was Cregan's play, and would avoid it. 'But *The Quest!* That says action, *white heat*... Isn't Bradford the forge of the white heat of theatre writing? Shakespeare, she declared, would never have written *Lear* without Marlowe and Webster snapping at his heels. Now you! You've got Brenton, Hampton, with their fangs at your tendons, *but it's not a dogfight*, I have to tell them. Never feel you have to lacerate each other to get the prize, even if the mob have bets on you! It's a bumper display of fire-cracking plays. You write a good one, Hare writes a better one, you write a better one still. Ban the bomb, so we should! But no one can ban nuclear fission from the theatre. Do you even *like* Hare's plays?' I told her I'd seen *Knuckle* and liked it very much. 'Could you do a better one?' she volleyed. 'About money? He tells you money corrupts and we know that. But it's the *way* he tells it. That's what the critics didn't like - some *upstart* changing the language. Could you change not only the language but the *style*, so it doesn't *look* like a play. That would fox the bastards!'

She took a sip of her tea, then rose, went to the door and yelled down the stairs: 'Biscuits! Vanessa!' Then sat down again, mischievous:

'Second productions are always lesser. If that's the rule, don't break it, *change* it. Or was there another reason you didn't want to go to Edinburgh?'

'I *do* want to go to Edinburgh.'

'You look exhausted.'

(I wish people wouldn't say that.)

I could feel my face cracking. She must have seen it, but instead of comforting, she said: 'Use it! You've just had the worst critical response, at the Bush: *Faint praise!* So what if you're exhausted? You don't know your best energy till you've been shattered emotionally. Hare was the same. I told him: Fuck the critics! They *want* you to fail. They want to *break your spirit!*'

RECASTING

I've just had a long conversation with Hugh Wooldridge. The voice is just as it was forty-five years ago. He says he is stouter now with silvery hair and a certain stiffness in the joints, but in my mind he is still the tall, urbane, non-acting thespian I rang that day from Peggy's office. We'd never met (or had we?). He knew so much about me from Chris, John Cumming, and a host of actors. Could I come to dinner, he insisted, *tonight*, at his mother's place, in Molyneux Street? 'Fear her not! You'll have seen her as Catherine de Medici in *Elizabeth R*, or in bed with Anna Massey in *The Right Honourable Gentleman*, or if you're considerably older than I think you are, as Ophelia, Viola, Miranda, Rosaline at the Vic and the Park... She's a dragon of course, but weren't you once a dragon for Digby Day, whom Mamma adores. She just loves to cook for bright young dragons!'

We met in a bar first. He had a juice, I had a beer. Let's do the business, he frowned, suddenly serious: Edinburgh! I said nothing was decided yet. You're at Lauriston? I said, that's the plan. Yippee! I was there last year. I love those priests. You know the entrance from the chapel into the hall is through the confessional. Confess your sins and you're in! I said it's not sins, it's problems. It's madness even thinking of going there.

For a moment he was silent, staring at me with clear blue eyes:

'List them, the problems.'

'Half the cast can't come.'

'How many is half?'

'I don't know, five, four. Merlin, Bellicent, Galahad. It's less than half.'

'I know people you could use. You probably do too.'

'And Chris is only partially free.'

'How partial is partial?'

'He can come to Bradford to recast, but not rehearse. He can be in Edinburgh for tech and dress.'

'Get his dates down in writing. Next problem?'

'It's not really a problem, because I know you have the answer.'

'Lighting design. Cumming can't come. But I can.'

'If we're on. Because there's one insurmountable problem. Our composer won't be there and even if he were, there's no organ in the hall.'

Hugh stood up: Do you have change? I gave him my change. He went to the pay-phone, dialled, someone answered, they had a short conversation; he went to the bar, bought more beer, more juice.

'Thomas Attlee,' he sat down, 'old friend from school, he's coming to dinner. He does hard rock, soft rock, jazz, you name it, and he has his own Hammond organ.'

We walked to Molyneux Street. I had to skip to keep up with him. He was talking all the way, about Thomas - you'd never know from the look of him, but take away the tenebrous locks and hippy beads, and he's the spit of Uncle Clem. He didn't start the Welfare State, or give India its independence, but he has composed, with me directing, a new musical, a revue, a mini-opera and several songs, which he will play for you tonight.

I don't remember the dinner. Was his mother even there? I think we had a take-away and a load more beer. I remember listening to Thomas on Hugh's father's piano - once tinkled on, said Hugh, by the fingers of Sibelius. Pa was the composer John Wooldridge; you haven't heard of him. He survived bomber command then died in a car crash sixteen years ago. I think I laughed; I was drunk. I was saying: 'Thomas! I will personally hump your Hammond up to Edinburgh, if you will play the music for *The Quest* and compose for the cruise-ship-of-fools revue *which I am even now writing in my head!* And Hugh, You-hoo, Hughie-Hugh, will you light-design both shows and direct the latter, so help me Galahad!

I crashed on the couch. In the morning, Hugh's mother made us omelettes with cheese. Margaretta Scott, soon to storm the boards as a 'dreadnought' Lady Bracknell, was asking, as she thrust my omelette to fluff up under the grill, if I would please write her something *new,* to do at the Court - a *Godot* for girls! I said sure, and I did, a two-hander about a time-bomb. And I directed it, said Hugh on the phone, forty-five years later. No, *I* did, I said, and it closed the Theatre Upstairs! Wasn't it the one, said Hugh, where she entered from the balcony down a water-chute? No, I said, that was another one, at the Arts. I did six plays that year. And it wasn't your Ma, it was Tammy Ustinov, and Chris directed it. You did the lighting. Ah yes, sang Hugh, as Maurice Chevalier from *Gigi, Ah remember... eet... vell.*

He came up to Bradford to discuss the revue and help with recasting. Out of the rottenness of despair, new actors were emerging like grubs transforming into nymphs and butterflies. Or a spider in the case of Merlin. We'd lost Arnie Kinbrum who had been playing him as a Jewish stage manager. Another actor, if we could find one, would never hold the show together. Then in dropped Raven James Iqbal like an arachnid. A wild-man acrobat, he would go on to join the circus. He played Merlin as a shaman mouthing mystic spells, that whipped the company into line. Till Galahad came. Pete Brent had played him like a cricketer in whites, coming to chivvy up a losing team. It didn't occur to me that Galahad could as easily be dark. I'd wanted to give Pied a part but he was in Yugoslavia. Now suddenly he was back. His sleepy eyes smiling, his black hair hanging in dreads, he might not seem your Purest Knight. But imagine his journeys, horrors he's vanquished, revelations he's been scorched by; then clothe him in white, white armour, white cloak, and how 'other' would that be! As the Piper, he just had to step onto the stage, like a flame in red and yellow, for the rats to shriek and the kids to scream, as he led them to their deaths. As Melchior in *Spring Awakening,* he could rape a child, provoke suicide, be sent to borstal, yet survive to 'learn all the world has to offer'. Galahad could be Pied's next step and he was up for it. As a young lecturer in Yugoslav Studies, he had just returned from the country which like Camelot was a patchwork of warring tribes, just about held together by a waning ruler. His ability to inspire both wonder and terror, as he transmits a sense of civil war waiting to happen, would bring something *current* to the play, and send shivers down the spine. A dark knight in white clothing, he enters the hall as at the end of Act One...

> '... *the glorious, perhaps ruinous figure of the advancing Galahad, immaculate, himself clad in white samite, mystic, wonderful; these are things very remarkable in a student production.'* - Harold Hobson

*

For recasting Bellicent, paramour of Arthur and mother of Mordred, there was only one choice. I rang her. I said this was her chance to get to know the company as a *member* of the company. I said I'd heard she was good and I'd take her sight unseen, that's how desperate I was, ha! And honestly, I wasn't sore about Tom Wilkinson. He wasn't *my* nominee. He could bog off to Hollywood for all I cared!

I could hear thinking going on. I thought please don't say 'I'll get back to you'. We're hanging by a thread!

I could hear children's voices pleading: 'No Mummy! Don't! Think of *us*! We need a *holiday*!'

She said yes.

THE QUEST

Y ou come into a baronial hall, dimly lit, with banked seating on either side. An organ is playing; the hall is hushed. You climb to your seat and turning, see a crowd of shadows opposite like a swarm, ascending to their places. Expectation thickens the air. Your eyes adjust to the dimness. At the 'east' end, flame-red shafts of light slant through a stained-glass window onto a Round Table presided over by a throne-like 'Perilous' Chair. At the 'west' end, in deep shadow, a Sword is cemented in Stone, ready, you presume, to be drawn with ease by the destined king-to-be. You know the story but not how it will be told. All you know is this is Bradford, 'the most active student theatre in the country', with their third Festival programme, each more mammoth, more sensational, than the last; opening, cleverly you note, *before* the start of the main Festival, so as to attract national critics. You might recognise Harold Hobson of the *Sunday Times*, being helped out of his wheelchair by his assistant into his front-row seat. In the row behind, you might spot Michael Billington of the *Guardian*, exchanging pleasantries with Charles Lewson of the *Times*, B A Young of the *Financial Times,* John Barber of the *Telegraph,* Robert Cushman of the *Observer,* all hoping *The Quest* will be an improvement on the last Crane play - *Secrets* - which they'd collectively sat through, just a month ago, at the Bush. Behind them sits Allen Wright of the *Scotsman*, who would beg to take issue on the question of *Secrets*, having reviewed its original incarnation at the Traverse. Something of an expert in Crane plays, he reflects *The Quest* must be the seventh he has seen - *Crippen, The Tenant, Decent Things, The Blood Stream,*

Thunder, Secrets - each distinct in itself, a dramatic landmark in its own right; and behind *him*, ensconcing himself with a flourish, an impish-looking, tousle-haired fellow in cravat and velvet jacket, having been told about Crane, and keen to hail new talent, if not in the *Scotchman* (as he calls it) then the *Irish Times* for sure. Arthurian to his finger-tips, and Wildean, Joycean to the roots of his being, Owen Dudley Edwards, Reader in History at the University of Edinburgh, will become, in his words, the leading 'cranologist', seeing *The Quest* multiple times, interviewing the author and the Bradford company at length, studying the text in all its antecedents and wordplay, plus hunting down, seizing upon, reading, scrutinizing Crane's once and future catalogue.

But what you won't have seen, as the play gets going, as the Sword is eased from the Stone, and three Pilgrims kneel to the new King to be knighted, is the horror in the eyes of the newly dubbed Sir Tristram as through his visor he sees in the lightning flash that heralds the Coming of Arthur, two figures in uniform, one older, one younger, in the 'west end' entrance. He knows who they are, and what they portend. The question of the Licence came up yesterday, and he ignored it. The holy brothers had assured him the hall had a valid Entertainments Licence, which would be displayed in the foyer. Hugh Wooldridge, who had used the hall the year before, had said Entertainment covered only cabaret, concert, ceilidh, and choral singing. Any show involving actors dressing up, learning lines and *being dramatic*, was legally bound, on pain of closure and a fine, to display a valid THEATRE LICENCE; the acquiring of which, as revealed following a quick (anonymous) call to City Chambers, could take up to three weeks. As this would mean missing the Festival entirely, the only option was to go ahead, trusting to fate.

The younger officer seems poised to step forward to stop the show. The older officer is counselling restraint: there could be a riot. In addition to *The Quest* becoming the talk of the town, even before its opening, there is the politico-religious issue. As Dudley Edwards points out in his history of the Edinburgh Festival, *City of a Thousand Worlds*, 'the police owed some of their recruitment to the pious but secret order... of true-born Protestants, for whom the Jesuits remained a symbol of all they detested'. Softly softly catchee monks, the older officer seems to be saying to his militant colleague. Removing my helmet for the Coronation scene, I can see the smirk cross their faces. Bastards! They're enjoying it, without even buying tickets! As the newly-crowned Arthur goes royal-walk-about among the audience - 'And what do *you* do...? Have you come far...?' - I have to steer him away from chatting to the officers who are now chuckling, at least the older one is. The younger one seems to be gritting his teeth, either to stop himself guffawing, or to defy his colleague and step with full legal authority into the arena. But as one scene ends, so another begins. Wooden horses on wheels run charging, to audience cheers, down the track, unhorsing knights, causing mayhem. Then just as the actors are settling down to feast at the Round Table, and the officers exchange a glance, indicating now may be the moment, a ten-foot-tall green-garbed figure with a headsman's axe, comes between then, crying 'A BOON!' The officers shrink into the shadows. There will be no intervention. In my breaks I talk to our company manager John Wing and in the interval to Chris. As artists, as *jesters* to bureaucracy, we are immune to petty law. If forbidden to act, we *will act*. We're riding high at such speed, only an act of God can stop us, and He is with the Jesuits who, liable to be equally arraigned, are with *us*.

At the end of the show, when everyone is dead, except Gareth, and the audience are so stunned they don't applaud for a full minute; when slowly, out of the earth, the bodies rise, heads bowed, and the applause, the stamping, the bravoes are all over, and we're back in the dressing-room changing, celebrating, that's when I feel the black cloud falling around me, and anger that a flat-footed, poisonous pair of shits should pollute my happiness.

Wing comes to tell me to hurry up, I've been summoned. The officers are waiting in the foyer to talk to me. And Harold Hobson wants a word.

He was still in his seat. He looked crumpled and exhausted. He had one question. What were my sources? I said Tennyson mostly, but also Malory, *Gawain and the Green Knight*, even *Camelot*. It had all started, I supposed, when I won the poetry prize at school and chose *Knights of the Round Table* retold by Enid Blyton. We weren't allowed to read Blyton, so I kept my thumb over the author's name, when I was choosing, ha! The scourge of plagiarists and prats was fixing me with hooded eyes: 'When are you going to the National?' he asked with some scorn. I said: 'October. I think. I don't know. They might postpone.' As I watched his assistant help him into the wheelchair, I thought: well that, thank fuck, is my whole future down the pan, bar the pain and shame.

Then I went out to meet the officers.

*

At eight o'clock next morning, three Fellows, Past, Present and Future are standing on the steps of the City Chambers. The Fellow Past is primed to go in all guns blazing. The Fellow Present is still shell-shocked from the horror of last night. The Fellow Future, smartly dressed and silent, seems to be keeping her powder dry. 'Let me do the talking,' she says as they enter the Chambers and ask to see the clerk responsible for theatre licensing. They are told they will have to wait till ten o'clock. There's a coffee shop round the corner... They sit and wait ten seconds then Fellow Future jumps up and goes straight through to the stairs. 'Excuse *me!*' ejaculates the receptionist, but all three have vanished up the stairs like whippets. 'I hope we know where we're going,' says Past to Present. 'Her name was on the board on the wall,' says Future, 'Mrs McMullen, Licence and Permit Applications.' The door is open; we go straight in. She is sitting at a large desk, a small lady with neatly waved hair and piercing eyes, not unlike Janet in *Dr Finlay's Casebook.'* Will ye kindly go out again and *wait* till I say "Come in"?' We go out again. Should we knock? We knock. She says 'Come in'.

The rest can be left to Owen Dudley Edwards's account. He and the doughty Mrs McM were acquainted. Why only the previous week they had dined at the Doric in Market Street, at which repast Dudley Edwards's colleague Dr Peter Allen had enthused about the Bradford group and insisted on *The Quest* being top of Owen's ticket list. Thus Mrs McM, when the three Fellows knocked and came in, was (in Owen Dudley Edwards's words) *'not merely prepared to fight their cause… but to fight for it to the death. Trembling, the Bradford players cowered like some snake-hypnotised Andromeda as the lady of the City Chambers hurled her minions into the fray, tearing one magistrat from his sick-bed, grabbing another from the steps of an aeroplane, and with ultimate triumph thrusting an order to keep the hall open and in performance, into the very maw of the police.'*

*

If you've ever (writes John Lamb) *been in a show that was a really hot ticket, you'll know how exciting it is. People were fighting to get in. The theatre was so full for every performance that when you came on stage, it was like being hit by a wall of heat. We had authentic (but very hot) chain-mail costumes from Bermans and Nathans; my crown had be worn by Laurence Olivier in* Richard III. *Our venue was a large Victorian building, that had once seen barnstorming performances from Donald Wolfitt. Our set was laid out like a jousting arena, with banks of seats down each side. At one performance, Michael York came and sat, rather distractingly in the front row, causing most of the acting to be geared in his direction… Richard was a genius at publicity. We had superb lobby photos; we marched round the city in chain-mail promoting* The Quest; *we did radio interviews for the BBC and a television interview with Joan Bakewell in the Botanical Gardens… As soon as the reviews came out, Richard had them blown up and stuck outside the theatre, and the queues started to form. Harold Hobson in the* Sunday Times *hailed 'John Lamb's shining, golden, gallant and so-saddened King'. Michael Billington in the* Guardian *said people got so involved, they were shouting 'Come on Arthur!' like a football crowd.*

Robert Cushman in the Observer *said the battle was the best he had seen on any stage.* The Quest *won Richard yet another Fringe First which was presented by Esther Rantzen in a lunchtime ceremony where there was free gin and tonic... With the vanity and insecurity of all actors, I still treasure a letter from the* Irish Times *man in which he says 'I* cannot stress too highly what a sensitive performance you gave'... *Soon our fifteen minutes of fame were over and we were back in Bradford. The Festival had been the best fun you could have, in chain mail and a crown.*

There's a press photo showing a detail from one of the last moments in the last battle. Arthur is parrying a thrust from his brother Kay. Tristram is being skewered down the back of his neck, by Gareth. This is Mick's moment of triumph, finally gutting his pesky paramour, and mine in the ecstasy of death by love as the sword is driven home: the closest I ever got to anything physical with Mick, and it was repeated every night. From my position as a mangled corpse, I could at least take comfort in his lone survival as the dying King orders him to throw the sword into the lake. Twice he comes back and says he's done it, then has to admit he was lying. The third time he comes back, the King is dead and he tells the truth. He did throw it, as far as he could and it seemed an arm came out to catch it. But there's no one alive to hear him.

When we knew we would be performing again the next night, taking three hundred people on an unforgettable journey, the ending, though bleak, didn't seem so final. But on the last night, when Mick said (to no one): 'But there wasn't anybody there...' and the lights dimmed to black and there was silence, not even breathing; when gradually as the lights came up and we dragged ourselves, heads bowed, to standing, and the room erupted in applause, the sort of hand-hurting, throat-tearing applause, that most actors only dream of; as we relaxed into normal bowing and reprised the Knights and Ladies song with hurrahs and a jig; as the audience stood, every one of them clapping in time, and the house-lights came up, that's when I saw my parents: my mother biting her lip, trying not to cry; my father saying over and over 'Well done Wit... Well done Wit'. And I saw Peggy, in the front row, in her turban; I saw her wide eyes blink, like camera shutters, capturing the scene. And Owen Dudley Edwards, with his mane of black hair, roaring like a lion, and Andrew Cruickshank the new Chairman of the Festival Fringe Society, and Esther Rantzen presenter of this year's Fringe Firsts, and Caroline Blakiston, who two years ago (in *Villains*) I'd sprayed with blood from a sawn-off shotgun, and Juliet Cadzow, my bride in *Decent Things* and my love interest on Duna, and Phil Emanuel from the

Pool who had got me to Edinburgh in the first place. Then far away, just visible, on the back row, I spotted the one person to whom we surely owed everything, Mrs McMullen, who when complimented by Owen on her doughtiness in a great cause, had said: 'Well, we couldnae have the Jesuit Fathers in the dock, nor stop the wee lads' show'.

In the gap before the final performance of *Route*, I had time to talk to Peggy. She had spoken to Peter Hall, reciting *in italics* the final paragraph of Hobson's review of *The Quest*, where the undisputed *champion* of both Beckett *and* Pinter had said *he would shed no tear* if Hall were to *open the Olivier* with this *Austerlitz of a play!* But she held out *no hope*. Hall's response, with a sigh, had been that to open the Olivier with *anything* was becoming *an ever more distant dream*. Running the National in these stop-start times was like running *British Leyland.* Vilified by the press, under siege from the unions, the National, concluded Peggy, was *never going to move.* Frustration in this business was a *killer,* and she'd seen too many writers die! Why couldn't I stay at Bradford? Ayckbourn was still cutting his plays' teeth at Scarborough, before sending them to the West End. And before I could say: But Peggy, that's the very opposite of what you said before - she stared at me and blinked: Think dear, think seriously how to *structure your career;* then she was off to see a *dreadful* play by David Glade, did I know him?

I sat with my parents for the final *Route*, which my father found uproariously funny and my mother, recalling the dashed hopes of the migrant families on the *Ascania*, found worrying and upsetting. As the ship was going down and the company were singing *'We are sinking, we are sinking. Is this the end for you and me?'* I thought I saw Angie staring at me from the seating opposite. Later I picked up a note at the stage door, in her neat schoolgirl hand, congratulating me on the two plays and specially liking the Knobbly Knees Contest in *Route*, and in *Quest*, the line in Bellicent's pastiche of Good King Wenceslas '... *and tell him to put the fuel back,* exactly *where he found it!'* And tiny at the bottom, hardly readable, she added: 'Richard, there is still an "R"- shaped hole in my heart which will never heal. xxx.'

I had booked my parents into a small hotel run by an actor friend where they would stay two nights, then taking a detour to South Queensferry (my mother's birthplace), set off for Iona where Pa would enjoy a retreat with the Iona Community and Ma would enjoy the beach. They just had time to come backstage after the show, and while the actors were changing, Ma had a 'delightful conversation' with Hugh Wooldridge and Pa had a confidential chat with Thomas Attlee. 'Old Clem,' he enthused, 'was a great man. Don't tell Nan, but I voted for him *twice*, in preference to Winnie.' I said they didn't need to stay for the party, but corks were already popping and John

Lamb was presenting me (rather curtly I thought) with a farewell gift: a pewter cigarette-lighter in the shape of a medieval tower, accompanied by a poster which everyone had signed. In my speech, I said this wasn't good-bye. In my heart, I would never leave; nor in my lungs, which whenever I lit a fag with my new crenellated lighter, would get fogged up with longing. Yes physically I'd be in London, but the house I was buying, with the help of my parents (applause!), would be the corner of a foreign field that was forever Bradford. Anyone coming to London would be struck off my Christmas card list, if you *did not* come and stay. And there's always space at Shortlands, chipped in Mother, if any of you - such as *Hugh* - might need accommodation. But Mother, I interjected, Hugh *lives* in London! (Laughter). As they were going, Pa was saying, it was just like leaving a parish. You never knew there was so much love, and you wonder, too late, why you ever decided to go. Why *did* I decide? Could I think again, as Peggy suggested, about *structuring my career*? Chris had always argued against falling into the trap of the National just as I was maturing as a writer. I wished he was here now, to talk it through. Could we turn time back? Could Theatre, like Superman, grasp hold of the earth and ratchet it back to before I'd given my notice? I'd written a piece for *Javelin* outlining a programme for the following year, so bold, it capped everything I'd done so far; only to see it capped two months later, by an even bolder programme proposed by my Successor. Was this why I was always trying to deny her existence, why I've never named her in this book, even though *she* was the one who led the posse to City Chambers, even though *she* was getting better reviews and more laughs as Bellicent than Jackie N ever did. I could accept her hidden behind her shades, but when she took them off, I looked away. I made no attempt to befriend her children, as Johns Lamb and Wing did. I even wished for them to be badly behaved so I could yell at them, but they were good; they knew how to behave in a theatre, and were only bolshie when tired, as we all were. Christ! And what was happening to John Lamb? The more he grew into Arthur, the further he seemed to grow away from me. He was casting himself as the linchpin in the company, even inviting Fellows Present and Future to a weekend, after Edinburgh, on his father's boat on the Isle of Wight, so we could 'get to know each other and effect the handover'. I told him that most definitely was *not going to happen*. Was that why, after being so fulsome in his notes to me, ever since he joined the Group - Scrabble jibes, offers of puns etc for the play - was that the reason for his curtness when handing me the gift? Was that why, on the poster, all he had written was *Thank you, J Lamb*? I'm looking at the poster now, still vital and of the moment after nearly half a century, because the writing was done in the emotion of the last performance. It reads like hand-shakes, hugs and sobs, as a golden era ends. There are love notes here, past regrets, future promises. *All my blotless kisses*, says Paul N-L (Lancelot), now a fixture with Mrs Merce (Leonora) who says: *Come up and see us sometime! Luv, kisses and hugs*. And Guinevere, now pregnant and blooming (though I didn't know this at the time), says: *Thank you for so much, and a lot more besides! xx*. And Mick (Gareth from *Quest*, Albert Ross from *Route* and Ernst who has the gay kissing scene in *Spring Awakening)* writes in big, loopy letters: *Pssssssttt ... I'll let you know. Mick. PS: I won't be sad about it...* And in the bottom corner, in a scrawly hand - I'd forgotten he'd come up with the stage crew - a little *memento mori* that even now sets me tingling: *Once was not enough, best of luck, love Fred (Shipley).*

When I asked Lamb, now retired from the Foreign Office and living in Uruguay, if he would write up his memories of 1974, back came enough material, with illustrations, for a small book. It seemed what had come over as curtness was his diplomat's way of bottling personal feelings, just as Arthur tried to keep his emotions under wraps when the Table was being pulled apart. Other signatories of the poster that I kept in touch with after leaving, included Blob (Mordred), now Professor of Computing at the University of Victoria, Canada; Effie (Lynette) who rented a room from me in Clapham, worked front of house at the National, became a teacher, got married. And...

PIED

He was my last and closest friend at Bradford and the most distant. He had travelled to remote places and studied harsh political systems, as if no boundary was uncrossable, but his home was always Bradford. With his tangled hair, squished face and puffy eyes, he could be Afro, Oriental, Hispanic, never English; yet he loved cricket and Wodehouse. He could talk ten to the dozen on silly subjects, then pitch into serious politics, then walk on in silence. When they told me he was dead, I found a contact and phoned. He'd gone 'off the radar', working in admin, having stepped down from the chairmanship of the Bradford Civic, still travelling and coming home; married twice with children who were now married with children. His voice had the lightness and pensiveness of forty years ago. He was a phantom in a time-warp. I felt if I saw him now, grizzled and grandfatherly, not sleek and sleepy-eyed, he would fade out and I would too. He was for ever the young musician, playing guitar, singing songs, who I'd propelled into show-stopping roles as an actor. He came up with me to Edinburgh before the Festival to do publicity and tramping the streets we talked about two plays he'd written which I wanted to put on as last-minute lunchtimes at Lauriston: *But...* about bureaucracy running out of control, and *The Last Train* about the exit route from Yugoslavia in 1940 bringing death, not salvation. He was a traveller to dark places, and a story-teller when he got home. His plays had *a frighteningly true ring of reality... weaving a lively aura of suspense with the threads of rumour ...*' (Scotsman).

His songs tell of no man's land, blindness, the need to travel, the crossing into new states:

Release my hand in no man's land,
Return to the gods you understand,
For I must travel further.
Through the frontier gate to a different state,
I'd throw the dice, enbrace my fate.
I'll live with the new order.
I will cross the eastern border

FINALE

Your World is round,
as your Table is round
and it rolls right back
to where it started.
- Guinevere, The Quest

GOING ON

I'm driving the five-tonner heading south out of Edinburgh. When a show ends, I always need to be doing something active, to head off the black dog. So it was perfect, last night, at the post-post-party-party, when the two techies who were to share the driving in the morning, were lamenting having to stay 'on the wagon', and I said to them: 'Look, the skips don't have to be in London till Tuesday. Let me drive, I need to. You can meet me in the loading bay tomorrow when you're back, then take it on from there.' Then fixing the pick-up time with Thomas who had arranged to travel in the cab, and with anyone else who wanted to take up the spare place - 'I'll take it!' said Effie - I scooted off to Norman's.

Norman always pours a Glenfiddich when I come in and we chat for a few moments. Last night though, it was so late, he and Morag had gone to bed. I've known Norman since '71 when I was in *High Living* for STV and we got talking in the canteen. He said, though his work was mainly in Glasgow, his home was in Edinburgh and I should let him know if I ever needed a *pillie fa ma wee heid.*

There was the bottle and glass on the table under a low light. I helped myself and flopped in the chair. The malt slipped down like quicksilver, sweet mercury poisoning, and I was unconscious in minutes. I slept badly. I dreamt that a dog was licking my face, infecting me with viral nostalgia, which is incurable.

We're speeding down the A7 towards Gorebridge. It's mid-day. There are clouds in the sky but not from the weather. In the wing mirror, I see black dust being kicked up by the hellhound who is gaining on us. We can pull ahead as long as there are no roadworks or accidents, and we keep talking about the present, the immediate future, never the past.

'Why the hurry?' says Thomas.

'Don't get caught for speeding,' says Effie.

'Michael Barnes,' I reply. 'The lean guy with the staring eyes. He's the director of the Belfast Festival. He saw both shows and wants to take them as they are, to the library where Chris and I did *Secrets* last year. It's the perfect space, like a banquetting hall, and it could also be a boat. But I told him we could never retain the cast and anyway wasn't Chris doing the Barker plays, and wasn't I supposed to be starting at the National?'

'*Are* you starting at the National?' says Thomas.

'I thought you said you were postponing for a year and staying in Bradford,' says Effie.

We drive on in silence. We're nearing Galashiels. The air is clearing. We *could* do Belfast. I could ring Michael tonight. He said he needed an answer by yesterday for the publicity. We'd be headlining the Festival. But I'd been cagey, mouthing excuses till he shrugged and walked away, signalling the loss was mine not his, and in two seconds I'd be running after him. Michael, I said, running after him, let me talk to Chris and the National and the company. Give me a day, give me a week. I'm at a crossroads in my career. And I'm thinking, maybe I *should* take the National as the sinecure it's turning out to be, and do what Peter Hall does all the time, bunking off to direct operas etc. Michael said if we couldn't retain the cast, there were plenty of local actors, from both sides of the Ulster divide. We could do what Arthur did and summon knights and ladies from across the land in the cause of peace.

We're passing Melrose and heading onto the A68 towards Jedburgh. We haven't had lunch and could stop for a burger and at the same time get all *questy* in the ruins of Jedburgh Abbey. But I'm against it. In the absence of more discussion on Belfast and the future, Effie and Thomas are getting nostalgic over Lauriston: Michael York grinning in the front row, when everything seemed to be geared in his direction; then everyone downing too much gin at the Awards lunch, and me getting mad at them later for slurring their lines: the only time they'd ever seen me lose my rag - it was impressive!

We pass straight through Jedburgh. I'm not going to stop. Black clouds are returning, with heavy drops of rain, like the spittle of Cerberus. We could give him the slip by taking a wrong turning. There's a detour into the past, beyond nostalgia, that I've been wanted to take. It's not far off our route, but there's a way to go yet. I'm not going to mention it, but the thought of it spurs me on. We're making good time. The sun is trying to break through. And soon we're over the border, surfing the see-saw of Northumberland, to Hadrian's Wall. Can we stop here? says Thomas. I'm famished, says Effie. So we stop for a snack. I'm getting sleepy: the Wall, the outer reach of the old Roman Empire, over which Bellicent and her boys must have crossed coming down from Orkney. A man with a dog enters the cafe. Let's press on, I insist: Consett, Bishop Auckland, Darlington, merging onto the A1. They're dozing. They don't notice, when instead of veering *west* towards Leeds, I go *east* on the A63 towards Selby, Thorpe Willoughby, Osgodby... Are we there yet? murmurs Effie. Have we gone wrong? blinks Thomas, as we turn down what seems like a *lane*. Things are bumping in the back. Are the horses, the table, the skips coming loose? Is the Hammond okay? Can we check, says Thomas. Where are you taking us? says Effie. We're taking a detour,' I say, to the village where I grew up. Before the dawn of time.

We're coming into Howden and instead of the direct route, I'm taking the road less travelled via Gilberdyke to Blacktoft, where the Humber Estuary washes in. We chunter through Yokefleet, passing Beeton's farm, till there, across the marshland, we see it: the Vicarage: vast, blushing red, alone against the weather, a bastion guarding the village. Tell the Brontes they were lucky! Their ceilings were low, their rooms were snug. We had rain running down the *insides* of walls, stone flags, bare boards, no curtains, just blinds from the war. I was going to stop and walk up through the front garden to the porch, ring the bell and ask, as a ghost from before the dawn of time, if I could take a peak into the playroom, the front kitchen, the Hitler room, the bedroom where I nearly died. But it's not my house. Close up, it looks softer, warmer. The drive has been tarmacked. There are no mole-hills on the lawn. The swing, the black tree and the kitchen garden have all gone. It would spoil the memory to go in; the house looks empty anyway. We pass the church - it looks locked - and the old church and the graveyard, past Mrs Durham's house, her garden gravelled over, no roses round the door, and the forge and the school, both now private houses, very private, silent.

'Where are the children?' says Effie.

'Where are the people?' says Thomas.

We pull up by the shop and Milson's house. Wait here a moment, I tell them. The shop door still rings the same jingly bell. Mrs Thompson is at the till.

'Why, it's Wretched!' she exclaims. 'How are you love? My goodness! Maurice! Margaret! It's Wretched Crane! All grown up!'

I tell them we're just passing through from Edinburgh. How's Miss Wilson? Is she still here? Go and see, she says. Go round the back as you always used to.

I return to the truck. Effie and Thomas hop down. I tell them we're going to see Miss Wilson, who taught me to read, write, count and sing. We walk down the passageway to the back of Milson's long, thin house. Through the window we can see her in her chair, asleep, in her knitted woollen dress, her hair short and shiny-white, white hair-grips gripping the curls. I tap the window. She doesn't stir. She must be ninety I whisper. She might die from shock. I tap louder. Oh God... She opens her eyes, turn to us, turns away, puts on her grey-framed glasses, sees three faces looking in. She's going to tell us to go away. She doesn't know me. We shouldn't have come. She's standing now, tall as a small poplar tree, just as she was twenty-five years ago when I would come for tea and my singing lesson. I would tap on the window, she would get up, go to the kitchen and let me in. She lets us in. Hello Richard. Will you introduce me to your friends? Then I notice something truly odd. The table in the dining-room is set for tea, with four places: the best Clarice Cliff tea service, the triple-decker cake-server filled with fairy-cakes, and the tea-pot shaped like a house. She was expecting us! Milson! I bend to kiss her lightly on the cheek. I'm taller than you now! This is Fiona, but we call her Effie, and this is Thomas Attlee. Don't mind the hippy hair. Underneath, he's the very spit of his Uncle Clem the Prime Minister. Milson laughs her ho-ho-ho laugh (with a short 'o'), bids us sit at table, takes the tea-pot shaped like a house, into the kitchen to the kettle which is already boiling.

'How did she know we were coming?' says Effie.

'Can we cool it with the Prime Minister thing?' says Thomas.

'How did you know we were coming?' I ask Milson as she re-enters with the filled tea-pot now clothed in a knitted cosy.

'I was dreaming,' she says, 'that you would come with two friends, so I laid the table for four, filled the kettle and fell asleep again! Ho-ho-ho!'

Now we're all sitting down, I'm asking her about the village. She says the vicarage, the forge and the school have all been sold, but the shop is still there, and also the pub, but they too will have to close. It's as if the slow closure of business, the distancing of faith - the vicar now lives in a small house in Blacktoft - the relocation of children to larger, urban schools, the gradual sedation of Laxton into a dormitory for Goole, have cast a deathly peace over the village; which Milson accepts. This is her last tea party, table laid, kettle filled in advance. When we've gone, she will be free at last to drift away. I notice she has a large lump on her hand, like a fungus. When I ask her about it, she says she's noticed it too. It seems to be growing. It's not too painful but it has stopped her playing the piano. Perhaps after tea, we should all go through to the front room and Thomas can play. He has the long, strong fingers of fine pianist, and perhaps Effie, who has a rich tone when speaking, will sing. She says this noticing that the boy with the fingers and the girl with the rich tone, have been nibbling at their fairy-cakes and giggling, as with pinkie poised, they raise their tea-cups to sip the tea. Perhaps Effie may even sing for her tea, says Milson. This was how should used to react when we were being silly at school, but there's something sinister about it now, something predatory and unMilson-like, as if someone is *playing* being Milson, and suddenly I get it! The strategy behind the tight smile, the pursed lips that then break into the short 'o' laugh, through the tiny aperture of the mouth. Here is a black dog in little-old-lady clothing, concealing fangs! and not Milson at all. I want to get back on the road, but Effie is singing, *a capella*, the song for Elaine and we're struck silent, as when the Red Knight entered carrying the drowned child:

> A still, small voice spake unto me:
> Thou are so full of misery.
> Were it not better not to be?

Thine anguish will not let thee sleep
Nor any train of reason keep.
Thou canst not think but thou must weep.

No one has noticed the sky darkening, the rain pattering on the window and the old man looking in. We should never have come here. So far from a detour to give nostalgia the slip, this was a trap and we've fallen into it. And now they're rising and going through to the front room. I'm looking at the man in the window as into a mirror. When he's faded out, leaving only his tears running down the glass, I get up, but it's not easy. I'm heavy with age. I have to drag my feet like lead weights. I am six, I am twenty-nine, I am seventy-four. I go through to the front room. Thomas is playing, Effie is singing, one of the jolly songs from *Route,* and Milson is joining in with her spirited *vibrato.* I want to sing too, but no sound comes. When I speak, it's like a record played at the wrong speed: 'I'm s-o-r-r-y. We have to l-e-a-v-e.'

*

I'm driving west, towards Leeds. Effie and Thomas are asleep. Rain is tipping down making visibility almost nil. I'm straining to see anything beyond the swish of the wipers. All the time I'm thinking, we ought to go back. Milson has *dentures*, not fangs! I remember them clicking in the old days when she sang and they clicked again today. She taught me to read, write, count and sing. I owe her everything and she's dying. But I don't feel sad. I could crack my face and spill tears, but *as an actor.* I am a ghost. I play parts. I can whistle up a storm. I am the moment of collision between past and future. Blink and you miss me. Blink and you capture the moment I created. The swish of the curtain of rain induces dreams. I'm standing in the wings. There was a time when the wall between actor and audience, was unbreached. Now we have traverse, thrust, in-the-round, promenade. Has a trick been lost? The divide between 'them and us' makes humans *super.* That's why actors who play kings, when you see them on chat shows or meet them, are *awfully* disappointing. But put them in the wings, behind swagged velure and they'll tell you, even in a long run, it still spooks you. The mob who will howl for your head if you blow it, are holding their breath. The *tricoteuses* (Hobson, Billington, Barber...) are knitting your shroud. The click of the needles. The click of the wipers. If all the world's a stage, we're at the end of Part One. Part Two is not written. I'm going to have to blag it. Teachers from Milson and Mr Ludo to Peggy and JRB, have taught me to make a high art of blagging, which is all theatre is: persuading that you exist as the person you are not and being applauded for it. If all the world's a fantasy castle, and once, long ago, you scaled the heights -

Remember me? I wrote *The Quest* and acted in it too! - if all the world is repetition, decline, frustration, oblivion, shouldn't you have quit by now? '*The half-made actors, I've seen them,*' said Mr Bernau, '*trading hope for envy, ambition for bitchiness...*' If all the world's a shit-house, and you've cruised the cubicles for too many years, isn't there a reckoning to come? We could have played three weeks! We could have filled every night! An extra ten thousand could have seen my work, including JRB and Peter Hall. We could have transferred to London and rocked the theatre scene. Michael York as Arthur! David Essex and Julie Covington prised from *Godspell* to play Lancelot and Guinevere! I could have gone to the National as a force to be reckoned with, instead of a northern curiosity whose excellence, being hearsay, must be proved all over again. Last night at the flat during the party, I said to Fred: That was nice what you wrote, but you shouldn't count on me. I'm a shit. And his sheep-face cracked. I could go to sleep now and miss the lash of the rain. Let a child step into the road. Screech the brakes. Send all of us piling through the windscreen. I have the power to kill; or to go on going on. No one knows we ever met. We are such stuff as nightmares are made of.

'Are you okay?' says Effie.

'Why have we stopped?' says Thomas.

'I thought I saw something,' I reply. 'But I imagined it.'

*

We're coming into Bradford. The sky has cleared. It's still light. We'll head for the loading bay, leave the keys with the porters and I'll scoot off for one last night at 279. Nye Hall is moving in, painting the black walls white. He's in the attic. All my stuff is in bundles in the downstairs room. I can sleep in David's room. He left two weeks ago. I have to be in Edinburgh for the AGM on Saturday, but till then I'm free. John Lamb has invited me and the Susseccor for a couple of days on his father's boat on the Isle of Wight. I know I said categorically I wouldn't go, but the weather may turn. It may be my destiny. Once and Future Fellows should have a handover on the water. As Lamb said, I could give her the lowdown on *Javelin* and Arts Advisory, then after a fish supper and a glass or two of the finest wine, just lie out on deck under a blaze of stars, and tell our stories.

THE END

Acknowledgements

... and now, finally, seven years on, I'm through, and it's time to roll the credits. For an actor, who needs a live audience making a noise, it's been uniquely silent. The progress - part pilgrim, part rake - has defied Bunyan and Hogarth. I've skimmed the Slough of Despond, and phut-phutted over the Delectable Mountains; I've been libidinous and transgressive, but never sunk into gambling hell or died in Bedlam. As a ghost, who must act, I've learnt to blend life with art, slip from first to third person, flay the bear and go berserk in its hot-blooded skin. I've learnt that time is elastic and will twang back on you, if you're lucky, making the book less a memoir, more an essay in remembering. I've pegged the present to the past and space-walked into the future. I've made people say things they never said (but might have done), and filled what-ifs and gaps-between with invention and imagining. But one thing is certain. Everything you've read here is true (up to a point). All that happens happened, but not always in the right order. Any resemblance to persons living or dead in essential, even when names have been changed (Batty, Flopsy, Serena...) and characters merged.

For all its unreliability, a thesis-sized programme of research has gone into *Ghost Boy*. For the politics of the period, I read Andy Beckett's *When The Lights Went Out* by (Faber 2009) and *Supermac: The Life Of Harold Macmillan* by Richard Thorpe (Random House 2010); for Repton School in my father's time, Roald Dahls's *Boy* (Cape 1984); for Cambridge in the sixties, Clive James's *May Week Was In June* (Macmillan 1991); for the Edinburgh Festival and Fringe, Owen Dudley Edwards's *City Of A Thousand Worlds* (Mainstream 1991); for an intimate portrait of Peggy Ramsay, Simon Callow's *Love Is Where It Falls* (Nick Hern 2007); for the Brontes, Daphne Du Maurier's *The Infernal World Of Branwell Bronte* (Gollancz 1960) and *Take Courage: Anne Bronte And The Art Of Life* by Samantha Ellis (Chatto 2017); for the Bounty, Donald A Maxton's *The Mutiny On HMS Bounty* (McFarland 2008); for the National Theatre *The Peter Hall Diaries* (Hamish Hamilton 1983), *The Diaries of Kenneth Tynan* (ed John Lahr, Bloomsbury 2001), John Russell Brown's *Free Shakespeare* (Applause 1974), *In Two Minds*, Kate Bassett's biography of Jonathan Miller (Oberon Books 2010) and Michael Blakemore's *Stage Blood* (Faber 2013); plus biographies of Laurence Olivier (Terry Coleman, Bloomsbury 2005), Bette Davis (Ed Sikov, Aurum 2007); Peter Ustinov's *Dear Me* (Heinemann 1977) and *Gielgud's Letters* (ed Richard Mangan, Weidenfeld 2004). Films revisited include *The Four Feathers, The Night Of The Hunter, Los Olvidados, Orphee, Bonnie and Clyde, Spartacus* and *They Shoot Horses Don't They?* I also discovered videos of *The Duna Bull* and *Villains* (Ep 4 *Chas*). Music to set the mood by, came from Glenn Miller (*Blue Evening*), Nat King Cole (*When I Fall In Love)*, the Beatles (*Girl)*, Bobby Hebb (*Sunny*), George Harrison (*My Sweet Lord*), the Rolling Stones (*Angie*), and Annie Lennox and the African Children's Choir (*The Coventry Carol*).

But the great joy of researching *Ghost Boy*, has been tracking down friends, hearing voices on the phone that haven't changed in fifty years, setting trails that snake back into the era of Gestetner and Quink, and one Sunday in 2011, walking into a sea of faces from Class of '58 at St John's School Leatherhead: wrinklier, balder, but in attitude unchanged, as if they'd never left the building. This was the spark that flamed into the idea for a memoir which then crackled into a seven-year sleuthing project.

People I must thank include Nigel Pittman who lived a parallel life through the period and read and responded to the draft script as a 'general reader'; likewise Lynne Truss and Kerry Lee Crabbe who read early sections and gave enthusiastic feedback. Nigel Pegram, former pupil of The Old Ride gave me lowdown on the Flynns, which led to information and photos from the archives of Brighton College. My uncle, Bob Twidle, sent memories of the Twidle grandparents and the seafaring Harbords. I read Aunt Elfrida's biography of Uncle Mo, and the WW1 diaries and poems of Uncle Wilfred. I went through the 'ammo box' letters with my mother, as a memory project when her mind was fading, and the life-time of letters I'd written to her, which she returned to me. My sisters, Elizabeth, Judith and Monica, helped add detail and colour to the Yorkshire, Birmingham and Jamaica sections, and in December 2014, I met up with the cast of the 1966 Footlights Revue. Andy Mayer, Tim Davies, Jane Barry, Richard Syms and Chris Mohr, then read and responded to the Cambridge sections. Angie Wrapson and Michael Church covered Notting Hill Gate and Islington. Cherith Mellor remembered Nottingham; Juliet Cadzow refreshed the memories of Scotland; Greg Philo, Alan Bridger, Blob Wyvill, John Lamb and John Waller recalled Bradford adventures, overarching all of whom were David Edgar, Howard Brenton, Chris Mitchell and Chris Parr. I owe Parr the biggest thankyou for calling me out as an actor, then making me convert the acting into writing, while blazing a trail for me to follow.

And finally my thanks and best love to those closest to me: to my wife Faynia for putting up with a moody writer in the attic for seven years, then reading the work-in-progress and giving valued feedback, and to my sons Leo and Sam, for seizing on the book and responding immediately, in detail and with wonder.

Richard Crane
Brighton

RICHARD CRANE is an actor and playwright. He was the first Resident Dramatist at the National Theatre; Literary Manager at the Royal Court; Fellow in Creative Writing, University of Leicester; Visiting Writing Fellow, University of East Anglia; Lecturer in Creative and Dramatic Writing, University of Sussex and Writer in Residence, HM Prison Bedford. Nine of his plays have won Edinburgh Festival Fringe First Awards, including *Thunder, The Quest, Vanity, Satan's Ball, Pushkin, Rolling the Stone.* Other plays include *Brothers Karamazov,* starring Alan Rickman, Edinburgh Festival and West End; *Mutiny!,* with David Essex, Piccadilly Theatre London; *Venus and Superkid* with Milton Reame-James, Arts Theatre and Roundhouse London; *The Possessed,* with Yuri Lyubimov and Alfred Schnittke, Odeon Paris, Almeida London; *Gogol,* Royal Court London, Traverse Edinburgh, Moscow, New York; *Clownmaker,* Edinburgh, London, New York and *Bloody Neighbours,* National Theatre. He is co-Founder and Associate Director of Brighton Theatre. He is married to the director Faynia Williams. They have four children and four grandchildren. Richard's plays are published by Heinemann, Chappell's Music, Samuel French and Oberon Books; recordings by Phonogram, Telstar and Stage Door Records. He lives in Brighton.